ACCESS FOR THE HANDICAPPED

The Barrier-Free Regulations for Design and Construction in all 50 States

ACCESS FOR THE HANDICAPPED

The Barrier-Free Regulations
for Design and Construction
in all 50 States

Peter S. Hopf, AIA
and
John A. Raeber, AIA

VNR VAN NOSTRAND REINHOLD COMPANY

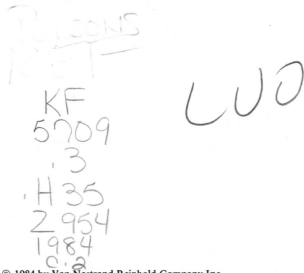
Published by Van Nostrand Reinhold Company Inc.
135 West 50th Street
New York, New York 10020

Van Nostrand Reinhold Company Limited
Molly Millars Lane
Wokingham, Berkshire RG11 2PY, England

Van Nostrand Reinhold
480 Latrobe Street
Melbourne, Victoria 3000, Australia

Macmillan of Canada
Division of Gage Publishing Limited
164 Commander Boulevard
Agincourt, Ontario M1S 3C7, Canada

15 14 13 12 11 10 9 8 7 6 5 4 3 2 1

Library of Congress Cataloging in Publication Data

Hopf, Peter S., 1929–
  Access for the handicapped.

  Includes index.
  1. Architecture and the physically handicapped—
Law and legislation—United States—States. I. Raeber,
John A. (John Arthur) II. Title.
KF5709.3.H35Z954 1984   343.73′07872042   83–10650
ISBN 0–442–23545–3   347.3037872042

PREFACE

Physically handicapped individuals are anxious to be useful members of our society. Unless our buildings and facilities are accessible and usable by them, however, they may not be able to function as such, or may not be able to operate as independently as they would be otherwise.

Recent public recognition of the needs of the physically handicapped has resulted in updating of previously existing standards, and in the passing of laws which mandate that buildings and facilities be made barrier-free. The design professional or builder involved with the planning or construction of new or altered buildings is already faced with the task of complying with innumerable governmental regulations on many subjects which vary from locality to locality. The relatively recent inclusion of accessiblity regulations has now added still another element with which the designer or builder must be familiar.

The principal purpose of this book is therefore to make this new data available with maximum ease and in as "painless" a form as possible. Since the design professions use the graphic medium on a daily basis, we feel that this is a natural "language" with which to communicate the country's principal accessibility regulations. While some communities and/or agencies may have further regulations beyond those included in federal and state laws, we believe that being knowledgeable about the latter is a necessary key step to awareness and compliance with the principal regulations in the field of accessibility. We have therefore limited the contents of this book to federal and state standards, as well as the main national standards.

Design criteria for making facilities suitable for use by the physically handicapped is a subject of continuing research by sociologists, psychologists, and others knowledgeable in the field—especially the handicapped themselves. Discussions on the subject frequently elicit differing opinions—often with the observation that the laws are not sufficiently far-reaching. We have deliberately kept this book limited to the confines of the regulations themselves, and have not strayed into the field of opinion or recommendations (unless so stated in the regulations themselves).

This Preface is therefore the place for the recommendation that is most frequently heard: the regulations should only be considered as a minimum legal requirement, and designers, through a creative thinking process and in consultation with specialists in the field, can do much to further enhance a building's use by the handicapped.

The agencies and persons who have—directly or indirectly—contributed to this book are too numerous to mention individually. Data and information was furnished by the enforcement agencies in all of the 50 states, and we owe them our appreciation and wish to thank them collectively for their help and assistance. They also reviewed the material in the State-by-State summaries and provided us with the most up-to-date revisions in their respective jurisdictions. Their cooperation has been very helpful in making the book as accurate as possible.

We also acknowledge the courtesies extended to us by the International Conference of Building Officials (ICBO), the Building Officials & Code Administrators International, Inc. (BOCA), and the American National Standards Institute (ANSI).

The bulk of the book's contents are graphics. They were drawn by Donald C. Akerland and Thomas S. Lee.

Finally, we are deeply indebted to the prodigious work of our wives: Edith Hopf and Sandi Raeber. In addition to furnishing much-needed moral support, they provided the in-depth research, codifying, checking, and coordination that was needed to ensure the timely and accurate completion of the book.

Peter S. Hopf, AIA
John A. Raeber, AIA

CONTENTS

ACCESS FOR THE HANDICAPPED

The Barrier-Free Regulations
for Design and Construction
in all 50 States

SECTION 1
HOW TO USE THIS BOOK

THE NEEDS OF THE HANDICAPPED

Providing access for the handicapped is often considered by the able-bodied as "someone else's problem." Although the physically handicapped person passing us on the street may get a glance of sympathy, what is often really on our minds is: "I sure am glad that's not me."

How little it would take to convert the able-bodied "us" into a handicapped "them"!

A broken leg, a heart attack, an automobile accident, a punctured eardrum, an eye infection, or medical surgery could instantly change our able-bodied status into one with a physical handicap.

The numbers are staggering. The National Center for Health Statistics has estimated that over 67 million Americans suffer from limiting physical conditions and would benefit from a more accessible environment, and an additional 20 million over the age of 65 are estimated to be limited in mobility. Thus, physical barriers are limiting the activities of more than one out of four Americans. The California Department of Rehabilitation indicates that 10% of the population between 16 and 65 is disabled, as does the U.S. Census. Statistics for Ohio show a state disability rate of 9.1%. South Carolina estimates 10.2% of its working age population and 39.2% of persons 65 and over as being disabled.

While there may be variances and lack of agreement on precise disablement data, there can be no doubt that the numbers of disabled Americans are, indeed, enormous. Paradoxically, our very way of life can be considered to be a major contributor to the large numbers of handicapped persons. The increasingly longer life spans which we enjoy due to medical advances result, in turn, in an increasing number of persons afflicted with the physical infirmities of old age. Similarly, 50 years ago, only a small percentage of persons survived major damage such as spinal cord injury. Today, while medical miracles are often life-giving, they do so at the risk of physical impairment. In the past, the probability of survival of severely damaged newborn babies—and therefore the chance for reaching maturity—was small. With an increasing survival rate today, the need for mobility assistance has increased.

The term "handicapped" generally refers to those persons who have some form of disability which prevents them, to some degree, from functioning normally in our society. Traditionally, the handicapped have not been very visible and have often required the assistance of another person in some way.

Today, the emphasis is on independent mobility and functioning in the mainstream of society. Most definitions of the handicapped include those who may suffer from the problems discussed below.

ARCHITECTURAL ACCESSIBILITY AND BARRIER REMOVAL

Architectural accessibility and barrier removal are concerned with the physical conditions of the environment, buildings, public accommodations, means of transportation, housing, and the streets.

For physically handicapped persons, problems of architectural accessibility arise in several contexts. First to be provided is access to buildings and facilities in order to exercise the rights of citizenship, including petitioning government. Second is to secure the services offered by government and the private sector in the locations they are made available. Third, both in terms of public and private buildings, accessibility opens the opportunity to employment. Fourth, in relationship to one's private life, accessible housing affects the capacity of individuals to live in a particular locality and enjoy a home environment which is both supportive of particular needs of handicapped persons and is safe. Fifth, accessibility relates to the mobility of the physically handicapped individual on the streets, in moving into and out of buildings, in being accommodated on transportation vehicles in order to get to work and fulfill professional responsibilities, and in traveling about to experience recreation and a full social life and visit friends and family.

Concern regarding architectural accessibility and barrier removal is reflected in federal and state laws. Federal legislation establishes architectural requirements for federal facilities and federally assisted programs and activities. State legislative requirements may affect state and local government buildings and facilities; buildings and facilities constructed or renovated with financial assistance from state and local governments; public buildings, including buildings into which the public is invited as a part of the regular course of business; public accommodations, which usually include amusements, parks, restaurants, transportation terminals, and lodging facilities; public housing; and private housing.

THE STANDARDS

Significant first steps in recognizing the need for making facilities accessible to the handicapped occurred in May 1959, when the American Standards Association, at the request of the President's Committee on Employment of Physically Handicapped, called a general conference of those groups concerned with the problem. The Committee and the National Society for Crippled Children and Adults were designated as co-sponsors of the project, which was approved by the Construction Standards Board. The ASA Sectional Committee on Facilities in Public Buildings for Persons with Physical Handicaps, A117, published the first standard in 1961.

This committee had a membership of over 40 organizations, both public and private. It included representatives of labor, architects, engineers, hospitals, hotels, blind persons, religious groups, municipal organizations, and federal agencies. Published as ANSI (American National Standards Institute, Inc.) A117.1, it is considered as the cornerstone of standards to make "buildings and facilities used by the public accessible to, and functional for, the physically handicapped, to, through, and within their doors without loss of function, space or facility where the general public is concerned."

Many of the federal regulations and much of the state legislation since then have been significantly affected by these ANSI standards and they have been frequently, either in total, or to a large extent, incorporated into pertinent statutes or administrative regulations. ANSI reaffirmed these standards in 1971.

By March 1980, ANSI had completely revised the standards and published them as ANSI A117.1—1980. "American National Standard Specifications for Making Buildings and Facilities Accessible to and Usable by Physically Handicapped People." Drastically changed from its previous edition, and much more comprehensive and specific, the new edition replaced and superseded the previous version. Gradually, this revised version is being incorporated into state legislation, but it will be several years before references to the 1961 standard will have been completely deleted from the statutes.

The ANSI 1980 standards are, at this writing, the most frequently utilized national standards, followed by the 1961 version. Other national standard codes, such as the 1978 BOCA code and the Uniform Building Code, also include special provisions for handicapped persons. These latter codes have been adopted in total or on a partial basis by several states, but their heaviest use is by local communities. It is not possible, in one comprehensive volume, to list all of the communities using these codes, but the provisions of those codes have nevertheless been included in this book.

Closely paralleling the ANSI 1980 standard are the guidelines of the Architectural and Transportation Barriers Compliance Board of the Federal Government. Section 502 of the Rehabilitation Act of 1973 (29 USC 792) established the Architectural and Transportation Barriers Compliance Board (ATBCB) as an independent Federal agency to insure compliance with standards required under the Architectural Barriers Act of 1968.

Congress had found that compliance with the Architectural Barriers Act had been spotty and that enforcement of accessibility standards was necessary to fulfill the Congressional commitment to afford handicapped individuals the opportunity to move freely and integrate themselves in society. In 1978, Congress expanded the responsibilities of the ATBCB and required it to "establish minimum guidelines and requirements for standards issued pursuant to the . . . Architectural Barriers Act of 1968." Based on the minimum guidelines and requirements issued by ATBCB, four federal agencies—the Department of Defense, the General Services Administration, the Department of Housing and Urban Development, and the United States Postal Service—are to prescribe standards for the design, construction, and alteration of certain federal and federally assisted buildings to "insure, whenever possible, that physically handicapped persons will have ready access to, and use of, such buildings." While each of the four agencies has standards uniquely applicable to their own functions, they were to be revised to conform to the ATBCB minimum guidelines. As of the date of this writing, that had not been accomplished.

While these federal agencies have not incorporated these guidelines, as yet, two states—Delaware and Arkansas—have, with some very minor exceptions, adopted the ATBCB minimum guidelines. They are therefore also included in this book.

Finally, some states, such as California, have issued their own state standards, unique and different from any of the foregoing.

APPLICABILITY

The applicability of the handicapped provisions of adopted statutes and regulations varies from state to state. Virtually all, however, require compliance with their standards for publicly funded facilities—either those of the state or any of its political subdivisions or agencies. Many are applicable, as well, to privately funded public buildings, and some, such as California, extend to nearly every type of building in the state. Definitions of "public buildings" also vary from state to state, but are usually defined as those facilities used by the general public. The State-by-State Listing of Regulations in this book provides a summary of individual state application requirements.

Most state regulations refer to *minimum* requirements, and they should be considered as such. While our knowledge of the needs of the handicapped will undoubtedly continue to grow, this book has stayed strictly within the confines of the minimum state requirements and does not address any additional recommendations for further enhancing the viability of facilities for use by the physically handicapped. The minimum code requirements normally do not require everything in a building to comply. Most codes require access to a building (normally described as at least one primary travel route and point of access), and then, within a building require access to all facilities within the building (i.e., all floors, meeting rooms, toilets, etc.). Within specialized spaces such as toilets, the normal requirement is to provide at least one of each type. Thus, in most states, not all entrance doors, water closets, and telephones are required to comply. It will normally suffice, for example, to provide at least one accessible way to get into a building, and then once inside, to provide access to at least one toilet per floor, and then at least one complying fixture of each type within each accessible toilet.

Most codes also require complying elements, such as parking stalls, entrances, toilets, telephones, etc., to be identified, almost universally, by the International Symbol of Accessibility.

Exempted from most state requirements are one- and two-family residences. Requirements for other housing and lodging facilities, such as hotels, motels, multiple dwellings, etc., vary. Some states require nothing, while others require a minimum percentage of each type of unit either to comply or to be made adaptable (such as having built-in support for bathroom grab bars).

USING THIS BOOK

The principal purpose of this book is to provide a comprehensive, easily usable reference manual showing the application and technical requirements to comply with state regulations on handicapped accessibility.

The state-by-state summary of code requirements has been digested from the laws and regulations of all of the states as they were available at the time of manuscript preparation. While it has been uniformly arranged for all of the states and therefore should enable the user to make a comparative review between all of the states, it is not intended to be used for in-depth legal purposes, nor is it intended to provide a complete recitation of all of the elements in the various state laws. Its aim is to provide an overview of the main elements of all of the states. For those who require a copy of the specific state regulations, they may be obtained from the sources indicated at the end of each state listing.

Similarly, the graphic portion of this book has been prepared with the same purpose: to provide quickly accessible, easily readable, comprehensive and uniformly arranged information on specific requirements for all of the states. Obviously, the material is the authors' interpretation of the various regulations and has neither implicit nor explicit sanction of the respective jurisdictions.

Since regulations change periodically, users are encouraged to contact the sources for additional information listed at the end of each state's description of the regulations for the most up-to-date information.

While the book has attempted to include all the regulations of the states, it should be noted that some states have additional specific requirements for specialized functions. These include facilities such as libraries, schools, multiple dwellings, hospitals, etc. Because of the relatively limited application of such specific uses, they are not included herein. Again, the individual state agencies can be contacted for this information. While individual state requirements for these special building types are not included, the section entitled "Special Building Types" shows the pertinent requirements of ATBCB and ANSI—1980. They can be applied to the pertinent jurisdictions.

The graphics have generally been arranged according to the following sequence:

1. They follow the travel route of a person as he or she approaches a building and then enters it for a specific purpose. This arrangement is the pattern used by most states and national standards.

2. Each topic first shows those states using ANSI—1980 standards, then those which have adopted the 1961 version, and then by other national standards. The final grouping under each topic are those states which have adopted variations of the national standards or which have adopted their own regulations. Since many states have adopted similar regulations, illustrations depicting the regulations of multiple states are listed first.

SECTION 2
STATE-BY-STATE LISTING
OF
REGULATIONS

ALABAMA

Legislation and/or Regulations:

Act No. 224—1965; Act No. 1210—1975; amendment, eff. 1/1/76.

Applicability:

Buildings and facilities used by the public which are constructed in whole or in part by the use of state, county, or municipal funds, or the funds of any political subdivision of the state.

Exemptions:

State Fire Marshal and the Director of the State Building Commission, each with the concurrence of the other, can grant waivers of a particular standard when, in their joint opinion, following a specification or standard would be unreasonably costly and impractical or that an alternative facility is reasonably available.

Enforcement:

State Fire Marshal.

Remarks:

Responsibility for reviewing architectural plans and specifications for buildings to which the act applies is:

a. Where state school funds are utilized—the State Board of Education and the State Building Commission;
b. Where other state funds are utilized—the State Building Commission:
c. Where funds of counties, municipalities or other political subdivisions are utilized—the governing bodies thereof and the State Building Commission.

Each such reviewing authority is authorized to adopt and enforce rules and regulations prescribing additional standards based on standards prescribed by the American National Standards Institute for making buildings and facilities accessible to and functional for the physically handicapped.

Additional Information:

State Fire Marshal
445 South McDonough Street
Montgomery, Alabama 36104
(205) 832-5844

ALASKA

Legislation and/or Regulations:

AS 35.10.015, Architectural Barrier Regulations; Alaska Administrative Code 17 AAC 50.010—Construction of Public Buildings Accessible to Physically Handicapped.

Applicability:

1. The design and construction of new buildings and facilities; including both rooms and spaces; site improvements; and public walks.
2. Remodeling, alterations, and rehabilitation of existing construction.
3. Permanent, temporary, and emergency conditions.
4. Both owned and leased buildings and facilities as required by AS 35.10.015.

Exemptions:

1. Facilities or portions thereof used solely for the storage and/or repair of heavy equipment or aircraft.
2. Facilities or portions thereof housing mechanical and electrical equipment.
3. Facilities or portions thereof used solely for bulk storage.

Additions, remodeling, alterations, or rehabilitation may be made to any facility without requiring the entire facility to comply with all requirements of the standards, provided additions, remodeling, alterations, or rehabilitation conform to that required by the standards for a new facility.

Enforcement:

Commissioner, Department of Transportation and Public Facilities or his duly authorized representative.

Remakrs:

Alaska has adopted ANSI A117.1 (1980), with some minor amendments by the Department of Transportation and Public Facilities.

Additional Information:

Department of Transportation and Public Facilities
Division of General Design and Construction
4111 Aviation Drive—Pouch 6900
Anchorage, Alaska 99502
(907) 266-1580

ARIZONA

Legislation and/or Regulations:

Revised statutes sec. 34–401 et seq (1979).

Applicability:

All buildings and facilities used by the public which are constructed in whole or in part by the use of state funds, or the funds of any political subdivision of the state and to all places of public accommodation (i.e., public places of entertainment, amusement, recreation, where food or beverages are sold for consumption on the premises, etc.), including temporary or emergency construction.

Also applicable to elevators in all public buildings and accommodations which have more than one floor level designed, constructed, substantially altered, or undergoing major repairs from and after July 1, 1979.

Exemptions:

Enforcement:

a. Where state funds are utilized:

The state agency responsible for planning and supervising the constructing of such state buildings or facilities.

b. Where state school funds are utilized:

For constructing buildings or facilities for a state university or college, the Arizona Board of Regents.

For constructing buildings or facilities for a junior college, the Governing Body of the Junior College District.

For constructing buildings or facilities for a common school or high school, the Governing Body of the Common School or High School District.

c. Where funds of counties, municipalities or other political subdivisions of the state are utilized for construction of buildings or facilities therefore, the governing bodies thereof.

Remarks:

The text of the standards in the revised statutes generally follows the text of ANSI A117.1 (1961).

Non-compliance by a contractor with the standards and specifications may constitute grounds for suspension or revocation of the contractor's license.

Additional Information:

Division of Building Codes
1645 West Jefferson Street
Phoenix, Arizona 85007
(602) 271-4072

ARKANSAS

Legislation and/or Regulations:

Arkansas Statutes 14–627 et seq (Legislative Act No. 122) as amended by Act 860 and 804 of 1979.

Applicability:

All buildings of assembly, educational institutions, and office buildings which are constructed in whole or in part by the use of state funds, or the funds of any instrumentality of the state.

Exemptions:

Where compliance is impractical in the opinion of the enforcing agency.

Enforcement:

Arkansas State Building Services.

Remarks:

Arkansas has incorporated large portions of the Architectural Transportation Barriers Compliance Board (ATBCB) Guidelines except where state law exceeds guidelines.

Additional Information:

Arkansas State Building Services
700 Medical Arts Building
12th and Marshall Streets
Little Rock, Arkansas 72202
(501) 371-1833

CALIFORNIA

Legislation and/or Regulations:

California Government Code, sec. 4450 et seq (Access to Publicly Funded Public Accommodations by Physically Handicapped Persons); California Administrative Code, sec 7250 et seq (Facilities for Handicapped Persons); California Health and Safety Code, sec 19955 et seq (Access to Privately Funded Public Accommodations by Physically Handicapped Persons).

Applicability:

Buildings, structures, sidewalks, curbs, and related facilities constructed in California by the use of state, county, or municipal funds, or the funds of any political subdivision of the state. Applies to such buildings and facilities intended for use by the public, which have any reasonable availability to, or usage by, physically handicapped persons, including all facilities used for education and instruction including the University of California, the California State University and Colleges, and the various community college districts, which are constructed in whole or in part by the use of state, county, or municipal funds, or the funds of any political subdivision of the state.

Buildings, structures, and facilities, occupied 50% or more, which are leased, rented, contracted, sublet, or hired for periods in excess of two years by any municipal, county, or state division of government, or special district shall be made accessible to and usable by the physically handicapped. Exceptions to this paragraph may be made upon application to, and approval by, the Department of Rehabilitation.

Also covered are public accommodations or facilities constructed in California with private funds. "Public accommodation or facilities" means a building, structure, facility, complex, or improved area which is used by the general public and includes auditoriums, hospitals, theaters, restaurants, hotels, motels, stadiums, convention centers, office buildings, shopping centers, religious facilities, parks, campgrounds, to mention only a few. Both publicly and privately funded housing is also included where apartments (three or more units) are being built. Only one- and two-family units and condominiums are excluded without justifying some form of hardship.

Except as otherwise provided by law, buildings, structures, sidewalks, curbs, and related facilities subject to the provisions of this chapter, shall conform to the building standards published in the State Building Standards Code. Buildings, structures, sidewalks, curbs, and related facilities subject to the provisions of this chapter shall conform to the regulations of the State Architect encompassed in Title 24.

Remodeling work is also required to comply in both publicly and privately-funded facilities. When remodeling costs more than $50,000 (an escalation factor is provided), the path of travel to the area being remodeled, the means of egress, related sanitary facilities, drinking fountains, and public telephones are also required to be made accessible. Less stringent alternates may be allowed for remodeling work as long as access is provided. Where legal or physical constraints prevent access, an appeal is required.

Exemptions:

Administrative authorities designated under "Enforcement" may grant exceptions from the literal requirements of the building standards published in the State Building Standards Code relating to access for the physically handicapped or the other regulations adopted pursuant to this section or permit the use of other methods or materials, but only when it is clearly evident that equivalent facilitation and protection are thereby secured. Where access cannot be provided due to legal or physical constraints, an appeal is required.

Enforcement:

By the Director of the Department of General Services where state funds are utilized for any project or where funds of counties, municipalities, or other political subdivisions are utilized for the construction of elementary, secondary, or community college projects.

By the governing bodies thereof where funds of counties, municipalities, or other political subdivisions are utilized except as otherwise provided above.

By the building department of every city, county, or city and county within its territorial area where private funds are utilized.

Remarks:

California uses regulations prepared by the Office of the State Architect. Where state funds for any building or facility subject to this chapter, or where funds of counties, municipalities, or other political subdivision are utilized for the construction of elementary, secondary, or community college buildings and facilities subject to this chapter, no contract shall be awarded until the Department of General Services has issued written approval stating that the plans and specifications comply with the intent of this chapter.

Additional Information:

State of California
Department of Rehabilitation, Mobility Barriers Section
830 "K" Street Mall
Sacramento, California 95814
(916) 445-3897

State of California
Office of the State Architect
Handicapped Compliance Division
1500 5th Street
Sacramento, California 95814

COLORADO

Legislation and/or Regulations:

1973 Colorado Revised Statutes, Title 9, Art. 5, sec. 9–5–101 through 9–5–110.

Applicability:

All buildings and facilities used by the public which are constructed in whole or in part by the use of state, county, or municipal funds, or the funds of any political subdivision of the state. The intent is to make all buildings and facilities covered by the act accessible to, and functional for, the physically handicapped to, through, and within their doors, without loss of function, space, or facility where the general public is concerned. Requirements apply to permanent buildings.

Exemptions:

Where the authority responsible for the proper construction for the particular governmental department, agency, or unit determines that full compliance with any particular standard or specification is impracticable or unnecessary. Exemption is based on undue hardship on the taxpayers of the governmental unit liable for the cost of compliance in relation to the benefits to the physically handicapped that might be derived from compliance.

Enforcement:

Where state funds are utilized—the State Buildings Division.

Where funds of counties, municipalities, or other political subdivisions are utilized—the governing bodies thereof.

Remarks:

Colorado uses ANSI A117.1 (1980) with minor modifications.

Additional Information:

State Buildings Division
617 State Services Building
1525 Sherman Street
Denver, Colorado 80203
(303) 839-2626

CONNECTICUT

Legislation and/or Regulations:

Connecticut general statutes sec. 19–295A and 19–395L; Connecticut Building Code, Article 21.

Applicability:

All new buildings and building elements constructed under permits issued, and all buildings or building elements constructed or substantially renovated by the state, and the municipality or any other political subdivision of the state. The purpose is to insure accessibility thereto and use by the physically handicapped.

Exemptions:

1. Use Group A, High Hazard Buildings.
2. Use Group B-1, "Storage, Moderate."
3. Use Group B-2, "Storage, Low."
4. Use Group L-1, Residential-Hotels, having fewer than 25 units.
5. Use Group L-2, Residential Multi-Family, having fewer than 25 units.
6. Use Group L-3, "Residential, One- and Two-Family."
7. Use Group E regarding renovations, additions or alterations to existing buildings above the street floor being converted to Use Group E, Business Buildings, provided: (a) each story above the street floor contains less than 2,500 square feet of usable area per floor; and (b) the street floor is renovated or altered to comply with the required handicapped provisions.

Enforcement:

State Building Inspector and State Building Code Standards Committee; Department of Transportation for curb cuts.

Additional Information:

State Building Inspector
Bureau of Public Works
294 Colony Street
Meriden, Connecticut 06450
(203) 238-6011

DELAWARE

Legislation and/or Regulation:

Title 29, Chapter 73 (7/79).

Applicability:

Any facility, or part of any facility and any alteration thereto, which, after July 13, 1979 is:

1. Constructed by or on behalf of the state;
2. Is leased or rented in whole or in part by the state;
3. Is financed in whole or in part by the state or by bonds guaranteed in whole or in part by the state.

Not applicable to any facility designated by the board of electors of any county as a polling place for any election for any official for the state.

Purpose:

To enable handicapped members of society to make use of public facilities with the maximum of safety and independence by providing for the implementation of standards for the elimination of architectural barriers. Chapter is to be construed liberally to achieve that purpose.

Plans, specifications and designs are to be submitted to the Architectural Accessibility Board for approval prior to construction and/or leasing.

Exemptions:

Granted by the Architectural Accessibility Board in writing for "good and sufficient reason."

Enforcement:

By negotiation with the Architectural Accessibility Board; if no solution for compliance is agreed upon, by the Attorney General.

Remarks

The detailed standards adopted by Delaware, effective June 1, 1981, very closely parallel the standards of the federal Architectural and Transportation Barriers Compliance Board.

Additional Information:

Architectural Accessibility Board
P.O. Box 1401
O'Neill Building
Dover, Delaware 19901
(302) 736-4160

FLORIDA

Legislation and/or Regulations:

Chapter 553, Part V, Florida Statutes, (sec 553.45 through 553.48), as amended by 78-235 and 78-333, Laws of Florida—for buildings not owned, nor financed by the state.

Chapter 255.21, Florida Statutes, and Department of General Services Chapter 13D-1 for governmental facilities.

For Non-Government-Funded Buildings and Facilities

Applicability:

Entrances and exits at the first floor or ground floor for licensed business establishments conducting business with the general public and to which the general public is invited. (Not applicable to buildings or facilities existing, under construction, or under contract for construction on October 1, 1974.)

All new buildings, as defined in this part, except those specifically exempted, which the general public may frequent, live in, or work in shall be made accessible as required.

Exemptions:

Building maintenance and storage areas where only employees have occasion to enter and within which work cannot reasonably be performed by the handicapped, unless such areas provide the only path between areas normally used by the handicapped.

Buildings having accessibility at habitable grade levels where no elevator is provided shall not be required to comply at floors above such levels if facilities normally sought and used by the public in such buildings are accessible to and usable by the physically handicapped at such habitable grade levels.

Residential Occupancies:

Two-story and three-story buildings with less than 49 units, having accessibility at habitable grade levels, shall not be required to comply at floors above such levels except where an elevator is provided. Twenty-five percent of the total number of living units shall comply; provided that accessory facilities such as pools, patios, sauna rooms, recreational buildings, laundry rooms, and similar areas shall comply.

Within living units, hallways having no walk-through openings in the sidewalls may be less than 44 inches wide, but no less than 36 inches wide.

Within living units, toilet rooms providing 29-inch clear passage need not comply.

One- and two-family dwellings are exempted from this part.

Handrails shall not be required on ramps 7 feet or less that are integral with walkways, platforms, courtyards, or other paved areas, where the sides of such ramps are protected by curbs or flared sides.

Individual modifications of, or exception from, the literal requirements, may be granted by the Florida Board of Building Codes and Standards in cases of unnecessary or extreme hardship.

Remarks:

Florida has adopted ANSI A117.1—1961 (r 1971), with modifications, for non-government-funded buildings and facilities.

For Government-funded Buildings and Facilities

Applicability:

Any building or facility intended for use by the general public which, in whole or in part, is constructed or altered, or operated as a lessee, by or on behalf of the state or any political subdivision, municipality, or special district thereof, or any public administrative board or authority of the state. Remodeled or altered buildings or facilities:

a. The entire building or facility shall conform with all of the standards if the cost of remodeling or alterations exceeds 50% of the fair market value of the building or facility.
b. The remodeled part of the building or facility shall conform with all of the standards if the cost of the remodeling or alterations is between 20% and 50% of the fair market value of the building or facility.

c. The doors, entrances, exits and public toilet rooms in the remodeled part of the building or facility shall conform with the standards if the cost of remodeling or alterations is less than 20% of the fair market value of the building or facility.

d. Conformance with the standards is not required if the cost of remodeling or altering is less than 20% of the fair market value of the building or facility, or any load bearing structure is not altered, or if the remodeling or alterations are only for the purpose of decor or maintenance of the building or facility.

Exemptions:

In the case of government funded buildings and facilities, by the governmental agency or department responsible for compliance with the standards for the following reasons:

a. The general public and the physically disabled will not, except under extraordinary circumstances, be users of the facility or services of the agency or agencies housed in the building or facility.

b. The services which would be housed in the building or facility covered by the application for modification or waiver are housed to the extent necessary to serve the physically disabled in other facilities which do conform to the standards for special facilities for the disabled.

c. For other reasons at the discretion of the governmental agency or department responsible for compliance with the standards.

Enforcement:

County or municipal buildings or facilities—each county or municipality.

Schools and community colleges—the Department of Education.

State buildings—the Department of General Services, Division of Building Construction and Property Management.

Additional Information:

For non-government-funded buildings or facilities:

Bureau of Housing and Community Development
Division of Local Resource Management
2571 Executive Center Circle, East
Tallahassee, Florida 32301
(904) 488-1536

For government-funded buildings and facilities:

Bureau of Construction
Department of General Services
State of Florida
12 Larson Building
Tallahassee, Florida 32301
(904) 488-6680

GEORGIA

Legislation and/or Regulations:

Sec. 91-1104 through 91-1125.

Applicability:

All government buildings, public buildings, and facilities constructed or substantially renovated after the effective date of the law (eff. 7/1/77). The intent of the law is to eliminate, insofar as possible, unnecessary physical barriers encountered by handicapped or elderly persons whose ability to participate in the social and economic life of Georgia is needlessly restricted when such persons cannot readily use government buildings and facilities used by the public.

The only standards applicable to rental apartment complexes and temporary lodging facilities are to require each entrance to such building, and all doors providing entrance to and within said units to be of a width usable by individuals in wheelchairs, and to the parking standards set forth.

The law applies to permanent buildings, and to temporary or emergency construction.

Exemptions:

By the Safety Fire Commissioner or (where applicable) the Board of Regents of the University System, or the local governing authority having jurisdiction over the building, upon receipt of a sworn written statement that full compliance with a particular standard or specification is impractical, and if there is substantial compliance to the maximum extent practical.

The law shall not be construed to require the equipment and facilities for handicapped persons specified by the law to be provided in public buildings which are not ordinarily open to and used by the general public.

The provisions of the law do not apply to a private single-family residence, duplex, triplex, or condominium.

Enforcement:

a. The Safety Fire Commissioner, except as noted.
b. The Board of Regents with respect to all properties under its jurisdiction.
c. Local governing authorities with respect to public buildings, which include all buildings, structures, streets, sidewalks, walkways, and access thereto, used by the public or in which handicapped or elderly persons may be employed that are constructed or substantially renovated by the use of private funds, including rental complexes of 20 units or more originally constructed after July 1, 1978, and temporary lodging facilities of 20 units or more, which are under their jurisdiction.

Remarks:

Georgia's regulations are closely patterned after ANSI A117.1—1961.

Additional Information:

State Building Administrative Board
166 Pryor Street, S.W.
Atlanta, Georgia 30303
(404) 656-3930

HAWAII

Legislation and/or Regulations:

Revised statutes sec. 103-50 (1969).

Applicability:

Public buildings and facilities by the state or any political subdivision.

Remarks:

Hawaii uses ANSI A117.1—1980.

Additional Information:

Commission on the Handicapped
Old Federal Building
335 Merchant Street
Honolulu, Hawaii 96813
(808) 548-7606

IDAHO

Legislation and/or Regulations:

Code sec. 39-3201 et seq; sec 40-527.

Applicability:

Buildings built by state and local funds, public accommodations, facilities used primarily by the general public as a place of gathering or amusement, including auditoriums or stadiums, streets, curbs, and parking facilities.

Enforcement:

Division of Public Works, and agency funding and/or supervising construction.

Remarks:

Idaho uses ANSI A117.1—1980.

Additional Information:

Administrator for the Division of Public Works
650 West State
Boise, Idaho 83720
(808) 334-3453.

ILLINOIS

Legislation and/or Regulations:

Illinois Facilities for the Handicapped Act, Illinois revised statutes, Chapter 111 1/2, sec. 3701 et seq, and *Accessibility Standards Illustrated* as revised to date.

Applicability:

All public buildings and site facilities of a permanent or temporary nature, open to and usable by the public, including new construction, remodeling, rehabilitation, and historic preservation. A public building is one which is open or used by the general public and may be publicly owned (owned or leased by the state or a political subdivision) or may be privately owned and used as a place of gathering or amusement, such as theaters, restaurants, hotels, or stadiums. Included are office buildings and factories, excluding below grade and second floors less than 15,000 square feet.

New buildings shall be fully accessible per the standards. When public buildings are remodeled for reasons other than accessibility, they shall be made accessible to the extent defined in the standards so that the percentage of the gross floor building area is equal to the remodeling cost divided by the building replacement cost.

Basic accessibility includes parking space, entrance walk, entrance door, horizontal and vertical circulation to all public spaces, notification of emergency, emergency egress provisions, and toilet facilities.

Exemptions:

a. One- and two-family residences.
b. Second and third floors of apartment buildings not served by elevators.
c. Privately owned and financed apartment buildings.
d. Buildings owned/leased by the federal government.

Enforcement:

Publicly-owned buildings (State of Illinois or one of its political subdivisions): the Contracting Authority.

Privately-owned buildings: building permit issuing official.

Remarks:

The Capital Development Board publishes a comprehensively-written and illustrated pamphlet entitled *Accessibility Standards Illustrated*. Numerous specific applications and details are shown therein which have not been shown in this book.

Additional Information:

Capital Development Board
401 South Spring Street
Springfield, Illinois 62706
(217) 782-8529

INDIANA

Legislation and/or Regulations:

Indiana code 1971, I.C. 22-11-1-10, amended; Indiana Construction Rules and Regulations, 1981 Edition, Volume One; 660 I.A.C. 1-1.

Applicability:

"Places of employment and public buildings, and other buildings and structures and their related site improvements as those improvements affect accessibility to the physically handicapped. . . ."

Exemptions:

Provisions need not apply to buildings or areas within buildings which are frequented only by employees and where the work within such areas cannot reasonably be performed by the handicapped unless such areas lie in the path of egress from areas normally used by the handicapped.

Buildings having accessibility at habitable grade levels, where no public elevator is provided, shall not be required to comply at floors above such levels if facilities normally sought and used by the public in such buildings are available at said grade level.

Enforcement:

State Fire Marshal for exiting (Chapter 33).

Administrative Building Council—for accessibility.

Remarks:

Indiana has adopted the 1979 Uniform Building Code with modifications.

Additional Information:

Administrative Building Council
State Building Commissioner
429 North Pennsylvania Street
Indianapolis, Indiana 46204
(317) 633-5433

Indiana State Fire Marshal's Office
100 North Senate Avenue
Room 502, State Office Building
Indianapolis, Indiana 46204
(317) 232-2222

IOWA

Legislation and/or Regulations:

Iowa Administrative Code, 680, Chapter 16. Division 7; Iowa Code, Chapters 103A and 104A.

Applicability:

All buildings, temporary or permanent, and their site facilities, including streets used by the public. Also applicable to multiple-dwelling unit buildings containing five or more individual dwelling units. Rehabilitation and renovation projects shall be made to comply whenever the projects are required by a local building code or the state building code to meet requirements of new construction. The rules and regulations are intended to make all buildings and facilities used by the public accessible to, and functional for, the physically handicapped, to, through, and within their doors, without loss of function, space, or facility where the general public is concerned.

The standards apply to all buildings intended for use by the general public.

Enforcement:

Building Code Commissioner enforces Chapter 104A.

Remarks:

Many of the ANSI A117.1—1980 standards have been adopted. Other Code requirements (sec 601D9) require curb cutouts and ramps in all new curbs constructed at any point along a street which gives access to a crosswalk. Sec 601E6 of the Code requires special identification devices for motor vehicles used by the handicapped and provides for on-street and off-street parking in cities or other political subdivisions.

Additional Information:

Iowa State Building Code
Dept. of Public Safety
Wallace State Office Building
Des Moines, Iowa 50319
(515) 281-3807

KANSAS

Legislation and/or Regulations:

K.S.A 58-1301 et seq; K.S.A. 79-32, 175; (1981).

Applicability:

All public buildings and facilities in Kansas, and additions thereto, and all governmental buildings and facilities, and additions thereto shall conform to ANSI specifications which were approved by ANSI March 3, 1980 (ANSI A117.1—1980), and as may be modified by rules and regulations adopted by the secretary of administration.

Any such building or facility, or addition thereto, to which the provisions of this section were applicable prior to July 1, 1981, shall be governed by the provisions of this section which were in effect on the date the contract for the construction or renovation of such building or facility was entered into.

A building or facility for which a standard has been waived or modified pursuant to K.S.A. 1980 Supp. 58-1307 shall be deemed to conform to the standards established if such building or facility conforms to all such standards which have not been waived or modified and to any modified standard approved for such building or facility pursuant to K.S.A. 1980 Supp. 58-1307.

School buildings shall conform with the requirements of the 1979 edition of the Uniform Building Code, 1979 Uniform Mechanical Code. Electric wiring shall conform to the requirements of the 1981 issue of the National Electric Code. Minimum plumbing requirements shall meet the 1979 edition of the Uniform Plumbing Code.

The construction of mobile, modular, portable or relocatable school buildings shall meet the requirements of the 1976 edition of the Life Safety Code of N.F.P.A. Minimum plumbing requirements shall meet the 1979 edition of the Uniform Plumbing Code.

The construction of all school buildings shall include reasonable provisions for making buildings and facilities accessible to, and usable by, the physically handicapped, as approved by the State Board of Education.

Exemptions:

By waiver or modification of the person, agency, or governing body responsible for enforcement, upon application that full compliance with any standard is impractical or unreasonable.

Enforcement:

a. For all school building construction or renovation: the State Board of Education, by plan approval.
b. For all construction or renovation for which state funds are utilized: the Secretary of Administration.
c. For all construction or renovation where funds of a county, municipality, or other political subdivision are utilized: the governing body thereof or an agency thereof designated by the governing body.
d. For all other construction or renovation of buildings or facilities which are subject to the provisions of the act: the county or district attorney of the county in which the building or facility is located.

Remarks:

Public building or facility is defined as any building, structure, recreational area, street, curbing, or sidewalk, and access thereto, which is used by the public, or in which physically handicapped persons may be employed, and which is constructed, purchased, leased, or rented by the use of private funds. It includes rental apartment complexes and temporary lodging facilities which contain 20 units or more, except that the provisions of the act apply only to 10% of those units and do not apply to recreational facilities which are provided by an apartment complex or temporary lodging facility for the use of its tenants and lodgers.

The definition includes any entrance to or accommodation in any building, structure, or recreational area described above which is available for use by the public or employees, including bathrooms, toilet stalls, dining areas, drinking fountains, phone booths, and lodging rooms or quarters.

Governmental building or facility is similarly defined (excluding the rental apartment complex and temporary lodging facilities section), which is constructed, purchased, leased, or rented in whole or in part by moneys appropriated by the state or any political subdivision thereof, to the extent not required otherwise by federal law.

Kansas provides a tax credit for making all or any part of a taxpayer's principal dwelling accessible to the handicapped (K.S.A. 79-32, 176).

Statute incorporates ANSI A117.1—1961 by reference.

Additional Information:

Architectural Division
Department of Administration
State Office Building
Topeka, Kansas 66612
(913) 296-3811

KENTUCKY

Legislation and/or Regulations:

KRS Chapter 198B; 815 KAR 7:060.

Applicability:

New construction: The regulation is mandatory to and in all buildings and facilities, including both rooms and spaces, site improvements, exterior facilities and public walks, as follows:

1. Storage, miscellaneous, and temporary occupancies in which the total occupant load is in excess of 100 persons or 20,000 square feet or 3 stories.
2. Factory and industrial occupancies in which the total occupant load is in excess of 100 persons or 20,000 square feet.
3. Business occupancies in which the total occupant load is in excess of 100 persons or 10,000 square feet.
4. Mercantile occupancies in which the total occupancy load is in excess of 100 persons, 3,000 square feet of consumer area or 10,000 square feet of total floor area.
5. Churches, parochial and private schools, and other similar non-public assembly type occupancies in which the total occupant load is in excess of 250 persons or 3,200 square feet.
6. Assembly occupancies (other than those in subsection 5) in which the total occupant load is in excess of 50 persons or 1,500 square feet total area.
7. Residential occupancies, with the exception of single-family dwellings, duplexes, and multi-family housing projects of less than 25 dwelling units.
8. Institutional occupancies, with the exception of child day care facilities providing care for less than 13 children.
9. All buildings and facilities which are leased or owned by the state, county, city, or other municipal corporations, regardless of type of use, occupant load or total square footage.
10. Any establishment which is physically located within any building or facility otherwise covered by this section, or which is physically located within the premises of any such covered establishment, and which also holds itself out as serving patrons of such covered establishments.
11. All gasoline service stations, regardless of size or occupant capacity.
12. Any building with an occupant load, occupancy type, or size not listed in this section shall be exempt from the requirements of this regulation as a "small business concern."

Existing Buildings:

a. Alterations and repairs may be made to any structure without requiring other areas of the existing structure to comply, provided such new work conforms to that of a new structure.
b. Additions to an existing facility shall comply with the standards established; however, the existing portion need not comply provided such addition does not result in decreased accessibility.
c. Remodeling involving major structural changes to a building shall require full compliance with all applicable provisions.
d. All buildings or facilities owned or leased by state, city, or county governmental bodies shall be accessible and shall not be considered a "small business concern."

Exemptions:

One- and two-family dwellings which are single-family detached units or duplexes.

Multi-family residential buildings or projects consisting of 24 units or less.

The restoration or authentic reconstruction of buildings designated as historic properties by the Kentucky Heritage Commission or the National Register of Historic Places.

Any building with an occupant load, occupancy type, or size not listed in this section shall be exempt from the requirements of this regulation as a "small business concern."

Modification of the technical provisions may be allowed where such modification provides equal facilitation.

Enforcement:

By the local building official or state building official having plan review and inspection responsibility under the Kentucky Building Code. Enforcing authority is the Department of Housing, Buildings, and Construction Division of Building Codes Enforcement.

Remarks:

Kentucky's accessibility standard is based on ANSI A117.1—1980.

Additional Information:

Department of Housing, Buildings, and
Construction
Division of Building Codes Enforcement
U.S. 127 South
Frankfort, Kentucky 40601
(502) 564-8090

Elevators Division
(502) 564-3626

LOUISIANA

Legislation and/or Regulations:

R.S. 40:1731 et seq (rev. 1981).

Applicability:

New public facilities or governmental facilities (defined as one for which a construction contract has been signed on or after January 1, 1978).

A public facility means a building, structure, or improved area to which the general public customarily has access or utilizes for purposes of education, employment, transportation, recreation; for the purchase, rental, or acquisition of goods and services; or housing other than privately owned one- or two-family dwellings. A public facility does not include a governmental facility.

A governmental facility means a building, structure, or improved area utilized for purposes of education, employment, housing other than privately owned one- and two-family dwellings, transportation, or recreation or for the purchase, rental, or acquisition of goods or services and which is:

a. Owned by, or on behalf of, the state or its political subdivisions.
b. Leased or rented in whole or in part by the state or its political subdivisions after January 1, 1978. A public facility which is the subject of a lease or rental agreement before September 9, 1977 shall not be required to meet ANSI standards contained in this Part for the term of the existing lease or rental agreement but shall be brought into compliance before a lease or rental agreement is renewed. However, no elevator will be required to be installed in existing facilities where services provided therein are made conveniently available to all physically handicapped persons.
c. Financed in whole or in part by a grant or loan made or guaranteed by the state or its political subdivisions after September 9, 1977.
d. Constructed, purchased, leased, or rented in whole or in part by the use of federal funds except as otherwise provided by federal law.

Exceptions to the Foregoing:

1. Building maintenance, freight loading, and storage areas where only employees have occasion to enter and within which the work cannot reasonably be performed by any handicapped individual, unless such areas provide the only path between areas normally used by the public.
2. Public facilities which are utilized for the purchase, rental, acquisition of goods and services with five thousand square feet or less per floor, which are accessible at habitable grade levels shall not be required to comply at floors above such levels except where an elevator is to be provided.
3. Public facilities for accommodation (i.e., hotels, motels, apartment buildings, dormitories, resort lodges, and such other uses) which are two-story and three-story buildings with less than forty-nine units, which are accessible at habitable grade levels, shall not be required to comply at floors above such levels except where an elevator is provided. Such facilities for accommodation containing less than fifteen dwelling units are exempted from the requirements except that the use area openings, passageways to exits, and exit discharge areas of such facilities for accommodation shall be at least thirty inches wide in compliance with ANSI standards. The requirements shall apply to at least 5% or at least one dwelling unit in complexes of 15 dwelling units or more.

All public and governmental facilities constructed or remodeled in accordance with ANSI standards which are in compliance therewith, shall display the international symbol of accessibility indicating the location of such facilities.

Exemptions:

By the State Fire Marshal in cases of practical difficulty or unnecessary hardship, but only when it is clearly evident that equivalent facilitation or protection is secured.

Enforcement:

State Fire Marshal and local building code authorities and health authorities.

Remarks:

Existing governmental facilities shall be altered so as to comply with ANSI standards no later than January 1, 1982 except in those situations where such compliance is not practicably feasible or economically reasonable as determined by the State Fire Marshal in consultation with the office of rehabilitative services. However, no elevator will be required to be installed in existing facilities where services provided therein are made conveniently available to all physically handicapped facilities.

Section shall not be construed to require the remodeling of public facilities solely to provide accessibility and usability to the physically handicapped when alterations would not otherwise be undertaken.

Additional Information:

Office of Human Development
Division of Vocational Rehabilitation
2097 Beaumont Drive
Baton Rouge, Louisiana 70806
(504) 925-4967

State Fire Marshal
325 Loyola Street
Room 109
New Orleans, Louisiana 70112
(504) 568-5500

MAINE

Legislation and/or Regulations:

25 MRSA sec. 2701 et seq; 5 MRSA sec. 4591 et seq.

Applicability:

Public accommodations and places of employment constructed, remodeled, or enlarged after January 1, 1982:

a. Buildings and facilities constructed specifically as a place of public accommodation, or when the estimated total costs for remodeling or enlarging an existing building exceeds $250,000.

b. Buildings and facilities constructed specifically as a place of employment, or when the estimated total costs for remodeling or enlarging an existing building exceeds $100,000.

c. Structures to which the public customarily has access and utilizes, and which is constructed, in whole or in part, with funds of the state or its political subdivisions; or a structure specifically intended as: (1) a place where five persons or more will be employed; or (2) public housing (a building which includes a minimum of ten family units), and which is constructed, in whole or in part with either state or federal funds.

d. All construction, remodeling, and enlarging begun after January 1, 1982 of buildings subject to this chapter shall comply with the standards.

Existing Facilities:

a. Buildings or facilities constructed specifically as a place of public accommodation on or after September 1, 1974, but before January 1, 1982, or when the estimated costs for remodeling or enlarging an existing building exceeds $250,000 and the remodeling or enlarging is begun before January 1, 1982 shall meet the required standards.

b. Any building or facility constructed specifically as a place of employment on or after September 1, 1974, but before January 1, 1982, or when the estimated total costs for remodeling or enlarging an existing building exceed $100,000, and the remodeling or enlarging is begun before January 1, 1982, shall comply with the public accommodation requirements relating to walks, entries, restroom facilities, and doors.

Enforcement:

The state, county, or municipal authority who reviews the plans for any building covered by this chapter.

Where state funds are used, including for space in buildings rented or leased by the state pursuant to agreements concluded with effective dates of January 1, 1982, or later, the Director of Public Improvements; except in respect to elementary and secondary school buildings, it shall be the Commissioner of Educational and Cultural Services.

Remarks:

Maine uses ANSI A117.1—1980.

Additional Information:

Bureau of Public Improvements
State Office Building
Augusta, Maine 04333
(207) 289-2881

Department of Educational and Cultural Services
State House Station 23
Augusta, Maine 04333
(207) 289-2321

MARYLAND

Legislation and/or Regulations:

Article 41, sec. 257JK, Annotated Code of Maryland.

Applicability:

All levels and areas of new buildings, structures, facilities, and sites constructed for use by employees or the general public except:

1. Public buildings, structures, or improved areas leased to or owned by the state or its political subdivisions where work is to be performed under regulations of the Department of General Services;
2. One- or two-family dwelling units, use group R3 and R4, sec. 209;
3. Miscellaneous and temporary buildings, use group T, sec. 211.

All additions to existing buildings, structures, facilities, and sites shall be considered new construction and shall comply with the requirements of sec. 106.4.

Whenever the use or occupancy of an existing building or structure or portion of it is changed, the building or structure or portion shall be brought into conformity with the requirements for new buildings in accordance with sec. 105, except for existing town or row type houses where the location of an entrance is such that installation of a ramp, as specified under Regulation .04, would not be possible.

Buildings, structures, facilities, or sites which are to be repaired, remodeled, or rehabilitated in excess of 50% of their current physical value (to be determined by the building official or the Department of Economic and Community Development) shall comply with the requirements of this Code, except for existing town or row type houses where the location of entrances is such that installation of ramps as specified under Regulation .04 would not be possible.

Exemptions:

By the Director, Division of Codes Administration, Department of Economic and Community Development for hardship because of nature of use, occupancy, or other factors. It shall be considered only when the application for a building permit has been reviewed and denied by the local authority on specific grounds under this Code.

Enforcement:

By the local subdivision or other public agencies having jurisdiction over buildings, structures, facilities, or sites.

Remarks:

Maryland has incorporated sections of the Building Officials and Code Administrators International Basic Building Code (BOCA), 1978 Edition. Reference to sections 105, 106, 109, 202, 209, 211, 315, 610, 612, 615, 616, 625, and 1217 are cross-referenced to that Code.

Additional Information:

Division of Codes Administration
Department of Economic and Community Development
2525 Riva Road
Annapolis, Maryland 21401
(301) 269-2701

MASSACHUSETTS

Legislation and/or Regulations:

General Laws Chapter 22, sec. 13A; 521 CMR 1.00 et seq.

Applicability:

Construction, reconstruction, alterations, remodeling, and change of use, of all public buildings and privately financed buildings open and used by the public. Five percent of the units in lodging or residential facilities for hire, rent, or lease, containing 20 or more units.

Public buildings are defined as those constructed by the commonwealth or any political subdivision thereof with public funds and open to public use, including but not limited to those constructed by public housing authorities, the Massachusetts Port Authority, the Massachusetts Parking Authority, The Massachusetts Turnpike Authority, the Massachusetts Bay Transportation Authority, or building authorities of any public educational institution, or their successors; and privately financed buildings that are open to and used by the public.

Buildings that are open to and used by the public include, but are not limited to, transportation terminals, institutional buildings, commercial buildings exceeding two stories in height in which more than 40 persons are employed, buildings having places of assembly of a capacity of more than 150 persons, hotels, motels, dormitories, public parking garages or lots with a capacity of 25 or more automobiles, public sidewalks and ways, public areas of apartment buildings and condominiums containing 12 or more units and of funeral homes, and rest rooms and public areas of shopping centers and restaurants.

Exemptions:

By the Architectural Barriers Board for a modification of, or substitution for, rules or regulations for cases of impracticability.

The Board may vary the applicability of the Regulations in the following instances:

1. Where the requirements of public toilet rooms may be impractical, private toilet or lavatory rooms may be allowed.
2. If the function or service performed on upper floors in buildings is also available on an accessible level, a variance on the requirements for an elevator may be granted.
3. Where private offices, power maintenance, or other such private areas in an otherwise public building, which because of their intended use, are normally not open to and used by the public, they may be exempted.
4. A government building not open to public use and used by the public, such as a power plant or garage for government vehicles, may be exempted.
5. When a building is occupied for two or more uses not included in the same use group, the provisions applying to each use shall apply to such parts of the building, whether horizontally or vertically, as come within that use. In case of conflicting provisions, the regulations securing the greater accessibility for the handicapped shall apply. If a building has multi-purpose use, the regulations shall apply to the entire building by virtue of the combined use if any one of the uses is within the jurisdiction of the Board.
6. For historical buildings owned or protected by the government, the Board may allow alternate accessibility.
7. A building owned, controlled, or operated by a private club or organization which is not ordinarily open to the general public may be exempted from the regulations to those portions of the premises which are not open to public use.

Enforcement:

Architectural Barriers Board; state and local building inspectors.

Remarks:

In addition to those illustrated in this book, Massachusetts has special requirements for governmental facilities, commercial buildings, shopping centers, restaurants, funeral homes, lodging or residential facilities, hotels, motels, educational institutions, health facilities, recreational facilities, detention facilities, and transportation terminals.

Additional Information:

Architectural Barriers Board
Room 1319
McCormack State Office Building
1 Ashburton Place
Boston, Massachusetts 02108
(617) 727-6257

MICHIGAN

Legislation and/or Regulations:

Michigan Compiled Laws: sec. 125.1351 et seq; sec. 125.1501 et seq; Michigan Administrative Code R 408.30101 et seq.

Applicability:

Applies to all levels and areas used by the general public, employees, persons visiting or on the premises for any reason, and to all use groups except R-3, R-4, and T. Areas of a building or structure, such as mechanical equipment rooms, machine rooms, and penthouses housing equipment, may be excluded from the requirements. Buildings and structures, and facilities within buildings and structures, meeting the requirements for barrier-free design shall be clearly identified with the international symbol of accessibility for the handicapped.

Use group R-1: At least one bedroom unit for every 25 bedroom units or fraction thereof in use group R-1 buildings shall be made accessible to, and usable by, physically handicapped persons. The bedroom units allocated for the physically handicapped shall be proportionately distributed throughout the range of size and price of the total bedroom units.

Use group R-2: In addition to multiple dwellings in this use group, the requirements for barrier-free design shall apply to complexes and group housing. The requirements shall not apply to dormitories, lodging houses, and boarding houses having accommodations for less than 20 individuals. At least one dwelling unit for every 25 dwelling units, or fraction thereof, shall be accessible to, and usable by, physically handicapped persons, and shall be proportionately distributed throughout the ranges of sizes of the total dwelling units.

Exemptions:

By the Barrier-Free Design Board.

Also, repairs, alterations, and additions necessary for the preservation, restoration, or continued use of an existing building or structure which has been designated by the Michigan history division, department of state, as being on the national register of historic places or the state register of historic sites, or the building or structure is eligible for either register.

Enforcement:

By the building official (normally the county or one or more of its governmental subdivisions)

Remarks:

Subject to a number of exceptions, the Michigan building code has incorporated the provisions of the BOCA Basic Building Code, 1978 Edition.

Additional Information:

Bureau of Construction Codes
State Secondary Complex
7150 Harris Drive
P.O. Box 30015
Lansing, Michigan 48909
(517) 322-1701

MINNESOTA

Legislation and/or Regulations:

Minnesota statutes ann., sec. 471.465 et seq; MCAR sec. 1.15501 et seq.

Applicability:

All buildings except the following:

1. Group R-3, Group R Division 4 and M Occupancies.
2. Temporary buildings.
3. Buildings not exceeding 150 square feet in floor area need not be provided with sanitation facilities for the handicapped specified in 2 MCAR sec. 1.15503.
4. One-story buildings, other than service stations, not exceeding 2,000 square feet in floor area need not be provided with sanitation facilities for the handicapped specified in 2 MCAR sec. 1.15503 when approved by the Building Official.
5. Floors of buildings not used by the general public and on which handicapped persons cannot be employed because of the nature of the work.
6. Group R-1 Occupancies in which dwelling units are individually owned, sanitation facilities for the handicapped specified in 2 MCAR sec. 1.15503 and other facilities for the handicapped specified in 2 MCAR sec. 1.15504 need not be provided.

Enforcement:

Commissioner of Administration (Building Codes Division).

Additional Information:

Department of Administration
Division of Building Codes and Standards
408 Metro Square Building
St. Paul, Minnesota 55101
(612) 296-4626

MISSISSIPPI

Legislation and/or Regulations:

Code ann. sec. 43-6-101 et seq.

Applicability:

All buildings of assembly, educational institutions, office buildings, or other public buildings constructed in whole or in part by the use of state, county, or municipal funds, or the funds of any instrumentality of the state, except where such compliance is impractical in the opinion of the State Board of Health.

The State Building Commission, the boards of supervisors, the governing authorities of each municipality, and the governing authorities of all political subdivisions of the state, pursuant to an order of the state board of health, shall cause to be constructed such entrance ramps to facilitate ingress and egress in each public building under the supervision of the said governing bodies.

Exemptions:

By the State Board of Health for cases of impracticability.

Enforcement:

State Board of Health.

Additional Information:

State Board of Health
2413 North First Street
P.O. Box 1700
Jackson, Mississippi 39205
(601) 354-6646

MISSOURI

Legislation and/or Regulations:

Missouri revised statutes, Chapter 8, sec. 8.610 et seq.

Applicability:

All buildings and facilities for public use and assembly constructed in whole or in part by the use of state funds, or the funds of any political subdivision of the state.

New construction and improvements (except those for which contracts have been entered into prior to August 13, 1976) in public parks, recreational areas, and rest areas, constructed or supported wholly or partially by public funds, shall be planned and executed in a manner that will enable handicapped persons and senior citizens to share, as fully as practicable, in the enjoyment of these areas and facilities. Opportunities to participate in fishing, picnicking, sunbathing, and other outdoor recreational pursuits shall be provided as fully as practicable. Facilities shall be equipped with such devices as are necessary for appropriate use by handicapped and senior citizens.

Any repair or maintenance of any building, facility, or other property of the state of Missouri undertaken after September 28, 1973, involving the use of federal funds or other federal assistance shall, whenever practicable, conform to the standards.

Exemptions:

Any building or facility for which the contract for planning or design was awarded prior to September 28, 1973.

Deviations from the standards may be permitted where conformance is impractical and where the method, material, and dimension used in lieu thereof does not create a hazard.

Permission to deviate from the standards may be granted only by the commissioner of administration.

Enforcement:

1. Where state school funds are utilized—the state department of elementary and secondary education.
2. Where state funds are utilized—the division, agency, or instrumentality of the state having jurisdictional control of the design function of the work.
3. Where funds of counties, municipalities, or other political subdivisions are utilized—the governing bodies thereof.

Additional Information:

Department of Elementary and Secondary Education
P.O. Box 480
Jefferson City, Missouri 65102
(314) 751-4212

MONTANA

Legislation and/or Regulations:

Montana code ann., sec. 50-60-201 and 50-60-203.

Applicability:

For buildings and facilities utilizing state or local funds.

For buildings covered by state code enforcement program, the requirements are enforced in all buildings except residential buildings containing less than five dwelling units and private garages or storage buildings for the owner's own use.

When local government enforces the code, it applies to all structures.

Enforcement:

Department of Administration, Building Codes Division; local governments certified by the state to enforce the codes.

Remarks:

Montana uses the provisions contained in the Uniform Building Code, which have been incorporated by reference. State code is the maximum-minimum code to be used by all levels of government enforcing the code.

Additional Information:

Department of Administration
Building Codes Division
Capitol Station
Helena, Montana 59620
(406) 449-3933

NEBRASKA

Legislation and/or Regulations:

Revised state statutes sec. 72-1101 et seq.

Applicability:

All buildings and facilities used by the public which are constructed or remodeled in whole or in part by the use of state, county or municipal funds, or the funds of any political subdivision of the state. After January 1, 1977, such standards shall apply to all buildings and facilities which shall be constructed or remodeled within Nebraska and where the public is invited to enter or remain upon the premises as business invitees.

Where remodeling projects require expenditures exceeding 50% of the replacement value of the structure over any consecutive three-year period, the total structure shall comply with the required provisions. If remodeling projects are less than 50% of the replacement value of that structure, the area being remodeled shall comply.

Exemptions:

By the Public Buildings Safety Advisory Committee for reasons of impracticability.

The provisions do not apply to buildings, structures, or installations, or portions thereof, used for agricultural purposes or heavy industry including but not limited to repair shops, railroad yards and any other business or industrial building where the presence of handicapped persons could or would tend to place them in a position of potential hazard to their person, but shall apply to any separate portions of such buildings, structures, or installations where managerial functions are conducted if the entry to, and presence of, handicapped persons in such separate portions of such buildings, structures or, installations would not tend to place them in a position of potential hazard to their person.

Enforcement:

The State Fire Marshal; appropriate officials of local political subdivisions responsible for review and approval of building plans.

Additional Information:

State Fire Marshal
State Office Building—6th Floor
P.O. Box 94677
Lincoln, Nebraska 68509
(402) 471-2027

NEVADA

Legislation and/or Regulations:

Nevada revised statutes sec. 338.180.

"A Guidebook to: The Minimum Federal Requirements for Accessible Designs" adopted pursuant to NRS sec. 338.180.

Applicability:

All buildings and facilities used by the public insofar as possible. All public buildings and facilities by the state or by a political subdivision, district, authority, board, or public corporation or entity of the state shall provide facilities and features for the physically handicapped so that buildings normally used by the public are constructed with entrance ramps, toilet facilities, drinking fountains, doors, and public telephones accessible to and usable by the physically handicapped.

Enforcement:

Nevada Public Works Board.

Remarks:

Nevada requires buildings and facilities to conform to the American Standard specifications effective when the plans and specifications are approved, as published by the American Standards Association.

Additional Information:

State of Nevada Public Works Board
505 East King Street
Carson City, Nevada 89710
(702) 885-4870

NEW HAMPSHIRE

Legislation and/or Regulations:

Revised statutes ann. 275-C; the Architectural Barrier-Free Design Code for the State of New Hampshire.

Applicability:

Construction or substantial rehabilitation of publicly funded buildings or one partially or fully funded with federal, state, county, or municipal funds.

Educational institutions, which include public schools, universities, and other publicly funded institutions, devoted to the education of New Hampshire citizens and others.

Dormitories.

Publicly funded health institutions or facilities in which people suffering from physical limitations because of health or age are harbored for medical or other care or treatment, including, but not limited to, hospitals, clinics, sanatoriums, boarding or rest homes, convalescent or nursing homes, rehabilitation centers, alcohol and drug detoxification centers, community health centers, and mental health centers.

Publicly funded recreational facilities including, but not limited to, rinks, swimming pools, gymnasiums, arenas, stadiums, and other such facilities.

Parks, campsites, and roadside parks which are publicly funded.

Areas of detention facilities open to the public in detention facilities including, but not limited to, those publicly funded buildings designed for the detention of people under restraint including, but not limited to, jails, prisons, reformatories, mental rehabilitation facilities, and similar uses. Inaccessible secure areas are exempt provided that separate, secure accessible areas are available to the physically handicapped detained person.

Exemptions:

Waivers, substitutions, or modifications by the Permanent Subcommittee on Architectural Barrier-Free Design of the Governor's Commission for the Handicapped for reasons of historic preservation requirements or compelling public interest.

Enforcement:

By local or state agencies having jurisdiction over a given project. Local, state, or federal Codes, if more stringent than the standards, will take precedence and apply.

Additional Information:

Governor's Commission for the Handicapped
6 Loudon Road
Concord, New Hampshire 03301
(603) 271-2773

NEW JERSEY

Legislation and/or Regulations:

Statutes ann. sec. 52:32-1 et seq; sec. 52:32-4 et seq; sec. 52:32-5 et seq; sec. 52:32-11 et seq; sec. 52-14 et seq.

Uniform Construction Code, Chapter 23, Title 5, New Jersey Administrative Code.

Barrier-Free Design Regulations (7/15/77) and Revision #1 (1/15/79).

Applicability:

Construction or remodeling of all buildings, structures and facilities used by the general public except:

1. One- to four-family residences (self-contained units independently constructed or separated from similar units by party walls, fire walls, or separation walls).
2. Townhouses (privately owned or rented dwelling units of two or more levels of living space where the separation between levels is more than 12 inches).
3. Warehouse storage areas.
4. All buildings classified as hazardous occupancies.
5. Historic buildings (existing buildings identified and classified by the state and or local government authority as historic buildings) subject to the approval of the Board of Appeals when making provisions for the handicapped cannot be accomplished without major alteration or changing of the character of the building.
6. A building permit issued under valid construction regulations prior to the effective date of these regulations shall remain valid, and the construction of any building or structure may be completed pursuant to and in accordance with said permit. The construction of any building or structure started before the promulgation of these regulations that did not, as of the date of the beginning of the construction, require a construction permit, may be completed without a construction permit.

Exemptions:

In cases of practical difficulty, exceptions may be granted from the specific requirements and specifications, or other methods and materials may be used, but only when it is clearly evident that equivalent facilitation and protection for the physically handicapped are thereby secured.

Appeals may be granted by the established board of appeals in the case of municipal enforcing agencies, or by the appointed hearing official if the Department of Community Affairs is the enforcing agency, or the State Treasurer (attention: Director, Division of Building and Construction) with respect to buildings of the state of New Jersey, owned by the state, and any of its departments, divisions, bureaus, boards, councils, authorities, or other agencies.

Note: Appeals and variations are outlined in sec. 5:23-2.10 and 5:23-2.4 of the Uniform Construction Code.

Enforcement:

Any municipality that has established jurisdiction for code enforcement, or the State Department of Community Affairs in the case of municipalities that have relinquished jurisdiction.

The Department of the Treasury, Division of Building and Construction, with respect to all buildings constructed or remodeled by the state of New Jersey, owned by the state, and any of its departments, divisions, bureaus, boards, councils, authorities, or other agencies.

Additional Information:

State of New Jersey
Department of Community Affairs
Division of Housing
Bureau of Construction Code Enforcement
620 West State Street
CN 805
Trenton, New Jersey 08625
(609) 292-6364

New Jersey Construction Code Regulations and Barrier-Free Design Regulations with Amendment may be ordered from:

New Jersey Department of Community Affairs
Bureau of Construction Code Enforcement
CN 800 PUBLICATION
Trenton, New Jersey 08625
Attention: Publications

NEW MEXICO

Legislation and/or Regulations:

Statutes ann. sec. 60-13-44.D,G; sec. 15-3-7,8; sec. 67-3-64.

Applicability:

Any public buildings constructed through expenditures of state, county, or municipal funds, including temporary or emergency conditions.

All commercial projects shall comply with the 1979 Edition of the Uniform Building Code.

Exemptions:

Exceptions for commercial projects as contained in the 1979 Uniform Building Code.

Enforcement:

Director of the Property Control Division, Department of Finance, Construction and Industries Commission.

Enforcement for commercial projects: Construction Industries Commission.

Remarks:

New Mexico has adopted ANSI A117.1—1980 with some minor modifications.

Additional Information:

General Construction Bureau
Construction Industries Division
Bataan Memorial Building
Santa Fe, New Mexico 87503
(505) 827-5571

NEW YORK

Legislation and/or Regulations:

Public Building Law sec. 50 et seq; Executive Law sec. 370 et seq; Highway Law sec. 330, sec. 51 and 52.

New York State Building Construction Code, and amendments to the State Building Construction Code C215(824) et seq.

Applicability:

All buildings shall be provided with an exterior accessible route, interior accessible route, usable spaces, accessible elements and facilities. Spaces and rooms intended for the general public and occupant use shall be accessible, including: business spaces, mercantile spaces, industrial spaces, assembly spaces, institutional spaces, toilet rooms, bathrooms, bathing facilities, and shower rooms.

Where seating, tables, and work surfaces are provided in usable spaces, at least one, and not less than 5%, shall comply with ANSI A117.1—1980 requirements.

Where storage facilities such as cabinets, shelves, closets, or drawers are provided in usable spaces, at least one storage facility of each type shall comply with ANSI A117.1—1980 requirements.

Exceptions:

1. For assembly occupancies having a mezzanine or balcony which provides the same view as the main floor, accessibility to the mezzanine or balcony shall not be required, provided toilet rooms are on the main floor.
2. For restaurants, dining rooms, and similar occupancies having the same services on levels other than the main floor, accessibility to such levels shall not be required, provided that toilet rooms are on the main floor.
3. For buildings in which the intended use is the storage of goods or merchandise, the only requirement shall be accessibility at the primary entrance.

Enforcement:

Commissioner of Housing; State Building Code Council. The body with design approval authority shares responsibilities.

Additional Information:

State Building Code Council
Two World Trade Center
New York, New York 10047
(212) 488-7126

Division of Housing and Community Renewal
Two World Trade Center
New York, New York 10047

NORTH CAROLINA

Legislation and/or Regulations:

General statutes sec. 143-138; North Carolina State Building Code.

Applicability:

The standard applies to all buildings and facilities regulated by the North Carolina State Building Code, with the exception of single- and two-family detached dwellings in accordance with the following:

Residential—A (Sleeping Occupancy)—Apartments, hotels, motels, dormitories as specifically provided for.

Business—B—B-1 (Office Occupancy)—All these buildings except that the requirements may be waived by the enforcing authority where the code makes these requirements applicable for small buildings which are already built. B-2 (Shopping)—Mercantile stores and shopping centers.

Schools—C (Educational Facilities)—Applies to all buildings and as specifically provided for with respect to residential requirements.

Jails, Prisons, Mental Hospitals, Orphanages, and Nursing Homes and Hospitals—D—Applies to all public areas and as specifically provided for with respect to residential requirements.

Assembly—E—Stadiums, Grandstands, Theaters, Dance Halls, Skating Rinks, etc.—Applies to all public areas of these buildings and as specifically provided. Assembly areas which are raised above the floor or on an incline need not meet the requirements, provided spectator areas which are accessible for the handicapped are designed as part of such an assembly.

Storage—F—Airplane Hangars, Garages, and Warehouses.

Industrial—G—Industrial Plants—applies to all these buildings except that the requirements may be waived by the enforcing authority for garages with attendants, heavy storage or industrial areas, and other similar type occupancies.

The standard is mandatory on all new construction of buildings and facilities as defined and identified. The addition of a wing unit to an existing facility shall be considered new construction, of and by itself, and would therefore be mandated under the standard.

The standard is not mandatory for the restoration or authentic reconstruction of a historic structure designated by the State Preservation Officer pursuant to General Statutes 121.8 and N.C.A.C. 4G.0600.

Enforcement:

Local enforcement officer in cooperation with the State Commissioner of Insurance and other State Officials with responsibility under G.S. 143-139.

Additional Information:

Engineering and Building Codes Division
North Carolina Department of Insurance
P.O. Box 26387
Raleigh, North Carolina 27611
(919) 733-3901

NORTH DAKOTA

Legislation and/or Regulations:

North Dakota Century Code sec. 48-02-19; sec. 23-13-12, 13; sec. 40-31-01.1; sec. 39-01-15.

Applicability:

All public buildings and facilities constructed, in whole or in part, from funds of the state or of its political subdivisions, except:

1. Institutions under the supervision and control of the Board of Higher Education, provided, however, that at least two institutions of higher education shall be so constructed or remodeled so as to make all programs offered therein accessible as required.
2. Areas, offices, or levels of public buildings not used for activities open to members of the general public.

Exemptions:

By the State Construction Superintendent in cases of practical difficulty, unnecessary hardship, or extreme differences.

Enforcement:

State Construction Superintendent.

Remarks:

North Dakota has adopted ANSI A117.1—1961.

Additional Information:

Superintendent of Construction
Department of State
State Capitol Building
Bismarck, North Dakota 58505
(701) 224-2905

OHIO

Legislation and/or Regulations:

Ohio Revised Code sec. 3781.111; Ohio Administrative Code rule 4101:2-5-15.

Applicability:

All buildings or portions thereof open to the public except:

Nontransient residential structures, including industrialized (factory-built) units, one-, two-, and three-family dwelling units, townhouses, and condominiums, *or*

Commercial establishments containing less than 10,000 square feet.

Lodging facilities owned by the state or any political subdivision of the state are considered in compliance if 10% of the units are accessible.

Enforcement:

Municipal or county building inspection departments certified by the Board of Building Standards. In non-certified areas, the State Division of Factory and Building Inspection.

Remarks:

As of July 1, 1982, Ohio uses the 1981 BOCA Code, updated to sec. 515 with 1982 supplement.

Additional Information:

Board of Building Standards
Department of Industrial Relations
2323 West Fifth Avenue
Columbus, Ohio 43216
(614) 466-3316

OKLAHOMA

Legislation and/or Regulations:

Statutes ann. 61 sec. 11 et seq.

Applicability:

Buildings and facilities built by state or local funds. Includes new or altered buildings that increase floor area by 25% or more within a 12-month period.

Enforcement:

State Board of Public Affairs.

Remarks:

Oklahoma has adopted ANSI A117.1—1961 (except for elevators).

Additional Information:

State Board of Public Affairs
306 State Capitol Building
Oklahoma City, Oklahoma 73105
(405) 521-2111

OREGON

Legislation and/or Regulations:

Oregon revised statutes 447.210 et seq and 456.750 et seq.

Applicability:

Every government or public building or portion thereof. Where there is a conflict between a general requirement and a specific requirement for an individual occupancy, the specific requirement shall be applicable.

Government buildings include all buildings and structures defined in ORS 447.210 to 447.280 used by the public which are constructed, purchased, leased, or rented in whole or part by the use of state, county, or municipal funds, or the funds of any political subdivision of the state; and to the extent not required otherwise by federal law or regulations or not beyond the power of the state to regulate, all buildings and structures used by the public which are constructed, purchased, leased, or rented in whole or in part by the use of federal funds.

Public buildings (privately owned and publicly used) as they relate to architectural barriers, include all buildings and structures used by the public that are constructed, purchased, leased, or rented in whole or in part by the use of private funds where the building or structure has a ground area of more than 4,000 square feet or is more than 20 feet in height from the top surface of the lowest flooring to the highest interior overhead finish of the building or structure.

Exceptions:

1. No need to apply to more than 5% of the dwelling units or guest rooms of any Group R, Division 1 Occupancy building classified as government or public buildings.
2. Not applicable in buildings unless classified as government or public buildings, as defined above.
3. Existing government or public buildings, except that existing architectural barriers, in the area of work, shall be removed, in part or in total, to a cost not to exceed 25% of the value of the work being done within any 12-month period, in government and public buildings.

Exemptions:

By the municipal appeals board, where full compliance with a particular architectural barrier standard or specification is impractical in that it would defeat the purpose of the project proposed or in process.

Enforcement:

Department of Commerce.

Remarks:

Oregon has adopted many of the provisions against barriers contained in the 1979 edition of the Uniform Building Code.

Additional Information:

Building Codes Division
Department of Commerce
Labor and Industries Building
Salem, Oregon 97310
(503) 378-8086

PENNSYLVANIA

Legislation and/or Regulations:

The Handicapped Act, Act 235, Act of September 1, 1965, P.L. 459, 71 Purdon Statutes sec. 1455.1 et seq.

Applicability:

All buildings of assembly, educational institutions, and office buildings which are constructed in whole or in part by the use of Commonwealth funds, or the funds of any instrumentality of the Commonwealth. All buildings which are leased by the Commonwealth or an instrumentality of the Commonwealth by reason of a lease executed after December 31, 1974.

Also applies to privately owned department stores, theaters, retail stores, sports arenas, and restaurants with sit-down interior dining facilities constructed after the effective date of the act (October 2, 1974). *Exception:* those containing less than 2,800 square feet of usable floor space, and those for which contracts for the planning and/or design have been awarded prior to the effective date of the amending act.

Exemptions:

By the Secretary of Labor and Industry (with advice of an Advisory Board).

Enforcement:

Department of Labor and Industry.

Additional Information:

Division of Buildings
Bureau of Occupational and Industrial Safety
Department of Labor and Industry
Labor and Industry Building
7th and Forester Streets
Harrisburg, Pennsylvania 17120
(717) 787-3806

RHODE ISLAND

Legislation and/or Regulations:

Rhode Island State Building Code, Regulation SBC-7 (November 1, 1981).

Applicability:

All buildings and portions thereof of use groups A (assembly), B (business), F (factory), I (institutional), M (mercantile), and S (storage). Exceptions:

1. Mechanical, storage and similar types of incidental space.
2. Mezzanines and balconies, provided accessible accommodations are available at the main level and the services are similar.
3. Use groups R-3, R-4, and T.
4. Special access requirements for R-1 and R-2 use:
   a. Residential (R-1) use: Bedroom units required by Table 1.4 in use group R-1 (residential, hotels) buildings shall be made accessible to physically handicapped persons. The bedroom units allocated for the physically handicapped shall be proportionately distributed throughout all types of units. Access to additional floors without public facilities is not required.
   b. Residential (R-2) use: All new dwelling units in use group R-2 (residential, multi-family) buildings, required to be accessible in Table 315.2, shall be designed to the space and equipment criteria for the physically handicapped. The dwelling units so designed shall be proportionately distributed throughout all types of units. Laundry and storage facilities, if provided, shall be accessible. Access to additional floors without public spaces is not required.

Dwelling units (residential, multi-family) required to be accessible in R-2 buildings shall be of the adaptable type. The design shall include all space requirements, structural supports, or equipment supplies so that when rented, the unit can be made to comply with the accessibility criteria of this standard, which pertains to the specific disability of the person(s) renting said unit. The cost to make the dwelling unit's facilities (i.e., kitchen, bath, cabinets, etc.) accessible shall be borne by the owner.

When said (residential, multi-family) R-2 building is rented to 60% of any new units constructed, the owner may rent the adaptable dwelling unit for other than handicapped usage without accessible features.

Exemptions:

–

Enforcement:

Local Building Official

Remarks:

Rhode Island has adopted ANSI A 117.1–1980, with some minor modifications.

Additional information:

Department of Community Affairs
Building Commissioner
12 Humbert Street
North Providence, Rhode Island 02911
(401) 277–3033

Table 1.4.   Accessible Units

R-1 NUMBER OF BEDROOM UNITS	R-2 NUMBER OF DWELLING UNITS	REQUIRED NUMBER OF ACCESSIBLE UNITS
	Up to 25	0
Up to 24	25 to 49	1
25 to 49	50 to 99	2
50 to 74	100 to 149	3*
75 to 99	200 to 299	4*
100 to 124	300 to 399	5*
Over 125	Over 400	4% of bedroom units or fraction thereof*

* Proportionately distribute throughout all types of units.

SOUTH CAROLINA

Legislation and/or Regulations:

Code of Laws of South Carolina, sec. 10-5-210 et seq.

Applicability:

All buildings and facilities used by the public for purposes of commerce, employment, recreation, education, and other normal and essential functions (permanent and temporary or emergency conditions). *Not applicable:* private residences, except where defined as public buildings.

Applies to all new construction and renovation which structurally affects at least 35% of a building's or facility's gross area or external appurtenances, or a combination of such renovation projects over a period of 18 months, as follows:

a. Comply with for the total structure and external areas if renovation involves structural revisions and if construction or renovation of a building or facility constitutes 35% of the total gross area and external grounds and appurtenances.
b. Renovation projects involving only painting, carpeting, partition revisions, or other surface revisions to buildings, regardless of their scope of effect, do not constitute structural renovation as herein applied.
c. Compliance is not mandatory if renovation does not constitute at least 35% of the building or facility structure.
d. Building or facility additions to existing structures shall be treated as separate buildings or facilities or new construction, and such additions shall comply with the Standard.

Exceptions:

a. Floors above grade of any building where such building does not exceed 7,500 square feet in area per floor, where accessibility is provided at grade floor levels, and elevator service is not provided.
b. If the incremental construction cost to conform a building exceeds 7% of the total estimated or renovation costs, the provisions do not apply to the construction or renovation of that building on the floors above grade and shall not apply so as to require the expenditure of more than 7% of the total construction or renovation cost on floors on grade level.
c. Agricultural buildings.

d. Only 5% (but no less than one living unit) of the total number of dwelling units for rent, lease, or hire are required to comply. Common facilities shall be accessible.
e. Hallways within dwelling units having no walk-through openings in the sidewalls may be less than 44 inches wide, but shall not be less than 36 inches wide.
f. Toilet rooms within dwelling units providing 29-inch clear passage need not comply with other toilet room provisions, except that the units shall be usable.

Exemptions:

By the South Carolina Board for Barrier-Free Design of the State Budget and Control Board if:

a. The purpose of the Standard can be fulfilled by an acceptable alternative design; or
b. The incremental construction cost to conform exceeds 7% of the total construction or renovation costs; or
c. Occupancy and employment practices would generally exclude the use of a structure by handicapped persons due to hazards and employment requirements; or
d. Usage or size of structures would have minimal impact in facilitating the handicapped; or
e. The building involved is identified or classified by national or state jurisdiction as an "historic building," in which case no more than one accessible entrance may be required except that no such entrance may be required for so-called house museums.

By Special Review Agents (same as shown for "Enforcement," below) for state owned or leased facilities, elementary-secondary public school facilities, and health care facilities.

In areas of the state where building codes have been adopted and Boards of Adjustments and Appeals established in accordance with the Standard Building Code, such boards may carry out their normal function concerning code requirements for facilities for the handicapped.

Enforcement:

By local building officials, where such officials are appointed by municipal or county bodies.

By Chief Fire Inspectors, where local building officials are not appointed.

In the absence of either of the foregoing, by the Director of Technical Services of the State Budget and Control Board.

By the State Engineer, State Budget and Control Board, for state-owned or leased facilities.

By the Director, Office of School Planning and Building, State Department of Education, for public elementary-secondary school facilities.

By the Chief, Bureau of Health Facilities Engineering, State Department of Health and Environmental Control, for health care facilities.

Remarks:

South Carolina has adopted the provisions of sec. 508 of the Standard Building Code and ANSI A117.1—1961 (R 1971). Where there are conflicts between these, the mandatory provisions of the Standard Building Code shall be observed and used.

South Carolina provides tax deductions to private owners of public facilities for the removal of access barriers. Refer to S. C. Code of Laws 1976, sec. 12-7-700 (16).

Additional Information:

South Carolina Board for Barrier-Free Design
300 Gervais Street
Columbia, South Carolina 29201
(803) 758-2469

SOUTH DAKOTA

Legislation and/or Regulations:

SDCL 5-14-12 et seq.

Applicability:

All buildings and facilities used by the public which are constructed in whole or in part by the use of state, county, or municipal funds, or the funds of any political subdivision of the state. Applies to all such buildings and facilities constructed in South Dakota after July 1, 1965, or any remodeling, alteration or addition to any such buildings after July 1, 1975 from any of these funds or any combination thereof.

Exemptions:

By the authority responsible for the proper construction for the particular governmental department, agency, or unit concerned for reasons of impracticability.

Enforcement:

The administrator in charge of, and authorized to contract for, new construction, remodeling, alteration, or addition on behalf of the political subdivision involved.

Remarks:

South Dakota has adopted ANSI A117.1—1961.

Additional Information:

Bureau of Administration
State Building #2
Pierre, South Dakota 57501
(605) 773-3696

TENNESSEE

Legislation and/or Regulations:

Code ann. sec 53-2544 et seq.

Applicability:

Any public building, the construction of which is commenced after July 1, 1970.

All auditoriums, theaters, gymnasiums, stadiums, and other public entertainment facilities must provide accommodations in level or nearly level locations from which persons confined in wheelchairs may see and hear the offered entertainment as well as persons regularly seated in the facility.

Exemptions:

By local building inspector for reasons of cost or impracticability.

Enforcement:

Agency which has primary responsibility for design of public buildings.

Remarks:

Tennessee has adopted the minimum specifications contained in the 1976 Edition of *An Illustrated Handbook of the Handicapped* section of the North Carolina State Building Code (see North Carolina).

Additional Information:

Department of Insurance
Division of Fire Prevention
Sudekum Building, 4th Floor
6th and Church
Nashville, Tennessee 37219
(605) 741-2981

TEXAS

Legislation and/or Regulations:

Article 7 of Article 601b, Vernons Texas Civil Statutes, as amended.

Applicability:

Public buildings if public funds are used in the construction of a building. Land donations by governmental units or any other use of public lands on which buildings or facilities are constructed shall be deemed to be funded in part by public funds even though structures on that land are constructed with private funds.

Buildings constructed with private funds but which were constructed for the primary purpose of donating or deeding to a public entity.

Privately owned buildings and facilities identified in the Act that are leased or rented to state agencies. *Exceptions:* If space to be leased will not be used by the public, and there is improbable employment of the aged, handicapped, or disabled persons because of the physical requirements of the work or the nature and function of the facility. The agency shall submit pertinent data to the State Purchasing and General Services Commission for such cases on such impracticability, which the Commission will review and set out such standards and specifications which are considered practical.

Privately owned buildings and facilities identified in the Act.

For privately funded buildings and facilities, the regulations pertain only to new construction and are not applicable in renovation projects.

Exemptions:

For public buildings: by the State Purchasing and General Services Commission for reasons of impracticability.

Enforcement:

State Purchasing and General Services Commission with the assistance of the appropriate agencies, public officials. The Board of Regents has jurisdiction for buildings under the jurisdiction of the University of Texas.

Remarks:

With some minor modifications, Texas regulations closely parallel ANSI A117.1—1980.

Additional Information:

State Purchasing and General Services Commission
Architectural Barriers Section
L.B.J. Building
P.O. Box 13047, Capitol Station
Austin, Texas 78711
(512) 475-2622

UTAH

Legislation and/or Regulations:

Code ann. sec. 26-27-1 et seq.

Applicability:

All buildings and facilities used by the public which are constructed or remodeled in whole or in part by the use of state, county, or municipal funds, or the funds of any political subdivision of the state. *Exceptions:* buildings or facilities, or portions thereof, not intended for public use including, but not limited to, caretaker dwellings, paint shops and spray painting rooms, service buildings, heating plants; balconies and bleachers with fixed seating and reviewing stands in Groups A, B, and E; privately-owned hotels, motels, schools, and institutional residential buildings and facilities; individual privately owned residential dwellings, condominiums, and residential projects created with the intent to be sold to the aged and/or physically handicapped; individual privately owned residential dwellings, condominiums, and residential projects created with the intent to be sold, rented, or leased primarily to the aged and/or physically handicapped. (Note: Although not required to comply, Utah recommends applying minimum design criteria to the latter three privately owned facilities. Details can be obtained from the Utah State Building Board.)

The Act applies to permanent as well as temporary or emergency construction.

Remodeling or alteration of the foregoing buildings or facilities are included where such remodeling or alteration affects areas in which there are architectural barriers for the physically handicapped. If the remodeling involves less than 50% of the space of the building or facility, only the areas being remodeled need to comply. If such remodeling involves 50% or more of the space of the building or facility the entire building or facility shall be brought into compliance.

Enforcement:

1. Where state school funds are utilized—State Board of Education.
2. Where state funds are utilized—Utah State Building Board.
3. Where funds of counties, municipalities, or other political subdivisions are utilized—by the governing board of the county or municipality in which the building or facility is located.

Additional Information:

Department of Administrative Services
Division of Facilities Construction and
   Management
4110 State Office Building
Salt Lake City, Utah 84114
(801) 533-5561

VERMONT

Legislation and/or Regulations:

Vermont statutes ann. Title 18 sec. 1322; Title 3, Chapter 25.

Applicability:

All buildings and facilities used by the public. Included are permanent, temporary, or emergency conditions. It does not apply to private residences.

Buildings used by the public include churches, courthouses, jails, municipal rooms, state and county institutions, railroad stations, school buildings, school and society halls, hotels, restaurants, and buildings rented for tenements, boarders and roomers, and places of amusement, factories, mills, workshops, or buildings in which persons are employed, and shall include all buildings used as nurseries, convalescent homes, homes for the aged, and tents and outdoor structures used for a public assembly.

Exemptions:

By the Architectural Barrier Compliance Board for buildings not normally used by handicapped persons, or if compliance with specific standards would be prohibitively costly in relation to the normal costs of the total project.

Enforcement:

Department of Labor and Industry.

Additional Information:

Department of Labor and Industry
Fire Prevention Section
State Office Building
Montpelier, Vermont 05602
(802) 828-2106

VIRGINIA

Legislation and/or Regulations:

Code sec. 2.1-514 et seq; sec. 15.1-381. Addendum 1, Art. 5, sec. 515.0 et seq. Uniform Statewide Building Code, 1981.

Applicability:

Any building or facility, including temporary and emergency construction, used by the public which is constructed in whole or in part or altered by use of state, county, or municipal funds, or the funds of any political subdivision of the state.

Exemptions:

Modifications to the code may be granted by the local building official; decision of local building official may be appealed to the local Appeals Board, then the State Building Code Technical Review Board.

In buildings with an area of 1,000 square feet or less, constructed with the first floor elevated above grade level, these provisions may be waived where access is considered impractical by the building official.

In buildings of two or more stories where the total area of all floors is less than 12,000 square feet, only the first grade level floor shall be required to comply with these provisions.

Buildings of use group A accommodating less than 50 persons, and buildings of other use groups with an area of 1,000 square feet or less, shall be required to comply with the building access provisions of the referenced standard.

Enforcement:

State Board of Housing and Community Development.

Remarks:

Virginia's Uniform Statewide Building Code has incorporated the provisions of the BOCA Basic Building Code, 1978 Edition. Accepted engineering practice standards include ANSI A117.1—1980.

Additional Information:

Department of Housing and Community Development
Office of Uniform Building Code
205 North Fourth Street
Richmond, Virginia 23219
(804) 786-5041

WASHINGTON

Legislation and/or Regulations:

Revised Code of Washington 19.27 (State Building Code Act); Chapter 70.92 (Provisions in Buildings for Aged and Handicapped); Washington Administrative Code 51-12 (State Regulations for Barrier-Free Facilities).

Applicability:

All Groups A, B, E, H, I, and R-1 occupancy (as defined in the Uniform Building Code, 1979 Edition) buildings, structures, or portions thereof, which are constructed, remodeled, or rehabilitated.

Exceptions:

1. Additions, alterations, or repairs may be made to any building or structure without requiring the existing building or structure to comply with all the requirements of this code; provided that where substantial alterations occur, these regulations shall apply.
2. Any portion of a building or structure in respect to which the administrative authority deems, after considering all circumstances applying thereto, that full compliance is unreasonable.
3. Buildings or portions thereof not customarily occupied by humans.
4. Apartment houses with ten or fewer units.

Exemptions:

By the administrative authority of any jurisdiction for reasons of impracticability.

Subject to decision of Board of Appeals as specified in the Uniform Building Code.

Enforcement:

City and County Building Departments.

Remarks:

Washington uses the provisions of the 1979 Uniform Building Code and ANSI 1980, supplemented by additional standards.

Additional Information:

Planning & Community Affairs Agency
Ninth & Columbia Building
MS/GH-51
Olympia, Washington 98504
(206) 754-1243

WEST VIRGINIA

Legislation and/or Regulations:

Art 10F, Chapter 18, Code of West Virginia.

Applicability:

All public buildings and/or facilities.

Exceptions:

1. Apartment houses with less than twenty units, row houses, and rooming houses.
2. Convents and monasteries.
3. Jails and other places of detention.
4. Garages, hangars, and boat houses.
5. All buildings classified as hazardous occupancies.
6. Warehouses.
7. Buildings specifically built for field service purposes such as, but not limited to, conservation fire towers, fish hatcheries, or tree nursery buildings.
8. Residence halls at colleges or universities which have at least two other resident halls for men and two other resident halls for women so constructed as to allow physically handicapped persons reasonable means of access to and use of such buildings.

Exemptions:

By the Director, Division of Vocational Rehabilitation, West Virginia State Board of Vocational Education, for reasons of impracticability or financial hardship.

Enforcement:

Director, Division of Vocational Rehabilitation, West Virginia State Board of Vocational Education.

Remarks:

Apartment buildings with 20 units or more shall have one out of every 10 of each type of unit designed for the physically handicapped.

Requirements for specific buildings are given below.

Additional Information:

State Board of Vocational Education
Division of Vocational Rehabilitation
State Capitol Building
Charleston, West Virginia 25305

Requirements for Specific Buildings

FACILITY	ACCESSIBLE ENTRANCE	ELEVATORS TO ALL PUBLIC FLOORS	ACCESSIBLE RESTROOMS	REACHABLE WATER FOUNTAINS AND PHONES
Transportation Terminals	X	X	X	X
Auditoriums	X	X	X	X
Apartment Houses	X	X	X	
Bowling Alleys	X		X	X
Churches	X	X	X	
Stadiums	X		X	
Conference Centers	X	X	X	X
Restaurants	X		X	
Theaters	X	X	X	X
Schools	X	X	X	X
Hotels and Motels	X		X	X
Gasoline Stations	X		X	
Hospitals and Clinics	X	X	X	X
Libraries	X	X	X	X
Court Houses, City and County Buildings	X	X	X	X
Office Buildings	X	X with 3 or more floors	X	X
Small Retail Stores	X	X		
Food Stores	X			
Banks	X			
Cleaners, Hairdressing and Other Service Shops	X			
Museums	X	X	X	X
Quick Food Shops	X			

WISCONSIN

Legislation and/or Regulations:

Wisconsin Statutes sec. 101.13; Ind. 52.04, 52.041 and 52.042 Wisconsin Administrative Code.

Applicability:

All new public buildings and places of employment shall be provided with access to a primary floor, interior circulation, and toilet facilities. Included are government-owned buildings, factories, office and mercantile buildings, theaters and assembly halls, places of abode, day care centers, health care facilities, places of detention, garage occupancies, and open parking structures.

Exceptions:

Mechanical equipment rooms, maintenance equipment and other storage rooms, janitor closets, storage warehouses, saw and feed mills, motion picture booths, portable bleachers, and similar occupancies determined by the Department of Industry, Labor, and Human Relations.

If the total gross area of the building, including all floors, is 20,000 square feet or less, interior circulation is required to a primary floor and throughout at least two-thirds of that floor area. Access is not required to a mezzanine if duplicate facilities to those provided on the mezzanine are located on an accessible floor. Access is required to employee facilities (i.e., lunch rooms, change rooms, and locker rooms).

If the total gross area of the building, including all floors, is greater than 20,000 square feet, interior circulation is required to all floors and to at least two-thirds of the total area of each floor. Access is required to any floor level containing the only facility of its kind. Access is not required to a mezzanine if duplicate facilities to those provided on the mezzanine are located on an accessible floor. Multiple-use buildings with a total gross area greater than 20,000 square feet, including all floors, shall comply with the criteria for each specific use. Interior circulation is required to and throughout at least two-thirds of each specific use area.

Multiple-use buildings with a total gross area of 20,000 square feet or less, including all floors, shall be provided with a means of access to and throughout at least two-thirds of the total area of the primary floor. Government-owned buildings and dental and medical clinics and offices shall comply with the criteria established for each specific use.

Floors used entirely for storage or mechanical purposes need not be included in determining the total gross area.

All existing public buildings or places of employment, and all additions, shall be provided with access to a primary floor, interior circulation, and toilet facilities in accordance with the percentage of gross interior area of a building being remodeled, added to, or both.

(Section Ind. 52.04 Wis. Adm. Code contains numerous specific details for individual circumstances. Refer to this Code for such details. Section Ind. 52.041 and 52.042 relate to requirements of access, interior circulation, and toilet facilities for new and existing health care facilities.)

Exemptions:

The Wisconsin Administrative Code (Chapters 50–64) does not apply to the following types of buildings:

1. One and two-family dwellings;
2. Buildings used exclusively for farming purposes;
3. Buildings used for housing of livestock or for other agricultural purposes;
4. Temporary buildings used exclusively for construction purposes, not exceeding two stories in height, and not used as living quarters;
5. Buildings located on Indian reservation land held in trust by the United States.

Enforcement:

Department of Industry, Labor, and Human Relations, Division of Safety and Buildings.

Additional Information:

Wisconsin Department of Industry, Labor, and Human Relations
Post Office Box 7969
Madison, Wisconsin 53707
(608) 266-8982

WYOMING

Legislation and/or Regulations:

Statutes sec. 35-13-101 et seq.

Applicability:

Public buildings, or additions thereto, for general public use, built by the state or any governmental subdivision or any school district or other public administrative body within the state.

Exemptions:

By the State Fire Marshal in consultation with the Director of Vocational Rehabilitation, the Director of Governor's Committee for the Employment of the Handicapped, and the State Safety Engineer.

Enforcement:

The State Fire Marshal or the City Engineer having appropriate jurisdiction.

Additional Information:

State Fire Marshal
720 West 18th Street
Cheyenne, Wyoming 82002
(307) 777-7288

SECTION 3
TECHNICAL COMPLIANCE

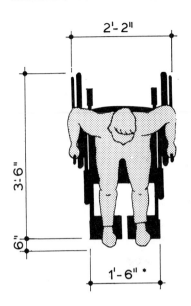
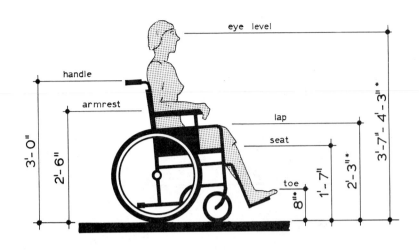

DIMENSIONS OF ADULT-SIZED WHEELCHAIRS

Basis of standard — ANSI 1980 — Appendix and others	APPLICABILITY			
	ALA	● LA	OHIO	GUAM
	● ALASKA	● MAINE	OKLA	PR
	ARIZ	MD	ORE	VIR IS
Notes —	ARK	MASS	PA	DC
(This data is not part of ANSI A 117.1-1980, but is included for information purposes only).	CAL	MICH	● RI	
(*)Data not applicable in Texas.	● COLO	MINN	SC	
	CONN	MISS	SD	FED'L FUNDS
	DEL	MO	TENN	
	FLA	MONT	● TEXAS	
	GA	NEB	UTAH	
	● HAWAII	● NEV	● VT	
	● IDAHO	NH	● VA	
	ILL	NJ	WASH	
	IND	● NM	W VA	
	IOWA	● NY	WIS	OTHER
	KANS	NC	WYO	
	KY	ND		

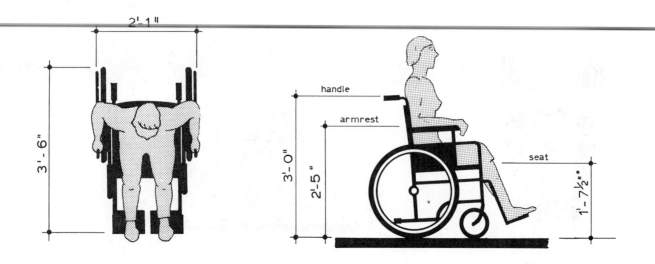

DIMENSIONS OF ADULT-SIZED WHEELCHAIRS

Basis of standard —	APPLICABILITY			
ANSI 1961 — 3.1 and others	● ALA	LA	OHIO	GUAM
	ALASKA	MAINE	● OKLA	PR
	● ARIZ	MD	ORE	VIR IS
	ARK	MASS	PA	DC
Notes —	CAL	MICH	RI	
(*)1'-4½" in West Virginia	COLO	MINN	● SC	
	CONN	MISS	● SD	FED'L
	DEL	MO	TENN	FUNDS
	FLA	MONT	TEXAS	
	● GA	● NEB	UTAH	
	HAWAII	NEV	VT	
	IDAHO	NH	VA	
	ILL	● NJ	WASH	
	IND	NM	● W VA	
	● IOWA	NY	WIS	OTHER
	● KANS	NC	WYO	
	KY	● ND		

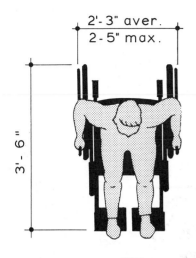

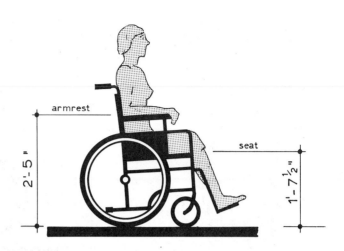

DIMENSIONS OF ADULT-SIZED WHEELCHAIRS

Basis of standard — North Carolina State Building Code and others	APPLICABILITY			
	ALA	LA	OHIO	GUAM
	ALASKA	MAINE	OKLA	PR
	ARIZ	MD	ORE	VIR IS
Notes —	ARK	MASS	PA	DC
	CAL	MICH	RI	
	COLO	MINN	SC	
	CONN	MISS	SD	FED'L
	DEL	MO	● TENN	FUNDS
	FLA	MONT	TEXAS	
	GA	NEB	UTAH	
	HAWAII	NEV	VT	
	IDAHO	NH	VA	
	ILL	NJ	WASH	
	IND	NM	W VA	
	IOWA	NY	WIS	OTHER
	KANS	● NC	WYO	
	KY	ND		

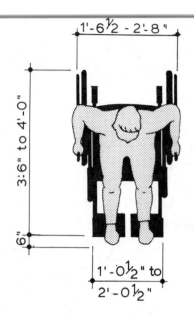

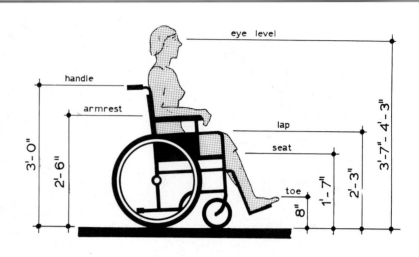

DIMENSIONS OF ADULT-SIZED WHEELCHAIRS

Basis of standard —	APPLICABILITY			
Capital Development Board	ALA	LA	OHIO	GUAM
	ALASKA	MAINE	OKLA	PR
	ARIZ	MD	ORE	VIR IS
Notes —	ARK	MASS	PA	DC
	CAL	MICH	RI	
	COLO	MINN	SC	
	CONN	MISS	SD	FED'L
	DEL	MO	TENN	FUNDS
	FLA	MONT	TEXAS	
	GA	NEB	UTAH	
	HAWAII	NEV	VT	
	IDAHO	NH	VA	
	● ILL	NJ	WASH	
	IND	NM	W VA	
	IOWA	NY	WIS	OTHER
	KANS	NC	WYO	
	KY	ND		

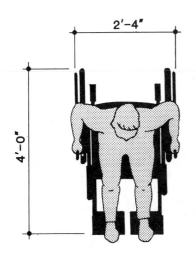

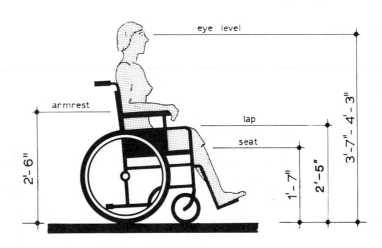

DIMENSIONS OF ADULT-SIZED WHEELCHAIRS

Basis of standard —	APPLICABILITY			
521 CMR Architectural Barriers Board	ALA	LA	OHIO	GUAM
	ALASKA	MAINE	OKLA	PR
	ARIZ	MD	ORE	VIR IS
Notes —	ARK	● MASS	PA	DC
	CAL	MICH	RI	
	COLO	MINN	SC	
	CONN	MISS	SD	FED'L
	DEL	MO	TENN	FUNDS
	FLA	MONT	TEXAS	
	GA	NEB	UTAH	
	HAWAII	NEV	VT	
	IDAHO	NH	VA	
	ILL	NJ	WASH	
	IND	NM	W VA	
	IOWA	NY	WIS	OTHER
	KANS	NC	WYO	
	KY	ND		

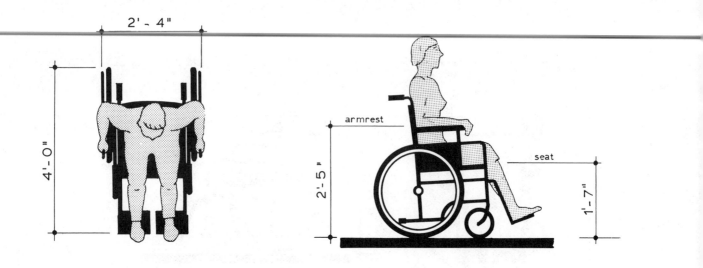

DIMENSIONS OF ADULT-SIZED WHEELCHAIRS

Basis of standard — Architectural Barrier Free Design Code	APPLICABILITY			
	ALA	LA	OHIO	GUAM
	ALASKA	MAINE	OKLA	PR
	ARIZ	MD	ORE	VIR IS
Notes —	ARK	MASS	PA	DC
	CAL	MICH	RI	
	COLO	MINN	SC	
	CONN	MISS	SD	FED'L FUNDS
	DEL	MO	TENN	
	FLA	MONT	TEXAS	
	GA	NEB	UTAH	
	HAWAII	NEV	VT	
	IDAHO	● NH	VA	
	ILL	NJ	WASH	
	IND	NM	W VA	
	IOWA	NY	WIS	OTHER
	KANS	NC	WYO	
	KY	ND		

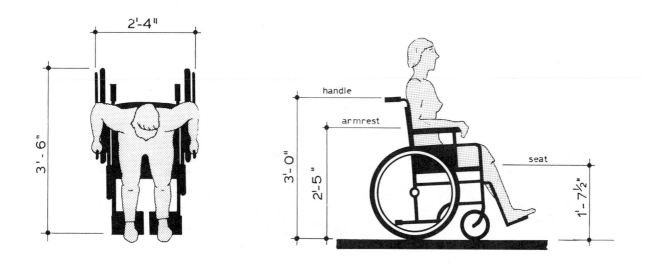

DIMENSIONS OF ADULT-SIZED WHEELCHAIRS

Basis of standard —	APPLICABILITY			
Structural Specialty Code	ALA	LA	OHIO	GUAM
	ALASKA	MAINE	OKLA	PR
	ARIZ	MD	● ORE	VIR IS
Notes —	ARK	MASS	PA	DC
Minimum turning radius = 42″	CAL	MICH	RI	
	COLO	MINN	SC	
	CONN	MISS	SD	FED'L
	DEL	MO	TENN	FUNDS
	FLA	MONT	TEXAS	
	GA	NEB	UTAH	
	HAWAII	NEV	VT	
	IDAHO	NH	VA	
	ILL	NJ	WASH	
	IND	NM	W VA	
	IOWA	NY	WIS	OTHER
	KANS	NC	WYO	
	KY	ND		

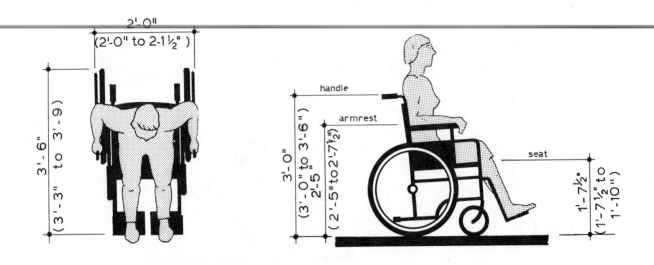

DIMENSIONS OF ADULT-SIZED WHEELCHAIRS

Basis of standard — Utah State Building Board Planning and Design Criteria	APPLICABILITY			
	ALA	LA	OHIO	GUAM
	ALASKA	MAINE	OKLA	PR
	ARIZ	MD	ORE	VIR IS
Notes — Motorized chairs are as wide as 2'-5" with a 6" allowance for additional equipment	ARK	MASS	PA	DC
	CAL	MICH	RI	
	COLO	MINN	SC	
	CONN	MISS	SD	FED'L FUNDS
	DEL	MO	TENN	
	FLA	MONT	TEXAS	
	GA	NEB	● UTAH	
	HAWAII	NEV	VT	
	IDAHO	NH	VA	
	ILL	NJ	WASH	
	IND	NM	W VA	
	IOWA	NY	WIS	OTHER
	KANS	NC	WYO	
	KY	ND		

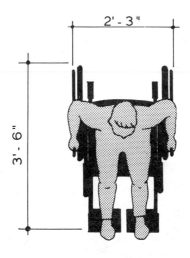

DIMENSIONS OF ADULT –SIZED WHEELCHAIRS

Basis of standard —	APPLICABILITY			
Wisconsin Administrative Code	ALA	LA	OHIO	GUAM
	ALASKA	MAINE	OKLA	PR
	ARIZ	MD	ORE	VIR IS
Notes —	ARK	MASS	PA	DC
	CAL	MICH	RI	
	COLO	MINN	SC	
	CONN	MISS	SD	FED'L FUNDS
	DEL	MO	TENN	
	FLA	MONT	TEXAS	
	GA	NEB	UTAH	
	HAWAII	NEV	VT	
	IDAHO	NH	VA	
	ILL	NJ	WASH	
	IND	NM	W VA	
	IOWA	NY	● WIS	OTHER
	KANS	NC	WYO	
	KY	ND		

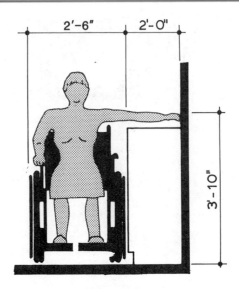

2'-6"   2'-0"

3'-10"

MAXIMUM SIDE REACH OVER OBSTRUCTION

Basis of standard —	APPLICABILITY			
ANSI 1980 — 4.2.6 and others	ALA	● LA	OHIO	GUAM
	● ALASKA	● MAINE	OKLA	PR
	ARIZ	MD	ORE	VIR IS
	ARK	MASS	PA	DC
Notes —	● CAL	MICH	● RI	
Data applies if clear floor space allows parallel approach.	● COLO	MINN	SC	
Texas: max. height of built-in lavatories 3'-1"; max. side reach across top: 1'-8"	CONN	MISS	SD	FED'L FUNDS
	DEL	MO	TENN	
	FLA	MONT	● TEXAS	
	GA	NEB	UTAH	
	● HAWAII	● NEV	● VT	
	● IDAHO	NH	● VA	
	ILL	NJ	WASH	
	IND	● NM	W VA	
	IOWA	● NY	WIS	OTHER
	KANS	NC	WYO	
	● KY	ND		

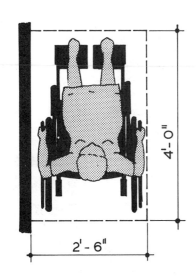

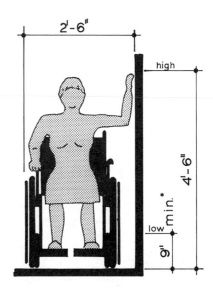

CLEAR FLOOR SPACE PARALLEL APPROACH

HIGH AND LOW SIDE REACH LIMITS

Basis of standard — ANSI 1980 — 4.2.6 and others	APPLICABILITY			
	ALA	● LA	OHIO	GUAM
	● ALASKA	● MAINE	OKLA	PR
	ARIZ	MD	ORE	VIR IS
Notes — Data applies if clear floor space allows parallel approach. (*) 12″ min. in Texas	● ARK	MASS	PA	DC
	● CAL	MICH	● RI	
	● COLO	MINN	SC	
	CONN	MISS	SD	● FED'L FUNDS
	● DEL	MO	TENN	
	FLA	MONT	● TEXAS	
	GA	NEB	UTAH	
	● HAWAII	● NEV	● VT	
	● IDAHO	NH	● VA	
	ILL	NJ	WASH	
	IND	● NM	W VA	
	IOWA	● NY	WIS	OTHER
	KANS	NC	WYO	
	KY	ND		

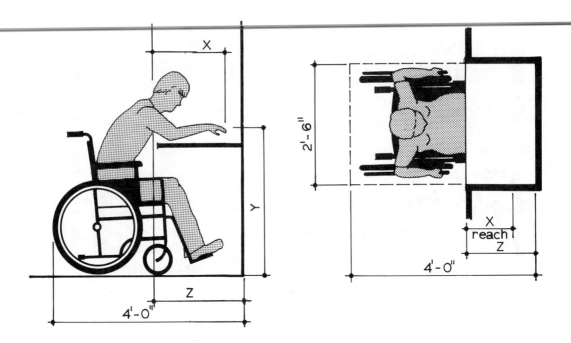

MAXIMUM FORWARD REACH OVER AN OBSTRUCTION

Basis of standard —	APPLICABILITY			
ANSI 1980 — 4.2.5 and others	ALA	● LA	OHIO	GUAM
	● ALASKA	● MAINE	OKLA	PR
	ARIZ	MD	ORE	VIR IS
	ARK	MASS	PA	DC
Notes —	● CAL	MICH	● RI	
If the high forward reach is over an obstruction the following data applies:	● COLO	MINN	SC	
$x = 25''$ max.; $z \geqslant x$.	CONN	MISS	SD	FED'L
When $x < 20''$, then y shall be 48″ max.	DEL	MO	TENN	FUNDS
When $x = 20''$ to $25''$, then y shall be 44″ max.	FLA	MONT	● TEXAS	
	GA	NEB	UTAH	
	● HAWAII	● NEV	● VT	
	● IDAHO	NH	● VA	
	ILL	NJ	WASH	
	IND	● NM	W VA	
	IOWA	● NY	WIS	OTHER
	KANS	NC	WYO	
	● KY	ND		

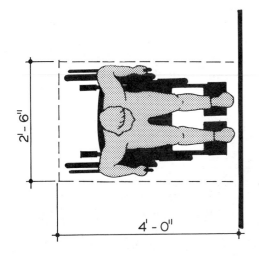

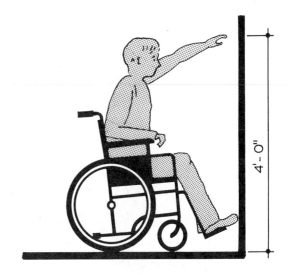

HIGH FORWARD REACH LIMIT

Basis of standard — ANSI 1980 — 4.2.5 and others	APPLICABILITY			
	ALA	● LA	OHIO	GUAM
	● ALASKA	● MAINE	OKLA	PR
	ARIZ	MD	ORE	VIR IS
	ARK	MASS	PA	DC
Notes —	● CAL	MICH	● RI	
Data applies if clear floor space only allows forward approach to an object.	● COLO	MINN	SC	
	CONN	MISS	SD	FED'L
	DEL	MO	TENN	FUNDS
	FLA	MONT	● TEXAS	
	GA	NEB	UTAH	
	● HAWAII	● NEV	● VT	
	● IDAHO	NH	● VA	
	ILL	NJ	WASH	
	IND	● NM	W VA	
	IOWA	● NY	WIS	OTHER
	KANS	NC	WYO	
	KY	ND		

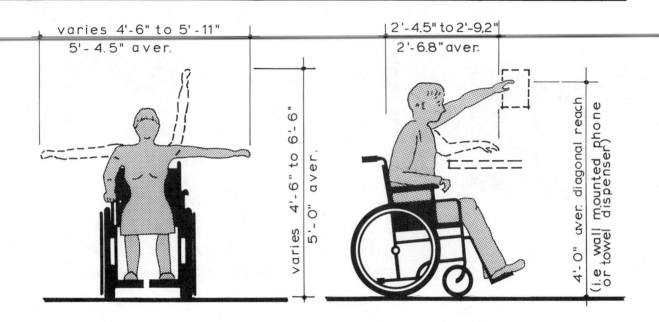

THE INDIVIDUAL FUNCTIONING IN A WHEELCHAIR

Basis of standard — ANSI 1961 — 3.3 and others	APPLICABILITY			
	● ALA	LA	OHIO	GUAM
	ALASKA	MAINE	● OKLA	PR
	● ARIZ	MD	ORE	VIR IS
Notes — Data shown is for adults.	ARK	MASS	PA	DC
	CAL	MICH	RI	
	COLO	MINN	● SC	
	CONN	MISS	● SD	FED'L
	DEL	MO	● TENN	FUNDS
	FLA	MONT	TEXAS	
	● GA	● NEB	UTAH	
	HAWAII	NEV	VT	
	IDAHO	NH	VA	
	ILL	● NJ	WASH	
	IND	NM	● W VA	
	● IOWA	NY	WIS	OTHER
	● KANS	● NC	WYO	
	KY	● ND		

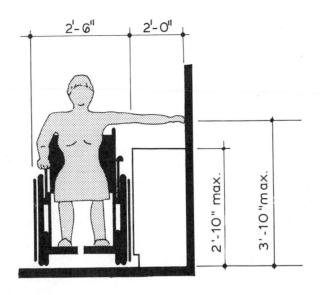

2'-6"   2'-0"

2'-10" max.

3'-10" max.

MAXIMUM SIDE REACH OVER OBSTRUCTION

Basis of standard —	APPLICABILITY			
ATBCB § 1190.40 and others	ALA	LA	OHIO	GUAM
	ALASKA	MAINE	OKLA	PR
	ARIZ	MD	ORE	VIR IS
Notes —	● ARK	MASS	PA	DC
Data applies if clear floor space allows parallel approach.	CAL	MICH	RI	
	COLO	MINN	SC	
	CONN	MISS	SD	● FED'L FUNDS
	● DEL	MO	TENN	
	FLA	MONT	TEXAS	
	GA	NEB	UTAH	
	HAWAII	NEV	VT	
	IDAHO	NH	VA	
	ILL	NJ	WASH	
	IND	NM	W VA	
	IOWA	NY	WIS	OTHER
	KANS	NC	WYO	
	KY	ND		

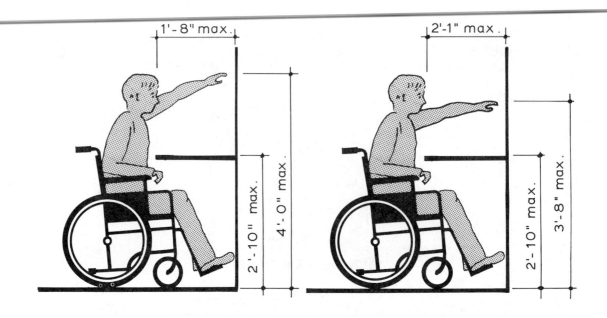

REACH OVER AN OBSTRUCTION

Basis of standard — ATBCB § 1190.40 and others	APPLICABILITY			
	ALA	LA	OHIO	GUAM
	ALASKA	MAINE	OKLA	PR
	ARIZ	MD	ORE	VIR IS
● ARK	MASS	PA	DC
	CAL	MICH	RI	
	COLO	MINN	SC	
	CONN	MISS	SD	● FED'L FUNDS
● DEL	MO	TENN	
	FLA	MONT	TEXAS	
	GA	NEB	UTAH	
	HAWAII	NEV	VT	
	IDAHO	NH	VA	
	ILL	NJ	WASH	
	IND	NM	W VA	
	IOWA	NY	WIS	OTHER
	KANS	NC	WYO	
	KY	ND		

Notes —

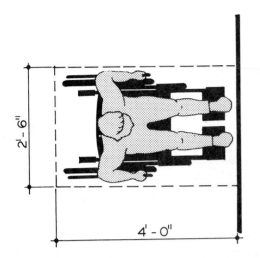

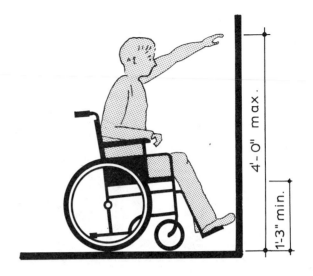

FORWARD   REACH   LIMIT

Basis of standard — ATBCB § 1190.40 and others	APPLICABILITY			
	ALA	LA	OHIO	GUAM
	ALASKA	MAINE	OKLA	PR
	ARIZ	MD	ORE	VIR IS
Notes — ● ARK	MASS	PA	DC
Data applies if clear floor space only allows for a forward approach to object.	CAL	MICH	RI	
	COLO	MINN	SC	
	CONN	MISS	SD	● FED'L FUNDS
	● DEL	MO	TENN	
	FLA	MONT	TEXAS	
	GA	NEB	UTAH	
	HAWAII	NEV	VT	
	IDAHO	NH	VA	
	ILL	NJ	WASH	
	IND	NM	W VA	
	IOWA	NY	WIS	OTHER
	KANS	NC	WYO	
	KY	ND		

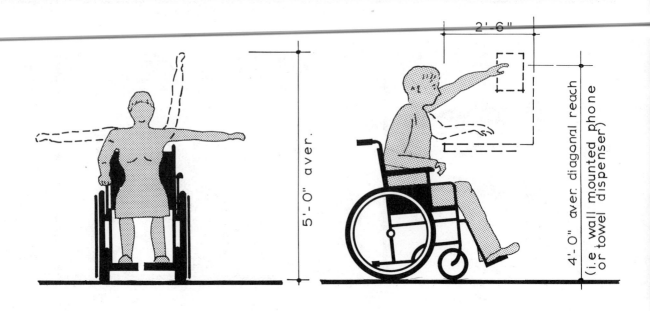

THE INDIVIDUAL FUNCTIONING IN A WHEELCHAIR

Basis of standard —	APPLICABILITY			
Mass. — 521 CMR 1.00 Architectural Barriers Board and	ALA	LA	OHIO	GUAM
N.H. — Architectural Barrier Free Design Code	ALASKA	MAINE	OKLA	PR
	ARIZ	MD	ORE	VIR IS
Notes —	ARK	● MASS	PA	DC
	CAL	MICH	RI	
	COLO	MINN	SC	
	CONN	MISS	SD	FED'L
	DEL	MO	TENN	FUNDS
	FLA	MONT	TEXAS	
	GA	NEB	UTAH	
	HAWAII	NEV	VT	
	IDAHO	● NH	VA	
	ILL	NJ	WASH	
	IND	NM	W VA	
	IOWA	NY	WIS	OTHER
	KANS	NC	WYO	
	KY	ND		

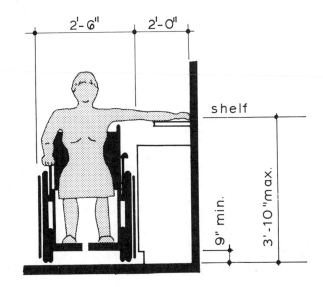

MAXIMUM SIDE REACH OVER OBSTRUCTION

Basis of standard —	APPLICABILITY			
Capital Development Board	ALA	LA	OHIO	GUAM
	ALASKA	MAINE	OKLA	PR
	ARIZ	MD	ORE	VIR IS
Notes —	ARK	MASS	PA	DC
	CAL	MICH	RI	
	COLO	MINN	SC	
	CONN	MISS	SD	FED'L
	DEL	MO	TENN	FUNDS
	FLA	MONT	TEXAS	
	GA	NEB	UTAH	
	HAWAII	NEV	VT	
	IDAHO	NH	VA	
	● ILL	NJ	WASH	
	IND	NM	W VA	
	IOWA	NY	WIS	OTHER
	KANS	NC	WYO	
	KY	ND		

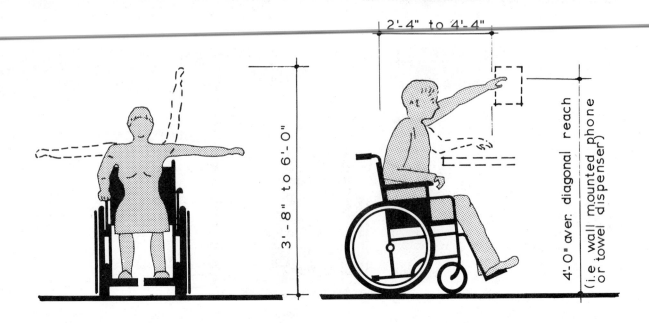

2'-4" to 4'-4"

3'-8" to 6'-0"

4'-0" aver. diagonal reach
(i.e. wall mounted phone
or towel dispenser)

THE INDIVIDUAL FUNCTIONING IN A WHEELCHAIR

Basis of standard — Capital Development Board	APPLICABILITY			
	ALA	LA	OHIO	GUAM
	ALASKA	MAINE	OKLA	PR
	ARIZ	MD	ORE	VIR IS
Notes —	ARK	MASS	PA	DC
	CAL	MICH	RI	
	COLO	MINN	SC	
	CONN	MISS	SD	FED'L
	DEL	MO	TENN	FUNDS
	FLA	MONT	TEXAS	
	GA	NEB	UTAH	
	HAWAII	NEV	VT	
	IDAHO	NH	VA	
	● ILL	NJ	WASH	
	IND	NM	W VA	
	IOWA	NY	WIS	OTHER
	KANS	NC	WYO	
	KY	ND		

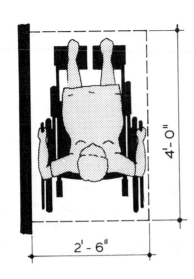

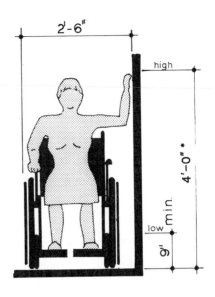

CLEAR FLOOR SPACE PARALLEL APPROACH

HIGH AND LOW SIDE REACH LIMITS

Basis of standard —	APPLICABILITY			
815 KAR 7:060	ALA	LA	OHIO	GUAM
	ALASKA	MAINE	OKLA	PR
	ARIZ	MD	ORE	VIR IS
	ARK	MASS	PA	DC
Notes —	CAL	MICH	RI	
(*)If over an object up to 24″ wide, high side reach shall be 3′-10″.	COLO	MINN	SC	
	CONN	MISS	SD	FED'L FUNDS
	DEL	MO	TENN	
	FLA	MONT	TEXAS	
	GA	NEB	UTAH	
	HAWAII	NEV	VT	
	IDAHO	NH	VA	
	ILL	NJ	WASH	
	IND	NM	W VA	
	IOWA	NY	WIS	OTHER
	KANS	NC	WYO	
	● KY	ND		

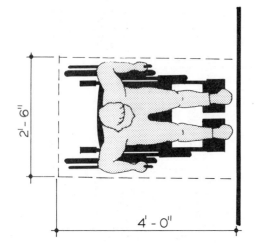
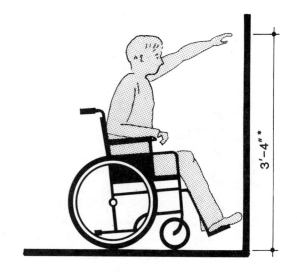

HIGH FORWARD REACH LIMIT

Basis of standard — 815 KAR 7:060	APPLICABILITY			
	ALA	LA	OHIO	GUAM
	ALASKA	MAINE	OKLA	PR
	ARIZ	MD	ORE	VIR IS
	ARK	MASS	PA	DC
	CAL	MICH	RI	
	COLO	MINN	SC	
	CONN	MISS	SD	FED'L FUNDS
	DEL	MO	TENN	
	FLA	MONT	TEXAS	
	GA	NEB	UTAH	
	HAWAII	NEV	VT	
	IDAHO	NH	VA	
	ILL	NJ	WASH	
	IND	NM	W VA	
	IOWA	NY	WIS	OTHER
	KANS	NC	WYO	
	● KY	ND		

Notes —

(*)According to Figure 2 of the Kentucky Code the high forward reach over an object less than 20″ deep is 48″ and over an object 20″ to 25″ deep is 44″, both of which conflict with the requirement under Section 4, item (5) which limits the high forward reach to 40″.

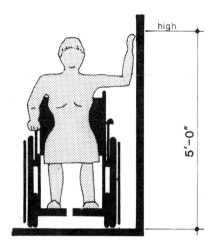

5'-0"

HIGH AND LOW
SIDE REACH LIMITS

Basis of standard —	APPLICABILITY			
521 CMR 1.00 Architectural Barriers Board	ALA	LA	OHIO	GUAM
	ALASKA	MAINE	OKLA	PR
	ARIZ	MD	ORE	VIR IS
Notes —	ARK	● MASS	PA	DC
	CAL	MICH	RI	
	COLO	MINN	SC	
	CONN	MISS	SD	FED'L FUNDS
	DEL	MO	TENN	
	FLA	MONT	TEXAS	
	GA	NEB	UTAH	
	HAWAII	NEV	VT	
	IDAHO	NH	VA	
	ILL	NJ	WASH	
	IND	NM	W VA	
	IOWA	NY	WIS	OTHER
	KANS	NC	WYO	
	KY	ND		

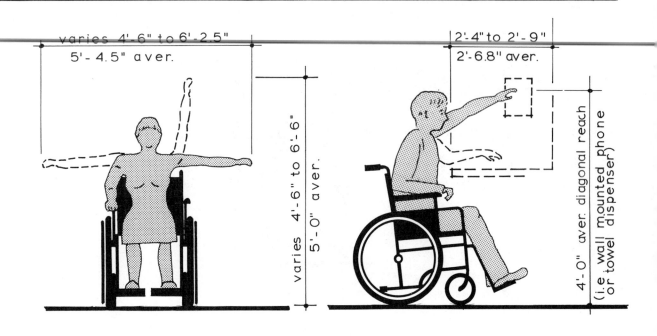

varies 4'-6" to 6'-2.5"
5'-4.5" aver.

2'-4" to 2'-9"
2'-6.8" aver.

varies 4'-6" to 6'-6"
5'-0" aver.

4'-0" aver. diagonal reach
(i.e wall mounted phone or towel dispenser)

THE INDIVIDUAL FUNCTIONING IN A WHEELCHAIR

Basis of standard — Utah State Building Board Planning and Design Criteria	APPLICABILITY			
	ALA	LA	OHIO	GUAM
	ALASKA	MAINE	OKLA	PR
	ARIZ	MD	ORE	VIR IS
	ARK	MASS	PA	DC
	CAL	MICH	RI	
	COLO	MINN	SC	
	CONN	MISS	SD	FED'L FUNDS
Notes —	DEL	MO	TENN	
	FLA	MONT	TEXAS	
	GA	NEB	● UTAH	
	HAWAII	NEV	VT	
	IDAHO	NH	VA	
	ILL	NJ	WASH	
	IND	NM	W VA	
	IOWA	NY	WIS	OTHER
	KANS	NC	WYO	
	KY	ND		

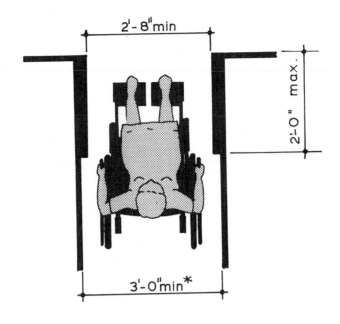

2'- 8"min

2'-0" max.

3'-0"min*

MINIMUM CLEAR WIDTH FOR SINGLE WHEELCHAIR

Basis of standard —	APPLICABILITY			
ANSI 1980 — 4.2.1 and 4.3.3 and others	ALA	● LA	OHIO	GUAM
	● ALASKA	● MAINE	OKLA	PR
	ARIZ	MD	ORE	VIR IS
Notes —	● ARK	MASS	PA	DC
Dimensions shown indicate the minimum clear width of an accessible route. Texas: min.: 3′ -8″.	CAL	MICH	● RI	
	● COLO	MINN	SC	
	CONN	MISS	SD	● FED'L FUNDS
	● DEL	MO	TENN	
	FLA	MONT	TEXAS	
	GA	NEB	UTAH	
	● HAWAII	● NEV	● VT	
	● IDAHO	NH	● VA	
	● ILL	NJ	WASH	
	IND	● NM	W VA	
	● IOWA	● NY	WIS	OTHER
	KANS	NC	WYO	
	KY	ND		

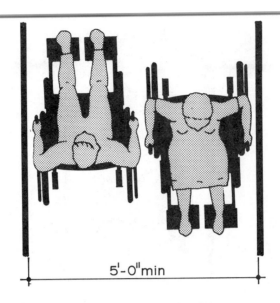

5'-0"min

MINIMUM CLEAR WIDTH FOR TWO WHEELCHAIRS

Basis of standard — ANSI 1980 — 4.2.2 and 4.3.4 and others	APPLICABILITY			
	● ALA	● LA	OHIO	GUAM
	● ALASKA	● MAINE	OKLA	PR
	ARIZ	MD	ORE	VIR IS
	● ARK	MASS	PA	DC
	● CAL	MICH	● RI	
Notes — For accessible routes less than 60″ wide, provide min. 60″ x 60″ passing space (or T-intersection of 2 corridors) at reasonable intervals not to exceed 200′.	● COLO	MINN	SC	
	CONN	MISS	SD	● FED'L FUNDS
	● DEL	MO	TENN	
	FLA	MONT	TEXAS	
	GA	● NEB	UTAH	
	● HAWAII	● NEV	● VT	
	● IDAHO	NH	● VA	
	ILL	NJ	WASH	
	IND	● NM	W VA	
	IOWA	● NY	WIS	OTHER
	KANS	NC	WYO	
	● KY	ND		

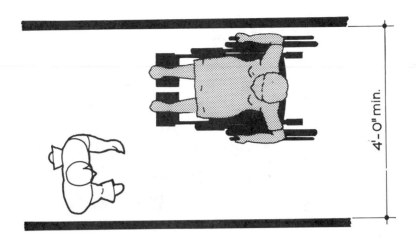

MINIMUM PASSAGE WIDTH FOR ONE WHEELCHAIR
AND ONE AMBULATORY PERSON

Basis of standard — ANSI 1980 — Appendix and others	APPLICABILITY			
	ALA	● LA	OHIO	GUAM
	● ALASKA	● MAINE	OKLA	PR
	ARIZ	MD	ORE	VIR IS
Notes —	ARK	MASS	PA	DC
This data is not part of ANSI A 117.1 — 1980, but is included for information purposes only.	CAL	MICH	● RI	
	● COLO	MINN	SC	
	CONN	MISS	SD	FED'L
	DEL	MO	TENN	FUNDS
	FLA	MONT	● TEXAS	
	GA	NEB	UTAH	
	● HAWAII	● NEV	● VT	
	● IDAHO	NH	● VA	
	● ILL	NJ	WASH	
	IND	● NM	W VA	
	IOWA	● NY	WIS	OTHER
	KANS	NC	WYO	
	KY	ND		

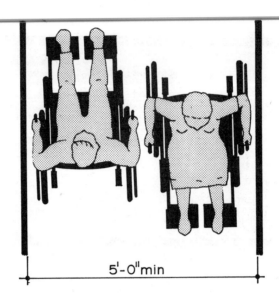

MINIMUM CLEAR WIDTH FOR TWO WHEELCHAIRS

Basis of standard — ANSI 1961 — 3.2.3 and others	APPLICABILITY			
	ALA	LA	OHIO	GUAM
	ALASKA	MAINE	● OKLA	PR
	● ARIZ	MD	● ORE	VIR IS
Notes —	ARK	MASS	PA	DC
	CAL	MICH	RI	
	COLO	MINN	● SC	
	CONN	MISS	● SD	FED'L FUNDS
	DEL	MO	● TENN	
	FLA	MONT	● TEXAS	
	● GA	NEB	UTAH	
	HAWAII	NEV	VT	
	IDAHO	● NH	VA	
	● ILL	● NJ	WASH	
	IND	NM	● W VA	
	● IOWA	NY	WIS	OTHER
	● KANS	● NC	WYO	
	KY	● ND		

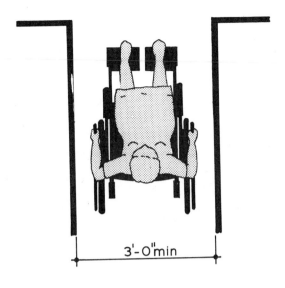

MINIMUM CLEAR WIDTH FOR SINGLE WHEELCHAIR

Basis of standard — CAC Title 24 Part 2. Notes —	APPLICABILITY			
	ALA	LA	OHIO	GUAM
	ALASKA	MAINE	OKLA	PR
	ARIZ	MD	ORE	VIR IS
	ARK	MASS	PA	DC
	● CAL	MICH	RI	
	COLO	MINN	SC	
	CONN	MISS	SD	FED'L FUNDS
	DEL	MO	TENN	
	FLA	MONT	TEXAS	
	GA	NEB	UTAH	
	HAWAII	NEV	VT	
	IDAHO	NH	VA	
	ILL	NJ	WASH	
	IND	NM	W VA	
	IOWA	NY	WIS	OTHER
	KANS	NC	WYO	
	KY	ND		

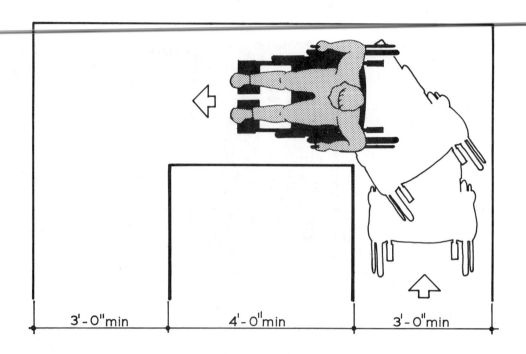

90° TURN

3'-0"min   4'-0"min   3'-0"min

Basis of standard —
ANSI 1980 — 4.3.3 and others

Notes —

APPLICABILITY			
ALA	● LA	OHIO	GUAM
● ALASKA	● MAINE	OKLA	PR
ARIZ	MD	ORE	VIR IS
● ARK	MASS	PA	DC
CAL	MICH	● RI	
● COLO	MINN	SC	
CONN	MISS	SD	● FED'L FUNDS
● DEL	MO	TENN	
FLA	MONT	● TEXAS	
GA	NEB	UTAH	
● HAWAII	● NEV	● VT	
● IDAHO	NH	● VA	
ILL	NJ	WASH	
IND	● NM	W VA	
● IOWA	● NY	WIS	OTHER
KANS	NC	WYO	
KY	ND		

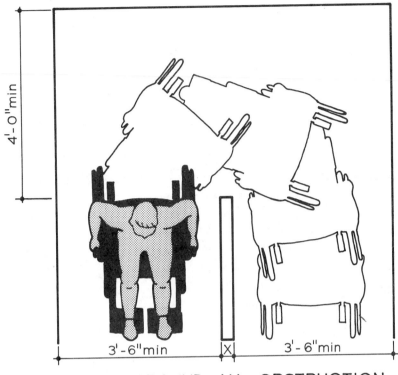

4'-0"min

3'-6"min   X   3'-6"min

TURNS AROUND AN OBSTRUCTION

Basis of standard —	APPLICABILITY			
ANSI 1980 — 4.3.3	ALA	● LA	OHIO	GUAM
	● ALASKA	● MAINE	OKLA	PR
	ARIZ	MD	ORE	VIR IS
Notes —	● ARK	MASS	PA	DC
Dimensions shown apply when x = 48″ max.	CAL	MICH	● RI	
	● COLO	MINN	SC	
	CONN	MISS	SD	● FED'L FUNDS
	● DEL	MO	TENN	
	FLA	MONT	● TEXAS	
	GA	NEB	UTAH	
	● HAWAII	● NEV	● VT	
	● IDAHO	NH	● VA	
	● ILL	NJ	WASH	
	IND	● NM	W VA	
	● IOWA	● NY	WIS	OTHER
	KANS	NC	WYO	
	KY	ND		

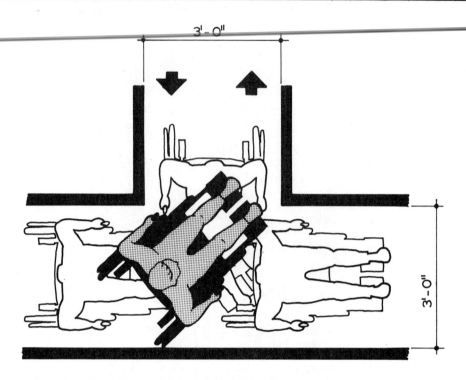

WHEELCHAIR TURNING SPACE

Basis of standard — ANSI 1980 − 4.2.3 and others	APPLICABILITY			
	ALA	● LA	OHIO	GUAM
	● ALASKA	● MAINE	OKLA	PR
	ARIZ	MD	ORE	VIR IS
	ARK	MASS	PA	DC
Notes — Dimensions shown are for a 180° turn in a T-shaped space. Texas: clearance of 4'-6" x 5'-2" are also satisfactory to make a 180° turn.	CAL	MICH	● RI	
	● COLO	MINN	SC	
	CONN	MISS	SD	FED'L FUNDS
	DEL	MO	TENN	
	FLA	MONT	● TEXAS	
	GA	NEB	UTAH	
	● HAWAII	● NEV	● VT	
	● IDAHO	NH	● VA	
	ILL	NJ	WASH	
	IND	● NM	W VA	
	● IOWA	● NY	WIS	OTHER
	KANS	NC	WYO	
	● KY	ND		

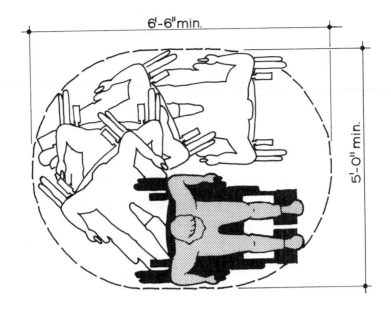

SPACE NEEDED FOR SMOOTH U-TURN IN A WHEELCHAIR

Basis of standard — ANSI 1980 — Appendix	APPLICABILITY			
	ALA	● LA	OHIO	GUAM
	● ALASKA	● MAINE	OKLA	PR
	ARIZ	MD	ORE	VIR IS
	ARK	MASS	PA	DC
	CAL	MICH	● RI	
	● COLO	MINN	SC	
	CONN	MISS	SD	FED'L FUNDS
	DEL	MO	TENN	
	FLA	MONT	TEXAS	
	GA	NEB	UTAH	
	● HAWAII	● NEV	● VT	
	● IDAHO	NH	● VA	
	ILL	NJ	WASH	
	IND	● NM	W VA	
	IOWA	● NY	WIS	OTHER
	KANS	NC	WYO	
	KY	ND		

Notes —

This data is not part of ANSI A 117.1 — 1980. The dimensions shown hereon will enable many people to turn without repeated tries and bumping into surrounding objects, so that U-turns can be made without difficulty.

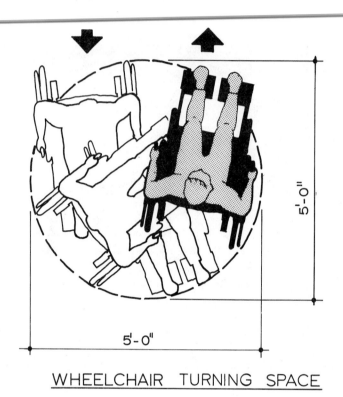

5'-0"

5'-0"

WHEELCHAIR TURNING SPACE

Basis of standard —	APPLICABILITY			
ANSI 1980 – 4.2.3 ANSI 1961 – 3.2.2 and various other state regulations	● ALA	● LA	OHIO	GUAM
	● ALASKA	● MAINE	● OKLA	PR
	● ARIZ	MD	ORE	VIR IS
Notes —	ARK	MASS	PA	DC
Dimensions shown are for a 180° turn. (ANSI 1961-: The fixed turning radius of a standard wheelchair wheel to wheel, is 18″. The fixed turning radius, front structure to rear structure, is 31.5″.)	CAL	MICH	● RI	
	● COLO	MINN	● SC	
	● CONN	MISS	● SD	● FED'L FUNDS
	● DEL	MO	TENN	
	FLA	MONT	● TEXAS	
	● GA	● NEB	UTAH	
	● HAWAII	● NEV	● VT	
	● IDAHO	● NH	● VA	
	ILL	● NJ	WASH	
	IND	● NM	● W VA	
	● IOWA	● NY	WIS	OTHER
	● KANS	NC	WYO	
	● KY	● ND		

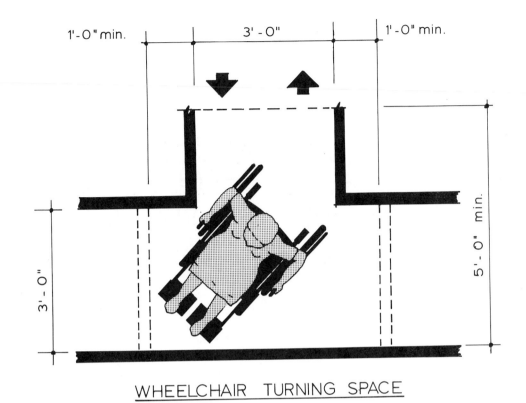

1'-0" min.   3'-0"   1'-0" min.

3'-0"

5'-0" min.

WHEELCHAIR TURNING SPACE

Basis of standard — ATBCB 1190.40 and others	APPLICABILITY			
	ALA	LA	OHIO	GUAM
	ALASKA	MAINE	OKLA	PR
	ARIZ	MD	ORE	VIR IS
● ARK	MASS	PA	DC	
	CAL	MICH	RI	
Notes —	COLO	MINN	SC	
Dimensions shown are for a 180° turn in a T-shaped space.	CONN	MISS	SD	● FED'L FUNDS
	● DEL	MO	TENN	
	FLA	MONT	TEXAS	
	GA	NEB	UTAH	
	HAWAII	NEV	VT	
	IDAHO	NH	VA	
	ILL	NJ	WASH	
	IND	NM	W VA	
	IOWA	NY	WIS	OTHER
	KANS	NC	WYO	
	KY	ND		

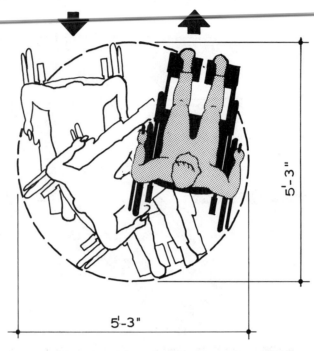

AVERAGE   WHEELCHAIR   TURNING   SPACE

Basis of standard —	APPLICABILITY			
North Carolina State Building Code	ALA	LA	OHIO	GUAM
	ALASKA	MAINE	OKLA	PR
	ARIZ	MD	ORE	VIR IS
Notes —	ARK	MASS	PA	DC
The fixed turning radius, front structure to rear structure, is 36″. The average turning space required is 63″ x 63″ . In an area with open ends, such as a corridor, a minimum of 54″ between walls would permit a 360° turn.	CAL	MICH	RI	
	COLO	MINN	SC	
	CONN	MISS	SD	FED'L
	DEL	MO	● TENN	FUNDS
	FLA	MONT	TEXAS	
	GA	NEB	UTAH	
	HAWAII	NEV	VT	
	IDAHO	NH	VA	
	ILL	NJ	WASH	
	IND	NM	W VA	
	IOWA	NY	WIS	OTHER
	KANS	● NC	WYO	
	KY	ND		

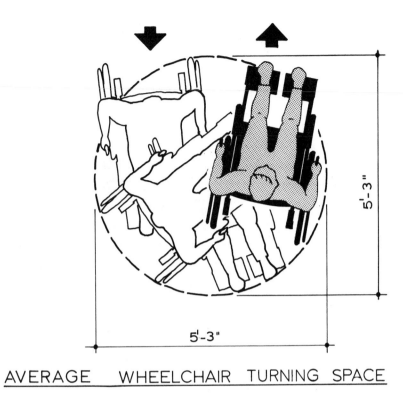

5'-3"

5'-3"

AVERAGE   WHEELCHAIR   TURNING   SPACE

Basis of standard —	APPLICABILITY			
Various	ALA	LA	OHIO	GUAM
	ALASKA	MAINE	OKLA	PR
	ARIZ	MD	ORE	VIR IS
Notes —	ARK	MASS	PA	DC
Average fixed turning radius, front structure to rear structure is 31.5″, requiring a 63″ x 63″ turning space. Utah: Fixed turning radius of a standard wheelchair is 36″ requiring an average 72″ x 72″ turning space.	CAL	MICH	RI	
	COLO	MINN	SC	
	CONN	MISS	SD	FED'L FUNDS
	DEL	MO	TENN	
	FLA	MONT	TEXAS	
	GA	NEB	● UTAH	
	HAWAII	NEV	VT	
	IDAHO	NH	VA	
	● ILL	NJ	WASH	
	IND	NM	W VA	
	IOWA	NY	WIS	OTHER
	KANS	NC	WYO	
	KY	ND		

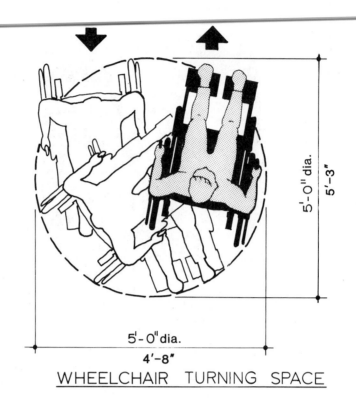

5'-0" dia.

5'-3"

5'-0" dia.

4'-8"

WHEELCHAIR TURNING SPACE

Basis of standard —	APPLICABILITY			
CAC Title 24, Part 2	ALA	LA	OHIO	GUAM
	ALASKA	MAINE	OKLA	PR
	ARIZ	MD	ORE	VIR IS
Notes —	ARK	MASS	PA	DC
The 4'-8" x 5'-3" turning space is an alternate.	● CAL	MICH	RI	
	COLO	MINN	SC	
	CONN	MISS	SD	FED'L FUNDS
	DEL	MO	TENN	
	FLA	MONT	TEXAS	
	GA	NEB	UTAH	
	HAWAII	NEV	VT	
	IDAHO	NH	VA	
	ILL	NJ	WASH	
	IND	NM	W VA	
	IOWA	NY	WIS	OTHER
	KANS	NC	WYO	
	KY	ND		

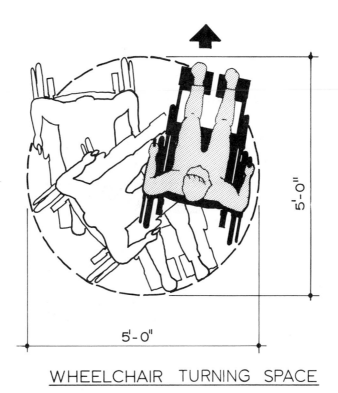

WHEELCHAIR TURNING SPACE

Basis of standard —	APPLICABILITY			
521 CMR Architectural Barriers Board	ALA	LA	OHIO	GUAM
	ALASKA	MAINE	OKLA	PR
	ARIZ	MD	ORE	VIR IS
Notes —	ARK	● MASS	PA	DC
Required for a 360° turn	CAL	MICH	RI	
	COLO	MINN	SC	
	CONN	MISS	SD	FED'L
	DEL	MO	TENN	FUNDS
	FLA	MONT	TEXAS	
	GA	NEB	UTAH	
	HAWAII	NEV	VT	
	IDAHO	NH	VA	
	ILL	NJ	WASH	
	IND	NM	W VA	
	IOWA	NY	WIS	OTHER
	KANS	NC	WYO	
	KY	ND		

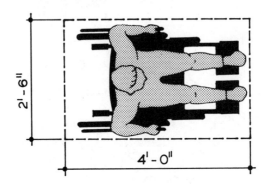

2'-6"

4'-0"

CLEAR FLOOR SPACE

Basis of standard — ANSI 1980 — 4.2.4.1 and others	APPLICABILITY			
	ALA	● LA	OHIO	GUAM
	● ALASKA	● MAINE	OKLA	PR
	ARIZ	MD	ORE	VIR IS
Notes — One full unobstructed side of clear floor or ground space shall adjoin or overlap an accessible route or adjoin another wheelchair clear floor space.	● ARK	MASS	PA	DC
	● CAL	MICH	RI	
	● COLO	MINN	SC	
	CONN	MISS	SD	● FED'L FUNDS
	● DEL	MO	TENN	
	FLA	MONT	● TEXAS	
	GA	NEB	UTAH	
	● HAWAII	● NEV	● VT	
	● IDAHO	NH	● VA	
	ILL	NJ	WASH	
	IND	● NM	W VA	
	IOWA	● NY	WIS	OTHER
	KANS	NC	WYO	
	● KY	ND		

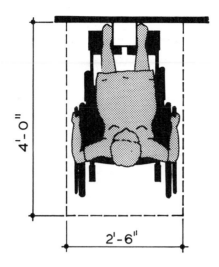

4'-0"

2'-6"

FORWARD   APPROACH

Basis of standard —	APPLICABILITY			
ANSI 1980 − 4.2.4.1 and others	ALA	● LA	OHIO	GUAM
	● ALASKA	● MAINE	OKLA	PR
	ARIZ	MD	ORE	VIR IS
Notes —	● ARK	MASS	PA	DC
Clear floor or ground space for wheelchairs may be part of the knee space required under some objects. One full unobstructed side of clear floor or ground space shall adjoin or overlap an accessible route or adjoin another wheelchair clear floor space.	● CAL	MICH	RI	
	● COLO	MINN	SC	
	CONN	MISS	SD	● FED'L FUNDS
	● DEL	MO	TENN	
	FLA	MONT	TEXAS	
	GA	NEB	UTAH	
	● HAWAII	● NEV	● VT	
	● IDAHO	NH	● VA	
	ILL	NJ	WASH	
	IND	● NM	W VA	
	IOWA	● NY	WIS	OTHER
	KANS	NC	WYO	
	● KY	ND		

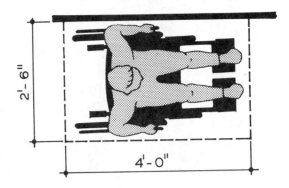

PARALLEL APPROACH

Basis of standard —	APPLICABILITY			
ANSI 1980 — 4.2.4.1 and others	ALA	● LA	OHIO	GUAM
	● ALASKA	● MAINE	OKLA	PR
	ARIZ	MD	ORE	VIR IS
Notes —	● ARK	MASS	PA	DC
Clear floor or ground space for wheelcharis may be part of the knee space required under some objects. One full unobstructed side of clear floor or ground space shall adjoin or overlap an accessible route or adjoin another wheelchair clear floor space.	● CAL	MICH	RI	
	● COLO	MINN	SC	
	CONN	MISS	SD	● FED'L FUNDS
	● DEL	MO	TENN	
	FLA	MONT	TEXAS	
	GA	NEB	UTAH	
	● HAWAII	● NEV	● VT	
	● IDAHO	NH	● VA	
	ILL	NJ	WASH	
	IND	● NM	W VA	
	IOWA	● NY	WIS	OTHER
	KANS	NC	WYO	
	● KY	ND		

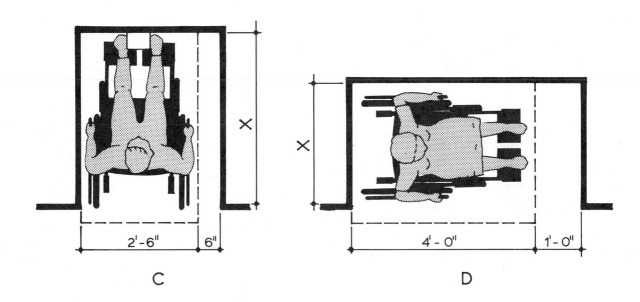

C   D

ADDITIONAL MANEUVERING CLEARANCES FOR ALCOVES

Basis of standard — ANSI 1980 — 4.2.4.2 and others	APPLICABILITY			
	ALA	● LA	OHIO	GUAM
	● ALASKA	● MAINE	OKLA	PR
	ARIZ	MD	ORE	VIR IS
Notes — For situation "C", if x > 24″, provide additional 6″ maneuvering clearance	● ARK	MASS	PA	DC
For situation "D" if x > 15″, provide additional 12″ maneuvering clearance	● CAL	MICH	● RI	
Diagrams apply to clear space in alcoves or where otherwise confined on all or part of three sides.	● COLO	MINN	SC	
	CONN	MISS	SD	● FED'L FUNDS
	● DEL	MO	TENN	
	FLA	MONT	● TEXAS	
	GA	NEB	UTAH	
	● HAWAII	● NEV	● VT	
	● IDAHO	NH	● VA	
	ILL	NJ	WASH	
	IND	● NM	W VA	
	IOWA	● NY	WIS	OTHER
	KANS	NC	WYO	
	● KY	ND		

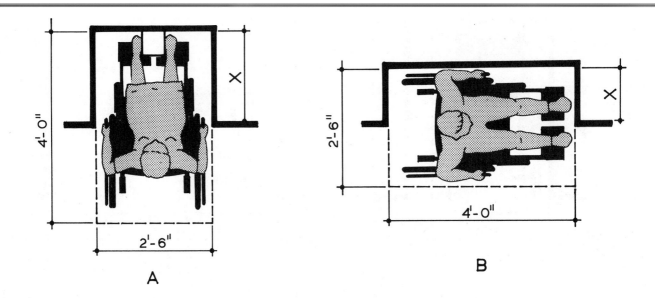

A

B

CLEAR FLOOR SPACE IN ALCOVES

Basis of standard —	APPLICABILITY			
ANSI 1980 — 4.2.4.2 and others	ALA	● LA	OHIO	GUAM
	● ALASKA	● MAINE	OKLA	PR
	ARIZ	MD	ORE	VIR IS
Notes —	● ARK	MASS	PA	DC
For situation "A", x = 24″ max.	● CAL	MICH	● RI	
For situation "B", x = 15″ max.	● COLO	MINN	SC	
Diagrams apply to clear space in alcoves or where otherwise confined on all or part of three sides.	CONN	MISS	SD	● FED'L FUNDS
	● DEL	MO	TENN	
	FLA	MONT	● TEXAS	
	GA	NEB	UTAH	
	● HAWAII	● NEV	● VT	
	● IDAHO	NH	● VA	
	ILL	NJ	WASH	
	IND	● NM	W VA	
	IOWA	● NY	WIS	OTHER
	KANS	NC	WYO	
	● KY	ND		

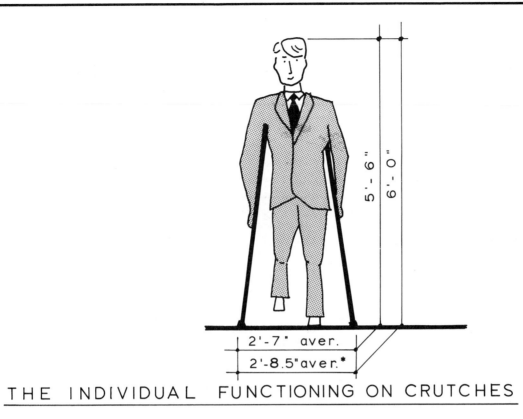

5'-6"
6'-0"

2'-7" aver.
2'-8.5"aver.*

THE INDIVIDUAL FUNCTIONING ON CRUTCHES

Basis of standard —	APPLICABILITY			
ANSI 1961 — 3.4 and others	● ALA	LA	OHIO	GUAM
	ALASKA	MAINE	● OKLA	PR
	● ARIZ	MD	ORE	VIR IS
	ARK	MASS	PA	DC
	CAL	MICH	RI	
Notes —	COLO	MINN	● SC	
(*)Texas: Crutches: 2'-8" wide	● CONN	MISS	● SD	FED'L
Walkers: 2'-4" wide	DEL	MO	● TENN	FUNDS
Cane reach, side-to-side: 2'-8"	FLA	MONT	● TEXAS	
	● GA	● NEB	● UTAH	
	HAWAII	NEV	VT	
	IDAHO	NH	VA	
	ILL	● NJ	WASH	
	IND	NM	● W VA	
	● IOWA	NY	WIS	OTHER
	● KANS	● NC	WYO	
	KY	● ND		

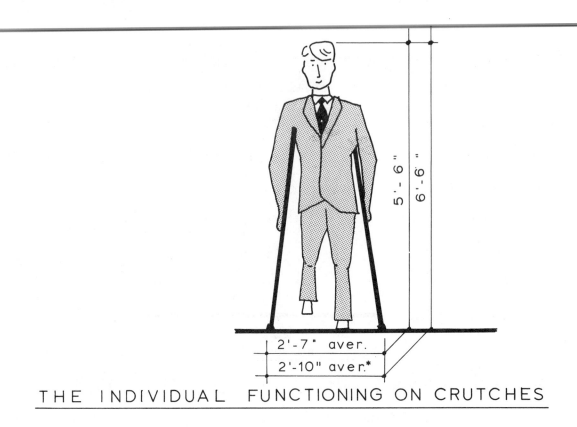

5'-6"

6'-6"

2'-7" aver.

2'-10" aver.*

THE INDIVIDUAL FUNCTIONING ON CRUTCHES

Basis of standard —	APPLICABILITY			
Various	ALA	LA	OHIO	GUAM
	ALASKA	MAINE	OKLA	PR
	ARIZ	MD	ORE	VIR IS
Notes —	ARK	MASS	PA	DC
(*) 3'-0″ in Illinois.	CAL	MICH	RI	
	COLO	MINN	SC	
	CONN	MISS	SD	FED'L
	DEL	MO	TENN	FUNDS
	FLA	MONT	TEXAS	
	GA	NEB	UTAH	
	HAWAII	NEV	VT	
	IDAHO	● NH	VA	
	● ILL	NJ	WASH	
	IND	NM	W VA	
	IOWA	NY	WIS	OTHER
	KANS	NC	WYO	
	KY	ND		

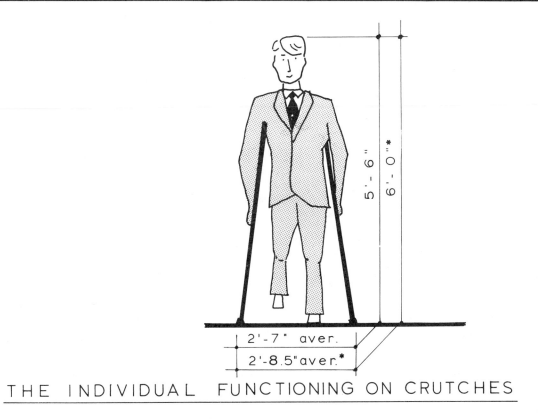

5'-6"

6'-0"*

2'-7" aver.

2'-8.5"aver.*

THE INDIVIDUAL FUNCTIONING ON CRUTCHES

Basis of standard — 521 CMR Architectural Barriers Board	APPLICABILITY			
	ALA	LA	OHIO	GUAM
	ALASKA	MAINE	OKLA	PR
	ARIZ	MD	ORE	VIR IS
Notes — (*)6'-6" height — 2'10" aver.	ARK	● MASS	PA	DC
	CAL	MICH	RI	
	COLO	MINN	SC	
	CONN	MISS	SD	FED'L FUNDS
	DEL	MO	TENN	
	FLA	MONT	TEXAS	
	GA	NEB	UTAH	
	HAWAII	NEV	VT	
	IDAHO	NH	VA	
	ILL	NJ	WASH	
	IND	NM	W VA	
	IOWA	NY	WIS	OTHER
	KANS	NC	WYO	
	KY	ND		

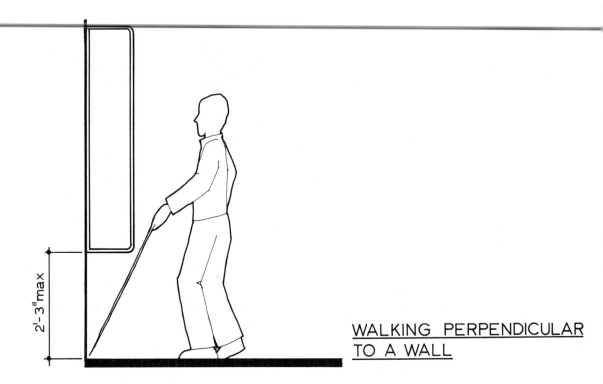

2'-3"max

WALKING PERPENDICULAR
TO A WALL

Basis of standard — ANSI 1980 — 4.4.1 and others	APPLICABILITY			
	ALA	● LA	OHIO	GUAM
	● ALASKA	● MAINE	OKLA	PR
	ARIZ	MD	ORE	VIR IS
Notes — In this configuration, mounted objects may protrude any amount.	ARK	MASS	PA	DC
	CAL	MICH	● RI	
	● COLO	MINN	SC	
	CONN	MISS	SD	● FED'L FUNDS
	● DEL	MO	TENN	
	FLA	MONT	TEXAS	
	GA	NEB	UTAH	
	● HAWAII	● NEV	● VT	
	● IDAHO	NH	● VA	
	ILL	NJ	WASH	
	IND	● NM	W VA	
	IOWA	● NY	WIS	OTHER
	KANS	NC	WYO	
	● KY	ND		

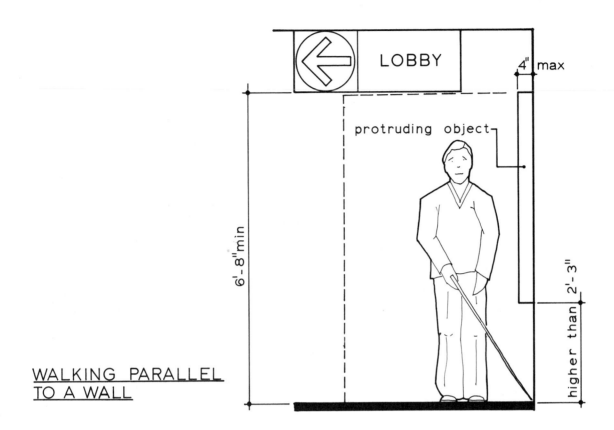

LOBBY

protruding object

4" max

6'-8" min

higher than 2'-3"

WALKING PARALLEL
TO A WALL

Basis of standard —	APPLICABILITY			
ANSI 1980 — 4.4.1 and 4.4.2 and others	ALA	● LA	OHIO	GUAM
	● ALASKA	● MAINE	OKLA	PR
	ARIZ	MD	ORE	VIR IS
	● ARK	MASS	PA	DC
	● CAL	MICH	● RI	
	● COLO	MINN	SC	
Notes —	CONN	MISS	SD	● FED'L FUNDS
Applies to objects projecting from walls up to 6'-8" height. Min. headroom of walks, halls, corridors, passageways, aisles or other circulation spaces = 80". (Federal, Arkansas, and Delaware requirements limit objects fixed to wall at 2'-0" long.)	● DEL	MO	TENN	
	FLA	MONT	● TEXAS	
	GA	NEB	UTAH	
	● HAWAII	● NEV	● VT	
	● IDAHO	NH	● VA	
	ILL	NJ	● WASH	
	IND	● NM	W VA	
	IOWA	● NY	WIS	OTHER
	KANS	NC	WYO	
	● KY	ND		

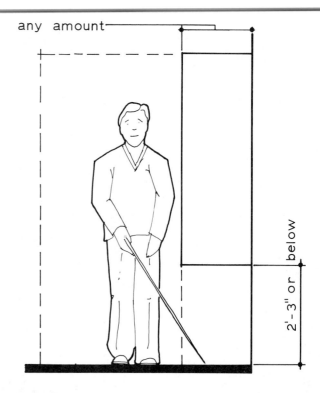

any amount

2'-3" or below

WALKING PARALLEL
TO A WALL

Basis of standard — ANSI 1980 — 4.4.1 and others	APPLICABILITY			
	ALA	● LA	OHIO	GUAM
	● ALASKA	● MAINE	OKLA	PR
	ARIZ	MD	ORE	VIR IS
Notes —	ARK	MASS	PA	DC
	● CAL	MICH	● RI	
	● COLO	MINN	SC	
	CONN	MISS	SD	● FED'L FUNDS
	● DEL	MO	TENN	
	FLA	MONT	● TEXAS	
	GA	NEB	UTAH	
	● HAWAII	● NEV	● VT	
	● IDAHO	NH	● VA	
	ILL	NJ	WASH	
	IND	● NM	W VA	
	IOWA	● NY	WIS	OTHER
	KANS	NC	WYO	
	● KY	ND		

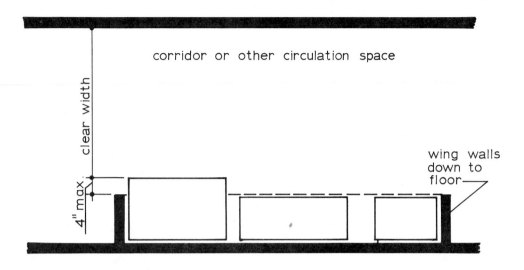

EXAMPLE OF PROTECTION AROUND WALL-MOUNTED OBJECTS AND MEASUREMENTS OF CLEAR WIDTHS

Basis of standard —	APPLICABILITY			
ANSI 1980 – 4.4.1 and others	ALA	● LA	OHIO	GUAM
	● ALASKA	● MAINE	OKLA	PR
	ARIZ	MD	ORE	VIR IS
Notes —	● ARK	MASS	PA	DC
Protruding objects shall not reduce the clear width of	● CAL	MICH	● RI	
an accessible route or maneuvering space. Illustration	● COLO	MINN	SC	
shows protruding objects hanging on wall with leading	CONN	MISS	SD	● FED'L FUNDS
edges above 27". (Additional protection is not	● DEL	MO	TENN	
required between objects hanging between wing walls.)	FLA	MONT	TEXAS	
	GA	NEB	UTAH	
	● HAWAII	● NEV	● VT	
	● IDAHO	NH	● VA	
	ILL	NJ	WASH	
	IND	● NM	W VA	
	IOWA	● NY	WIS	OTHER
	KANS	NC	WYO	
	● KY	ND		

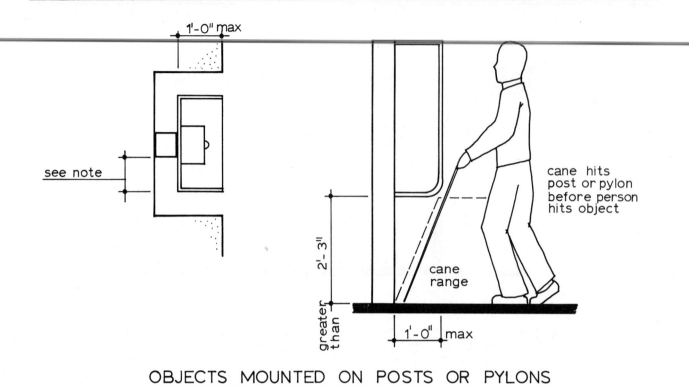

1'-0" max

see note

2'-3"

greater than

cane range

1'-0" max

cane hits post or pylon before person hits object

OBJECTS MOUNTED ON POSTS OR PYLONS

Basis of standard —	APPLICABILITY			
ANSI 1980 — 4.4.1 and others	ALA	● LA	OHIO	GUAM
	● ALASKA	● MAINE	OKLA	PR
	ARIZ	MD	ORE	VIR IS
Notes —	● ARK	MASS	PA	DC
Pylon-to-end overhang can be greater than 12″ because no one can approach the object from this direction.	● CAL	MICH	● RI	
	● COLO	MINN	SC	
	CONN	MISS	SD	● FED'L FUNDS
	● DEL	MO	TENN	
	FLA	MONT	● TEXAS	
	GA	NEB	UTAH	
	● HAWAII	● NEV	● VT	
	● IDAHO	NH	● VA	
	ILL	NJ	WASH	
	IND	● NM	W VA	
	IOWA	● NY	WIS	OTHER
	KANS	NC	WYO	
	● KY	ND		

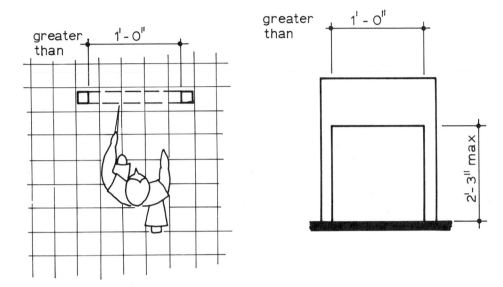

FREE - STANDING OVERHANGING OBJECTS

Basis of standard —	APPLICABILITY			
ANSI 1980 — 4.4.1 and others	ALA	● LA	OHIO	GUAM
	● ALASKA	● MAINE	OKLA	PR
	ARIZ	MD	ORE	VIR IS
Notes —	● ARK	MASS	PA	DC
Calif. — Illustrative only, not part of the regulations.	● CAL	MICH	● RI	
	● COLO	MINN	SC	
	CONN	MISS	SD	● FED'L FUNDS
	● DEL	MO	TENN	
	FLA	MONT	TEXAS	
	GA	NEB	UTAH	
	● HAWAII	● NEV	● VT	
	● IDAHO	NH	● VA	
	ILL	NJ	WASH	
	IND	● NM	W VA	
	IOWA	● NY	WIS	OTHER
	KANS	NC	WYO	
	KY	ND		

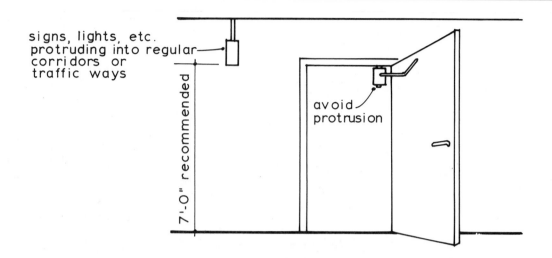

signs, lights, etc. protruding into regular corridors or traffic ways

7'-0" recommended

avoid protrusion

P R O T R U S I O N S

Basis of standard — ANSI 1961 – 5.13.4 and others	APPLICABILITY			
	● ALA	LA	OHIO	GUAM
	ALASKA	MAINE	● OKLA	PR
	ARIZ	MD	ORE	VIR IS
Notes —	ARK	MASS	PA	DC
Nebraska, South Carolina, Arizona, West Virginia, Georgia, and Connecticut requires 7'-0" min. clear height.	CAL	MICH	● RI	
	COLO	MINN	● SC	
New Jersey: Objects below 7'-0" should not project more than 6" into corridors, exitways, or traffic ways used by the general public.	● CONN	MISS	● SD	FED'L FUNDS
	DEL	MO	TENN	
	FLA	MONT	TEXAS	
	● GA	● NEB	● UTAH	
	HAWAII	NEV	VT	
	IDAHO	NH	VA	
	ILL	NJ	WASH	
	IND	NM	● W VA	
	IOWA	NY	WIS	OTHER
	● KANS	NC	WYO	
	KY	● ND		

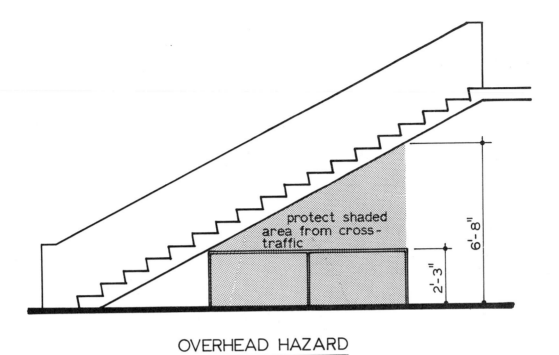

OVERHEAD HAZARD

Basis of standard — ATBCB 1190.50 and others	APPLICABILITY			
	ALA	LA	OHIO	GUAM
	ALASKA	MAINE	OKLA	PR
	ARIZ	MD	ORE	VIR IS
	● ARK	MASS	PA	DC
Notes —	● CAL	MICH	RI	
If vertical clearance of area adjoining accessible route is reduced to less than 6'-8", provide a barrier to warn blind or visually impaired persons.	COLO	MINN	SC	
	CONN	MISS	SD	● FED'L
	● DEL	MO	TENN	FUNDS
	FLA	MONT	TEXAS	
	GA	NEB	UTAH	
	HAWAII	NEV	VT	
	IDAHO	NH	VA	
	ILL	NJ	WASH	
	IND	NM	W VA	
	IOWA	NY	WIS	OTHER
	KANS	NC	WYO	
	KY	ND		

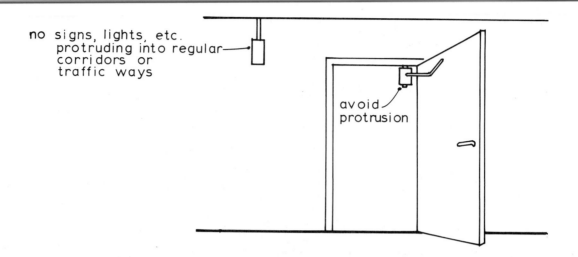

no signs, lights, etc.
protruding into regular
corridors or
traffic ways

avoid
protrusion

P R O T R U S I O N S

Basis of standard —	APPLICABILITY			
BOCA 1978	ALA	LA	● OHIO	GUAM
	ALASKA	MAINE	OKLA	PR
	ARIZ	MD	ORE	VIR IS
Notes —	ARK	MASS	PA	DC
Do not locate manholes or floor access panels in the line of egress which reduce clearance of less than 32″.	CAL	MICH	RI	
	COLO	MINN	SC	
	CONN	MISS	SD	FED'L FUNDS
	DEL	MO	TENN	
	FLA	MONT	TEXAS	
	GA	NEB	UTAH	
	HAWAII	NEV	VT	
	IDAHO	NH	● VA	
	ILL	NJ	WASH	
	IND	NM	W VA	
	IOWA	NY	WIS	OTHER
	KANS	NC	WYO	
	KY	ND		

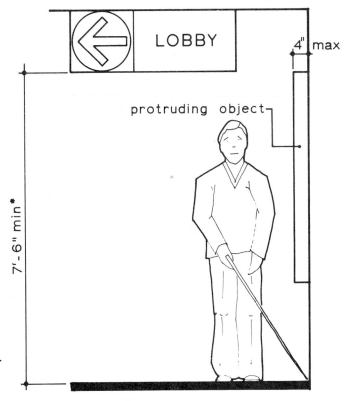

LOBBY

4" max

7'-6" min*

protruding object

WALKING PARALLEL
TO A WALL

Basis of standard —	APPLICABILITY			
Capital Development Board	ALA	LA	OHIO	GUAM
	ALASKA	MAINE	OKLA	PR
	ARIZ	MD	ORE	VIR IS
Notes —	ARK	MASS	PA	DC
Illinois and Indiana: For protrusions in excess of 4″: continue to floor or to within 8″ of floor; or recess; or enclose by wing halls. Such protected areas shall have contrasting floor texture and color. Applies also to post mounted furniture. Illinois: For emergency exit signs: may have bottom, 6'-6″ above floor where low ceiling heights prohibit placement above 7'-6″. (*) Indiana: 6'-6″	CAL	MICH	RI	
	COLO	MINN	SC	
	CONN	MISS	SD	FED'L FUNDS
	DEL	MO	TENN	
	FLA	MONT	TEXAS	
	GA	NEB	UTAH	
	HAWAII	NEV	VT	
	IDAHO	NH	VA	
	● ILL	NJ	WASH	
	● IND	NM	W VA	
	IOWA	NY	WIS	OTHER
	KANS	NC	WYO	
	KY	ND		

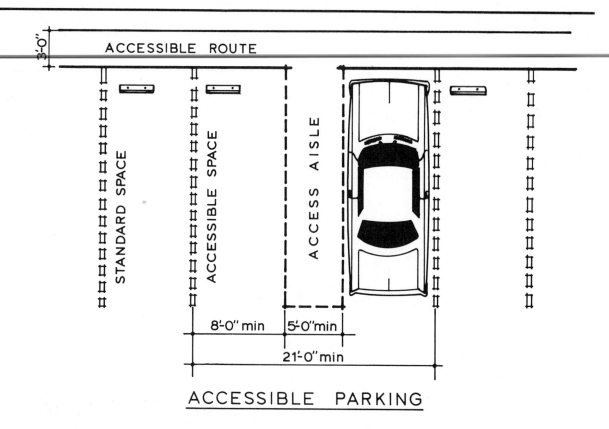

ACCESSIBLE PARKING

Basis of standard — ANSI 1980 — and others	APPLICABILITY			
	ALA	● LA	OHIO	GUAM
	● ALASKA	● MAINE	OKLA	PR
	ARIZ	MD	ORE	VIR IS
	● ARK	MASS	PA	DC
	CAL	MICH	● RI	
	● COLO	MINN	SC	
	CONN	MISS	SD	● FED'L FUNDS
	● DEL	MO	TENN	
	FLA	MONT	TEXAS	
	GA	NEB	UTAH	
	● HAWAII	● NEV	● VT	
	● IDAHO	NH	VA	
	ILL	NJ	WASH	
	IND	● NM	W VA	
	IOWA	NY	WIS	OTHER
	KANS	NC	WYO	
	KY	ND		

Notes —

Locate on shortest possible accessible route to accessible building entrance. Two accessible parking spaces may share a common access aisle. Car overhangs shall not reduce clear width of accessible circulation route. Designate accessible parking spaces by a sign showing symbol of accessibility. Do not obscure sign by parked vehicle. Federal requires 9'-6" min. vertical clearance at passenger loading zones. In Arkansas, refer to Act 772 of 1979 for details.

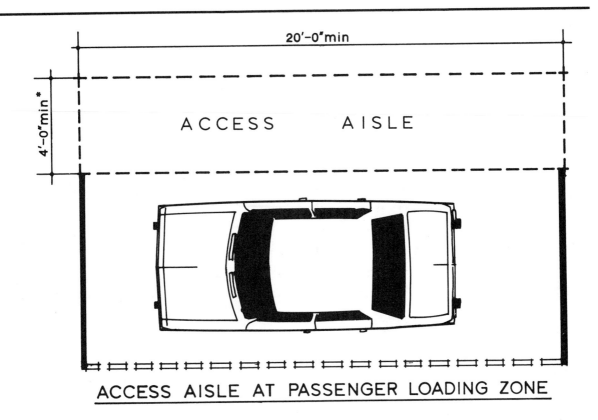

20'-0"min

4'-0"min *

ACCESS   AISLE

ACCESS AISLE AT PASSENGER LOADING ZONE

Basis of standard —	APPLICABILITY			
ANSI 1980 — 4.6.5 and others	ALA	● LA	OHIO	GUAM
	● ALASKA	● MAINE	OKLA	PR
	ARIZ	MD	ORE	VIR IS
	● ARK	MASS	PA	DC
	CAL	MICH	● RI	
Notes —	● COLO	MINN	SC	
If there are curbs between the access aisle and the vehicle pull-up space, provide complying curb ramp. If passenger loading zones are provided, a reasonable number, but at least one, shall comply with requirements. Federal, Arkansas and Delaware require 9'-6" vertical clearance. (In Arkansas, refer to Act 772 of 1979 for details.) (*)44" in Texas.	CONN	MISS	SD	● FED'L FUNDS
	● DEL	MO	TENN	
	FLA	MONT	TEXAS	
	GA	NEB	UTAH	
	● HAWAII	● NEV	● VT	
	● IDAHO	NH	● VA	
	ILL	NJ	WASH	
	IND	● NM	W VA	
	IOWA	● NY	WIS	OTHER
	KANS	NC	WYO	
	● KY	ND		

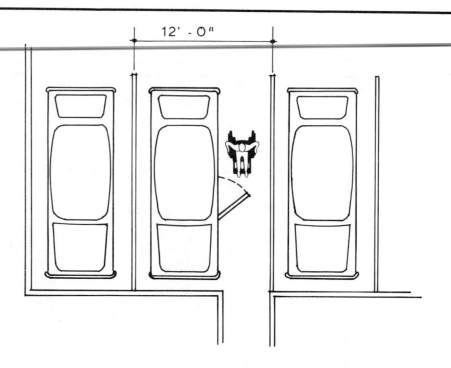

12' - 0"

PARKING LOTS

Basis of standard — ANSI 1961 — 4.3 and others	APPLICABILITY			
	ALA	LA	OHIO	GUAM
	ALASKA	MAINE	● OKLA	PR
	● ARIZ	MD	ORE	VIR IS
	ARK	MASS	PA	DC
	CAL	MICH	RI	
	COLO	MINN	● SC	
	CONN	MISS	● SD	FED'L
Notes —	DEL	MO	TENN	FUNDS
Set aside accessible spaces, approximate to the facility, and identify for use by individuals with physical disabilities. Plan with care so that individuals in wheelchairs or using braces and crutches are not compelled to wheel or walk behind parked cars. Distribute spaces for use by disabled in accord with frequency and persistency of parking needs.	FLA	MONT	TEXAS	
	● GA	NEB	UTAH	
	HAWAII	NEV	VT	
	IDAHO	NH	VA	
	ILL	NJ	WASH	
W. Va. min: 1 reserved space plus one per 50 spaces.	IND	NM	● W VA	
	IOWA	NY	WIS	OTHER
	● KANS	NC	WYO	
	KY	● ND		

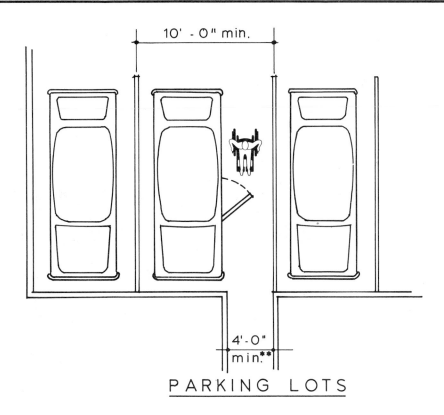

10' - 0" min.

4'-0" min.**

PARKING LOTS

Basis of standard —	APPLICABILITY			
BOCA — 1978 and others	ALA	LA	● OHIO	GUAM
	ALASKA	MAINE	OKLA	PR
	ARIZ	MD	ORE	VIR IS
Notes —	ARK	MASS	PA	DC
Identify spaces by signs.* Locate as close as possible to building entrance.	CAL	● MICH	● RI	
	COLO	MINN	SC	
	CONN	MISS	SD	FED'L FUNDS
	DEL	MO	TENN	
	FLA	MONT	TEXAS	
	GA	NEB	UTAH	
	HAWAII	NEV	VT	
	IDAHO	NH	VA	
	ILL	NJ	WASH	
	IND	NM	W VA	
	IOWA	NY	WIS	OTHER
	KANS	NC	WYO	
	KY	ND		

Notes —
Identify spaces by signs.*
Locate as close as possible to building entrance.

Total parking in lot	Required number of accessible spaces
Up to 25	1
26 to 50	2
51 to 75	3
76 to 100	4
101 to 150	5
151 to 200	6
201 to 300	7
301 to 400	8
401 to 500	9
501 to 1000	2% of total
Over 1000	20 plus 1 for each 100 over 1,000

(*)Michigan specifies approx. 6' height.
(**)Rhode Island: 3'-0".

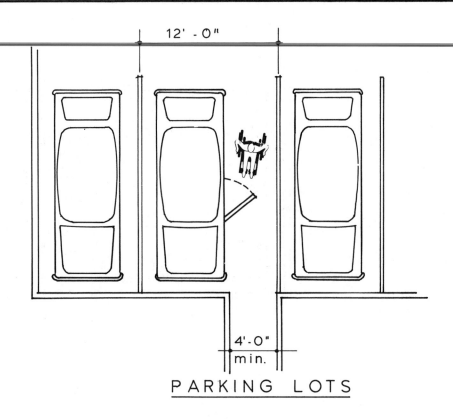

12' - 0"

4'-0"
min.

PARKING LOTS

Basis of standard —	APPLICABILITY			
BOCA – 1978	ALA	LA	OHIO	GUAM
	ALASKA	MAINE	OKLA	PR
Notes —	ARIZ	● MD	ORE	VIR IS
Identify spaces by 8′ high sign. If sign is against	ARK	MASS	PA	DC
building or location inaccessible to vehicular or	CAL	MICH	RI	
pedestrian traffic, mount min. 6′ above grade.	COLO	MINN	SC	
Conform size, lettering and coloring to require-	CONN	MISS	SD	FED'L
ments of Federal Highway Administration. Max.	DEL	MO	TENN	FUNDS
grade for spaces: 5%. Locate as close as possible	FLA	MONT	TEXAS	
to building entrances.	GA	NEB	UTAH	
	HAWAII	NEV	VT	
	IDAHO	NH	VA	
	ILL	NJ	WASH	
	IND	NM	W VA	
	IOWA	NY	WIS	OTHER
	KANS	NC	WYO	
	KY	ND		

Total parking in lot	Required number of accessible spaces
Up to 25	1
26 to 50	2
51 to 75	3
76 to 100	4
101 to 150	5
151 to 200	6
201 to 300	7
301 to 400	8
401 to 500	9
501 to 1000	2% of total
Over 1000	20 plus 1 for each 100 over 1,000

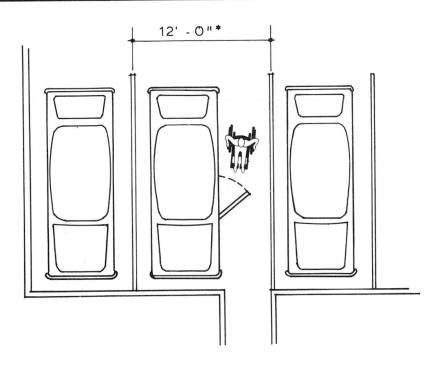

12' - 0" *

PARKING LOTS

Basis of standard —	APPLICABILITY			
State Building Code and others	ALA	LA	OHIO	GUAM
	ALASKA	MAINE	OKLA	PR
	ARIZ	MD	● ORE	VIR IS
Notes —	ARK	MASS	PA	DC
Provide at least 1 space per 50 spaces or fraction	CAL	MICH	RI	
thereof, and identify. Locate as near as practicable	COLO	● MINN	SC	
to accessible building entrance.	CONN	MISS	SD	FED'L
(*)North Carolina and Tennessee require 12'-6".	DEL	MO	● TENN	FUNDS
Oregon applies regulation to government and public	FLA	MONT	TEXAS	
buildings and publicly maintained parking facilities.	GA	● NEB	UTAH	
	HAWAII	NEV	VT	
	IDAHO	NH	VA	
	ILL	NJ	WASH	
	IND	NM	W VA	
	IOWA	NY	WIS	OTHER
	KANS	● NC	WYO	
	KY	ND		

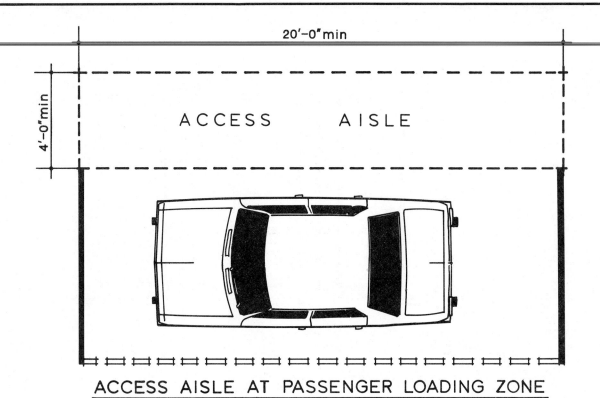

20'-0"min

4'-0"min

ACCESS   AISLE

ACCESS AISLE AT PASSENGER LOADING ZONE

Basis of standard —	APPLICABILITY			
Iowa Administrative Code and others	ALA	LA	OHIO	GUAM
	ALASKA	MAINE	OKLA	PR
	ARIZ	MD	ORE	VIR IS
	ARK	MASS	PA	DC
Notes —	CAL	MICH	RI	
Washington: Loading zones and drop-off zones shall have long dimension abutting an accessible route of travel. Where separated by curbs, provide curb-cuts or ramps. Passenger drop-off zones min. 12' wide by 25' long.	COLO	MINN	SC	
	CONN	MISS	SD	FED'L
	DEL	MO	TENN	FUNDS
	FLA	MONT	TEXAS	
	GA	NEB	UTAH	
	HAWAII	NEV	VT	
	IDAHO	NH	VA	
	ILL	NJ	● WASH	
	IND	NM	W VA	
	● IOWA	NY	WIS	OTHER
	KANS	NC	WYO	
	KY	ND		

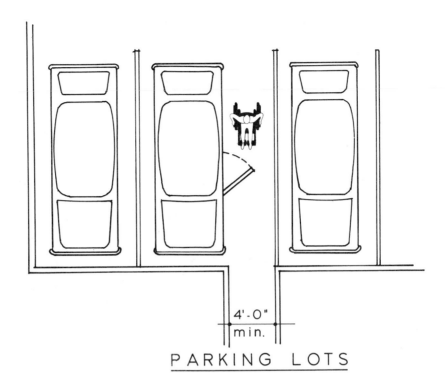

4'-0" min.

PARKING LOTS

Basis of standard —	APPLICABILITY			
Act 235, P.L. 348 (Pa.) and others	ALA	LA	OHIO	GUAM
	ALASKA	MAINE	OKLA	PR
	ARIZ	MD	ORE	VIR IS
Notes —	ARK	MASS	● PA	DC
Provide at least one parking area at grade level of the building or provide ramps at curbs or steps between the parking area and the building.	CAL	MICH	RI	
	COLO	MINN	SC	
	CONN	● MISS	SD	FED'L
	DEL	MO	TENN	FUNDS
	FLA	MONT	TEXAS	
	GA	NEB	UTAH	
	HAWAII	NEV	VT	
	IDAHO	NH	VA	
	ILL	NJ	WASH	
	IND	NM	W VA	
	IOWA	NY	WIS	OTHER
	KANS	NC	WYO	
	KY	ND		

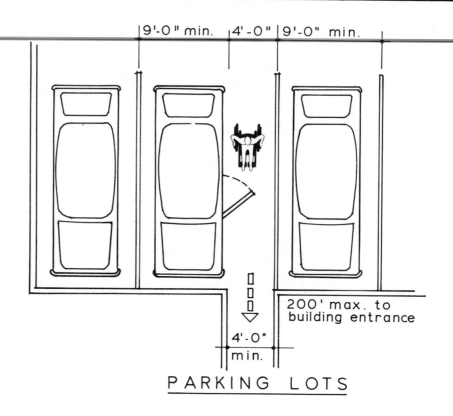

9'-0" min.   4'-0"   9'-0" min.

200' max. to
building entrance

4'-0"
min.

P A R K I N G   L O T S

Basis of standard — Barrier Free Design Standard	APPLICABILITY			
	● ALA	LA	OHIO	GUAM
	ALASKA	MAINE	OKLA	PR
	ARIZ	MD	ORE	VIR IS
	ARK	MASS	PA	DC
	CAL	MICH	RI	
	COLO	MINN	SC	
	CONN	MISS	SD	FED'L FUNDS
	DEL	MO	TENN	
	FLA	MONT	TEXAS	
	GA	NEB	UTAH	
	HAWAII	NEV	VT	
	IDAHO	NH	VA	
	ILL	NJ	WASH	
	IND	NM	W VA	
	IOWA	NY	WIS	OTHER
	KANS	NC	WYO	
	KY	ND		

Notes —

Identify spaces with wheelchair symbol. Locate spaces within 200' of building entrance.

Total parking in lot	Required number of accessible spaces
Up to 25	1
26 to 50	2
51 to 75	3
76 to 100	4
101 to 150	5
151 to 200	6
201 to 300	7
301 to 400	8
401 to 500	9
501 to 1,000	2% of total
Over 1,000	20 plus 1 for each 100 over 1,000

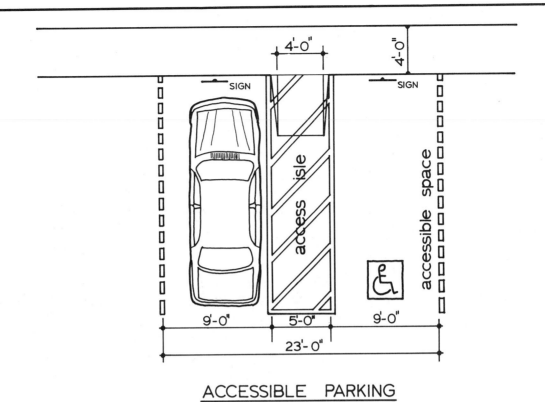

ACCESSIBLE   PARKING

Basis of standard —	APPLICABILITY			
CAC Title 24, Part 2	ALA	LA	OHIO	GUAM
	ALASKA	MAINE	OKLA	PR
Notes —	ARIZ	MD	ORE	VIR IS
1. Signage: 3′ square symbol in space; 70 sq. in. sign with symbol at front of space; 17″ × 22″ sign stating illegally parked cars will be towed, at space or entry to off-street parking.	ARK	MASS	PA	DC
	● CAL	MICH	RI	
2. Curb ramp may not protrude more than 5′-0″ into space.	COLO	MINN	SC	
3. Space to be level within ¼″ per foot.	CONN	MISS	SD	FED'L
4. Wheelchairs cannot be required to pass behind any car other than their own.	DEL	MO	TENN	FUNDS
	FLA	MONT	TEXAS	
5. Total Number of Number of handicapped	GA	NEB	UTAH	
Parking Spaces parking spaces required	HAWAII	NEV	VT	
1- 40 1	IDAHO	NH	VA	
41- 80 2	ILL	NJ	WASH	
81-120 3	IND	NM	W VA	
121-160 4	IOWA	NY	WIS	OTHER
161-300 5	KANS	NC	WYO	
301-400 6	KY	ND		
401-500 7				
Over 500 1 for each 200 additional spaces provided				

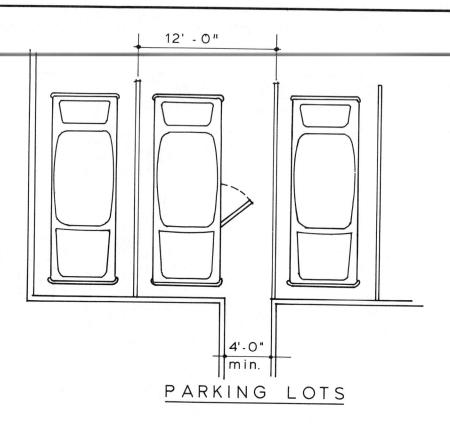

12' - 0"

4'-0"
min.

PARKING LOTS

Basis of standard —	APPLICABILITY			
Department of General Services	ALA	LA	OHIO	GUAM
	ALASKA	MAINE	OKLA	PR
	ARIZ	MD	ORE	VIR IS
Notes —	ARK	MASS	PA	DC
Applies to government facilities. Min. spaces: 2, plus 2 for each 300 public parking spaces. Provide 1/2 for physically disabled persons in wheelchairs, and 1/2 for other physically disabled persons. Add one space of each of these two types in the ratio and number established by the using agency. For Physical Restoration Rehabilitation, provide a min. of 4 such spaces of which 3 shall be for physically disabled persons in wheelchairs. Diagram shows space for physically disabled persons in wheelchairs. Provide ramp for elevation change from parking area to walk. Designate spaces as appropriate: PARKING FOR DISABLED PERSONS ONLY or PARKING FOR WHEELCHAIR DRIVERS ONLY and with International Wheelchair Symbol of accessibility.	CAL	MICH	RI	
	COLO	MINN	SC	
	CONN	MISS	SD	FED'L FUNDS
	DEL	MO	TENN	
	● FLA	MONT	TEXAS	
	GA	NEB	UTAH	
	HAWAII	NEV	VT	
	IDAHO	NH	VA	
	ILL	NJ	WASH	
	IND	NM	W VA	
	IOWA	NY	WIS	OTHER
	KANS	NC	WYO	
	KY	ND		

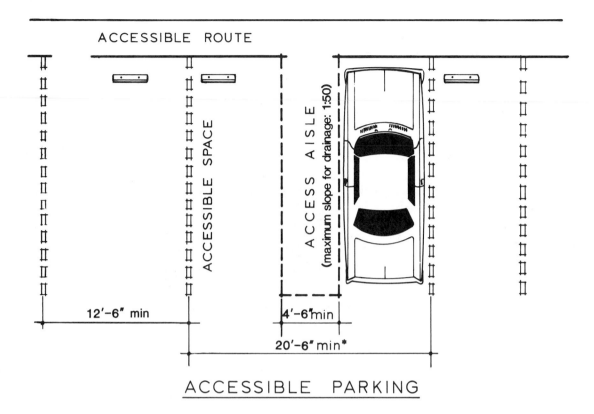

ACCESSIBLE ROUTE

ACCESSIBLE SPACE

ACCESS AISLE (maximum slope for drainage: 1:50)

12'-6" min

4'-6" min

20'-6" min*

ACCESSIBLE PARKING

Basis of standard —	APPLICABILITY			
Capital Development Board	ALA	LA	OHIO	GUAM
	ALASKA	MAINE	OKLA	PR
	ARIZ	MD	ORE	VIR IS
Notes —	ARK	MASS	PA	DC
Locate handicapped spaces or a passenger loading zone as close as possible to the shortest accessible path of travel to each building.	CAL	MICH	RI	
	COLO	MINN	SC	
Total No. of parking spaces Number of parking spaces for disabled drivers	CONN	MISS	SD	FED'L FUNDS
	DEL	MO	TENN	
1-400 Min. = 2 or 2% of total provided, whichever is the greatest	FLA	MONT	TEXAS	
401 and above 8 plus 1% of the total above 401	GA	NEB	UTAH	
For curbs at parking, provide curb ramps. In structures provide 8'-0" min. headroom with 6' wide access aisle (may extend into circulation route); clearance to be provided is for half the number of handicapped spaces shown on above table. See next page.	HAWAII	NEV	VT	
	IDAHO	NH	VA	
	● ILL	NJ	WASH	
	IND	NM	W VA	
(*)Permissible where entry can be gained by car going in forward or in reverse.	IOWA	NY	WIS	OTHER
	KANS	NC	WYO	
	KY	ND		

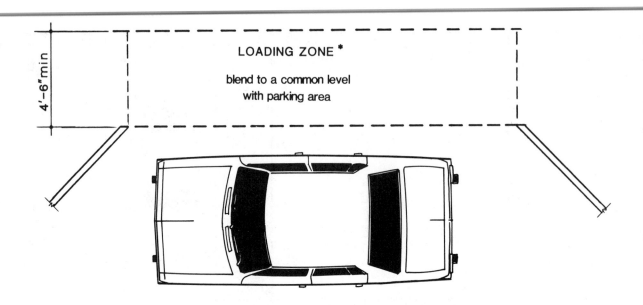

PASSENGER LOADING ZONE

Basis of standard —	APPLICABILITY			
Capital Development Board	ALA	LA	OHIO	GUAM
	ALASKA	MAINE	OKLA	PR
	ARIZ	MD	ORE	VIR IS
Notes —	ARK	MASS	PA	DC
See note, on preceeding page. Provide all spaces on an accessible level for multi-story parking structures without elevators. Mark parking spaces with International Symbol for accessibility on walls or poles (7'-6" to bottom). (*)Loading zone surface shall contrast in color and texture to the surrounding surfaces.	CAL	MICH	RI	
	COLO	MINN	SC	
	CONN	MISS	SD	FED'L
	DEL	MO	TENN	FUNDS
	FLA	MONT	TEXAS	
	GA	NEB	UTAH	
	HAWAII	NEV	VT	
	IDAHO	NH	VA	
	● ILL	NJ	WASH	
	IND	NM	W VA	
	IOWA	NY	WIS	OTHER
	KANS	NC	WYO	
	KY	ND		

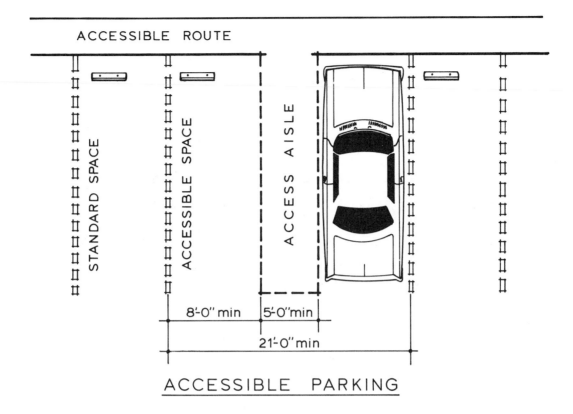

ACCESSIBLE ROUTE

STANDARD SPACE

ACCESSIBLE SPACE

ACCESS AISLE

8'-0" min 5'-0" min

21'-0" min

ACCESSIBLE PARKING

Basis of standard —	APPLICABILITY			
Indiana Amendments to Uniform Building Code	ALA	LA	OHIO	GUAM
	ALASKA	MAINE	OKLA	PR
Notes —	ARIZ	MD	ORE	VIR IS
Locate as close as possible to elevators, ramps, walkways and accessible entrances. In parking garages provide 7'-6" unobstructed ceiling height for physically handicapped parking spaces.	ARK	MASS	PA	DC
	CAL	MICH	RI	
	COLO	MINN	SC	
Parking spaces for handicapped	CONN	MISS	SD	FED'L FUNDS
	DEL	MO	TENN	
Total spaces in lot Required number of reserved spaces	FLA	MONT	TEXAS	
0 to 7 0	GA	NEB	UTAH	
8 to 25 1	HAWAII	NEV	VT	
26 to 50 2	IDAHO	NH	VA	
51 to 75 3	ILL	NJ	WASH	
76 to 100 4	● IND	NM	W VA	
101 to 150 5	IOWA	NY	WIS	OTHER
151 to 200 6	KANS	NC	WYO	
201 to 300 7	KY	ND		
301 to 400 8				
401 to 500 9				
501 to 1000 2% of total				
Over 1000 20 plus 1 for each 100 over 1000				

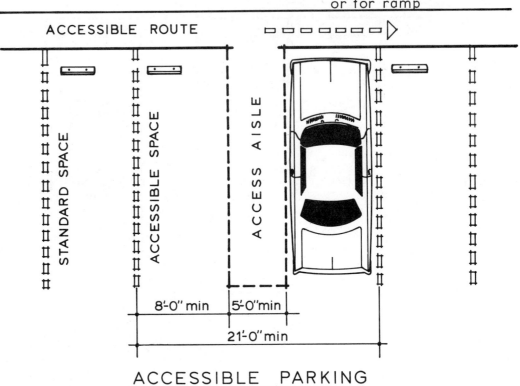

max. distance to entrance: 200' for 1:30 max. slope
100' for more than 1:30 slope
or for ramp

ACCESSIBLE ROUTE

STANDARD SPACE

ACCESSIBLE SPACE

ACCESS AISLE

8'-0" min   5'-0" min

21'-0" min

ACCESSIBLE PARKING

Basis of standard —	APPLICABILITY			
Iowa Administrative Code	ALA	LA	OHIO	GUAM
	ALASKA	MAINE	OKLA	PR
	ARIZ	MD	ORE	VIR IS
Notes —	ARK	MASS	PA	DC
Identify spaces with international symbol of the handicapped. Locate spaces as close as possible to accessible path of travel. Provide firm surface with 1:50 max slope. Two accessible parking spaces may share a common access aisle.	CAL	MICH	RI	
	COLO	MINN	SC	
	CONN	MISS	SD	FED'L
	DEL	MO	TENN	FUNDS
	FLA	MONT	TEXAS	
	GA	NEB	UTAH	
	HAWAII	NEV	VT	
	IDAHO	NH	VA	
	ILL	NJ	WASH	
	IND	NM	W VA	
	● IOWA	NY	WIS	OTHER
	KANS	NC	WYO	
	KY	ND		

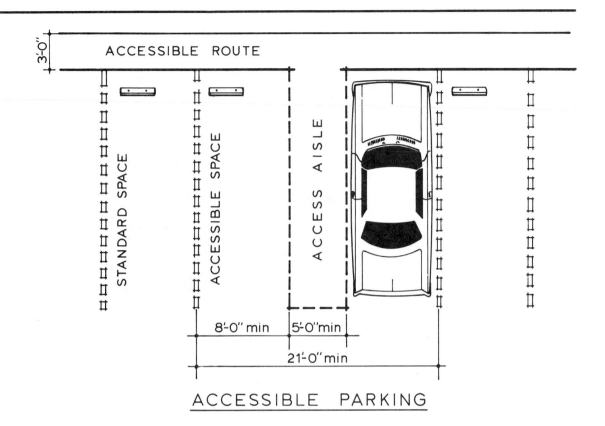

ACCESSIBLE ROUTE

3'-0"

STANDARD SPACE

ACCESSIBLE SPACE

ACCESS AISLE

8'-0" min   5'-0" min

21'-0" min

ACCESSIBLE PARKING

Basis of standard —	APPLICABILITY			
815 KAR 7:060	ALA	LA	OHIO	GUAM
	ALASKA	MAINE	OKLA	PR
	ARIZ	MD	ORE	VIR IS
Notes —	ARK	MASS	PA	DC
Minimum accessible parking spaces required:	CAL	MICH	RI	
	COLO	MINN	SC	
1 to 25 1	CONN	MISS	SD	FED'L
26 to 50 2	DEL	MO	TENN	FUNDS
51 to 75 3	FLA	MONT	TEXAS	
76 to 100 4	GA	NEB	UTAH	
101 to 150 5	HAWAII	NEV	VT	
151 to 200 6	IDAHO	NH	VA	
201 to 300 7	ILL	NJ	WASH	
301 to 400 8	IND	NM	W VA	
401 to 500 9	IOWA	NY	WIS	OTHER
501 or over ... 2% of total – 20 plus 1 for each 200 over 1000	KANS	NC	WYO	
	● KY	ND		

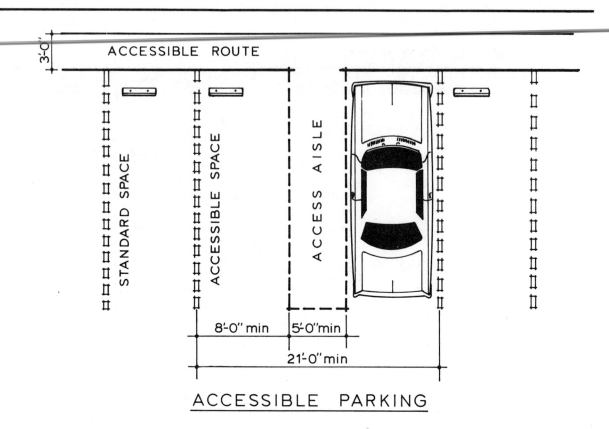

3'-0"

ACCESSIBLE ROUTE

STANDARD SPACE

ACCESSIBLE SPACE

ACCESS AISLE

8'-0" min   5'-0" min

21'-0" min

ACCESSIBLE PARKING

Basis of standard —	APPLICABILITY			
Act 625, 1977 Louisiana legislature	ALA	● LA	OHIO	GUAM
	ALASKA	MAINE	OKLA	PR
	ARIZ	MD	ORE	VIR IS
Notes —	ARK	MASS	PA	DC
Special minimum requirements for new (after 1/1/78) governmental or public facilities:	CAL	MICH	RI	
3 spaces in immediate vicinity of a physical rehabilitation center	COLO	MINN	SC	
1 space for each 300 publicly owned and operated parking lot spaces.	CONN	MISS	SD	FED'L FUNDS
	DEL	MO	TENN	
Locate accessible to curb ramp or curb cut to allow access to facility served. Diagonal or perpendicular spaces min. 12' wide. Parallel parking spaces at beginning or end of a block or adjacent to alley entrances.	FLA	MONT	TEXAS	
	GA	NEB	UTAH	
	HAWAII	NEV	VT	
	IDAHO	NH	VA	
	ILL	NJ	WASH	
	IND	NM	W VA	
	IOWA	NY	WIS	OTHER
	KANS	NC	WYO	
	KY	ND		

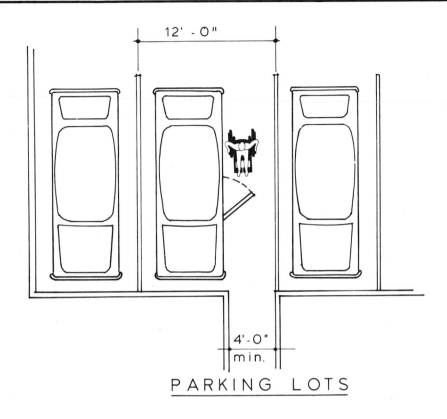

PARKING LOTS

Basis of standard —	APPLICABILITY			
Architectural Barriers Board	ALA	LA	OHIO	GUAM
	ALASKA	MAINE	OKLA	PR
	ARIZ	MD	ORE	VIR IS
Notes —	ARK	● MASS	PA	DC
Lots and public parking garages with a capacity of 25 or more automobiles:	CAL	MICH	RI	
	COLO	MINN	SC	
All spaces Special spaces	CONN	MISS	SD	FED'L
25 1 space	DEL	MO	TENN	FUNDS
26-40 5% but not less than 2				
41-100 4% but not less than 3	FLA	MONT	TEXAS	
101-200 3% but not less than 4	GA	NEB	UTAH	
201-500 2% but not less than 6				
501-1000 1.5% but not less than 10	HAWAII	NEV	VT	
1000-2000 1% but not less than 15	IDAHO	NH	VA	
2001-5000 .075% but not less than 20				
5001- .050% but not less than 30	ILL	NJ	WASH	
Provide curb ramp at sidewalks. Identify spaces with	IND	NM	W VA	
"International Symbol of Accessibility" at a min 6'	IOWA	NY	WIS	OTHER
and max. ht. of 10' above ground or floor. Slope parking surface max 5%.	KANS	NC	WYO	
	KY	ND		

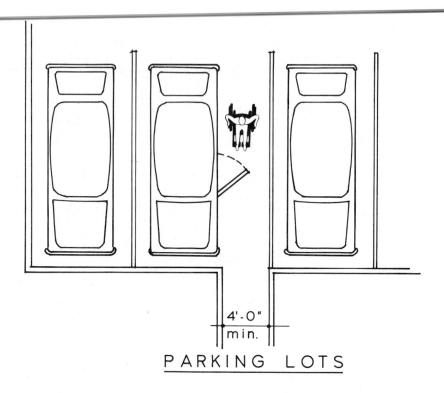

4'-0"
min.

PARKING LOTS

Basis of standard —	APPLICABILITY			
Missouri Revised Statutes, Ch. 8	ALA	LA	OHIO	GUAM
	ALASKA	MAINE	OKLA	PR
	ARIZ	MD	ORE	VIR IS
Notes —	ARK	MASS	PA	DC
Where parking is provided, there shall be a walk or ramp, not interrupted by steps or curbs, from at least one parking area to the building or facility.	CAL	MICH	RI	
	COLO	MINN	SC	
	CONN	MISS	SD	FED'L FUNDS
	DEL	● MO	TENN	
	FLA	MONT	TEXAS	
	GA	NEB	UTAH	
	HAWAII	NEV	VT	
	IDAHO	NH	VA	
	ILL	NJ	WASH	
	IND	NM	W VA	
	IOWA	NY	WIS	OTHER
	KANS	NC	WYO	
	KY	ND		

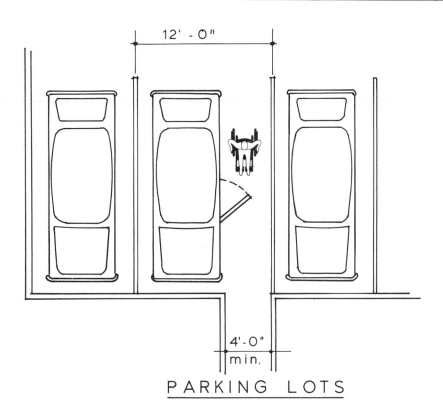

12' - 0"

4' - 0"
min.

PARKING LOTS

Basis of standard —	APPLICABILITY			
Architectural Barrier Free Code of New Hampshire	ALA	LA	OHIO	GUAM
	ALASKA	MAINE	OKLA	PR
	ARIZ	MD	ORE	VIR IS
Notes —	ARK	MASS	PA	DC
Locate closest to the designated primary accessible entrance(s) and identify with International Symbol of Access and sign that space or pair of spaces are reserved for the physically handicapped located between 6'-8" and 10'-0" to bottom edge. Required spaces:	CAL	MICH	RI	
	COLO	MINN	SC	
	CONN	MISS	SD	FED'L FUNDS
	DEL	MO	TENN	
	FLA	MONT	TEXAS	
	GA	NEB	UTAH	
	HAWAII	NEV	VT	
	IDAHO	● NH	VA	
	ILL	NJ	WASH	
	IND	NM	W VA	
	IOWA	NY	WIS	OTHER
	KANS	NC	WYO	
	KY	ND		

All spaces   Special spaces   but not less than
  1-25   1
  26-80   5%   2 spaces
  81-200   3%   4 spaces
 201-500   2%   6 spaces
  501 +   1.5%   10 spaces

Max. slope of surface: 1 in 20.

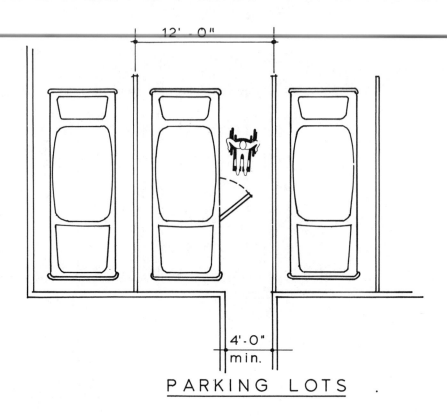

12' - 0"

4'-0"
min.

PARKING LOTS   .

Basis of standard —	APPLICABILITY			
Barrier Free Design Regulations	ALA	LA	OHIO	GUAM
	ALASKA	MAINE	OKLA	PR
	ARIZ	MD	ORE	VIR IS
Notes —	ARK	MASS	PA	DC
Minimum number under control of state, county or municipality or parking authority: 1% of the total	CAL	MICH	RI	
spaces, but not less than 2 in location most accessible	COLO	MINN	SC	
to the building it serves. All other cases where park-	CONN	MISS	SD	FED'L
ing lots are provided for public buildings:	DEL	MO	TENN	FUNDS
Total parking in lot Number of accessible spaces	FLA	MONT	TEXAS	
Up to 50 1	GA	NEB	UTAH	
51 to 200 2	HAWAII	NEV	VT	
Over 200 1%	IDAHO	NH	VA	
If designated space is more than 200' from the princi-	ILL	● NJ	WASH	
pal accessible entrance, provide drop-off area within	IND	NM	W VA	
100' of entrance. Standard parking space parallel to	IOWA	NY	WIS	OTHER
curb is acceptable if it provides sufficient space for	KANS	NC	WYO	
handicapped to enter and exit automobile on to	KY	ND		

Minimum number under control of state, county or
municipality or parking authority: 1% of the total
spaces, but not less than 2 in location most accessible
to the building it serves. All other cases where parking lots are provided for public buildings:
Total parking in lot   Number of accessible spaces
      Up to 50   1
      51 to 200   2
      Over 200   1%
If designated space is more than 200' from the principal accessible entrance, provide drop-off area within
100' of entrance. Standard parking space parallel to
curb is acceptable if it provides sufficient space for
handicapped to enter and exit automobile on to
paved surface with sufficient area and affords route
of travel accessibility to building.

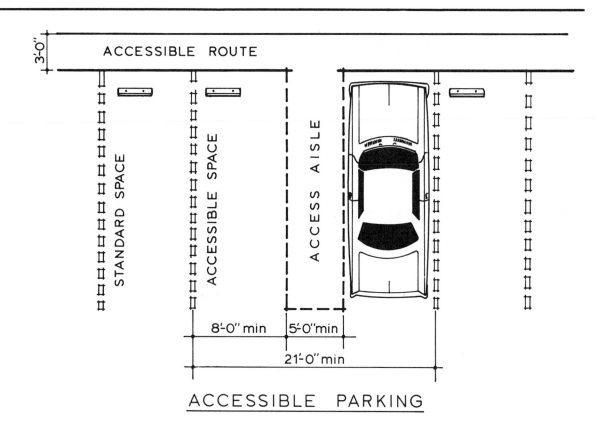

ACCESSIBLE PARKING

Basis of standard —	APPLICABILITY			
C 215-3	ALA	LA	OHIO	GUAM
	ALASKA	MAINE	OKLA	PR
Notes —	ARIZ	MD	ORE	VIR IS
For shopping centers or a facility having at least five separate retail stores and at least 20 public off-street parking spaces, a minimum of 5 percent of such spaces or 10 such spaces, whichever is less, shall be for use by the physically handicapped. (Chapter 20S-Laws of 1981.)	ARK	MASS	PA	DC
	CAL	MICH	RI	
	COLO	MINN	SC	
	CONN	MISS	SD	FED'L FUNDS
Table C 215-3 (I-824.3)—Required number of parking spaces	DEL	MO	TENN	
	FLA	MONT	TEXAS	
	GA	NEB	UTAH	
	HAWAII	NEV	VT	
	IDAHO	NH	VA	
	ILL	NJ	WASH	
	IND	NM	W VA	
	IOWA	● NY	WIS	OTHER
	KANS	NC	WYO	
	KY	ND		

Table C 215-3 (I-824.3)—Required number of parking spaces

Total parking spaces in lot or garage	Number of accessible parking spaces
1 to 25	1
26 to 50	2
51 to 75	3
76 to 100	4
101 to 150	5
151 to 200	6
201 to 300	7
301 to 400	8
401 to 500	9
501 to 1000	2% of total
Over 1000	20 plus 1 for each 100 over 1000

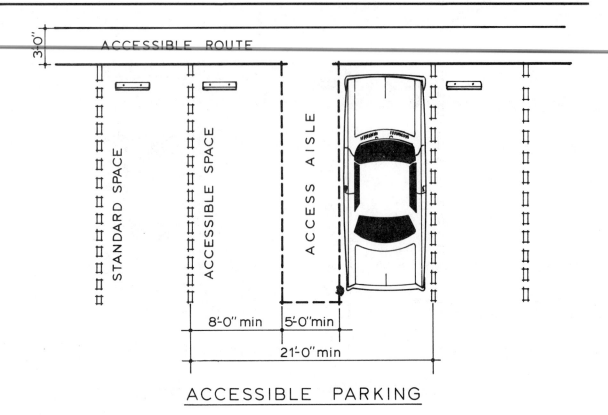

ACCESSIBLE PARKING

Basis of standard — State Purchasing and General Services Commission	APPLICABILITY			
	ALA	LA	OHIO	GUAM
	ALASKA	MAINE	OKLA	PR
	ARIZ	MD	ORE	VIR IS
Notes —	ARK	MASS	PA	DC
Locate on shortest possible accessible route to accessible building entrance. Two accessible parking spaces may share a common access aisle. Car overhangs shall not reduce clear width of accessible circulation route. Designate accessible parking spaces by a sign showing symbol of accessibility. Do not obscure sign by parked vehicle. Max slope: 1:50 in any direction.	CAL	MICH	RI	
	COLO	MINN	SC	
	CONN	MISS	SD	FED'L
	DEL	MO	TENN	FUNDS
	FLA	MONT	● TEXAS	
	GA	NEB	UTAH	
	HAWAII	NEV	VT	
	IDAHO	NH	VA	
	ILL	NJ	WASH	
	IND	NM	W VA	
	IOWA	NY	WIS	OTHER
	KANS	NC	WYO	
	KY	ND		

Total parking spaces available / Minimum number of accessible spaces

Total parking spaces available	Minimum number of accessible spaces
1–50	1
51–100	2
101–300	3
301–500	5
Over 500	1.0% of total

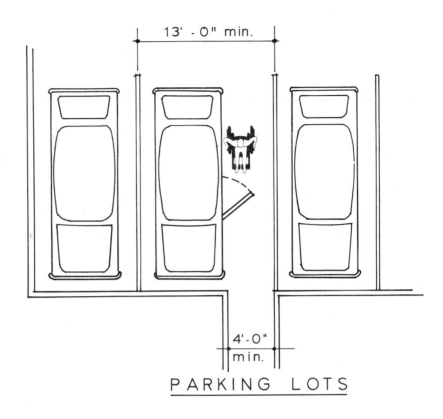

13' - 0" min.

4'- 0"
min.

PARKING LOTS

Basis of standard —	APPLICABILITY			
Utah State Building Board	ALA	LA	OHIO	GUAM
	ALASKA	MAINE	OKLA	PR
	ARIZ	MD	ORE	VIR IS
Notes —	ARK	MASS	PA	DC
Locate as near as possible to main public or primary building entrance and identify. (See also page on passenger zone).	CAL	MICH	RI	
	COLO	MINN	SC	
Total number of spaces Required accessible spaces	CONN	MISS	SD	FED'L FUNDS
0 to 100 2% or a minimum of one	DEL	MO	TENN	
101 to 200 2 plus 1% over 100				
201 to 500 3 plus .5% over 200	FLA	MONT	TEXAS	
501 to 1000 5 plus .25% over 500	GA	NEB	● UTAH	
1001 to 5000 7 plus .125% over 1000				
5001 to over 12 plus .075% over 5000	HAWAII	NEV	VT	
Stripe adjacent 4' wide passenger loading zone by colored diagonal markings 4" wide and 6" apart.	IDAHO	NH	VA	
	ILL	NJ	WASH	
Access to hardsurfaced walkway by level surface or curb cut and curb ramp.	IND	NM	W VA	
	IOWA	NY	WIS	OTHER
	KANS	NC	WYO	
	KY	ND		

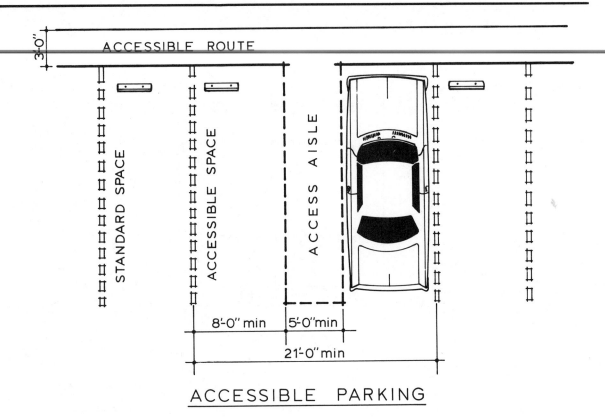

ACCESSIBLE PARKING

Basis of standard —	APPLICABILITY			
Uniform Statewide Building Code	ALA	LA	OHIO	GUAM
	ALASKA	MAINE	OKLA	PR
	ARIZ	MD	ORE	VIR IS
Notes —	ARK	MASS	PA	DC
(a) Where parking is provided, a minimum of 3 percent of the spaces shall meet the requirements of the standard. The spaces shall be identified by above grade signs as reserved for physically handicapped persons. The signs shall have the lower edge of the sign no lower than 4 feet above grade, nor higher than 7 feet above grade. Inclined approaches shall be provided to allow convenient access, and where curbed areas access exceed 100 feet in length, such approaches shall be provided at intervals not exceeding 100 feet. Where several curbed areas require access on the same premises, inclined approaches shall be arranged to allow convenient access from one curbed area to another.	CAL	MICH	RI	
	COLO	MINN	SC	
	CONN	MISS	SD	FED'L
	DEL	MO	TENN	FUNDS
	FLA	MONT	TEXAS	
	GA	NEB	UTAH	
	HAWAII	NEV	VT	
	IDAHO	NH	● VA	
	ILL	NJ	WASH	
	IND	NM	W VA	
	IOWA	NY	WIS	OTHER
	KANS	NC	WYO	
	KY	ND		

ACCESSIBLE ROUTE

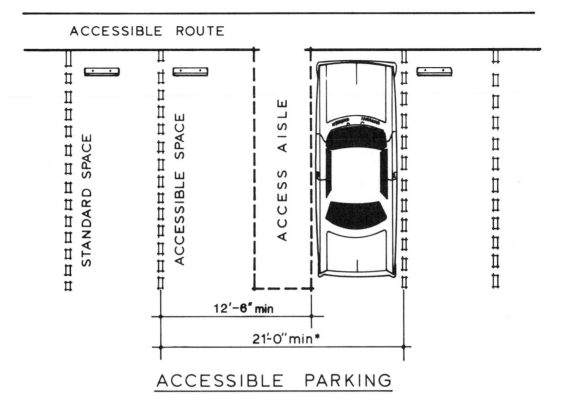

STANDARD SPACE

ACCESSIBLE SPACE

ACCESS AISLE

12'-6" min

21'-0" min*

ACCESSIBLE   PARKING

Basis of standard — Building Code Advisory Council	APPLICABILITY			
	ALA	LA	OHIO	GUAM
	ALASKA	MAINE	OKLA	PR
	ARIZ	MD	ORE	VIR IS
Notes — Provide min. of one, or 2%, whichever is greater if capacity is 200 or fewer, and one accessible space for every 100 spaces over 200, but not less than 1 space for each accessible or adaptable dwelling unit. Locate to provide least distance to accessible facilities served. Max slope 1:50. Identify with International symbol of access at head of parking space, centered 4' to 5' high, bearing words "Legal Permit Required" (*) Assumes 4'-0" min. access aisle between two adjacent spaces.	ARK	MASS	PA	DC
	CAL	MICH	RI	
	COLO	MINN	SC	
	CONN	MISS	SD	FED'L FUNDS
	DEL	MO	TENN	
	FLA	MONT	TEXAS	
	GA	NEB	UTAH	
	HAWAII	NEV	VT	
	IDAHO	NH	VA	
	ILL	NJ	● WASH	
	IND	NM	W VA	
	IOWA	NY	WIS	OTHER
	KANS	NC	WYO	
	KY	ND		

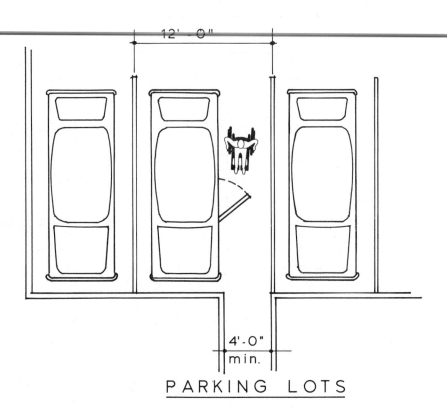

12' - 0"

4'-0"
min.

PARKING LOTS

Basis of standard —	APPLICABILITY			
Ind. 52.04, 6 Wisconsin Administrative Code	ALA	LA	OHIO	GUAM
	ALASKA	MAINE	OKLA	PR
	ARIZ	MD	ORE	VIR IS
Notes —	ARK	MASS	PA	DC
Where parking spaces are provided, designate and provide at rate of 2% of total number of parking spaces, with min. of one. Identify accessible spaces with International Symbol of Accessibility and direct persons to the accessible entrance(s). Locate as close to building entrance as possible. Parking spaces in a parking ramp shall be located as close as possible to the main ramp entrance, to an accessible public walk, or to an accessible elevator.	CAL	MICH	RI	
	COLO	MINN	SC	
	CONN	MISS	SD	FED'L
	DEL	MO	TENN	FUNDS
	FLA	MONT	TEXAS	
	GA	NEB	UTAH	
	HAWAII	NEV	VT	
	IDAHO	NH	VA	
	ILL	NJ	WASH	
	IND	NM	W VA	
	IOWA	NY	● WIS	OTHER
	KANS	NC	WYO	
	KY	ND		

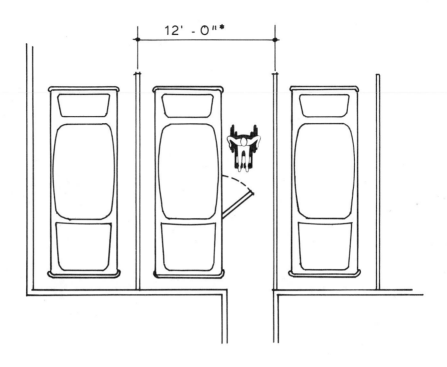

12' - 0"*

PARKING LOTS

Basis of standard —	APPLICABILITY			
Basics of Barrier Free Design	ALA	LA	OHIO	GUAM
	ALASKA	MAINE	OKLA	PR
	ARIZ	MD	ORE	VIR IS
Notes —	ARK	MASS	PA	DC
Reserve at least 2% of available spaces for the physically handicapped in public building parking lots. Spaces to be clearly designated by signs or as near as possible to building entrances. Locate on a level surface and plan in a manner so as not to require a person in a wheelchair or using crutches or braces to move behind parked cars or in the flow of traffic. (*) 13'-0" preferred.	CAL	MICH	RI	
	COLO	MINN	SC	
	CONN	MISS	SD	FED'L FUNDS
	DEL	MO	TENN	
	FLA	MONT	TEXAS	
	GA	NEB	UTAH	
	HAWAII	NEV	VT	
	IDAHO	NH	VA	
	ILL	NJ	WASH	
	IND	NM	W VA	
	IOWA	NY	WIS	OTHER
	KANS	NC	● WYO	
	KY	ND		

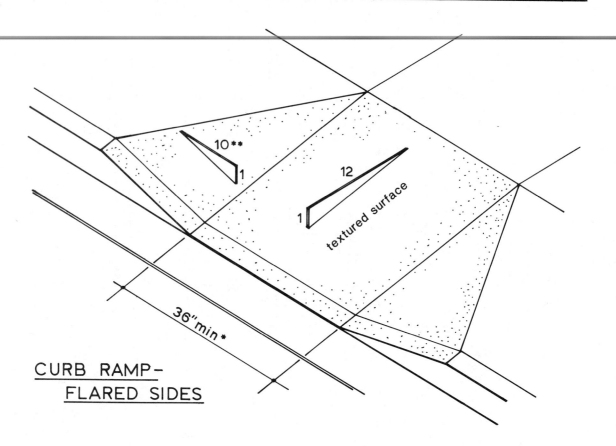

CURB RAMP-
FLARED SIDES

Basis of standard —	APPLICABILITY			
ANSI 1980 — 4.7 and others	ALA	● LA	OHIO	GUAM
	● ALASKA	● MAINE	OKLA	PR
	ARIZ	MD	ORE	VIR IS
	ARK	MASS	PA	DC
Notes —	CAL	MICH	● RI	
Provide curb ramps wherever an accessible route crosses a curb. Slopes shown are maximum. Refer to ramp rise of projection tables under "Ramps" for additional data. Provide flared sides where pedestrians must walk across ramp.	● COLO	MINN	SC	
	CONN	MISS	SD	FED'L
	DEL	MO	TENN	FUNDS
(*)Virginia: Requires 48″ min.	FLA	MONT	TEXAS	
(**)Washington: max. 1:12, max. curb ramp cross slope: 1:50, contrasting surface texture.	GA	NEB	UTAH	
	● HAWAII	● NEV	● VT	
	● IDAHO	NH	● VA	
	ILL	NJ	● WASH	
	IND	● NM	W VA	
	IOWA	● NY	WIS	OTHER
	KANS	NC	WYO	
	● KY	ND		

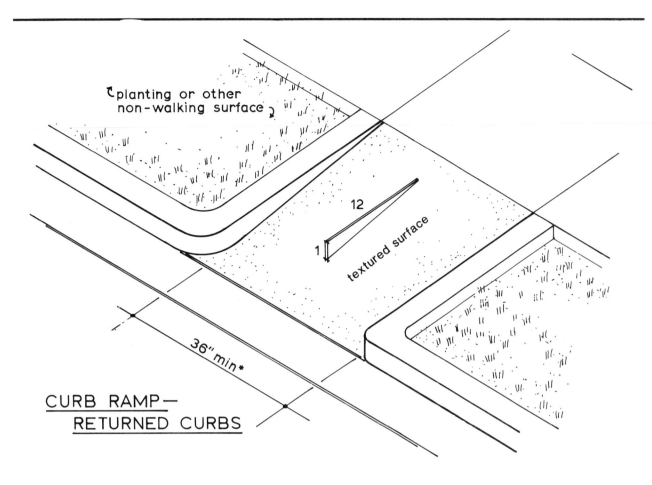

planting or other
non-walking surface

12

1

textured surface

36" min*

CURB RAMP—
RETURNED CURBS

Basis of standard —	APPLICABILITY			
ANSI 1980 — 4.7 and others	ALA	● LA	OHIO	GUAM
	● ALASKA	● MAINE	OKLA	PR
	ARIZ	MD	ORE	VIR IS
Notes —	ARK	MASS	PA	DC
See notes on preceding pages	CAL	MICH	● RI	
	● COLO	MINN	SC	
	CONN	MISS	SD	FED'L
	DEL	MO	TENN	FUNDS
	FLA	MONT	TEXAS	
	GA	NEB	UTAH	
	● HAWAII	● NEV	● VT	
	● IDAHO	NH	● VA	
	ILL	NJ	WASH	
	IND	● NM	W VA	
	IOWA	● NY	WIS	OTHER
	KANS	NC	WYO	
	● KY	ND		

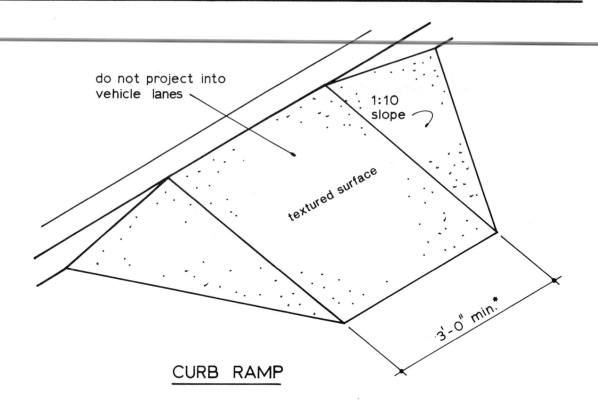

do not project into vehicle lanes

1:10 slope

textured surface

3'-0" min.*

CURB RAMP

Basis of standard — ANSI 1980 — and others	APPLICABILITY			
	ALA	● LA	OHIO	GUAM
	● ALASKA	● MAINE	OKLA	PR
	ARIZ	MD	ORE	VIR IS
Notes —	● ARK	MASS	PA	DC
Locate built-up ramps so that they do not project into vehicular traffic lanes	CAL	MICH	● RI	
(*)Applies to Federal, Arkansas, and Delaware	● COLO	MINN	SC	
	CONN	MISS	SD	● FED'L FUNDS
	● DEL	MO	TENN	
	FLA	MONT	TEXAS	
	GA	NEB	UTAH	
	● HAWAII	● NEV	● VT	
	● IDAHO	NH	VA	
	ILL	NJ	WASH	
	IND	● NM	W VA	
	IOWA	● NY	WIS	OTHER
	KANS	NC	WYO	
	● KY	ND		

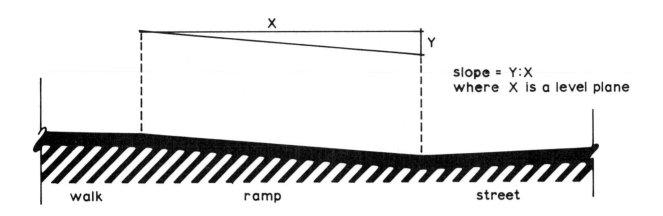

slope = Y:X
where X is a level plane

walk   ramp   street

MEASUREMENT OF CURB RAMP SLOPES

Basis of standard —	APPLICABILITY			
ANSI 1980 — 4.7 and others	ALA	● LA	OHIO	GUAM
	● ALASKA	● MAINE	OKLA	PR
	ARIZ	MD	ORE	VIR IS
Notes —	ARK	MASS	PA	DC
Provide curb ramps wherever an accessible route crosses a curb, complying with slopes shown min. width = 3'-0" exclusive of flared sides. Locate built-up curb ramps so that they do not project into vehicular traffic lanes	CAL	MICH	● RI	
	● COLO	MINN	SC	
	CONN	MISS	SD	FED'L FUNDS
	DEL	MO	TENN	
	FLA	MONT	● TEXAS	
	GA	NEB	UTAH	
	● HAWAII	● NEV	● VT	
	● IDAHO	NH	VA	
	ILL	NJ	WASH	
	IND	● NM	W VA	
	IOWA	● NY	WIS	OTHER
	KANS	NC	WYO	
	● KY	ND		

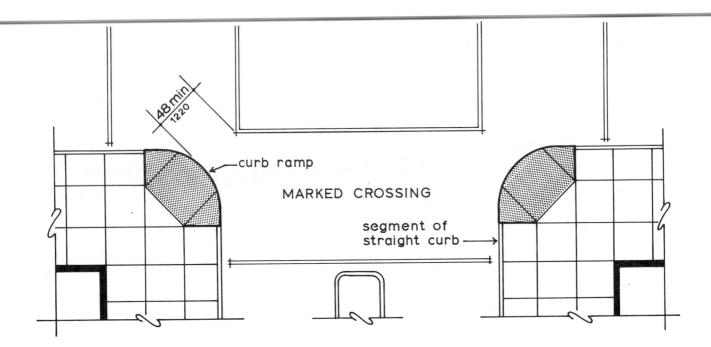

48 min
1220

curb ramp

MARKED CROSSING

segment of
straight curb

DIAGONAL • FLARED CURB RAMP

Basis of standard —	APPLICABILITY			
ANSI 1980 — 4.7.10 and others	ALA	● LA	OHIO	GUAM
	● ALASKA	● MAINE	OKLA	PR
	ARIZ	MD	ORE	VIR IS
Notes —	● ARK	MASS	PA	DC
Segment of straight curb within marked crossing: 2'-0" min.	CAL	MICH	● RI	
	● COLO	MINN	SC	
	CONN	MISS	SD	● FED'L FUNDS
	● DEL	MO	TENN	
	FLA	MONT	TEXAS	
	GA	NEB	UTAH	
	● HAWAII	● NEV	● VT	
	● IDAHO	NH	● VA	
	ILL	NJ	WASH	
	IND	● NM	W VA	
	IOWA	● NY	WIS	OTHER
	KANS	NC	WYO	
	● KY	ND		

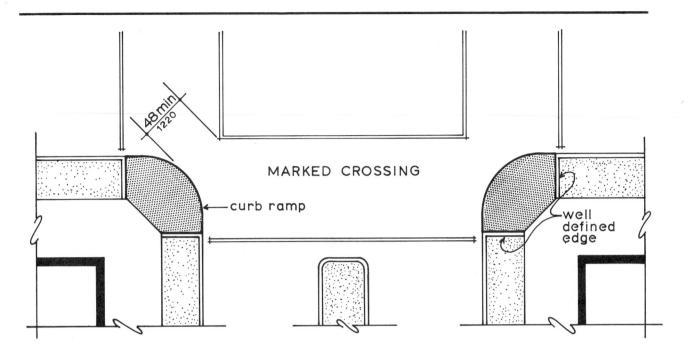

48 min
1220

MARKED CROSSING

curb ramp

well defined edge

DIAGONAL·RETURNED CURB RAMP

Basis of standard —	APPLICABILITY			
ANSI 1980 — 4.7.10 and others	ALA	● LA	OHIO	GUAM
	● ALASKA	● MAINE	OKLA	PR
	ARIZ	MD	ORE	VIR IS
Notes —	● ARK	MASS	PA	DC
	CAL	MICH	● RI	
	● COLO	MINN	SC	
	CONN	MISS	SD	● FED'L FUNDS
	● DEL	MO	TENN	
	FLA	MONT	TEXAS	
	GA	NEB	UTAH	
	● HAWAII	● NEV	● VT	
	● IDAHO	NH	VA	
	ILL	NJ	WASH	
	IND	● NM	W VA	
	IOWA	● NY	WIS	OTHER
	KANS	NC	WYO	
	● KY	ND		

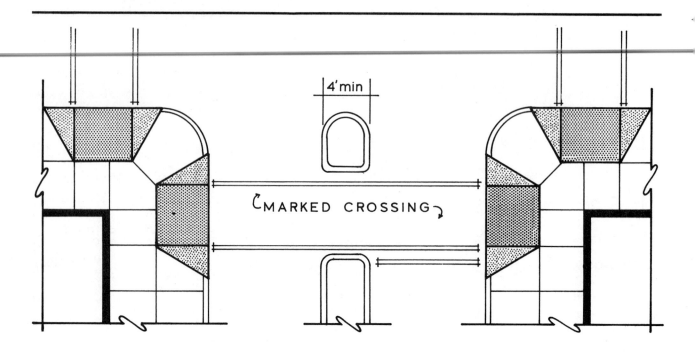

CURB RAMP WITH FLARED SIDES

Basis of standard — ANSI 1980 — 4.7 and others	APPLICABILITY			
	ALA	● LA	OHIO	GUAM
	● ALASKA	● MAINE	OKLA	PR
	ARIZ	MD	ORE	VIR IS
Notes —	● ARK	MASS	PA	DC
Locate curb ramps to prevent obstruction by parked vehicles and locate wholly within markings (excluding any flared sides). Raised islands in crossings shall be cut through at street level or lane curb ramps to provide min. 4'-0" wide level area. Provide tactile warning texture extending full width and depth of ramp, including any flares.	CAL	MICH	● RI	
	● COLO	MINN	SC	
	CONN	MISS	SD	● FED'L
	● DEL	MO	TENN	FUNDS
	FLA	MONT	TEXAS	
	GA	NEB	UTAH	
	● HAWAII	● NEV	● VT	
	● IDAHO	NH	VA	
	ILL	NJ	WASH	
	IND	● NM	W VA	
	IOWA	● NY	WIS	OTHER
	KANS	NC	WYO	
	● KY	ND		

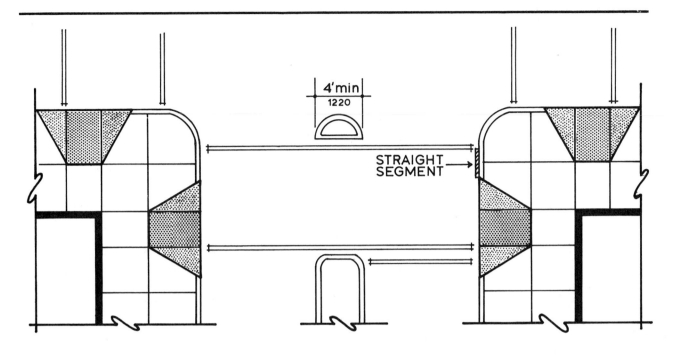

CURB RAMP WITH FLARED SIDES

Basis of standard —	APPLICABILITY			
ANSI 1980 — 4.7 and others	ALA	● LA	OHIO	GUAM
	● ALASKA	● MAINE	OKLA	PR
	ARIZ	MD	ORE	VIR IS
Notes —	● ARK	MASS	PA	DC
See notes on preceding page	CAL	MICH	● RI	
	● COLO	MINN	SC	
	CONN	MISS	SD	● FED'L FUNDS
	● DEL	MO	TENN	
	FLA	MONT	TEXAS	
	GA	NEB	UTAH	
	● HAWAII	● NEV	● VT	
	● IDAHO	NH	VA	
	ILL	NJ	WASH	
	IND	● NM	W VA	
	IOWA	● NY	WIS	OTHER
	KANS	NC	WYO	
	● KY	ND		

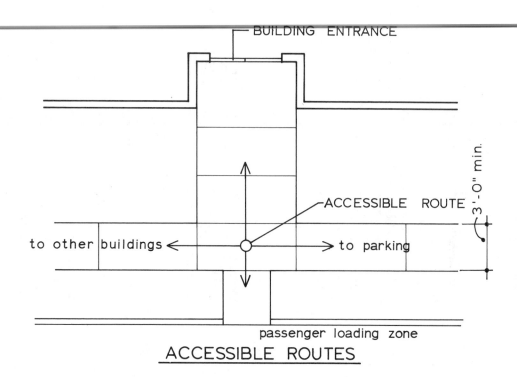

ACCESSIBLE ROUTES

Basis of standard — ANSI 1980 – 4.3 and others	APPLICABILITY			
	ALA	● LA	OHIO	GUAM
	● ALASKA	● MAINE	OKLA	PR
	ARIZ	MD	ORE	VIR IS
	ARK	MASS	PA	DC
	CAL	MICH	● RI	
	● COLO	MINN	SC	
	CONN	MISS	SD	FED'L
	DEL	MO	TENN	FUNDS
	FLA	MONT	● TEXAS	
	GA	NEB	UTAH	
	● HAWAII	● NEV	● VT	
	● IDAHO	NH	● VA	
	ILL	NJ	WASH	
	IND	● NM	W VA	
	IOWA	● NY	WIS	OTHER
	KANS	NC	WYO	
	● KY	ND		

Notes —

Provide at least one accessible route from location shown. At least one accessible route shall connect all accessible spaces and elements and with all accessible dwelling units within the building or facility.

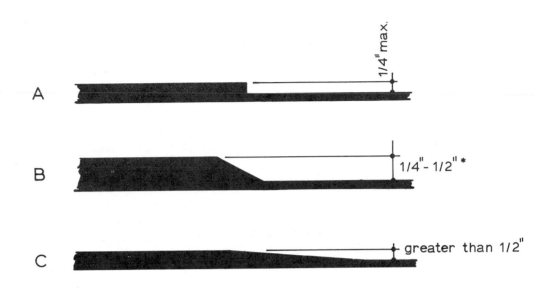

A

1/4" max.

B

1/4"- 1/2" *

C

greater than 1/2"

CHANGES IN LEVEL

Basis of standard — ANSI 1980 — 4.5.2 and others	APPLICABILITY			
	ALA	● LA	OHIO	GUAM
	● ALASKA	● MAINE	OKLA	PR
	ARIZ	MD	ORE	VIR IS
Notes — Condition A requires no edge treatment Condition B requires bevel with 1:2 max. slope Condition C requires ramp complying with appropriate requirements. Texas: Range for condition "B" is 1/4" to 3/4", condition "C" is not applicable (*)Washington: requires 1:4 bevel.	● ARK	MASS	PA	DC
	● CAL	MICH	● RI	
	● COLO	MINN	SC	
	CONN	MISS	SD	● FED'L
	● DEL	MO	TENN	FUNDS
	FLA	MONT	● TEXAS	
	GA	NEB	UTAH	
	● HAWAII	● NEV	● VT	
	● IDAHO	NH	● VA	
	ILL	NJ	● WASH	
	IND	● NM	W VA	
	IOWA	● NY	WIS	OTHER
	KANS	NC	WYO	
	● KY	ND		

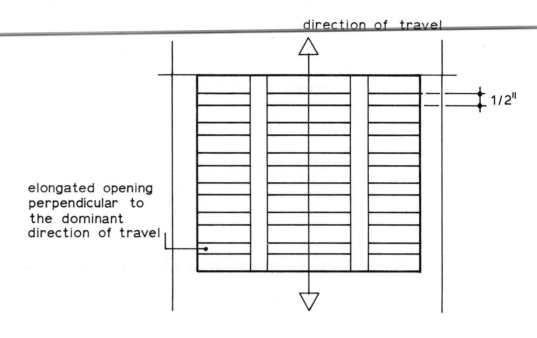

direction of travel

elongated opening
perpendicular to
the dominant
direction of travel

1/2"

GRATINGS

Basis of standard —	APPLICABILITY			
ANSI 1980 — 4.5.4 and others	ALA	● LA	OHIO	GUAM
	● ALASKA	● MAINE	OKLA	PR
	ARIZ.	MD	ORE	VIR IS
Notes —	● ARK	● MASS	PA	DC
Washington: max. vertical surface change: 1/8″	● CAL	MICH	● RI	
Iowa and Utah: max. 1/4″ vertical surface change	● COLO	MINN	SC	
New Jersey: permits 3/4″ max. opening in any	CONN	MISS	SD	● FED'L FUNDS
direction, with grid flush with the surrounding surface.	● DEL	MO	TENN	
California: Requires gratings to be off the path of	FLA	MONT	● TEXAS	
travel, but when unavoidable, allows 1/2″ maximum	GA	NEB	● UTAH	
opening in direction of travel.	● HAWAII	● NEV	● VT	
	● IDAHO	NH	● VA	
	ILL	● NJ	● WASH	
	IND	● NM	W VA	
	● IOWA	● NY	WIS	OTHER
	KANS	NC	WYO	
	● KY	ND		

max. pile height : 1/2"

edge trim

CARPET

Basis of standard — ANSI 1980 – 4.5.3 and others	APPLICABILITY			
	ALA	● LA	OHIO	GUAM
	● ALASKA	● MAINE	OKLA	PR
	ARIZ	MD	ORE	VIR IS
	● ARK	MASS	PA	DC
	CAL	MICH	● RI	
	● COLO	MINN	SC	
	CONN	MISS	SD	● FED'L
	● DEL	MO	TENN	FUNDS
	FLA	MONT	TEXAS	
	GA	NEB	UTAH	
	● HAWAII	● NEV	● VT	
	● IDAHO	NH	● VA	
	● ILL	● NJ	● WASH	
	IND	● NM	W VA	
	IOWA	● NY	WIS	OTHER
	KANS	NC	WYO	
	● KY	ND		

Notes —

Severely attach carpet or carpet tile
Illinois does not have a max. pile height, but requires lowpile, tightweave and firm underlayment, prohibiting heavily patterned carpet, expecially stripes, on stairs. Also, requires max 1:2 slope for carpet trim.
Washington and New Jersey do not specify max. pile height.

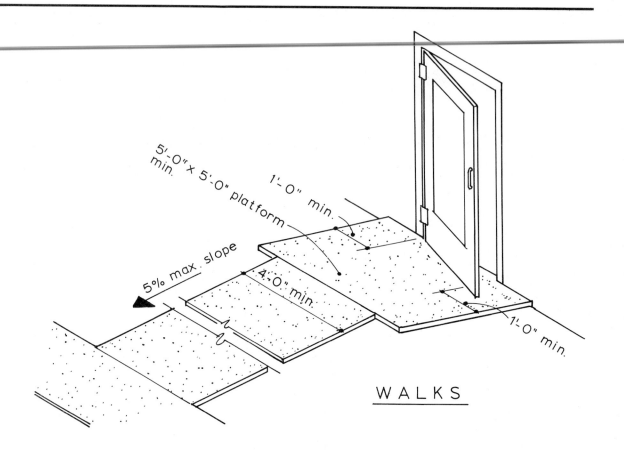

5'-0" x 5'-0" platform min.

1'-0" min.

5% max. slope

4'-0" min.

1'-0" min.

WALKS

Basis of standard — ANSI 1961 — 4.2 and others	APPLICABILITY			
	ALA	LA	OHIO	GUAM
	ALASKA	MAINE	● OKLA	PR
	● ARIZ	MD	ORE	VIR IS
	ARK	MASS	● PA	DC
	CAL	MICH	RI	
	COLO	MINN	● SC	
	CONN	● MISS	● SD	FED'L
	DEL	MO	TENN	FUNDS
	● FLA	MONT	TEXAS	
	● GA	NEB	UTAH	
	HAWAII	NEV	VT	
	IDAHO	NH	VA	
	ILL	NJ	WASH	
	IND	NM	● W VA	
	IOWA	NY	WIS	OTHER
	● KANS	NC	WYO	
	KY	● ND		

Notes —

Walks to have continuing common surface, not interrupted by steps or abrupt level changes. Platform shown may be 3'-0" deep and 5'-0" wide if door does not swing on to the platform or toward the walk. Walks of near maximum grade should have level areas if of considerable length. Walks or driveways should have level areas at intervals. Walks or driveways should have a nonslip surface and blend with adjacent areas to a common level.

Florida: Applies to non-government financed facilities. Increase 1'-0" to 1'-6" for government facilities.

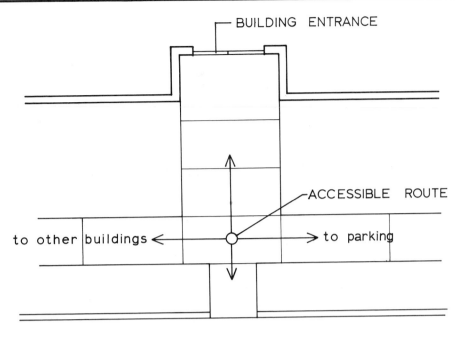

BUILDING ENTRANCE

ACCESSIBLE ROUTE

to other buildings ←   → to parking

ACCESSIBLE ROUTES

Basis of standard — ANSI 1961 — 5.2 and others	APPLICABILITY			
	● ALA	LA	OHIO	GUAM
	ALASKA	MAINE	● OKLA	PR
	ARIZ	MD	ORE	VIR IS
	ARK	● MASS	PA	DC
	CAL	MICH	RI	
	COLO	MINN	● SC	
	● CONN	MISS	● SD	FED'L
	DEL	MO	TENN	FUNDS
	● FLA	MONT	TEXAS	
	● GA	NEB	UTAH	
	HAWAII	NEV	VT	
	IDAHO	NH	VA	
	ILL	● NJ	WASH	
	IND	● NM	W VA	
	● IOWA	NY	WIS	OTHER
	● KANS	NC	WYO	
	KY	● ND		

Notes —
At least one primary entrance to each building shall be usable by individuals in wheelchairs. At least one entrance usable by individuals in wheelchairs shall be on a level that would make the elevators accessible. Florida: Provide curb cuts or ramps, or both.

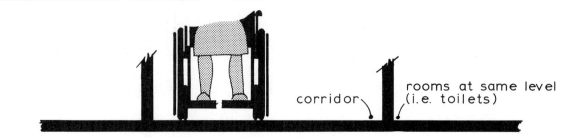

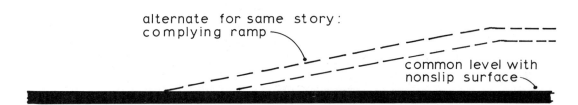

FLOORS ON A GIVEN STORY

Basis of standard —	APPLICABILITY			
ANSI 1961 — 5.5 and others	● ALA	LA	OHIO	GUAM
	ALASKA	● MAINE	● OKLA	PR
	● ARIZ	MD	ORE	VIR IS
Notes —	ARK	● MASS	● PA	DC
Utah excepts: Balconies with fixed seating, small buildings and residences with platform lifts.	CAL	MICH	RI	
South Carolina: Permits max. 1″ height difference between adjoining surfaces.	COLO	MINN	● SC	
New Jersey: Permits max. 2′-8″ height difference and	● CONN	● MISS	● SD	FED'L FUNDS
10% max. usable net area for raised or depressed areas in lobbies, restaurants, cocktail lounges and	DEL	● MO	● TENN	
theaters, with ramps this may be exceeded.	● FLA	MONT	TEXAS	
Exemptions from same level requirements balconies,	● GA	● NEB	UTAH	
bleachers, raised or depressed areas not normally open to the general public.	HAWAII	NEV	● VT	
	IDAHO	NH	● VA	
	ILL	● NJ	● WASH	
	IND	● NM	W VA	
	● IOWA	NY	WIS	OTHER
	● KANS	● NC	WYO	
	KY	● ND		

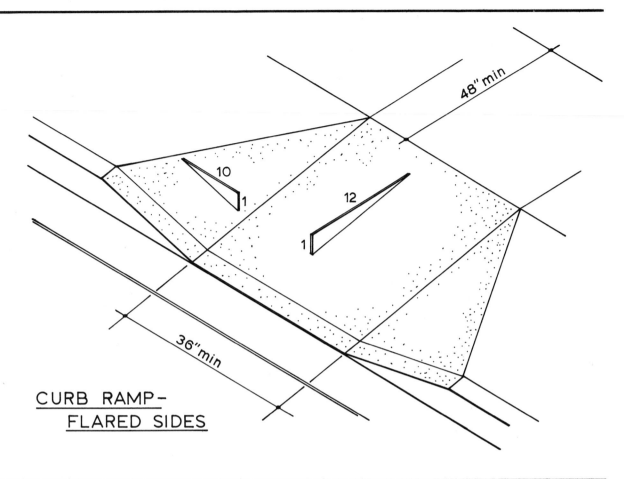

CURB RAMP-
FLARED SIDES

Basis of standard — ATBCB — § 1190.70 and others	APPLICABILITY			
	ALA	LA	OHIO	GUAM
	ALASKA	MAINE	OKLA	PR
	ARIZ	MD	ORE	VIR IS
● ARK	MASS	PA	DC
	CAL	MICH	RI	
	COLO	MINN	SC	
	CONN	MISS	SD	● FED'L FUNDS
● DEL	MO	TENN	
	FLA	MONT	TEXAS	
	GA	NEB	UTAH	
	HAWAII	NEV	VT	
	IDAHO	NH	VA	
	ILL	NJ	WASH	
	IND	NM	W VA	
	IOWA	NY	WIS	OTHER
	KANS	NC	WYO	
	KY	ND		

Notes —

Provide curbramps wherever an accessible route crosses a curb. Slopes shown are maximum. Refer to ramp rise and projection tables under "Ramps" for additional data. Provide flared sides if where pedestrians must walk across ramp.

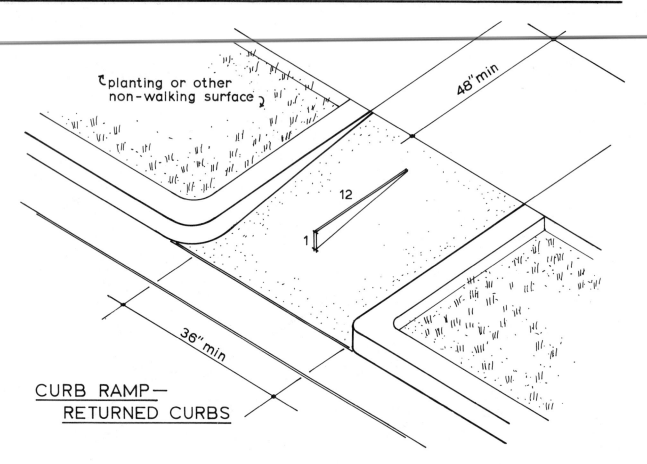

planting or other
non-walking surface

48" min

12

1

36" min

CURB RAMP—
RETURNED CURBS

Basis of standard — ATBCB – § 1190.70	APPLICABILITY			
	ALA	LA	OHIO	GUAM
	ALASKA	MAINE	OKLA	PR
	ARIZ	MD	ORE	VIR IS
● ARK	MASS	PA	DC	
	CAL	MICH	RI	
	COLO	MINN	SC	
	CONN	MISS	SD	● FED'L FUNDS
● DEL	MO	TENN		
	FLA	MONT	TEXAS	
	GA	NEB	UTAH	
	HAWAII	NEV	VT	
	IDAHO	NH	VA	
	ILL	NJ	WASH	
	IND	NM	W VA	
	IOWA	NY	WIS	OTHER
	KANS	NC	WYO	
	KY	ND		

Notes —

See notes on preceding pages

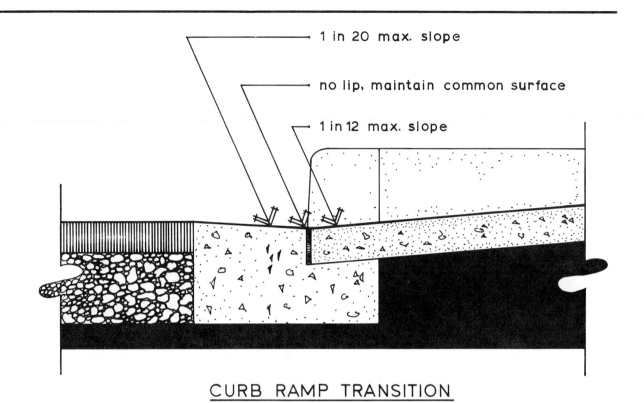

1 in 20 max. slope

no lip, maintain common surface

1 in 12 max. slope

CURB RAMP TRANSITION

Basis of standard — ATBCB 1190.70 e8 and others	APPLICABILITY			
	ALA	LA	OHIO	GUAM
	ALASKA	MAINE	OKLA	PR
	ARIZ	MD	ORE	VIR IS
Notes — ● ARK	MASS	PA	DC
Transitions from ramps to walks, gutters, or streets shall be flush and free of abrupt changes. Curbs ramps with less than a 6″ rise do not require handrails. (6″ rise max. not applicable in Delaware.)	CAL	MICH	RI	
	COLO	MINN	SC	
	CONN	MISS	SD	● FED'L
	● DEL	MO	TENN	FUNDS
	FLA	MONT	TEXAS	
	GA	NEB	UTAH	
	HAWAII	NEV	VT	
	IDAHO	NH	VA	
	ILL	NJ	WASH	
	IND	NM	W VA	
	IOWA	NY	WIS	OTHER
	KANS	NC	WYO	
	KY	ND		

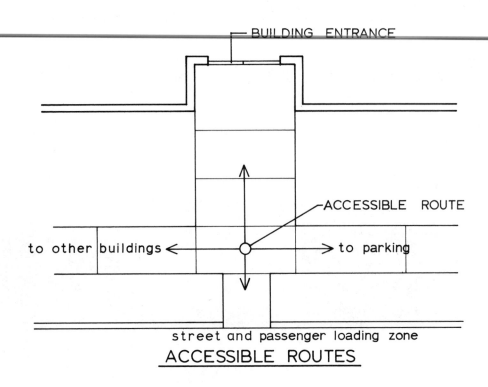

ACCESSIBLE ROUTES

Basis of standard — ATBCB 1190.31 and others	APPLICABILITY			
	ALA	LA	OHIO	GUAM
	ALASKA	MAINE	OKLA	PR
	ARIZ	MD	ORE	VIR IS
Notes —	● ARK	MASS	PA	DC
Provide at least one accessible route connecting an accessible building entrance with elements shown and all accessible spaces, rooms and elements within the building or facility.	CAL	MICH	RI	
	COLO	MINN	SC	
	CONN	MISS	SD	FED'L FUNDS
A service entrance shall not be the sole accessible entrance unless it is the only entrance as in a factory or a garage.	● DEL	MO	TENN	●
	FLA	MONT	TEXAS	
	GA	NEB	UTAH	
	HAWAII	NEV	VT	
	IDAHO	NH	VA	
	ILL	NJ	WASH	
	IND	NM	W VA	
	IOWA	NY	WIS	OTHER
	KANS	NC	WYO	
	KY	ND		

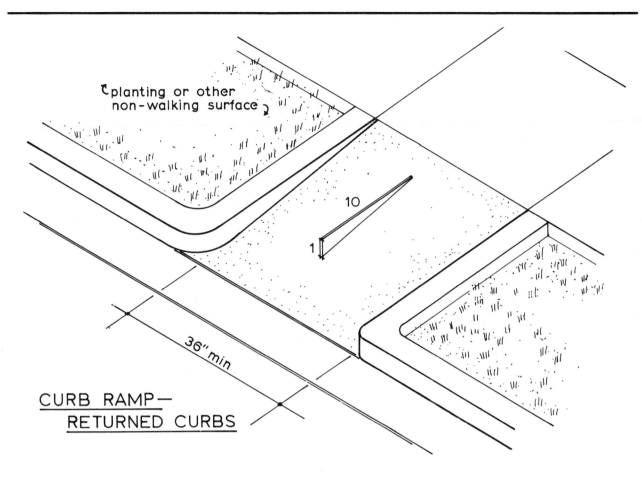

ℓ planting or other non-walking surface ℐ

10

1

36" min

CURB RAMP— RETURNED CURBS

Basis of standard — BOCA — 1978	APPLICABILITY			
	ALA	LA	● OHIO	GUAM
	ALASKA	MAINE	OKLA	PR
	ARIZ	MD	ORE	VIR IS
Notes —	ARK	MASS	PA	DC
Maximum slopes:	CAL	MICH	RI	
	COLO	MINN	SC	
	CONN	MISS	SD	FED'L
	DEL	MO	TENN	FUNDS
	FLA	MONT	TEXAS	
	GA	NEB	UTAH	
	HAWAII	NEV	VT	
	IDAHO	NH	● VA	
	ILL	NJ	WASH	
	IND	NM	W VA	
	IOWA	NY	WIS	OTHER
	KANS	NC	WYO	
	KY	ND		

Notes —

Maximum slopes:

Slope	Max. Horiz. Projection for Rampways	Max. Horiz. Projection of Each Run
1:8 or less	2'	2'
1:10 or less	8'	8'
1:12 or less	60'	30'
1:16 or less	40'	160'

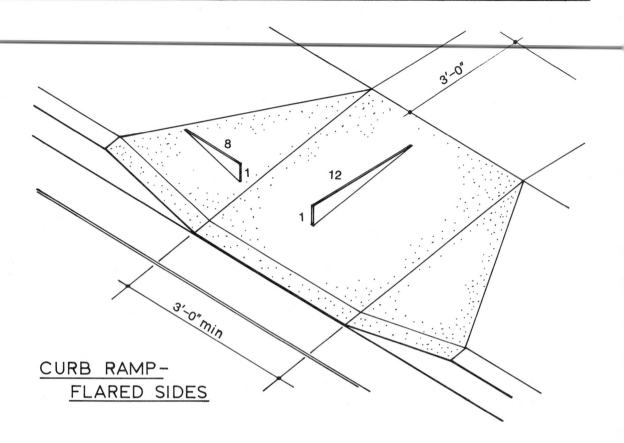

CURB RAMP-
FLARED SIDES

Basis of standard — BOCA – 1978	APPLICABILITY			
Notes — See preceding page for slope data. Provide flared sides with max. 1:10 slope if walkwidth is less than 3'-0" wide. All other flares shall be 1:8 or less.	ALA	LA	● OHIO	GUAM
	ALASKA	MAINE	OKLA	PR
	ARIZ	MD	ORE	VIR IS
	ARK	MASS	PA	DC
	CAL	MICH	RI	
	COLO	MINN	SC	
	CONN	MISS	SD	FED'L FUNDS
	DEL	MO	TENN	
	FLA	MONT	TEXAS	
	GA	NEB	UTAH	
	HAWAII	NEV	VT	
	IDAHO	NH	● VA	
	ILL	NJ	WASH	
	IND	NM	W VA	
	IOWA	NY	WIS	OTHER
	KANS	NC	WYO	
	KY	ND		

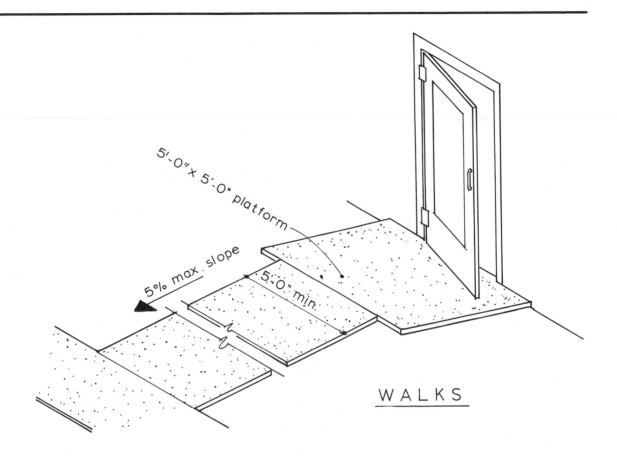

5'-0" x 5'-0" platform

5% max. slope

5'-0" min.

WALKS

Basis of standard —	APPLICABILITY			
BOCA 1978 and Construction Code Commission General Rules	ALA	LA	● OHIO	GUAM
	ALASKA	MAINE	OKLA	PR
	ARIZ	● MD	ORE	VIR IS
	ARK	MASS	PA	DC
Notes —	CAL	● MICH	RI	
For practical difficulties, gradient may be changed but not to exceed ramp requirements, in which case comply with BOCA ramp requirements. Provide at least one primary entrance at grade floor level uninterrupted by steps or abrupt level changes.	COLO	MINN	SC	
	CONN	MISS	SD	FED'L FUNDS
	DEL	MO	TENN	
	FLA	MONT	TEXAS	
	GA	NEB	UTAH	
	HAWAII	NEV	VT	
	IDAHO	NH	● VA	
	ILL	NJ	WASH	
	IND	NM	W VA	
	IOWA	NY	WIS	OTHER
	KANS	NC	WYO	
	KY	ND		

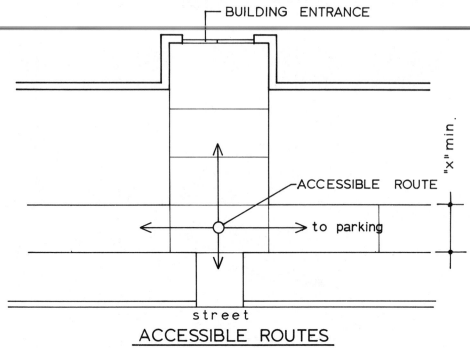

ACCESSIBLE ROUTES

Basis of standard —	APPLICABILITY			
BOCA 1978 and others	ALA	LA	● OHIO	GUAM
	ALASKA	MAINE	OKLA	PR
	ARIZ	MD	ORE	VIR IS
	ARK	MASS	PA	DC
	CAL	MICH	RI	
	COLO	MINN	SC	
	● CONN	MISS	SD	FED'L FUNDS
	DEL	MO	TENN	
	FLA	MONT	TEXAS	
	GA	NEB	UTAH	
	HAWAII	NEV	VT	
	IDAHO	NH	● VA	
	ILL	NJ	WASH	
	IND	NM	W VA	
	IOWA	NY	WIS	OTHER
	KANS	NC	WYO	
	KY	ND		

Notes —

Provide at least one primary accessible entrance to each new building or structure, uninterrupted by steps or abrupt grade changes. Max. gradient: 1′ in 20′. At least one entrance shall be on a level to make elevators accessible to individuals in wheelchairs.

x min. = 5′-0″
      = 4′-0″ in Connecticut

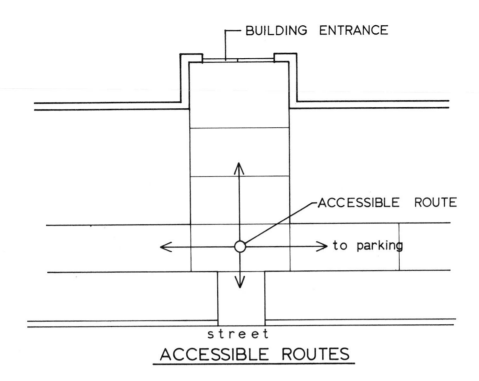

BUILDING ENTRANCE

ACCESSIBLE ROUTE

to parking

street

ACCESSIBLE ROUTES

Basis of standard —	APPLICABILITY			
BOCA – 1978	ALA	LA	● OHIO	GUAM
	ALASKA	MAINE	OKLA	PR
	ARIZ	MD	ORE	VIR IS
Notes —	ARK	MASS	PA	DC
Provide interior access to all floor levels required to be accessible for the physically handicapped by complying ramps or elevators, and access to all points on each floor level by means of complying passageways, corridors, and doorways.	CAL	MICH	RI	
	COLO	MINN	SC	
	CONN	MISS	SD	FED'L FUNDS
	DEL	MO	TENN	
Rhode-Island exception to second floor interior access: two-story motels and hotels; two-story office buildings whose story is 10,000 sq. ft. or less with the exception of two-story state and municipal buildings and all medical office buildings.	FLA	MONT	TEXAS	
	GA	NEB	UTAH	
	HAWAII	NEV	VT	
	IDAHO	NH	● VA	
	ILL	NJ	WASH	
	IND	NM	W VA	
	IOWA	NY	WIS	OTHER
	KANS	NC	WYO	
	KY	ND		

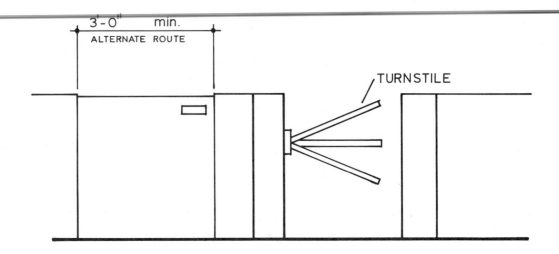

3'-0"   min.

ALTERNATE ROUTE

TURNSTILE

TURNSTILES

Basis of standard —	APPLICABILITY			
BOCA — 1978 and others	ALA	LA	● OHIO	GUAM
	ALASKA	MAINE	OKLA	PR
	ARIZ	● MD	ORE	VIR IS
Notes —	ARK	● MASS	PA	DC
Provide clearly marked alternate routes for buildings utilizing turnstiles to control traffic.	CAL	MICH	● RI	
Indiana & Maryland: Provide at least one checkout lane on each floor 3'-0" min. wide for buildings which include such lanes.	COLO	MINN	SC	
	CONN	MISS	SD	FED'L
	DEL	MO	TENN	FUNDS
	FLA	MONT	TEXAS	
	GA	NEB	UTAH	
	HAWAII	NEV	VT	
	IDAHO	NH	● VA	
	ILL	NJ	WASH	
	● IND	NM	W VA	
	IOWA	NY	WIS	OTHER
	KANS	NC	WYO	
	KY	ND		

TABLE NO. 33-A — MINIMUM EGRESS AND ACCESS REQUIREMENTS

USE[1]	MINIMUM OF TWO EXITS OTHER THAN ELEVATORS ARE REQUIRED WHERE NUMBER OF OCCUPANTS IS OVER	SQUARE FEET PER OCCUPANT[9]	ACCESS BY MEANS OF A RAMP OR AN ELEVATOR MUST BE PROVIDED FOR THE PHYSICALLY HANDICAPPED AS INDICATED[2]
1. Aircraft Hangars (No Repair)	10	500	Yes
2. Auction Rooms	30	7	Yes
3. Assembly Areas, Concentrated Use (without fixed seats) Auditoriums Bowling Alleys (Assembly areas) Churches and Chapels Dance Floors Lodge Rooms Reviewing Stands Stadiums	50	7	Yes[3,4]
4. Assembly Areas, Less-concentrated Use Conference Rooms Dining Rooms Drinking Establishments Exhibit Rooms Gymnasiums Lounges Skating Rinks Stages	50	15	Yes[3]
5. Children's Homes and Homes for the Aged	5	80	Yes[5]
6. Classrooms	50	20	Yes[5]
7. Dormitories	10	50	No[6]
8. Dwellings	10	300	Yes[6]
9. Garage, Parking	30	200	
10. Hospitals and Sanitariums-Nursing Homes	5	80	Yes[5]
11. Hotels and Apartments	10	200	Yes[8]
12. Kitchen — Commercial	30	200	No
13. Library Reading Room	50	50	Yes[3]
14. Locker Rooms	30	50	Yes
15. Mechanical Equipment Room	30	300	No
16. Nurseries for Children (Day-care)	6	50	Yes

Basis of standard —

Uniform Building Code

Notes —

Main exits from buildings requiring access by the physically handicapped, as listed in Table No. 33-A, shall be usable by individuals in wheelchairs and be on a level that would make the elevators accessible where provided. When a corridor or exterior exit balcony is accessible to an elevator, changes in elevation of the floor shall be made by means of a ramp. See next page for continuation.

APPLICABILITY			
ALA	LA	OHIO	GUAM
ALASKA	MAINE	OKLA	PR
ARIZ	MD	ORE	VIR IS
ARK	MASS	PA	DC
CAL	MICH	RI	
COLO	MINN	SC	
CONN	MISS	SD	FED'L FUNDS
DEL	MO	TENN	
FLA	● MONT	TEXAS	
GA	NEB	UTAH	
HAWAII	NEV	VT	
IDAHO	NH	VA	
ILL	NJ	● WASH	
● IND	NM	W VA	
IOWA	NY	WIS	OTHER
KANS	NC	WYO	
KY	ND		

USE[1]	MINIMUM OF TWO EXITS OTHER THAN ELEVATORS ARE REQUIRED WHERE NUMBER OF OCCUPANTS IS OVER	SQUARE FEET PER OCCUPANT[9]	ACCESS BY MEANS OF A RAMP OR AN ELEVATOR MUST BE PROVIDED FOR THE PHYSICALLY HANDICAPPED AS INDICATED[2]
17. Offices	30	100	Yes[5]
18. School Shops and Vocational Rooms	50	50	Yes
19. Stores — Retail Sales Rooms			
Basement	[7]	20	Yes
Ground Floor	50	30	Yes
Upper Floors	10	50	Yes
20. Warehouses	30	300	No
21. All Others	50	100	

1. Refer to Sections 3318 and 3319 for other specific requirements.
2. Elevators shall not be construed as providing a required exit.
3. Access to secondary areas on balconies or mezzanines may be by stairs only, except when such secondary areas contain the only available toilet facilities.
4. Reviewing stands, grandstands and bleachers need not comply.
5. Access to floors other than that closest to grade may be by stairs only, except when the only available toilet facilities are on other levels.
6. Access to floors other than that closest to grade and to garages used in connection with apartment houses may be by stairs only.
7. See Section 3302 for basement exit requirements.
8. See Section 1213 for access to buildings and facilities in hotels and apartments.
9. This table shall not be used to determine working space requirements per person.

Basis of standard —	APPLICABILITY			
Uniform Building Code	ALA	LA	OHIO	GUAM
	ALASKA	MAINE	OKLA	PR
	ARIZ	MD	ORE	VIR IS
Notes —	ARK	MASS	PA	DC
See preceeding page for notes	CAL	MICH	RI	
	COLO	MINN	SC	
Washington: deletes footnotes 5 + 6.	CONN	MISS	SD	FED'L FUNDS
Indiana: For item 20 (Warehouses) change "NO" to "YES", and add footnote 5. Footnotes 3 and 5 end with "... by stairs only." Delete footnotes 8 and 9.	DEL	MO	TENN	
Provide new footnote 8: "See Table 5-E and Section 1314, Construction Rules and Regulations, Administrative Building Council, 1978 Edition.	FLA	● MONT	TEXAS	
	GA	NEB	UTAH	
	HAWAII	NEV	VT	
	IDAHO	NH	VA	
	ILL	NJ	● WASH	
	● IND	NM	W VA	
	IOWA	NY	WIS	OTHER
	KANS	NC	WYO	
	KY	ND		

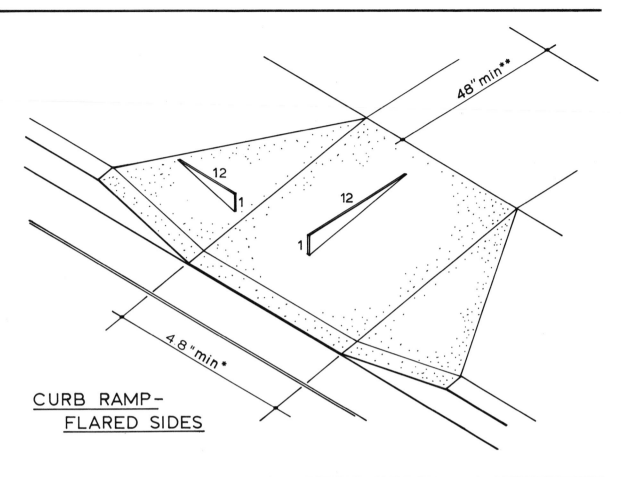

CURB RAMP—
FLARED SIDES

Basis of standard —	APPLICABILITY			
Various	ALA	LA	OHIO	GUAM
	ALASKA	MAINE	OKLA	PR
	ARIZ	● MD	ORE	VIR IS
Notes —	ARK	MASS	PA	DC
Gradients shown are maximum.	CAL	● MICH	RI	
(*)North Carolina: 3'-4", sides flared 2'-0" wide.	COLO	MINN	SC	
Provide min. of two per lineal block, except one	CONN	MISS	SD	FED'L
may be provided between each radius point of a	DEL	MO	TENN	FUNDS
street turn out of an intersection if adequate	FLA	MONT	TEXAS	
provisions are made to prevent vehicular traffic	GA	NEB	UTAH	
from encroaching on the ramp.	HAWAII	NEV	VT	
(**)Indiana: 5'-0"	IDAHO	NH	VA	
	ILL	NJ	WASH	
	● IND	NM	W VA	
	IOWA	NY	WIS	OTHER
	KANS	● NC	WYO	
	KY	ND		

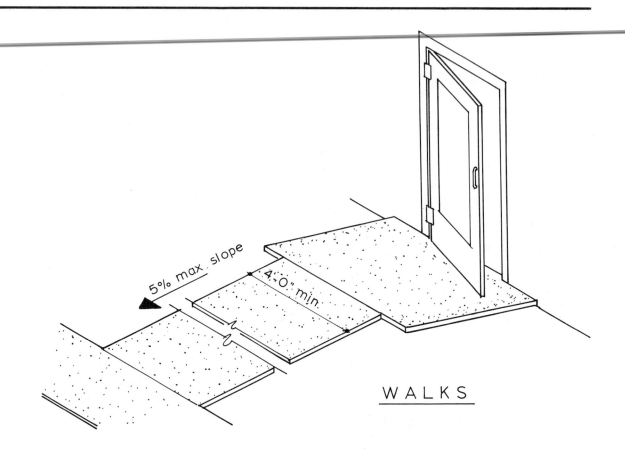

WALKS

Basis of standard —	APPLICABILITY			
Various	ALA	LA	OHIO	GUAM
	ALASKA	MAINE	OKLA	PR
	ARIZ	MD	ORE	VIR IS
Notes —	ARK	MASS	PA	DC
Iowa: Max height of surface change: 1/4″, max. slope 1:50 for at least 4′-0″ in front of accessible entrances.	CAL	MICH	RI	
	COLO	● MINN	SC	
	● CONN	MISS	SD	FED'L FUNDS
	DEL	MO	TENN	
	FLA	MONT	TEXAS	
	GA	NEB	UTAH	
	HAWAII	NEV	VT	
	IDAHO	NH	VA	
	ILL	NJ	WASH	
	IND	NM	W VA	
	● IOWA	NY	WIS	OTHER
	KANS	NC	WYO	
	KY	ND		

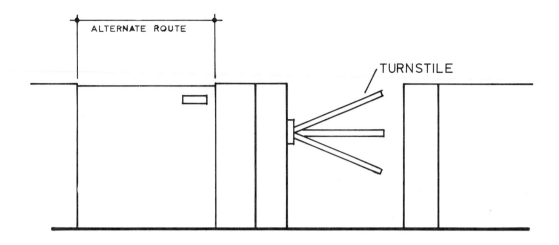

ALTERNATE ROUTE

TURNSTILE

TURNSTILES

Basis of standard —	APPLICABILITY			
Capital Development Board and others	ALA	LA	OHIO	GUAM
	ALASKA	MAINE	OKLA	PR
	ARIZ	MD	ORE	VIR IS
Notes —	ARK	MASS	PA	DC
Illinois, Washington, New Jersey: Provide alternate access immediately next to turnstile or narrow gate. Illinois: Provide at least one check out aisle 2'-8" min. clear with 3'-0" max. height counter top in all shops, stores, etc.	CAL	MICH	RI	
	COLO	MINN	SC	
	CONN	MISS	SD	FED'L FUNDS
	DEL	MO	TENN	
	FLA	MONT	TEXAS	
	GA	NEB	UTAH	
	HAWAII	NEV	VT	
	IDAHO	NH	VA	
	● ILL	● NJ	● WASH	
	IND	NM	W VA	
	IOWA	NY	WIS	OTHER
	KANS	NC	WYO	
	KY	ND		

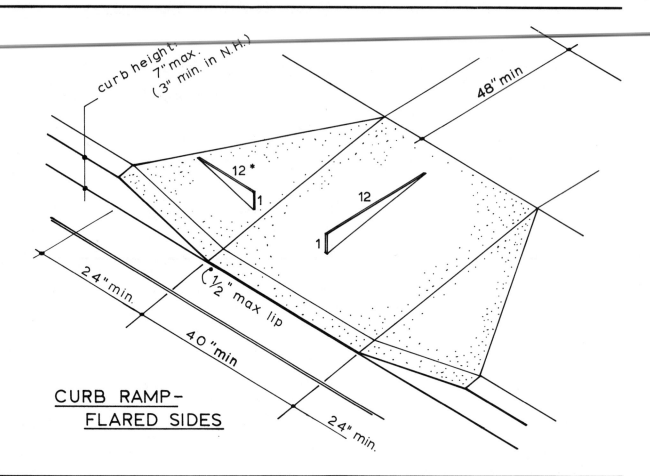

curb height:
7" max.
(3" min. in N.H.)

48" min

12 *

1

12

1

24" min.

(½" max lip

40" min

24" min.

CURB RAMP-
FLARED SIDES

Basis of standard —	APPLICABILITY			
Mass Architectural Barrier Board 521 CMR and others	ALA	LA	OHIO	GUAM
	ALASKA	MAINE	OKLA	PR
	ARIZ	MD	ORE	VIR IS
Notes —	ARK	● MASS	PA	DC
Roughen ramp surface, including sides. (Indicate that travel is not permitted by 40" fences or railings in N. H.). Provide sidewalk ramps at each corner of each intersection and at all other street crossings as close as possible to apex of intersection. Also provide if driveways have side curbs.	CAL	MICH	RI	
	COLO	MINN	SC	
	CONN	MISS	SD	FED'L
	DEL	MO	TENN	FUNDS
	FLA	MONT	TEXAS	
(*)Flare where sidewalks are too narrow for curbed ramp.	GA	NEB	UTAH	
	HAWAII	NEV	VT	
	IDAHO	● NH	VA	
	ILL	NJ	WASH	
	IND	NM	W VA	
	IOWA	NY	WIS	OTHER
	KANS	NC	WYO	
	KY	ND		

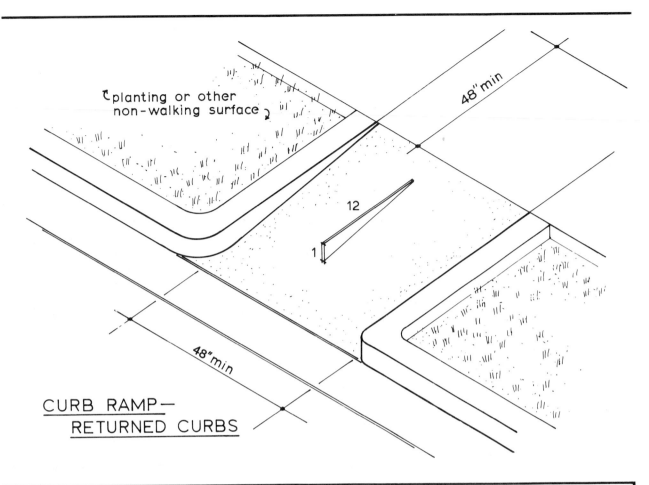

CURB RAMP—
RETURNED CURBS

Basis of standard —	APPLICABILITY			
Art. 10F, Chapt. 18, Code of West Virginia and others	ALA	LA	OHIO	GUAM
	ALASKA	MAINE	OKLA	PR
	ARIZ	MD	ORE	VIR IS
	ARK	MASS	PA	DC
Notes —	CAL	MICH	RI	
West Virginia: Min. 2 curb cuts per lineal block, located at intersections. Surface to be non-slip, use different type of material as identification for the blind.	COLO	MINN	SC	
	CONN	MISS	SD	FED'L FUNDS
	DEL	MO	TENN	
	FLA	MONT	TEXAS	
	GA	● NEB	UTAH	
	HAWAII	NEV	VT	
	IDAHO	NH	VA	
	ILL	NJ	WASH	
	IND	NM	● W VA	
	IOWA	NY	WIS	OTHER
	KANS	NC	WYO	
	KY	ND		

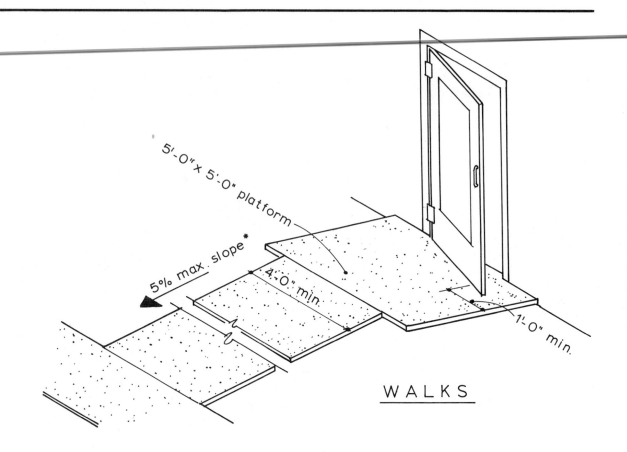

5'-0" x 5'-0" platform

5% max. slope *

4'-0" min.

1'-0" min.

W A L K S

Basis of standard —	APPLICABILITY			
North Carolina State Building Code	ALA	LA	OHIO	GUAM
	ALASKA	MAINE	OKLA	PR
	ARIZ	MD	ORE	VIR IS
Notes —	ARK	MASS	PA	DC
Walks to have continuous common surface not interrupted by steps or abrupt level changes greater than 1/2". At driveways or parking lots, blend to a common level with curb cuts with 5% max gradient. (*)May be 8.33% with handrails.	CAL	MICH	RI	
	COLO	MINN	SC	
	CONN	MISS	SD	FED'L FUNDS
	DEL	MO	● TENN	
	FLA	MONT	TEXAS	
	GA	NEB	UTAH	
	HAWAII	NEV	VT	
	IDAHO	NH	VA	
	ILL	NJ	WASH	
	IND	NM	W VA	
	IOWA	NY	WIS	OTHER
	KANS	● NC	WYO	
	KY	ND		

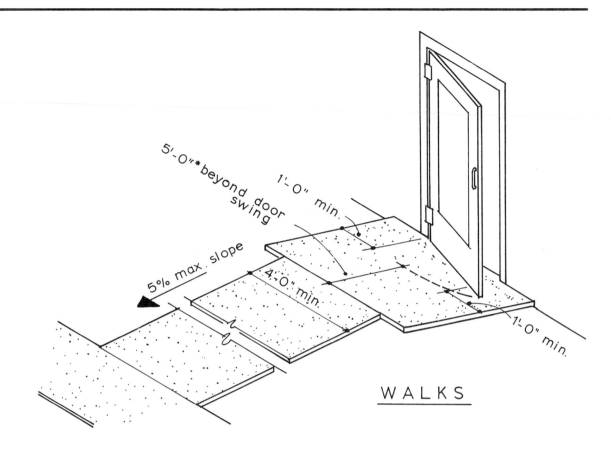

5'-0"* beyond door swing

1'-0" min.

5% max. slope

4'-0" min.

1'-0" min.

W A L K S

Basis of standard —	APPLICABILITY			
Barrier-Free Design Standard	● ALA	LA	OHIO	GUAM
	ALASKA	MAINE	OKLA	PR
	ARIZ	MD	ORE	VIR IS
Notes —	ARK	MASS	PA	DC
Walks to have continuous surface uninterrupted by steps or abrupt level changes. Level where possible, with max. gradient of 5%. Level rest areas at 60' max. if gradient exceeds 3%. Firm, fixed non-slip materials. If gratings cannot be avoided, max. opening = 3/4". Where grade drops abruptly within 3' of walk, provide 32" high handrails. (*)If door does not swing onto platform it may be 5' wide x 3' deep.	CAL	MICH	RI	
	COLO	MINN	SC	
	CONN	MISS	SD	FED'L FUNDS
	DEL	MO	TENN	
	FLA	MONT	TEXAS	
	GA	NEB	UTAH	
	HAWAII	NEV	VT	
	IDAHO	NH	VA	
	ILL	NJ	WASH	
	IND	NM	W VA	
	IOWA	NY	WIS	OTHER
	KANS	NC	WYO	
	KY	ND		

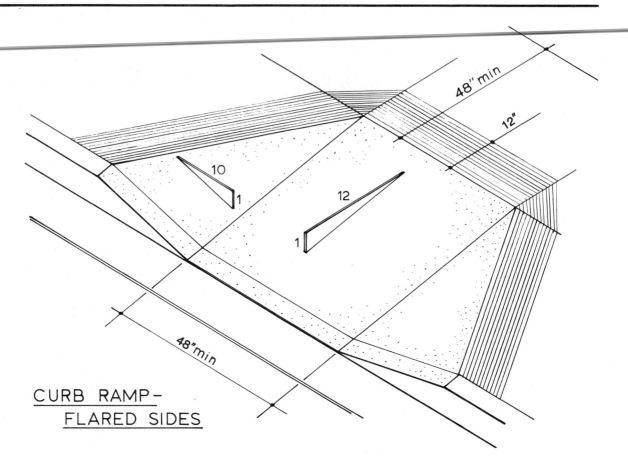

CURB RAMP-
FLARED SIDES

Basis of standard —	APPLICABILITY			
CAC Title 24, Part 2	ALA	LA	OHIO	GUAM
	ALASKA	MAINE	OKLA	PR
	ARIZ	MD	ORE	VIR IS
Notes —	ARK	MASS	PA	DC
Provide 12″ wide indicator for the blind, 1/4″ x 1/4″ grooves 3/4″ on center.	● CAL	MICH	RI	
Provide 1/2″ beveled lip at juncture of curb ramp and street.	COLO	MINN	SC	
	CONN	MISS	SD	FED'L FUNDS
	DEL	MO	TENN	
	FLA	MONT	TEXAS	
	GA	NEB	UTAH	
	HAWAII	NEV	VT	
	IDAHO	NH	VA	
	ILL	NJ	WASH	
	IND	NM	W VA	
	IOWA	NY	WIS	OTHER
	KANS	NC	WYO	
	KY	ND		

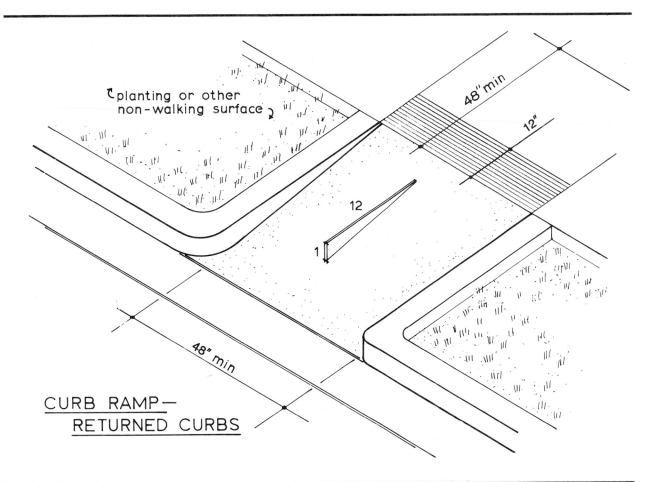

planting or other
non-walking surface

48" min

12"

12

1

48" min

CURB RAMP—
RETURNED CURBS

Basis of standard —	APPLICABILITY			
CAC Title 24, Part 2	ALA	LA	OHIO	GUAM
	ALASKA	MAINE	OKLA	PR
	ARIZ	MD	ORE	VIR IS
Notes —	ARK	MASS	PA	DC
Provide 12″ wide indicator for the blind, 1/4″ x 1/4″	● CAL	MICH	RI	
grooves 3/4″ on center.	COLO	MINN	SC	
Provide 1/2″ beveled lip at juncture of curb ramp and	CONN	MISS	SD	FED'L
street.	DEL	MO	TENN	FUNDS
	FLA	MONT	TEXAS	
	GA	NEB	UTAH	
	HAWAII	NEV	VT	
	IDAHO	NH	VA	
	ILL	NJ	WASH	
	IND	NM	W VA	
	IOWA	NY	WIS	OTHER
	KANS	NC	WYO	
	KY	ND		

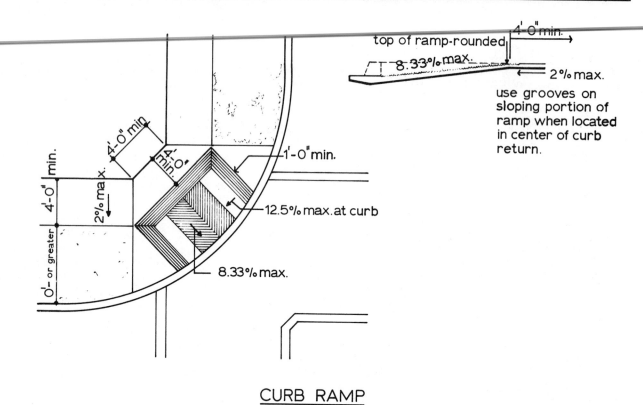

CURB RAMP

Basis of standard — CAC Title 24, Part 2	APPLICABILITY			
	ALA	LA	OHIO	GUAM
	ALASKA	MAINE	OKLA	PR
	ARIZ	MD	ORE	VIR IS
	ARK	MASS	PA	DC
Notes — Where curb cuts are at center of intersection provide chevron "v" grooves 1-1/2" on center.	● CAL	MICH	RI	
	COLO	MINN	SC	
	CONN	MISS	SD	FED'L FUNDS
	DEL	MO	TENN	
	FLA	MONT	TEXAS	
	GA	NEB	UTAH	
	HAWAII	NEV	VT	
	IDAHO	NH	VA	
	ILL	NJ	WASH	
	IND	NM	W VA	
	IOWA	NY	WIS	OTHER
	KANS	NC	WYO	
	KY	ND		

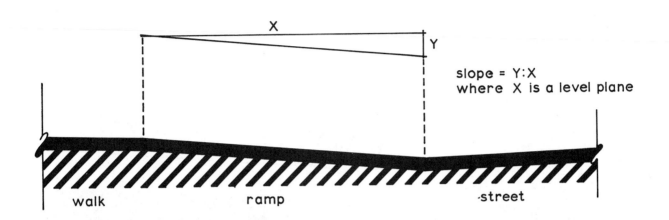

X

Y

slope = Y:X
where X is a level plane

walk   ramp   -street

MEASUREMENT OF CURB RAMP SLOPES

Basis of standard — CAC Title 24, Part 2	APPLICABILITY			
	ALA	LA	OHIO	GUAM
	ALASKA	MAINE	OKLA	PR
	ARIZ	MD	ORE	VIR IS
	ARK	MASS	PA	DC
Notes —	● CAL	MICH	RI	
	COLO	MINN	SC	
	CONN	MISS	SD	FED'L
	DEL	MO	TENN	FUNDS
	FLA	MONT	TEXAS	
	GA	NEB	UTAH	
	HAWAII	NEV	VT	
	IDAHO	NH	VA	
	ILL	NJ	WASH	
	IND	NM	W VA	
	IOWA	NY	WIS	OTHER
	KANS	NC	WYO	
	KY	ND		

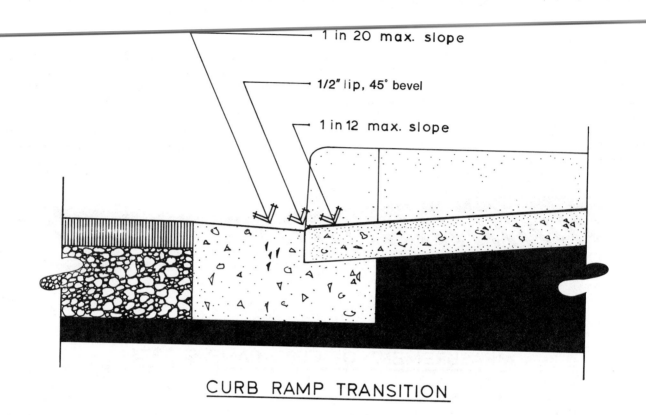

1 in 20 max. slope

1/2" lip, 45° bevel

1 in 12 max. slope

CURB RAMP TRANSITION

Basis of standard —	APPLICABILITY			
CAC Title 24, Part 2	ALA	LA	OHIO	GUAM
	ALASKA	MAINE	OKLA	PR
	ARIZ	MD	ORE	VIR IS
Notes —	ARK	MASS	PA	DC
	● CAL	MICH	RI	
	COLO	MINN	SC	
	CONN	MISS	SD	FED'L
	DEL	MO	TENN	FUNDS
	FLA	MONT	TEXAS	
	GA	NEB	UTAH	
	HAWAII	NEV	VT	
	IDAHO	NH	VA	
	ILL	NJ	WASH	
	IND	NM	W VA	
	IOWA	NY	WIS	OTHER
	KANS	NC	WYO	
	KY	ND		

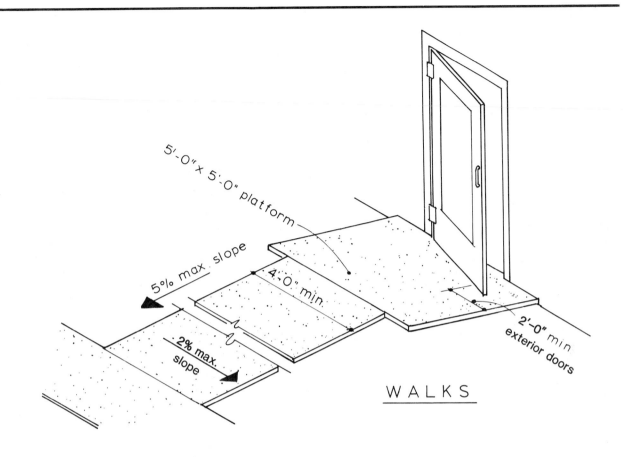

WALKS

Basis of standard —	APPLICABILITY			
CAC Title 24, Part 2	ALA	LA	OHIO	GUAM
	ALASKA	MAINE	OKLA	PR
	ARIZ	MD	ORE	VIR IS
	ARK	MASS	PA	DC
Notes —	● CAL	MICH	RI	
	COLO	MINN	SC	
	CONN	MISS	SD	FED'L FUNDS
	DEL	MO	TENN	
	FLA	MONT	TEXAS	
	GA	NEB	UTAH	
	HAWAII	NEV	VT	
	IDAHO	NH	VA	
	ILL	NJ	WASH	
	IND	NM	W VA	
	IOWA	NY	WIS	OTHER
	KANS	NC	WYO	
	KY	ND		

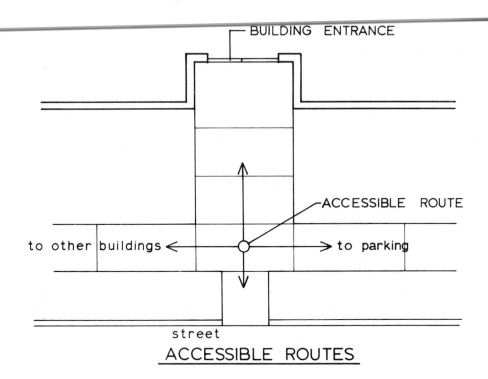

ACCESSIBLE ROUTES

Basis of standard — CAC Title 24, Part 2	APPLICABILITY			
	ALA	LA	OHIO	GUAM
	ALASKA	MAINE	OKLA	PR
	ARIZ	MD	ORE	VIR IS
Notes —	ARK	MASS	PA	DC
New construction: All primary entrances shall be accessible.	● CAL	MICH	RI	
Remodelling: At least one entrance shall be accessible.	COLO	MINN	SC	
	CONN	MISS	SD	FED'L
	DEL	MO	TENN	FUNDS
	FLA	MONT	TEXAS	
	GA	NEB	UTAH	
	HAWAII	NEV	VT	
	IDAHO	NH	VA	
	ILL	NJ	WASH	
	IND	NM	W VA	
	IOWA	NY	WIS	OTHER
	KANS	NC	WYO	
	KY	ND		

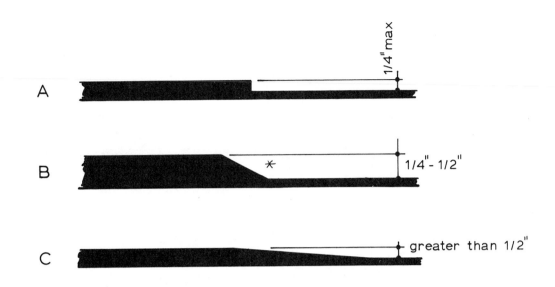

CHANGES IN LEVEL

Basis of standard — CAC Title 24, Part 2	APPLICABILITY			
	ALA	LA	OHIO	GUAM
	ALASKA	MAINE	OKLA	PR
	ARIZ	MD	ORE	VIR IS
Notes —	ARK	MASS	PA	DC
"C" requires a 1:12 slope (8.33%).	● CAL	MICH	RI	
	COLO	MINN	SC	
	CONN	MISS	SD	FED'L FUNDS
	DEL	MO	TENN	
	FLA	MONT	TEXAS	
	GA	NEB	UTAH	
	HAWAII	NEV	VT	
	IDAHO	NH	VA	
	ILL	NJ	WASH	
	IND	NM	W·VA	
	IOWA	NY	WIS	OTHER
	KANS	NC	WYO	
	KY	ND		

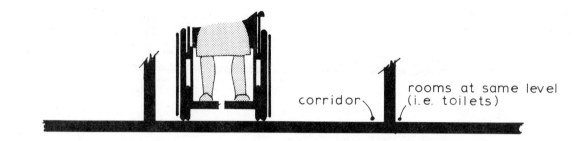

corridor

rooms at same level
(i.e. toilets)

alternate for same story:
complying ramp,
lift or elevator

common level with
nonslip surface

FLOORS ON A GIVEN STORY

Basis of standard — CAC Title 24, Part 2	APPLICABILITY			
	ALA	LA	OHIO	GUAM
	ALASKA	MAINE	OKLA	PR
	ARIZ	MD	ORE	VIR IS
	ARK	MASS	PA	DC
	● CAL	MICH	RI	
	COLO	MINN	SC	
	CONN	MISS	SD	FED'L FUNDS
	DEL	MO	TENN	
	FLA	MONT	TEXAS	
	GA	NEB	UTAH	
	HAWAII	NEV	VT	
	IDAHO	NH	VA	
	ILL	NJ	WASH	
	IND	NM	W VA	
	IOWA	NY	WIS	OTHER
	KANS	NC	WYO	
	KY	ND		

Basis of standard —
CAC Title 24, Part 2

Notes —
Restaurants may have up to 25% of the dining area on an inaccessible level.

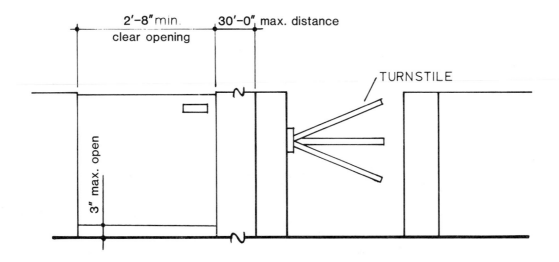

2'-8" min. clear opening

30'-0" max. distance

TURNSTILE

3" max. open

TURNSTILES

Basis of standard —	APPLICABILITY			
CAC Title 24, Part 2	ALA	LA	OHIO	GUAM
	ALASKA	MAINE	OKLA	PR
	ARIZ	MD	ORE	VIR IS
Notes —	ARK	MASS	PA	DC
Audible alarms are not allowed on gates.	● CAL	MICH	RI	
Gates shall be openable with maximum 5 lb. pressure.	COLO	MINN	SC	
	CONN	MISS	SD	FED'L FUNDS
	DEL	MO	TENN	
	FLA	MONT	TEXAS	
	GA	NEB	UTAH	
	HAWAII	NEV	VT	
	IDAHO	NH	VA	
	ILL	NJ	WASH	
	IND	NM	W VA	
	IOWA	NY	WIS	OTHER
	KANS	NC	WYO	
	KY	ND		

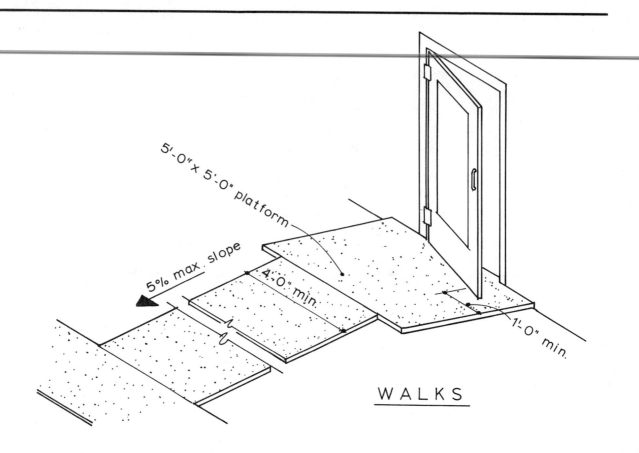

5'-0" X 5'-0" platform

5% max. slope

4'-0" min.

1'-0" min.

WALKS

Basis of standard —	APPLICABILITY			
Connecticut Building Code	ALA	LA	OHIO	GUAM
	ALASKA	MAINE	OKLA	PR
	ARIZ	MD	ORE	VIR IS
Notes —	ARK	MASS	PA	DC
Platform may be 3'-0" deep by 5'-0" wide if door does not swing onto platform or toward walk.	CAL	MICH	RI	
	COLO	MINN	SC	
	● CONN	MISS	SD	FED'L FUNDS
	DEL	MO	TENN	
	FLA	MONT	TEXAS	
	GA	NEB	UTAH	
	HAWAII	NEV	VT	
	IDAHO	NH	VA	
	ILL	NJ	WASH	
	IND	NM	W VA	
	IOWA	NY	WIS	OTHER
	KANS	NC	WYO	
	KY	ND		

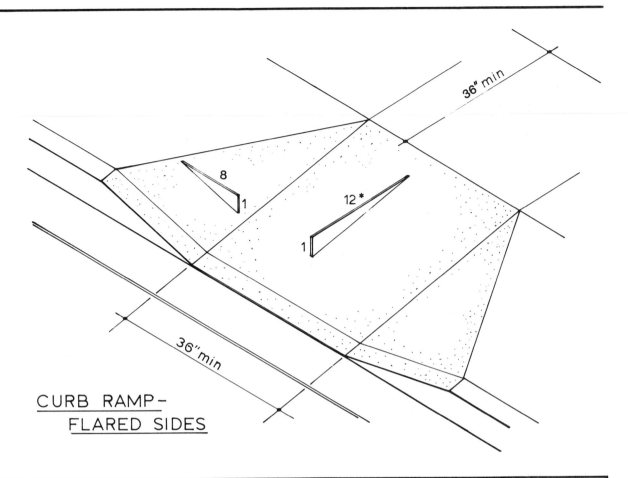

CURB RAMP –
FLARED SIDES

Basis of standard —	APPLICABILITY			
Capital Development Board	ALA	LA	OHIO	GUAM
	ALASKA	MAINE	OKLA	PR
	ARIZ	MD	ORE	VIR IS
Notes —	ARK	MASS	PA	DC
Blend to a common level at adjoining surfaces. Whole curb ramp shall contrast in color and texture to surrounding walk surface. Surfaces of curb ramps shall be joint free and slip-resistant, located to minimize conflicts between pedestrians and vehicles. (*)May be 1:8 max. in existing sidewalks if more gradual slope is impossible.	CAL	MICH	RI	
	COLO	MINN	SC	
	CONN	MISS	SD	FED'L FUNDS
	DEL	MO	TENN	
	FLA	MONT	TEXAS	
	GA	NEB	UTAH	
	HAWAII	NEV	VT	
	IDAHO	NH	VA	
	● ILL	NJ	WASH	
	IND	NM	W VA	
	IOWA	NY	WIS	OTHER
	KANS	NC	WYO	
	KY	ND		

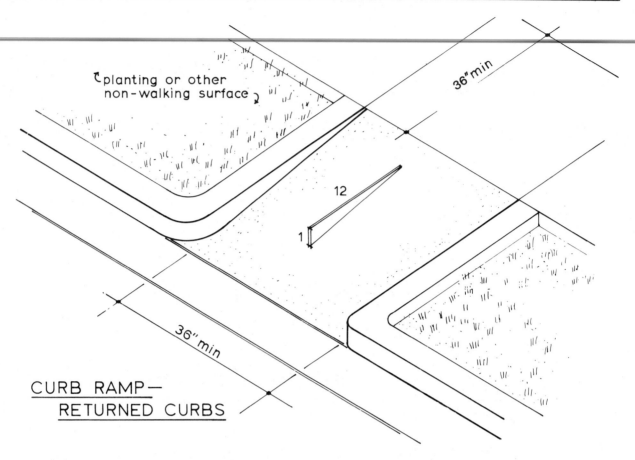

CURB RAMP—
RETURNED CURBS

Basis of standard —	APPLICABILITY			
Capital Development Board	ALA	LA	OHIO	GUAM
	ALASKA	MAINE	OKLA	PR
	ARIZ	MD	ORE	VIR IS
Notes —	ARK	MASS	PA	DC
See notes on preceding page.	CAL	MICH	RI	
	COLO	MINN	SC	
	CONN	MISS	SD	FED'L
	DEL	MO	TENN	FUNDS
	FLA	MONT	TEXAS	
	GA	NEB	UTAH	
	HAWAII	NEV	VT	
	IDAHO	NH	VA	
	● ILL	NJ	WASH	
	IND	NM	W VA	
	IOWA	NY	WIS	OTHER
	KANS	NC	WYO	
	KY	ND		

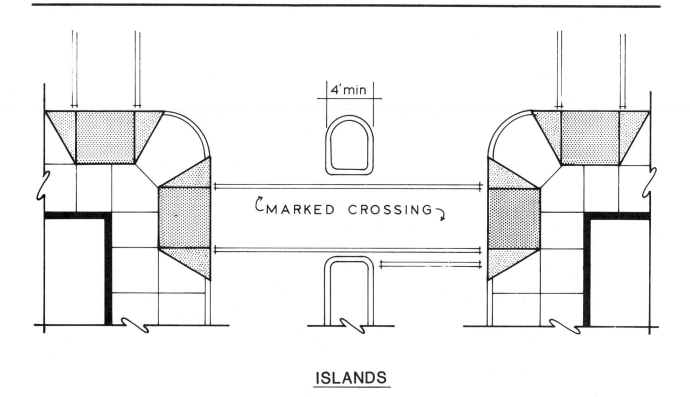

ISLANDS

Basis of standard —	APPLICABILITY			
Capital Development Board	ALA	LA	OHIO	GUAM
	ALASKA	MAINE	OKLA	PR
	ARIZ	MD	ORE	VIR IS
Notes —	ARK	MASS	PA	DC
Street crossings shall be considered as continuations of walks and sidewalks. Blend crossings with islands to a common level. Surface of cross walk at island to have a different color and texture. Provide a support device to steady people with balance problems (may be guardrail or pole). Pedestrian overpasses and underpasses shall be accessible paths of travel and shall comply to requirements.	CAL	MICH	RI	
	COLO	MINN	SC	
	CONN	MISS	SD	FED'L FUNDS
	DEL	MO	TENN	
	FLA	MONT	TEXAS	
	GA	NEB	UTAH	
	HAWAII	NEV	VT	
	IDAHO	NH	VA	
	● ILL	NJ	WASH	
	IND	NM	W VA	
	IOWA	NY	WIS	OTHER
	KANS	NC	WYO	
	KY	ND		

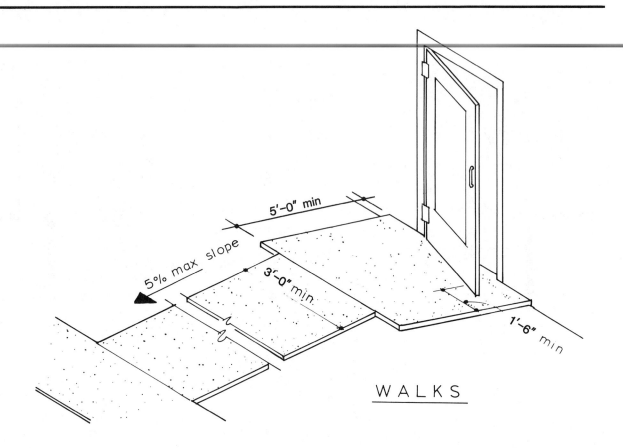

5'-0" min

5% max slope

3'-0" min

1'-6" min

WALKS

Basis of standard —	APPLICABILITY			
Capital Development Board	ALA	LA	OHIO	GUAM
	ALASKA	MAINE	OKLA	PR
	ARIZ	MD	ORE	VIR IS
Notes —	ARK	MASS	PA	DC
For gradients steeper than 5%, conform to ramp requirements (max. allowable = 8.33%). For max. 5% sustained gradients provide min. 5' long rest areas at 100' intervals. Cross slope or crowning of walks between 1:50 and 1:100. Max slope in front of door for drainage: 1:50.	CAL	MICH	RI	
	COLO	MINN	SC	
	CONN	MISS	SD	FED'L FUNDS
	DEL	MO	TENN	
	FLA	MONT	TEXAS	
	GA	NEB	UTAH	
	HAWAII	NEV	VT	
	IDAHO	NH	VA	
	● ILL	NJ	WASH	
	IND	NM	W VA	
	IOWA	NY	WIS	OTHER
	KANS	NC	WYO	
	KY	ND		

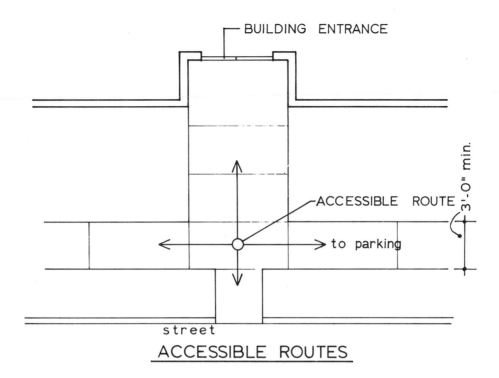

ACCESSIBLE ROUTES

Basis of standard —	APPLICABILITY			
Capital Development Board	ALA	LA	OHIO	GUAM
	ALASKA	MAINE	OKLA	PR
	ARIZ	MD	ORE	VIR IS
Notes —	ARK	MASS	PA	DC
For high incidence of people in wheelchairs or using walking aids, min. walk width: 5'-0". Walks less than 5'-0" wide: provide 5'-0" width min. with 7'-0" min. length at max. 10' o.c. intervals. Walks not to be interrupted by abrupt level changes, firm, stable, without slipping hazards. Max. joints 1/2" wide, flush with adjoining surfaces. Provide tactile clue, curb or railing when a hazardous area occurs alongside a walk or pedestrian area. All major entrances (exits) to buildings and rooms shall be accessible.	CAL	MICH	RI	
	COLO	MINN	SC	
	CONN	MISS	SD	FED'L
	DEL	MO	TENN	FUNDS
	FLA	MONT	TEXAS	
	GA	NEB	UTAH	
	HAWAII	NEV	VT	
	IDAHO	NH	VA	
	● ILL	NJ	WASH	
	IND	NM	W VA	
	IOWA	NY	WIS	OTHER
	KANS	NC	WYO	
	KY	ND		

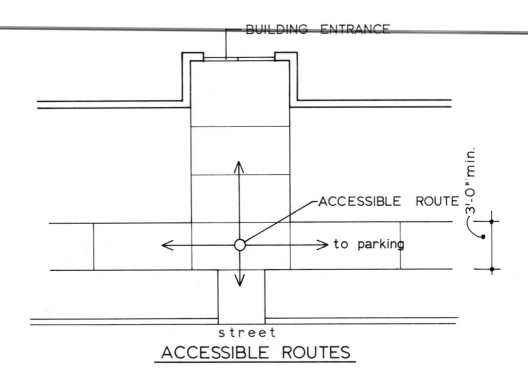

BUILDING ENTRANCE

ACCESSIBLE ROUTE

to parking

3'-0" min.

street

ACCESSIBLE ROUTES

Basis of standard —	APPLICABILITY			
Capital Development Board	ALA	LA	OHIO	GUAM
	ALASKA	MAINE	OKLA	PR
	ARIZ	MD	ORE	VIR IS
Notes —	ARK	MASS	PA	DC
All accessible spaces in a building or facility shall be served from an accessible entrance by at least one path of travel without stairs or escalators. Serve all accessible areas in building. Provide accessible means of emergency egress or a place of refuge from all accessible spaces. (Illinois permits alternatives which include ANSI-complying horizontal exits, fire-resistive elevator lobbies, elevators meeting administrative authority approval as a means of egress, or enclosed ANSI-complying stairways. Refer to details in code.)	CAL	MICH	RI	
	COLO	MINN	SC	
	CONN	MISS	SD	FED'L
	DEL	MO	TENN	FUNDS
	FLA	MONT	TEXAS	
	GA	NEB	UTAH	
	HAWAII	NEV	VT	
	IDAHO	NH	VA	
	● ILL	NJ	WASH	
	IND	NM	W VA	
	IOWA	NY	WIS	OTHER
	KANS	NC	WYO	
	KY	ND		

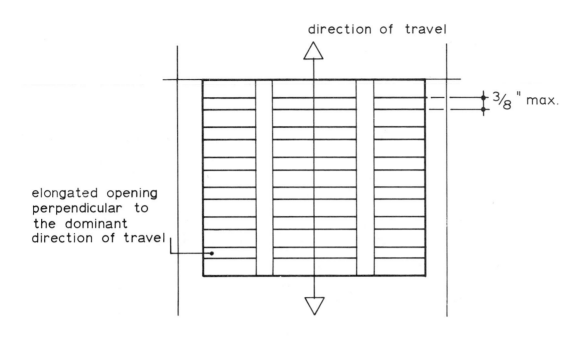

direction of travel

3/8" max.

elongated opening
perpendicular to
the dominant
direction of travel

GRATINGS

Basis of standard —	APPLICABILITY			
Capital Development Board	ALA	LA	OHIO	GUAM
	ALASKA	MAINE	OKLA	PR
	ARIZ	MD	ORE	VIR IS
Notes —	ARK	MASS	PA	DC
Max. vertical height change on solid manhole covers: 1/4″	CAL	MICH	RI	
	COLO	MINN	SC	
	CONN	MISS	SD	FED'L FUNDS
	DEL	MO	TENN	
	FLA	MONT	TEXAS	
	GA	NEB	UTAH	
	HAWAII	NEV	VT	
	IDAHO	NH	VA	
	● ILL	NJ	WASH	
	IND	NM	W VA	
	IOWA	NY	WIS	OTHER
	KANS	NC	WYO	
	KY	ND		

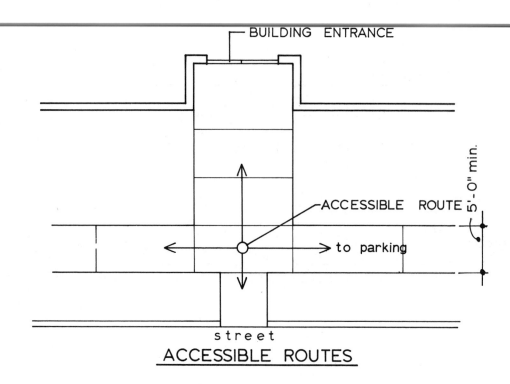

ACCESSIBLE ROUTES

Basis of standard —	APPLICABILITY			
Indiana Amendments to Uniform Building Code	ALA	LA	OHIO	GUAM
	ALASKA	MAINE	OKLA	PR
	ARIZ	MD	ORE	VIR IS
Notes —	ARK	MASS	PA	DC
Provide at least one primary entrance at each grade floor level uninterrupted by steps or abrupt level changes exceeding 1/2″ max. gradient: 1:20, max. cross slope: 1:50. Provide complying curb cuts or curb approaches for curbs. Exceptions: Buildings frequented only by employees where work cannot reasonably be performed by the handicapped (unless such areas lie in path of egress normally used by handicapped) and for buildings without public elevators for floors above grade levels used by the public if facilities normally sought by the public are available at grade levels.	CAL	MICH	RI	
	COLO	MINN	SC	
	CONN	MISS	SD	FED'L FUNDS
	DEL	MO	TENN	
	FLA	MONT	TEXAS	
	GA	NEB	UTAH	
	HAWAII	NEV	VT	
	IDAHO	NH	VA	
	ILL	NJ	WASH	
	● IND	NM	W VA	
	IOWA	NY	WIS	OTHER
	KANS	NC	WYO	
	KY	ND		

TABLE NO. 5-E — PRESCRIBED OCCUPANT AREA LOADING AND ACCESS REQUIREMENT FOR PHYSICALLY HANDICAPPED

USE	SQUARE FEET PER OCCUPANT	ACCESS BY MEANS OF A LEVEL ENTRY. RAMP OR AN ELEVATOR MUST BE PROVIDED FOR THE PHYSICALLY HANDICAPPED AS INDICATED
Aircraft Hangers (No Repair)	500	Yes
Auction Rooms	7	Yes
Assembly Areas Concentrated Use (without fixed seats) Auditoriums Bowling Alleys (Assembly areas) Churches and Chapels Dance Floors Lodge Rooms Reviewing Stands Stadiums	7	Yes Access to secondary areas on balconies or mezzanine may be by stairs only, except when the only available toilet facilities are on other levels. Reviewing stands, grandstands and bleachers need not comply.
Assembly Areas Less-concentrated Use Conference Rooms Dining Rooms Drinking Establishments Exhibit Rooms Gymnasiums Lounges Stages	15	Yes Access to secondary areas on balconies or mezzanines may be by stairs only, except when the only available toilet facilities are on other levels.
Childrens Homes and Homes for the Aged	80	Yes Access to floors other than that closest to grade may be by stairs only, except when the only available toilet facilities are on other levels; third story and above shall be accessible.
Classrooms	20	Yes
Dormitories	50	Yes Access to floors other than that closest to grade may be by stairs only, except when the only available toilet facilities are on other levels; third story and above shall be accessible.
Dwellings	300	No
Garage, Parking	200	Yes Access to floors other than that closest to grade may be by stairs only, except when the only available toilet facilities are on other levels; third story and above shall be accessible. (See Section 512 for accessible parking space requirements.)

Basis of standard —
Indiana Amendments to Uniform Building Code

Notes —
Continued on following page

APPLICABILITY			
ALA	LA	OHIO	GUAM
ALASKA	MAINE	OKLA	PR
ARIZ	MD	ORE	VIR IS
ARK	MASS	PA	DC
CAL	MICH	RI	
COLO	MINN	SC	
CONN	MISS	SD	FED'L FUNDS
DEL	MO	TENN	
FLA	MONT	TEXAS	
GA	NEB	UTAH	
HAWAII	NEV	VT	
IDAHO	NH	VA	
ILL	NJ	WASH	
● IND	NM	W VA	
IOWA	NY	WIS	OTHER
KANS	NC	WYO	
KY	ND		

TABLE NO. 5-E — Continued

USE	SQUARE FEET PER OCCUPANT	ACCESS BY MEANS OF A LEVEL ENTRY. RAMP OR AN ELEVATOR MUST BE PROVIDED FOR THE PHYSICALLY HANDICAPPED AS INDICATED
Hospitals and Sanitariums Nursing Homes	80	Yes
Hotels and Apartments	200	Yes See Section 1213.
Kitchens-Commercial	200	No
Library Reading Room	50	Yes Access to secondary areas on balconies or mezzanine may be by stairs only, except when the only available toilet facilities are on other levels.
Locker Rooms	50	Yes
Mechanical Equipment Room	300	No
Nurseries for Children (Day-Care)	50	Yes
Offices	100	Yes Access to floors other than that closest to grade may be by stairs only, except when the only available toilet facilities are on other levels; third story and above shall be accessible.
School Shops and Vocational	50	Yes
Skating Rinks	50 on the skating area; 15 on the deck	Yes Access to floors other than that closest to grade may be by stairs only, except when the only available toilet facilities are on other levels; third story and above shall be accessible.
Stores — Retail Sales Rooms		
Basement	20	Yes
Ground Floor	30	Yes
Upper Floors	50	Yes
Swimming Pools	50 for the pool area; 15 on the deck	Yes Access to floors other than that closest to grade may be by stairs only, except when the only available toilet facilities are on other levels; third story and above shall be accessible.
Transitory Commercial Mobile Structure	100	No
Warehouses	300	Yes Access to floors other than that closest to grade may be by stairs only, except when the only available toilet facilities are on other levels; third story and above shall be accessible.
All others	100	To be determined by the administrative authority.

Basis of standard —
Indiana Amendments to Uniform Building Code

Notes —
Continued from preceding page

APPLICABILITY			
ALA	LA	OHIO	GUAM
ALASKA	MAINE	OKLA	PR
ARIZ	MD	ORE	VIR IS
ARK	MASS	PA	DC
CAL	MICH	RI	
COLO	MINN	SC	
CONN	MISS	SD	FED'L FUNDS
DEL	MO	TENN	
FLA	MONT	TEXAS	
GA	NEB	UTAH	
HAWAII	NEV	VT	
IDAHO	NH	VA	
ILL	NJ	WASH	
● IND	NM	W VA	
IOWA	NY	WIS	OTHER
KANS	NC	WYO	
KY	ND		

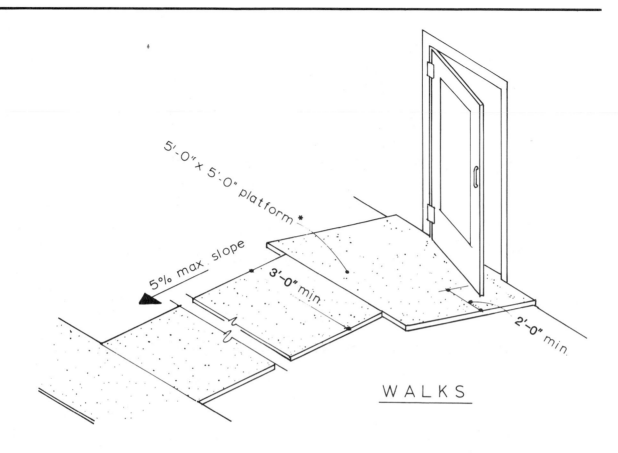

5'-0" x 5'-0" platform *

5% max. slope

3'-0" min.

2'-0" min.

WALKS

Basis of standard —	APPLICABILITY			
815 KAR 7:060	ALA	LA	OHIO	GUAM
	ALASKA	MAINE	OKLA	PR
	ARIZ	MD	ORE	VIR IS
Notes —	ARK	MASS	PA	DC
(*)Where approach to landing has slope exceeding 1:20, platform shall extend minimum 42″ beyond swing of door.	CAL	MICH	RI	
	COLO	MINN	SC	
	CONN	MISS	SD	FED'L
	DEL	MO	TENN	FUNDS
	FLA	MONT	TEXAS	
	GA	NEB	UTAH	
	HAWAII	NEV	VT	
	IDAHO	NH	VA	
	ILL	NJ	WASH	
	IND	NM	W VA	
	IOWA	NY	WIS	OTHER
	KANS	NC	WYO	
	● KY	ND		

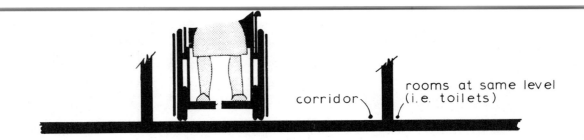

corridor

rooms at same level
(i.e. toilets)

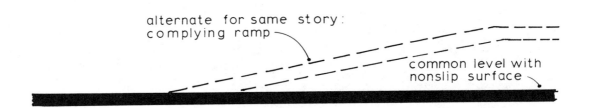

alternate for same story:
complying ramp

common level with
nonslip surface

FLOORS ON A GIVEN STORY

Basis of standard — 815 KAR 7:060	APPLICABILITY			
	ALA	LA	OHIO	GUAM
	ALASKA	MAINE	OKLA	PR
	ARIZ	MD	ORE	VIR IS
Notes —	ARK	MASS	PA	DC
	CAL	MICH	RI	
	COLO	MINN	SC	
	CONN	MISS	SD	FED'L FUNDS
	DEL	MO	TENN	
	FLA	MONT	TEXAS	
	GA	NEB	UTAH	
	HAWAII	NEV	VT	
	IDAHO	NH	VA	
	ILL	NJ	WASH	
	IND	NM	W VA	
	IOWA	NY	WIS	OTHER
	KANS	NC	WYO	
	● KY	ND		

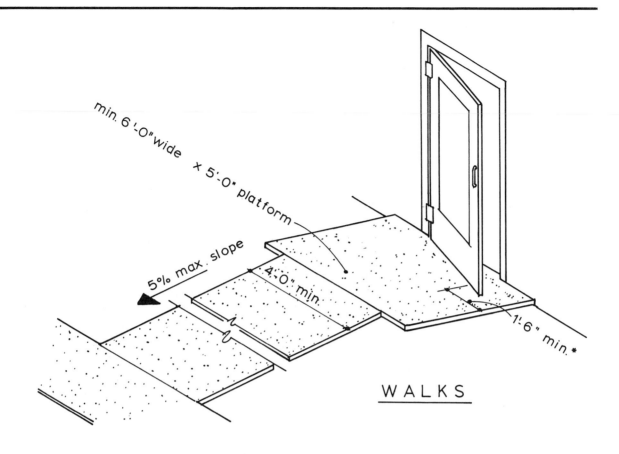

WALKS

Basis of standard —	APPLICABILITY			
Architectural Barriers Board	ALA	LA	OHIO	GUAM
	ALASKA	MAINE	OKLA	PR
	ARIZ	MD	ORE	VIR IS
Notes —	ARK	● MASS	PA	DC
Provide continuous common surface not interrupted	CAL	MICH	RI	
by steps or abrupt level changes greater than 1/2″;	COLO	MINN	SC	
non-slip surface. Where walk sides drop sharply,	CONN	MISS	SD	FED'L
provide min. 1′-0″ wide flat shoulder with texture	DEL	MO	TENN	FUNDS
different than sidewalk with max. 1:4 slope. Where	FLA	MONT	TEXAS	
slope is greater than 1:4 protect by a curb or other	GA	NEB	UTAH	
reasonable barrier.	HAWAII	NEV	VT	
(*)2′-0″ preferred.	IDAHO	NH	VA	
	ILL	NJ	WASH	
	IND	NM	W VA	
	IOWA	NY	WIS	OTHER
	KANS	NC	WYO	
	KY	ND		

edge trim

DOOR MAT

Basis of standard — Architectural Barriers Board	APPLICABILITY			
	ALA	LA	OHIO	GUAM
	ALASKA	MAINE	OKLA	PR
	ARIZ	MD	ORE	VIR IS
Notes — Max. door mat height: 1/2″. Carpet shall be high density, low pile, non-absorbent, stretched tautly, and securely anchored at all open edges. Ht. of edging strip: 3/8″ max. Padding: max. 1/4″ thick.	ARK	● MASS	PA	DC
	CAL	MICH	RI	
	COLO	MINN	SC	
	CONN	MISS	SD	FED'L
	DEL	MO	TENN	FUNDS
	FLA	MONT	TEXAS	
	GA	NEB	UTAH	
	HAWAII	NEV	VT	
	IDAHO	NH	VA	
	ILL	NJ	WASH	
	IND	NM	W VA	
	IOWA	NY	WIS	OTHER
	KANS	NC	WYO	
	KY	ND		

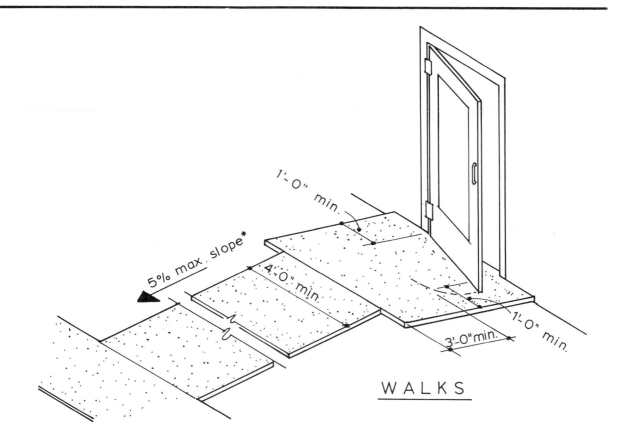

WALKS

Basis of standard — Missouri Revised Statutes, Ch. 8	APPLICABILITY			
	ALA	LA	OHIO	GUAM
	ALASKA	MAINE	OKLA	PR
	ARIZ	MD	ORE	VIR IS
	ARK	MASS	PA	DC
	CAL	MICH	RI	
	COLO	MINN	SC	
	CONN	MISS	SD	FED'L FUNDS
	DEL	● MO	TENN	
	FLA	MONT	TEXAS	
	GA	NEB	UTAH	
	HAWAII	NEV	VT	
	IDAHO	NH	VA	
	ILL	NJ	WASH	
	IND	NM	W VA	
	IOWA	NY	WIS	OTHER
	KANS	NC	WYO	
	KY	ND		

Notes —
Walks to be of a continuing common surface not interrupted by steps or abrupt level changes. Blend to a common level when crossing other walks, driveways or parking areas. Level of walk area outside public doorways to be at the same level as the area inside the door.

(*)Unless the parallel and adjacent public thoroughfare gradient is greater, in which case the walk gradient shall conform to the gradient of such parallel and adjacent thoroughfare.

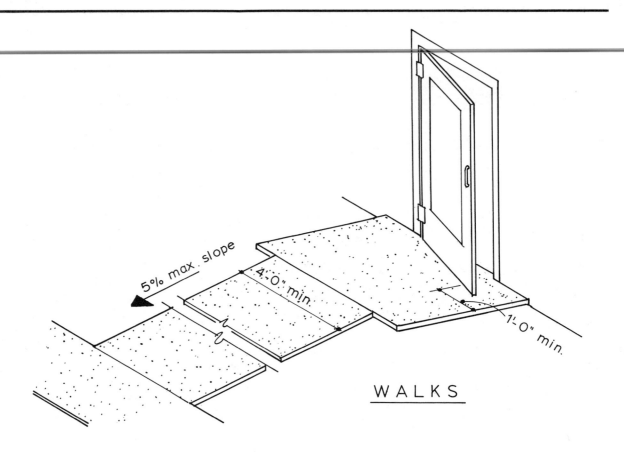

5% max. slope

4'-0" min.

1'-0" min.

WALKS

Basis of standard —	APPLICABILITY			
State of Nebraska Provisions for the Handicapped	ALA	LA	OHIO	GUAM
	ALASKA	MAINE	OKLA	PR
	ARIZ	MD	ORE	VIR IS
Notes —	ARK	MASS	PA	DC
Walks to have continuing common level, not interrupted by steps or abrupt level changes. If slope is greater than 5%, it is considered a ramp and handrail and other provisions for ramps apply. Vertical level changes greater than 1/2″ are hazardous.	CAL	MICH	RI	
	COLO	MINN	SC	
	CONN	MISS	SD	FED'L FUNDS
	DEL	MO	TENN	
	FLA	MONT	TEXAS	
	GA	● NEB	UTAH	
	HAWAII	NEV	VT	
	IDAHO	NH	VA	
	ILL	NJ	WASH	
	IND	NM	W VA	
	IOWA	NY	WIS	OTHER
	KANS	NC	WYO	
	KY	ND		

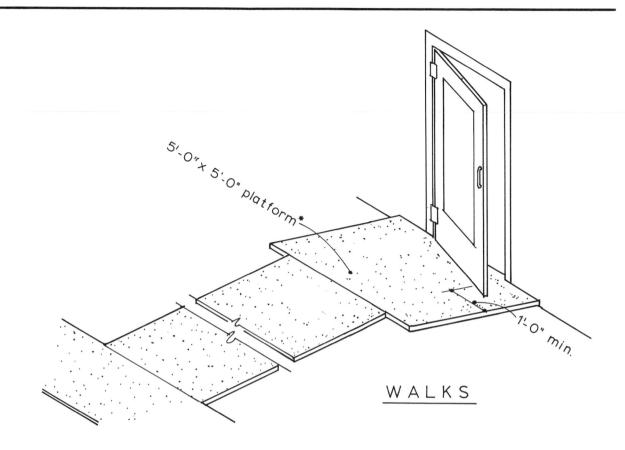

5'-0" x 5'-0" platform *

1'-0" min.

W A L K S

Basis of standard —	APPLICABILITY			
State of Nebraska Provisions for the Handicapped	ALA	LA	OHIO	GUAM
	ALASKA	MAINE	OKLA	PR
	ARIZ	MD	ORE	VIR IS
Notes —	ARK	MASS	PA	DC
Where rail is required, dimensions shall be inside to inside rail dimension. Provide at least one primary entrance usable by individuals in wheelchairs. One entrance shall be on a level making elevators accessible.	CAL	MICH	RI	
	COLO	MINN	SC	
	CONN	MISS	SD	FED'L FUNDS
	DEL	MO	TENN	
(*)May be 5'-0" wide by 3'-0" deep if door does not swing toward platform.	FLA	MONT	TEXAS	
	GA	● NEB	UTAH	
	HAWAII	NEV	VT	
	IDAHO	NH	VA	
	ILL	NJ	WASH	
	IND	NM	W VA	
	IOWA	NY	WIS	OTHER
	KANS	NC	WYO	
	KY	ND		

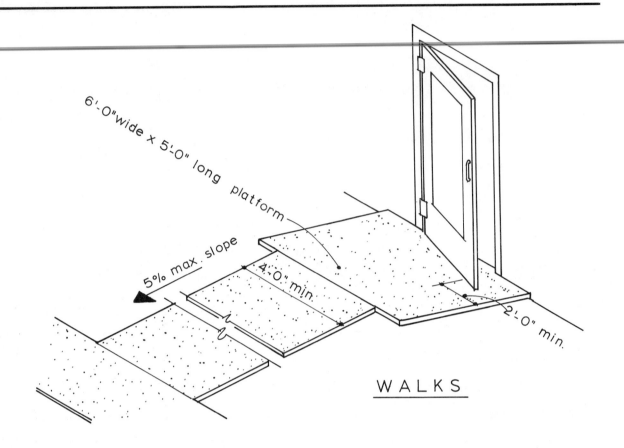

6'-0" wide x 5'-0" long platform

5% max. slope

4'-0" min.

2'-0" min.

WALKS

Basis of standard —	APPLICABILITY			
Architectural Barrier Free Design Code for the State of New Hampshire	ALA	LA	OHIO	GUAM
	ALASKA	MAINE	OKLA	PR
	ARIZ	MD	ORE	VIR IS
	ARK	MASS	PA	DC
	CAL	MICH	RI	
	COLO	MINN	SC	
Notes —	CONN	MISS	SD	FED'L FUNDS
Designated primary entrance shall be accessible by persons in wheelchairs. Designate primary accessible entrance at facility entrances which are not accessible. Accessible entrances to be on a level to provide egress from elevators. Secure door mats higher than 1/2″, or recess. Max. grate opening: 1/2″. Protrusions into entranceways not permitted. Min. height: 6′-8″. Speed for door closers: four to six seconds. Protect sides of walks by 1′-0″ min. shoulder with a texture other than sidewalk and an adjacent slope of 1:4 max. if sides of walk drop sharply. For slopes exceeding 1: 1:4, protect with 4″ min curb or other reasonable barrier.	DEL	MO	TENN	
	FLA	MONT	TEXAS	
	GA	NEB	UTAH	
	HAWAII	NEV	VT	
	IDAHO	● NH	VA	
	ILL	NJ	WASH	
	IND	NM	W VA	
	IOWA	NY	WIS	OTHER
	KANS	NC	WYO	
	KY	ND		

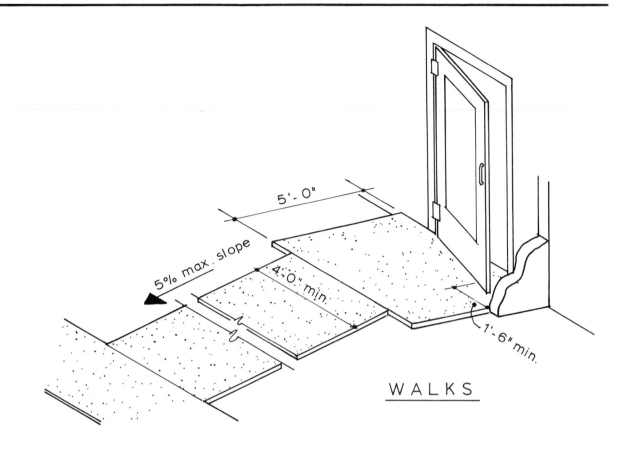

5'- 0"

5% max. slope

4'-0" min.

1'- 6" min.

WALKS

Basis of standard —	APPLICABILITY			
Barrier Free Design Regulations	ALA	LA	OHIO	GUAM
	ALASKA	MAINE	OKLA	PR
	ARIZ	MD	ORE	VIR IS
Notes —	ARK	MASS	PA	DC
Slopes over 5% shall comply with ramp requirements.	CAL	MICH	RI	
Continuing surface not interrupted by steps or abrupt	COLO	MINN	SC	
level changes. Intersections with other walks,	CONN	MISS	SD	FED'L
driveways, parking lots or streets, when constituting a	DEL	MO	TENN	FUNDS
route of travel for handicapped, shall be set at	FLA	MONT	TEXAS	
common level or blend to a common level with curb	GA	NEB	UTAH	
cuts or ramps. Surface: non-slip. Provide level rest	HAWAII	NEV	VT	
areas every 60' when grade is between 3% and 5%.	IDAHO	NH	VA	
Max. drainage transverse slope: 3/16″ per foot.	ILL	● NJ	WASH	
Provide protection where drop in grade exceeds 8″	IND	NM	W VA	
within 3′ of sidewalk.	IOWA	NY	WIS	OTHER
	KANS	NC	WYO	
	KY	ND		

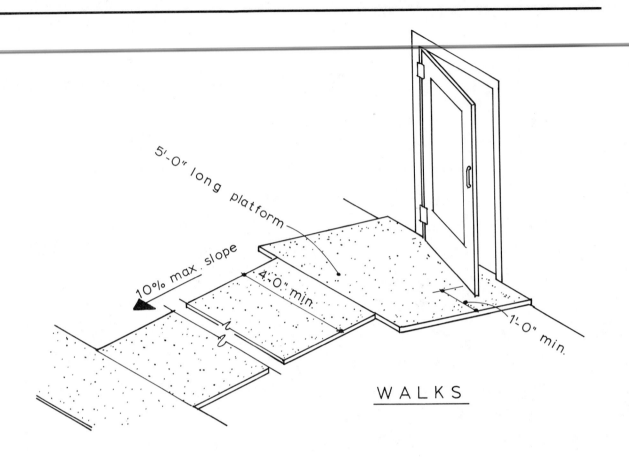

5'-0" long platform

10% max. slope

4'-0" min.

1'-0" min.

WALKS

Basis of standard — Structural Specialty Code	APPLICABILITY			
	ALA	LA	OHIO	GUAM
	ALASKA	MAINE	OKLA	PR
	ARIZ	MD	● ORE	VIR IS
	ARK	MASS	PA	DC
Notes — Walks to be hard surfaced of a continuing common surface not interrupted by abrupt changes in elevation.	CAL	MICH	RI	
	COLO	MINN	SC	
	CONN	MISS	SD	FED'L FUNDS
	DEL	MO	TENN	
	FLA	MONT	TEXAS	
	GA	NEB	UTAH	
	HAWAII	NEV	VT	
	IDAHO	NH	VA	
	ILL	NJ	WASH	
	IND	NM	W VA	
	IOWA	NY	WIS	OTHER
	KANS	NC	WYO	
	KY	ND		

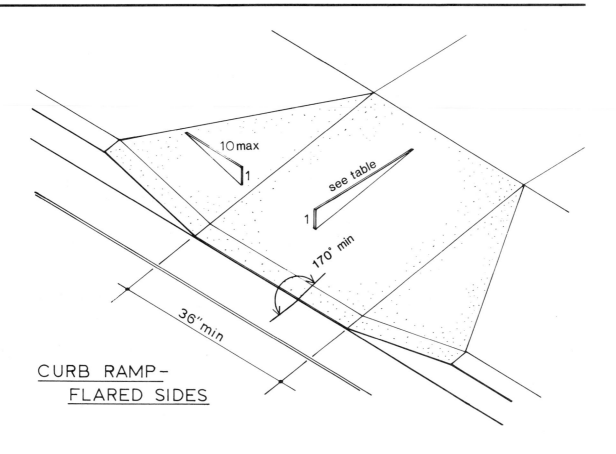

CURB RAMP-
FLARED SIDES

Basis of standard —	APPLICABILITY			
State Purchasing and General Services Commission	ALA	LA	OHIO	GUAM
	ALASKA	MAINE	OKLA	PR
	ARIZ	MD	ORE	VIR IS
Notes —	ARK	MASS	PA	DC
Locate so they are not obstructed by parked vehicles nor intrude into vehicular traffic lanes. Surface to be	CAL	MICH	RI	
slip resistant. For slopes less than 1:10 provide	COLO	MINN	SC	
surface texture that significantly contrasts with surrounding surfaces. Flare sides where curb ramps	CONN	MISS	SD	FED'L FUNDS
intersect pedestrian walks. Curb ramps 4'-0" wide or	DEL	MO	TENN	
wider are not required to have flared or protected sides. Max. slope and rise:	FLA	MONT	● TEXAS	
	GA	NEB	UTAH	
	HAWAII	NEV	VT	
	IDAHO	NH	VA	
	ILL	NJ	WASH	
	IND	NM	W VA	
	IOWA	NY	WIS	OTHER
	KANS	NC	WYO	
	KY	ND		

		Max. horizontal
Max slope	Max. rise	projection (run)
1:6	3"	1'-6"
1:8	7"	4'-8"
1:9	8"	6'-0"
1:10	9"	8'-0"
1:12	2'-6"	30'-0"
1:14	2'-10"	40'-0"
1:16	3'-8"	60'-0"

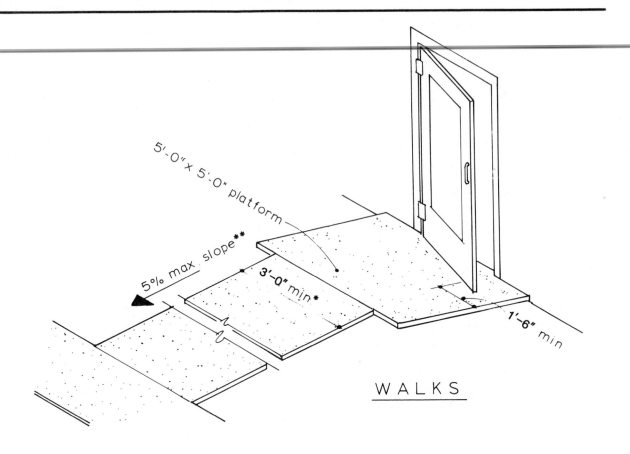

WALKS

Basis of standard —	APPLICABILITY			
State Purchasing and General Services Commission	ALA	LA	OHIO	GUAM
	ALASKA	MAINE	OKLA	PR
	ARIZ	MD	ORE	VIR IS
Notes —	ARK	MASS	PA	DC
Walks to have continuous common surface not interrupted by steps or abrupt level changes. Level changes up to 3/4″ with beveled edges are acceptable. Firm, stable, slip-resistant, regular surface. No protrusions reducing clear width to less than 3′-0″. Overhead clearance: 6′-8″ min.	CAL	MICH	RI	
	COLO	MINN	SC	
	CONN	MISS	SD	FED'L FUNDS
	DEL	MO	TENN	
(*)Use 3′-8″ for lengths in excess of 30′.	FLA	MONT	● TEXAS	
(**)6% max slope permitted where less than 30′ long.	GA	NEB	UTAH	
	HAWAII	NEV	VT	
	IDAHO	NH	VA	
	ILL	NJ	WASH	
	IND	NM	W VA	
	IOWA	NY	WIS	OTHER
	KANS	NC	WYO	
	KY	ND		

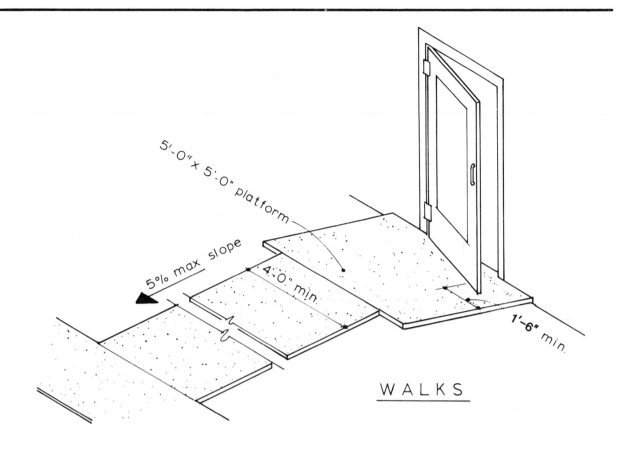

5'-0" x 5'-0" platform

5% max slope

4'-0" min.

1'-6" min.

WALKS

Basis of standard —	APPLICABILITY			
Utah State Building Board	ALA	LA	OHIO	GUAM
	ALASKA	MAINE	OKLA	PR
	ARIZ	MD	ORE	VIR IS
Notes —	ARK	MASS	PA	DC
Slopes over 5% are considered as ramps. Provide	CAL	MICH	RI	
continuous common surface not interrupted by steps	COLO	MINN	SC	
or abrupt level changes greater than 1/2″. Blend to	CONN	MISS	SD	FED'L
common level by means of curb cuts and slopes with				FUNDS
max. gradient of 12.5%. Max. cross slope: 1/8″/ft.	DEL	MO	TENN	
For gradients exceeding 5% provide rest areas at 30′	FLA	MONT	TEXAS	
max. intervals.	GA	NEB	● UTAH	
(*)1'-0″ for interior doors.	HAWAII	NEV	VT	
	IDAHO	NH	VA	
	ILL	NJ	WASH	
	IND	NM	W VA	
	IOWA	NY	WIS	OTHER
	KANS	NC	WYO	
	KY	ND		

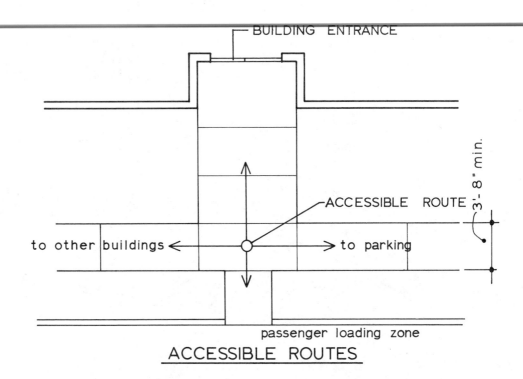

ACCESSIBLE ROUTES

Basis of standard — Building Code Advisory Council	**APPLICABILITY**			
	ALA	LA	OHIO	GUAM
	ALASKA	MAINE	OKLA	PR
	ARIZ	MD	ORE	VIR IS
Notes — A walk surface less than 5'-0" wide shall have unobstructed passing space, 5' x 5' min. at 200' max. intervals. Max. slope for shoulders: 1:50 for 3' min., with same grade at accessible route of travel. Max slope and cross-slope: 1:50. Max. expansion joint: 1/4", flush with surface. Blend curb cuts, roadways, etc. to a common surface. Provide 3'-0" high rail and 1'-6" mid rail where any portion of edge of accessible route is more than 8" above grade or which abuts hazardous area. Min. illumination: 5fc. Provide signs with International Symbol of Access at all primary public site entrance and every major junction along accessible routes indicating the direction to accessible destinations.	ARK	MASS	PA	DC
	CAL	MICH	RI	
	COLO	MINN	SC	
	CONN	MISS	SD	FED'L
	DEL	MO	TENN	FUNDS
	FLA	MONT	TEXAS	
	GA	NEB	UTAH	
	HAWAII	NEV	VT	
	IDAHO	NH	VA	
	ILL	NJ	● WASH	
	IND	NM	W VA	
	IOWA	NY	WIS	OTHER
	KANS	NC	WYO	
	KY	ND		

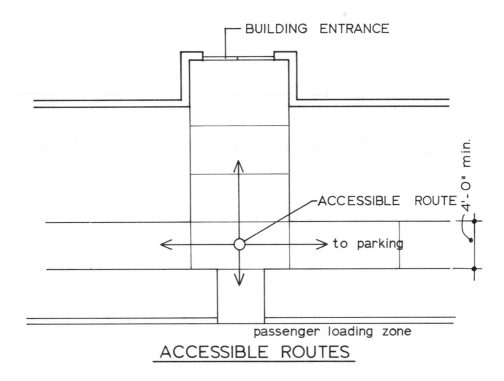

ACCESSIBLE ROUTES

Basis of standard — Art. 10F, Chapt. 18, Code of West Virginia	APPLICABILITY			
	ALA	LA	OHIO	GUAM
	ALASKA	MAINE	OKLA	PR
	ARIZ	MD	ORE	VIR IS
Notes —	ARK	MASS	PA	DC
Min. one primary entrance usable by individuals in	CAL	MICH	RI	
wheelchairs. Provide sign at primary entrance showing	COLO	MINN	SC	
location of secondary entrance for wheelchair entry.	CONN	MISS	SD	FED'L
At least one entrance available to wheelchair users				
that will make elevators accessible, which shall stop	DEL	MO	TENN	FUNDS
on all levels used by the general public. Provide ramps,	FLA	MONT	TEXAS	
elevators, or level entrance for all publicly funded	GA	NEB	UTAH	
facilities over one story used by the public and for all	HAWAII	NEV	VT	
public buildings over one story.	IDAHO	NH	VA	
	ILL	NJ	WASH	
	IND	NM	● W VA	
	IOWA	NY	WIS	OTHER
	KANS	NC	WYO	
	KY	ND		

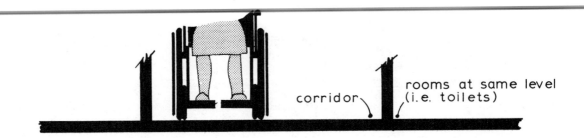

rooms at same level
(i.e. toilets)

corridor

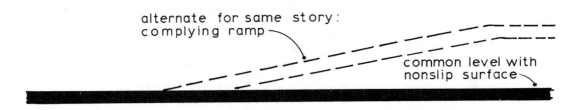

alternate for same story:
complying ramp

common level with
nonslip surface

FLOORS ON A GIVEN STORY

Basis of standard — Art 10F, Chapt. 18, Code of West Virginia		APPLICABILITY			
		ALA	LA	OHIO	GUAM
		ALASKA	MAINE	OKLA	PR
		ARIZ	MD	ORE	VIR IS
Notes — Primary corridors 5'-4" min width, level or connected by ramp. Floors to be non-slip. Floors at any one story all at one level or connected by ramp (there shall be no level difference between corridor and adjacent rooms). All educational facilities must be accessible by students and staff, including band, orchestra, choral, physical education and administrative offices.		ARK	MASS	PA	DC
		CAL	MICH	RI	
		COLO	MINN	SC	
		CONN	MISS	SD	FED'L FUNDS
		DEL	MO	TENN	
		FLA	MONT	TEXAS	
		GA	NEB	UTAH	
		HAWAII	NEV	VT	
		IDAHO	NH	VA	
		ILL	NJ	WASH	
		IND	NM	● W VA	
		IOWA	NY	WIS	OTHER
		KANS	NC	WYO	
		KY	ND		

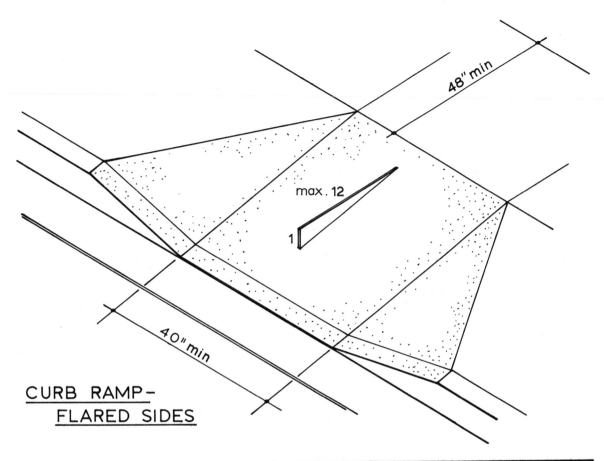

CURB RAMP-
FLARED SIDES

Basis of standard —	APPLICABILITY			
Ind. 52.04, Wisconsin Administrative Code	ALA	LA	OHIO	GUAM
	ALASKA	MAINE	OKLA	PR
	ARIZ	MD	ORE	VIR IS
	ARK	MASS	PA	DC
Notes —	CAL	MICH	RI	
Provide curb ramps where accessible walks cross driveways, parking facilities, streets or alleys, located to provide shortest line of travel from accessible parking to the accessible public entrance. Handrails not required for height differences of 8″ or less.	COLO	MINN	SC	
	CONN	MISS	SD	FED'L FUNDS
	DEL	MO	TENN	
	FLA	MONT	TEXAS	
	GA	NEB	UTAH	
	HAWAII	NEV	VT	
	IDAHO	NH	VA	
	ILL	NJ	WASH	
	IND	NM	W VA	
	IOWA	NY	● WIS	OTHER
	KANS	NC	WYO	
	KY	ND		

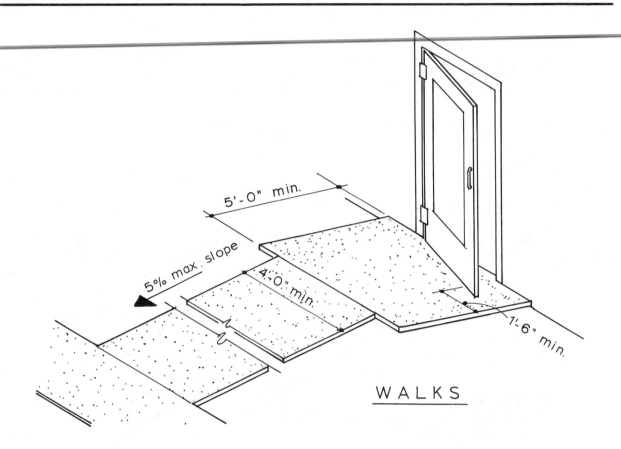

WALKS

Basis of standard —	APPLICABILITY			
Ind. 52.04, 6 Wisconsin Administrative Code	ALA	LA	OHIO	GUAM
	ALASKA	MAINE	OKLA	PR
	ARIZ	MD	ORE	VIR IS
	ARK	MASS	PA	DC
	CAL	MICH	RI	
	COLO	MINN	SC	
Notes —	CONN	MISS	SD	FED'L
Max. side slope = 1/4″ per foot.	DEL	MO	TENN	FUNDS
Provide rest platforms for slopes greater than 5% (but less than 8.3% or 1′ in 12′) at 30′ intervals and handrail on one side. For 8.3% slopes, comply as required for ramps. Provide handrails at walks where adjacent terrain exceeds 25% (1′ in 4′) on downward slope away from walk. Provide slip-resistant surface.	FLA	MONT	TEXAS	
	GA	NEB	UTAH	
	HAWAII	NEV	VT	
	IDAHO	NH	VA	
	ILL	NJ	WASH	
	IND	NM	W VA	
	IOWA	NY	● WIS	OTHER
	KANS	NC	WYO	
	KY	ND		

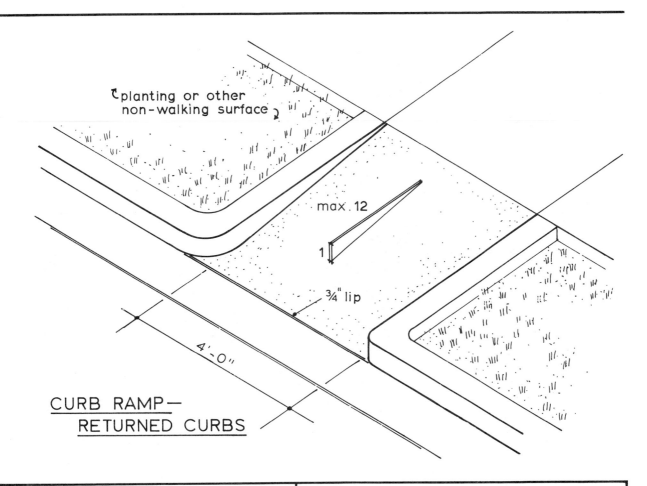

ℓ planting or other
non-walking surface

max. 12

1

¾" lip

4'-0"

CURB RAMP—
RETURNED CURBS

Basis of standard —	APPLICABILITY			
Basics of Barrier Free Design	ALA	LA	OHIO	GUAM
	ALASKA	MAINE	OKLA	PR
	ARIZ	MD	ORE	VIR IS
Notes —	ARK	MASS	PA	DC
Wyoming law requires min. of at least two ramps in every lineal block, intended for public use of all physically handicapped persons, including blind pedestrians whether public or private funds were used to construct the curb or sidewalk.	CAL	MICH	RI	
	COLO	MINN	SC	
	CONN	MISS	SD	FED'L FUNDS
	DEL	MO	TENN	
	FLA	MONT	TEXAS	
	GA	NEB	UTAH	
	HAWAII	NEV	VT	
	IDAHO	NH	VA	
	ILL	NJ	WASH	
	IND	NM	W VA	
	IOWA	NY	WIS	OTHER
	KANS	NC	● WYO	
	KY	ND		

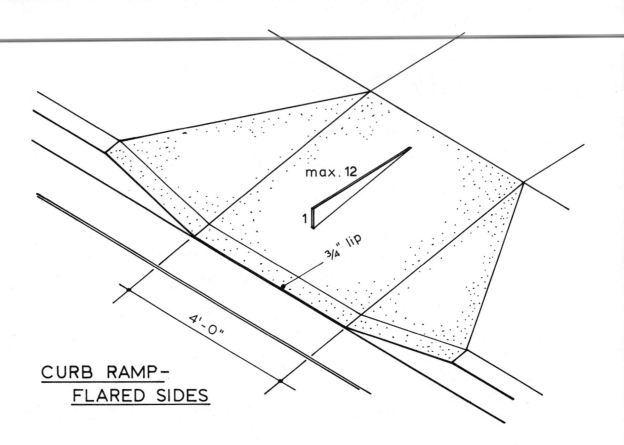

max. 12

1

3/4" lip

4'-0"

CURB RAMP-
FLARED SIDES

Basis of standard —	APPLICABILITY			
Basics of Barrier Free Design	ALA	LA	OHIO	GUAM
	ALASKA	MAINE	OKLA	PR
	ARIZ	MD	ORE	VIR IS
Notes —	ARK	MASS	PA	DC
See notes on preceding page.	CAL	MICH	RI	
	COLO	MINN	SC	
	CONN	MISS	SD	FED'L
	DEL	MO	TENN	FUNDS
	FLA	MONT	TEXAS	
	GA	NEB	UTAH	
	HAWAII	NEV	VT	
	IDAHO	NH	VA	
	ILL	NJ	WASH	
	IND	NM	W VA	
	IOWA	NY	WIS	OTHER
	KANS	NC	● WYO	
	KY	ND		

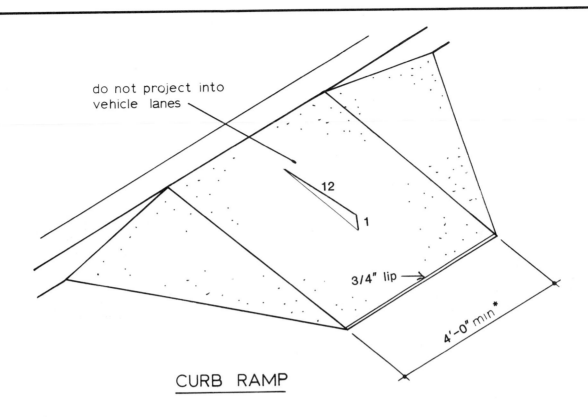

do not project into
vehicle lanes

12

1

3/4" lip →

4'-0" min *

CURB RAMP

Basis of standard —	APPLICABILITY			
Basics of Barrier Free Design	ALA	LA	OHIO	GUAM
	ALASKA	MAINE	OKLA	PR
	ARIZ	MD	ORE	VIR IS
	ARK	MASS	PA	DC
Notes —	CAL	MICH	RI	
See notes on preceding page.	COLO	MINN	SC	
	CONN	MISS	SD	FED'L
	DEL	MO	TENN	FUNDS
	FLA	MONT	TEXAS	
	GA	NEB	UTAH	
	HAWAII	NEV	VT	
	IDAHO	NH	VA	
	ILL	NJ	WASH	
	IND	NM	W VA	
	IOWA	NY	WIS	OTHER
	KANS	NC	● WYO	
	KY	ND		

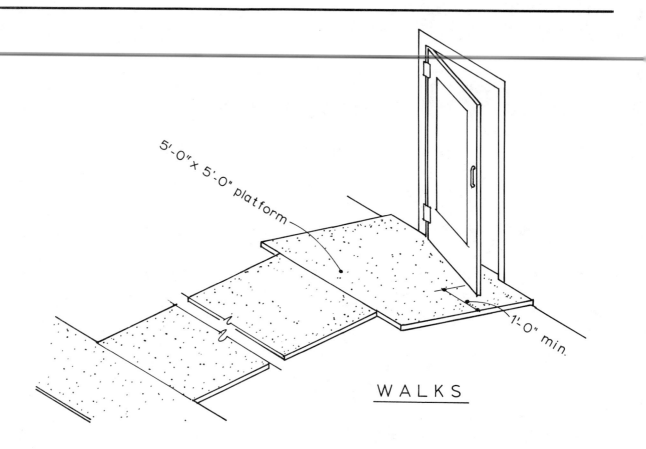

5'-0" x 5'-0" platform

1'-0" min.

WALKS

Basis of standard — The Basics of Barrier Free Design	APPLICABILITY			
	ALA	LA	OHIO	GUAM
	ALASKA	MAINE	OKLA	PR
	ARIZ	MD	ORE	VIR IS
Notes —	ARK	MASS	PA	DC
	CAL	MICH	RI	
	COLO	MINN	SC	
	CONN	MISS	SD	FED'L FUNDS
	DEL	MO	TENN	
	FLA	MONT	TEXAS	
	GA	NEB	UTAH	
	HAWAII	NEV	VT	
	IDAHO	NH	VA	
	ILL	NJ	WASH	
	IND	NM	W VA	
	IOWA	NY	WIS	OTHER
	KANS	NC	● WYO	
	KY	ND		

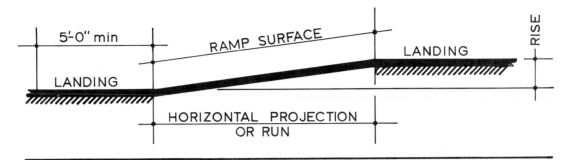

FOR SLOPE OF	MAXIMUM RISE inch	MAXIMUM HORIZONTAL PROJECTION foot
1:12	30	30
1:16	30	40
1:20	30	50

RAMP RISE & PROJECTION TABLE
NEW CONSTRUCTION

Basis of standard — ANSI 1980 – 4.8.2 and others	APPLICABILITY			
	ALA	● LA	OHIO	GUAM
	● ALASKA	● MAINE	OKLA	PR
	ARIZ	MD	ORE	VIR IS
Notes — Use least possible slope. Max. slope of new construction ramp = 1:12. Landing width min. = at least as wide as ramp leading to it. Min. landing size if ramp changes direction = 5'-0" x 5'-0".* Min. ramp clear width = 3'-0".	● ARK	MASS	PA	DC
	● CAL	MICH	● RI	
	● COLO	MINN	SC	
	CONN	MISS	SD	● FED'L FUNDS
(*)Calif.: Minimum landing size if ramp changes direction is 6'-0" in direction of travel. Bottom landing shall always be 6'-0".	● DEL	MO	TENN	
	FLA	MONT	TEXAS	
	GA	NEB	UTAH	
	● HAWAII	● NEV	● VT	
	● IDAHO	NH	● VA	
	ILL	NJ	WASH	
	IND	● NM	W VA	
	IOWA	● NY	WIS	OTHER
	KANS	NC	WYO	
	KY	ND		

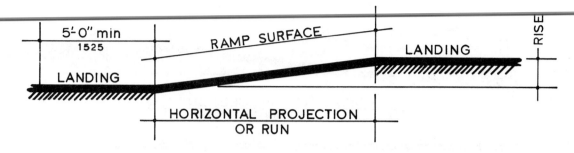

FOR SLOPE OF	MAXIMUM RISE		MAXIMUM HORIZONTAL PROJECTION	
	inch	mm	foot	m
1:10 to 1:8	3	75	2	0.6
1:12 to 1:10	6	150	5	1.5

RAMP RISE & PROJECTION TABLE
EXISTING CONSTRUCTION

Basis of standard — ANSI 1980 — 4.8.2 and others	APPLICABILITY			
	ALA	● LA	OHIO	GUAM
	● ALASKA	● MAINE	OKLA	PR
	ARIZ	MD	ORE	VIR IS
	ARK	MASS	PA	DC
	CAL	MICH	● RI	
	● COLO	MINN	SC	
	CONN	MISS	SD	● FED'L FUNDS
	DEL	MO	TENN	
	FLA	MONT	TEXAS	
	GA	NEB	UTAH	
	● HAWAII	● NEV	● VT	
	● IDAHO	NH	● VA	
	ILL	NJ	WASH	
	IND	● NM	W VA	
	IOWA	● NY	WIS	OTHER
	KANS	NC	WYO	
	KY	ND		

Notes —
Curb ramps and ramps on existing sites or in existing buildings may have slopes as shown if space limitations prohibit use of 1:12 or less.

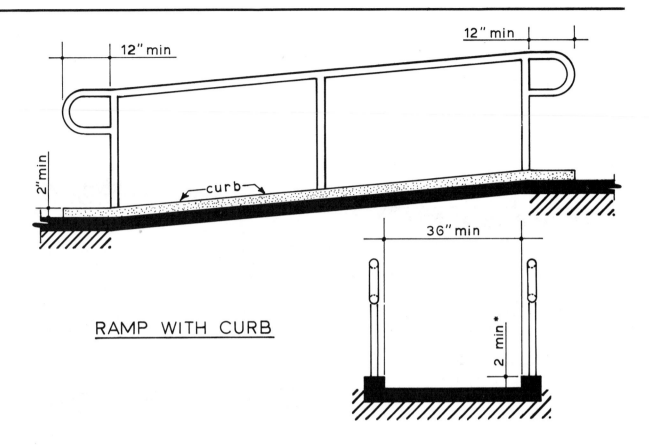

RAMP WITH CURB

Basis of standard — ANSI 1980 — 4.8 and others	APPLICABILITY			
	ALA	● LA	OHIO	GUAM
	● ALASKA	● MAINE	OKLA	PR
	ARIZ	MD	ORE	VIR IS
Notes — Illinois: handrails on both sides, 2'-6" to 2'-10" high, with a second set of handrails 2'-0" high in elementary schools, nursery schools and day care centers. The inside handrail on switchback or dog leg ramps shall be continuous and need not provide the 1'-0" extension except at the top and bottom of the ramp segment. Rails to be min. 1-1/2" clear of adjoining walls. (*)Calif.: Minimum curb height shall be 6". At ramps with handrails may use a guiderail centered at 3" instead of a curb. Curbs are required where there is a drop of more than 4".	ARK	MASS	PA	DC
	● CAL	MICH	RI	
	● COLO	MINN	SC	
	CONN	MISS	SD	FED'L FUNDS
	DEL	MO	TENN	
	FLA	MONT	● TEXAS	
	GA	NEB	UTAH	
	● HAWAII	● NEV	● VT	
	● IDAHO	NH	● VA	
	ILL	NJ	WASH	
	IND	● NM	W VA	
	IOWA	● NY	WIS	OTHER
	KANS	NC	WYO	
	KY	ND		

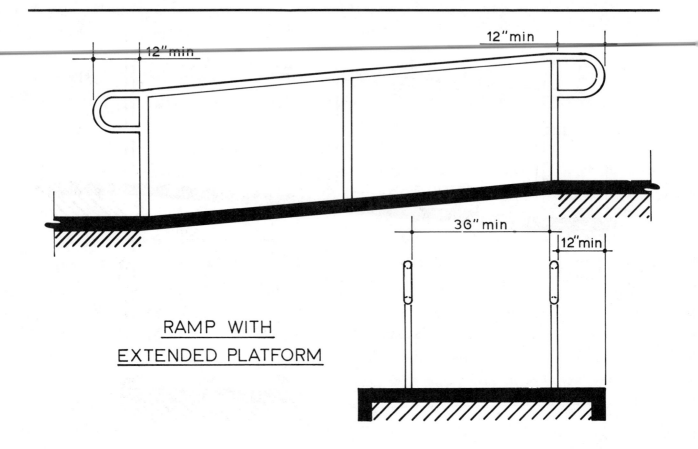

RAMP WITH
EXTENDED PLATFORM

Basis of standard —	APPLICABILITY			
ANSI 1980 — 4.8 and others	ALA	● LA	OHIO	GUAM
	● ALASKA	● MAINE	OKLA	PR
	ARIZ	MD	ORE	VIR IS
Notes —	ARK	MASS	PA	DC
	CAL	MICH	RI	
	● COLO	MINN	SC	
	CONN	MISS	SD	FED'L
	DEL	MO	TENN	FUNDS
	FLA	MONT	● TEXAS	
	GA	NEB	UTAH	
	● HAWAII	● NEV	● VT	
	● IDAHO	NH	● VA	
	● ILL	NJ	WASH	
	IND	● NM	W VA	
	IOWA	● NY	WIS	OTHER
	KANS	NC	WYO	
	KY	ND		

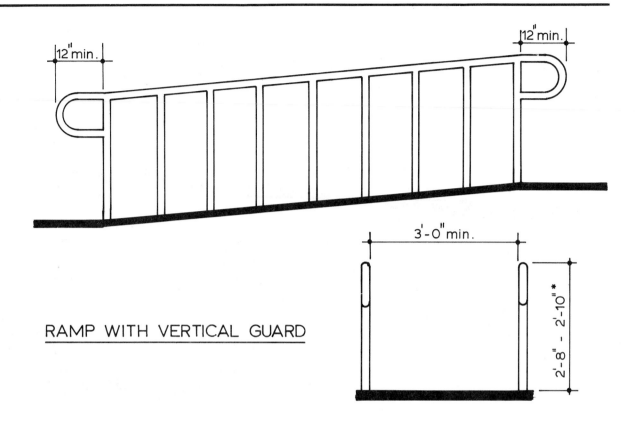

RAMP WITH VERTICAL GUARD

Basis of standard —	APPLICABILITY			
ANSI 1980 and others	ALA	● LA	OHIO	GUAM
	● ALASKA	● MAINE	OKLA	PR
	ARIZ	MD	ORE	VIR IS
	● ARK	MASS	PA	DC
Notes —	CAL	MICH	● RI	
(*)2'-8″ to 2'-10″ height applies only to Federal, Arkansas, and Delaware.	● COLO	MINN	SC	
	CONN	MISS	SD	● FED'L FUNDS
	● DEL	MO	TENN	
	FLA	MONT	TEXAS	
	GA	NEB	UTAH	
	● HAWAII	● NEV	● VT	
	● IDAHO	NH	● VA	
	ILL	NJ	WASH	
	IND	● NM	W VA	
	IOWA	● NY	WIS	OTHER
	KANS	NC	WYO	
	KY	ND		

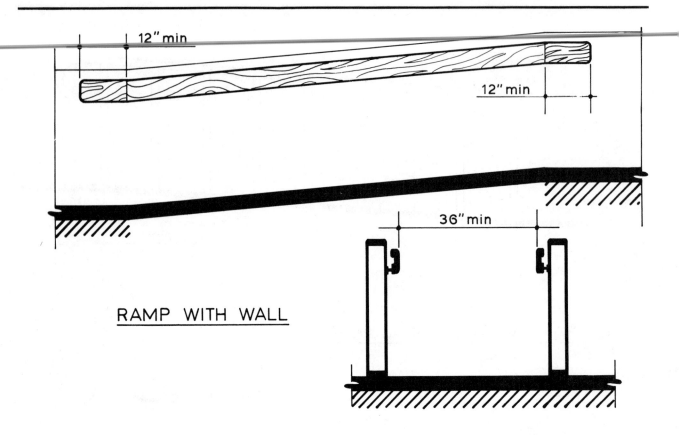

RAMP WITH WALL

Basis of standard —	APPLICABILITY			
ANSI 1980 — 4.8 and others	ALA	● LA	OHIO	GUAM
	● ALASKA	● MAINE	OKLA	PR
	ARIZ	MD	ORE	VIR IS
Notes —	ARK	MASS	PA	DC
	● CAL	MICH	● RI	
	● COLO	MINN	SC	
	CONN	MISS	SD	FED'L
	DEL	MO	TENN	FUNDS
	FLA	MONT	● TEXAS	
	GA	NEB	UTAH	
	● HAWAII	● NEV	● VT	
	● IDAHO	NH	● VA	
	ILL	NJ	WASH	
	IND	● NM	W VA	
	IOWA	● NY	WIS	OTHER
	KANS	NC	WYO	
	KY	ND		

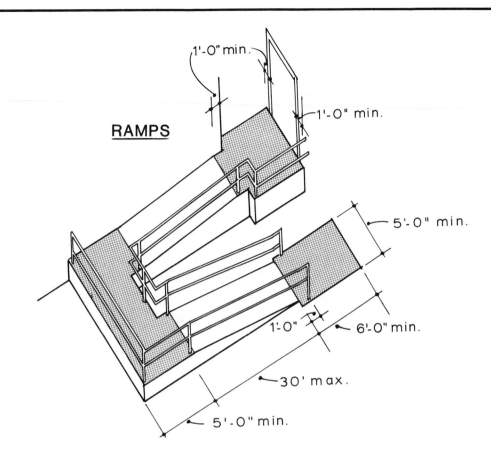

RAMPS

1'-0" min.
1'-0" min.
5'-0" min.
1'-0"
6'-0" min.
30' max.
5'-0" min.

Basis of standard —	APPLICABILITY			
ANSI 1961 — 5.1 and others	● ALA	LA	OHIO	GUAM
	ALASKA	MAINE	● OKLA	PR
	● ARIZ	MD	ORE	VIR IS
	ARK	MASS	PA	DC
Notes —	CAL	MICH	RI	
Max. slope = 1′ in 12′ (8.33%). Smooth handrails on at least one side, 2′-8″ high, preferably both sides extending 1′-0″ beyond top and bottom of ramp, conforming with ANSI A12. (Where codes specify handrails of heights other than 2′-8″ ANSI recommends two sets of handrails.) Ramp surface: non-slip. Level platform 5′ x 5′ at top if door swings onto platform or toward ramp (3′ x 5′ if door does not swing in that direction). Florida: Applies to non-government financed facilities.	COLO	MINN	● SC	
	● CONN	MISS	● SD	FED'L
	DEL	MO	TENN	FUNDS
	● FLA	MONT	TEXAS	
	● GA	NEB	UTAH	
	HAWAII	NEV	VT	
	IDAHO	NH	VA	
	ILL	NJ	WASH	
	IND	NM	W VA	
	IOWA	NY	WIS	OTHER
	● KANS	NC	WYO	
	KY	● ND		

RAMPS

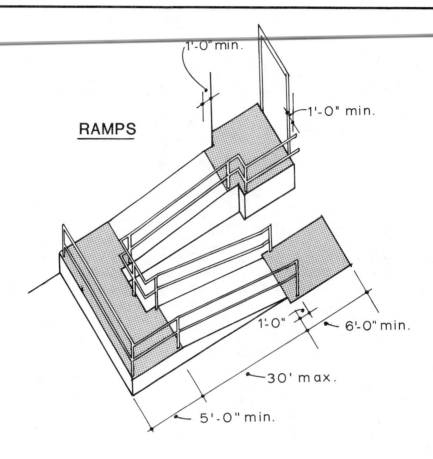

Basis of standard — ANSI 1961 and others	APPLICABILITY			
	ALA	LA	OHIO	GUAM
	ALASKA	MAINE	● OKLA	PR
	ARIZ	MD	ORE	VIR IS
	ARK	MASS	PA	DC
Notes —	CAL	MICH	RI	
	COLO	MINN	● SC	
Max. slope = 1′ in 12′ (8.33%) Handrails on at least one side, 2′-8″ high, preferably on both sides,	● CONN	MISS	● SD	FED'L
extending 1′-0″ beyond each end of ramp. Platforms: 5′ x 5′ min if door swings onto platform; 3′ deep x 5′	DEL	MO	TENN	FUNDS
wide if door does not swing onto platform. Ramp surface to be non-slip.	FLA	MONT	TEXAS	
W. Va.: Toeboard 2″ high, 4″ wide at open side.	GA	NEB	UTAH	
	HAWAII	NEV	VT	
	IDAHO	NH	VA	
	ILL	NJ	WASH	
	IND	NM	● W VA	
	IOWA	NY	WIS	OTHER
	● KANS	NC	WYO	
	KY	● ND		

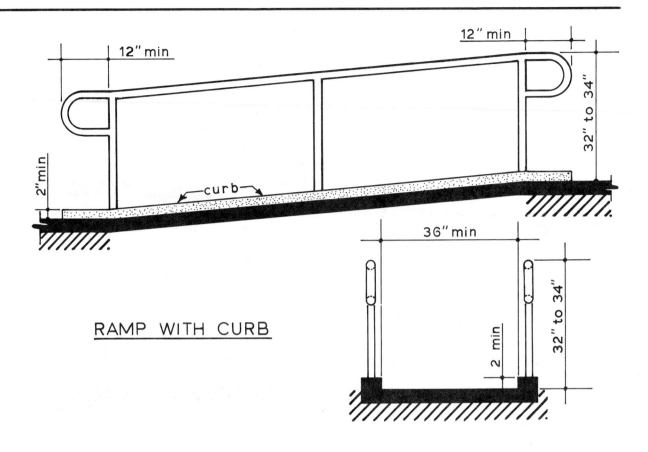

RAMP WITH CURB

Basis of standard —	APPLICABILITY			
ATBCB § 1190.70 and others	ALA	LA	OHIO	GUAM
	ALASKA	MAINE	OKLA	PR
	ARIZ	MD	ORE	VIR IS
● ARK	MASS	PA	DC
	CAL	MICH	● RI	
Notes —	COLO	MINN	SC	
Rhode Island: Handrails shall contain a min. of 4 rails. One shall be mounted 4″ max above ramp with top rail conforming to height dimension shown with 2 intermediate rails evenly spaced. If vertical rails are used the top and bottom rails will remain the same with 6″ max spacing between vertical rails. If rails are mounted on outside of ramp then provide 2-1/2″ toeguard. Toeguard shown in diagram may be substituted by a rail 4″ above ramp.	CONN	MISS	SD	● FED'L FUNDS
	● DEL	MO	TENN	
	FLA	MONT	TEXAS	
	GA	NEB	UTAH	
	HAWAII	NEV	VT	
	IDAHO	NH	VA	
	ILL	NJ	WASH	
	IND	NM	W VA	
	IOWA	NY	WIS	OTHER
	KANS	NC	WYO	
	KY	ND		

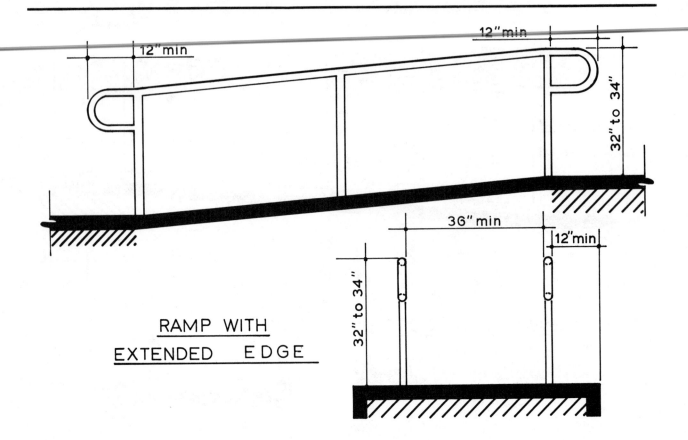

RAMP WITH
EXTENDED EDGE

Basis of standard —	APPLICABILITY			
ATBCB § 1190.70 and others	ALA	LA	OHIO	GUAM
	ALASKA	MAINE	OKLA	PR
	ARIZ	MD	ORE	VIR IS
Notes —	● ARK	MASS	PA	DC
	CAL	MICH	● RI	
	COLO	MINN	SC	
	CONN	MISS	SD	● FED'L FUNDS
	● DEL	MO	TENN	
	FLA	MONT	TEXAS	
	GA	NEB	UTAH	
	HAWAII	NEV	VT	
	IDAHO	NH	VA	
	ILL	NJ	WASH	
	IND	NM	W VA	
	IOWA	NY	WIS	OTHER
	KANS	NC	WYO	
	KY	ND		

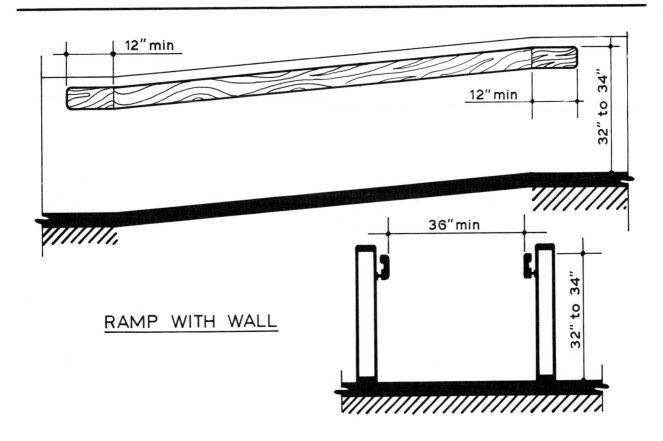

RAMP WITH WALL

Basis of standard —	APPLICABILITY			
ATBCB § 1190.70 and others	ALA	LA	OHIO	GUAM
	ALASKA	MAINE	OKLA	PR
	ARIZ	MD	ORE	VIR IS
● ARK	MASS	PA	DC
	CAL	MICH	RI	
Notes —	COLO	MINN	SC	
	CONN	MISS	SD	● FED'L FUNDS
	● DEL	MO	TENN	
	FLA	MONT	TEXAS	
	GA	NEB	UTAH	
	HAWAII	NEV	VT	
	IDAHO	NH	VA	
	ILL	NJ	WASH	
	IND	NM	W VA	
	IOWA	NY	WIS	OTHER
	KANS	NC	WYO	
	KY	ND		

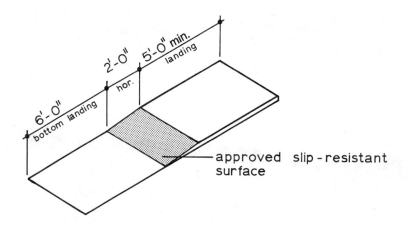

2'-0" MAXIMUM TOTAL RAMP LENGTH

RAMPS

Basis of standard —	APPLICABILITY			
BOCA 1978	ALA	LA	● OHIO	GUAM
	ALASKA	MAINE	OKLA	PR
	ARIZ	MD	ORE	VIR IS
Notes —	ARK	MASS	PA	DC
Above applies if slope is 12.5% (1:8) or less steep.	CAL	MICH	RI	
	COLO	MINN	SC	
	CONN	MISS	SD	FED'L FUNDS
	DEL	MO	TENN	
	FLA	MONT	TEXAS	
	GA	NEB	UTAH	
	HAWAII	NEV	VT	
	IDAHO	NH	VA	
	ILL	NJ	WASH	
	IND	NM	W VA	
	IOWA	NY	WIS	OTHER
	KANS	NC	WYO	
	KY	ND		

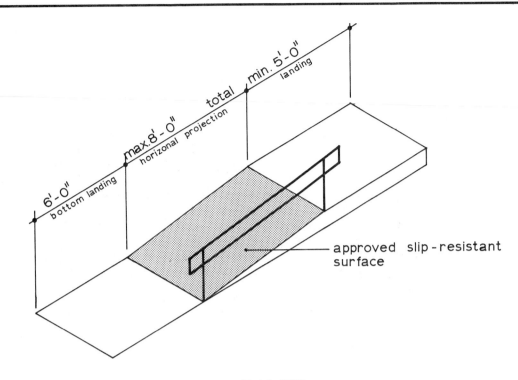

6'-0"
bottom landing

max. 8'-0"   total
horizonal projection

min. 5'-0"
landing

approved slip-resistant surface

RAMPS

Basis of standard —	APPLICABILITY			
BOCA 1978	ALA	LA	● OHIO	GUAM
	ALASKA	MAINE	OKLA	PR
	ARIZ	MD	ORE	VIR IS
Notes —	ARK	MASS	PA	DC
Above applies if slope is greater than 1:12 (8.3%) and less than, or equal to, 1:10 (10%). Provide handrail on at least one side for slopes greater than 1:12 between 2'-6" and 2'-10" high. Handrails shall be smooth and extend one foot beyond top and bottom of ramp and return to walls or posts at ends.	CAL	MICH	RI	
	COLO	MINN	SC	
	CONN	MISS	SD	FED'L FUNDS
	DEL	MO	TENN	
	FLA	MONT	TEXAS	
	GA	NEB	UTAH	
	HAWAII	NEV	VT	
	IDAHO	NH	VA	
	ILL	NJ	WASH	
	IND	NM	W VA	
	IOWA	NY	WIS	OTHER
	KANS	NC	WYO	
	KY	ND		

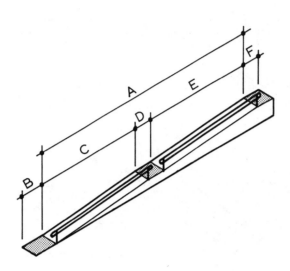

A. 60' maximum total horizonal projection (excluding landings)
B. 72" bottom landing
C. 30'-0" maximum horizontal projection
D. 60" landing
E. 30'-0" maximum horizontal projection
F. 60" landing

RAMPS

Basis of standard —	APPLICABILITY			
BOCA 1978	ALA	LA	● OHIO	GUAM
	ALASKA	MAINE	OKLA	PR
	ARIZ	MD	ORE	VIR IS
Notes —	ARK	MASS	PA	DC
Above applies if slope is greater than 1:16 (6.25%) and less than, or equal to, 1:12 (8.3%). Provide handrail on at least one side for slopes greater than 1:12 between 2'-6" and 2'-10" high. Handrails shall be smooth and extend one foot beyond top and bottom of ramp and return to walls or posts at ends. Slip resistant surfaces not required on slopes of 1:12 or less.	CAL	MICH	RI	
	COLO	MINN	SC	
	CONN	MISS	SD	FED'L FUNDS
	DEL	MO	TENN	
	FLA	MONT	TEXAS	
	GA	NEB	UTAH	
	HAWAII	NEV	VT	
	IDAHO	NH	VA	
	ILL	NJ	WASH	
	IND	NM	W VA	
	IOWA	NY	WIS	OTHER
	KANS	NC	WYO	
	KY	ND		

A. maximum total ramp length
   160' (excluding landings)
B. 72"
C. max. 40'-0"
D. 5'-0"

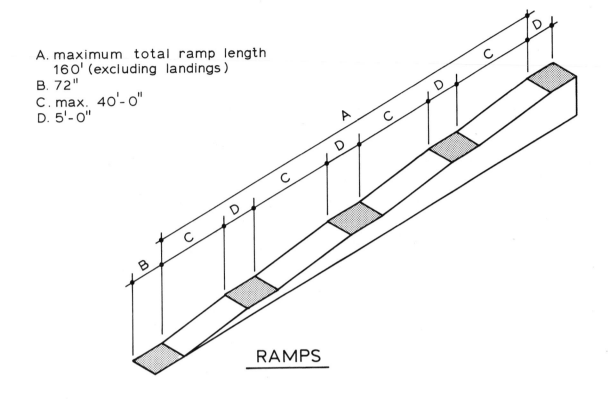

RAMPS

Basis of standard — BOCA 1978	APPLICABILITY			
	ALA	LA	● OHIO	GUAM
	ALASKA	MAINE	OKLA	PR
	ARIZ	MD	ORE	VIR IS
Notes — Above applies if slope is less than or equal to 1:16 (6.25%). Provide handrail on at least one side for slopes greater than 1:12 between 2'-6" and 2'-10" high. Handrails shall be smooth and extend one foot beyond top and bottom of ramp and return to walls or posts at ends.	ARK	MASS	PA	DC
	CAL	MICH	RI	
	COLO	MINN	SC	
	CONN	MISS	SD	FED'L FUNDS
	DEL	MO	TENN	
	FLA	MONT	TEXAS	
	GA	NEB	UTAH	
	HAWAII	NEV	VT	
	IDAHO	NH	VA	
	ILL	NJ	WASH	
	IND	NM	W VA	
	IOWA	NY	WIS	OTHER
	KANS	NC	WYO	
	KY	ND		

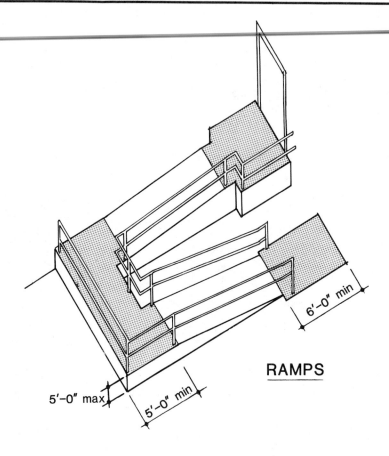

RAMPS

6'-0" min

5'-0" max

5'-0" min

Basis of standard —	APPLICABILITY			
Uniform Building Code and others	ALA	LA	OHIO	GUAM
	ALASKA	MAINE	OKLA	PR
	ARIZ	MD	ORE	VIR IS
Notes —	ARK	MASS	PA	DC
Ramps required by Table 33A shall not exceed slope of 1:12 (1:10 in Indiana). Slope of other ramps shall not exceed 1:8. Provide intermediate landing for each 5' of rise. Doors in any position shall not reduce minimum dimension to less than 3'-6" and shall not reduce the required width by more than 3-1/2" when fully open. Ramps having slopes exceeding 1:15 shall have handrails as required for stairways, except that intermediate handrails shall not be required. Indiana exempts handrail requirement for ramps 7' and less in length. Ramps used as exits shall conform to these requirements.	CAL	MICH	RI	
	COLO	MINN	SC	
	CONN	MISS	SD	FED'L
	DEL	MO	TENN	FUNDS
	FLA	● MONT	TEXAS	
	GA	NEB	UTAH	
	HAWAII	NEV	VT	
	IDAHO	NH	VA	
	ILL	NJ	WASH	
(*)For ramps exceeding 1:15 slope.	● IND	NM	W VA	
	IOWA	NY	WIS	OTHER
	KANS	NC	WYO	
	KY	ND		

RAMPS

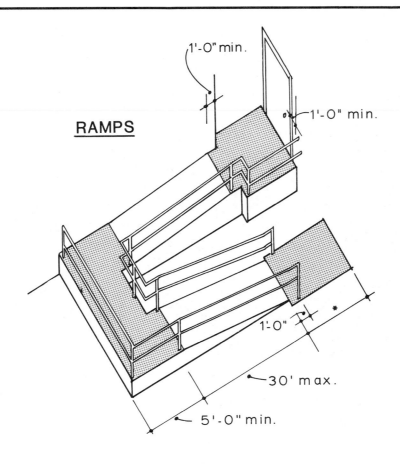

1'-0" min.

1'-0" min.

1'-0"

*

30' max.

5'-0" min.

Basis of standard —	APPLICABILITY			
North Carolina Building Code and others	ALA	LA	OHIO	GUAM
	ALASKA	MAINE	OKLA	PR
	ARIZ	MD	ORE	VIR IS
Notes —	ARK	MASS	PA	DC
Max. slope = 1′ in 12′ (8.33%). If ramp slopes 5% or less and there is no drop-off, no rails are required.	CAL	MICH	RI	
2′-8″ high rails are required on both ramp sides for	COLO	MINN	SC	
ramps with drop-off on one or both sides. 2′-8″ high	CONN	MISS	SD	FED'L
rails are required on one ramp side for slopes more than 5% with no drop-off. Surface: non-slip.	DEL	MO	● TENN	FUNDS
Straight ramp runs shall have 3′ long min. level	FLA	MONT	TEXAS	
platform at 30′ intervals.	GA	● NEB	UTAH	
(*)Nebraska: 6′ min. at bottom; min. ramp width: 4′-0″.	HAWAII	NEV	VT	
	IDAHO	NH	● VA	
	ILL	NJ	WASH	
	IND	NM	W VA	
	IOWA	NY	WIS	OTHER
	KANS	● NC	WYO	
	KY	ND		

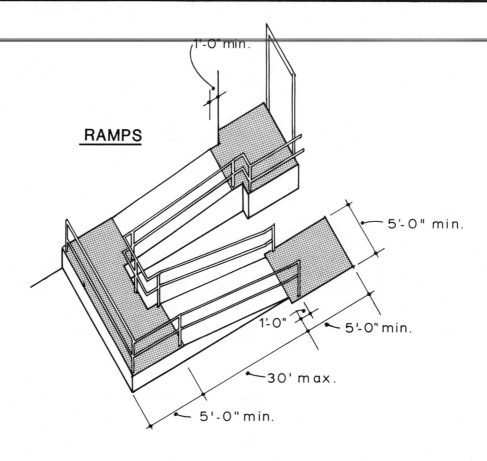

RAMPS

1'-0" min.

5'-0" min.

1'-0"

5'-0" min.

30' max.

5'-0" min.

Basis of standard —	APPLICABILITY			
Basics of Barrier Free Design and others	ALA	LA	OHIO	GUAM
	ALASKA	MAINE	OKLA	PR
	ARIZ	● MD	ORE	VIR IS
	ARK	MASS	PA	DC
Notes —	CAL	MICH	RI	
Min. ramp width: Maryland: 5'-0", Wyoming: 4'-0"	COLO	MINN	SC	
Max. slope 1:12. Provide handrail on both sides for	CONN	MISS	SD	FED'L
drop-offs and when slope exceeds 1:20. Height:	DEL	MO	TENN	FUNDS
2'-8" in Wyoming, min. 30" in Maryland. Top plat-	FLA	MONT	TEXAS	
form min. 5'-0" deep and 6'-0" wide in Wyoming,	GA	NEB	UTAH	
5'-0" wide in Maryland.	HAWAII	NEV	VT	
	IDAHO	NH	VA	
	ILL	NJ	WASH	
	IND	NM	W VA	
	IOWA	NY	WIS	OTHER
	KANS	NC	● WYO	
	KY	ND		

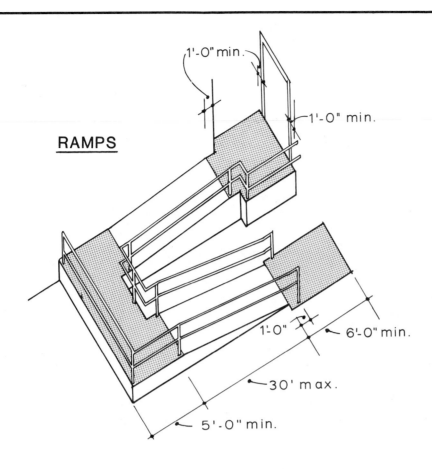

RAMPS

Basis of standard —	APPLICABILITY			
Various	ALA	LA	OHIO	GUAM
	ALASKA	MAINE	OKLA	PR
	ARIZ	MD	ORE	VIR IS
Notes —	ARK	MASS	● PA	DC
Max. slope = 1′ in 12′ (8.33%). Handrails on at least	CAL	MICH	RI	
one side, 2′-8″ high, preferably both sides extending	COLO	MINN	SC	
1′-0″ beyond top and bottom of ramp. Ramp width:	CONN	● MISS	SD	FED'L
min. 2′-8″ (inside clear), with non-slip surface.	DEL	MO	TENN	FUNDS
Platforms: 5′ x 5′ min. clear of door swings if door	FLA	MONT	TEXAS	
swings onto platform; 3′ deep x 5′ wide if door does	GA	NEB	UTAH	
not swing onto platform.	HAWAII	NEV	VT	
	IDAHO	NH	VA	
	ILL	NJ	WASH	
	IND	NM	W VA	
	IOWA	NY	WIS	OTHER
	KANS	NC	WYO	
	KY	ND		

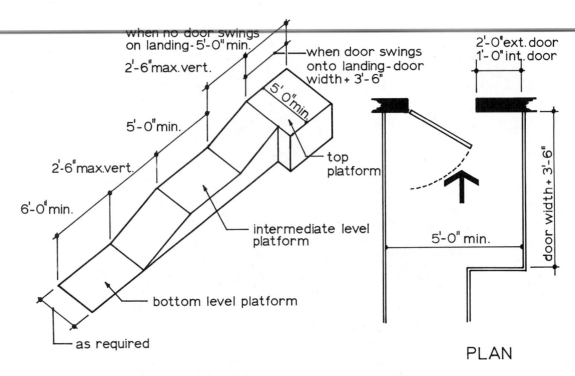

when no door swings
on landing-5'-0"min.

2'-6"max.vert.

5'-0"min.

2'-6"max.vert.

6'-0"min.

as required

when door swings
onto landing-door
width+3'-6"

5'-0"min.

top platform

intermediate level
platform

bottom level platform

2'-0"ext.door
1'-0"int.door

door width+3'-6"

5'-0" min.

PLAN

DOOR APPROACH AT LANDING

Basis of standard — CAC Title 24, Part 2	APPLICABILITY			
	ALA	LA	OHIO	GUAM
	ALASKA	MAINE	OKLA	PR
	ARIZ	MD	ORE	VIR IS
Notes —	ARK	MASS	PA	DC
	● CAL	MICH	RI	
	COLO	MINN	SC	
	CONN	MISS	SD	FED'L FUNDS
	DEL	MO	TENN	
	FLA	MONT	TEXAS	
	GA	NEB	UTAH	
	HAWAII	NEV	VT	
	IDAHO	NH	VA	
	ILL	NJ	WASH	
	IND	NM	W VA	
	IOWA	NY	WIS	OTHER
	KANS	NC	WYO	
	KY	ND		

RAMPS

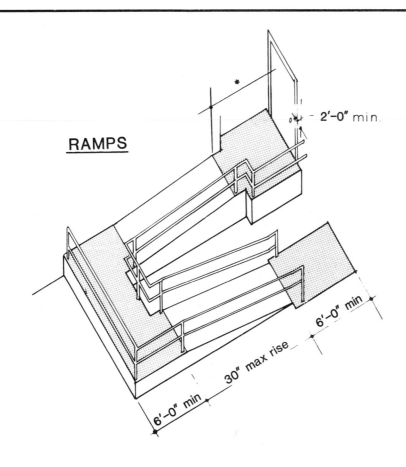

2'-0" min.

30" max rise

6'-0" min

6'-0" min

Basis of standard — CAC Title 24, Part 2	APPLICABILITY			
	ALA	LA	OHIO	GUAM
	ALASKA	MAINE	OKLA	PR
	ARIZ	MD	ORE	VIR IS
	ARK	MASS	PA	DC
Notes — (*)If door swings onto landing: provide landing equal to the door width plus 3'-6".	● CAL	MICH	RI	
	COLO	MINN	SC	
	CONN	MISS	SD	FED'L
	DEL	MO	TENN	FUNDS
	FLA	MONT	TEXAS	
	GA	NEB	UTAH	
	HAWAII	NEV	VT	
	IDAHO	NH	VA	
	ILL	NJ	WASH	
	IND	NM	W VA	
	IOWA	NY	WIS	OTHER
	KANS	NC	WYO	
	KY	ND		

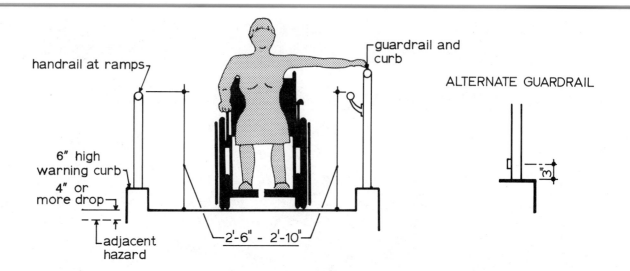

handrail at ramps

guardrail and curb

ALTERNATE GUARDRAIL

3"

6" high warning curb

4" or more drop

adjacent hazard

2'-6" - 2'-10"

HANDRAILS AND GUARDRAILS

Basis of standard — CAC Title 24, Part 2	APPLICABILITY			
	ALA	LA	OHIO	GUAM
	ALASKA	MAINE	OKLA	PR
	ARIZ	MD	ORE	VIR IS
Notes —	ARK	MASS	PA	DC
	● CAL	MICH	RI	
	COLO	MINN	SC	
	CONN	MISS	SD	FED'L FUNDS
	DEL	MO	TENN	
	FLA	MONT	TEXAS	
	GA	NEB	UTAH	
	HAWAII	NEV	VT	
	IDAHO	NH	VA	
	ILL	NJ	WASH	
	IND	NM	W VA	
	IOWA	NY	WIS	OTHER
	KANS	NC	WYO	
	KY	ND		

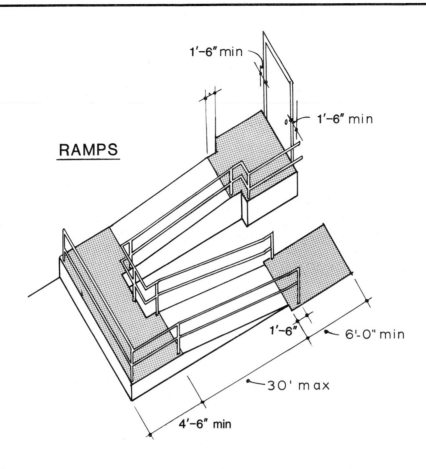

RAMPS

1'-6" min

1'-6" min

1'-6"

6'-0" min

30' max

4'-6" min

Basis of standard — Dept. of General Services	APPLICABILITY			
	ALA	LA	OHIO	GUAM
	ALASKA	MAINE	OKLA	PR
	ARIZ	MD	ORE	VIR IS
Notes — Applies to government facilities where ramp is above adjacent surface, provide curb and handrail on both sides, 2'-8" high. Min. ramp width between curbs: 2'-8". Do not penetrate ramps with manholes, cleanouts, etc. which would create a hazardous condition.	ARK	MASS	PA	DC
	CAL	MICH	RI	
	COLO	MINN	SC	
	CONN	MISS	SD	FED'L FUNDS
	DEL	MO	TENN	
	● FLA	MONT	TEXAS	
	GA	NEB	UTAH	
	HAWAII	NEV	VT	
	IDAHO	NH	VA	
	ILL	NJ	WASH	
	IND	NM	W VA	
	IOWA	NY	WIS	OTHER
	KANS	NC	WYO	
	KY	ND		

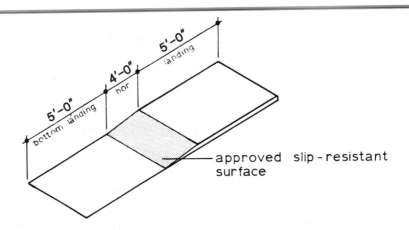

4'-0" MAXIMUM TOTAL RAMP LENGTH

RAMPS

Basis of standard —	APPLICABILITY			
Capital Development Board	ALA	LA	OHIO	GUAM
	ALASKA	MAINE	OKLA	PR
	ARIZ	MD	ORE	VIR IS
Notes — Allowable slope shown: 1:8; max. rise in single ramp segment: 6". Number of ramp segments permitted: 1. For curb ramps when site constraints prohibit 1:12 or 1:10 slope. May be used where existing physical constraints prevent construction of more gradually sloped ramps. Min. width: 3'-0"; where wheelchair passing can be expected on ramp, increase to 5'-0" min. width.	ARK	MASS	PA	DC
	CAL	MICH	RI	
	COLO	MINN	SC	
	CONN	MISS	SD	FED'L FUNDS
	DEL	MO	TENN	
	FLA	MONT	TEXAS	
	GA	NEB	UTAH	
	HAWAII	NEV	VT	
	IDAHO	NH	VA	
	● ILL	NJ	WASH	
	IND	NM	W VA	
	IOWA	NY	WIS	OTHER
	KANS	NC	WYO	
	KY	ND		

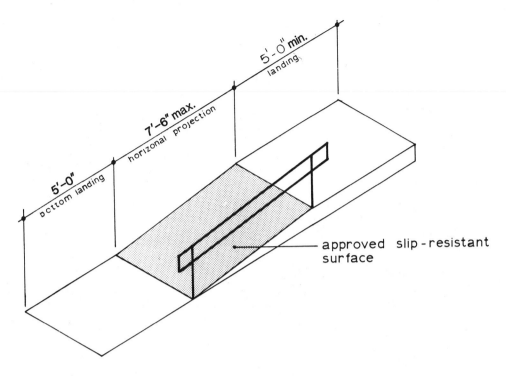

5'-0" min. landing

7'-6" max. horizonal projection

5'-0" bottom landing

approved slip-resistant surface

RAMPS

Basis of standard —	APPLICABILITY			
Capital Development Board	ALA	LA	OHIO	GUAM
	ALASKA	MAINE	OKLA	PR
	ARIZ	MD	ORE	VIR IS
Notes —	ARK	MASS	PA	DC
Allowable slope shown: 1:10 max. rise in single ramp	CAL	MICH	RI	
segment: 9″. Number of ramp segments permitted:	COLO	MINN	SC	
1. For curb ramps when site constraints prohibit	CONN	MISS	SD	FED'L
1:12 slope. May be used where existing physical	DEL	MO	TENN	FUNDS
constraints prevent construction of more gradually	FLA	MONT	TEXAS	
sloped ramps. Min. width: 3′-0″. Where wheelchair	GA	NEB	UTAH	
passing can be expected, increase to 5′-0″ min. width.	HAWAII	NEV	VT	
	IDAHO	NH	VA	
	● ILL	NJ	WASH	
	IND	NM	W VA	
	IOWA	NY	WIS	OTHER
	KANS	NC	WYO	
	KY	ND		

C. max   see below
D. 5'-0"

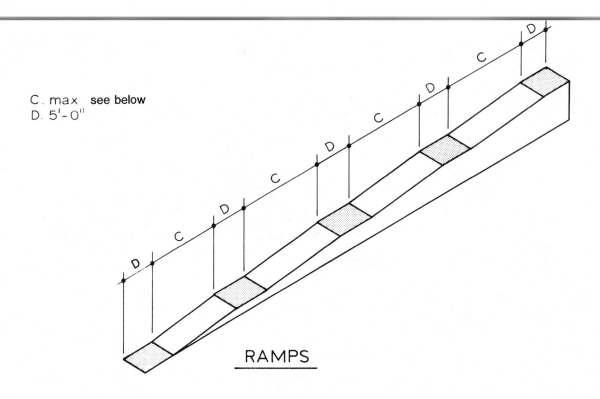

RAMPS

Basis of standard — Capital Development Board				

APPLICABILITY			
ALA	LA	OHIO	GUAM
ALASKA	MAINE	OKLA	PR
ARIZ	MD	ORE	VIR IS
ARK	MASS	PA	DC
CAL	MICH	RI	
COLO	MINN	SC	
CONN	MISS	SD	FED'L FUNDS
DEL	MO	TENN	
FLA	MONT	TEXAS	
GA	NEB	UTAH	
HAWAII	NEV	VT	
IDAHO	NH	VA	
● ILL	NJ	WASH	
IND	NM	W VA	
IOWA	NY	WIS	OTHER
KANS	NC	WYO	
KY	ND		

Notes —

Max slope:	1 single ramp sgement: "C" max. length:	Max rise:
1:12	30'	2'-6"
1:16	40'	2'-6"
1:20	50'	2'-6"

Use for new construction. Min. width: 3'-0". Where wheelchair passing can be expected on ramp, increase to 5'-0" min. width. Intermediate turning platforms min. 5'-0" long x 7'-0" wide for 180° maneuvering and 5'-0" x 5'-0" min. for 90° turns.

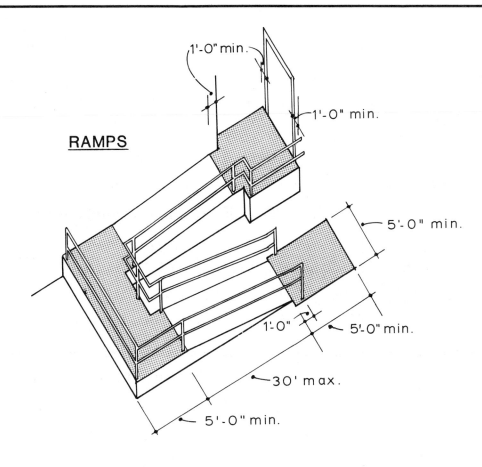

RAMPS

1'-0" min.

1'-0" min.

5'-0" min.

1'-0"

5'-0" min.

30' max.

5'-0" min.

Basis of standard —	APPLICABILITY			
Iowa Building Code	ALA	LA	OHIO	GUAM
	ALASKA	MAINE	OKLA	PR
	ARIZ	MD	ORE	VIR IS
	ARK	MASS	PA	DC
Notes —	CAL	MICH	RI	
Max. slope = 1' in 12' (8.33%). Smooth handrails on both sides, 2'-8" high. Dia. or width of gripping surface: 1-1/4" to 1-1/2". Space clear to wall: 1-1/2". Non-slip surface. Level platform at top 5' x 5' min. if door swings onto platform or 3' deep by 5' wide if door does not swing toward platform.	COLO	MINN	SC	
	CONN	MISS	SD	FED'L FUNDS
	DEL	MO	TENN	
	FLA	MONT	TEXAS	
	GA	NEB	UTAH	
	HAWAII	NEV	VT	
	IDAHO	NH	VA	
	ILL	NJ	WASH	
	IND	NM	W VA	
	● IOWA	NY	WIS	OTHER
	KANS	NC	WYO	
	KY	ND		

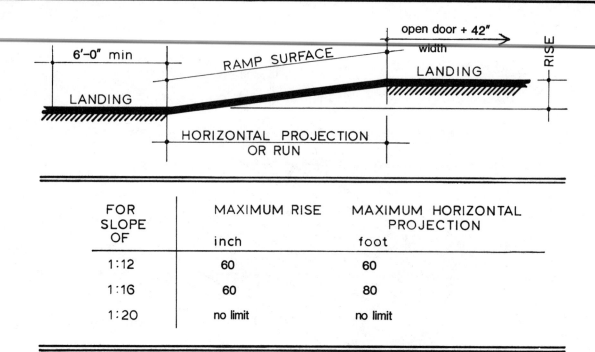

FOR SLOPE OF	MAXIMUM RISE inch	MAXIMUM HORIZONTAL PROJECTION foot
1:12	60	60
1:16	60	80
1:20	no limit	no limit

RAMP RISE & PROJECTION TABLE
NEW CONSTRUCTION

Basis of standard — 815 KAR 7:060	APPLICABILITY			
	ALA	LA	OHIO	GUAM
	ALASKA	MAINE	OKLA	PR
	ARIZ	MD	ORE	VIR IS
Notes —	ARK	MASS	PA	DC
	CAL	MICH	RI	
	COLO	MINN	SC	
	CONN	MISS	SD	FED'L FUNDS
	DEL	MO	TENN	
	FLA	MONT	TEXAS	
	GA	NEB	UTAH	
	HAWAII	NEV	VT	
	IDAHO	NH	VA	
	ILL	NJ	WASH	
	IND	NM	W VA	
	IOWA	NY	WIS	OTHER
	KANS	NC	WYO	
	● KY	ND		

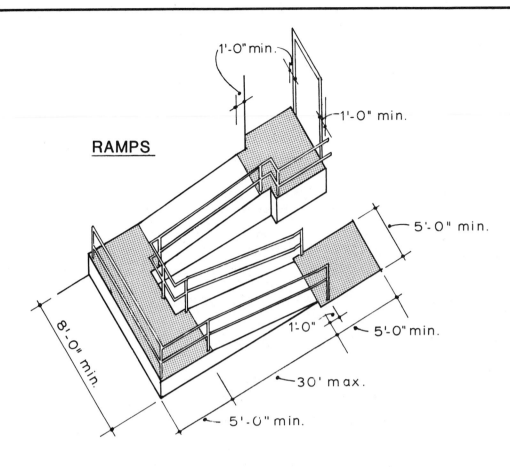

RAMPS

Basis of standard —	APPLICABILITY			
Maryland Building Code for the Handicapped	ALA	LA	OHIO	GUAM
	ALASKA	MAINE	OKLA	PR
	ARIZ	● MD	ORE	VIR IS
Notes —	ARK	MASS	PA	DC
Width: same as for walks. Max. slope: 1:12. 30″ min. high handrails where slope exceeds 1:20, required on one or both sides where sides of ramps are drop-offs above grade. Level areas for straight-run ramps maybe 3′-0″ long at 30′ max. intervals.	CAL	MICH	RI	
	COLO	MINN	SC	
	CONN	MISS	SD	FED'L FUNDS
	DEL	MO	TENN	
	FLA	MONT	TEXAS	
	GA	NEB	UTAH	
	HAWAII	NEV	VT	
	IDAHO	NH	VA	
	ILL	NJ	WASH	
	IND	NM	W VA	
	IOWA	NY	WIS	OTHER
	KANS	NC	WYO	
	KY	ND		

RAMPS

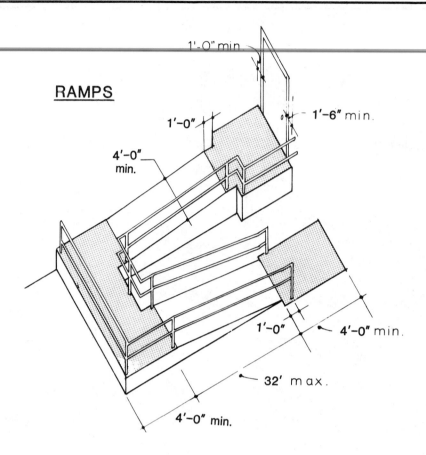

1'-0" min.

1'-6" min.

1'-0"

4'-0" min.

4'-0"
min.

1'-0"

4'-0" min.

32' max.

4'-0" min.

Basis of standard —	APPLICABILITY			
521 CMR Architectural Barriers Board	ALA	LA	OHIO	GUAM
	ALASKA	MAINE	OKLA	PR
	ARIZ	MD	ORE	VIR IS
Notes —	ARK	● MASS	PA	DC
For ramps required as a means of egress: Max. slope: 1:12; handrails on both sides 2'-9" high and 1'-7" high, extending 1'-6" beyond ramp top and bottom at a 3'-0" height (providing such extension does not create a hazard). Non-slip surface. No carpeting except high density, low pile, non-absorbant, stretched tautly, securely anchored, without padding. End path of travel carpet secured with edging strip max. 3/8" high. For rails, see also Grab Bars and Handrails under "Toilets". Circular ramps are not acceptable.	CAL	MICH	RI	
	COLO	MINN	SC	
	CONN	MISS	SD	FED'L FUNDS
	DEL	MO	TENN	
	FLA	MONT	TEXAS	
	GA	NEB	UTAH	
	HAWAII	NEV	VT	
	IDAHO	NH	VA	
	ILL	NJ	WASH	
	IND	NM	W VA	
	IOWA	NY	WIS	OTHER
	KANS	NC	WYO	
	KY	ND		

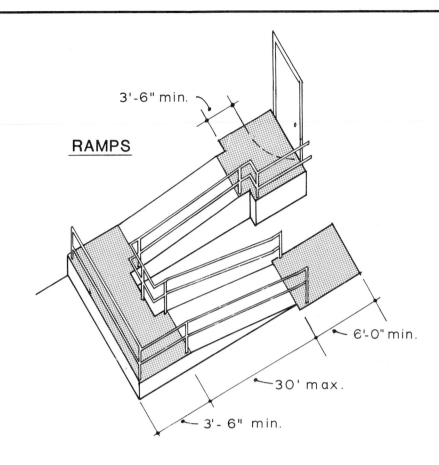

RAMPS

3'-6" min.

6'-0" min.

30' max.

3'-6" min.

Basis of standard —	APPLICABILITY			
BOCA — 1978	ALA	LA	OHIO	GUAM
	ALASKA	MAINE	OKLA	PR
	ARIZ	MD	ORE	VIR IS
Notes —	ARK	MASS	PA	DC
Provide interior access to required spaces by elevators or ramps. Maximum slopes:	CAL	● MICH	RI	
	COLO	MINN	SC	
	CONN	MISS	SD	FED'L FUNDS
	DEL	MO	TENN	
	FLA	MONT	TEXAS	
	GA	NEB	UTAH	
	HAWAII	NEV	VT	
	IDAHO	NH	VA	
	ILL	NJ	WASH	
	IND	NM	W VA	
	IOWA	NY	WIS	OTHER
	KANS	NC	WYO	
	KY	ND		

Notes —

Provide interior access to required spaces by elevators or ramps. Maximum slopes:

Slope	Max. horiz. projection for rampways	Max. horiz. projection of each run
1:8 or less	2'	2'
1:10 or less	8'	8'
1:12 or less	60'	30'
1:16 or less	160'	40'

Non-slip surfaces for slopes over 1:12. Provide guards at open sides. Width for egress: same as req'd. for corridors. Min. width for access but not for egress: 3'-8".

RAMPS

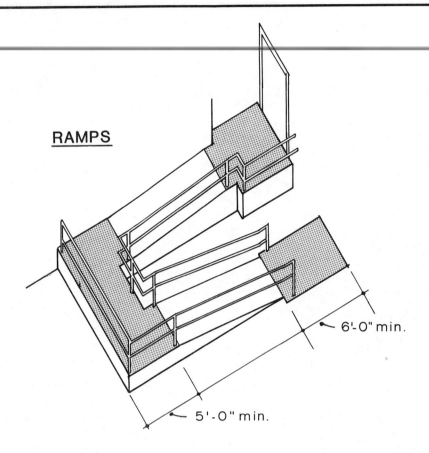

6'-0" min.

5'-0" min.

Basis of standard —	APPLICABILITY			
State Building Code	ALA	LA	OHIO	GUAM
	ALASKA	MAINE	OKLA	PR
	ARIZ	MD	ORE	VIR IS
Notes —	ARK	MASS	PA	DC
Surface: slip resistant. Max. slope: 1:12. Where vertical rise exceeds 2', provide intermediate landing max. 2'-6" vertically. Provide handrails and guardrails as required for stairs.	CAL	MICH	RI	
	COLO	● MINN	SC	
	CONN	MISS	SD	FED'L FUNDS
	DEL	MO	TENN	
	FLA	MONT	TEXAS	
	GA	NEB	UTAH	
	HAWAII	NEV	VT	
	IDAHO	NH	VA	
	ILL	NJ	WASH	
	IND	NM	W VA	
	IOWA	NY	WIS	OTHER
	KANS	NC	WYO	
	KY	ND		

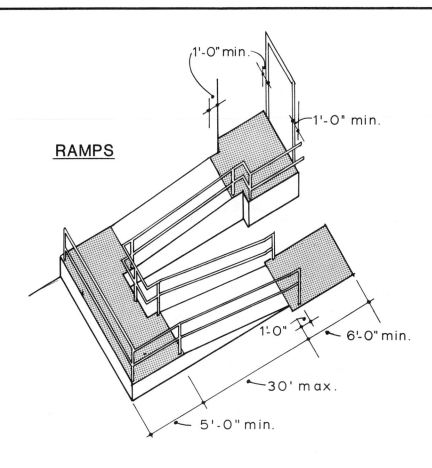

RAMPS

1'-0" min.

1'-0" min.

1'-0"

6'-0" min.

30' max.

5'-0" min.

Basis of standard —	APPLICABILITY			
Missouri Revised Statutes, Ch. 8	ALA	LA	OHIO	GUAM
	ALASKA	MAINE	OKLA	PR
	ARIZ	MD	ORE	VIR IS
	ARK	MASS	PA	DC
Notes —	CAL	MICH	RI	
Max. slope = 1′ in 12′. Min. width = 2′-8″ clear.	COLO	MINN	SC	
Handrails 2′-8″ on at least one side. Surface:	CONN	MISS	SD	FED'L
non-slip.	DEL	● MO	TENN	FUNDS
	FLA	MONT	TEXAS	
	GA	NEB	UTAH	
	HAWAII	NEV	VT	
	IDAHO	NH	VA	
	ILL	NJ	WASH	
	IND	NM	W VA	
	IOWA	NY	WIS	OTHER
	KANS	NC	WYO	
	KY	ND		

RAMPS

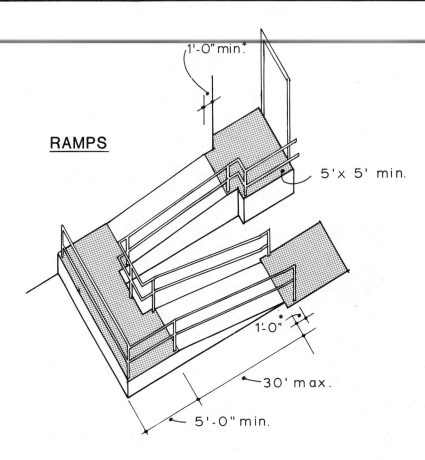

1'-0" min.*

5'x 5' min.

1'-0"*

30' max.

5'-0" min.

Basis of standard —				
Architectural Barrier Free Design Code	**APPLICABILITY**			
	ALA	LA	OHIO	GUAM
	ALASKA	MAINE	OKLA	PR
	ARIZ	MD	ORE	VIR IS
Notes —	ARK	MASS	PA	DC
Data applies to all ramps required as a means of egress.	CAL	MICH	RI	
Max. slope: 1:12. Min. width = 4'-0". Handrails: on	COLO	MINN	SC	
both sides at 2'-8" ht., min. 1-1/2", max. 2" o.d.,	CONN	MISS	SD	FED'L
basically round or oval with smooth surface and no	DEL	MO	TENN	FUNDS
sharp corners, 1-1/2" clear to wall. Non-slip surface;	FLA	MONT	TEXAS	
no carpet except secured low-pile.	GA	NEB	UTAH	
(*)Need not extend if safety hazard is caused.	HAWAII	NEV	VT	
	IDAHO	● NH	VA	
	ILL	NJ	WASH	
	IND	NM	W VA	
	IOWA	NY	WIS	OTHER
	KANS	NC	WYO	
	KY	ND		

RAMPS

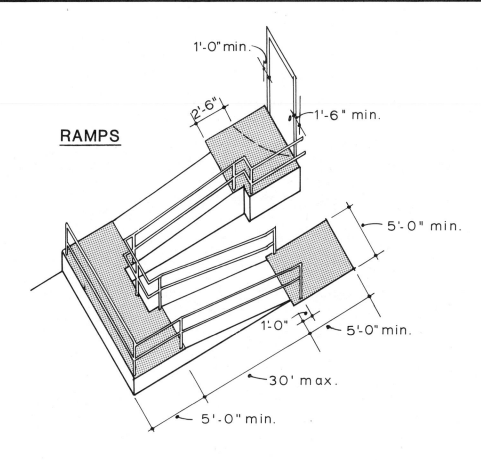

1'-0" min.

2'-6"

1'-6" min.

5'-0" min.

1'-0"

5'-0" min.

30' max.

5'-0" min.

Basis of standard — Barrier Free Design Regulations	APPLICABILITY			
	ALA	LA	OHIO	GUAM
	ALASKA	MAINE	OKLA	PR
	ARIZ	MD	ORE	VIR IS
Notes —	ARK	MASS	PA	DC
Max. slope = 1' in 12' (8.33%). Continuous handrails on both sides 2'-8" high extending 1'-0" beyond top and bottom of ramp. Handrails: 1-1/2" to 2" wide, 1-1/2" clear to wall or obstructions. Ramp surface: non-slip. Ramp width: 3'-6" min. clear.	CAL	MICH	RI	
	COLO	MINN	SC	
	CONN	MISS	SD	FED'L
	DEL	MO	TENN	FUNDS
	FLA	MONT	TEXAS	
	GA	NEB	UTAH	
	HAWAII	NEV	VT	
	IDAHO	NH	VA	
	ILL	● NJ	WASH	
	IND	NM	W VA	
	IOWA	NY	WIS	OTHER
	KANS	NC	WYO	
	KY	ND		

RAMPS

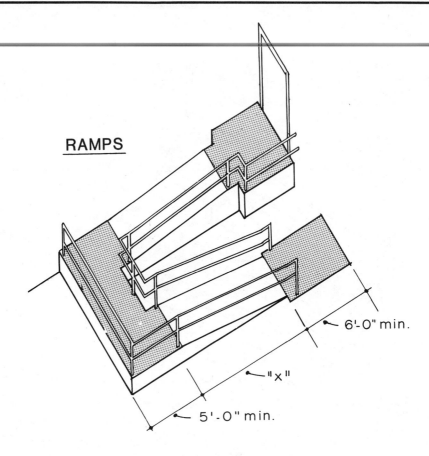

6'-0" min.

"x"

5'-0" min.

Basis of standard — Structural Specialty Code and Uniform Building Code	APPLICABILITY			
	ALA	LA	OHIO	GUAM
	ALASKA	MAINE	OKLA	PR
	ARIZ	MD	● ORE	VIR IS
Notes —	ARK	MASS	PA	DC
When slope is ... then max.	CAL	MICH	RI	
more than ... but less than ... "x" is	COLO	MINN	SC	
1 in 15 ... 1 in 12 ... 30′	CONN	MISS	SD	FED'L FUNDS
1 in 12 ... 1 in 10 ... 20′	DEL	MO	TENN	
1 in 10 ... 1 in 8 ... 10′	FLA	MONT	TEXAS	
Ranges steeper than 1 in 8 not permitted. Ranges required by Table 33-A of U.B.C. shall not exceed 1 in 12.	GA	NEB	UTAH	
	HAWAII	NEV	VT	
	IDAHO	NH	VA	
	ILL	NJ	WASH	
	IND	NM	W VA	
	IOWA	NY	WIS	OTHER
	KANS	NC	WYO	
	KY	ND		

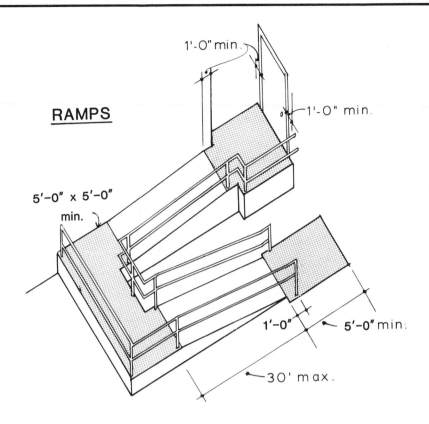

RAMPS

1'-0" min.

1'-0" min.

5'-0" x 5'-0" min.

1'-0"

5'-0" min.

30' max.

Basis of standard —	APPLICABILITY			
State Purchasing and General Services Commission	ALA	LA	OHIO	GUAM
	ALASKA	MAINE	OKLA	PR
	ARIZ	MD	ORE	VIR IS
Notes —	ARK	MASS	PA	DC
Accessible routes exceeding 5% slope (or 6% max. less than 30' long) are considered ramps. Min. clear width: 4'-0" (single runs not exceeding 30' long may be 3'-0"). Ramps with horizontal projection greater than 6'-0": Continuous handrails on both sides, between 2'-6" and 2'-10" high to support horizontal thrust of 50 lbs. per ft., 1-1/4" to 1-1/2" gripping surface, with 1-1/2" clearance. Slip resistant surface.	CAL	MICH	RI	
	COLO	MINN	SC	
	CONN	MISS	SD	FED'L FUNDS
	DEL	MO	TENN	
	FLA	MONT	● TEXAS	
	GA	NEB	UTAH	
Max. allowable slope · Max. rise · Max. horizontal projection	HAWAII	NEV	VT	
1:6 · 3" · 1'-6"	IDAHO	NH	VA	
1:8 · 7" · 4'-8"	ILL	NJ	WASH	
1:10 · 9" · 8'-0"	IND	NM	W VA	
1:12 · 2'-6" · 30'	IOWA	NY	WIS	OTHER
1:14 · 2'-10" · 40'	KANS	NC	WYO	
1:16 · 3'-8" · 60'	KY	ND		

RAMPS

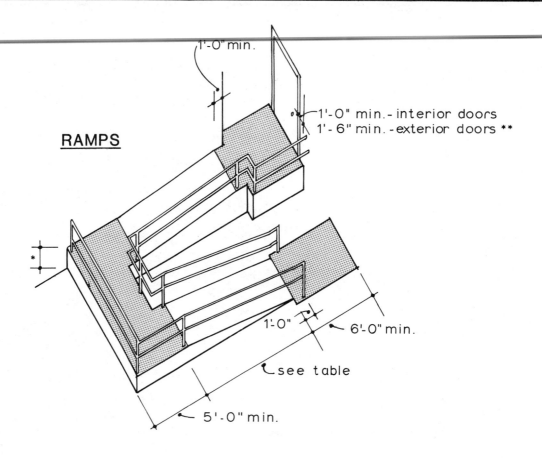

1'-0" min.

1'-0" min.-interior doors
1'-6" min.-exterior doors **

*

1'-0"

6'-0" min.

see table

5'-0" min.

Basis of standard —	APPLICABILITY			
Utah State Building Board Planning and Design Criteria	ALA	LA	OHIO	GUAM
	ALASKA	MAINE	OKLA	PR
	ARIZ	MD	ORE	VIR IS
Notes —	ARK	MASS	PA	DC
Maximum length and slopes for ramps	CAL	MICH	RI	
Max. horiz. projection per run (excluding landings) / Max. rise per run / Max. allowable slope	COLO	MINN	SC	
	CONN	MISS	SD	FED'L FUNDS
	DEL	MO	TENN	
	FLA	MONT	TEXAS	
	GA	NEB	● UTAH	
	HAWAII	NEV	VT	
	IDAHO	NH	VA	
	ILL	NJ	WASH	
	IND	NM	W VA	
	IOWA	NY	WIS	OTHER
	KANS	NC	WYO	
	KY	ND		

Notes —
Maximum length and slopes for ramps
Max. horiz.   Max.
projection per   rise   Max.
run (excluding   per   allowable
landings)   run   slope
    4'   6"   12.5% (1:8)
    8'   9"   10.0% (1:10)
    30'   30"   8.3% (1:12)
    60'   30"   5.0% (1:20)
Max. allowable slope for auditorium floors: 10.0%
For remodeled buildings and facilities, max. slope of
12.5% is permitted if other solutions are not feasible.
See following page for additional notes.

Basis of standard — Utah State Building Board Planning and Design Criteria	APPLICABILITY			
	ALA	LA	OHIO	GUAM
	ALASKA	MAINE	OKLA	PR
	ARIZ	MD	ORE	VIR IS
Notes —	ARK	MASS	PA	DC
See preceeding page. Handrail on one side, preferably two sides, required when ramp slope exceeds 5% or when there is a drop-off on either side. Height: 30″–34″. Non-slip floor with continuous walls or 4″ x 4″ curbs on each ramp side. Min. width: 4′-0″. (4″ high intermediate railing may be used in lieu of curb.) Min. 5′ x 5′ platform at top with door swinging onto ramp; 3′ x 5′ if door does not swing onto ramp. Interior ramp illumination 10fc min.; exterior ramps 5fc min. (*)More than 30″ height: provide 42″ high guardrails with 30″-34″ auxiliary handrails. (**)Remodeling with existing platforms: 12″ is o.k.	CAL	MICH	RI	
	COLO	MINN	SC	
	CONN	MISS	SD	FED'L FUNDS
	DEL	MO	TENN	
	FLA	MONT	TEXAS	
	GA	NEB	● UTAH	
	HAWAII	NEV	VT	
	IDAHO	NH	VA	
	ILL	NJ	WASH	
	IND	NM	W VA	
	IOWA	NY	WIS	OTHER
	KANS	NC	WYO	
	KY	ND		

RAMPS

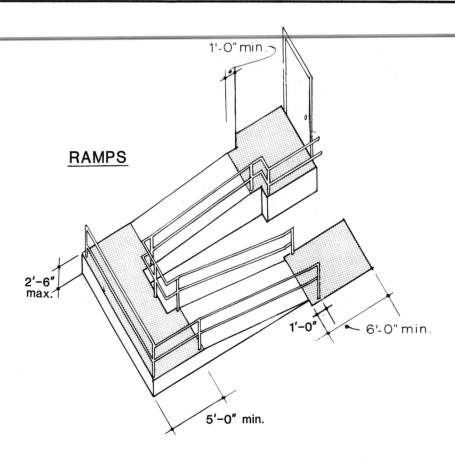

1'-0" min.

2'-6" max.

1'-0"

6'-0" min.

5'-0" min.

Basis of standard —	APPLICABILITY			
Building Code Advisory Council	ALA	LA	OHIO	GUAM
	ALASKA	MAINE	OKLA	PR
	ARIZ	MD	ORE	VIR IS
Notes —	ARK	MASS	PA	DC
Ramps steeper than 1 in 8 not permitted. Ramps	CAL	MICH	RI	
required by Table 33-A of UBC shall not exceed 1 in	COLO	MINN	SC	
12. For alterations max. rise of 3″ is permitted for	CONN	MISS	SD	FED'L
max. 1:8 slope, and 6″ for max. 1:10 slope. Provide				FUNDS
intermediate landing for each 2'-6″ of rise. No ramp	DEL	MO	TENN	
direction change except ramps with 30' min. inside	FLA	MONT	TEXAS	
diameter. Max. transverse slope: 1:50. Doors or	GA	NEB	UTAH	
gates shall not reduce min. landing dimension to less	HAWAII	NEV	VT	
than 3'-6″ nor the required width by more than 3-1/2″	IDAHO	NH	VA	
when fully open. Railings for ramps over 1:20: 2'-8″	ILL	NJ	● WASH	
to 3'-0″ high, 1-1/4″ to 2″ wide, both sides, 1-1/2″	IND	NM	W VA	
clear. Min. ramp width required by Table 33-A:	IOWA	NY	WIS	OTHER
3'-0″, width of other ramps as required for stairways.	KANS	NC	WYO	
	KY	ND		

RAMPS

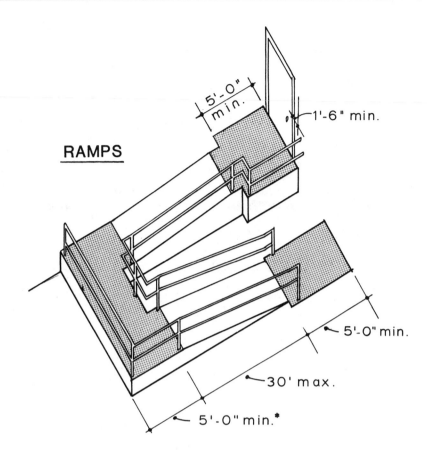

5'-0" min.

1'-6" min.

5'-0" min.

30' max.

5'-0" min.*

Basis of standard —	APPLICABILITY			
Ind. 52.04, 6 Wisconsin Administrative Code	ALA	LA	OHIO	GUAM
	ALASKA	MAINE	OKLA	PR
	ARIZ	MD	ORE	VIR IS
Notes —	ARK	MASS	PA	DC
Max. slope = 1' in 12'. Interior ramp with max. slope of 1' in 8' may be used for a max. height of 2'. Ramp width: 4'-0" of which a max. of 4" on each side maybe occupied by a handrail. Handrials: on each side, 2'-6" high (preferably 2'-8"); intermediate rails at midheight at unenclosed ramps; not required on interior ramps with slope of less than 1' in 20'. Surface: slip-resistant.	CAL	MICH	RI	
	COLO	MINN	SC	
	CONN	MISS	SD	FED'L FUNDS
	DEL	MO	TENN	
	FLA	MONT	TEXAS	
	GA	NEB	UTAH	
(*)Platforms not required on interior ramps with slope of less than 1' in 20'.	HAWAII	NEV	VT	
	IDAHO	NH	VA	
	ILL	NJ	WASH	
	IND	NM	W VA	
	IOWA	NY	● WIS	OTHER
	KANS	NC	WYO	
	KY	ND		

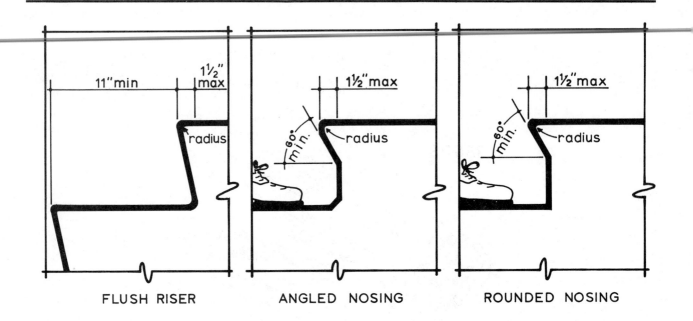

FLUSH RISER   ANGLED NOSING   ROUNDED NOSING

STAIR TREAD WIDTH & NOSINGS

Basis of standard —	APPLICABILITY			
ANSI 1980 — 4.9	ALA	● LA	OHIO	GUAM
	● ALASKA	● MAINE	OKLA	PR
	ARIZ	MD	ORE	VIR IS
	ARK	MASS	PA	DC
Notes —	● CAL	MICH	● RI	
Applicable to stairs connecting levels not connected by an elevator. All steps to have uniform riser heights and tread widths (11″ min.). Underside of nosings shall not be abrupt. Exception: These specifications are not mandatory for stairs within dwelling units. California: Required for all stairs except within dwelling units.	● COLO	MINN	SC	
	CONN	MISS	SD	FED'L FUNDS
	DEL	MO	TENN	
	FLA	MONT	● TEXAS	
	GA	NEB	UTAH	
	● HAWAII	● NEV	● VT	
	● IDAHO	NH	● VA	
	ILL	NJ	WASH	
	IND	● NM	W VA	
	● IOWA	● NY	WIS	OTHER
	KANS	NC	WYO	
	KY	ND		

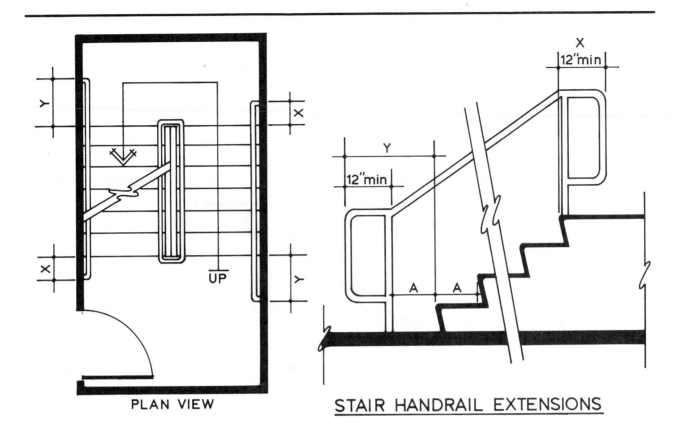

PLAN VIEW

STAIR HANDRAIL EXTENSIONS

Basis of standard — ANSI 1980 — 4.9.4	APPLICABILITY			
	ALA	● LA	OHIO	GUAM
	● ALASKA	● MAINE	OKLA	PR
	ARIZ	MD	ORE	VIR IS
	● ARK	MASS	PA	DC
	CAL	MICH	● RI	
	● COLO	MINN	SC	
	CONN	MISS	SD	● FED'L FUNDS
	● DEL	MO	TENN	
	FLA	MONT	● TEXAS	
	GA	NEB	UTAH	
	● HAWAII	● NEV	● VT	
	● IDAHO	NH	● VA	
	ILL	NJ	WASH	
	IND	● NM	W VA	
	● IOWA	● NY	WIS	OTHER
	KANS	NC	WYO	
	KY	ND		

Notes —

Refer also to "Grab Bars and Handrails" under "Equipment". Provide continuous handrails on both sides of all stairs. Inside handrail on switchback or 'dogleg stairs to be continuous. If rails are not continuous extend beyond top and bottom risers as shown, horizontal with floor. Clear space between rail and wall = 1-1/2″. Do not interrupt gripping surfaces by newel posts or other obstructions. Do not accumulate water on outside stairs or approaches. Texas: Mount rails between 2′-8″ and 2′-10″ high above leading tread edge. Support 50 lb. per ft.

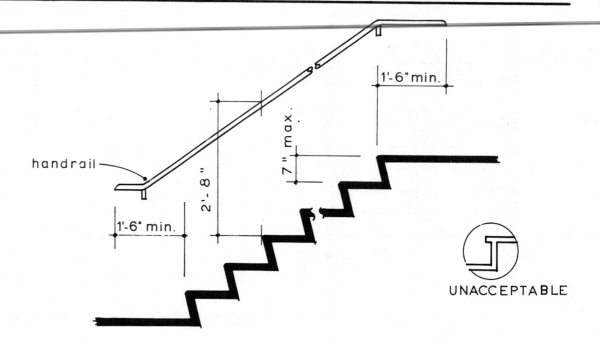

handrail

1'-6" min.

7" max.

2'-8"

1'-6" min.

UNACCEPTABLE

S T A I R S

Basis of standard — ANSI 1961 — 5.4 and others	APPLICABILITY			
	ALA	LA	OHIO	GUAM
	ALASKA	● MAINE	● OKLA	PR
	● ARIZ	MD	ORE	VIR IS
Notes —	ARK	MASS	● PA	DC
At least one hand rail shall extend at least 1'-6" beyond top and bottom steps. Design steps with recognized step formulas.	CAL	MICH	RI	
	COLO	MINN	● SC	
Florida: Applies to government facilities. Railings: max. dia.: 1½", 1½" clearance, supporting 250 lb. load. Non-slip surface. Exterior treads: 1'-2" wide min. if practicable.	● CONN	● MISS	● SD	FED'L FUNDS
	DEL	MO	TENN	
	● FLA	MONT	TEXAS	
Vermont: Stairs to conform to ANSI A9.1–1953. Handrails: 1½" od., 1½" clear of walls, not recessed.	GA	● NEB	UTAH	
	HAWAII	NEV	● VT	
	IDAHO	NH	VA	
	ILL	NJ	WASH	
	IND	NM	W VA	
	IOWA	NY	WIS	OTHER
	● KANS	NC	WYO	
	KY	● ND		

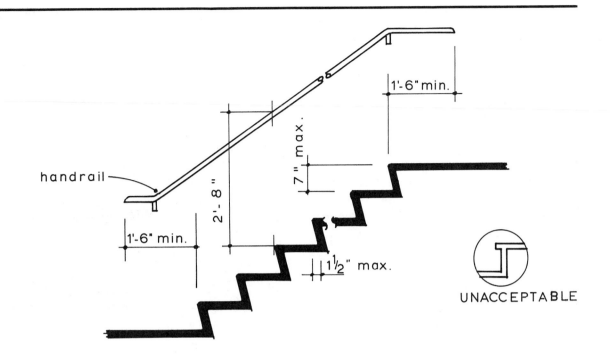

handrail

1'-6" min.

7" max.

2'-8"

1'-6" min.

1½" max.

UNACCEPTABLE

S T A I R S

Basis of standard —	APPLICABILITY			
ANSI 1961 — 5.4 and others	ALA	LA	OHIO	GUAM
	ALASKA	MAINE	● OKLA	PR
	ARIZ	MD	ORE	VIR IS
Notes —	ARK	MASS	PA	DC
Do not use abrupt nosing when stairs might require use by those with disabilities. Conform to ANSI A9.1-1953. Where codes specify handrails at heights other than 2'-8", it is recommended that two sets of rails be installed.	CAL	MICH	RI	
	COLO	MINN	● SC	
	CONN	MISS	● SD	FED'L FUNDS
	DEL	MO	TENN	
Florida: Applies to non-government financed facilities.	● FLA	MONT	TEXAS	
	● GA	NEB	UTAH	
	HAWAII	NEV	VT	
	IDAHO	NH	VA	
	ILL	NJ	WASH	
	IND	NM	W VA	
	IOWA	NY	WIS	OTHER
	● KANS	NC	WYO	
	KY	● ND		

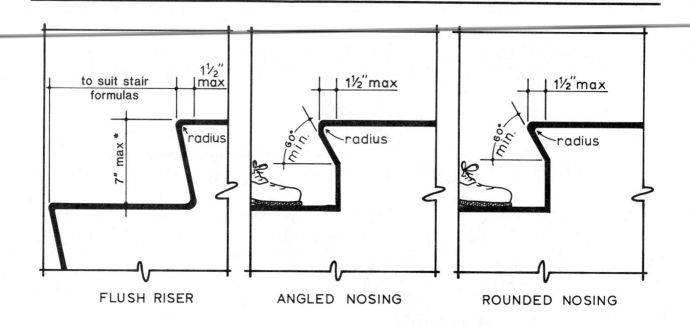

FLUSH RISER   ANGLED NOSING   ROUNDED NOSING

STAIR TREAD WIDTH & NOSINGS

Basis of standard — ATBCB 1190.80	APPLICABILITY			
	ALA	LA	OHIO	GUAM
	ALASKA	MAINE	OKLA	PR
	ARIZ	MD	ORE	VIR IS
Notes — Applies to stairs connecting levels not connected by an elevator. Max. radius of curvature at leading edge: ½″. Open risers not permitted; provide continuous handrails on both sides. (*)7½″ max. in Delaware	● ARK	MASS	PA	DC
	CAL	MICH	RI	
	COLO	MINN	SC	
	CONN	MISS	SD	
	● DEL	MO	TENN	● FED'L FUNDS
	FLA	MONT	TEXAS	
	GA	NEB	UTAH	
	HAWAII	NEV	VT	
	IDAHO	NH	VA	
	ILL	NJ	WASH	
	IND	NM	W VA	
	IOWA	NY	WIS	OTHER
	KANS	NC	WYO	
	KY	ND		

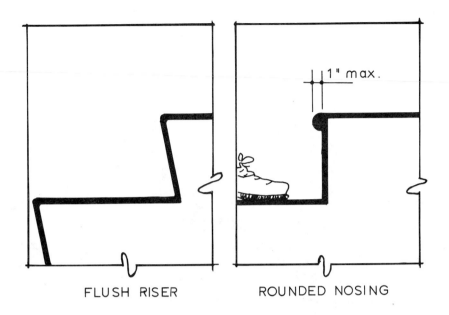

FLUSH RISER   ROUNDED NOSING

N O S I N G S

Basis of standard — Various	APPLICABILITY			
	ALA	LA	OHIO	GUAM
	ALASKA	MAINE	OKLA	PR
	ARIZ	MD	ORE	VIR IS
Notes —	ARK	MASS	PA	DC
	CAL	MICH	RI	
	COLO	● MINN	SC	
	CONN	MISS	SD	FED'L FUNDS
	DEL	MO	● TENN	
	FLA	MONT	TEXAS	
	GA	● NEB	UTAH	
	HAWAII	NEV	VT	
	IDAHO	NH	VA	
	ILL	NJ	WASH	
	IND	NM	W VA	
	IOWA	NY	WIS	OTHER
	KANS	● NC	WYO	
	KY	ND		

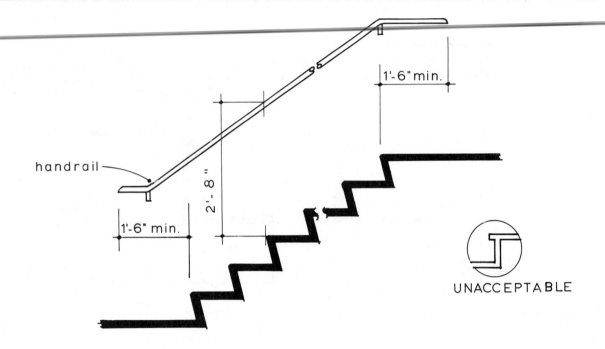

handrail

1'-6" min.

2'-8"

1'-6" min.

UNACCEPTABLE

<u>S T A I R S</u>

Basis of standard —	APPLICABILITY			
Basics of Barrier Free Design and others	ALA	LA	OHIO	GUAM
	ALASKA	MAINE	OKLA	PR
	ARIZ	MD	ORE	VIR IS
Notes —	ARK	MASS	PA	DC
Provide at least one continuous handrail. Extended handrails to be on the side of a continuing wall. Wyoming: Open risers not acceptable unless ramps, stairs or elevators are available on the same floor.	CAL	MICH	RI	
	COLO	MINN	SC	
	CONN	MISS	SD	FED'L FUNDS
	DEL	MO	● TENN	
	FLA	MONT	TEXAS	
	GA	NEB	UTAH	
	HAWAII	NEV	VT	
	IDAHO	NH	VA	
	ILL	NJ	WASH	
	IND	NM	W VA	
	IOWA	NY	WIS	OTHER
	KANS	● NC	● WYO	
	KY	ND		

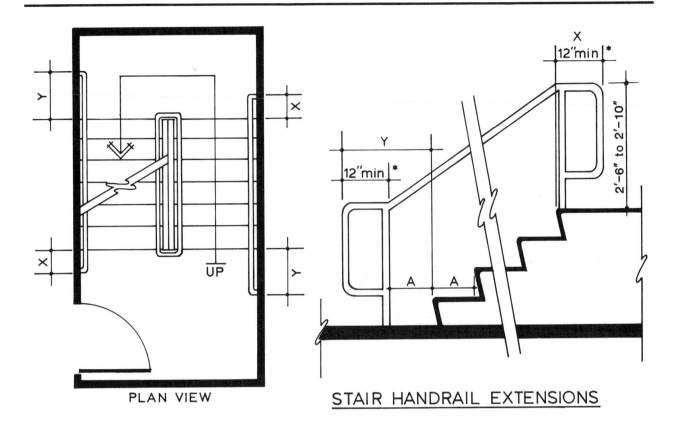

PLAN VIEW

STAIR HANDRAIL EXTENSIONS

Basis of standard —	APPLICABILITY			
Building Code Advisory Council and others	ALA	LA	OHIO	GUAM
	ALASKA	MAINE	OKLA	PR
	ARIZ	MD	● ORE	VIR IS
	ARK	MASS	PA	DC
Notes —	CAL	MICH	RI	
Provide railings on each side with intermediate hand-rail for stairways required to be more than 88″ in width. Private stairways 2′-6″ or less in height may have handrail on one side only. Return ends or terminate in newel posts or safety terminals. Provide an approved hatch openable to the exterior not less than 16 sq. ft. in area with a 2′ min. dimension for all interior stairways which extend to the top floor in any building four or more stories in height at the highest point of the stair shaft. (*)Oregon and Montana: 6″ min.	COLO	MINN	SC	
	CONN	MISS	SD	FED'L
	DEL	MO	TENN	FUNDS
	FLA	● MONT	TEXAS	
	GA	NEB	UTAH	
	HAWAII	NEV	VT	
	IDAHO	NH	VA	
	ILL	NJ	● WASH	
	IND	NM	W VA	
	IOWA	NY	WIS	OTHER
	KANS	NC	WYO	
	KY	ND		

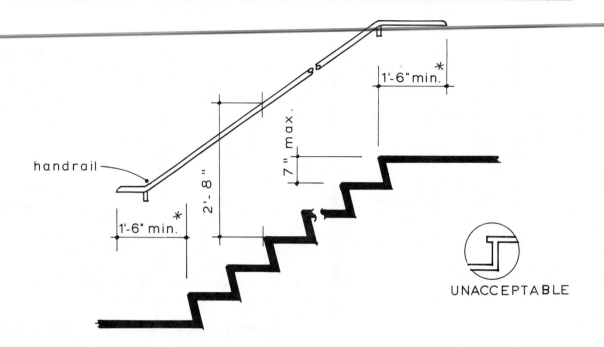

handrail

1'-6"min. *

7" max.

2'-8"

1'-6" min. *

UNACCEPTABLE

STAIRS

Basis of standard — Barrier Free Design Standard	APPLICABILITY			
	● ALA	LA	OHIO	GUAM
	ALASKA	MAINE	OKLA	PR
	ARIZ	MD	ORE	VIR IS
Notes — Min. width between handrails: 3'-6". Handrails: circular or oval, 1½″ to 2″ dia., non-slip finish on both sides of stairs. Treads: non-slip. Stairs must be well illuminated. Approaches and landings to be level. (*)For at least one handrail.	ARK	MASS	PA	DC
	CAL	MICH	RI	
	COLO	MINN	SC	
	CONN	MISS	SD	FED'L FUNDS
	DEL	MO	TENN	
	FLA	MONT	TEXAS	
	GA	NEB	UTAH	
	HAWAII	NEV	VT	
	IDAHO	NH	VA	
	ILL	NJ	WASH	
	IND	NM	W VA	
	IOWA	NY	WIS	OTHER
	KANS	NC	WYO	
	KY	ND		

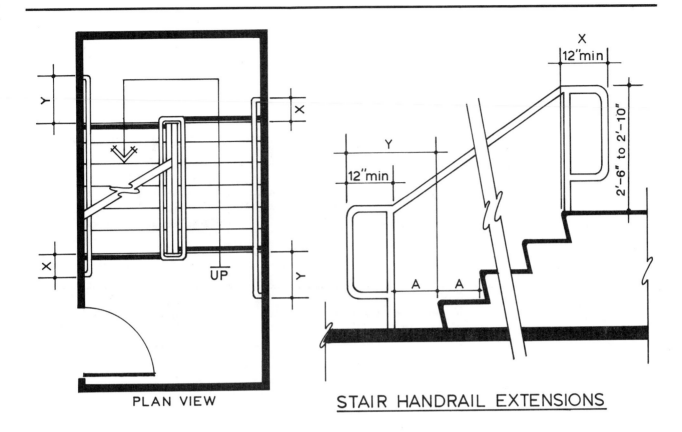

PLAN VIEW

STAIR HANDRAIL EXTENSIONS

Basis of standard — CAC Title 24, Part 2	APPLICABILITY			
	ALA	LA	OHIO	GUAM
	ALASKA	MAINE	OKLA	PR
	ARIZ	MD	ORE	VIR IS
Notes —	ARK	MASS	PA	DC
1. Inside handrail to be continuous and shall not extend into landing.	● CAL	MICH	RI	
	COLO	MINN	SC	
2. Exterior stairs: Provide 2″ wide contrasting stripe within 1″ of nosing at upper approach and every tread.	CONN	MISS	SD	FED'L FUNDS
	DEL	MO	TENN	
3. Interior stairs: Provide 2″ wide contrasting stripe within 1″ of nosing at upper approach and bottom tread of every flight of stairs.	FLA	MONT	TEXAS	
	GA	NEB	UTAH	
	HAWAII	NEV	VT	
	IDAHO	NH	VA	
	ILL	NJ	WASH	
	IND	NM	W VA	
	IOWA	NY	WIS	OTHER
	KANS	NC	WYO	
	KY	ND		

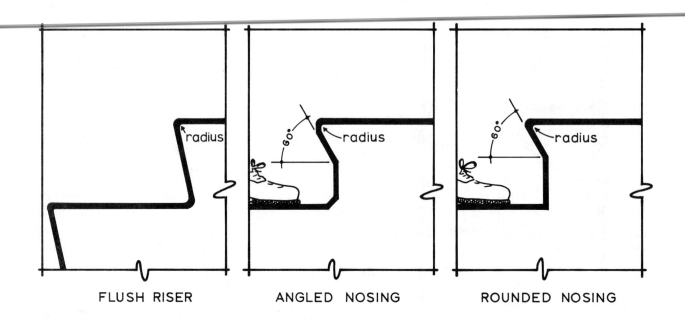

FLUSH RISER   ANGLED NOSING   ROUNDED NOSING

STAIR TREAD WIDTH & NOSINGS

Basis of standard — State of Connecticut Basic Building Code	APPLICABILITY			
	ALA	LA	OHIO	GUAM
	ALASKA	MAINE	OKLA	PR
	ARIZ	MD	ORE	VIR IS
	ARK	MASS	PA	DC
	CAL	MICH	RI	
	COLO	MINN	SC	
	● CONN	MISS	SD	FED'L
	DEL	MO	TENN	FUNDS
	FLA	MONT	TEXAS	
	GA	NEB	UTAH	
	HAWAII	NEV	VT	
	IDAHO	NH	VA	
	ILL	NJ	WASH	
	IND	NM	W VA	
	IOWA	NY	WIS	OTHER
	KANS	NC	WYO	
	KY	ND		

Notes —

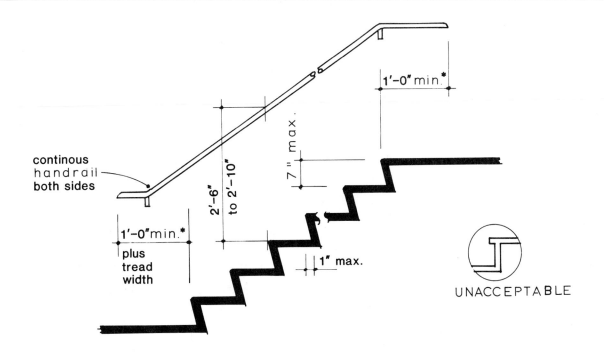

continous handrail both sides

1'-0" min.* plus tread width

2'-6" to 2'-10"

7" max.

1'-0" min.*

1" max.

UNACCEPTABLE

STAIRS

Basis of standard — Capital Development Board	APPLICABILITY			
	ALA	LA	OHIO	GUAM
	ALASKA	MAINE	OKLA	PR
	ARIZ	MD	ORE	VIR IS
Notes — Intermediate rails required for stairs wider than 7'-4" Provide second set of handrails 2'-0" high in elementary schools, nursery schools and day care centers. Handrail must return to wall or floor. No projection into stairway below 6'-8" except handrails, stair stringers and door hardware. Protect circulation space under a stair less than 7'-6" high. (*)Not applicable to exempted exit stairs and inside handrail on switchback or dogleg stairs.	ARK	MASS	PA	DC
	CAL	MICH	RI	
	COLO	MINN	SC	
	CONN	MISS	SD	FED'L FUNDS
	DEL	MO	TENN	
	FLA	MONT	TEXAS	
	GA	NEB	UTAH	
	HAWAII	NEV	VT	
	IDAHO	NH	VA	
	● ILL	NJ	WASH	
	IND	NM	W VA	
	IOWA	NY	WIS	OTHER
	KANS	NC	WYO	
	KY	ND		

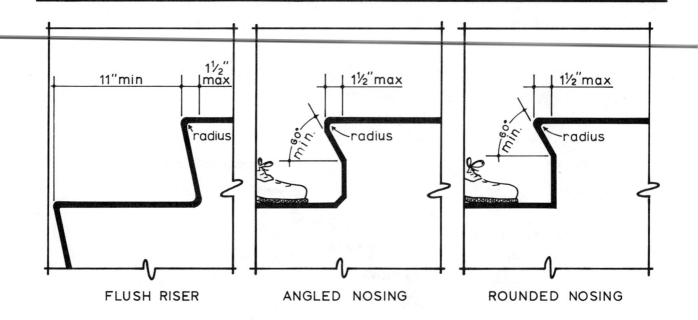

FLUSH RISER   ANGLED NOSING   ROUNDED NOSING

STAIR TREAD WIDTH & NOSINGS

Basis of standard — Capital Development Board	APPLICABILITY			
	ALA	LA	OHIO	GUAM
	ALASKA	MAINE	OKLA	PR
	ARIZ	MD	ORE	VIR IS
Notes —	ARK	MASS	PA	DC
Max. radius of curvature for leading edge of tread: ½". Edge of nosing shall be clearly distinguishable. Stair treads shall have non-slip surface.	CAL	MICH	RI	
	COLO	MINN	SC	
	CONN	MISS	SD	FED'L FUNDS
	DEL	MO	TENN	
	FLA	MONT	TEXAS	
	GA	NEB	UTAH	
	HAWAII	NEV	VT	
	IDAHO	NH	VA	
	● ILL	NJ	WASH	
	IND	NM	W VA	
	IOWA	NY	WIS	OTHER
	KANS	NC	WYO	
	KY	ND		

TREAD WIDTH IN FEET AND INCHES							RISER		THREAD WIDTH IN MM						
1'-2"	1'-1½"	1'-1"	1'-0½"	1'-0"	11½"	11"	INCHES	MM	279	292	305	318	330	343	356
						▬	7	178	▬						
			▬▬▬▬▬▬▬▬				6½	165	▬▬▬▬▬▬▬▬						
▬▬▬▬▬▬▬▬▬▬▬▬▬▬▬							6	152	▬▬▬▬▬▬▬▬▬▬▬▬▬▬▬						
	▬▬▬▬▬▬▬▬▬▬▬▬						5½	140	▬▬▬▬▬▬▬▬▬▬▬▬						
			▬▬▬▬▬				5	127	▬▬▬▬▬						
						▬	4½	114	▬						
						▬	4	102	▬						

ACCEPTABLE RANGE OF TREAD/RISER RELATIONSHIPS

Basis of standard —	APPLICABILITY			
Capital Development Board	ALA	LA	OHIO	GUAM
	ALASKA	MAINE	OKLA	PR
	ARIZ	MD	ORE	VIR IS
Notes —	ARK	MASS	PA	DC
Risers: min.: 4″, max.: 7″, tread to tread.	CAL	MICH	RI	
Treads: min. 11″ nosing to nosing. Comply with above chart. Exemption: Exit stairs required by	COLO	MINN	SC	
other codes, separated from other spaces by 1	CONN	MISS	SD	FED'L
hour rating may have 7½″ max. risers and 10″	DEL	MO	TENN	FUNDS
min. tread width. All risers and treads to have	FLA	MONT	TEXAS	
uniform dimensions on any given flight of stairs.	GA	NEB	UTAH	
Where stairway intersects a circulation path at right angles, set back first riser 2'-6″ min. from	HAWAII	NEV	VT	
circulation route. Locate tactile warning cues	IDAHO	NH	VA	
from edge of path of travel to top stair nosing	● ILL	NJ	WASH	
3'-0″ wide unless there is a perceivable difference in hardness between the tactile warning signal	IND	NM	W VA	
surface in which case the width of the signal shall	IOWA	NY	WIS	OTHER
be 2'-0″.	KANS	NC	WYO	
	KY	ND		

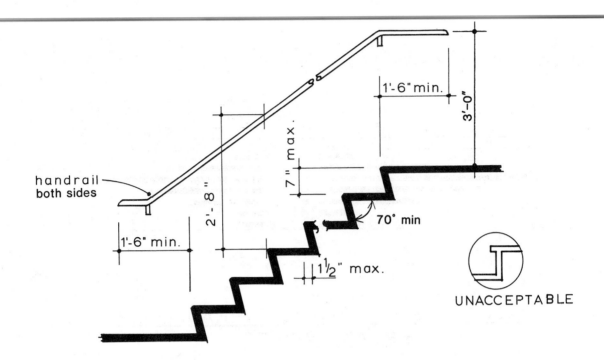

handrail both sides

1'-6" min.

2'-8"

1'-6" min.

7" max.

1½" max.

70° min

3'-0"

UNACCEPTABLE

STAIRS

Basis of standard —	APPLICABILITY			
521 CMR Architectural Barriers Board	ALA	LA	OHIO	GUAM
	ALASKA	MAINE	OKLA	PR
	ARIZ	MD	ORE	VIR IS
Notes —	ARK	● MASS	PA	DC
Stairs required as a means of egress by the State Building Code shall comply. No open risers. Treads to have non-slip surface. Exemption: Alterations of less than 25% of equalized assessed value where an elevator provides accessibility of all levels.	CAL	MICH	RI	
	COLO	MINN	SC	
	CONN	MISS	SD	FED'L FUNDS
	DEL	MO	TENN	
	FLA	MONT	TEXAS	
	GA	NEB	UTAH	
	HAWAII	NEV	VT	
	IDAHO	NH	VA	
	ILL	NJ	WASH	
	IND	NM	W VA	
	IOWA	NY	WIS	OTHER
	KANS	NC	WYO	
	KY	ND		

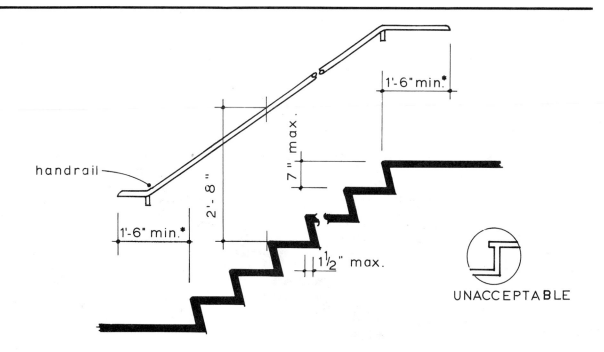

handrail

1'-6" min.*

7" max.

2'-8"

1'-6" min.*

1½" max.

UNACCEPTABLE

S T A I R S

Basis of standard — Missouri Revised Statutes, Ch. 8	APPLICABILITY			
	ALA	LA	OHIO	GUAM
	ALASKA	MAINE	OKLA	PR
	ARIZ	MD	ORE	VIR IS
Notes — Data applies to steps in public stairs reasonably expected to be used by persons with physical handicaps. Handrails on each side. Design steps with recognized step formulas. (*)Applies to at least one handrail unless such extension shall itself be a hazard.	ARK	MASS	PA	DC
	CAL	MICH	RI	
	COLO	MINN	SC	
	CONN	MISS	SD	FED'L FUNDS
	DEL	● MO	TENN	
	FLA	MONT	TEXAS	
	GA	NEB	UTAH	
	HAWAII	NEV	VT	
	IDAHO	NH	VA	
	ILL	NJ	WASH	
	IND	NM	W VA	
	IOWA	NY	WIS	OTHER
	KANS	NC	WYO	
	KY	ND		

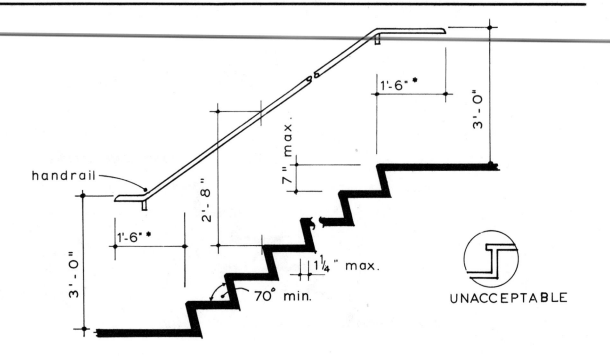

handrail

1'-6" *

3'-0"

7" max.

2'-8"

1'-6" *

3'-0"

1¼" max.

70° min.

UNACCEPTABLE

S T A I R S

Basis of standard —	APPLICABILITY			
	ALA	LA	OHIO	GUAM
	ALASKA	MAINE	OKLA	PR
	ARIZ	MD	ORE	VIR IS
Notes — Data applies to stairs required as a means of egress. Locate as close as possible to accessible entrance. Open risers are not permitted. Handrails on both sides. Provide additional lower handrail in buildings used primarily by small children at 2'-0" height. Handgrip portion of rails: 1½" to 2" o.d., basically round or oval or rounded rectangle max. 2" wide with ¾" radius, smooth surface without sharp corners 1½" wall clearance. Stair treads: non-slip surface. (*)Applies to wall rails wherever possible. Not needed if it causes hazard or if space does not permit.	ARK	MASS	PA	DC
	CAL	MICH	RI	
	COLO	MINN	SC	
	CONN	MISS	SD	FED'L FUNDS
	DEL	MO	TENN	
	FLA	MONT	TEXAS	
	GA	NEB	UTAH	
	HAWAII	NEV	VT	
	IDAHO	● NH	VA	
	ILL	NJ	WASH	
	IND	NM	W VA	
	IOWA	NY	WIS	OTHER
	KANS	NC	WYO	
	KY	ND		

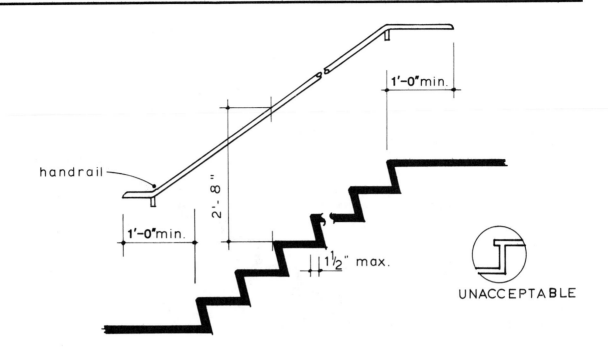

handrail

1'-0"min.

2'-8"

1'-0"min.

1½" max.

UNACCEPTABLE

STAIRS

Basis of standard —	APPLICABILITY			
Barrier Free Design Regulations	ALA	LA	OHIO	GUAM
	ALASKA	MAINE	OKLA	PR
	ARIZ	MD	ORE	VIR IS
	ARK	MASS	PA	DC
	CAL	MICH	RI	
	COLO	MINN	SC	
Notes —	CONN	MISS	SD	FED'L
Free standing handrails for required public stairs: 1½" to 2½" in width with 1½" to 2" clear to wall and/or support surface.	DEL	MO	TENN	FUNDS
	FLA	MONT	TEXAS	
	GA	NEB	UTAH	
	HAWAII	NEV	VT	
	IDAHO	NH	VA	
	ILL	● NJ	WASH	
	IND	NM	W VA	
	IOWA	NY	WIS	OTHER
	KANS	NC	WYO	
	KY	ND		

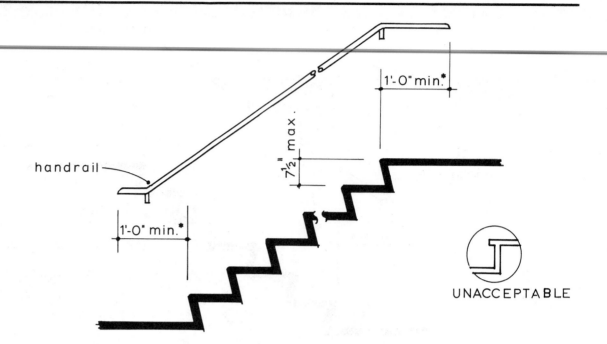

handrail

1'-0" min.*

$7\frac{1}{2}$" max.

1'-0" min.*

UNACCEPTABLE

STAIRS

Basis of standard — Uniform Building Code	APPLICABILITY			
	ALA	LA	OHIO	GUAM
	ALASKA	MAINE	OKLA	PR
	ARIZ	MD	ORE	VIR IS
Notes — Conform to Uniform Building Code and New Mexico Uniform Building Code. Conform steps, wherever possible, with existing step formulas. (*)At least one handrail.	ARK	MASS	PA	DC
	CAL	MICH	RI	
	COLO	MINN	SC	
	CONN	MISS	SD	FED'L FUNDS
	DEL	MO	TENN	
	FLA	MONT	TEXAS	
	GA	NEB	UTAH	
	HAWAII	NEV	VT	
	IDAHO	NH	VA	
	ILL	NJ	WASH	
	IND	● NM	W VA	
	IOWA	NY	WIS	OTHER
	KANS	NC	WYO	
	KY	ND		

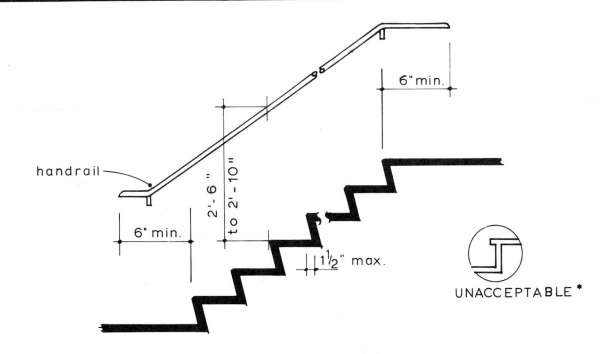

handrail

6" min.

6" min.

2'-6" to 2'-10"

1½" max.

UNACCEPTABLE *

STAIRS

Basis of standard —	APPLICABILITY			
Structural Specialty Code	ALA	LA	OHIO	GUAM
	ALASKA	MAINE	OKLA	PR
	ARIZ	MD	● ORE	VIR IS
	ARK	MASS	PA	DC
Notes —	CAL	MICH	RI	
Handrails required on each side, and except for private stairways, extend 6″ at top and bottom for one hand-rail, returning or terminating in newel posts or safety terminals. Handgrip: max. 2″ max. cross-section, 1¼″ min., with smooth surface and no sharp corners. (*)For stairs in government and public buildings.	COLO	MINN	SC	
	CONN	MISS	SD	FED'L
	DEL	MO	TENN	FUNDS
	FLA	MONT	TEXAS	
	GA	NEB	UTAH	
	HAWAII	NEV	VT	
	IDAHO	NH	VA	
	ILL	NJ	WASH	
	IND	NM	W VA	
	IOWA	NY	WIS	OTHER
	KANS	NC	WYO	
	KY	ND		

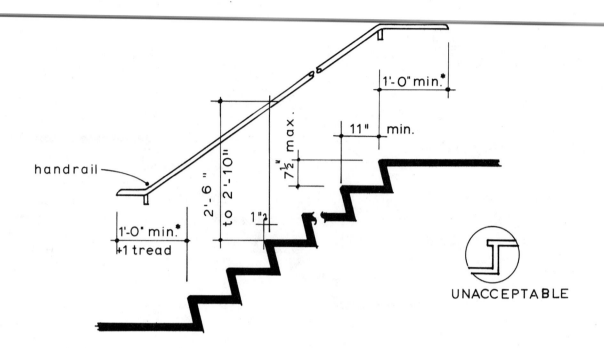

handrail

1'-0" min.*

11" min.

7½" max.

2'-6" to 2'-10"

1'-0" min.*
+1 tread

1"½

UNACCEPTABLE

STAIRS

Basis of standard — Utah State Building Board	APPLICABILITY			
	ALA	LA	OHIO	GUAM
	ALASKA	MAINE	OKLA	PR
	ARIZ	MD	ORE	VIR IS
Notes —	ARK	MASS	PA	DC
Handrails: At least one, smooth finish, 1¼" to 1½"	CAL	MICH	RI	
dia., 1½" space to wall. For children as principal	COLO	MINN	SC	
users, provide second set at 2'-0" height. Surface of	CONN	MISS	SD	FED'L
rails not to be interrupted by newel posts or other	DEL	MO	TENN	FUNDS
obstructions. Provide 2" wide abrasive floor warning	FLA	MONT	TEXAS	
strips within 3'-0" of stair top where halls empty	GA	NEB	● UTAH	
directly to open stairs.	HAWAII	NEV	VT	
(*)For at least one handrail.	IDAHO	NH	VA	
Exceptions: Remodeled facilities where existing con-	ILL	NJ	WASH	
ditions have: treads less than 11" and risers exceeding	IND	NM	W VA	
7½", handrails higher than 2'-6" to 2'-10", 12" hand-	IOWA	NY	WIS	OTHER
rail extension cannot be obtained for existing decora-	KANS	NC	WYO	
tive rails or would become a hazard.	KY	ND		

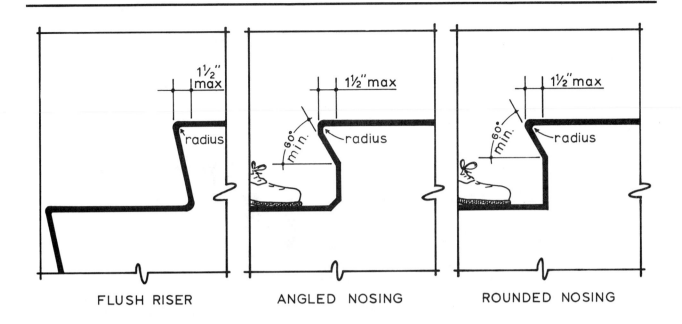

FLUSH RISER   ANGLED NOSING   ROUNDED NOSING

STAIR TREAD WIDTH & NOSINGS

Basis of standard — Building Code Advisory Council	APPLICABILITY			
	ALA	LA	OHIO	GUAM
	ALASKA	MAINE	OKLA	PR
	ARIZ	MD	ORE	VIR IS
	ARK	MASS	PA	DC
	CAL	MICH	RI	
	COLO	MINN	SC	
	CONN	MISS	SD	FED'L FUNDS
	DEL	MO	TENN	
	FLA	MONT	TEXAS	
	GA	NEB	UTAH	
	HAWAII	NEV	VT	
	IDAHO	NH	VA	
	ILL	NJ	● WASH	
	IND	NM	W VA	
	IOWA	NY	WIS	OTHER
	KANS	NC	WYO	
	KY	ND		

Notes —

For required stairs, nosings must be flush, non-slip, with ½" max. radius. Open risers prohibited except where floor areas are accessible by elevator.

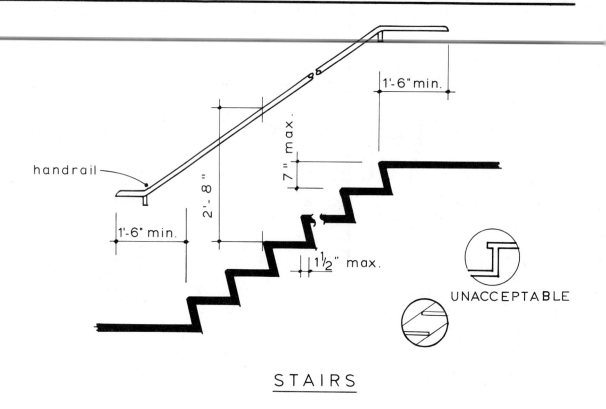

handrail

1'-6" min.

7" max.

2'-8"

1'-6" min.

1½" max.

UNACCEPTABLE

STAIRS

Basis of standard — Art 10F, Chapter 18, Code of West Virginia	APPLICABILITY			
	ALA	LA	OHIO	GUAM
	ALASKA	MAINE	OKLA	PR
	ARIZ	MD	ORE	VIR IS
	ARK	MASS	PA	DC
Notes —	CAL	MICH	RI	
Bevel at 45°, or round with ¾″ min. radius, undersides of nosings.	COLO	MINN	SC	
	CONN	MISS	SD	FED'L
	DEL	MO	TENN	FUNDS
	FLA	MONT	TEXAS	
	GA	NEB	UTAH	
	HAWAII	NEV	VT	
	IDAHO	NH	VA	
	ILL	NJ	WASH	
	IND	NM	● W VA	
	IOWA	NY	WIS	OTHER
	KANS	NC	WYO	
	KY	ND		

Basis of standard —	APPLICABILITY			
ANSI 1980 — 4.13 and others	ALA	● LA	OHIO	GUAM
	● ALASKA	● MAINE	OKLA	PR
	ARIZ	MD	ORE	VIR IS
Notes —	● ARK	MASS	PA	DC
1. Gates, including ticket gates, shall comply with requirements.	● CAL	MICH	● RI	
	● COLO	MINN	SC	
2. Revolving doors or turnstiles are not considered accessible doors.	CONN	MISS	SD	● FED'L FUNDS
3. In double-leaf doorways, at least one active leaf shall comply with requirements. (Federal requirements exempt double-leaf automatic doors if both leaves are automatic).	● DEL	MO	TENN	
	FLA	MONT	● TEXAS	
	GA	NEB	UTAH	
4. Maneuvering clearances shown on subsequent pages apply to non-automatic doors.	● HAWAII	● NEV	● VT	
	● IDAHO	NH	● VA	
	ILL	NJ	WASH	
	IND	● NM	W VA	
	IOWA	● NY	WIS	OTHER
	KANS	NC	WYO	
	● KY	ND		

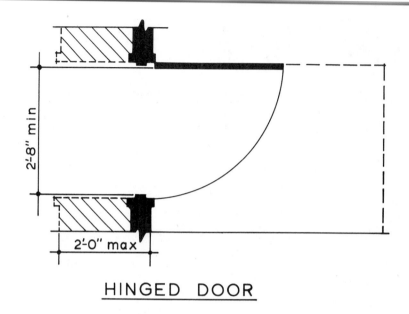

HINGED DOOR

Basis of standard — ANSI 1980 — 4.13.5 and ATBCB § 1190.130	APPLICABILITY			
	ALA	● LA	OHIO	GUAM
	● ALASKA	● MAINE	OKLA	PR
	ARIZ	MD	ORE	VIR IS
Notes — Openings more than 24″ in depth shall be 36″ wide. Texas: 2′-6″ clear door width is permitted if door opening depth is no greater than 8″, door swings open in excess of 90°, and a 5′ x 5′ clear area is provided on each side of doorway. Provide textured border on floor surface in front of dangerous area for openings without doors, 2′-0″ min. wide and long enough to cover the hazardous area.	● ARK	MASS	PA	DC
	CAL	MICH	● RI	
	● COLO	MINN	SC	
	CONN	MISS	SD	● FED'L FUNDS
	● DEL	MO	TENN	
	FLA	MONT	● TEXAS	
	GA	NEB	UTAH	
	● HAWAII	● NEV	● VT	
	● IDAHO	NH	● VA	
	ILL	NJ	WASH	
	IND	● NM	W VA	
	● IOWA	● NY	WIS	OTHER
	KANS	NC	WYO	
	● KY	ND		

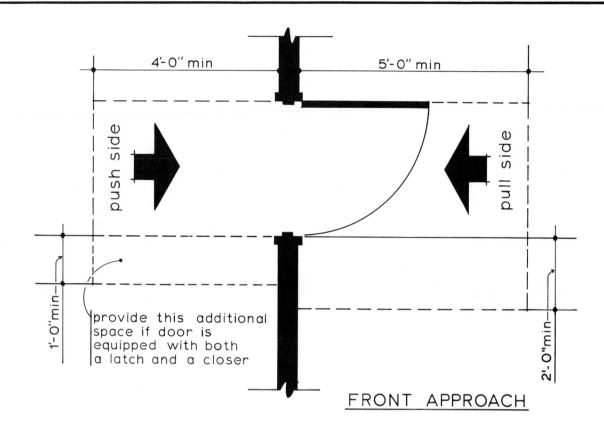

FRONT APPROACH

push side

pull side

4'-0" min

5'-0" min

1'-0" min

2'-0" min

provide this additional
space if door is
equipped with both
a latch and a closer

Basis of standard —	APPLICABILITY			
ANSI 1980 — 4.13.6	ALA	● LA	OHIO	GUAM
	● ALASKA	● MAINE	OKLA	PR
	ARIZ	MD	ORE	VIR IS
Notes —	ARK	MASS	PA	DC
Exemption from 1'-0" and 2'-0" latch side spaces: acute care hospital bedrooms for in-patients if door is at least 44" wide.	CAL	MICH	● RI	
	● COLO	MINN	SC	
	CONN	MISS	SD	FED'L FUNDS
	DEL	MO	TENN	
	FLA	MONT	TEXAS	
	GA	NEB	UTAH	
	● HAWAII	● NEV	● VT	
	● IDAHO	NH	● VA	
	ILL	NJ	WASH	
	IND	● NM	W VA	
	● IOWA	● NY	WIS	OTHER
	KANS	NC	WYO	
	● KY	ND		

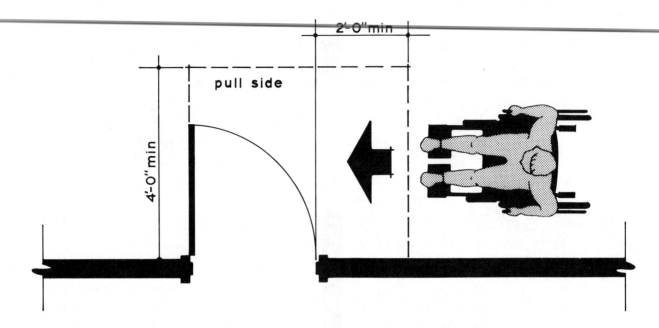

PULL SIDE LATCH APPROACH

Basis of standard —	APPLICABILITY			
ANSI 1980 — 4.13.6 and others	ALA	● LA	OHIO	GUAM
	● ALASKA	● MAINE	OKLA	PR
	ARIZ	MD	ORE	VIR IS
Notes —	● ARK	MASS	PA	DC
Increase 4'-0" min. to 5'-6" min. if door has closer.	CAL	MICH	● RI	
Exemption form 2'-0" latch side space: acute care	● COLO	MINN	SC	
hospital bedrooms for in-patients if door is at least	CONN	MISS	SD	FED'L
44" wide.	● DEL	MO	TENN	FUNDS
Above notes are not applicable in Federal, Arkansas,	FLA	MONT	● TEXAS	●
and Delaware.	GA	NEB	UTAH	
	● HAWAII	● NEV	● VT	
	● IDAHO	NH	● VA	
	ILL	NJ	WASH	
	IND	● NM	W VA	
	● IOWA	● NY	WIS	OTHER
	KANS	NC	WYO	
	● KY	ND		

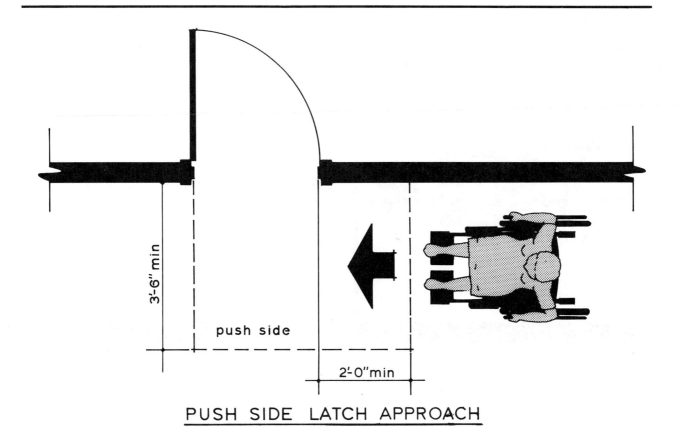

PUSH SIDE LATCH APPROACH

Basis of standard —	APPLICABILITY			
ANSI 1980 — 4.13.6 and others	ALA	● LA	OHIO	GUAM
	● ALASKA	● MAINE	OKLA	PR
	ARIZ	MD	ORE	VIR IS
	ARK	MASS	PA	DC
Notes —	CAL	MICH	● RI	
Increase 3'-6″ to 4'-0″ min. if door has closer. Exemption from 2'-0″ latch side space: acute care hospital bedrooms for in-patients if door is at least 44″ wide.	● COLO	MINN	SC	
	CONN	MISS	SD	FED'L FUNDS
	DEL	MO	TENN	
	FLA	MONT	● TEXAS	
	GA	NEB	UTAH	
	● HAWAII	● NEV	● VT	
	● IDAHO	NH	● VA	
	ILL	NJ	WASH	
	IND	● NM	W VA	
	● IOWA	● NY	WIS	OTHER
	KANS	NC	WYO	
	KY	ND		

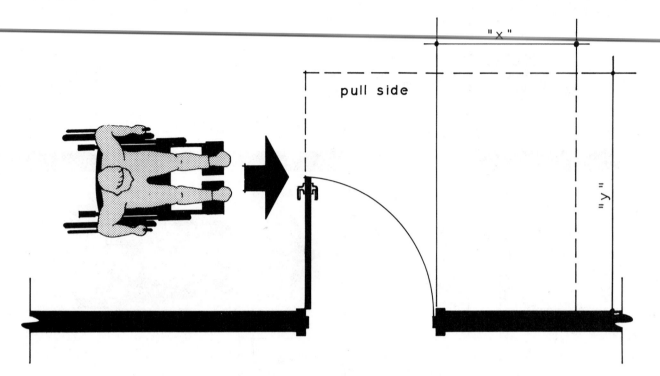

PULL SIDE HINGE APPROACH

Basis of standard —	APPLICABILITY			
ANSI 1980 — 4.13.6 and others	ALA	● LA	OHIO	GUAM
	● ALASKA	● MAINE	OKLA	PR
	ARIZ	MD	ORE	VIR IS
Notes —	ARK	MASS	PA	DC
X = 36″ min. if Y = 60″	CAL	MICH	● RI	
X = 42″ min. if Y = 54″	● COLO	MINN	SC	
Exemption from "X" latch side space: acute care	CONN	MISS	SD	FED'L
hospital bedrooms for in-patients if door is at least	DEL	MO	TENN	FUNDS
44″ wide.	FLA	MONT	● TEXAS	
	GA	NEB	UTAH	
	● HAWAII	● NEV	● VT	
	● IDAHO	NH	● VA	
	ILL	NJ	WASH	
	IND	● NM	W VA	
	● IOWA	● NY	WIS	OTHER
	KANS	NC	WYO	
	KY	ND		

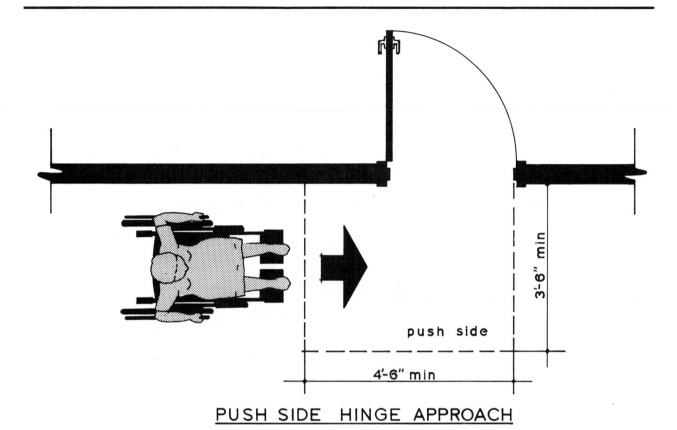

PUSH SIDE HINGE APPROACH

Basis of standard —	APPLICABILITY			
ANSI 1980 — 4.13.6 and others	ALA	● LA	OHIO	GUAM
	● ALASKA	● MAINE	OKLA	PR
	ARIZ	MD	ORE	VIR IS
	ARK	MASS	PA	DC
Notes —	CAL	MICH	● RI	
Increase 3'-6" dimension to 4'-0" min. if door has both latch and closer.	● COLO	MINN	SC	
	CONN	MISS	SD	FED'L
	DEL	MO	TENN	FUNDS
	FLA	MONT	● TEXAS	
	GA	NEB	UTAH	
	● HAWAII	● NEV	● VT	
	● IDAHO	NH	● VA	
	ILL	NJ	WASH	
	IND	● NM	W VA	
	● IOWA	● NY	WIS	OTHER
	KANS	NC	WYO	
	KY	ND		

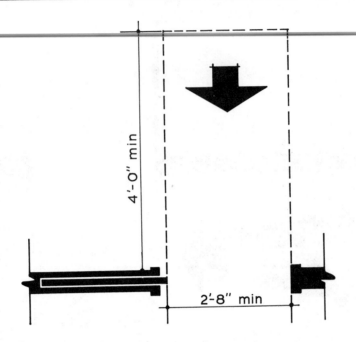

SLIDING DOOR

Basis of standard — ANSI 1980 — 4.13.5 and others	APPLICABILITY			
	ALA	● LA	OHIO	GUAM
	● ALASKA	● MAINE	OKLA	PR
	ARIZ	● MD	ORE	VIR IS
	ARK	MASS	PA	DC
Notes —	● CAL	MICH	● RI	
	● COLO	MINN	SC	
	CONN	MISS	SD	FED'L
	DEL	MO	TENN	FUNDS
	FLA	MONT	● TEXAS	
	GA	NEB	UTAH	
	● HAWAII	● NEV	● VT	
	● IDAHO	NH	● VA	
	ILL	NJ	WASH	
	IND	● NM	W VA	
	● IOWA	● NY	WIS	OTHER
	KANS	NC	WYO	
	● KY	ND		

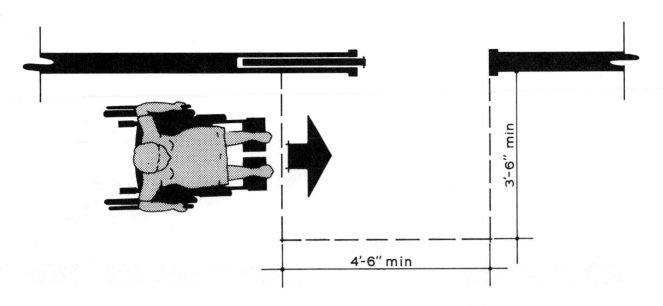

SLIDE SIDE APPROACH   SLIDING DOORS

Basis of standard —	APPLICABILITY			
ANSI 1980 – 4.13.6	ALA	● LA	OHIO	GUAM
	● ALASKA	● MAINE	OKLA	PR
	ARIZ	MD	ORE	VIR IS
	ARK	MASS	PA	DC
Notes —	CAL	MICH	● RI	
	● COLO	MINN	SC	
	CONN	MISS	SD	FED'L
	DEL	MO	TENN	FUNDS
	FLA	MONT	TEXAS	
	GA	NEB	UTAH	
	● HAWAII	● NEV	● VT	
	● IDAHO	NH	● VA	
	ILL	NJ	WASH	
	IND	● NM	W VA	
	● IOWA	● NY	WIS	OTHER
	KANS	NC	WYO	
	● KY	ND		

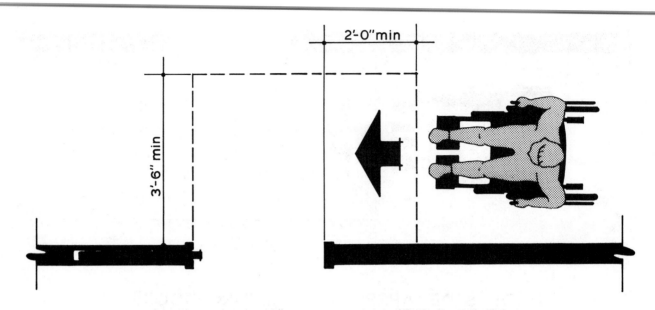

LATCH SIDE APPROACH   SLIDING DOORS

Basis of standard —			APPLICABILITY			
ANSI 1980 — 4.13.6			ALA	● LA	OHIO	GUAM
			● ALASKA	● MAINE	OKLA	PR
			ARIZ	MD	ORE	VIR IS
Notes —			ARK	MASS	PA	DC
Exemption from 2'-0" latch side space: acute care hospital bedrooms for in-patients if door is at least 44" wide.			CAL	MICH	● RI	
			● COLO	MINN	SC	
			CONN	MISS	SD	FED'L FUNDS
			DEL	MO	TENN	
			FLA	MONT	TEXAS	
			GA	NEB	UTAH	
			● HAWAII	● NEV	● VT	
			● IDAHO	NH	● VA	
			ILL	NJ	WASH	
			IND	● NM	W VA	
			● IOWA	● NY	WIS	OTHER
			KANS	NC	WYO	
			● KY	ND		

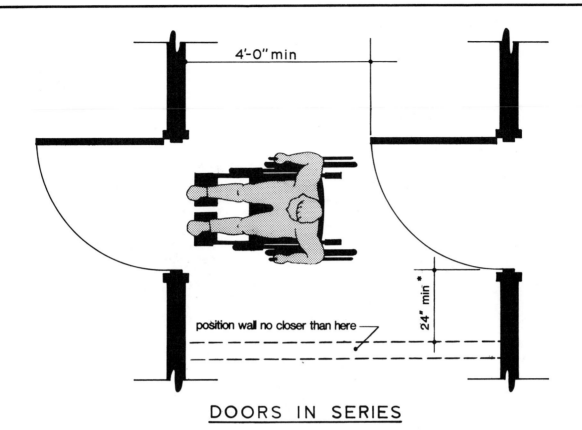

4'-0" min

24" min *

position wall no closer than here

DOORS IN SERIES

Basis of standard —	APPLICABILITY			
ANSI 1980 — 4.13.7 and others	ALA	● LA	OHIO	GUAM
	● ALASKA	● MAINE	OKLA	PR
	ARIZ	MD	ORE	VIR IS
	ARK	MASS	PA	DC
Notes —	● CAL	MICH	● RI	
Swing either in the same direction or away from the space between the doors.	● COLO	MINN	SC	
(*)12″ for Iowa and Texas; 18″ for California.	CONN	MISS	SD	FED'L FUNDS
	DEL	MO	TENN	
	FLA	MONT	● TEXAS	
	GA	NEB	UTAH	
	● HAWAII	● NEV	● VT	
	● IDAHO	NH	● VA	
	ILL	NJ	WASH	
	IND	● NM	W VA	
	● IOWA	● NY	WIS	OTHER
	KANS	NC	WYO	
	● KY	ND		

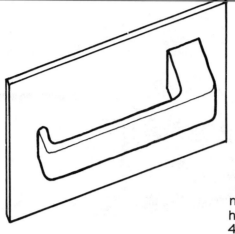

mount no operating
hardware higher than
4'-0" above finished
floor.*

HARDWARE

Basis of standard —	APPLICABILITY			
ANSI 1980 — and others	ALA	● LA	OHIO	GUAM
	● ALASKA	● MAINE	OKLA	PR
	ARIZ	MD	ORE	VIR IS
Notes —	● ARK	MASS	PA	DC
Handles, pulls, locks, latches and other operating devices on accessible doors shall have a shape easy to grasp with one hand without requiring twisting of the wrist, tight grasping or pinching to operate. Acceptable designs include lever operated hardware, push-type mechanisms and U-shaped handles. For sliding doors, operating hardware shall be exposed and usable from both sides when fully open. Federal, Arkansas and Delaware: Hardware 4'-0" above floor (exception: mortise and surface mounted bolts to secure inactive leaf of double leaf door without center mullion may be mounted at any height). (*)California: 3'-8" maximum.	● CAL	MICH	● RI	
	● COLO	MINN	SC	
	CONN	MISS	SD	● FED'L FUNDS
	● DEL	MO	TENN	
	FLA	MONT	TEXAS	
	GA	NEB	UTAH	
	● HAWAII	● NEV	● VT	
	● IDAHO	NH	● VA	
	ILL	NJ	WASH	
	IND	● NM	W VA	
	IOWA	● NY	WIS	OTHER
	KANS	NC	WYO	
	● KY	ND		

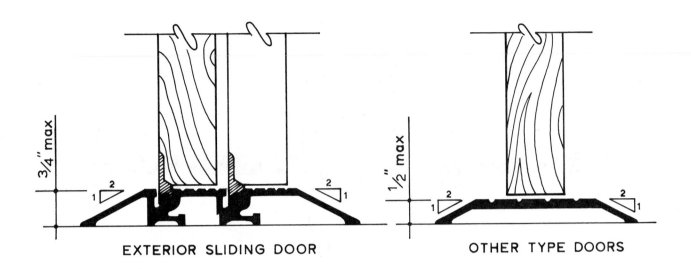

3/4" max

1/2" max

EXTERIOR SLIDING DOOR

OTHER TYPE DOORS

THRESHOLDS AT DOORWAYS

Basis of standard — ANSI 1980 — 4.13.8 and others	APPLICABILITY			
	ALA	● LA	OHIO	GUAM
	● ALASKA	● MAINE	OKLA	PR
	ARIZ	MD	ORE	VIR IS
Notes —	● ARK	MASS	PA	DC
Texas: ¾″ max. height applies when doors remain open during passage such as doors without closers, sliding doors, and automatic doors.	CAL	MICH	● RI	
	● COLO	MINN	SC	
	CONN	MISS	SD	● FED'L FUNDS
	● DEL	MO	TENN	
	FLA	MONT	● TEXAS	
	GA	NEB	UTAH	
	● HAWAII	● NEV	● VT	
	● IDAHO	NH	● VA	
	ILL	NJ	WASH	
	IND	● NM	W VA	
	IOWA	● NY	WIS	OTHER
	KANS	NC	WYO	
	● KY	ND		

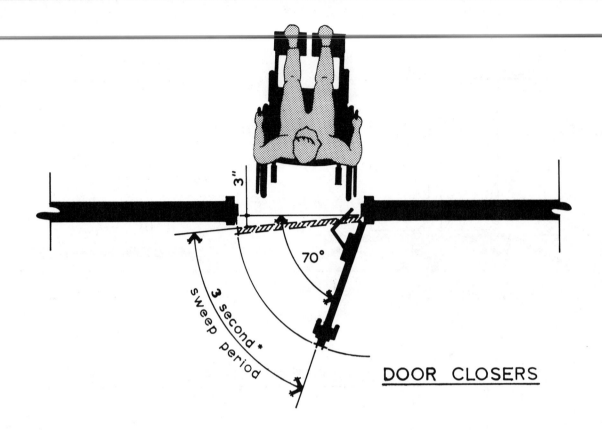

3"

70°

3 second *
sweep period

DOOR CLOSERS

Basis of standard —	APPLICABILITY			
ANSI 1980 — 4.13.10 and others	ALA	● LA	OHIO	GUAM
	● ALASKA	● MAINE	OKLA	PR
	ARIZ	MD	ORE	VIR IS
Notes —	● ARK	MASS	PA	DC
Closing time shown is minimum required.	CAL	MICH	● RI	
(*)Federal, Delaware, and Arkansas: 5 second sweep	● COLO	MINN	SC	
period.	CONN	MISS	SD	● FED'L FUNDS
	● DEL	MO	TENN	
	FLA	MONT	● TEXAS	
	GA	NEB	UTAH	
	● HAWAII	● NEV	● VT	
	● IDAHO	NH	● VA	
	ILL	NJ	WASH	
	IND	● NM	W VA	
	IOWA	● NY	WIS	OTHER
	KANS	NC	WYO	
	● KY	ND		

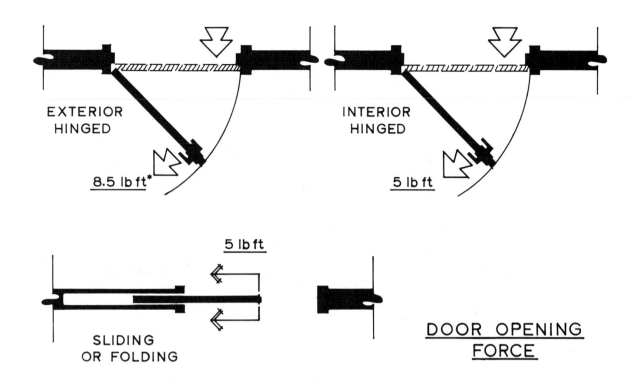

EXTERIOR HINGED

8.5 lb ft*

INTERIOR HINGED

5 lb ft

5 lb ft

SLIDING OR FOLDING

DOOR OPENING FORCE

Basis of standard — ANSI 1980 — 4.13.11 and others	APPLICABILITY			
	ALA	● LA	OHIO	GUAM
	● ALASKA	● MAINE	OKLA	PR
	ARIZ	MD	ORE	VIR IS
	● ARK	MASS	PA	DC
	● CAL	MICH	● RI	
	● COLO	MINN	SC	
	CONN	MISS	SD	● FED'L FUNDS
	● DEL	MO	TENN	
	FLA	MONT	● TEXAS	
	GA	NEB	UTAH	
	● HAWAII	● NEV	● VT	
	● IDAHO	NH	● VA	
	ILL	NJ	WASH	
	IND	● NM	W VA	
	IOWA	● NY	WIS	OTHER
	KANS	NC	WYO	
	● KY	ND		

Notes —

Forces shown are maximum to push or pull a door open. Fire doors shall have the minimum opening force allowable by the appropriate administrative authority.
(*)Not applicable to Federal, Delaware, or Arkansas.

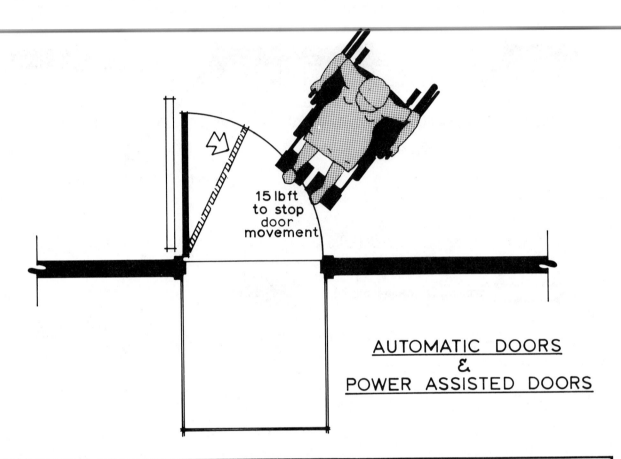

AUTOMATIC DOORS
&
POWER ASSISTED DOORS

Basis of standard —		APPLICABILITY			
ANSI 1980 — 4.13.12 and others		ALA	● LA	OHIO	GUAM
		● ALASKA	● MAINE	OKLA	PR
		ARIZ	MD	ORE	VIR IS
		● ARK	MASS	PA	DC
Notes —		CAL	MICH	● RI	
Comply with provisions of ANSI A 156.10 — 1979. Slowly opening, low-powered, automatic doors shall not open to backcheck faster than 3 seconds. 15 lb. ft. to stop doors applies to automatic doors. (Federal, Delaware and Arkansas requirements: comply with ANSI A 156.10 — latest edition; no opening to backcheck in less than 5 seconds; max. 150 lbs. to stop door movement.)		● COLO	MINN	SC	
		CONN	MISS	SD	● FED'L FUNDS
		● DEL	MO	TENN	
		FLA	MONT	TEXAS	
		GA	NEB	UTAH	
		● HAWAII	● NEV	● VT	
		● IDAHO	NH	● VA	
		ILL	NJ	WASH	
		IND	● NM	W VA	
		IOWA	● NY	WIS	OTHER
		KANS	NC	WYO	
		● KY	ND		

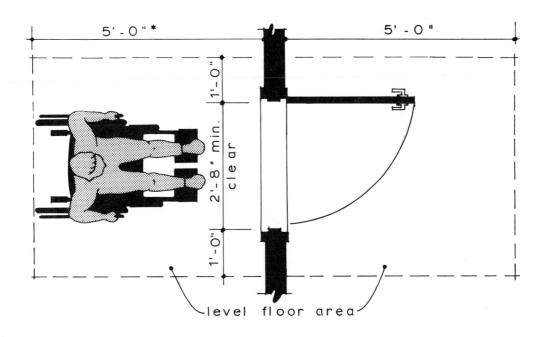

Basis of standard —	APPLICABILITY			
ANSI 1961 — 5.3	ALA	LA	OHIO	GUAM
	ALASKA	MAINE	● OKLA	PR
	ARIZ	MD	ORE	VIR IS
Notes —	ARK	MASS	PA	DC
Doors shall be operable by a single effort. (Two leaf doors are not usable by those with disabilities unless they operate by a single effort or unless one of the leaves is at least in conformance with the above diagram.) Avoid sharp inclines and abrupt level changes at doorsills. As much as possible, thresholds shall be flush with floor. Data applies to interior and exterior doorways. Conforming automatic doors are acceptable. Provide 16″ high kickplates or make doors to safely withstand damage from crutches, wheelchairs, etc. (*)May be 3′-0″ in W. Va.	CAL	MICH	RI	
	COLO	MINN	● SC	
	CONN	MISS	● SD	FED'L FUNDS
	DEL	MO	TENN	
	● FLA	MONT	TEXAS	
	● GA	NEB	UTAH	
	HAWAII	NEV	VT	
	IDAHO	NH	VA	
	ILL	NJ	WASH	
	IND	NM	● W VA	
	IOWA	NY	WIS	OTHER
	● KANS	NC	WYO	
	KY	● ND		

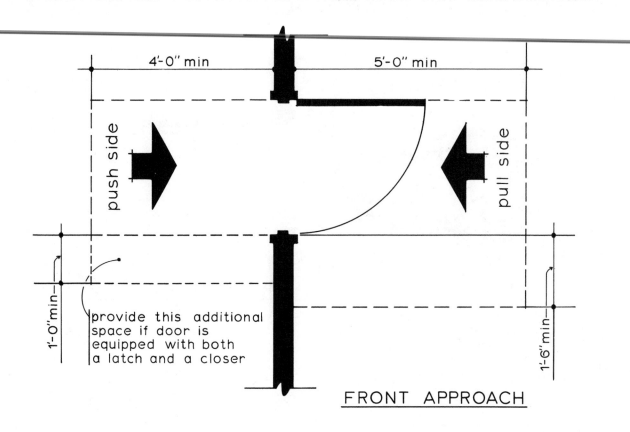

4'-0" min

5'-0" min

push side

pull side

1'-0" min

provide this additional
space if door is
equipped with both
a latch and a closer

1'-6" min

FRONT APPROACH

Basis of standard —	APPLICABILITY			
ATBCB § 1190.130 and others	ALA	LA	OHIO	GUAM
	ALASKA	MAINE	OKLA	PR
	ARIZ	MD	ORE	VIR IS
Notes —	● ARK	MASS	PA	DC
Exemption from 1'-6" latch side space: acute care hospital bedrooms if door is at least 3'-8" wide (not applicable to Texas).	CAL	MICH	RI	
	COLO	MINN	SC	
	CONN	MISS	SD	● FED'L FUNDS
	● DEL	MO	TENN	
	FLA	MONT	● TEXAS	
	GA	NEB	UTAH	
	HAWAII	NEV	VT	
	IDAHO	NH	VA	
	ILL	NJ	WASH	
	IND	NM	W VA	
	IOWA	NY	WIS	OTHER
	KANS	NC	WYO	
	KY	ND		

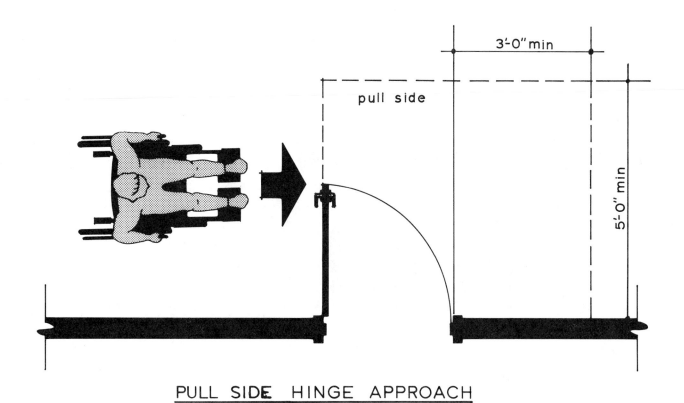

PULL SIDE HINGE APPROACH

Basis of standard — ATBCB § 1190.130 and others	APPLICABILITY			
	ALA	LA	OHIO	GUAM
	ALASKA	MAINE	OKLA	PR
	ARIZ	MD	ORE	VIR IS
Notes — Michigan: Entrance doors only.	● ARK	MASS	PA	DC
	CAL	● MICH	RI	
	COLO	MINN	SC	
	CONN	MISS	SD	● FED'L FUNDS
	● DEL	MO	TENN	
	FLA	MONT	TEXAS	
	GA	NEB	UTAH	
	HAWAII	NEV	VT	
	IDAHO	NH	VA	
	ILL	NJ	WASH	
	IND	NM	W VA	
	IOWA	NY	WIS	OTHER
	KANS	NC	WYO	
	KY	ND		

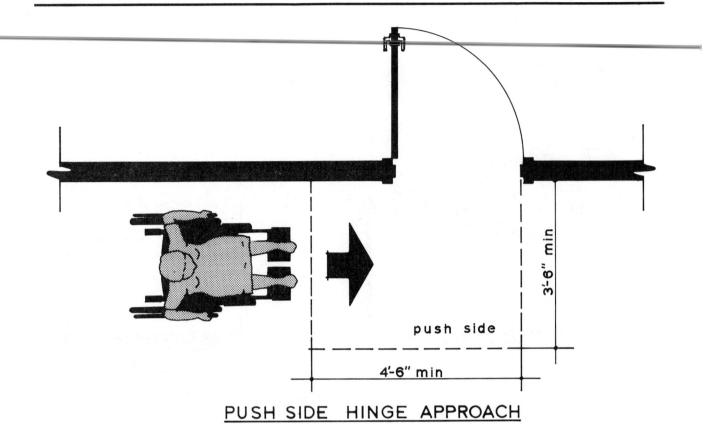

PUSH SIDE HINGE APPROACH

Basis of standard — ATBCB § 1190.130	APPLICABILITY			
	ALA	LA	OHIO	GUAM
	ALASKA	MAINE	OKLA	PR
	ARIZ	MD	ORE	VIR IS
● ARK	MASS	PA	DC
	CAL	MICH	RI	
	COLO	MINN	SC	
	CONN	MISS	SD	● FED'L FUNDS
● DEL	MO	TENN	
	FLA	MONT	TEXAS	
	GA	NEB	UTAH	
	HAWAII	NEV	VT	
	IDAHO	NH	VA	
	ILL	NJ	WASH	
	IND	NM	W VA	
	IOWA	NY	WIS	OTHER
	KANS	NC	WYO	
	KY	ND		

Notes —

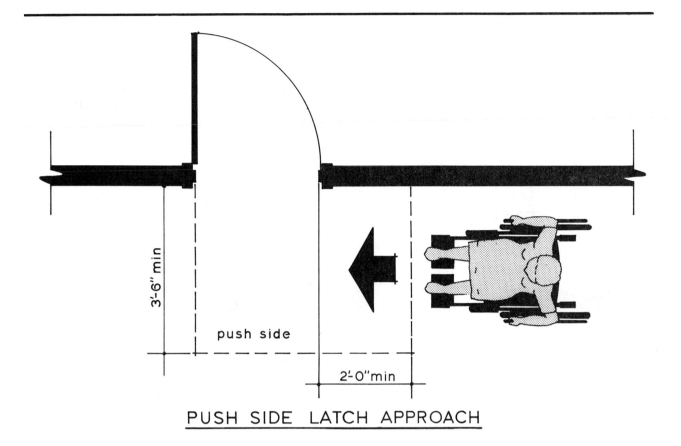

PUSH SIDE LATCH APPROACH

Basis of standard — ATBCB § 1190.130 and others	APPLICABILITY			
	ALA	LA	OHIO	GUAM
	ALASKA	MAINE	OKLA	PR
	ARIZ	MD	ORE	VIR IS
● ARK	MASS	PA	DC
Notes —	● ARK	MASS	PA	DC
	CAL	MICH	RI	
	COLO	MINN	SC	
	CONN	MISS	SD	● FED'L FUNDS
	● DEL	MO	TENN	
	FLA	MONT	TEXAS	
	GA	NEB	UTAH	
	HAWAII	NEV	VT	
	IDAHO	NH	VA	
	ILL	NJ	WASH	
	IND	NM	W VA	
	IOWA	NY	WIS	OTHER
	KANS	NC	WYO	
	KY	ND		

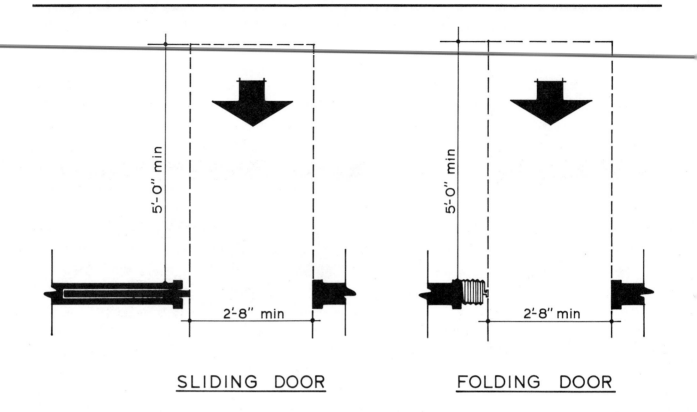

SLIDING DOOR   FOLDING DOOR

Basis of standard — ATBCB § 1190.130 and others	APPLICABILITY			
	ALA	LA	OHIO	GUAM
	ALASKA	MAINE	OKLA	PR
	ARIZ	MD	ORE	VIR IS
Notes — ● ARK	MASS	PA	DC
5'-0" dimension applies to front approach.	CAL	MICH	RI	
	COLO	MINN	SC	
	CONN	MISS	SD	
	● DEL	MO	TENN	● FED'L FUNDS
	FLA	MONT	TEXAS	
	GA	NEB	UTAH	
	HAWAII	NEV	VT	
	IDAHO	NH	VA	
	ILL	NJ	WASH	
	IND	NM	W VA	
	IOWA	NY	WIS	OTHER
	KANS	NC	WYO	
	KY	ND		

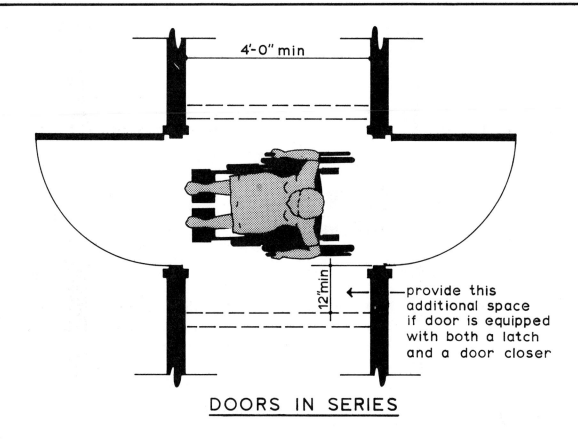

4'-0" min

12" min

provide this
additional space
if door is equipped
with both a latch
and a door closer

DOORS IN SERIES

Basis of standard —	APPLICABILITY			
ATBCB § 1190.130 and others	ALA	LA	OHIO	GUAM
	ALASKA	MAINE	OKLA	PR
	ARIZ	MD	ORE	VIR IS
	● ARK	MASS	PA	DC
Notes —	CAL	MICH	RI	
Opposing doors shall not swing towards each other into the intervening space.	COLO	MINN	SC	
	CONN	MISS	SD	● FED'L FUNDS
	● DEL	MO	TENN	
	FLA	MONT	TEXAS	
	GA	NEB	UTAH	
	HAWAII	NEV	VT	
	IDAHO	NH	VA	
	ILL	NJ	WASH	
	IND	NM	W VA	
	● IOWA	NY	WIS	OTHER
	KANS	NC	WYO	
	KY	ND		

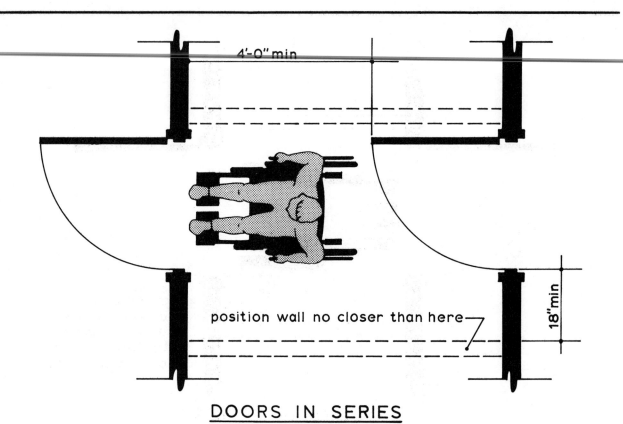

4'-0" min

position wall no closer than here

18"min

DOORS IN SERIES

Basis of standard — ATBCB § 1190.130 and others	APPLICABILITY			
	ALA	LA	OHIO	GUAM
	ALASKA	MAINE	OKLA	PR
	ARIZ	MD	ORE	VIR IS
● ARK	MASS	PA	DC
	CAL	MICH	RI	
	COLO	MINN	SC	
	CONN	MISS	SD	● FED'L FUNDS
● DEL	MO	TENN	
	FLA	MONT	TEXAS	
	GA	NEB	UTAH	
	HAWAII	NEV	VT	
	IDAHO	NH	VA	
● ILL	NJ	WASH	
	IND	NM	W VA	
	IOWA	NY	WIS	OTHER
	KANS	NC	WYO	
	KY	ND		

Notes —
Opposing doors shall not swing towards each other into the intervening space.
Illinois: Hinge single doors hung in series on same side.

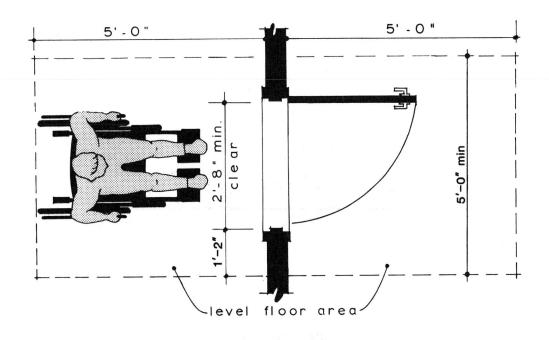

5' - 0"

5' - 0"

2' - 8" min. clear

1'-2"

5'-0" min

level floor area

Basis of standard — BOCA 1978	APPLICABILITY			
	ALA	LA	● OHIO	GUAM
	ALASKA	MAINE	OKLA	PR
	ARIZ	MD	ORE	VIR IS
Notes —	ARK	MASS	PA	DC
Ohio: max. slope in any direction for grade floor exitways 1:50 in any direction; center level area in doorway. Where changes in elevation exist in exitway access corridors, exitways or exitway discharge, use ramps when difference in elevation is less than 12″. 8″ max. step down is permitted by BOCA for exterior doors not required for the physically handicapped and aged.	CAL	MICH	RI	
	COLO	MINN	SC	
	CONN	MISS	SD	FED'L FUNDS
	DEL	MO	TENN	
	FLA	MONT	TEXAS	
	GA	NEB	UTAH	
	HAWAII	NEV	VT	
	IDAHO	NH	VA	
	ILL	NJ	WASH	
	IND	NM	W VA	
	IOWA	NY	WIS	
	KANS	NC	WYO	OTHER
	KY	ND		

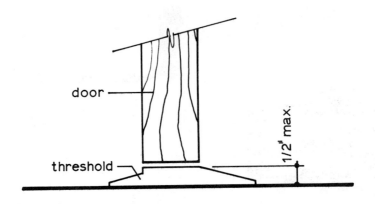

door

threshold

1/2" max.

DOORWAY GRADING

Basis of standard —	APPLICABILITY			
BOCA 1978 and others	ALA	LA	● OHIO	GUAM
	ALASKA	MAINE	OKLA	PR
	ARIZ	● MD	ORE	VIR IS
Notes —	ARK	MASS	PA	DC
Detail applies to grade floor exitways.	CAL	MICH	RI	
Florida: Applies to non-government financed facilities.	COLO	MINN	SC	
	CONN	MISS	SD	FED'L
	DEL	MO	TENN	FUNDS
	● FLA	MONT	TEXAS	
	GA	NEB	UTAH	
	HAWAII	NEV	VT	
	IDAHO	NH	VA	
	ILL	NJ	WASH	
	IND	NM	W VA	
	IOWA	NY	WIS	OTHER
	KANS	NC	WYO	
	KY	ND		

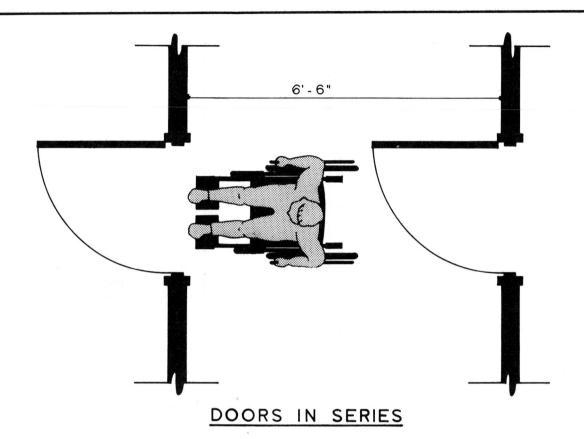

DOORS IN SERIES

Basis of standard —	APPLICABILITY			
North Carolina State Building Code and various others.	● ALA	LA	OHIO	GUAM
	ALASKA	MAINE	OKLA	PR
	ARIZ	MD	ORE	VIR IS
Notes —	ARK	MASS	PA	DC
Depth may be 5'-0″ in Utah if both doors swing out of the vestibule. Applies to doors other than those which are electronically controlled in Wisconsin.	CAL	MICH	RI	
	COLO	MINN	● SC	
	CONN	MISS	SD	FED'L FUNDS
	DEL	MO	● TENN	
	FLA	MONT	TEXAS	
	GA	NEB	● UTAH	
	HAWAII	NEV	VT	
	IDAHO	NH	VA	
	ILL	NJ	WASH	
	IND	NM	● W VA	
	IOWA	NY	● WIS	OTHER
	KANS	● NC	WYO	
	KY	ND		

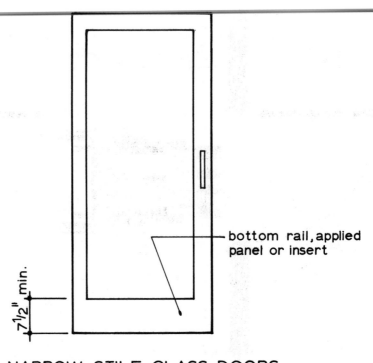

bottom rail, applied
panel or insert

7½" min.

NARROW STILE GLASS DOORS

Basis of standard —	APPLICABILITY			
North Carolina State Building Code and others	ALA	LA	OHIO	GUAM
	ALASKA	MAINE	OKLA	PR
	ARIZ	MD	ORE	VIR IS
Notes —	ARK	MASS	PA	DC
	CAL	MICH	RI	
	COLO	MINN	SC	
	CONN	MISS	SD	FED'L
	DEL	MO	● TENN	FUNDS
	FLA	MONT	TEXAS	
	GA	NEB	UTAH	
	HAWAII	NEV	VT	
	IDAHO	NH	● VA	
	ILL	NJ	WASH	
	IND	NM	W VA	
	IOWA	NY	WIS	OTHER
	KANS	● NC	WYO	
	● KY	ND		

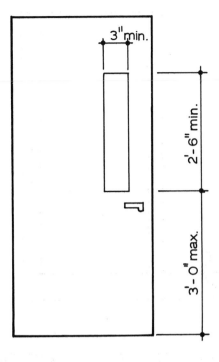

VISION PANELS

Basis of standard —	APPLICABILITY			
North Carolina State Building Code and others	ALA	LA	OHIO	GUAM
	ALASKA	MAINE	OKLA	PR
	ARIZ	MD	ORE	VIR IS
Notes —	ARK	MASS	PA	DC
	CAL	MICH	RI	
	COLO	MINN	SC	
	CONN	MISS	SD	FED'L
	DEL	MO	● TENN	FUNDS
	FLA	MONT	TEXAS	
	GA	NEB	● UTAH	
	HAWAII	NEV	VT	
	IDAHO	NH	VA	
	ILL	● NJ	WASH	
	IND	NM	W VA	
	IOWA	NY	WIS	OTHER
	KANS	● NC	WYO	
	KY	ND		

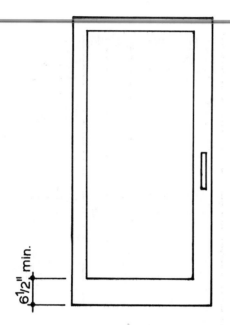

6½" min.

STILE AND RAIL GLASS DOORS

Basis of standard — Utah State Building Board and others	APPLICABILITY			
	ALA	LA	OHIO	GUAM
	ALASKA	MAINE	OKLA	PR
	ARIZ	MD	ORE	VIR IS
Notes —	ARK	MASS	PA	DC
Preferred kickplate: 8″ high.	CAL	MICH	RI	
Exceptions: fully automatic doors.	COLO	MINN	SC	
Wyoming requires 16″ high kickplate.	CONN	MISS	SD	FED'L
Illinois requires 10″ high smooth uninterrupted	DEL	MO	TENN	FUNDS
bottom of doors (automatic doors are exempted).	FLA	MONT	TEXAS	
	GA	NEB	● UTAH	
	HAWAII	NEV	VT	
	IDAHO	NH	VA	
	● ILL	NJ	WASH	
	IND	NM	W VA	
	IOWA	NY	WIS	OTHER
	KANS	NC	● WYO	
	KY	ND		

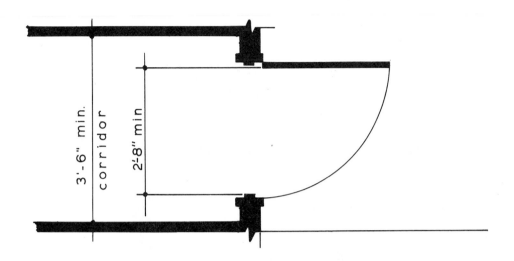

HINGED DOOR

Basis of standard — North Carolina State Building Code	APPLICABILITY			
	ALA	LA	OHIO	GUAM
	ALASKA	MAINE	OKLA	PR
	ARIZ	MD	ORE	VIR IS
Notes — Doors operate by single effort. Max. pressure required for door closers = 15 lbs. Two leaf doors are not usable unless they meet above requirements and one leaf provides min. 2′-8″ clear opening. Floor on inside and outside of doorway to be level min. 5′ from door and extend one foot beyond side from which door opens. Exterior thresholds max. edge height = ¾″ and beveled. Interior thresholds to be flush with floor or beveled at max. 5% slope with max. edge height of ½″.	ARK	MASS	PA	DC
	CAL	MICH	RI	
	COLO	MINN	SC	
	CONN	MISS	SD	FED'L FUNDS
	DEL	MO	● TENN	
	FLA	MONT	TEXAS	
	GA	NEB	UTAH	
	HAWAII	NEV	VT	
	IDAHO	NH	● VA	
	ILL	NJ	WASH	
	IND	NM	W VA	
	IOWA	NY	WIS	OTHER
	KANS	● NC	WYO	
	KY	ND		

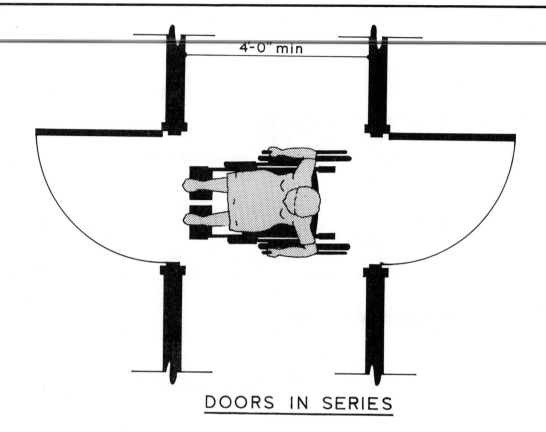

4'-0" min

DOORS IN SERIES

Basis of standard — Structural Specialty Code and others	APPLICABILITY			
	ALA	LA	OHIO	GUAM
	ALASKA	MAINE	OKLA	PR
	ARIZ	● MD	● ORE	VIR IS
Notes — Oregon: when providing access for the physically handicapped, self-closing exit doors shall be openable with 8 lbs. max. force. Self-opening devices are preferable. Protect bottom 18″ of door with a kickplate. Max. threshold height: ½″. Exception: when door opens onto a stair landing, conform to UBC Sec. 3305(g). Identify doors and exitways suitable for use by the handicapped.	ARK	MASS	PA	DC
	CAL	MICH	RI	
	COLO	MINN	SC	
	CONN	MISS	SD	FED'L FUNDS
	DEL	MO	TENN	
	FLA	MONT	TEXAS	
	GA	NEB	UTAH	
	HAWAII	NEV	VT	
	IDAHO	NH	VA	
	ILL	NJ	WASH	
	IND	NM	W VA	
	IOWA	NY	WIS	OTHER
	KANS	NC	WYO	
	KY	ND		

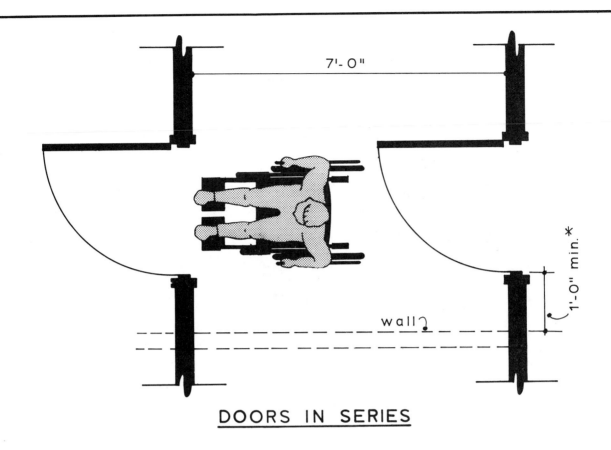

DOORS IN SERIES

Basis of standard — State Building Code and others	APPLICABILITY			
	ALA	LA	OHIO	GUAM
	ALASKA	MAINE	OKLA	PR
	ARIZ	MD	ORE	VIR IS
Notes — (*)2'-0" at primary public entrance in New Hampshire.	ARK	MASS	PA	DC
	CAL	MICH	RI	
	COLO	● MINN	SC	
	CONN	MISS	SD	FED'L FUNDS
	DEL	MO	TENN	
	FLA	MONT	TEXAS	
	GA	NEB	UTAH	
	HAWAII	NEV	VT	
	IDAHO	● NH	VA	
	ILL	NJ	WASH	
	IND	NM	W VA	
	IOWA	NY	WIS	OTHER
	KANS	NC	WYO	
	KY	ND		

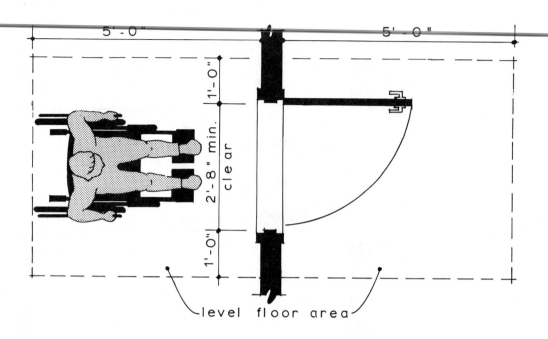

5'-0"   5'-0"

1'-0"

2'-8" min. clear

1'-0"

level floor area

Basis of standard — State Building Code and others	APPLICABILITY			
	ALA	LA	OHIO	GUAM
	ALASKA	MAINE	OKLA	PR
	ARIZ	MD	ORE	VIR IS
	ARK	MASS	PA	DC
Notes — For Missouri: provide at least one public entrance conforming to data in diagram; data applies to public doors which shall be operable by a single effort.	CAL	MICH	● RI	
	COLO	MINN	SC	
	CONN	MISS	SD	FED'L FUNDS
	DEL	● MO	TENN	
	FLA	MONT	TEXAS	
	GA	NEB	UTAH	
	HAWAII	NEV	VT	
	IDAHO	NH	VA	
	ILL	NJ	WASH	
	IND	NM	W VA	
	IOWA	NY	WIS	OTHER
	KANS	NC	WYO	
	KY	ND		

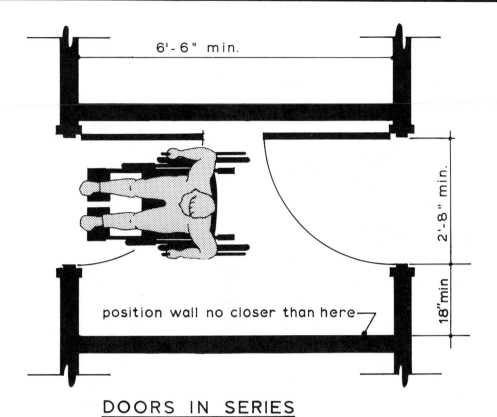

DOORS IN SERIES

Basis of standard —	APPLICABILITY			
Barrier Free Design and others	ALA	LA	OHIO	GUAM
	ALASKA	MAINE	OKLA	PR
	ARIZ	MD	ORE	VIR IS
Notes —	ARK	MASS	PA	DC
New Jersey: all doors shall swing in same direction.	CAL	MICH	RI	
	COLO	MINN	● SC	
	CONN	MISS	SD	FED'L
	DEL	MO	TENN	FUNDS
	FLA	MONT	TEXAS	
	GA	NEB	UTAH	
	HAWAII	NEV	VT	
	IDAHO	NH	VA	
	ILL	● NJ	WASH	
	IND	NM	W VA	
	IOWA	NY	WIS	OTHER
	KANS	NC	WYO	
	KY	ND		

The diagram labels read: 6'-6" min. (top width), 2'-8" min. and 18" min. (right side), and "position wall no closer than here".

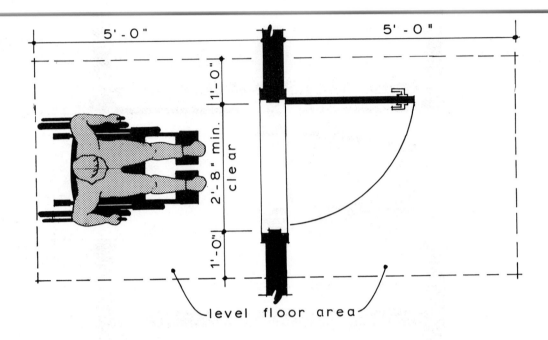

level floor area

Basis of standard —	APPLICABILITY			
Standards for Making Public Facilities Accessible to the Physically Handicapped (N.M.) and others.	ALA	LA	OHIO	GUAM
	ALASKA	MAINE	OKLA	PR
	ARIZ	MD	ORE	VIR IS
	ARK	MASS	● PA	DC
	CAL	MICH	RI	
Notes —	COLO	MINN	SC	
Avoid sharp inclines and abrupt level changes. Thresholds shall be flush with floor as much as possible.	CONN	MISS	SD	FED'L FUNDS
	DEL	MO	TENN	
	FLA	MONT	TEXAS	
	GA	NEB	UTAH	
	HAWAII	NEV	VT	
	IDAHO	NH	VA	
	ILL	NJ	WASH	
	IND	● NM	W VA	
	IOWA	NY	WIS	OTHER
	KANS	NC	WYO	
	KY	ND		

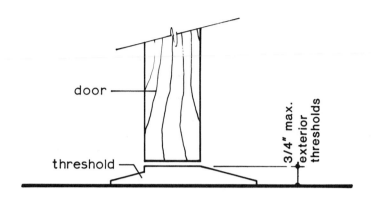

door

threshold

3/4" max. exterior thresholds

DOORWAY GRADING

Basis of standard —	APPLICABILITY			
North Carolina State Building Code	ALA	LA	OHIO	GUAM
	ALASKA	MAINE	OKLA	PR
	ARIZ	MD	ORE	VIR IS
Notes —	ARK	MASS	PA	DC
(*)Interior thresholds shall be flush with floor or beveled 5% max. slope with a max. height of 1".	CAL	MICH	RI	
	COLO	MINN	SC	
	CONN	MISS	SD	FED'L FUNDS
	DEL	MO	● TENN	
	FLA	MONT	TEXAS	
	GA	NEB	UTAH	
	HAWAII	NEV	VT	
	IDAHO	NH	VA	
	ILL	NJ	WASH	
	IND	NM	W VA	
	IOWA	NY	WIS	OTHER
	KANS	● NC	WYO	
	KY	ND		

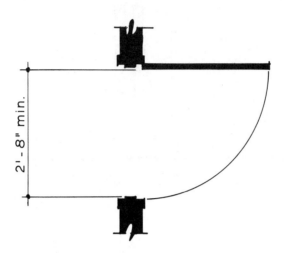

HINGED DOOR

Basis of standard — Barrier Free Design Standard	APPLICABILITY			
	● ALA	LA	OHIO	GUAM
	ALASKA	MAINE	OKLA	PR
	ARIZ	MD	ORE	VIR IS
Notes —	ARK	MASS	PA	DC
Doors to operate by single effort. Max. pressure required (including closer) = 8 lbs. Time delay of closing mechanism = 4 to 6 seconds. Two leaf doors not acceptable unless they meet above requirements and one leaf provides min. 2'-8" clear opening. Floor on inside and outside of doorway to be level min. 5' from door swing and 1' beyond each side of door. Thresholds to be flush with floor or beveled both sides with max. 8% slope. Automatic doors are desirable. Sliding doors are acceptable (avoid recessed handles).	CAL	MICH	RI	
	COLO	MINN	SC	
	CONN	MISS	SD	FED'L
	DEL	MO	TENN	FUNDS
	FLA	MONT	TEXAS	
	GA	NEB	UTAH	
	HAWAII	NEV	VT	
	IDAHO	NH	VA	
	ILL	NJ	WASH	
	IND	NM	W VA	
	IOWA	NY	WIS	OTHER
	KANS	NC	WYO	
	KY	ND		

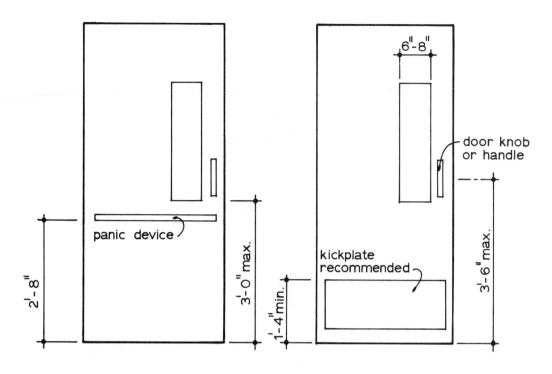

VISION PANELS AND HARDWARE

Basis of standard —	APPLICABILITY			
Barrier Free Design Standard	● ALA	LA	OHIO	GUAM
	ALASKA	MAINE	OKLA	PR
	ARIZ	MD	ORE	VIR IS
Notes —	ARK	MASS	PA	DC
Provide vision panel at all swinging doors. Knurl door handles and knobs in danger areas as warning to the blind.	CAL	MICH	RI	
	COLO	MINN	SC	
	CONN	MISS	SD	FED'L
	DEL	MO	TENN	FUNDS
	FLA	MONT	TEXAS	
	GA	NEB	UTAH	
	HAWAII	NEV	VT	
	IDAHO	NH	VA	
	ILL	NJ	WASH	
	IND	NM	W VA	
	IOWA	NY	WIS	OTHER
	KANS	NC	WYO	
	KY	ND		

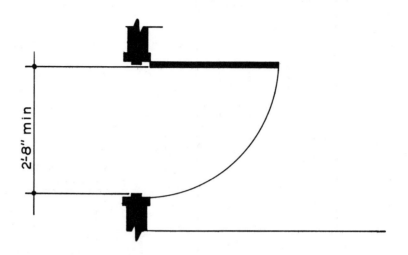

2'-8" min

HINGED DOOR

Basis of standard —	APPLICABILITY			
Arizona Revised Statutes	ALA	LA	OHIO	GUAM
	ALASKA	MAINE	OKLA	PR
	● ARIZ	MD	ORE	VIR IS
Notes —	ARK	MASS	PA	DC
Floor on inside and outside of each doorway shall be level 5′ from the door in the direction the door swings and shall extend one foot beyond each side of door. Avoid sharp inclines and abrupt level changes at door sills. Thresholds shall be flush with floor as much as practicable. Doors to be operable by a single effort. Avoid low-hanging door closers within the opening of a doorway when the door is open or that protrude hazardously into regular corridors or traffic ways when the door is closed.	CAL	MICH	RI	
	COLO	MINN	SC	
	CONN	MISS	SD	FED'L FUNDS
	DEL	MO	TENN	
	FLA	MONT	TEXAS	
	GA	NEB	UTAH	
	HAWAII	NEV	VT	
	IDAHO	NH	VA	
	ILL	NJ	WASH	
	IND	NM	W VA	
	IOWA	NY	WIS	OTHER
	KANS	NC	WYO	
	KY	ND		

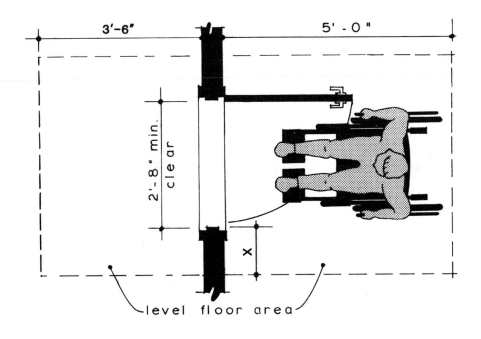

level floor area

Basis of standard —	APPLICABILITY			
CAC Title 24, Part 2	ALA	LA	OHIO	GUAM
	ALASKA	MAINE	OKLA	PR
	ARIZ	MD	ORE	VIR IS
Notes —	ARK	MASS	PA	DC
"X" = 24″ for exterior doors; 18″ for interior doors.	● CAL	MICH	RI	
	COLO	MINN	SC	
	CONN	MISS	SD	FED'L FUNDS
	DEL	MO	TENN	
	FLA	MONT	TEXAS	
	GA	NEB	UTAH	
	HAWAII	NEV	VT	
	IDAHO	NH	VA	
	ILL	NJ	WASH	
	IND	NM	W VA	
	IOWA	NY	WIS	OTHER
	KANS	NC	WYO	
	KY	ND		

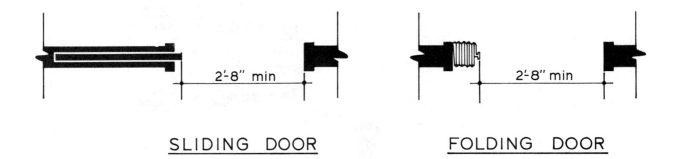

SLIDING   DOOR   FOLDING   DOOR

Basis of standard —	APPLICABILITY			
CAC Title 24, Part 2	ALA	LA	OHIO	GUAM
	ALASKA	MAINE	OKLA	PR
	ARIZ	MD	ORE	VIR IS
Notes —	ARK	MASS	PA	DC
	● CAL	MICH	RI	
	COLO	MINN	SC	
	CONN	MISS	SD	FED'L
	DEL	MO	TENN	FUNDS
	FLA	MONT	TEXAS	
	GA	NEB	UTAH	
	HAWAII	NEV	VT	
	IDAHO	NH	VA	
	ILL	NJ	WASH	
	IND	NM	W VA	
	IOWA	NY	WIS	OTHER
	KANS	NC	WYO	
	KY	ND		

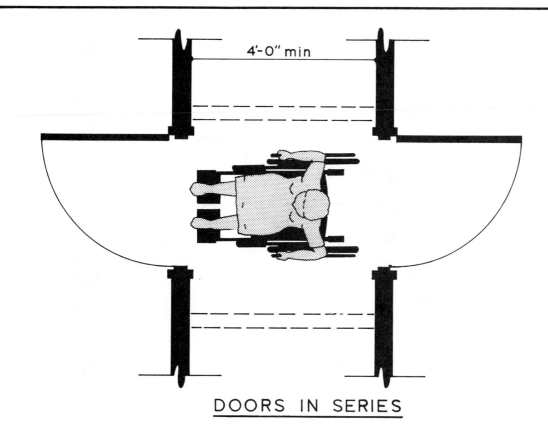

DOORS IN SERIES

Basis of standard — CAC Title 24, Part 2	APPLICABILITY			
	ALA	LA	OHIO	GUAM
	ALASKA	MAINE	OKLA	PR
	ARIZ	MD	ORE	VIR IS
Notes —	ARK	MASS	PA	DC
	● CAL	MICH	RI	
	COLO	MINN	SC	
	CONN	MISS	SD	FED'L FUNDS
	DEL	MO	TENN	
	FLA	MONT	TEXAS	
	GA	NEB	UTAH	
	HAWAII	NEV	VT	
	IDAHO	NH	VA	
	ILL	NJ	WASH	
	IND	NM	W VA	
	IOWA	NY	WIS	OTHER
	KANS	NC	WYO	
	KY	ND		

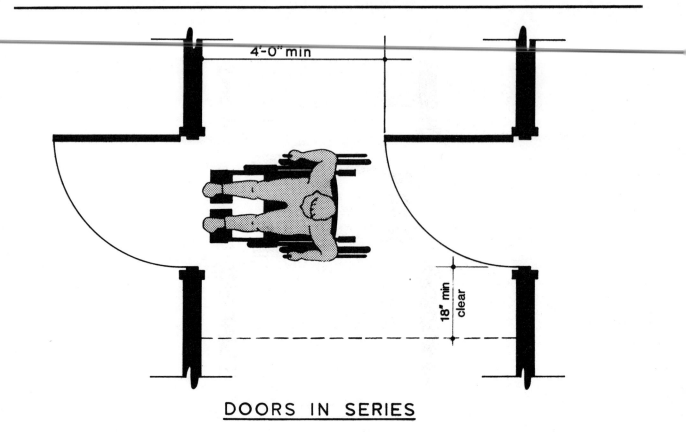

4'-0" min

18" min clear

DOORS IN SERIES

Basis of standard — CAC Title 24, Part 2	APPLICABILITY			
	ALA	LA	OHIO	GUAM
	ALASKA	MAINE	OKLA	PR
	ARIZ	MD	ORE	VIR IS
	ARK	MASS	PA	DC
Notes —	● CAL	MICH	RI	
	COLO	MINN	SC	
	CONN	MISS	SD	FED'L FUNDS
	DEL	MO	TENN	
	FLA	MONT	TEXAS	
	GA	NEB	UTAH	
	HAWAII	NEV	VT	
	IDAHO	NH	VA	
	ILL	NJ	WASH	
	IND	NM	W VA	
	IOWA	NY	WIS	OTHER
	KANS	NC	WYO	
	KY	ND		

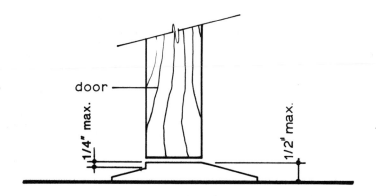

THRESHOLDS

Basis of standard — CAC Title 24, Part 2	APPLICABILITY			
	ALA	LA	OHIO	GUAM
	ALASKA	MAINE	OKLA	PR
	ARIZ	MD	ORE	VIR IS
Notes — Maximum vertical face on a threshold shall be ¼″.	ARK	MASS	PA	DC
	● CAL	MICH	RI	
	COLO	MINN	SC	
	CONN	MISS	SD	FED'L FUNDS
	DEL	MO	TENN	
	FLA	MONT	TEXAS	
	GA	NEB	UTAH	
	HAWAII	NEV	VT	
	IDAHO	NH	VA	
	ILL	NJ	WASH	
	IND	NM	W VA	
	IOWA	NY	WIS	OTHER
	KANS	NC	WYO	
	KY	ND		

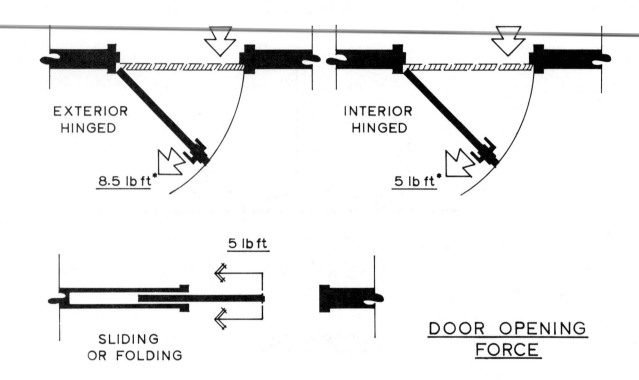

EXTERIOR HINGED

INTERIOR HINGED

8.5 lb ft*

5 lb ft*

5 lb ft

SLIDING OR FOLDING

DOOR OPENING FORCE

Basis of standard — CAC Title 24, Part 2	APPLICABILITY			
	ALA	LA	OHIO	GUAM
	ALASKA	MAINE	OKLA	PR
	ARIZ	MD	ORE	VIR IS
Notes — (*)Fire rated doors are required to have a 15 lb. pressure for life safety.	ARK	MASS	PA	DC
	● CAL	MICH	RI	
	COLO	MINN	SC	
	CONN	MISS	SD	FED'L FUNDS
	DEL	MO	TENN	
	FLA	MONT	TEXAS	
	GA	NEB	UTAH	
	HAWAII	NEV	VT	
	IDAHO	NH	VA	
	ILL	NJ	WASH	
	IND	NM	W VA	
	IOWA	NY	WIS	OTHER
	KANS	NC	WYO	
	KY	ND		

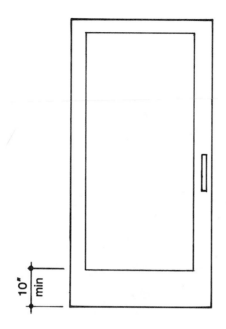

STILE AND RAIL GLASS DOORS

Basis of standard — CAC Title 24, Part 2	APPLICABILITY			
	ALA	LA	OHIO	GUAM
	ALASKA	MAINE	OKLA	PR
	ARIZ	MD	ORE	VIR IS
Notes — 10″ is required on push side only.	ARK	MASS	PA	DC
	● CAL	MICH	RI	
	COLO	MINN	SC	
	CONN	MISS	SD	FED'L FUNDS
	DEL	MO	TENN	
	FLA	MONT	TEXAS	
	GA	NEB	UTAH	
	HAWAII	NEV	VT	
	IDAHO	NH	VA	
	ILL	NJ	WASH	
	IND	NM	W VA	
	IOWA	NY	WIS	OTHER
	KANS	NC	WYO	
	KY	ND		

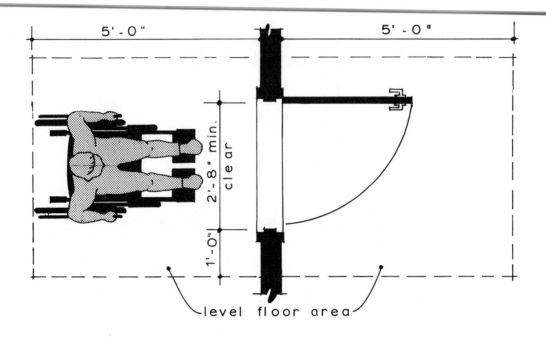

Basis of standard —	APPLICABILITY			
Connecticut Building Code	ALA	LA	OHIO	GUAM
	ALASKA	MAINE	OKLA	PR
	ARIZ	MD	ORE	VIR IS
Notes —	ARK	MASS	PA	DC
Doors to be operable with single effort. Two-leaf	CAL	MICH	RI	
doors are not acceptable unless they operate with	COLO	MINN	SC	
single effort or unless one of the two leaves comply.	● CONN	MISS	SD	FED'L
Provide 1′-4″ high kickplates or shall be made of	DEL	MO	TENN	FUNDS
material and finish to safely withstand abuse from	FLA	MONT	TEXAS	
canes, wheelchairs, etc. Avoid sharp inclines and	GA	NEB	UTAH	
abrupt level changes. As much as possible, thresh-	HAWAII	NEV	VT	
olds shall be flush with floor.	IDAHO	NH	VA	
	ILL	NJ	WASH	
	IND	NM	W VA	
	IOWA	NY	WIS	OTHER
	KANS	NC	WYO	
	KY	ND		

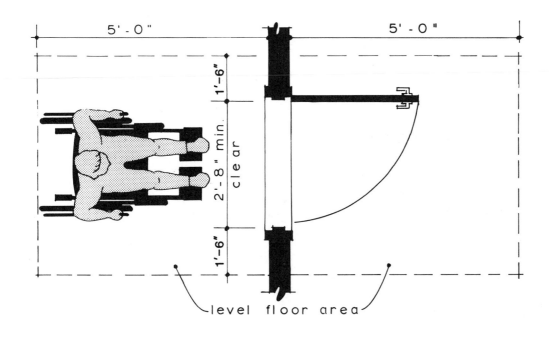

level floor area

Basis of standard —	APPLICABILITY			
Dept. of General Services	ALA	LA	OHIO	GUAM
	ALASKA	MAINE	OKLA	PR
	ARIZ	MD	ORE	VIR IS
Notes —	ARK	MASS	PA	DC
Florida: Applies to government facilities. Doors to be operable with single effort (max. recommended pressure: 8 lbs.). 2'-8" min. applies to at least one door of multiple leaf doors and at least one door immediately adjacent to a revolving door. Max. threshold height: ¾", with max. ¼" vertical rise. Max. height of doorknob height: 3'-0". Min. distance between doors (such as vestibules): 5'-0" corridor min.: 3'-8". Max wall hung or floor mounted projections: 1'-0".	CAL	MICH	RI	
	COLO	MINN	SC	
	CONN	MISS	SD	FED'L
	DEL	MO	TENN	FUNDS
	● FLA	MONT	TEXAS	
	GA	NEB	UTAH	
	HAWAII	NEV	VT	
	IDAHO	NH	VA	
	ILL	NJ	WASH	
	IND	NM	W VA	
	IOWA	NY	WIS	OTHER
	KANS	NC	WYO	
	KY	ND		

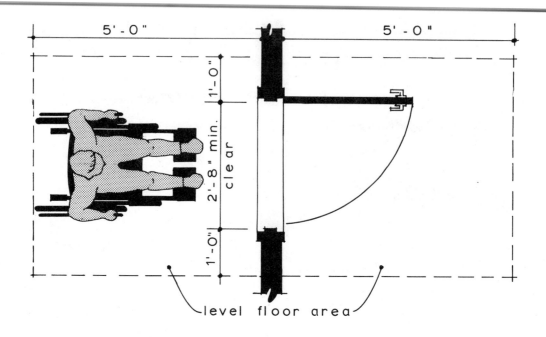

Basis of standard —	APPLICABILITY			
ANSI 1961 and Florida Board of Building Codes & Standards	ALA	LA	OHIO	GUAM
	ALASKA	MAINE	OKLA	PR
	ARIZ	MD	ORE	VIR IS
	ARK	MASS	PA	DC
	CAL	MICH	RI	
	COLO	MINN	SC	
Notes —	CONN	MISS	SD	FED'L FUNDS
Florida: Applies to non-government financed facilities. Avoid sharp inclines and abrupt changes at doorsills. Ramp changes in excess of ½″ at doorways requiring accessibility. All other walk-through openings: 2′-5″ min. clear width. Min. for corridors: 3′-8″ between walls when part of a required means of egress.	DEL	MO	TENN	
	● FLA	MONT	TEXAS	
	GA	NEB	UTAH	
	HAWAII	NEV	VT	
	IDAHO	NH	VA	
	ILL	NJ	WASH	
	IND	NM	W VA	
	IOWA	NY	WIS	OTHER
	KANS	NC	WYO	
	KY	ND		

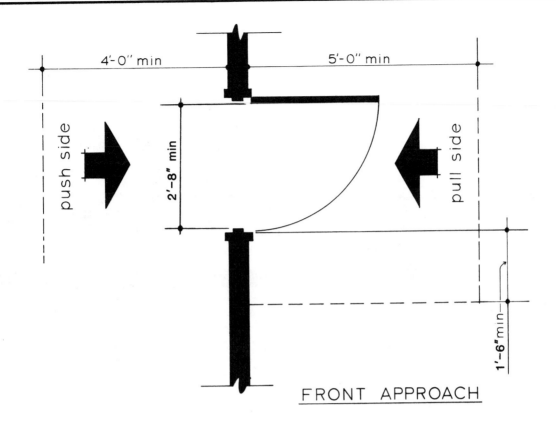

push side

pull side

4'-0" min

5'-0" min

2'-8" min

1'-6" min

FRONT APPROACH

Basis of standard —	APPLICABILITY			
Capital Development Board	ALA	LA	OHIO	GUAM
	ALASKA	MAINE	OKLA	PR
	ARIZ	MD	ORE	VIR IS
	ARK	MASS	PA	DC
	CAL	MICH	RI	
	COLO	MINN	SC	
	CONN	MISS	SD	FED'L
	DEL	MO	TENN	FUNDS
Notes —	FLA	MONT	TEXAS	
	GA	NEB	UTAH	
	HAWAII	NEV	VT	
	IDAHO	NH	VA	
	● ILL	NJ	WASH	
	IND	NM	W VA	
	IOWA	NY	WIS	OTHER
	KANS	NC	WYO	
	KY	ND		

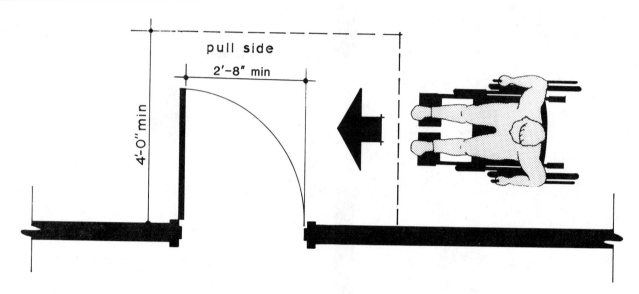

PULL SIDE LATCH APPROACH

Basis of standard — Capital Development Board	APPLICABILITY			
	ALA	LA	OHIO	GUAM
	ALASKA	MAINE	OKLA	PR
	ARIZ	MD	ORE	VIR IS
	ARK	MASS	PA	DC
	CAL	MICH	RI	
	COLO	MINN	SC	
	CONN	MISS	SD	FED'L
	DEL	MO	TENN	FUNDS
	FLA	MONT	TEXAS	
	GA	NEB	UTAH	
	HAWAII	NEV	VT	
	IDAHO	NH	VA	
● ILL	NJ	WASH	
	IND	NM	W VA	
	IOWA	NY	WIS	OTHER
	KANS	NC	WYO	
	KY	ND		

Notes —

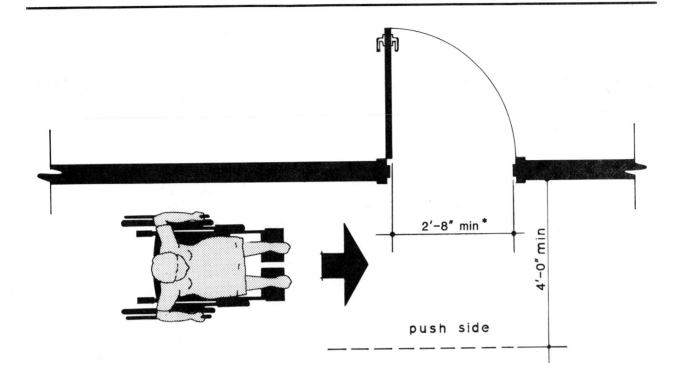

PUSH SIDE HINGE APPROACH

Basis of standard — Capital Development Board	APPLICABILITY			
	ALA	LA	OHIO	GUAM
	ALASKA	MAINE	OKLA	PR
	ARIZ	MD	ORE	VIR IS
	ARK	MASS	PA	DC
	CAL	MICH	RI	
	COLO	MINN	SC	
Notes —	CONN	MISS	SD	FED'L FUNDS
(*)May be 3'-6" in residential construction.	DEL	MO	TENN	
	FLA	MONT	TEXAS	
	GA	NEB	UTAH	
	HAWAII	NEV	VT	
	IDAHO	NH	VA	
	● ILL	NJ	WASH	
	IND	NM	W VA	
	IOWA	NY	WIS	OTHER
	KANS	NC	WYO	
	KY	ND		

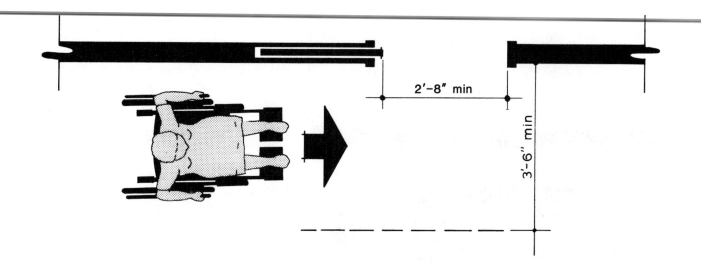

2'-8" min

3'-6" min

SLIDE SIDE APPROACH   SLIDING DOORS

Basis of standard — Capital Development Board	APPLICABILITY			
	ALA	LA	OHIO	GUAM
	ALASKA	MAINE	OKLA	PR
	ARIZ	MD	ORE	VIR IS
Notes — Folding doors use similar criteria. Hardware must be accessible in open and closed position (automatic doors are exempt.)	ARK	MASS	PA	DC
	CAL	MICH	RI	
	COLO	MINN	SC	
	CONN	MISS	SD	FED'L FUNDS
	DEL	MO	TENN	
	FLA	MONT	TEXAS	
	GA	NEB	UTAH	
	HAWAII	NEV	VT	
	IDAHO	NH	VA	
	● ILL	NJ	WASH	
	IND	NM	W VA	
	IOWA	NY	WIS	OTHER
	KANS	NC	WYO	
	KY	ND		

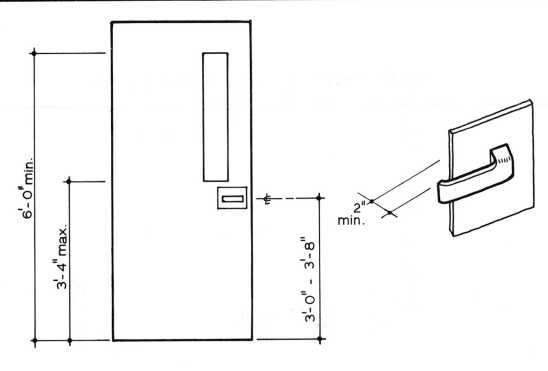

VISION PANELS

Basis of standard —	APPLICABILITY			
Capital Development Board	ALA	LA	OHIO	GUAM
	ALASKA	MAINE	OKLA	PR
	ARIZ	MD	ORE	VIR IS
Notes —	ARK	MASS	PA	DC
Doors to be operable without tight grasp, complex hand movements or exertion of great force. All manual doors to have lever design not requiring grasping and twisting of the wrist as the only means of operation; no sharp corners or edges; minimize catching of clothes on device. When door push plates are an integral part of the door stile, push plate shall be of a contrasting color. Where door opening device is a bar extending from stile to stile, the side of the bar to be pulled or pushed shall be distinguished with a color and texture change.	CAL	MICH	RI	
	COLO	MINN	SC	
	CONN	MISS	SD	FED'L FUNDS
	DEL	MO	TENN	
	FLA	MONT	TEXAS	
	GA	NEB	UTAH	
	HAWAII	NEV	VT	
	IDAHO	NH	VA	
	● ILL	NJ	WASH	
	IND	NM	W VA	
	IOWA	NY	WIS	OTHER
	KANS	NC	WYO	
	KY	ND		

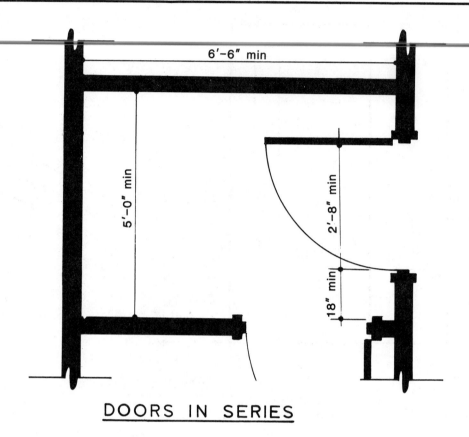

DOORS IN SERIES

Basis of standard — Capital Development Board	APPLICABILITY			
	ALA	LA	OHIO	GUAM
	ALASKA	MAINE	OKLA	PR
	ARIZ	MD	ORE	VIR IS
Notes —	ARK	MASS	PA	DC
	CAL	MICH	RI	
	COLO	MINN	SC	
	CONN	MISS	SD	FED'L
	DEL	MO	TENN	FUNDS
	FLA	MONT	TEXAS	
	GA	NEB	UTAH	
	HAWAII	NEV	VT	
	IDAHO	NH	VA	
	● ILL	NJ	WASH	
	IND	NM	W VA	
	IOWA	NY	WIS	OTHER
	KANS	NC	WYO	
	KY	ND		

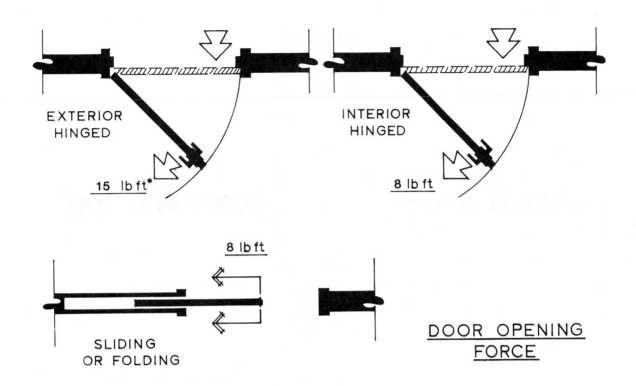

EXTERIOR HINGED

15 lb ft*

INTERIOR HINGED

8 lb ft

8 lb ft

SLIDING OR FOLDING

DOOR OPENING FORCE

Basis of standard — Capital Development Board	APPLICABILITY			
	ALA	LA	OHIO	GUAM
	ALASKA	MAINE	OKLA	PR
	ARIZ	MD	ORE	VIR IS
Notes —	ARK	MASS	PA	DC
Forces shown are applied perpendicular to door at the push/pull, or 2'-6" from the hinged side, whichever is furthest from the hinge. Force required to open a fire door shall be 12 lbf or the min. force needed to assure complete closing and latching of door. Door closers to comply with ANSI A 158.4 — 1972.	CAL	MICH	RI	
	COLO	MINN	SC	
	CONN	MISS	SD	FED'L FUNDS
	DEL	MO	TENN	
(*)If 15 lbf is exceeded, provide an automatic assist or an automatic door opener on at least one door at the major accessible entrance.	FLA	MONT	TEXAS	
	GA	NEB	UTAH	
	HAWAII	NEV	VT	
	IDAHO	NH	VA	
	● ILL	NJ	WASH	
	IND	NM	W VA	
	IOWA	NY	WIS	OTHER
	KANS	NC	WYO	
	KY	ND		

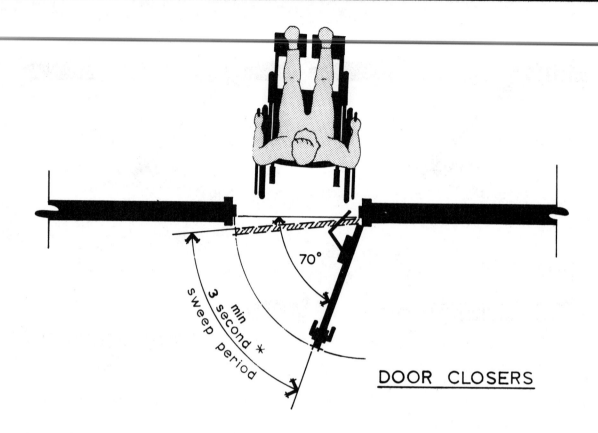

70°

min
3 second *
sweep period

DOOR CLOSERS

Basis of standard — Capital Development Board	APPLICABILITY			
	ALA	LA	OHIO	GUAM
	ALASKA	MAINE	OKLA	PR
	ARIZ	MD	ORE	VIR IS
Notes — Closers to have delay feature keeping door open for 5 sec. min. before beginning to close. Do not swing automatic doors into passing pedestrian traffic unless protective methods are used. Where automatic doors are opened with manually operated pressure plates, locate same within 4'-0" of door jamb and no higher than 3'-4".	ARK	MASS	PA	DC
	CAL	MICH	RI	
	COLO	MINN	SC	
	CONN	MISS	SD	FED'L FUNDS
	DEL	MO	TENN	
	FLA	MONT	TEXAS	
	GA	NEB	UTAH	
	HAWAII	NEV	VT	
	IDAHO	NH	VA	
	● ILL	NJ	WASH	
	IND	NM	W VA	
	IOWA	NY	WIS	OTHER
	KANS	NC	WYO	
	KY	ND		

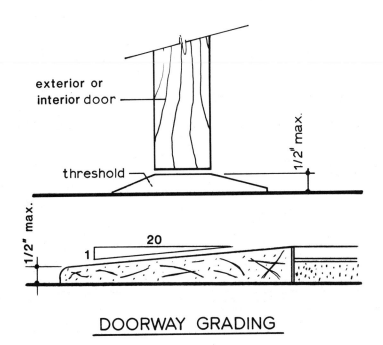

DOORWAY GRADING

Basis of standard — Capital Development Board	APPLICABILITY			
	ALA	LA	OHIO	GUAM
	ALASKA	MAINE	OKLA	PR
	ARIZ	MD	ORE	VIR IS
Notes — Thresholds with no vertical surface are preferred.	ARK	MASS	PA	DC
	CAL	MICH	RI	
	COLO	MINN	SC	
	CONN	MISS	SD	FED'L
	DEL	MO	TENN	FUNDS
	FLA	MONT	TEXAS	
	GA	NEB	UTAH	
	HAWAII	NEV	VT	
	IDAHO	NH	VA	
	● ILL	NJ	WASH	
	IND	NM	W VA	
	IOWA	NY	WIS	OTHER
	KANS	NC	WYO	
	KY	ND		

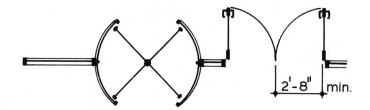

AN ACCESSIBLE ENTRANCE ALONGSIDE REVOLVING DOORS

Basis of standard —				
Capital Development Board				

	APPLICABILITY			
	ALA	LA	OHIO	GUAM
	ALASKA	MAINE	OKLA	PR
	ARIZ	MD	ORE	VIR IS
	ARK	MASS	PA	DC
	CAL	MICH	RI	
	COLO	MINN	SC	
	CONN	MISS	SD	FED'L FUNDS
	DEL	MO	TENN	
	FLA	MONT	TEXAS	
	GA	NEB	UTAH	
	HAWAII	NEV	VT	
	IDAHO	NH	VA	
●	ILL	NJ	WASH	
	IND	NM	W VA	
	IOWA	NY	WIS	OTHER
	KANS	NC	WYO	
	KY	ND		

Notes —

Place accessible entrance immediately to one side of revolving doors or turnstiles when they are provided. The accessible entrance doors shall have opening devices on both door faces and shall not be locked during regular business hours. Where more than one door is required at entrances, provide a left and right-handed door to give disabled persons choice of door to open. Where double doors are used, at least one leaf shall allow a 2'-8" clear opening. It is preferable that each leaf allow a 2'-8" min. clear opening.

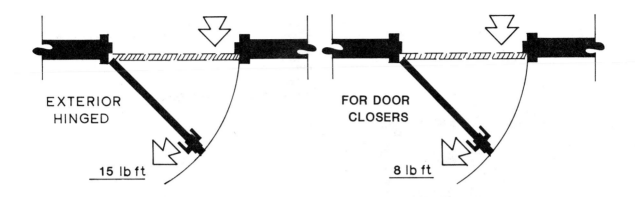

EXTERIOR
HINGED

FOR DOOR
CLOSERS

15 lb ft

8 lb ft

DOOR OPENING
FORCE

Basis of standard —	APPLICABILITY			
Indiana Amendments to Uniform Building Code	ALA	LA	OHIO	GUAM
	ALASKA	MAINE	OKLA	PR
	ARIZ	MD	ORE	VIR IS
Notes —	ARK	MASS	PA	DC
For fire doors, closing force must be adequate to assure automatic latching.	CAL	MICH	RI	
	COLO	MINN	SC	
	CONN	MISS	SD	FED'L FUNDS
	DEL	MO	TENN	
	FLA	MONT	TEXAS	
	GA	NEB	UTAH	
	HAWAII	NEV	VT	
	IDAHO	NH	VA	
	ILL	NJ	WASH	
	● IND	NM	W VA	
	IOWA	NY	WIS	OTHER
	KANS	NC	WYO	
	KY	ND		

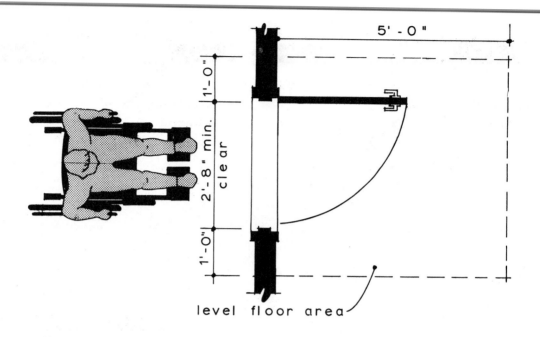

level floor area

Basis of standard — Iowa Administrative Code	APPLICABILITY			
	ALA	LA	OHIO	GUAM
	ALASKA	MAINE	OKLA	PR
	ARIZ	MD	ORE	VIR IS
	ARK	MASS	PA	DC
	CAL	MICH	RI	
	COLO	MINN	SC	
	CONN	MISS	SD	FED'L FUNDS
	DEL	MO	TENN	
	FLA	MONT	TEXAS	
	GA	NEB	UTAH	
	HAWAII	NEV	VT	
	IDAHO	NH	VA	
	ILL	NJ	WASH	
	IND	NM	W VA	
	● IOWA	NY	WIS	OTHER
	KANS	NC	WYO	
	KY	ND		

Notes —

Data applies to exterior and interior doors in areas accessible to physically handicapped. Max. threshold height: ¾″ for exterior doors, ½″ for interior doors. Max. force to open door: 8.5 pounds for exterior, 5.0 for interior hinged, folding or sliding doors. (Firedoors: min. allowed by local or state building code).
Handles, pulls, etc. to be easy to grasp & operate. For closers, adjust sweep at 70° open position to take 3 seconds to move to 3″ from latch. For specific door data refer to pages illustrating "ANSI – 1980", except that interior doors may have clear floor extension on the operating side only. ANSI 1980 applies to non-automatic doors.

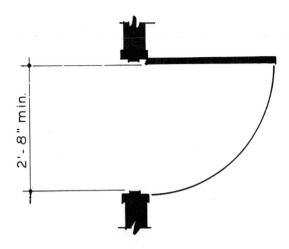

HINGED DOOR

Basis of standard — Annotated Code of Maryland, Article 49B	APPLICABILITY			
	ALA	LA	OHIO	GUAM
	ALASKA	MAINE	OKLA	PR
	ARIZ	● MD	ORE	VIR IS
Notes —	ARK	MASS	PA	DC
Doors openable by a single effort.	CAL	MICH	RI	
	COLO	MINN	SC	
	CONN	MISS	SD	FED'L
	DEL	MO	TENN	FUNDS
	FLA	MONT	TEXAS	
	GA	NEB	UTAH	
	HAWAII	NEV	VT	
	IDAHO	NH	VA	
	ILL	NJ	WASH	
	IND	NM	W VA	
	IOWA	NY	WIS	OTHER
	KANS	NC	WYO	
	KY	ND		

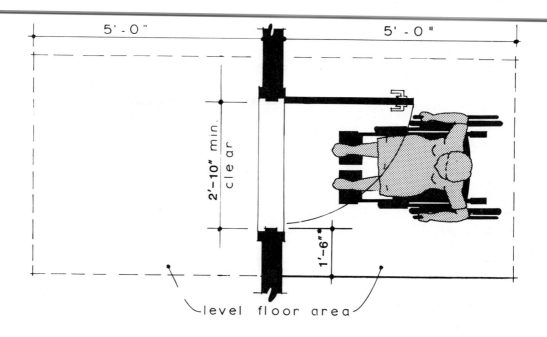

5'-0"   5'-0"

2'-10" min. clear

1'-6"

level floor area

Basis of standard —	APPLICABILITY			
521 CMR Architectural Barriers Board	ALA	LA	OHIO	GUAM
	ALASKA	MAINE	OKLA	PR
	ARIZ	MD	ORE	VIR IS
Notes —	ARK	● MASS	PA	DC
Min. door width: 3'-0" (includes walk-in closets).	CAL	MICH	RI	
Each door of a pair of doors shall be min. 3'-0" wide	COLO	MINN	SC	
or shall produce 2'-10" min. clear width.	CONN	MISS	SD	FED'L FUNDS
(*)2'-0" preferred.	DEL	MO	TENN	
	FLA	MONT	TEXAS	
	GA	NEB	UTAH	
	HAWAII	NEV	VT	
	IDAHO	NH	VA	
	ILL	NJ	WASH	
	IND	NM	W VA	
	IOWA	NY	WIS	OTHER
	KANS	NC	WYO	
	KY	ND		

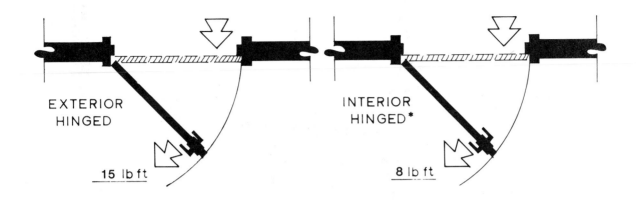

EXTERIOR
HINGED

15 lb ft

INTERIOR
HINGED*

8 lb ft

DOOR OPENING
FORCE

Basis of standard —	APPLICABILITY			
Architectural Barriers Board	ALA	LA	OHIO	GUAM
	ALASKA	MAINE	OKLA	PR
	ARIZ	MD	ORE	VIR IS
Notes — Doors requiring greater force to activate shall be equipped with compensating device to reduce operating force or be equipped with automatic opening device. Center door opening hardware 3'-0" to 3'-6" above floor. For means of egress use levers, push plates, pull bars, panic hardware, but not conventional door knobs or thumblatch pull devices; in paths of ingress doors to be operable with one hand. (*)For doors with self-closing feature.	ARK	● MASS	PA	DC
	CAL	MICH	RI	
	COLO	MINN	SC	
	CONN	MISS	SD	FED'L FUNDS
	DEL	MO	TENN	
	FLA	MONT	TEXAS	
	GA	NEB	UTAH	
	HAWAII	NEV	VT	
	IDAHO	NH	VA	
	ILL	NJ	WASH	
	IND	NM	W VA	
	IOWA	NY	WIS	OTHER
	KANS	NC	WYO	
	KY	ND		

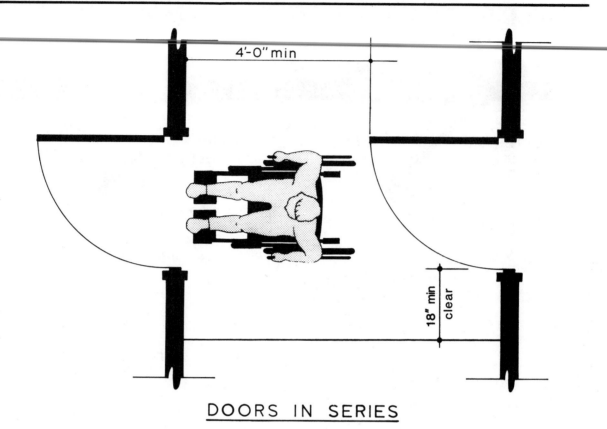

4'-0" min

18" min clear

DOORS IN SERIES

Basis of standard — Architectural Barriers Board	APPLICABILITY			
	ALA	LA	OHIO	GUAM
	ALASKA	MAINE	OKLA	PR
	ARIZ	MD	ORE	VIR IS
Notes —	ARK	● MASS	PA	DC
	CAL	MICH	RI	
	COLO	MINN	SC	
	CONN	MISS	SD	FED'L FUNDS
	DEL	MO	TENN	
	FLA	MONT	TEXAS	
	GA	NEB	UTAH	
	HAWAII	NEV	VT	
	IDAHO	NH	VA	
	ILL	NJ	WASH	
	IND	NM	W VA	
	IOWA	NY	WIS	OTHER
	KANS	NC	WYO	
	KY	ND		

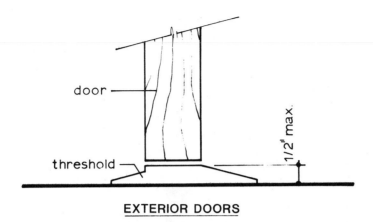

EXTERIOR DOORS

CHANGE IN FLOOR LEVEL

Basis of standard — 521 CMR Architectural Barriers Board	APPLICABILITY			
	ALA	LA	OHIO	GUAM
	ALASKA	MAINE	OKLA	PR
	ARIZ	MD	ORE	VIR IS
Notes — Interior thresholds shall be flush.	ARK	● MASS	PA	DC
	CAL	MICH	RI	
	COLO	MINN	SC	
	CONN	MISS	SD	FED'L FUNDS
	DEL	MO	TENN	
	FLA	MONT	TEXAS	
	GA	NEB	UTAH	
	HAWAII	NEV	VT	
	IDAHO	NH	VA	
	ILL	NJ	WASH	
	IND	NM	W VA	
	IOWA	NY	WIS	OTHER
	KANS	NC	WYO	
	KY	ND		

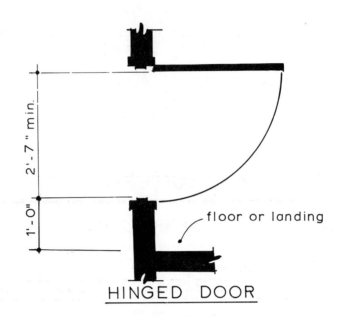

floor or landing

HINGED DOOR

Basis of standard —	APPLICABILITY			
State Building Code	ALA	LA	OHIO	GUAM
	ALASKA	MAINE	OKLA	PR
	ARIZ	MD	ORE	VIR IS
Notes —	ARK	MASS	PA	DC
Doors to be operable by a single effort with one hand. For two leaf doorways, at least one leaf shall comply. See UBC § 3303(d) for min. exit door width. Max. threshold height: ½″. Doors serving toilet rooms to be unlockable from either side.	CAL	MICH	RI	
	COLO	● MINN	SC	
	CONN	MISS	SD	FED'L FUNDS
	DEL	MO	TENN	
	FLA	MONT	TEXAS	
	GA	NEB	UTAH	
	HAWAII	NEV	VT	
	IDAHO	NH	VA	
	ILL	NJ	WASH	
	IND	NM	W VA	
	IOWA	NY	WIS	OTHER
	KANS	NC	WYO	
	KY	ND		

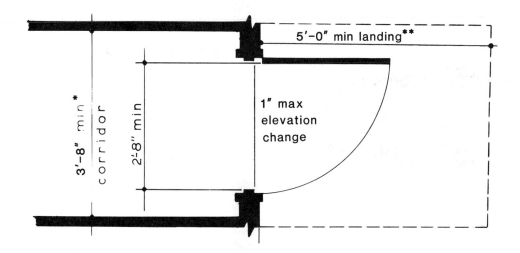

HINGED   DOOR

Basis of standard —	APPLICABILITY			
Uniform Building Code	ALA	LA	OHIO	GUAM
	ALASKA	MAINE	OKLA	PR
	ARIZ	MD	ORE	VIR IS
	ARK	MASS	PA	DC
Notes —	CAL	MICH	RI	
Required exit doorways shall permit door installation	COLO	MINN	SC	
of at least 3'-0" x 6'-8", opening at least 90°, with min.	CONN	MISS	SD	FED'L
clear exitway 2'-8" wide. Panic hardware, when in-	DEL	MO	TENN	FUNDS
stalled, to be mounted between 2'-6" and 3'-8" above	FLA	● MONT	TEXAS	
floor. Max. unlatching force applied in direction of	GA	NEB	UTAH	
travel: 15 lb. Revolving, sliding and overhead doors	HAWAII	NEV	VT	
shall not be used as required exits. Power operated	IDAHO	NH	VA	
doors complying with U.B.C. Standard No. 33-1 may	ILL	NJ	WASH	
be used for exit purposes.	IND	NM	W VA	
(*)Applies to occupant load of 10 or more. Regard-	IOWA	NY	WIS	OTHER
less of occupant load, corridors in Group R, Division	KANS	NC	WYO	
3 occupancies and within dwelling units in Group R,	KY	ND		
Division 1 occupancies shall have 3'-0" min. width.				
(**)May be 4'-0" when stair has a straight run.				

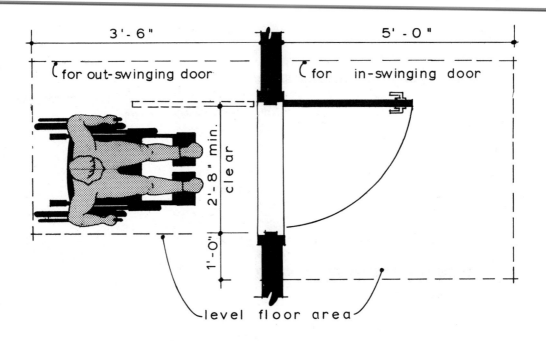

Basis of standard —	APPLICABILITY			
State of Nebraska Provisions for the Handicapped	ALA	LA	OHIO	GUAM
	ALASKA	MAINE	OKLA	PR
	ARIZ	MD	ORE	VIR IS
Notes —	ARK	MASS	PA	DC
Doors shall be operable by a single effort. Two-leaf doors must have one leaf with 2'-8" opening. Where practical thresholds shall be level with floor (max. = ½"). Use handles easy to grasp and operate. Swinging or sliding automatic doors are preferred. (*)1'-6" recommended.	CAL	MICH	RI	
	COLO	MINN	SC	
	CONN	MISS	SD	FED'L
	DEL	MO	TENN	FUNDS
	FLA	MONT	TEXAS	
	GA	● NEB	UTAH	
	HAWAII	NEV	VT	
	IDAHO	NH	VA	
	ILL	NJ	WASH	
	IND	NM	W VA	
	IOWA	NY	WIS	OTHER
	KANS	NC	WYO	
	KY	ND		

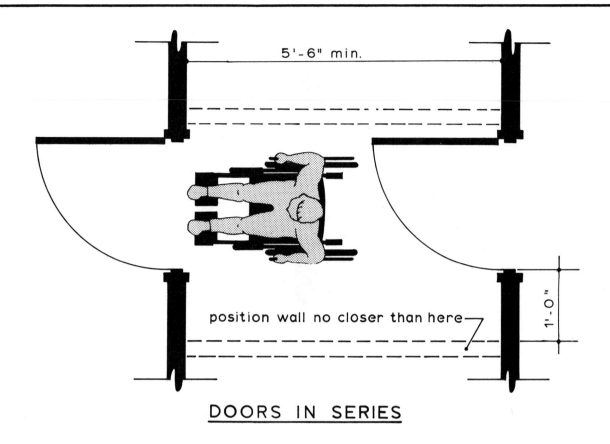

DOORS IN SERIES

Basis of standard —	APPLICABILITY			
State of Nebraska Provisions for the Handicapped	ALA	LA	OHIO	GUAM
	ALASKA	MAINE	OKLA	PR
	ARIZ	MD	ORE	VIR IS
Notes —	ARK	MASS	PA	DC
Space may be reduced to 5'-0" if 12" dimension is increased to 24".	CAL	MICH	RI	
	COLO	MINN	SC	
	CONN	MISS	SD	FED'L
	DEL	MO	TENN	FUNDS
	FLA	MONT	TEXAS	
	GA	● NEB	UTAH	
	HAWAII	NEV	VT	
	IDAHO	NH	VA	
	ILL	NJ	WASH	
	IND	NM	W VA	
	IOWA	NY	WIS	OTHER
	KANS	NC	WYO	
	KY	ND		

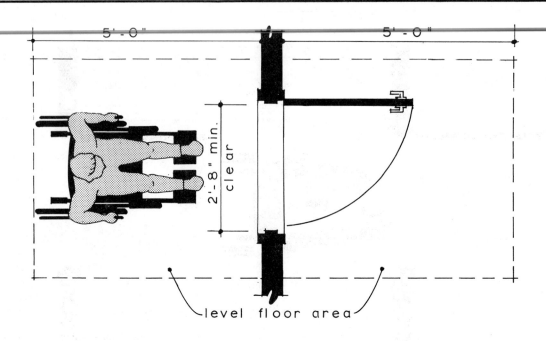

Basis of standard —	APPLICABILITY			
Architectural Barrier Free Design Code for the State of New Hampshire	ALA	LA	OHIO	GUAM
	ALASKA	MAINE	OKLA	PR
	ARIZ	MD	ORE	VIR IS
Notes —	ARK	MASS	PA	DC
Applicability: doorways required as a means of egress for the handicapped; doors; walk-in closet doors; each door of a pair of doors. Max. pressure to open: exterior doors: 15 lbs, interior doors with self-closing feature: 8 lbs. Automatic opening devices to have tactile warning for blind persons. Max threshold: exterior = ½″ beveled on both sides; interior = flush. Bevel strip to higher floor finish material with 1-in-4 bevel strip. Hardware height: 36″ to 42″. Do not use conventional door knobs or thumb latch pull devices. Hardware to be operated by single effort with one hand.	CAL	MICH	RI	
	COLO	MINN	SC	
	CONN	MISS	SD	FED'L
	DEL	MO	TENN	FUNDS
	FLA	MONT	TEXAS	
	GA	NEB	UTAH	
	HAWAII	NEV	VT	
	IDAHO	● NH	VA	
	ILL	NJ	WASH	
	IND	NM	W VA	
	IOWA	NY	WIS	OTHER
	KANS	NC	WYO	
	KY	ND		

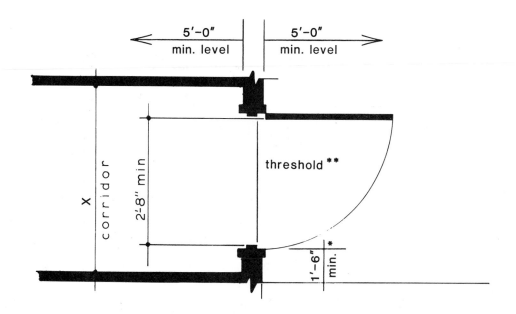

5'-0" min. level   5'-0" min. level

corridor   X

2'-8" min

threshold **

1'-6" min. *

HINGED DOOR

Basis of standard — Barrier Free Design Regulations	APPLICABILITY			
	ALA	LA	OHIO	GUAM
	ALASKA	MAINE	OKLA	PR
	ARIZ	MD	ORE	VIR IS
Notes —	ARK	MASS	PA	DC
Dimension "X":	CAL	MICH	RI	
5'-0" if door swings into corridor;	COLO	MINN	SC	
3'-6" if door does not swing into corridor and door openings are less than 3'-0";	CONN	MISS	SD	FED'L FUNDS
3'-0" if passage doors at corridor have 3'-0" clear opening and do not swing into corridor.	DEL	MO	TENN	
Max. push or pull force on door: 8 lbs (exempted are	FLA	MONT	TEXAS	
all doors having maximum push or pull per the	GA	NEB	UTAH	
governing code).	HAWAII	NEV	VT	
(*)Applies to pull side, including for inswinging doors.	IDAHO	NH	VA	
(**)Threshold: max. ¾" high, bevelled 45°.	ILL	● NJ	WASH	
	IND	NM	W VA	
	IOWA	NY	WIS	OTHER
	KANS	NC	WYO	
	KY	ND		

AN ACCESSIBLE ENTRANCE ALONGSIDE REVOLVING DOORS

Basis of standard —	APPLICABILITY			
Barrier Free Design Regulations	ALA	LA	OHIO	GUAM
	ALASKA	MAINE	OKLA	PR
	ARIZ	MD	ORE	VIR IS
Notes —	ARK	MASS	PA	DC
Where revolving doors are used, provide auxilliary hinged door adjacent to revolving door which shall remain unlocked whenever the revolving doors are unlocked.	CAL	MICH	RI	
	COLO	MINN	SC	
	CONN	MISS	SD	FED'L
	DEL	MO	TENN	FUNDS
	FLA	MONT	TEXAS	
	GA	NEB	UTAH	
	HAWAII	NEV	VT	
	IDAHO	NH	VA	
	ILL	● NJ	WASH	
	IND	NM	W VA	
	IOWA	NY	WIS	OTHER
	KANS	NC	WYO	
	KY	ND		

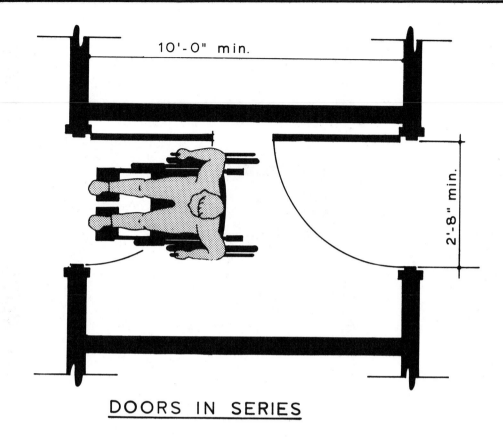

DOORS IN SERIES

Basis of standard —	APPLICABILITY			
Structural Specialty Code	ALA	LA	OHIO	GUAM
	ALASKA	MAINE	OKLA	PR
	ARIZ	MD	● ORE	VIR IS
	ARK	MASS	PA	DC
	CAL	MICH	RI	
	COLO	MINN	SC	
Notes —	CONN	MISS	SD	FED'L
Oregon: when providing access for the physically handicapped, self-closing exit doors shall be openable with 8 lbs. max. force. Self-opening devices are preferable. Protect bottom 18″ of door with a kickplate. Max. threshold height: ½″.	DEL	MO	TENN	FUNDS
	FLA	MONT	TEXAS	
	GA	NEB	UTAH	
Exception: when door opens onto a stair landing, conform to UBC Sec. 3305(g). Identify doors and exitways suitable for use by the handicapped.	HAWAII	NEV	VT	
	IDAHO	NH	VA	
	ILL	NJ	WASH	
	IND	NM	W VA	
	IOWA	NY	WIS	OTHER
	KANS	NC	WYO	
	KY	ND		

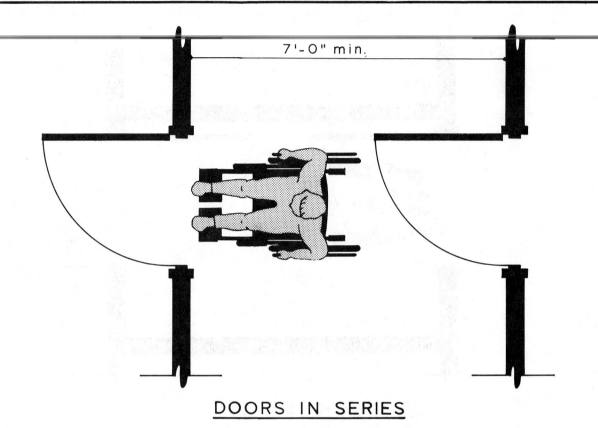

DOORS IN SERIES

Basis of standard —				
Structural Specialty Code				

Notes —				
Refer to notes on preceeding page				

APPLICABILITY			
ALA	LA	OHIO	GUAM
ALASKA	MAINE	OKLA	PR
ARIZ	MD	● ORE	VIR IS
ARK	MASS	PA	DC
CAL	MICH	RI	
COLO	MINN	SC	
CONN	MISS	SD	FED'L FUNDS
DEL	MO	TENN	
FLA	MONT	TEXAS	
GA	NEB	UTAH	
HAWAII	NEV	VT	
IDAHO	NH	VA	
ILL	NJ	WASH	
IND	NM	W VA	
IOWA	NY	WIS	OTHER
KANS	NC	WYO	
KY	ND		

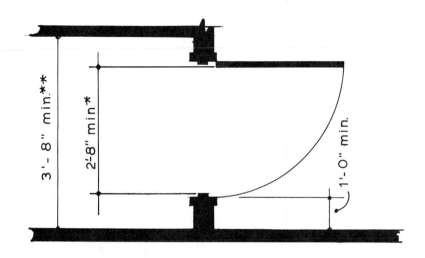

HINGED DOOR

Basis of standard — Barrier Free Design	APPLICABILITY			
	ALA	LA	OHIO	GUAM
	ALASKA	MAINE	OKLA	PR
	ARIZ	MD	ORE	VIR IS
Notes — Doors to operate by single effort. Min. 2'-8" door size also applies to one leaf of manually operated multiple leaf swinging doors. Floor inside and outside of each doorway to be essentially level for a distance of 5' from door. No sharp inclines or abrupt changes in level of floors. Thresholds flush with floor, max. mat. height 1". (*)Min. walk-through openings = 29" clear. (**)Min. dwelling unit hallways with no walk-thru openings in side walls = 36". Rooms without a 7' depth and a 5' x 5' turning space shall be equipped with outward swinging doors if hinged door leaves are installed.	ARK	MASS	PA	DC
	CAL	MICH	RI	
	COLO	MINN	● SC	
	CONN	MISS	SD	FED'L FUNDS
	DEL	MO	TENN	
	FLA	MONT	TEXAS	
	GA	NEB	UTAH	
	HAWAII	NEV	VT	
	IDAHO	NH	VA	
	ILL	NJ	WASH	
	IND	NM	W VA	
	IOWA	NY	WIS	OTHER
	KANS	NC	WYO	
	KY	ND		

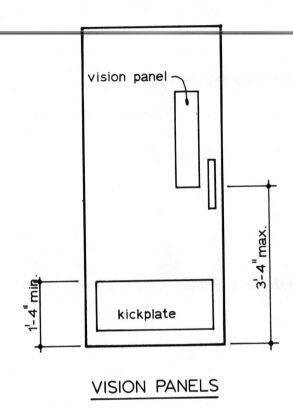

vision panel

kickplate

1'-4" min.

3'-4" max.

VISION PANELS

Basis of standard —	APPLICABILITY			
Barrier Free Deisgn	ALA	LA	OHIO	GUAM
	ALASKA	MAINE	OKLA	PR
	ARIZ	MD	ORE	VIR IS
	ARK	MASS	PA	DC
Notes —	CAL	MICH	RI	
	COLO	MINN	● SC	
	CONN	MISS	SD	FED'L
	DEL	MO	TENN	FUNDS
	FLA	MONT	TEXAS	
	GA	NEB	UTAH	
	HAWAII	NEV	VT	
	IDAHO	NH	VA	
	ILL	NJ	WASH	
	IND	NM	W VA	
	IOWA	NY	WIS	OTHER
	KANS	NC	WYO	
	KY	ND		

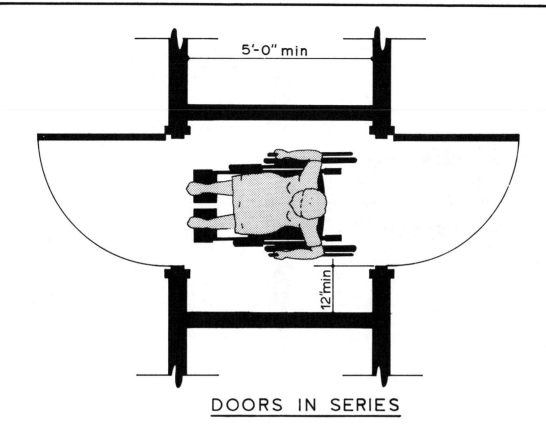

DOORS IN SERIES

Basis of standard — Barrier Free Design	APPLICABILITY			
	ALA	LA	OHIO	GUAM
	ALASKA	MAINE	OKLA	PR
	ARIZ	MD	ORE	VIR IS
Notes —	ARK	MASS	PA	DC
	CAL	MICH	RI	
	COLO	MINN	● SC	
	CONN	MISS	SD	FED'L FUNDS
	DEL	MO	TENN	
	FLA	MONT	TEXAS	
	GA	NEB	UTAH	
	HAWAII	NEV	VT	
	IDAHO	NH	VA	
	ILL	NJ	WASH	
	IND	NM	W VA	
	IOWA	NY	WIS	OTHER
	KANS	NC	WYO	
	KY	ND		

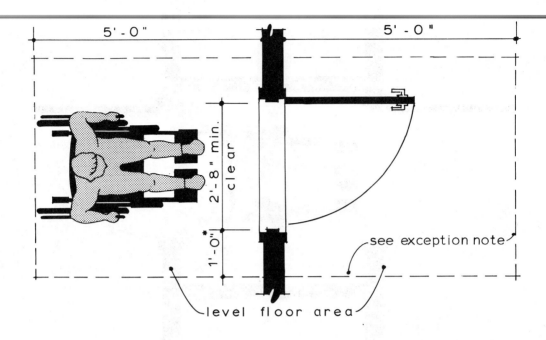

Basis of standard — Utah State Building Board	APPLICABILITY			
	ALA	LA	OHIO	GUAM
	ALASKA	MAINE	OKLA	PR
	ARIZ	MD	ORE	VIR IS
	ARK	MASS	PA	DC
	CAL	MICH	RI	
	COLO	MINN	SC	
	CONN	MISS	SD	FED'L
	DEL	MO	TENN	FUNDS
	FLA	MONT	TEXAS	
	GA	NEB	● UTAH	
	HAWAII	NEV	VT	
	IDAHO	NH	VA	
	ILL	NJ	WASH	
	IND	NM	W VA	
	IOWA	NY	WIS	OTHER
	KANS	NC	WYO	
	KY	ND		

Notes —
Data applies to exterior and interior doors leading to all public spaces. Two leaf doors are not usable unless one leaf operates with a single effort. Min. width for automatic doors: 36". Exception: remodelings where exist clear openings are 2'-5" wide. Threshold height: ¾" exterior beveled; interior ½" beveled. Max. bevel: 10%. For door closers, max. pressure to open = 8 lbs. with 3 second timing delay (5 lbs preferred). Exception note: 3'-8" hall or corridor width allowed where doors open onto but not into halls and corridors. (*)1'-6" min. required for all exterior entry and primary entry doors designated for handicapped user.

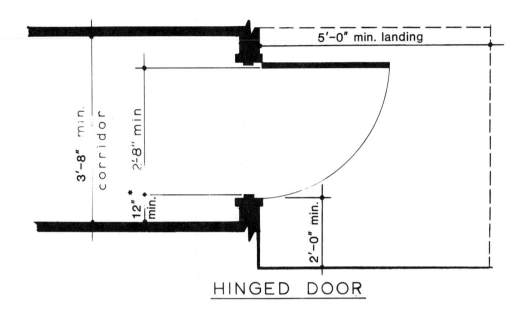

HINGED DOOR

Basis of standard —	APPLICABILITY			
Building Code Advisory Council	ALA	LA	OHIO	GUAM
	ALASKA	MAINE	OKLA	PR
	ARIZ	MD	ORE	VIR IS
Notes —	ARK	MASS	PA	DC
Min. height: 6'-7". Max. sill or threshold: ½".	CAL	MICH	RI	
Required exit doors: 3'-0" × 6'-8". Where doors open over landings, min. length: 5'-0". Minimum corridor	COLO	MINN	SC	
length: 4·0". Where corridor is longer than 50', pro-	CONN	MISS	SD	FED'L
vide, within its middle third, 5' × 5' unobstructed	DEL	MO	TENN	FUNDS
floor space. Every 200' of corridor shall be considered	FLA	MONT	TEXAS	
separately. Handrails and doors when fully open shall not reduce required width by more than 7". Trim	GA	NEB	UTAH	
may project into required width 1½" on each side.	HAWAII	NEV	VT	
Power operated doors to remain fully open for 6	IDAHO	NH	VA	
seconds before closing.	ILL	NJ	● WASH	
(*)When door is equipped with closer and latch.	IND	NM	W VA	
	IOWA	NY	WIS	OTHER
	KANS	NC	WYO	
	KY	ND		

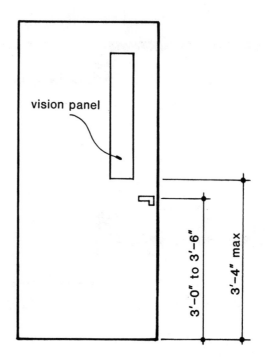

vision panel

3'-0" to 3'-6"

3'-4" max

Basis of standard —	APPLICABILITY			
Building Code Advisory Council	ALA	LA	OHIO	GUAM
	ALASKA	MAINE	OKLA	PR
	ARIZ	MD	ORE	VIR IS
Notes —	ARK	MASS	PA	DC
Touch switches for doors: 3'-0" above floor, and	CAL	MICH	RI	
between 1'-6" and 3'-0" horizontally from nearest	COLO	MINN	SC	
point of travel of the moving door. Other power	CONN	MISS	SD	FED'L
operated doors to be actuated no nearer than 3'-0"	DEL	MO	TENN	FUNDS
from nearest point of travel of the moving door.	FLA	MONT	TEXAS	
Locksets and latchsets to have lever or other devices	GA	NEB	UTAH	
permitting operation by wrist or arm pressure or	HAWAII	NEV	VT	
action.	IDAHO	NH	VA	
(*)Door pulls to be pulled at 3'-6" height.	ILL	NJ	● WASH	
	IND	NM	W VA	
	IOWA	NY	WIS	OTHER
	KANS	NC	WYO	
	KY	ND		

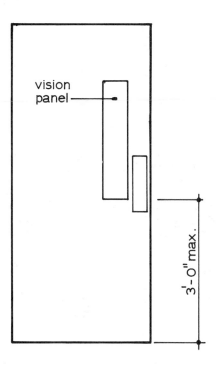

vision
panel

3'-0" max.

DOUBLE ACTING DOORS

Basis of standard —	APPLICABILITY			
Art 10F, Chapter 18, Code of West Virginia	ALA	LA	OHIO	GUAM
	ALASKA	MAINE	OKLA	PR
	ARIZ	MD	ORE	VIR IS
	ARK	MASS	PA	DC
Notes —	CAL	MICH	RI	
For all doors, max. 5/8″ edge height for door sills (flush recommended).	COLO	MINN	SC	
	CONN	MISS	SD	FED'L FUNDS
	DEL	MO	TENN	
	FLA	MONT	TEXAS	
	GA	NEB	UTAH	
	HAWAII	NEV	VT	
	IDAHO	NH	VA	
	ILL	NJ	WASH	
	IND	NM	● W VA	
	IOWA	NY	WIS	OTHER
	KANS	NC	WYO	
	KY	ND		

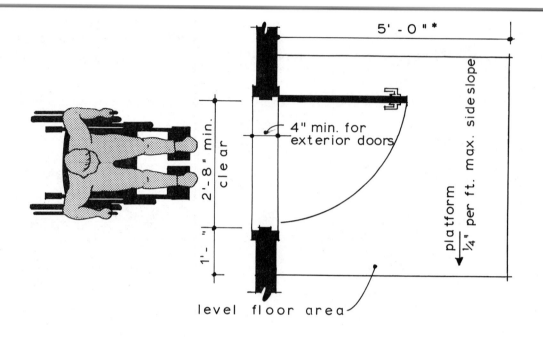

5'-0"*

2'-8" min. clear

1'-"

4" min. for exterior doors

platform ¼" per ft. max. side slope

level floor area

Basis of standard —	APPLICABILITY			
6 Wisconsin Administrative Code	ALA	LA	OHIO	GUAM
	ALASKA	MAINE	OKLA	PR
	ARIZ	MD	ORE	VIR IS
Notes —	ARK	MASS	PA	DC
Threshold heights: exterior 5/8" max.; weather-stripped 1"; interior 1/2". Bevel all thresholds for smooth unbroken surface.	CAL	MICH	RI	
	COLO	MINN	SC	
(*)May be 4'-0" when door swings inward.	CONN	MISS	SD	FED'L FUNDS
	DEL	MO	TENN	
	FLA	MONT	TEXAS	
	GA	NEB	UTAH	
	HAWAII	NEV	VT	
	IDAHO	NH	VA	
	ILL	NJ	WASH	
	IND	NM	W VA	
	IOWA	NY	● WIS	OTHER
	KANS	NC	WYO	
	KY	ND		

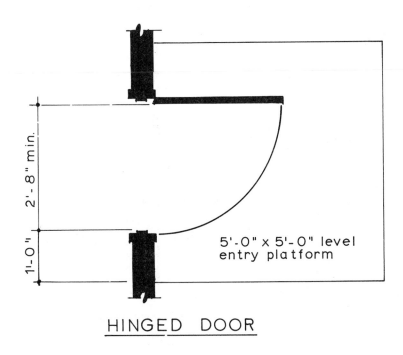

5'-0" x 5'-0" level
entry platform

2'-8" min.

1'-0"

HINGED DOOR

Basis of standard —	APPLICABILITY			
The Basics of Barrier Free Design	ALA	LA	OHIO	GUAM
	ALASKA	MAINE	OKLA	PR
	ARIZ	MD	ORE	VIR IS
Notes —	ARK	MASS	PA	DC
Max. pressure to open doors with closers: 15 lbs.	CAL	MICH	RI	
Time delay closers set to hold door open 12 seconds	COLO	MINN	SC	
and automatic doors are recommended. Max. thresh-	CONN	MISS	SD	FED'L
old heights: ¾" beveled with max. 5% slope at exterior	DEL	MO	TENN	FUNDS
doors; ½" at interior doors. Max. floor mat height·	FLA	MONT	TEXAS	
½".	GA	NEB	UTAH	
	HAWAII	NEV	VT	
	IDAHO	NH	VA	
	ILL	NJ	WASH	
	IND	NM	W VA	
	IOWA	NY	WIS	OTHER
	KANS	NC	● WYO	
	KY	ND		

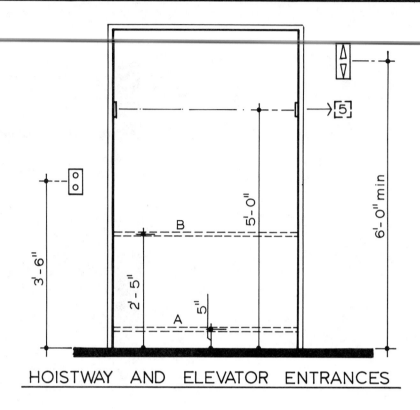

HOISTWAY AND ELEVATOR ENTRANCES

Basis of standard —	APPLICABILITY			
ANSI 1980 — 4.10, BOCA 1978, and others.	ALA	● LA	● OHIO	GUAM
	● ALASKA	● MAINE	OKLA	PR
	ARIZ	MD	ORE	VIR IS
	● ARK	MASS	PA	DC
	CAL	MICH	● RI	
	● COLO	MINN	SC	
	CONN	MISS	SD	● FED'L FUNDS
	● DEL	MO	● TENN	
	FLA	MONT	● TEXAS	
	GA	NEB	UTAH	
	● HAWAII	● NEV	● VT	
	● IDAHO	NH	● VA	
	● ILL	NJ	WASH	
	IND	● NM	W VA	
	IOWA	● NY	WIS	OTHER
	KANS	● NC	WYO	
	● KY	ND		

Notes —

Lines A and B show vertical locations of door reopening device not requiring contact. Reopening devices shall remain effective at least 20 seconds, and shall be provided to stop and reopen car and hoistway doors. Elevator doors shall open and close automatically. Both jambs of hoistway entrances to have raised or indented floor designations, or permanently applied plates, 60″ from floor, 2″ high (raised 0.30″ in Ohio). Door to be open min. 3 seconds.

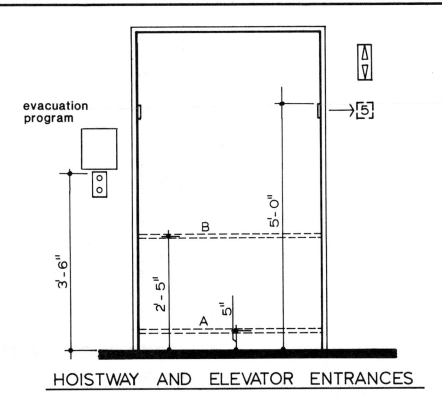

evacuation
program

3'-6"

2'-5"

5'-0"

5"

B

A

5

HOISTWAY   AND   ELEVATOR   ENTRANCES

Basis of standard —	APPLICABILITY			
Architectural Barrier Free Design Code and 521 CMR Architectural Barrier Board (Mass).	ALA	LA	OHIO	GUAM
	ALASKA	MAINE	OKLA	PR
	ARIZ	MD	ORE	VIR IS
Notes —	ARK	● MASS	PA	DC
Provide ramp or elevator to all levels for buildings with 2 or more levels. Provide reopening door device — lines A and B show electric eye locations. Non-contact device to hold doors open 3 seconds minimum. Non-contact device not required if timer is set to hold door open 6 seconds minimum at each stop. Call buttons:	CAL	MICH	RI	
	COLO	MINN	SC	
	CONN	MISS	SD	FED'L FUNDS
	DEL	MO	TENN	
	FLA	MONT	TEXAS	
	GA	NEB	UTAH	
	HAWAII	NEV	VT	
	IDAHO	● NH	VA	
	ILL	NJ	WASH	
	IND	NM	W VA	
	IOWA	NY	WIS	OTHER
	KANS	NC	WYO	
	KY	ND		

Notes —
Provide ramp or elevator to all levels for buildings
with 2 or more levels. Provide reopening door
device — lines A and B show electric eye locations.
Non-contact device to hold doors open 3 seconds
minimum. Non-contact device not required if
timer is set to hold door open 6 seconds minimum
at each stop. Call buttons:

Distance to center of furthest elevator	Minimum time from notification until doors start to close
5'-0"	4 seconds
10'-0"	7 seconds
15'-0"	10 seconds
20'-0"	13 seconds

Doors to be power-operated and automatic, self-
leveling to within ½" of floor. Jamb numbers for
floors: 2½" high, min., raised 1/8". Provide
audible hall signals — 1 sound for up, two for
down.

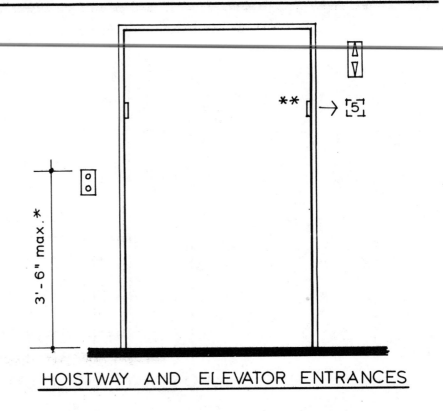

HOISTWAY AND ELEVATOR ENTRANCES

Basis of standard —	APPLICABILITY			
Wisconsin Administrative Code and others	ALA	LA	OHIO	GUAM
	ALASKA	MAINE	OKLA	PR
	ARIZ	MD	ORE	VIR IS
Notes —	ARK	MASS	PA	DC
(*)4'-0" max. in Wyoming.	CAL	MICH	RI	
(**) Raised letters and numerals in Wisconsin.	COLO	MINN	SC	
	CONN	MISS	SD	FED'L
	DEL	MO	TENN	FUNDS
	FLA	MONT	TEXAS	
	GA	NEB	UTAH	
	HAWAII	NEV	VT	
	IDAHO	NH	VA	
	ILL	NJ	WASH	
	IND	NM	W VA	
	IOWA	NY	● WIS	OTHER
	KANS	NC	● WYO	
	KY	ND		

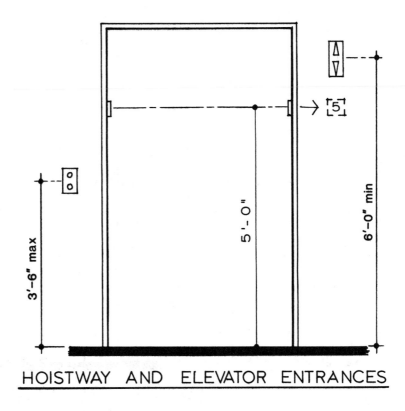

HOISTWAY AND ELEVATOR ENTRANCES

Basis of standard —	APPLICABILITY			
CAC Title 24, Part 2	ALA	LA	OHIO	GUAM
	ALASKA	MAINE	OKLA	PR
	ARIZ	MD	ORE	VIR IS
Notes —	ARK	MASS	PA	DC
Emboss number of floor on both sides of door casings on all floor in braille and arabic numerals. Hall signals sound once for upward travel, twice for down.	● CAL	MICH	RI	
	COLO	MINN	SC	
	CONN	MISS	SD	FED'L FUNDS
	DEL	MO	TENN	
	FLA	MONT	TEXAS	
	GA	NEB	UTAH	
	HAWAII	NEV	VT	
	IDAHO	NH	VA	
	ILL	NJ	WASH	
	IND	NM	W VA	
	IOWA	NY	WIS	OTHER
	KANS	NC	WYO	
	KY	ND		

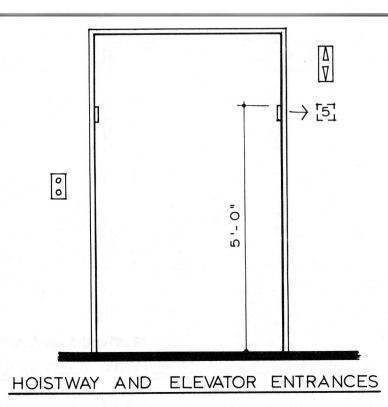

HOISTWAY AND ELEVATOR ENTRANCES

Basis of standard —	APPLICABILITY			
Connecticut Building Code — Art 21.	ALA	LA	OHIO	GUAM
	ALASKA	MAINE	OKLA	PR
	ARIZ	MD	ORE	VIR IS
Notes —	ARK	MASS	PA	DC
Provide tactile numbers for floor designation on the fixed point at the open side of the elevator door.	CAL	MICH	RI	
	COLO	MINN	SC	
	● CONN	MISS	SD	FED'L FUNDS
	DEL	MO	TENN	
	FLA	MONT	TEXAS	
	GA	NEB	UTAH	
	HAWAII	NEV	VT	
	IDAHO	NH	VA	
	ILL	NJ	WASH	
	IND	NM	W VA	
	IOWA	NY	WIS	OTHER
	KANS	NC	WYO	
	KY	ND		

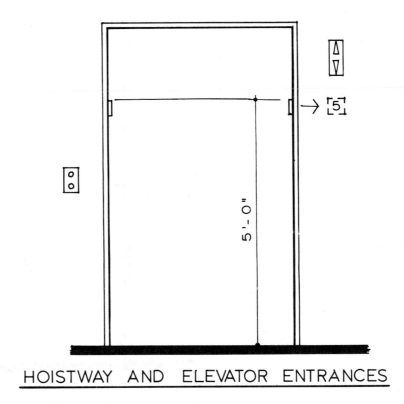

HOISTWAY AND ELEVATOR ENTRANCES

Basis of standard —	APPLICABILITY			
Maryland Building Code for the Handicapped	ALA	LA	OHIO	GUAM
	ALASKA	MAINE	OKLA	PR
	ARIZ	● MD	ORE	VIR IS
Notes —	ARK	MASS	PA	DC
Provide plates with 2″ high min., raised .030 inch numbers on a contrasting color background designating floor at both sides of each hoistway entrance. When elevators are required, identify one elevator as usable by the handicapped which shall comply with designated requirements.	CAL	MICH	RI	
	COLO	MINN	SC	
	CONN	MISS	SD	FED'L
	DEL	MO	TENN	FUNDS
	FLA	MONT	TEXAS	
	GA	NEB	UTAH	
	HAWAII	NEV	VT	
	IDAHO	NH	VA	
	ILL	NJ	WASH	
	IND	NM	W VA	
	IOWA	NY	WIS	OTHER
	KANS	NC	WYO	
	KY	ND		

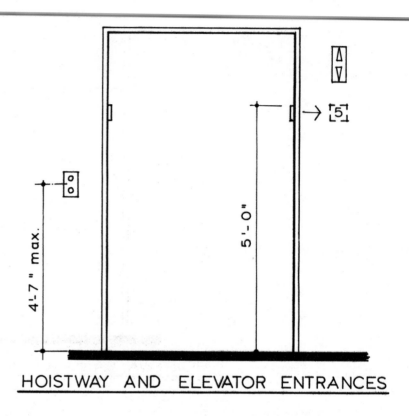

HOISTWAY AND ELEVATOR ENTRANCES

Basis of standard — Construction Code Commission.	APPLICABILITY			
	ALA	LA	OHIO	GUAM
	ALASKA	MAINE	OKLA	PR
	ARIZ	MD	ORE	VIR IS
Notes —	ARK	MASS	PA	DC
Floor designations to be metal tactile numbers on the fixed point at the open side of the elevator door, or on both sides when center opening doors are used. Provide an audible gong sound when elevator arrives at the ground floor landing where access to the building for the physically handicapped has been provided.	CAL	● MICH	RI	
	COLO	MINN	SC	
	CONN	MISS	SD	FED'L FUNDS
	DEL	MO	TENN	
	FLA	MONT	TEXAS	
	GA	NEB	UTAH	
	HAWAII	NEV	VT	
	IDAHO	NH	VA	
	ILL	NJ	WASH	
	IND	NM	W VA	
	IOWA	NY	WIS	OTHER
	KANS	NC	WYO	
	KY	ND		

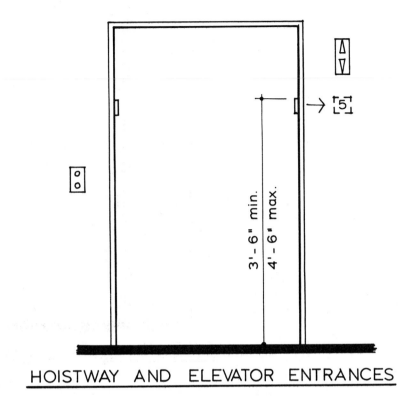

3'- 6" min.
4'- 6" max.

HOISTWAY AND ELEVATOR ENTRANCES

Basis of standard — State Building Code	APPLICABILITY			
	ALA	LA	OHIO	GUAM
	ALASKA	MAINE	OKLA	PR
	ARIZ	MD	ORE	VIR IS
Notes —	ARK	MASS	PA	DC
Provide tactile floor identification by raised or recessed numbers attached to elevator door jamb at each floor.	CAL	MICH	RI	
	COLO	● MINN	SC	
	CONN	MISS	SD	FED'L
	DEL	MO	TENN	FUNDS
	FLA	MONT	TEXAS	
	GA	NEB	UTAH	
	HAWAII	NEV	VT	
	IDAHO	NH	VA	
	ILL	NJ	WASH	
	IND	NM	W VA	
	IOWA	NY	WIS	OTHER
	KANS	NC	WYO	
	KY	ND		

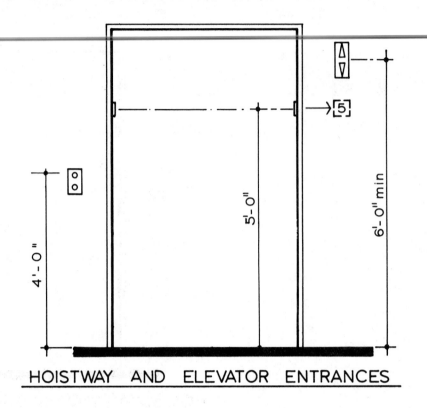

HOISTWAY AND ELEVATOR ENTRANCES

Basis of standard —	APPLICABILITY			
Nebraska Provisions for the Handicapped	ALA	LA	OHIO	GUAM
	ALASKA	MAINE	OKLA	PR
	ARIZ	MD	ORE	VIR IS
Notes —	ARK	MASS	PA	DC
Hall lantern: 2″ min. height for symbol, to light up a contrasting color. Accompany up direction with one audible signal, down with two audible signals. Mount floor designation on both sides of jamb, with 2½″ min. height numbers, raised 1/32″ min.	CAL	MICH	RI	
	COLO	MINN	SC	
	CONN	MISS	SD	FED'L FUNDS
	DEL	MO	TENN	
	FLA	MONT	TEXAS	
	GA	● NEB	UTAH	
	HAWAII	NEV	VT	
	IDAHO	NH	VA	
	ILL	NJ	WASH	
	IND	NM	W VA	
	IOWA	NY	WIS	OTHER
	KANS	NC	WYO	
	KY	ND		

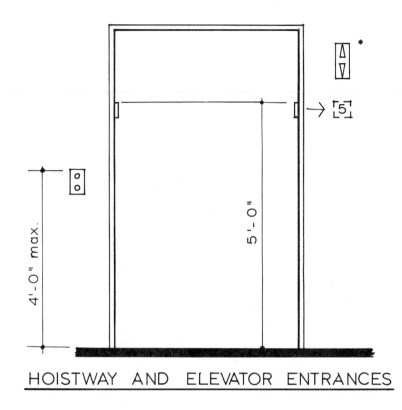

HOISTWAY AND ELEVATOR ENTRANCES

Basis of standard —	APPLICABILITY			
Utah State Building Board	ALA	LA	OHIO	GUAM
	ALASKA	MAINE	OKLA	PR
	ARIZ	MD	ORE	VIR IS
Notes —	ARK	MASS	PA	DC
Call buttons to have visual signals to indicate when call is registered. Audible signals required only for elevators serving three or more floors. Provide floor identification for all elevators serving three or more landings in braille and tactile arabic characters permantly anchored to door jambs with counter-sunk metal screws.	CAL	MICH	RI	
	COLO	MINN	SC	
	CONN	MISS	SD	FED'L FUNDS
	DEL	MO	TENN	
	FLA	MONT	TEXAS	
(*)Audible and visual signal, located to be visible from call button. Audible signal to sound once for up direction and twice for down direction.	GA	NEB	● UTAH	
	HAWAII	NEV	VT	
	IDAHO	NH	VA	
	ILL	NJ	WASH	
	IND	NM	W VA	
	IOWA	NY	WIS	OTHER
	KANS	NC	WYO	
	KY	ND		

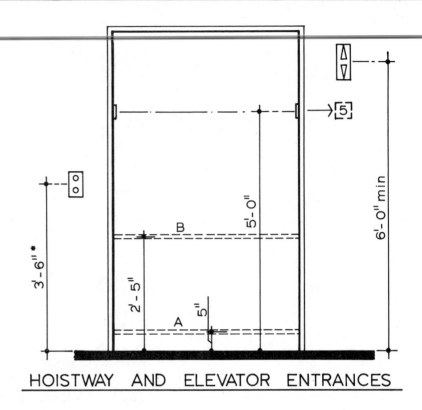

HOISTWAY   AND   ELEVATOR   ENTRANCES

Basis of standard —	APPLICABILITY			
ANSI 1980 — 4.10, BOCA 1978, and others.	ALA	● LA	● OHIO	GUAM
	● ALASKA	● MAINE	OKLA	PR
	ARIZ	MD	ORE	VIR IS
Notes —	● ARK	MASS	PA	DC
Visible and audible signal at each hoistway entrance: one sound for up, twice for down. Elevators to comply with ANSI A17.1–1978, and A17.1a–1979. Level to ½″ under zero loading. Features of visible signals: elements at least 2½″ in smallest dimension, signals visible from vicinity of hall call button. (In-car lanterns located in cars visible from vicinity of hall call buttons conforming to above requirements are acceptable). Provide visual signals for hall call buttons to show when calls are registered and answered. ¾″ min. dimension of call buttons. Up button on top. Vermont: Provide re-opening device at lines A and B. Door opening device to remain effective for 20 seconds min. (*)Texas: max. 4′-6″ for front approach, 4′-0″ for parallel approach.	CAL	MICH	● RI	
	● COLO	MINN	SC	
	CONN	MISS	SD	● FED'L FUNDS
	● DEL	MO	TENN	
	FLA	MONT	● TEXAS	
	GA	NEB	UTAH	
	● HAWAII	● NEV	● VT	
	● IDAHO	NH	● VA	
	● ILL	NJ	WASH	
	IND	● NM	W VA	
	IOWA	● NY	WIS	OTHER
	KANS	NC	WYO	
	● KY	ND		

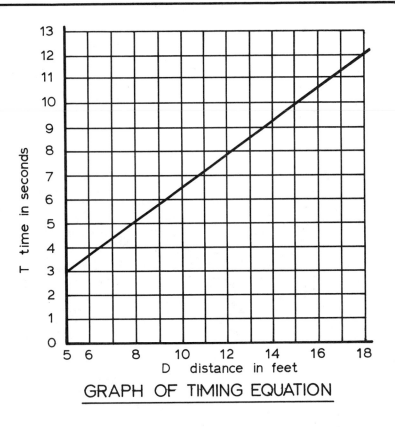

GRAPH OF TIMING EQUATION

Basis of standard —	APPLICABILITY			
ANSI 1980 – 4.10.7 and others	ALA	● LA	OHIO	GUAM
	● ALASKA	● MAINE	OKLA	PR
	ARIZ	MD	ORE	VIR IS
	ARK	MASS	PA	DC
Notes —	CAL	MICH	● RI	
Graph shows minimum acceptable time from notification that a car is answering a call until doors of that car start to close, calculated from T = D/1.5 ft/s or T = D/455 mm/s where T = total time in seconds, and D = distance from a point in the lobby or corridor 5'-0" (1525 mm) directly in front of the farthest call button controlling that car to the center line of its hoistway door. For cars with in-car lanterns, T begins when the lantern is visible from the vicinity of hall call buttons and an audible signal is sounded. Doors shall remain fully open for a 3 second minimum.	● COLO	MINN	SC	
	CONN	MISS	SD	FED'L FUNDS
	DEL	MO	TENN	
	FLA	MONT	● TEXAS	
	GA	NEB	UTAH	
	● HAWAII	● NEV	● VT	
	● IDAHO	NH	● VA	
	ILL	NJ	WASH	
	IND	● NM	W VA	
	IOWA	● NY	WIS	OTHER
	KANS	NC	WYO	
	● KY	ND		

distance	time
ft	sec
0 5	5
10	7
15	10
20	13

DOOR TIMING

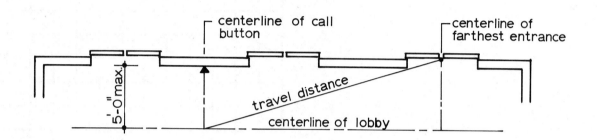

TRAVEL DISTANCE

Basis of standard —	APPLICABILITY			
ATBCB — 1190.100 and others	ALA	LA	OHIO	GUAM
	ALASKA	MAINE	OKLA	PR
	ARIZ	MD	ORE	VIR IS
Notes —	● ARK	MASS	PA	DC
Table shows minimum acceptable time from notification that a car is answering a hall call until doors of that car start to close. Establish travel distance from a point in the center of the corridor or lobby (max.: 5'-0") directly opposite the farthest hall button to the centerline of the farthest hoistway entrance. Doors shall remain fully open for a 5 second minimum (3 seconds in New Jersey and Vermont).	CAL	MICH	RI	
	COLO	MINN	SC	
	CONN	MISS	SD	● FED'L FUNDS
	● DEL	MO	TENN	
	FLA	MONT	TEXAS	
	GA	NEB	UTAH	
	HAWAII	NEV	VT	
	IDAHO	NH	VA	
	ILL	● NJ	WASH	
	IND	NM	W VA	
	IOWA	NY	WIS	OTHER
	KANS	NC	WYO	
	KY	ND		

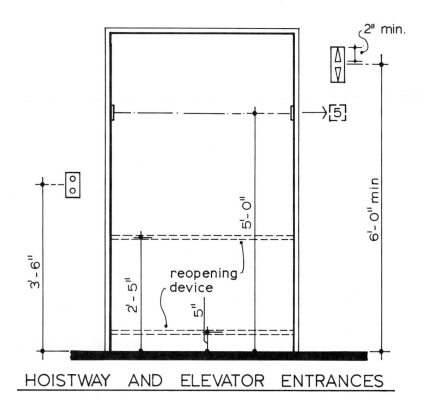

2" min.

5

6'-0" min

5'-0"

3'-6"

2'-5"

5"

reopening device

HOISTWAY AND ELEVATOR ENTRANCES

Basis of standard — North Carolina Building Code	APPLICABILITY			
	ALA	LA	OHIO	GUAM
	ALASKA	MAINE	OKLA	PR
	ARIZ	MD	ORE	VIR IS
Notes — Visible and audible signal at each hoistway entrance: one sound for up, twice for down. In-car lanterns located in jamb are acceptable. Floor designations on both jambs: on contrasting background, min. 2½" high, raised .030". Applied permanently attached plates are acceptable. Direction buttons: 3/4" min., raised, flush, or recessed with visual indications to show each call registered and extinguished when call is is answered. Max. depth of flush or recessed buttons: 3/8".	ARK	MASS	PA	DC
	CAL	MICH	RI	
	COLO	MINN	SC	
	CONN	MISS	SD	FED'L FUNDS
	DEL	MO	● TENN	
	FLA	MONT	TEXAS	
	GA	NEB	UTAH	
	HAWAII	NEV	VT	
	IDAHO	NH	VA	
	ILL	NJ	WASH	
	IND	NM	W VA	
	IOWA	NY	WIS	OTHER
	KANS	● NC	WYO	
	KY	ND		

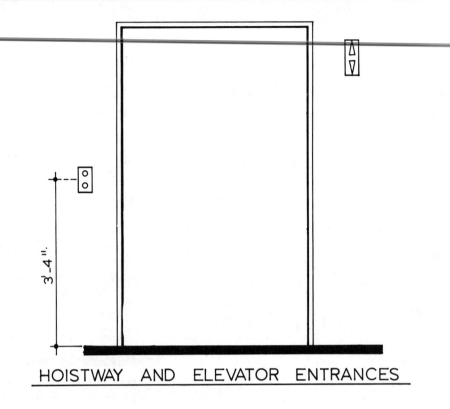

HOISTWAY   AND   ELEVATOR   ENTRANCES

Basis of standard — Barrier Free Design Standards	APPLICABILITY			
	● ALA	LA	OHIO	GUAM
	ALASKA	MAINE	OKLA	PR
	ARIZ	MD	ORE	VIR IS
Notes —	ARK	MASS	PA	DC
Lobby indicator signals:	CAL	MICH	RI	
Elevator going up: higher pitch sound	COLO	MINN	SC	
Elevator going down: lower pitch sound	CONN	MISS	SD	FED'L
	DEL	MO	TENN	FUNDS
	FLA	MONT	TEXAS	
	GA	NEB	UTAH	
	HAWAII	NEV	VT	
	IDAHO	NH	VA	
	ILL	NJ	WASH	
	IND	NM	W VA	
	IOWA	NY	WIS	OTHER
	KANS	NC	WYO	
	KY	ND		

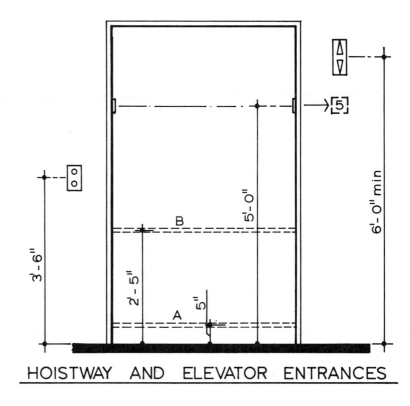

HOISTWAY AND ELEVATOR ENTRANCES

Basis of standard — Iowa Administrative Code	APPLICABILITY			
	ALA	LA	OHIO	GUAM
	ALASKA	MAINE	OKLA	PR
	ARIZ	MD	ORE	VIR IS
Notes —	ARK	MASS	PA	DC
	CAL	MICH	RI	
	COLO	MINN	SC	
	CONN	MISS	SD	FED'L
	DEL	MO	TENN	FUNDS
	FLA	MONT	TEXAS	
	GA	NEB	UTAH	
	HAWAII	NEV	VT	
	IDAHO	NH	VA	
	ILL	NJ	WASH	
	IND	NM	W VA	
	● IOWA	NY	WIS	OTHER
	KANS	NC	WYO	
	KY	ND		

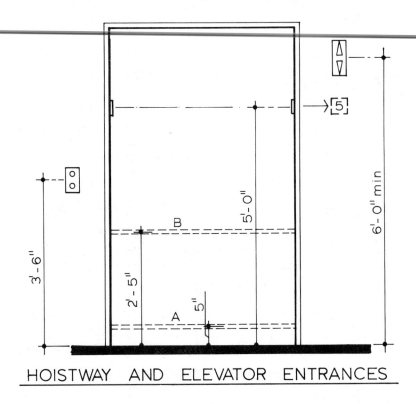

HOISTWAY AND ELEVATOR ENTRANCES

Basis of standard —	APPLICABILITY			
National Elevator Industry Inc. suggested minimum passenger elevator requirement for the handicapped.	ALA	LA	OHIO	GUAM
	ALASKA	MAINE	OKLA	PR
	ARIZ	MD	ORE	VIR IS
Notes —	ARK	MASS	PA	DC
Provide re-opening device at lines A and B. Door reopening device to remain effective for 6 seconds in New Jersey. Min. time for doors to remain fully open: 3 seconds. Hall call buttons: ¾″ min. raised, flush or recessed. Max. depth of flush or recessed button when operated: 3/8″. Provide visual indication to show each call registered and extinguished when call is answered. Visual signal hall lantern for each direction: 2½″ min. Audible signal to sound once for up, twice for down. Floor designations on both sides of each hoistway jamb: 2½″ min. high, raised (or embossed in N.J.) .030″ on contrasting color background.	CAL	MICH	RI	
	COLO	MINN	SC	
	CONN	MISS	SD	FED'L FUNDS
	DEL	MO	TENN	
	FLA	MONT	TEXAS	
	GA	NEB	UTAH	
	HAWAII	NEV	VT	
	IDAHO	NH	VA	
	ILL	● NJ	WASH	
	IND	NM	W VA	
	IOWA	NY	WIS	OTHER
	KANS	NC	WYO	
	KY	ND		

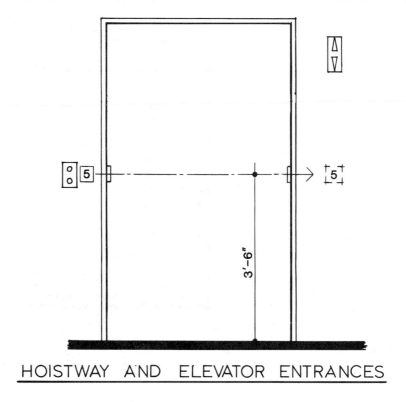

3'-6"

HOISTWAY AND ELEVATOR ENTRANCES

Basis of standard — Art 10F, Chap. 18, Code of West Virginia	APPLICABILITY			
	ALA	LA	OHIO	GUAM
	ALASKA	MAINE	OKLA	PR
	ARIZ	MD	ORE	VIR IS
Notes —	ARK	MASS	PA	DC
Provide raised numerals and locate 3'-6" high on each side of door casing and to the right of call buttons on each floor.	CAL	MICH	RI	
	COLO	MINN	SC	
	CONN	MISS	SD	FED'L FUNDS
	DEL	MO	TENN	
	FLA	MONT	TEXAS	
	GA	NEB	UTAH	
	HAWAII	NEV	VT	
	IDAHO	NH	VA	
	ILL	NJ	WASH	
	IND	NM	● W VA	
	IOWA	NY	WIS	OTHER
	KANS	NC	WYO	
	KY	ND		

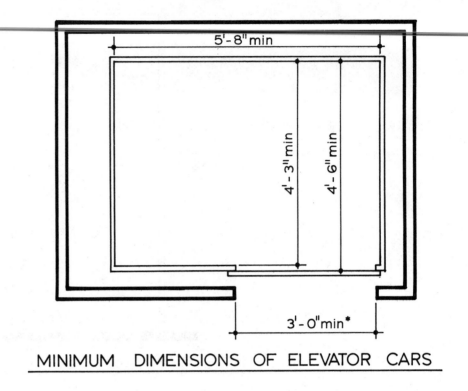

MINIMUM DIMENSIONS OF ELEVATOR CARS

Basis of standard —	APPLICABILITY			
ANSI 1980 – 4.10 and others	ALA	● LA	OHIO	GUAM
	● ALASKA	● MAINE	OKLA	PR
	ARIZ	MD	ORE	VIR IS
	ARK	MASS	PA	DC
Notes —	CAL	MICH	● RI	
For elevators with capacities of less than 2000 lb a minimum width of 54″ is allowed. A center opening door application may necessitate increasing the 5′-8″ dimension. Max. clearance between car platform sill and the edge of any hoistway landing = 1¼″. Floor leveling tolerance = ½″ max. Illinois: handrails on sidewalls, and preferably on side and rear walls to be mounted at between 2′-8″ and 3′-0″ height with 1½″ clearance. (*)Texas: 2′-8″ min.	● COLO	MINN	SC	
	CONN	MISS	SD	FED'L FUNDS
	DEL	MO	TENN	
	FLA	MONT	● TEXAS	
	GA	NEB	UTAH	
	● HAWAII	● NEV	● VT	
	● IDAHO	NH	● VA	
	● ILL	NJ	WASH	
	IND	● NM	W VA	
	IOWA	● NY	WIS	OTHER
	KANS	NC	WYO	
	● KY	ND		

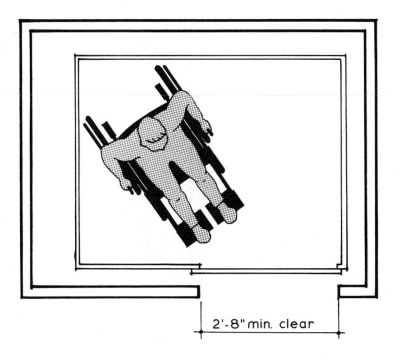

2'-8" min. clear

Basis of standard — ANSI 1961 – 5.9 and others.	APPLICABILITY			
	ALA	LA	OHIO	GUAM
	ALASKA	MAINE	● OKLA	PR
	ARIZ	MD	ORE	VIR IS
Notes — Elevators shall be accessible to, and usable by, the physically disabled on the level they use to enter the building, and at all levels normally used by the general public. Elevators shall allow for traffic as shown in "Human Data". Florida: applies to non-government financed facilities.	ARK	MASS	● PA	DC
	CAL	MICH	RI	
	COLO	MINN	● SC	
	CONN	MISS	● SD	FED'L FUNDS
	DEL	● MO	TENN	
	● FLA	MONT	TEXAS	
	● GA	NEB	UTAH	
	HAWAII	NEV	VT	
	IDAHO	NH	VA	
	ILL	NJ	WASH	
	IND	NM	W VA	
	IOWA	NY	WIS	OTHER
	● KANS	NC	WYO	
	KY	● ND		

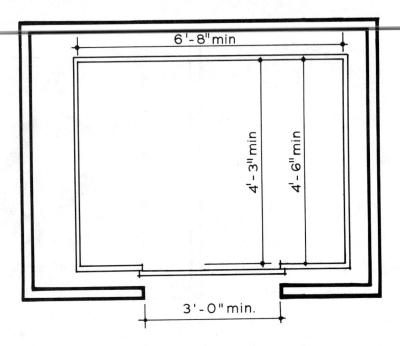

MINIMUM DIMENSIONS OF ELEVATOR CARS

Basis of standard — ATBCB 1190.100 and others	APPLICABILITY			
	ALA	LA	OHIO	GUAM
	ALASKA	MAINE	OKLA	PR
	ARIZ	MD	ORE	VIR IS
● ARK	MASS	PA	DC
	CAL	MICH	RI	
	COLO	MINN	SC	
	CONN	MISS	SD	● FED'L FUNDS
● DEL	MO	TENN	
	FLA	MONT	TEXAS	
	GA	NEB	UTAH	
	HAWAII	NEV	VT	
	IDAHO	NH	VA	
	ILL	NJ	WASH	
	IND	NM	W VA	
	IOWA	NY	WIS	OTHER
	KANS	NC	WYO	
	KY	ND		

Notes —
Exceptions: where existing shaft or structural elements prohibit strict compliance in alteration work, these dimensions may be reduced by the minimum amount necessary, but in no case shall they be less than 4'-0" by 4'-0". Max. clearance between car platform sill and the edge of any hoistway landing = 1¼".

Dimensions shown in diagram: 6'-8" min (width), 4'-3" min, 4'-6" min, 3'-0" min.

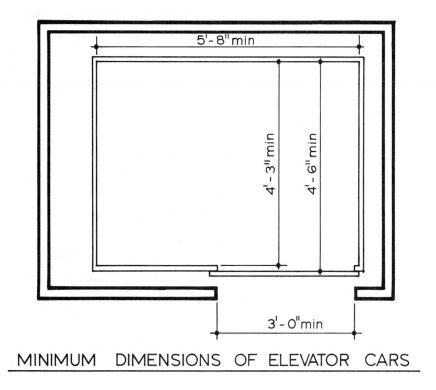

5'- 8"min

4'- 3" min

4'- 6" min

3'- 0"min

MINIMUM DIMENSIONS OF ELEVATOR CARS

Basis of standard — ATBCB 1190.100 and others.	APPLICABILITY			
	ALA	LA	OHIO	GUAM
	ALASKA	MAINE	OKLA	PR
	ARIZ	MD	ORE	VIR IS
Notes — See notes on preceding page.	● ARK	MASS	PA	DC
	CAL	MICH	RI	
	COLO	MINN	SC	
	CONN	MISS	SD	● FED'L FUNDS
	● DEL	MO	TENN	
	FLA	MONT	TEXAS	
	GA	NEB	UTAH	
	HAWAII	NEV	VT	
	IDAHO	NH	VA	
	ILL	NJ	WASH	
	IND	NM	W VA	
	IOWA	NY	WIS	OTHER
	KANS	NC	WYO	
	KY	ND		

5'-8"min**

4'-3"min

4'-6"min

3'-0"min *

MINIMUM DIMENSIONS OF ELEVATOR CARS

Basis of standard — Various	APPLICABILITY			
	ALA	LA	● OHIO	GUAM
	ALASKA	MAINE	OKLA	PR
	ARIZ	MD	ORE	VIR IS
Notes — (*)2'-8″ min. in New Hampshire, Ohio. (**)Ohio (BOCA 1978): where specifically authorized by local authorities for schools, institutions, and other buildings, 5'-4″ may be permitted.	ARK	MASS	PA	DC
	CAL	MICH	RI	
	COLO	MINN	SC	
	CONN	MISS	SD	FED'L FUNDS
	DEL	MO	TENN	
	FLA	MONT	TEXAS	
	GA	NEB	UTAH	
	HAWAII	NEV	VT	
	IDAHO	● NH	VA	
	ILL	NJ	WASH	
	IND	NM	W VA	
	● IOWA	NY	WIS	OTHER
	KANS	NC	WYO	
	KY	ND		

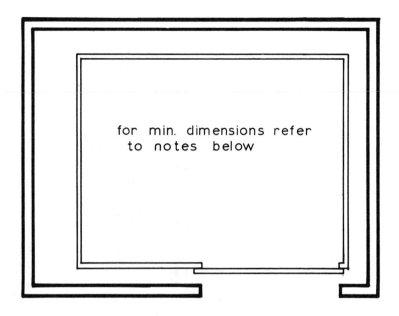

MINIMUM   DIMENSIONS   OF   ELEVATOR   CARS

Basis of standard —	APPLICABILITY			
North Carolina Building Code	ALA	LA	OHIO	GUAM
	ALASKA	MAINE	OKLA	PR
	ARIZ	MD	ORE	VIR IS
Notes —	ARK	MASS	PA	DC
Minimum dimensions of cab interior for elevators normally used by the public for buildings over three	CAL	MICH	RI	
stories high:	COLO	MINN	SC	
5'-0" X 5'-0" square, or	CONN	MISS	SD	FED'L
5'-3" X 4'-8" rectangular, or	DEL	MO	● TENN	FUNDS
6'-8" X 4'-3" rectangular.	FLA	MONT	TEXAS	
In buildings three stories or less, min. may be:	GA	NEB	UTAH	
6'-0" X 3'-8" min. 2000 lb. cap.	HAWAII	NEV	VT	
Elevators shall conform to building floor levels when stopped, with ½" tolerance.	IDAHO	NH	● VA	
	ILL	NJ	WASH	
	IND	NM	W VA	
	IOWA	NY	WIS	OTHER
	KANS	● NC	WYO	
	KY	ND		

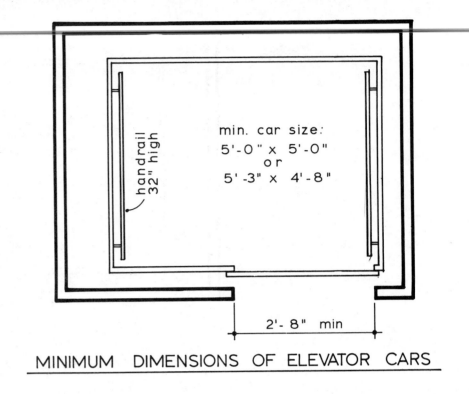

handrail 32" high

min. car size:
5'-0" x 5'-0"
or
5'-3" x 4'-8"

2'-8" min

MINIMUM DIMENSIONS OF ELEVATOR CARS

Basis of standard —	APPLICABILITY			
Barrier Free Design Standard	● ALA	LA	OHIO	GUAM
	ALASKA	MAINE	OKLA	PR
	ARIZ	MD	ORE	VIR IS
	ARK	MASS	PA	DC
Notes —	CAL	MICH	RI	
Operation shall be automatic with cab stopping precisely at floor levels with self-leveling feature. Provide doors with sensitive safety edge.	COLO	MINN	SC	
	CONN	MISS	SD	FED'L FUNDS
	DEL	MO	TENN	
	FLA	MONT	TEXAS	
	GA	NEB	UTAH	
	HAWAII	NEV	VT	
	IDAHO	NH	VA	
	ILL	NJ	WASH	
	IND	NM	W VA	
	IOWA	NY	WIS	OTHER
	KANS	NC	WYO	
	KY	ND		

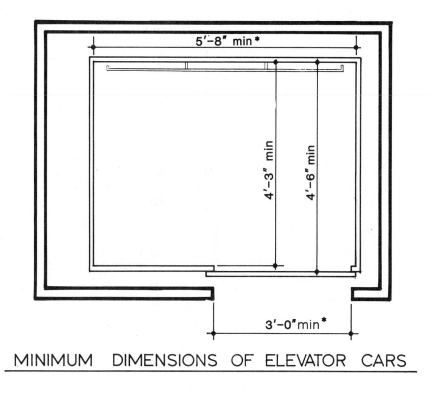

5'-8" min*

4'-3" min

4'-6" min

3'-0" min*

MINIMUM DIMENSIONS OF ELEVATOR CARS

Basis of standard — CAC Title 24, Part 2.	APPLICABILITY			
	ALA	LA	OHIO	GUAM
	ALASKA	MAINE	OKLA	PR
	ARIZ	MD	ORE	VIR IS
	ARK	MASS	PA	DC
	● CAL	MICH	RI	
	COLO	MINN	SC	
	CONN	MISS	SD	FED'L
	DEL	MO	TENN	FUNDS
	FLA	MONT	TEXAS	
	GA	NEB	UTAH	
	HAWAII	NEV	VT	
	IDAHO	NH	VA	
	ILL	NJ	WASH	
	IND	NM	W VA	
	IOWA	NY	WIS	OTHER
	KANS	NC	WYO	
	KY	ND		

Notes —

(*)4'-6" allowed where 50 persons or less; doors 2'-8".
At least one elevator is required to be 6'-8" wide with minimum 3'-6" door for ambulance stretcher, when elevators are required by Table 33A of the Uniform Building Code.
One handrail required in car at 2'-6" to 2'-10".

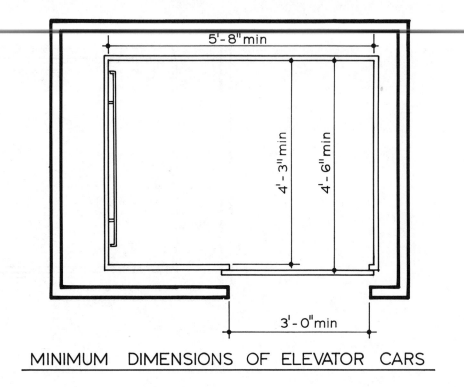

MINIMUM   DIMENSIONS   OF   ELEVATOR   CARS

Basis of standard — Connecticut Building Code — Art 21	APPLICABILITY			
	ALA	LA	OHIO	GUAM
	ALASKA	MAINE	OKLA	PR
	ARIZ	MD	ORE	VIR IS
	ARK	MASS	PA	DC
	CAL	MICH	RI	
	COLO	MINN	SC	
● CONN	MISS	SD	FED'L FUNDS
	DEL	MO	TENN	
	FLA	MONT	TEXAS	
	GA	NEB	UTAH	
	HAWAII	NEV	VT	
	IDAHO	NH	VA	
	ILL	NJ	WASH	
	IND	NM	W VA	
	IOWA	NY	WIS	OTHER
	KANS	NC	WYO	
	KY	ND		

Notes —
Provide at least one handrail min. 2'-6", max. 3'-0" above floor. Car and hoistway doors shall be automatically operated and shall be equipped with reopening devices.

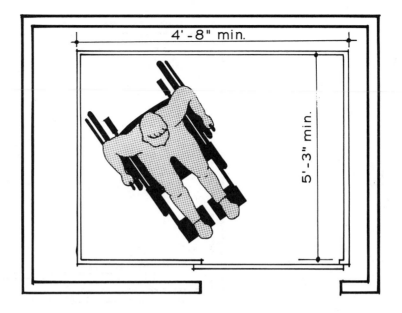

Basis of standard — Dept. of General Services	APPLICABILITY			
	ALA	LA	OHIO	GUAM
	ALASKA	MAINE	OKLA	PR
	ARIZ	MD	ORE	VIR IS
	ARK	MASS	PA	DC
	CAL	MICH	RI	
	COLO	MINN	SC	
	CONN	MISS	SD	FED'L FUNDS
	DEL	MO	TENN	
	● FLA	MONT	TEXAS	
	GA	NEB	UTAH	
	HAWAII	NEV	VT	
	IDAHO	NH	VA	
	ILL	NJ	WASH	
	IND	NM	W VA	
	IOWA	NY	WIS	OTHER
	KANS	NC	WYO	
	KY	ND		

Notes —

Florida: Applies to government facilities. Provide at least one complying elevator in public buildings more than one story high, serving all floors normally used by the public and employees. Minimum clear width to be 5'-0″ when depth is at least 5'-0″. Car floor to be level with building floor. Elevator doors to have sensitive edges in addition to any other sensing safety devices. Provide numbers, letters, and braille type the same type as elevator cabs on the right jamb of elevator entrance.

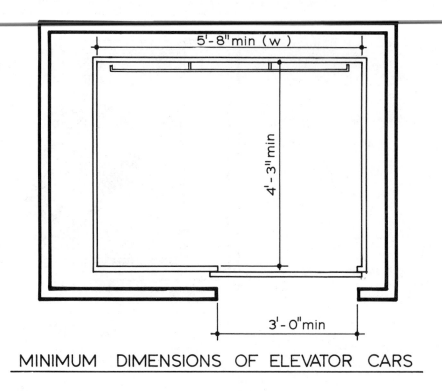

5'-8" min (w)

4'- 3" min

3'- 0" min

MINIMUM   DIMENSIONS   OF   ELEVATOR   CARS

Basis of standard —	APPLICABILITY			
Maryland Building Code for the Handicapped	ALA	LA	OHIO	GUAM
	ALASKA	MAINE	OKLA	PR
	ARIZ	● MD	ORE	VIR IS
Notes —	ARK	MASS	PA	DC
Capacity lbs. Min. w Clear opening door	CAL	MICH	RI	
Less than 2,500 5'-8" 3'-0"	COLO	MINN	SC	
2,500 or more 6'-8" 3'-6"	CONN	MISS	SD	FED'L
Rail at rear wall, to be smooth, 1½" min. clear of wall.	DEL	MO	TENN	FUNDS
2,000 lb elevator acceptable for 2 stories, 2,500 lb.	FLA	MONT	TEXAS	
for 3 stories.	GA	NEB	UTAH	
	HAWAII	NEV	VT	
	IDAHO	NH	VA	
	ILL	NJ	WASH	
	IND	NM	W VA	
	IOWA	NY	WIS	OTHER
	KANS	NC	WYO	
	KY	ND		

Capacity lbs. | Min. w | Clear opening door
Less than 2,500 | 5'-8" | 3'-0"
2,500 or more | 6'-8" | 3'-6"

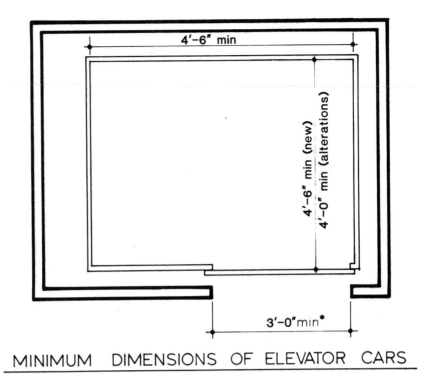

4'-6" min

4'-6" min (new)

4'-0" min (alterations)

3'-0"min*

MINIMUM DIMENSIONS OF ELEVATOR CARS

Basis of standard —	APPLICABILITY			
521 CMR Architectural Barriers Board	ALA	LA	OHIO	GUAM
	ALASKA	MAINE	OKLA	PR
	ARIZ	MD	ORE	VIR IS
Notes —	ARK	● MASS	PA	DC
Use ramps or elevators for buildings having two levels. Cars to be self-leveling with a plus or minus ½″ tolerance. Provide 3'-0″ high handrail on at least one wall with 1½″ clearance. Illumination at control panel and floor: 5 foot candles. Maximum closing speed one foot per second.	CAL	MICH	RI	
	COLO	MINN	SC	
	CONN	MISS	SD	FED'L FUNDS
	DEL	MO	TENN	
(*)2'-8″ allowed for alteration projects.	FLA	MONT	TEXAS	
	GA	NEB	UTAH	
	HAWAII	NEV	VT	
	IDAHO	NH	VA	
	ILL	NJ	WASH	
	IND	NM	W VA	
	IOWA	NY	WIS	OTHER
	KANS	NC	WYO	
	KY	ND		

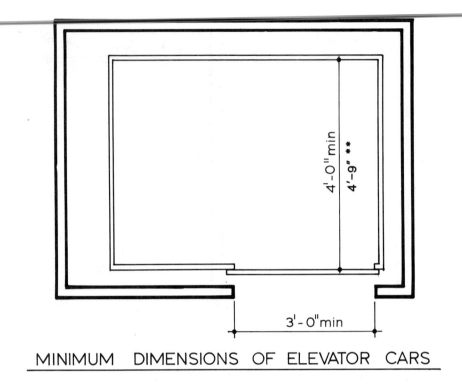

4'-0" min

4'-9" **

3'-0" min

MINIMUM DIMENSIONS OF ELEVATOR CARS

Basis of standard — Construction Code Commission	APPLICABILITY			
	ALA	LA	OHIO	GUAM
	ALASKA	MAINE	OKLA	PR
	ARIZ	MD	ORE	VIR IS
Notes —	ARK	MASS	PA	DC
Provide at least one handrail at normal handrail height in car. Doors to operate automatically. Leading edge of car doors to be equipped with door safety shoe reversing device and a light ray or other proximity reversing device.	CAL	● MICH	RI	
	COLO	MINN	SC	
	CONN	MISS	SD	FED'L FUNDS
(*)For not more than 3 stops, min. area = 22 sq. ft.	DEL	MO	TENN	
For all others, min. area = 25 sq. ft. with minimum	FLA	MONT	TEXAS	
dimension of 4'-7".	GA	NEB	UTAH	
	HAWAII	NEV	VT	
	IDAHO	NH	VA	
	ILL	NJ	WASH	
	IND	NM	W VA	
	IOWA	NY	WIS	OTHER
	KANS	NC	WYO	
	KY	ND		

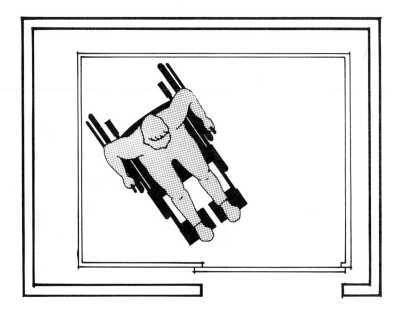

Basis of standard —	APPLICABILITY			
Public Building Facilities for the Handicapped	ALA	LA	OHIO	GUAM
	ALASKA	MAINE	OKLA	PR
	ARIZ	MD	ORE	VIR IS
Notes —	ARK	MASS	PA	DC
Where elevators are to be provided, at least one bank of elevators, or one single elevator if installed in single units, shall be accessible to, and usable by, the physically disabled at all levels normally used by the general public. Such bank of elevators, or single elevator, shall be designed to allow for traffic by wheelchairs.	CAL	MICH	RI	
	COLO	MINN	SC	
	CONN	● MISS	SD	FED'L FUNDS
	DEL	MO	TENN	
	FLA	MONT	TEXAS	
	GA	NEB	UTAH	
	HAWAII	NEV	VT	
	IDAHO	NH	VA	
	ILL	NJ	WASH	
	IND	NM	W VA	
	IOWA	NY	WIS	OTHER
	KANS	NC	WYO	
	KY	ND		

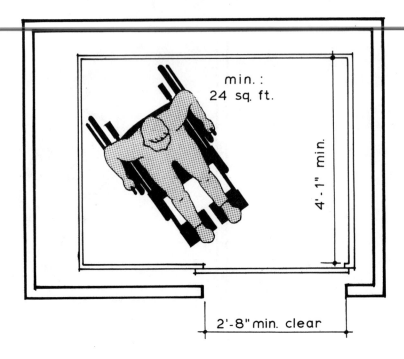

min.:
24 sq. ft.

4'-1" min.

2'-8" min. clear

Basis of standard —	APPLICABILITY			
	ALA	LA	OHIO	GUAM
	ALASKA	MAINE	OKLA	PR
	ARIZ	MD	ORE	VIR IS
Notes — Level to within ½″ of building floor levels.	ARK	MASS	PA	DC
	CAL	MICH	RI	
	COLO	MINN	SC	
	CONN	MISS	SD	FED'L FUNDS
	DEL	MO	TENN	
	FLA	MONT	TEXAS	
	GA	● NEB	UTAH	
	HAWAII	NEV	VT	
	IDAHO	NH	VA	
	ILL	NJ	WASH	
	IND	NM	W VA	
	IOWA	NY	WIS	OTHER
	KANS	NC	WYO	
	KY	ND		

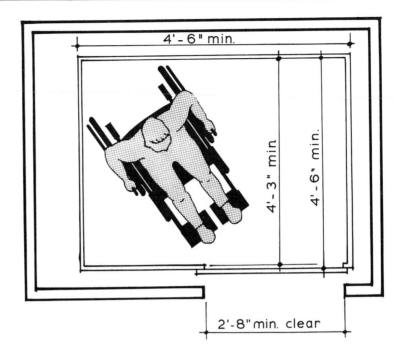

4'-6" min.

4'-3" min.

4'-6" min.

2'-8" min. clear

Basis of standard — Barrier Free Design Regulations .	**APPLICABILITY**			
	ALA	LA	OHIO	GUAM
	ALASKA	MAINE	OKLA	PR
	ARIZ	MD	ORE	VIR IS
Notes — Leveling tolerance: ½". Identify by plaque containing International Symbol of Access in relief. Located immediately adjacent to floor call button. Max. running clearance at threshold: 1¼". Provide 2'-8" high handrails, 1½" clear, at all sides except where doors occur. Min. illumination at controls and landing: 5 fc. Provide every multi-story building with accessible elevator except: business buildings with less than 6,000 sq ft. at other than the principal entrance level, mezzanines with less than 10,000 sq ft. in business and factory buildings, 1-4 family residences, multi-family apartment houses where elevator would serve no more than 4 dwelling units per floor, multi-family apartment buildings of less than 3 stories, two and three story hotels and motels with fewer than 80 units where first floor accommodations are provided barrier free.	ARK	MASS	PA	DC
	CAL	MICH	RI	
	COLO	MINN	SC	
	CONN	MISS	SD	FED'L FUNDS
	DEL	MO	TENN	
	FLA	MONT	TEXAS	
	GA	NEB	UTAH	
	HAWAII	NEV	VT	
	IDAHO	NH	VA	
	ILL	● NJ	WASH	
	IND	NM	W VA	
	IOWA	NY	WIS	OTHER
	KANS	NC	WYO	
	KY	ND		

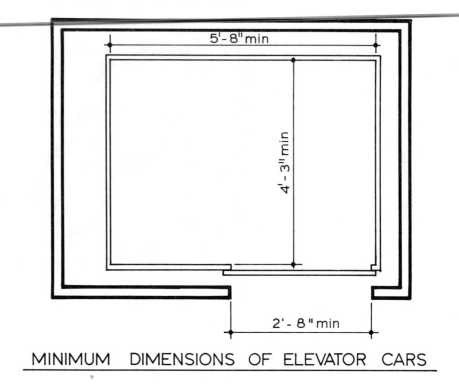

5'-8" min

4'-3" min

2'-8" min

MINIMUM DIMENSIONS OF ELEVATOR CARS

Basis of standard — Barrier Free Design	APPLICABILITY			
	ALA	LA	OHIO	GUAM
	ALASKA	MAINE	OKLA	PR
	ARIZ	MD	ORE	VIR IS
Notes — South Carolina utilizes minimal mandatory criteria, but lists preferred criteria. Both are shown on this page. Min. size for letters and numbers: 1½″ high, raised or recessed at least .0025″, plus braille. Floor call and change signals: visual and audible, differentiate up and down signals. Handrails 32″ above floor on all walls without doors with 1½″ min. wall clearance. 5′ high entrance identification on right jamb. Doors: power operated, sliding horizontal, sensitive safety edges or other reopening device. Automatic floor leveling differential = ½″ max.	ARK	MASS	PA	DC
	CAL	MICH	RI	
	COLO	MINN	● SC	
	CONN	MISS	SD	FED'L
	DEL	MO	TENN	FUNDS
	FLA	MONT	TEXAS	
	GA	NEB	UTAH	
	HAWAII	NEV	VT	
	IDAHO	NH	VA	
	ILL	NJ	WASH	
	IND	NM	W VA	
	IOWA	NY	WIS	OTHER
	KANS	NC	WYO	
	KY	ND		

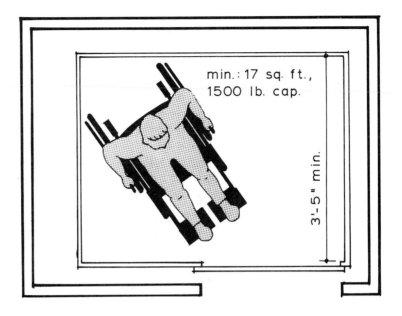

min.: 17 sq. ft.,
1500 lb. cap.

3'-5" min.

Basis of standard — Utah State Building Board	APPLICABILITY			
	ALA	LA	OHIO	GUAM
	ALASKA	MAINE	OKLA	PR
	ARIZ	MD	ORE	VIR IS
	ARK	MASS	PA	DC
	CAL	MICH	RI	
	COLO	MINN	SC	
	CONN	MISS	SD	FED'L FUNDS
	DEL	MO	TENN	
	FLA	MONT	TEXAS	
	GA	NEB	● UTAH	
	HAWAII	NEV	VT	
	IDAHO	NH	VA	
	ILL	NJ	WASH	
	IND	NM	W VA	
	IOWA	NY	WIS	OTHER
	KANS	NC	WYO	
	KY	ND		

Notes —

At least one elevator or interior ramp shall serve all floors and levels of publicly owned buildings above or below the main floor level. Operation shall be automatic, level to building floors with ½″ tolerance. 30″ to 34″ high handrails on side wall closest to control panel and across back wall, with 1½″ clearance to wall.

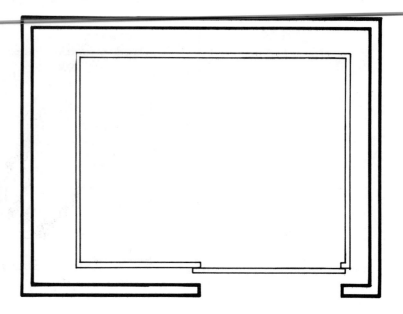

MINIMUM DIMENSIONS OF ELEVATOR CARS

Basis of standard —	APPLICABILITY			
Art 10F, Chapter 18, Code of West Virginia	ALA	LA	OHIO	GUAM
	ALASKA	MAINE	OKLA	PR
	ARIZ	MD	ORE	VIR IS
Notes —	ARK	MASS	PA	DC
Minimum cab size: space for one wheelchair and one ambulant individual. Provide exact leveling with floor level. Safety edge door with sensing device.	CAL	MICH	RI	
	COLO	MINN	SC	
	CONN	MISS	SD	FED'L
	DEL	MO	TENN	FUNDS
	FLA	MONT	TEXAS	
	GA	NEB	UTAH	
	HAWAII	NEV	VT	
	IDAHO	NH	VA	
	ILL	NJ	WASH	
	IND	NM	● W VA	
	IOWA	NY	WIS	OTHER
	KANS	NC	WYO	
	KY	ND		

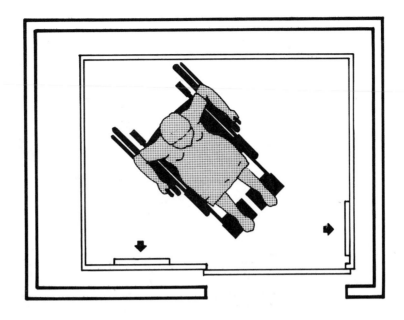

ALTERNATE LOCATIONS OF PANEL WITH SIDE OPENING DOOR

Basis of standard —	APPLICABILITY			
ANSI 1980 — 4.10 and others	ALA	● LA	OHIO	GUAM
	● ALASKA	● MAINE	OKLA	PR
	ARIZ	MD	ORE	VIR IS
Notes —	● ARK	MASS	PA	DC
	CAL	MICH	● RI	
	● COLO	MINN	SC	
	CONN	MISS	SD	● FED'L FUNDS
	● DEL	MO	TENN	
	FLA	MONT	TEXAS	
	GA	NEB	UTAH	
	● HAWAII	● NEV	● VT	
	● IDAHO	NH	● VA	
	● ILL	NJ	WASH	
	IND	● NM	W VA	
	● IOWA	● NY	WIS	OTHER
	KANS	NC	WYO	
	● KY	ND		

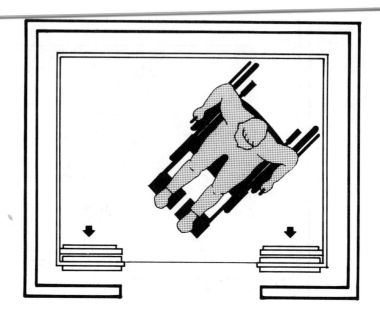

ALTERNATE LOCATIONS OF PANEL WITH CENTER OPENING DOOR

Basis of standard — ANSI 1980 — 4.10 and others	APPLICABILITY			
	ALA	● LA	OHIO	GUAM
	● ALASKA	● MAINE	OKLA	PR
	ARIZ	MD	ORE	VIR IS
Notes —	● ARK	MASS	PA	DC
	CAL	MICH	● RI	
	● COLO	MINN	SC	
	CONN	MISS	SD	● FED'L FUNDS
	● DEL	MO	TENN	
	FLA	MONT	● TEXAS	
	GA	NEB	UTAH	
	● HAWAII	● NEV	● VT	
	● IDAHO	NH	● VA	
	● ILL	NJ	WASH	
	IND	● NM	W VA	
	● IOWA	● NY	WIS	OTHER
	KANS	NC	WYO	
	● KY	ND		

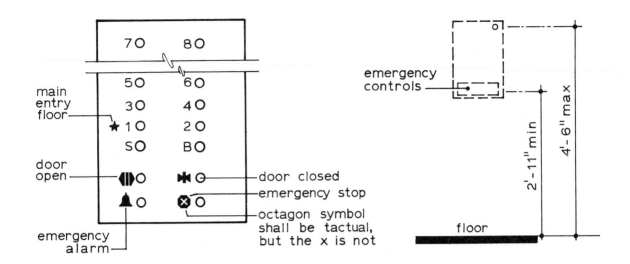

PANEL DETAIL   CONTROL HEIGHT

Basis of standard —	APPLICABILITY			
ANSI 1980 — 4.10 and others	ALA	● LA	OHIO	GUAM
	● ALASKA	● MAINE	OKLA	PR
	ARIZ	MD	ORE	VIR IS
	ARK	MASS	PA	DC
	● CAL	MICH	● RI	
	● COLO	MINN	SC	
	CONN	MISS	SD	FED'L FUNDS
	DEL	MO	TENN	
	FLA	MONT	TEXAS	
	GA	NEB	UTAH	
	● HAWAII	● NEV	● VT	
	● IDAHO	NH	● VA	
	● ILL	NJ	WASH	
	IND	● NM	W VA	
	IOWA	● NY	WIS	OTHER
	KANS	NC	WYO	
	● KY	ND		

Notes —

Button smallest dimension: ¾″. Buttons may be raised, flush or recessed. Designate all control buttons by raised or indented standard alphabet letters for letters, arabic characters for numerals, or standard symbols shown above and as required by ANSI A17.1–1978 and A17.1a–1979. Designate call button for main entry floor by raised or indented star at left of floor designation. Place all raised or indented designations immediately to left of applicable button. Permanently attached applied plates are acceptable. Provide floor buttons with visual indicators to show when each call is registered, which shall extinguish when each call is answered. Group emergency buttons at bottom of panels with center lines no lower than 2′-11″ above floor. California: Telephone maximum 4′-0″ with minimum 29″ cord.

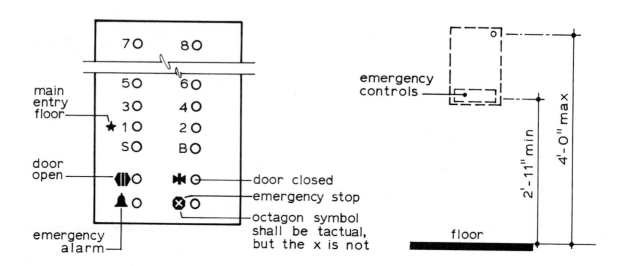

PANEL DETAIL   CONTROL HEIGHT

Basis of standard —	APPLICABILITY			
ATBCB 1190.100 and others	ALA	LA	OHIO	GUAM
	ALASKA	MAINE	OKLA	PR
	ARIZ	MD	ORE	VIR IS
Notes —	● ARK	MASS	PA	DC
See preceding page for notes.	CAL	MICH	RI	
Federal, Arkansas, and Delaware do not permit recessed buttons or designations. Control heights:	COLO	MINN	SC	
Federal and Arkansas permit 4'-6" max. height if	CONN	MISS	SD	
there is a substantial cost increase resulting from the	● DEL	MO	TENN	● FED'L FUNDS
4'-0" requirement; Delaware requires complying to	FLA	MONT	TEXAS	
"Human Data" (4'-0" for front reach, 4-6" for side	GA	NEB	UTAH	
reach).	HAWAII	NEV	VT	
	IDAHO	NH	VA	
	ILL	NJ	WASH	
	IND	NM	W VA	
	IOWA	NY	WIS	OTHER
	KANS	NC	WYO	
	KY	ND		

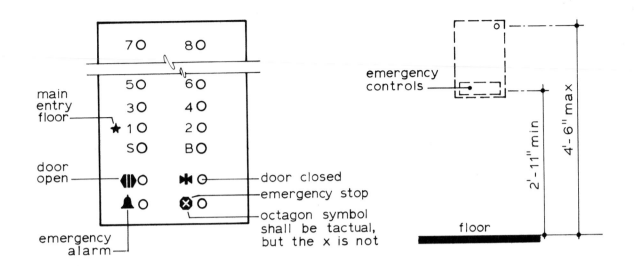

PANEL DETAIL   CONTROL   HEIGHT

Basis of standard —	APPLICABILITY			
BOCA − 1978 and others.	ALA	LA	● OHIO	GUAM
	ALASKA	MAINE	OKLA	PR
	ARIZ	MD	ORE	VIR IS
	ARK	MASS	PA	DC
Notes —	CAL	MICH	RI	
3/4″ min. floor registration buttons, exclusive of	COLO	MINN	SC	
border, raised, flush, or recessed. Max. depth of	CONN	MISS	SD	FED'L
flush or recessed buttons when operated: 3/8″.	DEL	MO	TENN	FUNDS
Provide visual indication to show each call registered	FLA	MONT	TEXAS	
and extinguished when answered. Provide workings	GA	NEB	UTAH	
adjacent and left of controls in a contrasting color	HAWAII	NEV	● VT	
background, min. 1/2″ high and raised or recessed	IDAHO	NH	VA	
.30″. Use symbols to readily identify essential con-	ILL	● NJ	WASH	
trols. New Jersey and Vermont: Telephones 4′-0″	IND	NM	W VA	
high max. with 3′-0″ min. cord. Provide markings	IOWA	NY	WIS	OTHER
1/2″ min. high, raised or recessed .030″ adjacent	KANS	NC	WYO	
to the control on a contrasting color background.	KY	ND		

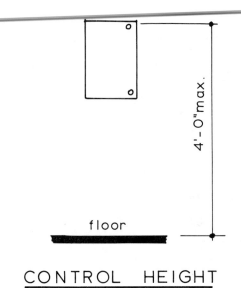

4'-0"max.

floor

CONTROL HEIGHT

Basis of standard — Art 10F, Chapt. 18, Code of West Virginia	APPLICABILITY			
	ALA	LA	OHIO	GUAM
	ALASKA	MAINE	OKLA	PR
	ARIZ	MD	ORE	VIR IS
Notes — Provide raised identification for controls. Florida: applies to government facilities. Identify controls by numbers and letters ½″ min. high and raised .025″ with square edges and adjacent braille immediately adjacent to the control.	ARK	MASS	PA	DC
	CAL	MICH	RI	
	COLO	MINN	SC	
	CONN	MISS	SD	FED'L
	DEL	MO	TENN	FUNDS
	● FLA	MONT	TEXAS	
	GA	NEB	UTAH	
	HAWAII	NEV	VT	
	IDAHO	NH	VA	
	ILL	NJ	WASH	
	IND	NM	● W VA	
	IOWA	NY	WIS	OTHER
	KANS	NC	WYO	
	KY	ND		

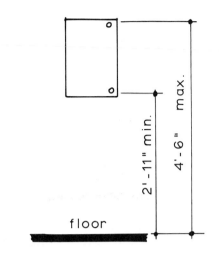

CONTROL HEIGHT

Basis of standard —	APPLICABILITY			
Architectural Barrier Free Design Code and others	ALA	LA	OHIO	GUAM
	ALASKA	MAINE	OKLA	PR
	ARIZ	MD	ORE	VIR IS
Notes —	ARK	● MASS	PA	DC
Dimensions shown are to button centerlines. Floor numbers, letters or symbols: 3/4″ in size, raised 1/8″ on contrasting background, located to left of floor buttons (not on the buttons). Braille letters or numbers may be used in addition to large raised letters. On every floor, post a written program to evacuate the physically handicapped above the hall buttons. Car position indicator, where provided, shall be located above control panel or door, illuminated on contrasting background. In addition, audible signals shall indicate passing floors. Massachussetts: provide telephone or two-way communications system at 4′-0″ max. height, where a service location is maintained in a building.	CAL	MICH	RI	
	COLO	MINN	SC	
	CONN	MISS	SD	FED'L FUNDS
	DEL	MO	TENN	
	FLA	MONT	TEXAS	
	GA	NEB	UTAH	
	HAWAII	NEV	VT	
	IDAHO	● NH	VA	
	ILL	NJ	WASH	
	IND	NM	W VA	
	IOWA	NY	WIS	OTHER
	KANS	NC	WYO	
	KY	ND		

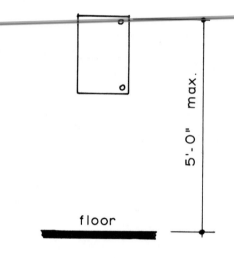

5'-0" max.

floor

CONTROL HEIGHT

Basis of standard — Various	APPLICABILITY			
	ALA	LA	● OHIO	GUAM
	ALASKA	MAINE	OKLA	PR
	ARIZ	MD	ORE	VIR IS
	ARK	MASS	PA	DC
	CAL	● MICH	RI	
	COLO	MINN	SC	
	CONN	MISS	SD	FED'L FUNDS
	DEL	MO	TENN	
	FLA	MONT	TEXAS	
	GA	NEB	UTAH	
	HAWAII	NEV	VT	
	IDAHO	NH	VA	
	ILL	NJ	WASH	
	IND	NM	W VA	
	IOWA	NY	WIS	OTHER
	KANS	NC	WYO	
	KY	ND		

Notes —
Michigan, Ohio, provide metal braille numbers adjacent to cab control buttons and switches.

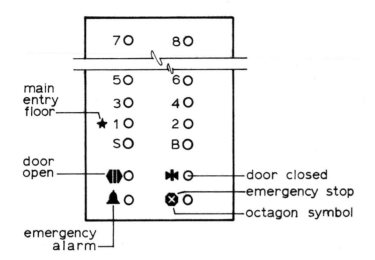

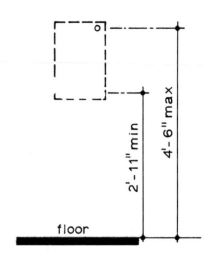

PANEL DETAIL
(shown configuration is not mandatory)

CONTROL HEIGHT

Basis of standard — North Carolina Building Code	APPLICABILITY			
	ALA	LA	OHIO	GUAM
	ALASKA	MAINE	OKLA	PR
	ARIZ	MD	ORE	VIR IS
	ARK	MASS	PA	DC
	CAL	MICH	RI	
	COLO	MINN	SC	
	CONN	MISS	SD	FED'L FUNDS
	DEL	MO	● TENN	
	FLA	MONT	TEXAS	
	GA	NEB	UTAH	
	HAWAII	NEV	VT	
	IDAHO	NH	VA	
	ILL	NJ	WASH	
	IND	NM	W VA	
	IOWA	NY	WIS	OTHER
	KANS	● NC	WYO	
	KY	ND		

Notes —

Provide car position indicator above operating panel or over opening of each car to show position of car in hoistway by indicator illumination on contrasting background and ½″ min. height. Also provide audible signal to tell passenger that car is stopping or passing a floor served by the elevator. In passenger elevators, all operating controls, buttons and emergency signaling devices shall be identified with raised arabic numerals or industry-recommended symbols to left of controls, at least ½″ high, raised or recessed .030″ min., permanently attached and on color contrasting background.

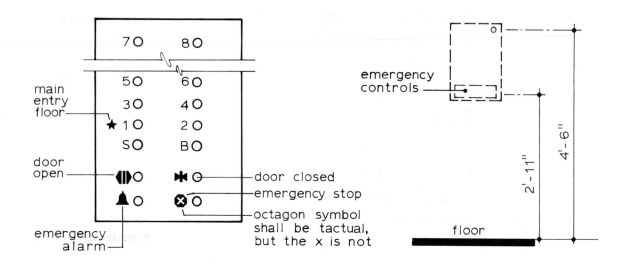

PANEL DETAIL   CONTROL HEIGHT

Basis of standard —	APPLICABILITY			
Arizona Revised Statutes sec. 34-406	ALA	LA	OHIO	GUAM
	ALASKA	MAINE	OKLA	PR
	● ARIZ	MD	ORE	VIR IS
	ARK	MASS	PA	DC
	CAL	MICH	RI	
	COLO	MINN	SC	
Notes —	CONN	MISS	SD	FED'L
Elevator control buttons shall have identifying features for the blind. Elevators shall allow for traffic by wheelchairs.	DEL	MO	TENN	FUNDS
	FLA	MONT	TEXAS	
	GA	NEB	UTAH	
	HAWAII	NEV	VT	
	IDAHO	NH	VA	
	ILL	NJ	WASH	
	IND	NM	W VA	
	IOWA	NY	WIS	OTHER
	KANS	NC	WYO	
	KY	ND		

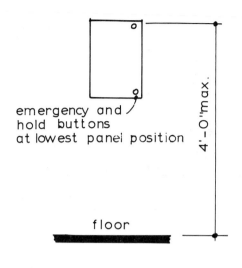

emergency and
hold buttons
at lowest panel position

4'-0"max.

floor

CONTROL   HEIGHT

Basis of standard —	APPLICABILITY			
Connecticut Building Code — Art 21 and others	ALA	LA	OHIO	GUAM
	ALASKA	MAINE	OKLA	PR
	ARIZ	MD	ORE	VIR IS
Notes —	ARK	MASS	PA	DC
Provide tactile numbers adjacent to all cab control buttons and switches. Locate "emergency" and "hold" buttons at lowest position on control panel.	CAL	MICH	RI	
	COLO	MINN	SC	
	● CONN	MISS	SD	FED'L FUNDS
	DEL	MO	TENN	
	FLA	MONT	TEXAS	
	GA	NEB	UTAH	
	HAWAII	NEV	VT	
	IDAHO	NH	VA	
	ILL	NJ	WASH	
	IND	NM	W VA	
	IOWA	NY	WIS	OTHER
	KANS	NC	WYO	
	KY	ND		

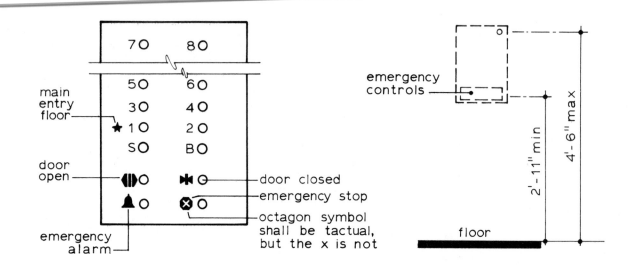

PANEL DETAIL   CONTROL HEIGHT

Basis of standard —	APPLICABILITY			
Iowa Administrative Code	ALA	LA	OHIO	GUAM
	ALASKA	MAINE	OKLA	PR
	ARIZ	MD	ORE	VIR IS
Notes —	ARK	MASS	PA	DC
	CAL	MICH	RI	
	COLO	MINN	SC	
	CONN	MISS	SD	FED'L
	DEL	MO	TENN	FUNDS
	FLA	MONT	TEXAS	
	GA	NEB	UTAH	
	HAWAII	NEV	VT	
	IDAHO	NH	VA	
	ILL	NJ	WASH	
	IND	NM	W VA	
	● IOWA	NY	WIS	OTHER
	KANS	NC	WYO	
	KY	ND		

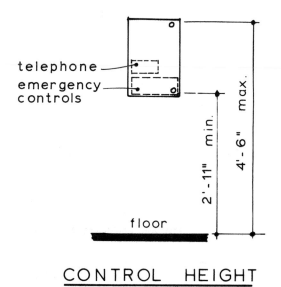

telephone
emergency
controls

2'-11" min.

4'-6" max.

floor

CONTROL HEIGHT

Basis of standard —	APPLICABILITY			
Maryland Building Code for the Handicapped	ALA	LA	OHIO	GUAM
	ALASKA	MAINE	OKLA	PR
	ARIZ	● MD	ORE	VIR IS
Notes —	ARK	MASS	PA	DC
Connect telephone directly to house phone unless it is a dial phone, in which case an emergency number shall be listed in a readily visible location. Min. telephone cord length: 3 feet. Letters or numbers shall be min. ½″ high block letters, raised .030″, with contrasting colors. Markings to be adjacent to the controls on a contrasting color background to the left of controls.	CAL	MICH	RI	
	COLO	MINN	SC	
	CONN	MISS	SD	FED'L FUNDS
	DEL	MO	TENN	
	FLA	MONT	TEXAS	
	GA	NEB	UTAH	
	HAWAII	NEV	VT	
	IDAHO	NH	VA	
	ILL	NJ	WASH	
	IND	NM	W VA	
	IOWA	NY	WIS	OTHER
	KANS	NC	WYO	
	KY	ND		

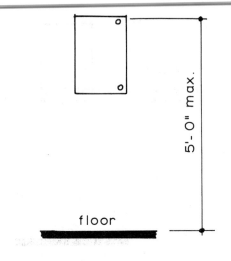

5'- 0" max.

floor

CONTROL HEIGHT

Basis of standard —	APPLICABILITY			
State Building Code	ALA	LA	OHIO	GUAM
	ALASKA	MAINE	OKLA	PR
	ARIZ	MD	ORE	VIR IS
Notes —	ARK	MASS	PA	DC
Provide tactile identification by raised or recessed letters, labels or plaques.	CAL	MICH	RI	
	COLO	● MINN	SC	
	CONN	MISS	SD	FED'L FUNDS
	DEL	MO	TENN	
	FLA	MONT	TEXAS	
	GA	NEB	UTAH	
	HAWAII	NEV	VT	
	IDAHO	NH	VA	
	ILL	NJ	WASH	
	IND	NM	W VA	
	IOWA	NY	WIS	OTHER
	KANS	NC	WYO	
	KY	ND		

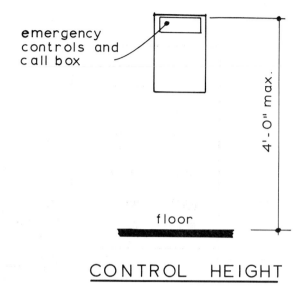

emergency controls and call box

floor

4'-0" max.

CONTROL   HEIGHT

Basis of standard — Nebraska Provisions for the Handicapped	APPLICABILITY			
	ALA	LA	OHIO	GUAM
	ALASKA	MAINE	OKLA	PR
	ARIZ	MD	ORE	VIR IS
Notes — Identify all controls by raised or notched information adjacent to or on the selection buttons. Preferred location of controls: sidewalls of the cab. Letters recessed or raised 1/32″ min., 1/2″ min. height. Visible signals 1/2″ min. height of contrasting color.	ARK	MASS	PA	DC
	CAL	MICH	RI	
	COLO	MINN	SC	
	CONN	MISS	SD	FED'L FUNDS
	DEL	MO	TENN	
	FLA	MONT	TEXAS	
	GA	● NEB	UTAH	
	HAWAII	NEV	VT	
	IDAHO	NH	VA	
	ILL	NJ	WASH	
	IND	NM	W VA	
	IOWA	NY	WIS	OTHER
	KANS	NC	WYO	
	KY	ND		

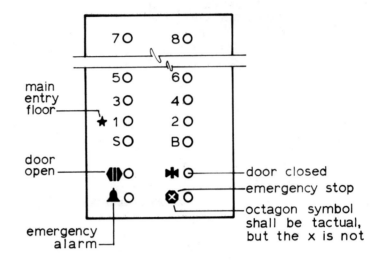

main
entry
floor

door
open ——— ⬤O ... ⬤O ——— door closed
⬤O ... ⊗O ——— emergency stop
——— octagon symbol
shall be tactual,
but the x is not

emergency
alarm ———

PANEL DETAIL

Basis of standard —	APPLICABILITY			
Structural Specialty Code	ALA	LA	OHIO	GUAM
	ALASKA	MAINE	OKLA	PR
	ARIZ	MD	● ORE	VIR IS
Notes —	ARK	MASS	PA	DC
Mark controls in compliance with national standards for use by the blind. Publicly used elevators shall provide for traffic by standard wheelchairs.	CAL	MICH	RI	
	COLO	MINN	SC	
	CONN	MISS	SD	FED'L
	DEL	MO	TENN	FUNDS
	FLA	MONT	TEXAS	
	GA	NEB	UTAH	
	HAWAII	NEV	VT	
	IDAHO	NH	VA	
	ILL	NJ	WASH	
	IND	NM	W VA	
	IOWA	NY	WIS	OTHER
	KANS	NC	WYO	
	KY	ND		

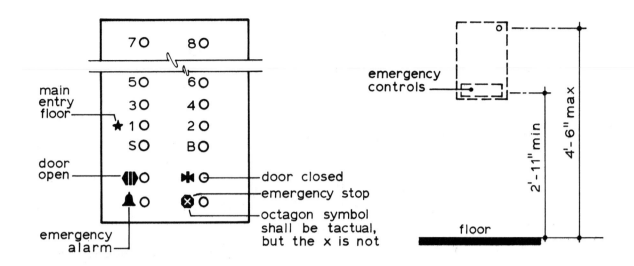

PANEL DETAIL

main
entry
floor

door
open — door closed

emergency stop

octagon symbol
shall be tactual,
but the x is not

emergency
alarm

CONTROL HEIGHT

emergency
controls

floor

2'-11" min

4'-6" max

Basis of standard —	APPLICABILITY			
Barrier Free Design	ALA	LA	OHIO	GUAM
	ALASKA	MAINE	OKLA	PR
	ARIZ	MD	ORE	VIR IS
	ARK	MASS	PA	DC
Notes —	CAL	MICH	RI	
Min. symbol height for central panels - ½", offset .0025". Adjacent braille symbols.	COLO	MINN	● SC	
	CONN	MISS	SD	FED'L
	DEL	MO	TENN	FUNDS
	FLA	MONT	TEXAS	
	GA	NEB	UTAH	
	HAWAII	NEV	VT	
	IDAHO	NH	VA	
	ILL	NJ	WASH	
	IND	NM	W VA	
	IOWA	NY	WIS	OTHER
	KANS	NC	WYO	
	KY	ND		

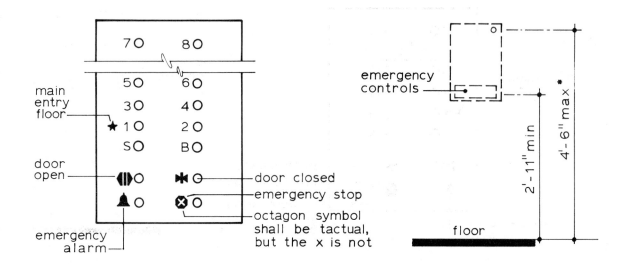

PANEL DETAIL   CONTROL HEIGHT

Basis of standard —	APPLICABILITY			
State Purchasing and General Services Commission	ALA	LA	OHIO	GUAM
	ALASKA	MAINE	OKLA	PR
Notes —	ARIZ	MD	ORE	VIR IS
Button smallest dimension: 3/4″, raised, flush, or recessed. Min. 5/8″ high designation for control buttons using standard alphabet letters, numerals or symbols. Designate call button for main entry floor with raised or idented star at left of floor designation. Place all raised or indented control button designations immediately at left of applicable button. Permanently attached applied plates are acceptable. Provide floor buttons with visual indicators to show when each call is registered which shall extinguish when each call is answered. Provide visual car position indicator over panel or door which illuminates and provides an audible sound (min. 50 dB, max. 1500 Hz) as car passes or stops at a floor served by the elevator. Visual indicator: 1/2″ min. high. If emergency two-way communication is provided and uses handset min. cord length: 2′-5″. Provide min. one handrail at rear wall 2′-8″ to 3′-0″ above floor with 1¼″ to 1½″ gripping surface, 1½″ clear. (*)4′-0″ for front approach.	ARK	MASS	PA	DC
	CAL	MICH	RI	
	COLO	MINN	SC	
	CONN	MISS	SD	FED'L FUNDS
	DEL	MO	TENN	
	FLA	MONT	● TEXAS	
	GA	NEB	UTAH	
	HAWAII	NEV	VT	
	IDAHO	NH	VA	
	ILL	NJ	WASH	
	IND	NM	W VA	
	IOWA	NY	WIS	OTHER
	KANS	NC	WYO	
	KY	ND		

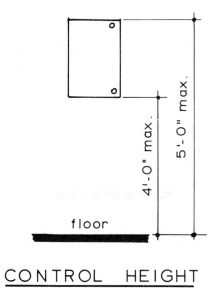

4'-0" max.

5'-0" max.

floor

CONTROL   HEIGHT

Basis of standard —	APPLICABILITY			
Utah State Building Board	ALA	LA	OHIO	GUAM
	ALASKA	MAINE	OKLA	PR
	ARIZ	MD	ORE	VIR IS
Notes —	ARK	MASS	PA	DC
Control panel buttons shall have both braille and	CAL	MICH	RI	
tactile alphabet characters for letters and arabic	COLO	MINN	SC	
characters for numbers or standard symbols. For	CONN	MISS	SD	FED'L
deep, narrow elevators, place control panel on the	DEL	MO	TENN	FUNDS
side wall within easy reach of a person in a wheel-	FLA	MONT	TEXAS	
chair. Provide visual and audible car position	GA	NEB	● UTAH	
indicator above control panel or over door. Audible	HAWAII	NEV	VT	
signals required only for elevators serving three or	IDAHO	NH	VA	
more floors.	ILL	NJ	WASH	
	IND	NM	W VA	
	IOWA	NY	WIS	OTHER
	KANS	NC	WYO	
	KY	ND		

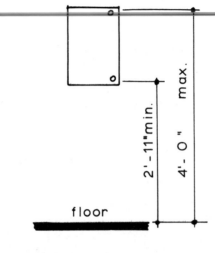

2'-11"min.

4'- 0 " max.

floor

CONTROL HEIGHT

Basis of standard —	APPLICABILITY			
Wisconsin Administrative Code	ALA	LA	OHIO	GUAM
	ALASKA	MAINE	OKLA	PR
	ARIZ	MD	ORE	VIR IS
Notes —	ARK	MASS	PA	DC
Provide raised letters and numerals on operating panel.	CAL	MICH	RI	
	COLO	MINN	SC	
	CONN	MISS	SD	FED'L
	DEL	MO	TENN	FUNDS
	FLA	MONT	TEXAS	
	GA	NEB	UTAH	
	HAWAII	NEV	VT	
	IDAHO	NH	VA	
	ILL	NJ	WASH	
	IND	NM	W VA	
	IOWA	NY	● WIS	OTHER
	KANS	NC	WYO	
	KY	ND		

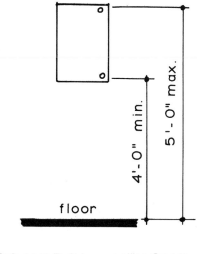

<u>CONTROL   HEIGHT</u>

Basis of standard —	APPLICABILITY			
Wyoming Statutes sec. 35-13-101	ALA	LA	OHIO	GUAM
	ALASKA	MAINE	OKLA	PR
	ARIZ	MD	ORE	VIR IS
Notes —	ARK	MASS	PA	DC
Control panels must be on the right side as viewed by a person inside the elevator, facing outward. All elevator buttons and controls must have a tactile identification beside them. Elevator floor levels must stop within a maximum of ½″ of building floor levels.	CAL	MICH	RI	
	COLO	MINN	SC	
	CONN	MISS	SD	FED'L FUNDS
	DEL	MO	TENN	
	FLA	MONT	TEXAS	
	GA	NEB	UTAH	
	HAWAII	NEV	VT	
	IDAHO	NH	VA	
	ILL	NJ	WASH	
	IND	NM	W VA	
	IOWA	NY	WIS	OTHER
	KANS	NC	● WYO	
	KY	ND		

Basis of standard —	APPLICABILITY			
Various	ALA	LA	OHIO	GUAM
	ALASKA	MAINE	OKLA	PR
	ARIZ	MD	ORE	VIR IS
Notes —	ARK	MASS	PA	DC
Most states require that toilets be designed for access by the physically handicapped and that at least one water closet, lavatory, mirror and accessory for each sex be provided in toilet rooms. Most states do not require urinals, but, where provided, at least one shall comply. Many states also require that accessible toilet rooms be identified as accessible by the handicapped.	CAL	MICH	RI	
	COLO	MINN	SC	
	CONN	MISS	SD	FED'L FUNDS
	DEL	MO	TENN	
	FLA	MONT	TEXAS	
	GA	NEB	UTAH	
	HAWAII	NEV	VT	
	IDAHO	NH	VA	
	ILL	NJ	WASH	
	IND	NM	W VA	
	IOWA	NY	WIS	● OTHER
	KANS	NC	WYO	
	KY	ND		

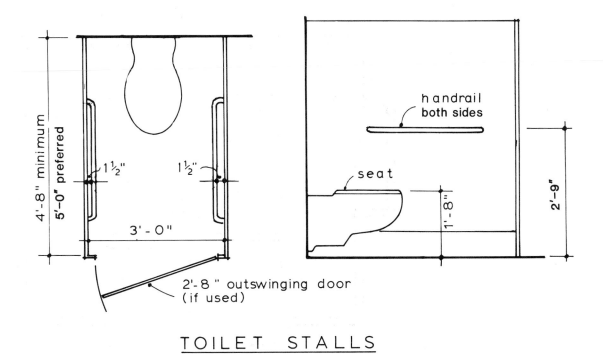

TOILET STALLS

Basis of standard —	APPLICABILITY			
ANSI 1961 — 5.6.2 and others	ALA	LA	OHIO	GUAM
	ALASKA	MAINE	● OKLA	PR
	● ARIZ	MD	ORE	VIR IS
	ARK	MASS	PA	DC
Notes —	CAL	MICH	RI	
Provide appropriate number of toilet rooms in accord with nature and use of a specific building or facility. Florida: applies to non-government financed facilities.	COLO	MINN	● SC	
	CONN	MISS	● SD	FED'L FUNDS
	DEL	MO	TENN	
	● FLA	MONT	TEXAS	
	● GA	NEB	UTAH	
	HAWAII	NEV	VT	
	IDAHO	NH	VA	
	ILL	NJ	WASH	
	IND	NM	W VA	
	IOWA	NY	WIS	OTHER
	● KANS	NC	WYO	
	KY	● ND		

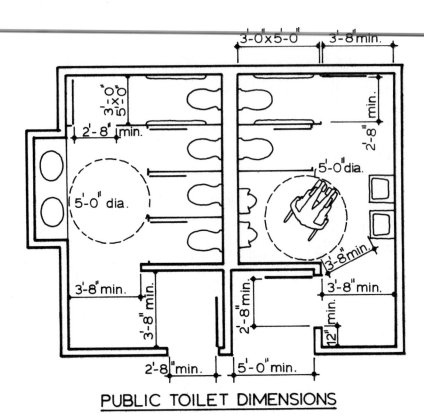

PUBLIC TOILET DIMENSIONS

Basis of standard — ANSI 1961 — 5.6.1, 3.2.2 and others	APPLICABILITY			
	ALA	LA	OHIO	GUAM
	ALASKA	MAINE	● OKLA	PR
	ARIZ	MD	ORE	VIR IS
Notes — Alternate to 5′ × 5′ space: 5′-3″ × 4′-8″ except for South Carolina where alternate is 4′-4″ × 6′-0″.	ARK	MASS	PA	DC
	CAL	MICH	RI	
	COLO	MINN	● SC	
	CONN	MISS	● SD	FED'L
	DEL	MO	TENN	FUNDS
	FLA	MONT	TEXAS	
	● GA	NEB	UTAH	
	HAWAII	NEV	VT	
	IDAHO	NH	VA	
	ILL	NJ	WASH	
	IND	NM	W VA	
	IOWA	NY	WIS	OTHER
	● KANS	NC	WYO	
	KY	● ND		

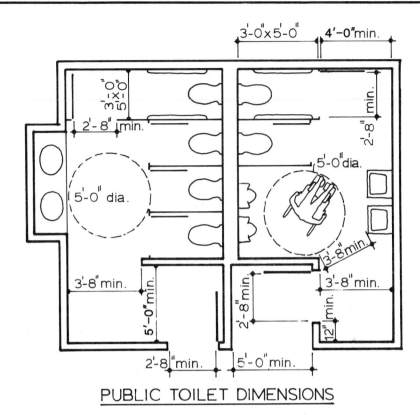

PUBLIC TOILET DIMENSIONS

Basis of standard —	APPLICABILITY			
BOCA 1978	ALA	LA	● OHIO	GUAM
	ALASKA	MAINE	OKLA	PR
	ARIZ	● MD	ORE	VIR IS
Notes —	ARK	MASS	PA	DC
Provide at least one water closet, lavatory and	CAL	MICH	RI	
miscellaneous accessories which are accessible.	COLO	MINN	SC	
Ohio, exceptions: if required fixtures are installed	CONN	MISS	SD	FED'L
in two or more toilet rooms for use by the same	DEL	MO	TENN	FUNDS
sex on the same floor, the Building Official may	FLA	MONT	TEXAS	
require that fixtures in only room comply for	GA	NEB	UTAH	
accessibility provided that room is conveniently	HAWAII	NEV	VT	
located and adequately marked for handicapped	IDAHO	NH	VA	
facilities. Maryland: at least one toilet room and	ILL	NJ	WASH	
one fixture of each type shall be accessible.	IND	NM	W VA	
	IOWA	NY	WIS	OTHER
	KANS	NC	WYO	
	KY	ND		

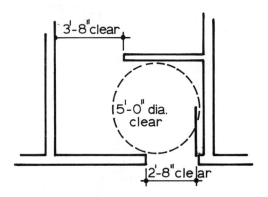

ACCESS TO TOILET ROOMS

Basis of standard — BOCA 1978	APPLICABILITY			
	ALA	LA	● OHIO	GUAM
	ALASKA	MAINE	OKLA	PR
	ARIZ	● MD	ORE	VIR IS
Notes —	ARK	MASS	PA	DC
	CAL	MICH	RI	
	COLO	MINN	SC	
	CONN	MISS	SD	FED'L FUNDS
	DEL	MO	TENN	
	FLA	MONT	TEXAS	
	GA	NEB	UTAH	
	HAWAII	NEV	VT	
	IDAHO	NH	VA	
	ILL	NJ	WASH	
	IND	NM	W VA	
	IOWA	NY	WIS	OTHER
	KANS	NC	WYO	
	KY	ND		

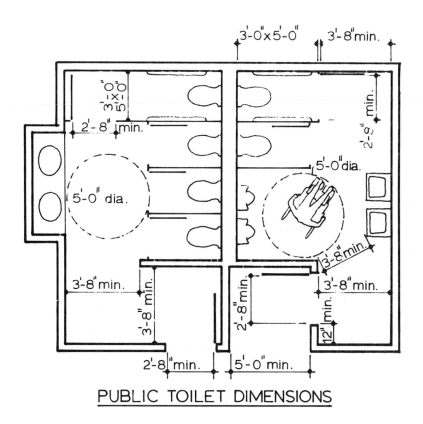

PUBLIC TOILET DIMENSIONS

Basis of standard —	APPLICABILITY			
Various	ALA	LA	OHIO	GUAM
	ALASKA	MAINE	OKLA	PR
	ARIZ	MD	ORE	VIR IS
Notes —	ARK	MASS	PA	DC
Provide min. one toilet room for each sex on each	CAL	MICH	RI	
floor, on same level as corridor floor. Indiana, Washington & Montana permit max. 1'-0" encroachment	COLO	MINN	SC	
on 5' circle. Montana exempts dwelling units and	CONN	MISS	SD	FED'L
guest rooms from 5' circle clearance. In Florida	DEL	MO	TENN	FUNDS
applicable to government facilities:	● FLA	● MONT	TEXAS	
	GA	NEB	UTAH	
	HAWAII	NEV	VT	
	IDAHO	NH	VA	
	ILL	● NJ	● WASH	
	● IND	NM	W VA	
	IOWA	NY	WIS	OTHER
	KANS	NC	WYO	
	KY	ND		

	A	B	C	D	E
Florida	—	4'-0"	4'-0"	3'-8"	—
Indiana	3'-8"	3'-8"	3'-8"	3'-8"	—
Montana	3'-8"	3'-8"	3'-8"	3'-8"	—
New Jersey	—	—	—	3'-6"	—
Washington	4'-0"	3'-8"	4'-0"	3'-8"	—

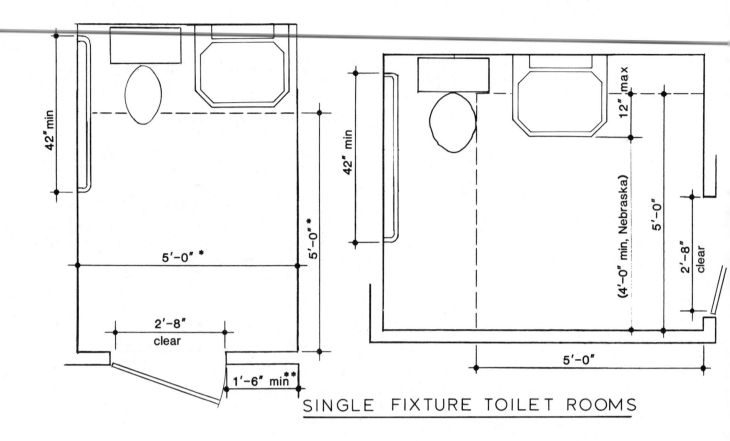

SINGLE FIXTURE TOILET ROOMS

Basis of standard — Various	APPLICABILITY			
	ALA	LA	OHIO	GUAM
	ALASKA	MAINE	OKLA	PR
	ARIZ	● MD	ORE	VIR IS
Notes — (*)3'-6" X 3'-6" in Maryland. (**)Applicable to New Jersey.	ARK	MASS	PA	DC
	CAL	MICH	RI	
	COLO	MINN	SC	
	CONN	MISS	SD	FED'L
	DEL	MO	TENN	FUNDS
	FLA	MONT	TEXAS	
	GA	● NEB	● UTAH	
	HAWAII	NEV	VT	
	IDAHO	NH	VA	
	ILL	● NJ	WASH	
	IND	NM	W VA	
	IOWA	NY	WIS	OTHER
	KANS	NC	WYO	
	KY	ND		

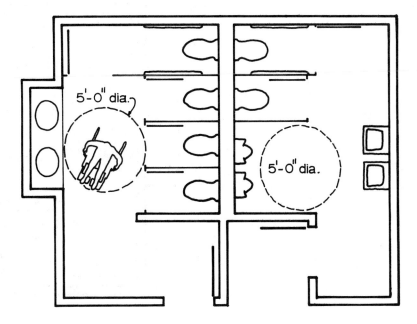

MINIMUM FIXTURES

Basis of standard —	APPLICABILITY			
North Carolina Building Code and others	ALA	LA	OHIO	GUAM
	ALASKA	MAINE	OKLA	PR
	ARIZ	MD	ORE	VIR IS
	ARK	MASS	PA	DC
Notes —	CAL	● MICH	RI	
Provide one toilet room each for men and women on every floor where toilet rooms are planned. Each building to have min. 2% of total fixtures of each type to comply. (*) = min. one fixture of each type. Toilet rooms with group facilities: min. one fixture of each type to comply. North Carolina, Tennessee, Virginia: toilet rooms with no group facilities (i.e., individual toilet rooms): considered as toilet stall as well as toilet room. At least one such room for men and one for women shall comply (urinals are not required).	COLO	MINN	SC	
	CONN	MISS	SD	FED'L
	DEL	MO	● TENN	FUNDS
	FLA	MONT	TEXAS	
	GA	NEB	UTAH	
	HAWAII	NEV	VT	
	IDAHO	NH	VA	
	ILL	NJ	WASH	
	IND	NM	W VA	
	IOWA	NY	WIS	OTHER
	KANS	● NC	WYO	
	KY	ND		

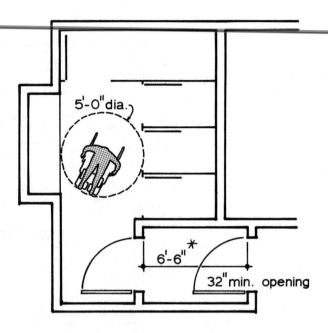

TOILET ROOM VESTIBULE

Basis of standard —		APPLICABILITY		
Various	● ALA	LA	OHIO	GUAM
	ALASKA	MAINE	OKLA	PR
	ARIZ	MD	ORE	VIR IS
Notes —	ARK	MASS	PA	DC
(*)Florida applicable to government facilities: 5'-0".	CAL	MICH	RI	
	COLO	MINN	SC	
	CONN	MISS	SD	FED'L
	DEL	MO	TENN	FUNDS
	● FLA	MONT	TEXAS	
	GA	NEB	UTAH	
	HAWAII	NEV	VT	
	IDAHO	NH	VA	
	ILL	● NJ	WASH	
	IND	NM	W VA	
	IOWA	NY	WIS	OTHER
	KANS	NC	WYO	
	KY	ND		

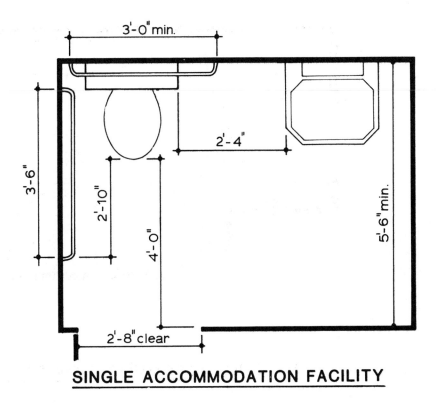

SINGLE ACCOMMODATION FACILITY

Basis of standard —	APPLICABILITY			
North Carolina Building Code	ALA	LA	OHIO	GUAM
	ALASKA	MAINE	OKLA	PR
	ARIZ	MD	ORE	VIR IS
	ARK	MASS	PA	DC
Notes —	CAL	MICH	RI	
Where total available floor space is particularly crucial, toespace under cabinets of no more than 6″ in depth and a min. of 8¾″ in height on any one side may supplant part of the 5′ × 5′ clear floor space. (Note for Virginia: if door swings in, provide min. 5′ × 5′ clear space beyond door swing).	COLO	MINN	SC	
	CONN	MISS	SD	FED'L FUNDS
	DEL	MO	● TENN	
	FLA	MONT	TEXAS	
	GA	NEB	UTAH	
	HAWAII	NEV	VT	
	IDAHO	NH	VA	
	ILL	NJ	WASH	
	IND	NM	W VA	
	IOWA	NY	WIS	OTHER
	KANS	● NC	WYO	
	KY	ND		

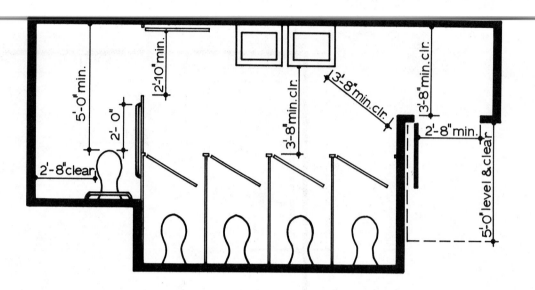

MULTIPLE ACCOMMODATION TOILET FACILITIES

Basis of standard — CAC Title 24, Part 2	APPLICABILITY			
	ALA	LA	OHIO	GUAM
	ALASKA	MAINE	OKLA	PR
	ARIZ	MD	ORE	VIR IS
	ARK	MASS	PA	DC
	● CAL	MICH	RI	
	COLO	MINN	SC	
	CONN	MISS	SD	FED'L FUNDS
	DEL	MO	TENN	
	FLA	MONT	TEXAS	
	GA	NEB	UTAH	
	HAWAII	NEV	VT	
	IDAHO	NH	VA	
	ILL	NJ	WASH	
	IND	NM	W VA	
	IOWA	NY	WIS	OTHER
	KANS	NC	WYO	
	KY	ND		

Notes —

Provide 3'-8" clear path to accessible water closet compartment, lavatories, urinal and accessories. Water closet compartment clearance is indicated for a side entry only.

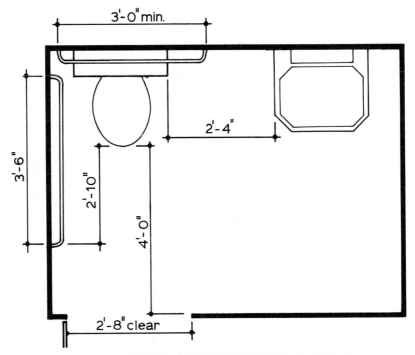

SINGLE ACCOMMODATION FACILITY

Basis of standard —	APPLICABILITY			
CAC Title 24, Part 2	ALA	LA	OHIO	GUAM
	ALASKA	MAINE	OKLA	PR
	ARIZ	MD	ORE	VIR IS
Notes —	ARK	MASS	PA	DC
Single accommodation facilities only, where only one person uses the room at a time; door has privacy lock.	● CAL	MICH	RI	
	COLO	MINN	SC	
	CONN	MISS	SD	FED'L
	DEL	MO	TENN	FUNDS
	FLA	MONT	TEXAS	
	GA	NEB	UTAH	
	HAWAII	NEV	VT	
	IDAHO	NH	VA	
	ILL	NJ	WASH	
	IND	NM	W VA	
	IOWA	NY	WIS	OTHER
	KANS	NC	WYO	
	KY	ND		

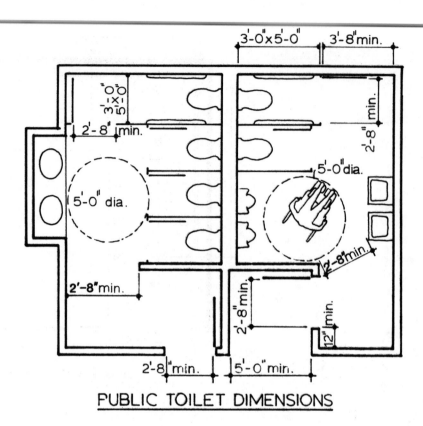

3'-0"x5'-0"   3'-8"min.

3'-0"x5'-0"

2'-8" min.

5'-0" dia.

2'-8" min.

5'-0" dia.

2'-8" min.

2'-8"min.

2'-8" min.

2'-8" min.   5'-0" min.

12" min.

PUBLIC TOILET DIMENSIONS

Basis of standard — Iowa Administrative Code	APPLICABILITY			
	ALA	LA	OHIO	GUAM
	ALASKA	MAINE	OKLA	PR
	ARIZ	MD	ORE	VIR IS
Notes —	ARK	MASS	PA	DC
Provide an appropriate number of water closets,	CAL	MICH	RI	
urinals (when provided) showers or bathtubs (when	COLO	MINN	SC	
provided), lavatories, mirrors, towel and disposal	CONN	MISS	SD	FED'L
fixtures and other dispensers at each floor level	DEL	MO	TENN	FUNDS
which is accessible to the physically handicapped.	FLA	MONT	TEXAS	
Toilet rooms and bathrooms shall have space to	GA	NEB	UTAH	
allow traffic for individuals in wheelchairs.	HAWAII	NEV	VT	
	IDAHO	NH	VA	
	ILL	NJ	WASH	
	IND	NM	W VA	
	● IOWA	NY	WIS	OTHER
	KANS	NC	WYO	
	KY	ND		

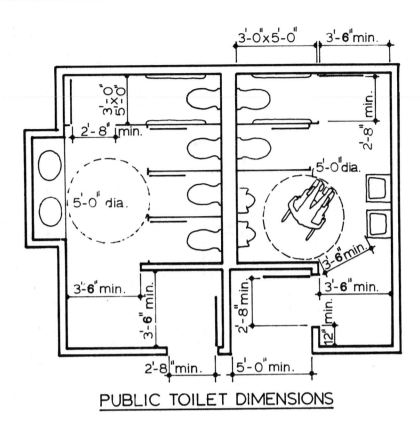

PUBLIC TOILET DIMENSIONS

Basis of standard —	APPLICABILITY			
Provisions for the Handicapped	ALA	LA	OHIO	GUAM
	ALASKA	MAINE	OKLA	PR
	ARIZ	MD	ORE	VIR IS
Notes —	ARK	MASS	PA	DC
Provide at least one fixture of each type complying with requirements.	CAL	MICH	RI	
	COLO	MINN	SC	
	CONN	MISS	SD	FED'L FUNDS
	DEL	MO	TENN	
	FLA	MONT	TEXAS	
	GA	● NEB	UTAH	
	HAWAII	NEV	VT	
	IDAHO	NH	VA	
	ILL	NJ	WASH	
	IND	NM	W VA	
	IOWA	NY	WIS	OTHER
	KANS	NC	WYO	
	KY	ND		

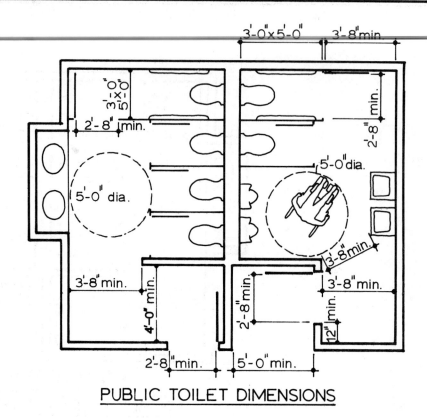

PUBLIC TOILET DIMENSIONS

Basis of standard — Architectural Barrier Free Design Code	APPLICABILITY			
	ALA	LA	OHIO	GUAM
	ALASKA	MAINE	OKLA	PR
	ARIZ	MD	ORE	VIR IS
Notes —	ARK	MASS	PA	DC
Measure 5′ X 5′ clearance 1′-0″ above floor. In toilet rooms required by other codes provide at least one complying water closet and lavatory.	CAL	MICH	RI	
	COLO	MINN	SC	
	CONN	MISS	SD	FED'L FUNDS
	DEL	MO	TENN	
	FLA	MONT	TEXAS	
	GA	NEB	UTAH	
	HAWAII	NEV	VT	
	IDAHO	● NH	VA	
	ILL	NJ	WASH	
	IND	NM	W VA	
	IOWA	NY	WIS	OTHER
	KANS	NC	WYO	
	KY	ND		

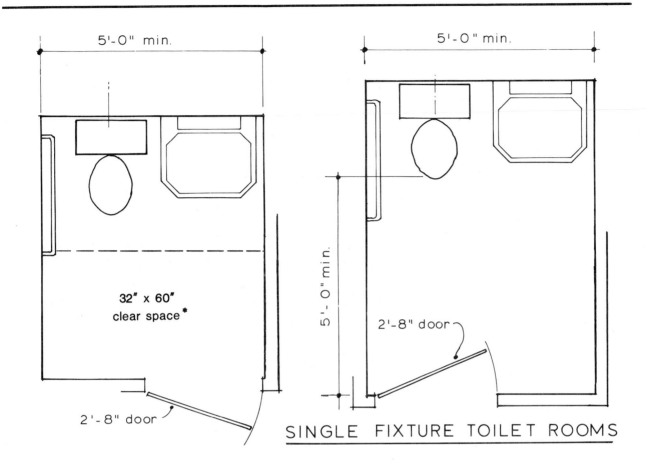

5'-0" min.

5'-0" min.

32" x 60"
clear space *

5'-0" min.

2'-8" door

2'-8" door

SINGLE FIXTURE TOILET ROOMS

Basis of standard —	APPLICABILITY			
Barrier Free Design Regulations	ALA	LA	OHIO	GUAM
	ALASKA	MAINE	OKLA	PR
	ARIZ	MD	ORE	VIR IS
Notes —	ARK	MASS	PA	DC
Maybe used where Uniform Construction Code permits installation of a single water closet and a single lavatory (does not apply where multiple rest rooms are provided). Horizontal grab bars 2'-9" above floor.	CAL	MICH	RI	
	COLO	MINN	SC	
	CONN	MISS	SD	FED'L FUNDS
	DEL	MO	TENN	
(*)Facilities limited to a 32" X 60" clear space are allowed in residential units and commercial facilities less than 6000 square feet gross area.	FLA	MONT	TEXAS	
	GA	NEB	UTAH	
	HAWAII	NEV	VT	
	IDAHO	NH	VA	
	ILL	● NJ	WASH	
	IND	NM	W VA	
	IOWA	NY	WIS	OTHER
	KANS	NC	WYO	
	KY	ND		

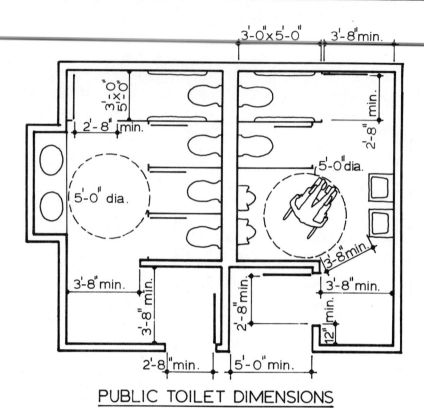

PUBLIC TOILET DIMENSIONS

Basis of standard —	APPLICABILITY			
Structural Specialty Code	ALA	LA	OHIO	GUAM
	ALASKA	MAINE	OKLA	PR
	ARIZ	MD	● ORE	VIR IS
Notes —	ARK	MASS	PA	DC
Provide at least one complying facility for each sex where access by the physically handicapped is required by Table 33A. Doors in any position may encroach on 5′ circle by not more than 12″.	CAL	MICH	RI	
	COLO	MINN	SC	
	CONN	MISS	SD	FED'L FUNDS
	DEL	MO	TENN	
	FLA	MONT	TEXAS	
	GA	NEB	UTAH	
	HAWAII	NEV	VT	
	IDAHO	NH	VA	
	ILL	NJ	WASH	
	IND	NM	W VA	
	IOWA	NY	WIS	OTHER
	KANS	NC	WYO	
	KY	ND		

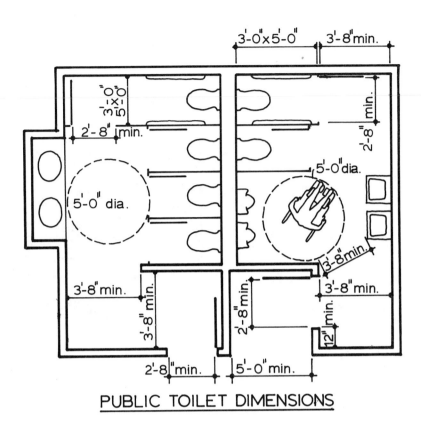

PUBLIC TOILET DIMENSIONS

Basis of standard —	APPLICABILITY			
Barrier Free Design	ALA	LA	OHIO	GUAM
	ALASKA	MAINE	OKLA	PR
	ARIZ	MD	ORE	VIR IS
Notes —	ARK	MASS	PA	DC
Provide min. one restroom each for males and females	CAL	MICH	RI	
on each floor marked by signs or symbols. Ramp	COLO	MINN	● SC	
abrupt changes in floor level in excess of 1″ at door-	CONN	MISS	SD	FED'L
ways. Provide appropriate number of lavatories with	DEL	MO	TENN	FUNDS
narrow aprons usable by wheelchaired individuals,	FLA	MONT	TEXAS	
or mount higher than normal to allow wheelchair	GA	NEB	UTAH	
approach to units.	HAWAII	NEV	VT	
	IDAHO	NH	VA	
	ILL	NJ	WASH	
	IND	NM	W VA	
	IOWA	NY	WIS	OTHER
	KANS	NC	WYO	
	KY	ND		

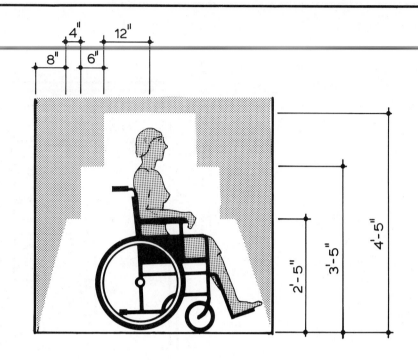

Basis of standard —	APPLICABILITY			
State Purchasing and General Services Commission	ALA	LA	OHIO	GUAM
	ALASKA	MAINE	OKLA	PR
	ARIZ	MD	ORE	VIR IS
Notes —	ARK	MASS	PA	DC
Where toilets are provided, provide at least one which complies. Where separate toilets are provided for	CAL	MICH	RI	
children and adults, comply with standards applicable to both. At least 20% of total restrooms for men and	COLO	MINN	SC	
women shall comply (except for unisex restrooms).	CONN	MISS	SD	FED'L FUNDS
For multi-level structures, locate so that handicapped	DEL	MO	TENN	
will not need to travel more than two floors to reach	FLA	MONT	● TEXAS	
accessible toilet (location on main entry level is recommended). Max. horizontal distance to at least	GA	NEB	UTAH	
one accessible room for each sex: 250 feet. Provide	HAWAII	NEV	VT	
min. 5′ X 5′ turning space in applicable toilet rooms.	IDAHO	NH	VA	
Overlap at fixtures for turning space permitted for	ILL	NJ	WASH	
clear space under fixtures complying with diagram	IND	NM	W VA	
above.	IOWA	NY	WIS	OTHER
	KANS	NC	WYO	
	KY	ND		

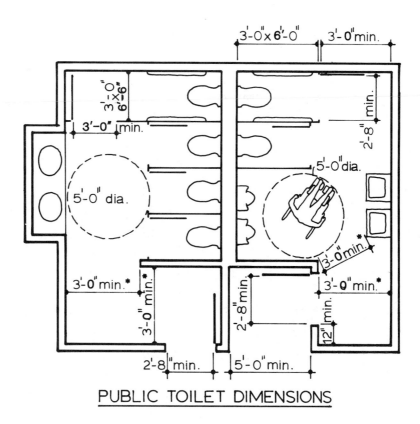

PUBLIC TOILET DIMENSIONS

Basis of standard —		APPLICABILITY		
Ind. 52.04, 6 Wisconsin Ad. Code	ALA	LA	OHIO	GUAM
	ALASKA	MAINE	OKLA	PR
	ARIZ	MD	ORE	VIR IS
Notes — Provide accessible toilets on a primary floor or accessible from a primary floor distributed as follows:	ARK	MASS	PA	DC
	CAL	MICH	RI	
	COLO	MINN	SC	
1. Accessible water closets at a rate of 10% of the total number of toilet facilities provided on each accessible floor, with a minimum of one for each sex.	CONN	MISS	SD	FED'L FUNDS
	DEL	MO	TENN	
	FLA	MONT	TEXAS	
2. One accessible toilet room in buildings accomodating 10 or less employees and less than 25 patrons per Ind 54.12(1) (a) 1.	GA	NEB	UTAH	
	HAWAII	NEV	VT	
(Also refer to Ind. 52.04 for other specific data for varied conditions.)	IDAHO	NH	VA	
(*)42″ preferred	ILL	NJ	WASH	
	IND	NM	W VA	
	IOWA	NY	● WIS	OTHER
	KANS	NC	WYO	
	KY	ND		

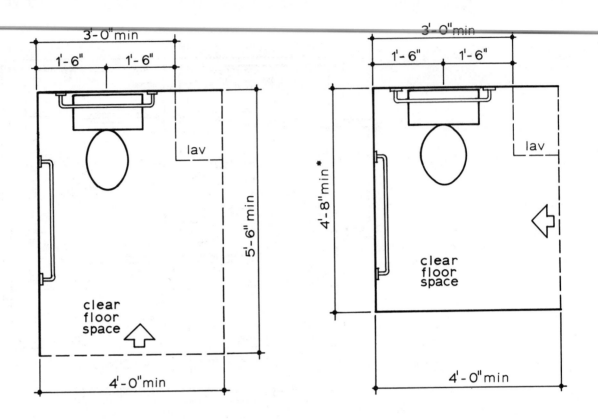

Basis of standard —	APPLICABILITY			
ANSI 1980 — 4.16.2 and others	ALA	● LA	OHIO	GUAM
	● ALASKA	● MAINE	OKLA	PR
	ARIZ	MD	ORE	VIR IS
Notes —	● ARK	MASS	PA	DC
Data shown is for water closets not in stalls. Clear floor space may be arranged to allow for left-handed or right-handed approach. Adaptable bathrooms use same dimensions shown.	CAL	MICH	● RI	
	● COLO	MINN	SC	
	CONN	MISS	SD	● FED'L FUNDS
(*)Federal Arkansas, and Delaware standards require 4'-11" for floor mounted water closet.	DEL	MO	TENN	
Illinois: shown for exposed flush valve conditions.	FLA	MONT	● TEXAS	
	GA	NEB	UTAH	
	● HAWAII	● NEV	● VT	
	● IDAHO	NH	● VA	
	● ILL	NJ	WASH	
	IND	● NM	W VA	
	● IOWA	● NY	WIS	OTHER
	KANS	NC	WYO	
	● KY	ND		

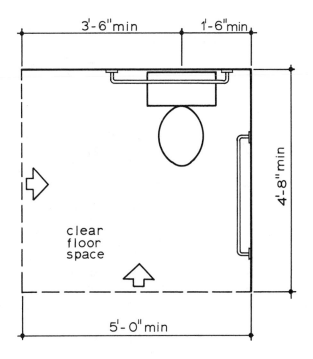

Basis of standard — ANSI 1980 — 4.16.2 and others	APPLICABILITY			
	ALA	● LA	OHIO	GUAM
	● ALASKA	● MAINE	OKLA	PR
	ARIZ	MD	ORE	VIR IS
	ARK	MASS	PA	DC
	CAL	MICH	● RI	
	● COLO	MINN	SC	
	CONN	MISS	SD	FED'L FUNDS
	DEL	MO	TENN	
	FLA	MONT	● TEXAS	
	GA	NEB	UTAH	
	● HAWAII	● NEV	● VT	
	● IDAHO	NH	● VA	
	ILL	NJ	WASH	
	IND	● NM	W VA	
	● IOWA	● NY	WIS	OTHER
	KANS	NC	WYO	
	● KY	ND		

Notes —

Data shown is for water closets not in stalls. Clear floor space may be arranged to allow for left-handed or right-handed approach. Adaptable bathrooms use similar dimensions shown.

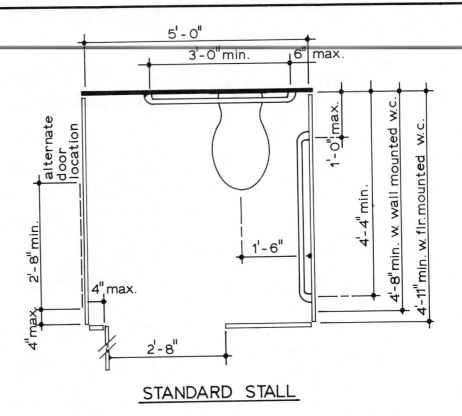

STANDARD STALL

Basis of standard —	APPLICABILITY			
ANSI 1980 — and others	ALA	● LA	OHIO	GUAM
	● ALASKA	● MAINE	OKLA	PR
	ARIZ	MD	ORE	VIR IS
Notes —	● ARK	MASS	PA	DC
Use wall mounted water closets for stall depth of 4'-8" or increase stall depth 3" to use floor mounted water closet. Stalls may have left or right-handed approach. Min. toe clearance for front and at least one side partition: 9". At least one complying stall in each toilet room is required in Alaska and Illinois. Provide 3'-6" min. in front of toilet stall door for these.	CAL	MICH	● RI	
	● COLO	MINN	SC	
	CONN	MISS	SD	● FED'L FUNDS
	● DEL	MO	TENN	
	FLA	MONT	TEXAS	
	GA	NEB	UTAH	
	● HAWAII	● NEV	● VT	
	● IDAHO	NH	● VA	
	● ILL	NJ	WASH	
	IND	● NM	W VA	
	● IOWA	● NY	WIS	OTHER
	KANS	NC	WYO	
	● KY	ND		

The diagram labels read:
5'-0", 3'-0" min., 6" max., 1'-0" max., 4'-4" min., 4'-8" min. w. wall mounted w.c., 4'-11" min. w. flr. mounted w.c., alternate door location, 2'-8" min., 4" max., 4" max., 1'-6", 2'-8"

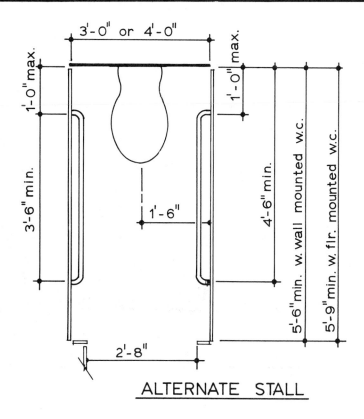

ALTERNATE STALL

Basis of standard —	APPLICABILITY			
ANSI 1980 and others.	ALA	● LA	OHIO	GUAM
	● ALASKA	● MAINE	OKLA	PR
	ARIZ	MD	ORE	VIR IS
	● ARK	MASS	PA	DC
Notes —	CAL	MICH	● RI	
Use wall mounted water closets for stall depth of 5'-6" or increase stall depth 3" to use floor mounted water closet. Stalls may have left- or right-handed approach. Min. toe clearance for front and at least one side wall: 9". Provide 3'-6" min. in front of toilet stall door. At least one complying stall in each toilet room is required in Alaska.	● COLO	MINN	SC	
	CONN	MISS	SD	● FED'L FUNDS
	● DEL	MO	TENN	
	FLA	MONT	TEXAS	
	GA	NEB	UTAH	
Kentucky: acceptable in existing buildings only.	● HAWAII	● NEV	● VT	
	● IDAHO	NH	● VA	
	● ILL	NJ	WASH	
	IND	● NM	W VA	
	● IOWA	● NY	WIS	OTHER
	KANS	NC	WYO	
	● KY	ND		

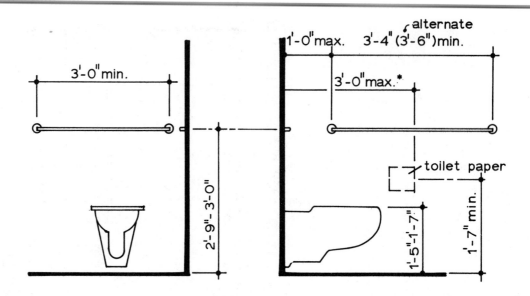

REAR WALL OF STANDARD STALL   SIDE WALLS

Basis of standard — ANSI 1980 — 4.17.6 and others	APPLICABILITY			
	ALA	● LA	OHIO	GUAM
	● ALASKA	● MAINE	OKLA	PR
	ARIZ	MD	ORE	VIR IS
Notes — Grab bars shall not obstruct required clear floor area, and shall comply with ANSI 4.26. Min. toe clearance for front and at least one side wall: 9″. Rhode Island: 3′-8″ max. to top of flush controls. (*)Locate 2′-10″ to center of tissue dispenser on side wall closest to toilet bowl, immediately below grab bar in Illinois.	● ARK	MASS	PA	DC
	CAL	MICH	● RI	
	● COLO	MINN	SC	
	CONN	MISS	SD	● FED'L FUNDS
	● DEL	MO	TENN	
	FLA	MONT	TEXAS	
	GA	NEB	UTAH	
	● HAWAII	● NEV	● VT	
	● IDAHO	NH	● VA	
	● ILL	NJ	WASH	
	IND	● NM	W VA	
	● IOWA	● NY	WIS	OTHER
	KANS	NC	WYO	
	KY	ND		

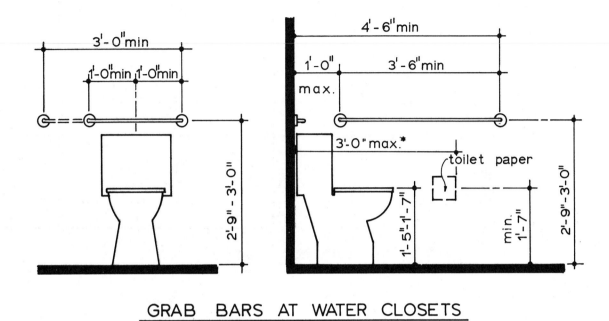

GRAB BARS AT WATER CLOSETS

Basis of standard — ANSI 1980 — 4.16 and others	APPLICABILITY			
	ALA	● LA	OHIO	GUAM
	● ALASKA	● MAINE	OKLA	PR
	ARIZ	MD	ORE	VIR IS
	● ARK	MASS	PA	DC
	CAL	MICH	● RI	
	● COLO	MINN	SC	
	CONN	MISS	SD	● FED'L FUNDS
Notes — Notes below not applicable to Iowa. For water closets in adaptable dwelling units see ANSI 4.34 (Dwelling Units). Provide controls for flush valves min. 44″ above floor mounted on wide side of toilet areas. (*)Federal requirement. Kentucky: flush controls maximum 40″ high; provide continuous feed toilet paper dispensers.	● DEL	MO	TENN	
	FLA	MONT	TEXAS	
	GA	NEB	UTAH	
	● HAWAII	● NEV	● VT	
	● IDAHO	NH	● VA	
	● ILL	NJ	WASH	
	IND	● NM	W VA	
	● IOWA	● NY	WIS	OTHER
	KANS	NC	WYO	
	● KY	ND		

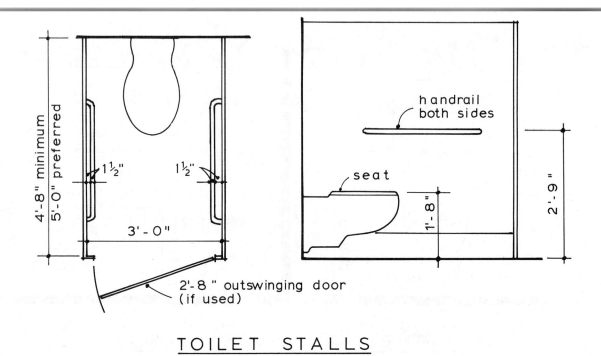

TOILET STALLS

Basis of standard —	APPLICABILITY			
ANSI 1961 — 5.6.2 and others	ALA	LA	OHIO	GUAM
	ALASKA	MAINE	OKLA	PR
	ARIZ	MD	ORE	VIR IS
Notes —	ARK	MASS	● PA	DC
Provide at least one toilet stall as shown.	CAL	MICH	RI	
	COLO	MINN	SC	
	CONN	● MISS	SD	FED'L
	DEL	● MO	TENN	FUNDS
	● FLA	MONT	TEXAS	
	GA	NEB	UTAH	
	HAWAII	NEV	VT	
	IDAHO	NH	VA	
	ILL	NJ	WASH	
	IND	NM	W VA	
	IOWA	NY	WIS	OTHER
	KANS	NC	WYO	
	KY	ND		

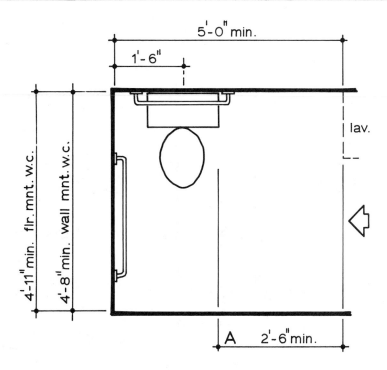

CLEAR FLOOR SPACE

Basis of standard —	APPLICABILITY			
ATBCB — 1190.150 and others	ALA	LA	OHIO	GUAM
	ALASKA	MAINE	OKLA	PR
	ARIZ	MD	ORE	VIR IS
● ARK	MASS	PA	DC
Notes —	CAL	MICH	RI	
Dimension A — provide 2'-6" min. clearance between water closet and in swinging door.	COLO	MINN	SC	
	CONN	MISS	SD	● FED'L FUNDS
	● DEL	MO	TENN	
	FLA	MONT	TEXAS	
	GA	NEB	UTAH	
	HAWAII	NEV	VT	
	IDAHO	NH	VA	
	ILL	NJ	WASH	
	IND	NM	W VA	
	IOWA	NY	WIS	OTHER
	KANS	NC	WYO	
	KY	ND		

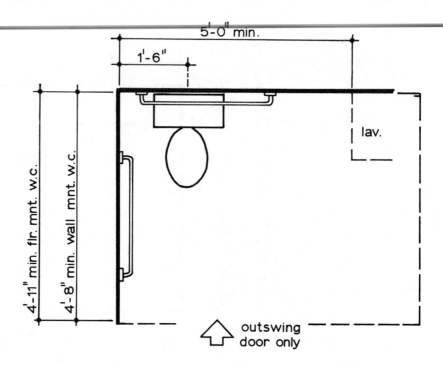

CLEAR FLOOR SPACE

Basis of standard —	APPLICABILITY			
ATBCB – 1190.150 and others	ALA	LA	OHIO	GUAM
	ALASKA	MAINE	OKLA	PR
	ARIZ	MD	ORE	VIR IS
Notes —	● ARK	MASS	PA	DC
	CAL	MICH	RI	
	COLO	MINN	SC	
	CONN	MISS	SD	● FED'L
	● DEL	MO	TENN	FUNDS
	FLA	MONT	TEXAS	
	GA	NEB	UTAH	
	HAWAII	NEV	VT	
	IDAHO	NH	VA	
	ILL	NJ	WASH	
	IND	NM	W VA	
	IOWA	NY	WIS	OTHER
	KANS	NC	WYO	
	KY	ND		

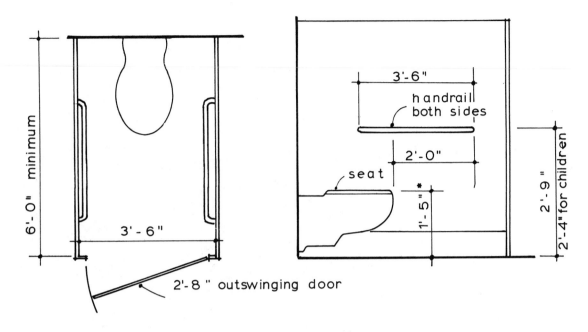

TOILET STALLS

Basis of standard —	APPLICABILITY			
BOCA 1978	ALA	LA	● OHIO	GUAM
	ALASKA	MAINE	OKLA	PR
	ARIZ	MD	ORE	VIR IS
Notes —	ARK	MASS	PA	DC
Provide 4'-0″ clear width between face of stall and a wall.	CAL	MICH	RI	
(*)1'-3″ for children; 1'-4″ to 1'-7″ in Ohio.	COLO	MINN	SC	
	CONN	MISS	SD	FED'L FUNDS
	DEL	MO	TENN	
	FLA	MONT	TEXAS	
	GA	NEB	UTAH	
	HAWAII	NEV	VT	
	IDAHO	NH	VA	
	ILL	NJ	WASH	
	IND	NM	W VA	
	IOWA	NY	WIS	OTHER
	KANS	NC	WYO	
	KY	ND		

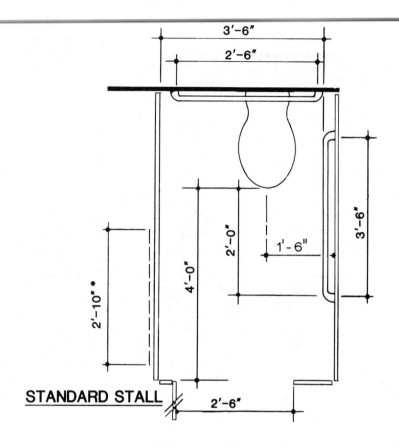

STANDARD STALL

Basis of standard —	APPLICABILITY			
Uniform Building Code	ALA	LA	OHIO	GUAM
	ALASKA	MAINE	OKLA	PR
	ARIZ	MD	● ORE	VIR IS
Notes —	ARK	MASS	PA	DC
Provide at least one facility for each sex on any floor where access by the physically handicapped is required by Table 33A. Provide 3'-8" min. wide access to compartments. Grab bars to have 1¼" to 1½" o.d., with 1½" clearance to wall (not required in Group R, Division 1 apartment houses), mounted 2'-8" to 2'-10" above floor. Dimensions are all minimum clear dimensions permitted. (*)Alternate door location. Indiana: use Table 5-E in lieu of Table 33A as the determinant of spaces where accessibility is required. Oregon: seat height 1'-6" to 1'-7" above floor.	CAL	MICH	RI	
	COLO	MINN	SC	
	CONN	MISS	SD	FED'L FUNDS
	DEL	MO	TENN	
	FLA	● MONT	TEXAS	
	GA	NEB	UTAH	
	HAWAII	NEV	VT	
	IDAHO	NH	VA	
	ILL	NJ	WASH	
	● IND	NM	W VA	
	IOWA	NY	WIS	OTHER
	KANS	NC	WYO	
	KY	ND		

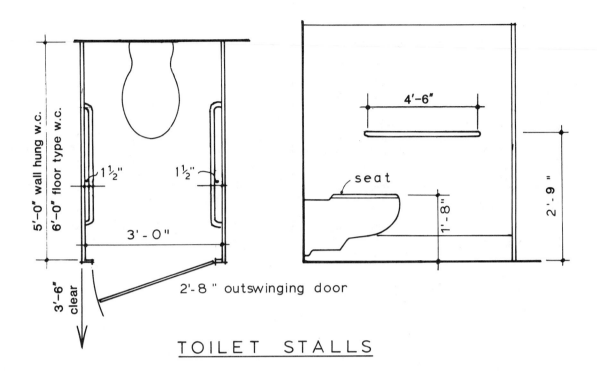

$1\frac{1}{2}$" $1\frac{1}{2}$"

3'-0"

5'-0" wall hung w.c.

6'-0" floor type w.c.

3'-6" clear

2'-8" outswinging door

4'-6"

seat

1'-8"

2'-9"

TOILET STALLS

Basis of standard —	APPLICABILITY			
North Carolina State Building Code	ALA	LA	OHIO	GUAM
	ALASKA	MAINE	OKLA	PR
	ARIZ	MD	ORE	VIR IS
Notes —	ARK	MASS	PA	DC
Secure grab bars at ends and center to support a 250 lb load.	CAL	MICH	RI	
	COLO	MINN	SC	
	CONN	MISS	SD	FED'L FUNDS
	DEL	MO	● TENN	
	FLA	MONT	TEXAS	
	GA	NEB	UTAH	
	HAWAII	NEV	VT	
	IDAHO	NH	VA	
	ILL	NJ	WASH	
	IND	NM	W VA	
	IOWA	NY	WIS	OTHER
	KANS	● NC	WYO	
	KY	ND		

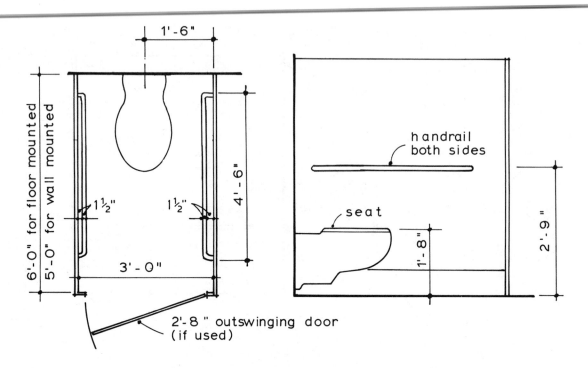

TOILET STALLS

Basis of standard —	APPLICABILITY			
Barrier Free Design Standard	● ALA	LA	OHIO	GUAM
	ALASKA	MAINE	OKLA	PR
	ARIZ	MD	ORE	VIR IS
Notes —	ARK	MASS	PA	DC
Rails: stainless steel or polished chrome, mounted at ends and center capable of supporting 250 lb. load. Clear space in front of door: 3'-6" deep, 3'-0" wide. Wyoming: max. height for operating mechanisms: 3'-4".	CAL	MICH	RI	
	COLO	MINN	SC	
	CONN	MISS	SD	FED'L FUNDS
	DEL	MO	TENN	
	FLA	MONT	TEXAS	
	GA	NEB	UTAH	
	HAWAII	NEV	VT	
	IDAHO	NH	VA	
	ILL	NJ	WASH	
	IND	NM	W VA	
	IOWA	NY	WIS	OTHER
	KANS	NC	● WYO	
	KY	ND		

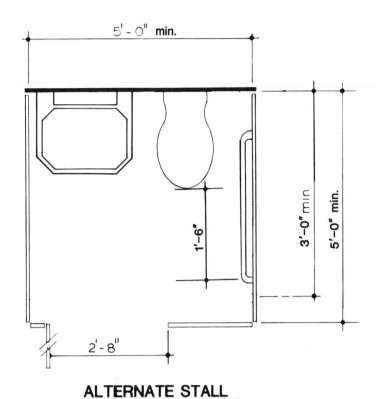

5'-0" min.

1'-6"

3'-0" min.

5'-0" min.

2'-8"

ALTERNATE STALL

Basis of standard —	APPLICABILITY			
North Carolina State Building Code	ALA	LA	OHIO	GUAM
	ALASKA	MAINE	OKLA	PR
	ARIZ	MD	ORE	VIR IS
Notes —	ARK	MASS	PA	DC
Grab bar height: 1'-1" above toilet seat. Clear floor area in front of stall: 3'-0" wide × 3'-6" deep.	CAL	MICH	RI	
	COLO	MINN	SC	
	CONN	MISS	SD	FED'L
	DEL	MO	● TENN	FUNDS
	FLA	MONT	TEXAS	
	GA	NEB	UTAH	
	HAWAII	NEV	VT	
	IDAHO	NH	VA	
	ILL	NJ	WASH	
	IND	NM	W VA	
	IOWA	NY	WIS	OTHER
	KANS	● NC	WYO	
	KY	ND		

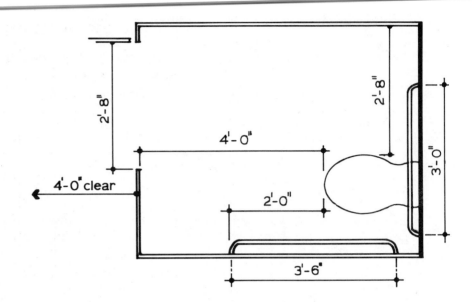

2'-8"

4'-0"

2'-8"

3'-0"

4'-0" clear

2'-0"

3'-6"

STANDARD FRONT ENTRY STALL

Basis of standard — CAC Title 24, Part 2.	APPLICABILITY			
	ALA	LA	OHIO	GUAM
	ALASKA	MAINE	OKLA	PR
	ARIZ	MD	ORE	VIR IS
Notes —	ARK	MASS	PA	DC
	● CAL	MICH	RI	
	COLO	MINN	SC	
	CONN	MISS	SD	FED'L FUNDS
	DEL	MO	TENN	
	FLA	MONT	TEXAS	
	GA	NEB	UTAH	
	HAWAII	NEV	VT	
	IDAHO	NH	VA	
	ILL	NJ	WASH	
	IND	NM	W VA	
	IOWA	NY	WIS	OTHER
	KANS	NC	WYO	
	KY	ND		

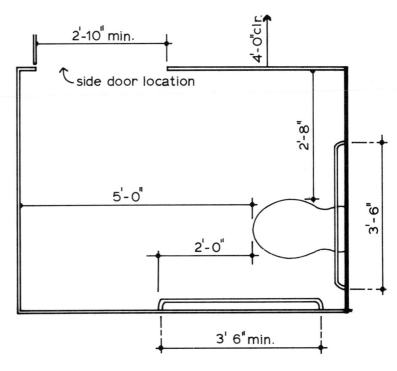

STANDARD SIDE ENTRY STALL

Basis of standard —	APPLICABILITY			
CAC Title 24, Part 2.	ALA	LA	OHIO	GUAM
	ALASKA	MAINE	OKLA	PR
	ARIZ	MD	ORE	VIR IS
	ARK	MASS	PA	DC
Notes —	● CAL	MICH	RI	
	COLO	MINN	SC	
	CONN	MISS	SD	FED'L
	DEL	MO	TENN	FUNDS
	FLA	MONT	TEXAS	
	GA	NEB	UTAH	
	HAWAII	NEV	VT	
	IDAHO	NH	VA	
	ILL	NJ	WASH	
	IND	NM	W VA	
	IOWA	NY	WIS	OTHER
	KANS	NC	WYO	
	KY	ND		

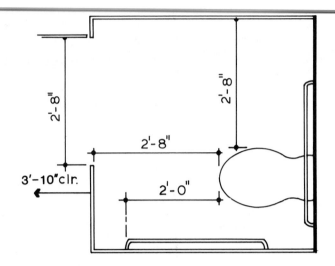

ALTERNATE STALL

Basis of standard — CAC Title 24, Part 2.	APPLICABILITY			
	ALA	LA	OHIO	GUAM
	ALASKA	MAINE	OKLA	PR
	ARIZ	MD	ORE	VIR IS
Notes — Allowed in existing buildings only.	ARK	MASS	PA	DC
	● CAL	MICH	RI	
	COLO	MINN	SC	
	CONN	MISS	SD	FED'L
	DEL	MO	TENN	FUNDS
	FLA	MONT	TEXAS	
	GA	NEB	UTAH	
	HAWAII	NEV	VT	
	IDAHO	NH	VA	
	ILL	NJ	WASH	
	IND	NM	W VA	
	IOWA	NY	WIS	OTHER
	KANS	NC	WYO	
	KY	ND		

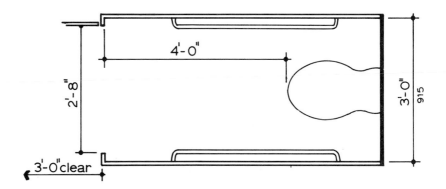

ALTERNATE STALL

Basis of standard — CAC Title 24, Part 2.	APPLICABILITY			
	ALA	LA	OHIO	GUAM
	ALASKA	MAINE	OKLA	PR
	ARIZ	MD	ORE	VIR IS
Notes — Allowed in existing buildings only.	ARK	MASS	PA	DC
	● CAL	MICH	RI	
	COLO	MINN	SC	
	CONN	MISS	SD	FED'L FUNDS
	DEL	MO	TENN	
	FLA	MONT	TEXAS	
	GA	NEB	UTAH	
	HAWAII	NEV	VT	
	IDAHO	NH	VA	
	ILL	NJ	WASH	
	IND	NM	W VA	
	IOWA	NY	WIS	OTHER
	KANS	NC	WYO	
	KY	ND		

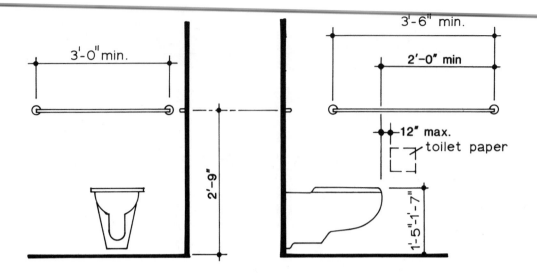

REAR WALL OF STANDARD STALL   SIDE WALLS

Basis of standard —	APPLICABILITY			
CAC Title 24, Part 2.	ALA	LA	OHIO	GUAM
	ALASKA	MAINE	OKLA	PR
	ARIZ	MD	ORE	VIR IS
Notes —	ARK	MASS	PA	DC
	● CAL	MICH	RI	
	COLO	MINN	SC	
	CONN	MISS	SD	FED'L FUNDS
	DEL	MO	TENN	
	FLA	MONT	TEXAS	
	GA	NEB	UTAH	
	HAWAII	NEV	VT	
	IDAHO	NH	VA	
	ILL	NJ	WASH	
	IND	NM	W VA	
	IOWA	NY	WIS	OTHER
	KANS	NC	WYO	
	KY	ND		

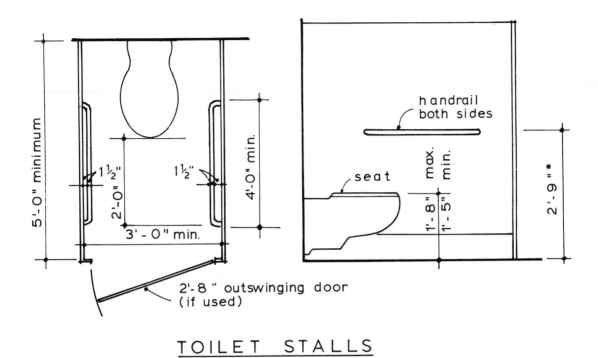

TOILET STALLS

Basis of standard — Basic Building Code	APPLICABILITY			
	ALA	LA	OHIO	GUAM
	ALASKA	MAINE	OKLA	PR
	ARIZ	MD	ORE	VIR IS
	ARK	MASS	PA	DC
	CAL	MICH	RI	
	COLO	MINN	SC	
	● CONN	MISS	SD	FED'L FUNDS
	DEL	MO	TENN	
	FLA	MONT	TEXAS	
	GA	NEB	UTAH	
	HAWAII	NEV	VT	
	IDAHO	NH	VA	
	ILL	NJ	WASH	
	IND	NM	W VA	
	IOWA	NY	WIS	OTHER
	KANS	NC	WYO	
	KY	ND		

Notes —

Clear space in front of door: 4'-0" × 4'-0" min. If only one water closet is required, use 1'-8" high model. Wall or floor mounted model may be used. Provide for narrow under structure that recedes sharply from the front.
(*)2'-4" for children, if provided.

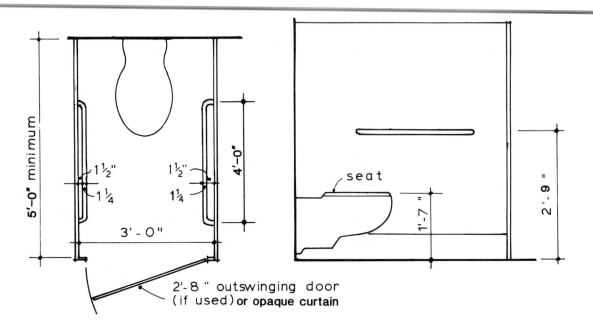

TOILET STALLS

Basis of standard — Dept. of General Services	APPLICABILITY			
	ALA	LA	OHIO	GUAM
	ALASKA	MAINE	OKLA	PR
	ARIZ	MD	ORE	VIR IS
Notes — For wall mounted water closets. Florida: applies to government facilities. Provide 3'-8" min. to wall opposite compartment door opening.	ARK	MASS	PA	DC
	CAL	MICH	RI	
	COLO	MINN	SC	
	CONN	MISS	SD	FED'L FUNDS
	DEL	MO	TENN	
	● FLA	MONT	TEXAS	
	GA	NEB	UTAH	
	HAWAII	NEV	VT	
	IDAHO	NH	VA	
	ILL	NJ	WASH	
	IND	NM	W VA	
	IOWA	NY	WIS	OTHER
	KANS	NC	WYO	
	KY	ND		

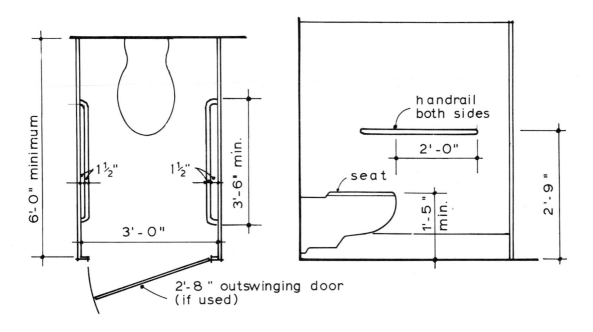

TOILET STALLS

Basis of standard — Maryland Building Code for the Handicapped	APPLICABILITY			
	ALA	LA	OHIO	GUAM
	ALASKA	MAINE	OKLA	PR
	ARIZ	● MD	ORE	VIR IS
Notes — Grab bars may have min. 1¼″ o.d. Anchor to withstand 300 lb. at center of bar. Water closets shall have narrow understructure receding sharply from the front. Seat mounted grab bars are acceptable if they do not encroach into the 3′-6″ square usable space. Provide 4′-0″ × 4′-0″ clear floor space in front of stall opening.	ARK	MASS	PA	DC
	CAL	MICH	RI	
	COLO	MINN	SC	
	CONN	MISS	SD	FED'L
	DEL	MO	TENN	FUNDS
	FLA	MONT	TEXAS	
	GA	NEB	UTAH	
	HAWAII	NEV	VT	
	IDAHO	NH	VA	
	ILL	NJ	WASH	
	IND	NM	W VA	
	IOWA	NY	WIS	OTHER
	KANS	NC	WYO	
	KY	ND		

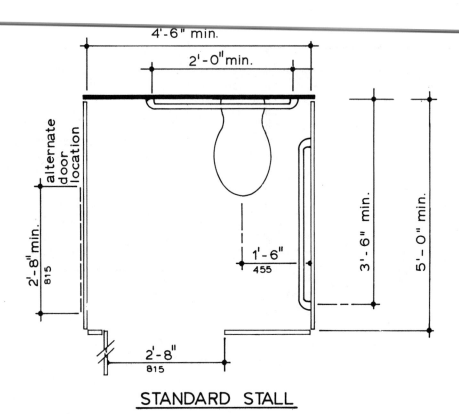

STANDARD STALL

Basis of standard —	APPLICABILITY			
Maryland Building Code for the Handicapped	ALA	LA	OHIO	GUAM
	ALASKA	MAINE	OKLA	PR
	ARIZ	● MD	ORE	VIR IS
Notes —	ARK	MASS	PA	DC
See notes on preceding page.	CAL	MICH	RI	
	COLO	MINN	SC	
	CONN	MISS	SD	FED'L
	DEL	MO	TENN	FUNDS
	FLA	MONT	TEXAS	
	GA	NEB	UTAH	
	HAWAII	NEV	VT	
	IDAHO	NH	VA	
	ILL	NJ	WASH	
	IND	NM	W VA	
	IOWA	NY	WIS	OTHER
	KANS	NC	WYO	
	KY	ND		

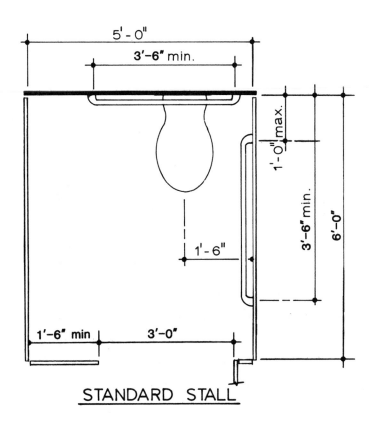

STANDARD STALL

Basis of standard —	APPLICABILITY			
Architectural Barriers Board	ALA	LA	OHIO	GUAM
	ALASKA	MAINE	OKLA	PR
	ARIZ	MD	ORE	VIR IS
	ARK	● MASS	PA	DC
	CAL	MICH	RI	
	COLO	MINN	SC	
	CONN	MISS	SD	FED'L FUNDS
	DEL	MO	TENN	
	FLA	MONT	TEXAS	
	GA	NEB	UTAH	
	HAWAII	NEV	VT	
	IDAHO	NH	VA	
	ILL	NJ	WASH	
	IND	NM	W VA	
	IOWA	NY	WIS	OTHER
	KANS	NC	WYO	
	KY	ND		

Notes —

Provide at least one complying stall in each public toilet room. Watercloset: narrow understructure, receding sharply, seat: 17″ to 19″ high. Grab bars: 1¼″ o.d., 1½″ clearance, 30″ high. Door: self-closing hinge, with lock 3'-0″ high. Max. coat hook height: 4'-6″ above floor.

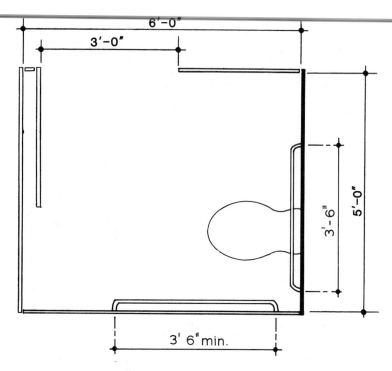

STANDARD SIDE ENTRY STALL

Basis of standard —	APPLICABILITY			
521 CMR Architectural Barriers Board	ALA	LA	OHIO	GUAM
	ALASKA	MAINE	OKLA	PR
	ARIZ	MD	ORE	VIR IS
Notes —	ARK	● MASS	PA	DC
	CAL	MICH	RI	
	COLO	MINN	SC	
	CONN	MISS	SD	FED'L
	DEL	MO	TENN	FUNDS
	FLA	MONT	TEXAS	
	GA	NEB	UTAH	
	HAWAII	NEV	VT	
	IDAHO	NH	VA	
	ILL	NJ	WASH	
	IND	NM	W VA	
	IOWA	NY	WIS	OTHER
	KANS	NC	WYO	
	KY	ND		

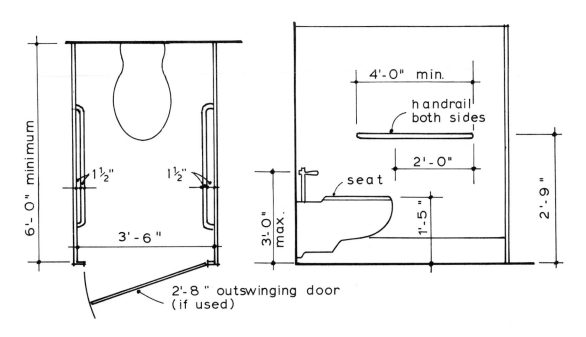

TOILET STALLS

Basis of standard —	APPLICABILITY			
Construction Code Commission general rules	**APPLICABILITY**			
	ALA	LA	OHIO	GUAM
	ALASKA	MAINE	OKLA	PR
	ARIZ	MD	ORE	VIR IS
Notes —	ARK	MASS	PA	DC
If opening is outside of stall, min. stall depth shall be 7'-0". Provide 4'-0" × 4'-0" min. clear space in front of stall opening. Anchor handrails to withstand 300 lb. force. Water closets shall have narrow understructure receding sharply from the front. Mount toilet paper holder so as not to impede wheelchair operation and within arm's reach of person using water closet.	CAL	● MICH	RI	
	COLO	MINN	SC	
	CONN	MISS	SD	FED'L FUNDS
	DEL	MO	TENN	
	FLA	MONT	TEXAS	
	GA	NEB	UTAH	
	HAWAII	NEV	VT	
	IDAHO	NH	VA	
	ILL	NJ	WASH	
	IND	NM	W VA	
	IOWA	NY	WIS	OTHER
	KANS	NC	WYO	
	KY	ND		

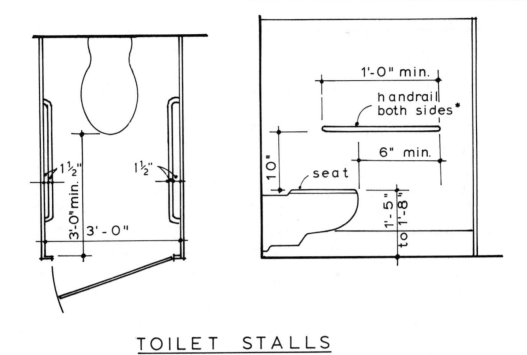

TOILET STALLS

Basis of standard —	APPLICABILITY			
State Building Code	ALA	LA	OHIO	GUAM
	ALASKA	MAINE	OKLA	PR
	ARIZ	MD	ORE	VIR IS
Notes —	ARK	MASS	PA	DC
(*)Provide grab bars at both sides or on one side and rear of toilet. Mounting of grab bars: horizontal — lowest point: 10″ above seat; extend min. 6″ in front of bowl; min. 12″ long. Vertical — 12″ from front of bowl; extend from 12″ above seat to 30″ above seat. Fasten securely to support min. 250 lb. load.	CAL	MICH	RI	
	COLO	● MINN	SC	
	CONN	MISS	SD	FED'L FUNDS
	DEL	MO	TENN	
	FLA	MONT	TEXAS	
	GA	NEB	UTAH	
	HAWAII	NEV	VT	
	IDAHO	NH	VA	
	ILL	NJ	WASH	
	IND	NM	W VA	
	IOWA	NY	WIS	OTHER
	KANS	NC	WYO	
	KY	ND		

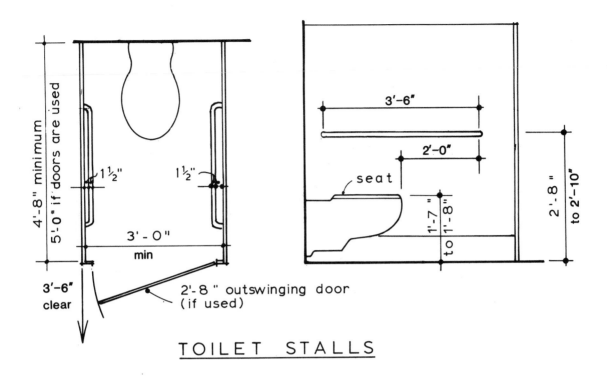

TOILET STALLS

Basis of standard —	APPLICABILITY			
Provisions for the Handicapped	ALA	LA	OHIO	GUAM
	ALASKA	MAINE	OKLA	PR
	ARIZ	MD	ORE	VIR IS
Notes —	ARK	MASS	PA	DC
	CAL	MICH	RI	
	COLO	MINN	SC	
	CONN	MISS	SD	FED'L FUNDS
	DEL	MO	TENN	
	FLA	MONT	TEXAS	
	GA	● NEB	UTAH	
	HAWAII	NEV	VT	
	IDAHO	NH	VA	
	ILL	NJ	WASH	
	IND	NM	W VA	
	IOWA	NY	WIS	OTHER
	KANS	NC	WYO	
	KY	ND		

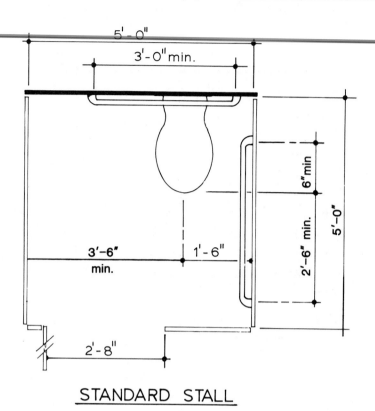

STANDARD STALL

Basis of standard —				
Architectural Barrier Free Design Code					

Basis of standard —	APPLICABILITY			
Architectural Barrier Free Design Code	ALA	LA	OHIO	GUAM
	ALASKA	MAINE	OKLA	PR
	ARIZ	MD	ORE	VIR IS
Notes —	ARK	MASS	PA	DC
Door: automatic self-closing hinge, or hinge pull device, lock: approx. 3'-0" high, coat hook: 4'-6" high. Grab bars: 1½" o.d., with 1½" clearance, 2'-6" high. Water closet: sharply receding under structure receding sharply, 1'-6" high seat.	CAL	MICH	RI	
	COLO	MINN	SC	
	CONN	MISS	SD	FED'L FUNDS
	DEL	MO	TENN	
	FLA	MONT	TEXAS	
	GA	NEB	UTAH	
	HAWAII	NEV	VT	
	IDAHO	● NH	VA	
	ILL	NJ	WASH	
	IND	NM	W VA	
	IOWA	NY	WIS	OTHER
	KANS	NC	WYO	
	KY	ND		

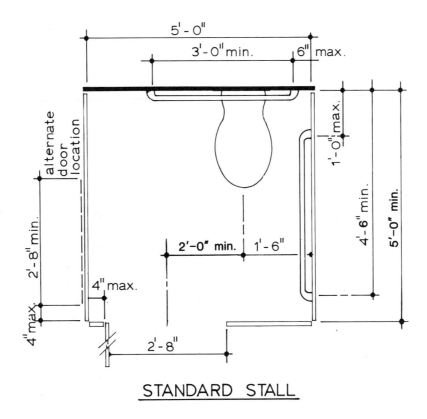

STANDARD STALL

Basis of standard —	APPLICABILITY			
Barrier Free Design Regulations	ALA	LA	OHIO	GUAM
	ALASKA	MAINE	OKLA	PR
	ARIZ	MD	ORE	VIR IS
Notes —	ARK	MASS	PA	DC
Provide 1¼″ to 1½″ wide grab bar, 2′-9″ high, 1½″ to 2″ clear of wall. Provide 3′-6″ min. from stall to opposite wall or other obstruction. Water closet to have 14″-15″ high overflow rim. Provide flushing mechanism other than foot operated. (If more than one barrier-free toilet room is provided for each sex in a building, provide toilet with seat at 1′-8″ high at alternate toilet rooms). Provide lever handled hardware with privacy latch. Distance from stall to opposite wall: 3′-6″ min.	CAL	MICH	RI	
	COLO	MINN	SC	
	CONN	MISS	SD	FED'L FUNDS
	DEL	MO	TENN	
	FLA	MONT	TEXAS	
	GA	NEB	UTAH	
	HAWAII	NEV	VT	
	IDAHO	NH	VA	
	ILL	● NJ	WASH	
	IND	NM	W VA	
	IOWA	NY	WIS	OTHER
	KANS	NC	WYO	
	KY	ND		

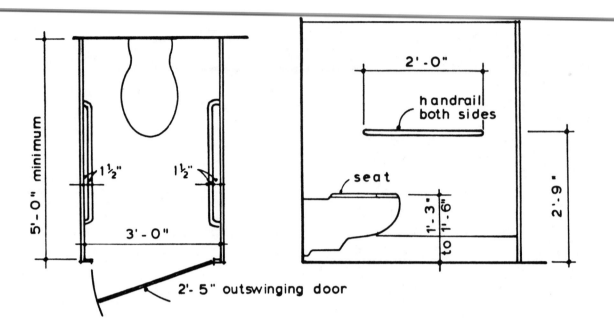

TOILET STALLS

Basis of standard —	APPLICABILITY			
Standard Building Code and ANSI 1961	ALA	LA	OHIO	GUAM
	ALASKA	MAINE	OKLA	PR
	ARIZ	MD	ORE	VIR IS
Notes —	ARK	MASS	PA	DC
Handrails to support 250 lbs. Provide 3'-8" unobstructed passage to stall.	CAL	MICH	RI	
	COLO	MINN	● SC	
	CONN	MISS	SD	FED'L FUNDS
	DEL	MO	TENN	
	FLA	MONT	TEXAS	
	GA	NEB	UTAH	
	HAWAII	NEV	VT	
	IDAHO	NH	VA	
	ILL	NJ	WASH	
	IND	NM	W VA	
	IOWA	NY	WIS	OTHER
	KANS	NC	WYO	
	KY	ND		

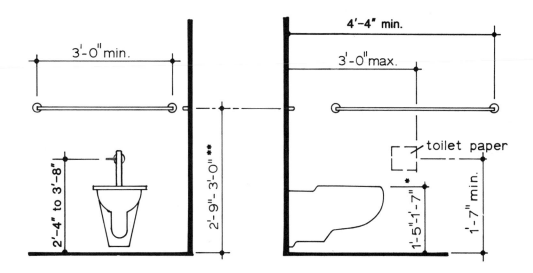

REAR WALL OF STANDARD STALL   SIDE WALLS

Basis of standard — State Purchasing and General Services Commission	APPLICABILITY			
	ALA	LA	OHIO	GUAM
	ALASKA	MAINE	OKLA	PR
	ARIZ	MD	ORE	VIR IS
	ARK	MASS	PA	DC
Notes —	CAL	MICH	RI	
(*)Height is to top of seat. For ages 5 thru 10 or 11 (Grades K thru 5 or 6): 1'-2" to 1'-3"; for ages 11 thru 14 or 15 (Grades 6 thru 8 or 9): 1'-3" to 1'-5".	COLO	MINN	SC	
(**)Grab bar height is to top. For ages 5 thru 10 or 11 (Grades K thru 5 or 6): 2'-4" to 2'-6" height; for ages 11 thru 14 or 15 (Grades 6 thru 8 or 9): 2'-6" to 2'-8" height.	CONN	MISS	SD	FED'L FUNDS
	DEL	MO	TENN	
	FLA	MONT	● TEXAS	
	GA	NEB	UTAH	
	HAWAII	NEV	VT	
	IDAHO	NH	VA	
	ILL	NJ	WASH	
	IND	NM	W VA	
	IOWA	NY	WIS	OTHER
	KANS	NC	WYO	
	KY	ND		

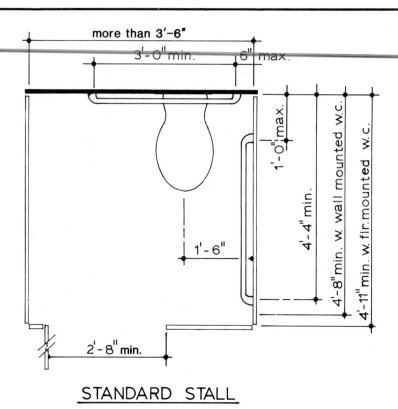

STANDARD STALL

Basis of standard — State Purchasing and General Services Commission	APPLICABILITY			
	ALA	LA	OHIO	GUAM
	ALASKA	MAINE	OKLA	PR
	ARIZ	MD	ORE	VIR IS
Notes — Min. toe clearance: 9″ (not required if stall depth is greater than 5′). Space in front of stall: 3′-4″ if door is 2′-8″, 3′-0″ if door is 3′-0″ (2′-6″ openings permitted if clear area 5′-0″ × 4′-0″ is provided in front of stall). Grab bars: outside dia. of 1¼″ to 1½″, 1½″ clearance to wall, able to support 250 lbs.	ARK	MASS	PA	DC
	CAL	MICH	RI	
	COLO	MINN	SC	
	CONN	MISS	SD	FED'L FUNDS
	DEL	MO	TENN	
	FLA	MONT	● TEXAS	
	GA	NEB	UTAH	
	HAWAII	NEV	VT	
	IDAHO	NH	VA	
	ILL	NJ	WASH	
	IND	NM	W VA	
	IOWA	NY	WIS	OTHER
	KANS	NC	WYO	
	KY	ND		

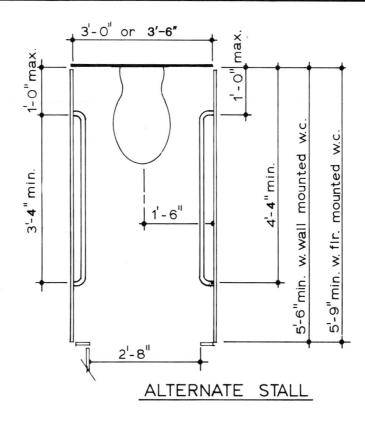

ALTERNATE STALL

Basis of standard —	APPLICABILITY			
State Purchasing and General Services Commission	ALA	LA	OHIO	GUAM
	ALASKA	MAINE	OKLA	PR
	ARIZ	MD	ORE	VIR IS
Notes —	ARK	MASS	PA	DC
See notes on preceding pages.	CAL	MICH	RI	
	COLO	MINN	SC	
	CONN	MISS	SD	FED'L
	DEL	MO	TENN	FUNDS
	FLA	MONT	● TEXAS	
	GA	NEB	UTAH	
	HAWAII	NEV	VT	
	IDAHO	NH	VA	
	ILL	NJ	WASH	
	IND	NM	W VA	
	IOWA	NY	WIS	OTHER
	KANS	NC	WYO	
	KY	ND		

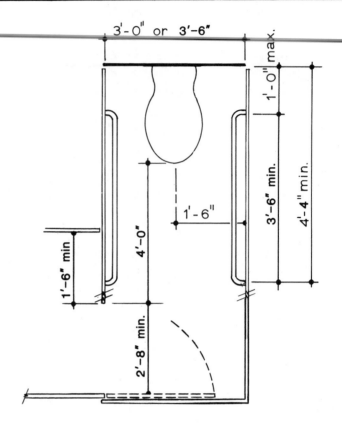

Basis of standard —	APPLICABILITY			
State Purchasing and General Services Commission	ALA	LA	OHIO	GUAM
	ALASKA	MAINE	OKLA	PR
	ARIZ	MD	ORE	VIR IS
Notes —	ARK	MASS	PA	DC
See notes on preceding page.	CAL	MICH	RI	
	COLO	MINN	SC	
	CONN	MISS	SD	FED'L
	DEL	MO	TENN	FUNDS
	FLA	MONT	● TEXAS	
	GA	NEB	UTAH	
	HAWAII	NEV	VT	
	IDAHO	NH	VA	
	ILL	NJ	WASH	
	IND	NM	W VA	
	IOWA	NY	WIS	OTHER
	KANS	NC	WYO	
	KY	ND		

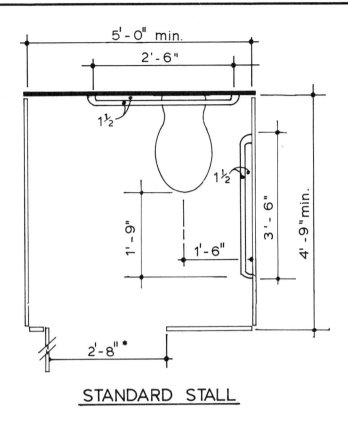

STANDARD STALL

Basis of standard — Utah State Building Board	APPLICABILITY			
	ALA	LA	OHIO	GUAM
	ALASKA	MAINE	OKLA	PR
	ARIZ	MD	ORE	VIR IS
	ARK	MASS	PA	DC
Notes — Provide 3'-6" deep by 5'-0" wide space outside of stall door. Top of seat 1'-3" to 1'-6" above floor. See following page for exceptions. Grab bars to support 250 lbs., height: 2'-8" from floor to top of bar. (*)Requires 2'-10" door.	CAL	MICH	RI	
	COLO	MINN	SC	
	CONN	MISS	SD	FED'L FUNDS
	DEL	MO	TENN	
	FLA	MONT	TEXAS	
	GA	NEB	● UTAH	
	HAWAII	NEV	VT	
	IDAHO	NH	VA	
	ILL	NJ	WASH	
	IND	NM	W VA	
	IOWA	NY	WIS	OTHER
	KANS	NC	WYO	
	KY	ND		

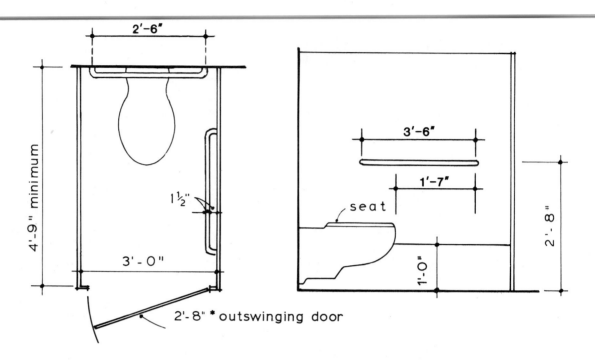

TOILET STALLS

Basis of standard —	APPLICABILITY			
Utah State Building Board	ALA	LA	OHIO	GUAM
	ALASKA	MAINE	OKLA	PR
	ARIZ	MD	ORE	VIR IS
Notes —	ARK	MASS	PA	DC
Stall size shown will be allowed only for remodeled facilities where the State Board of Health will not permit a reduction in fixtures and where it is not practical to enlarge the size of the toilet room. See preceding page for other conditions. Grab bars to support 250 lbs. Select water closet so under-structure will not interfere with close approach of wheelchair. Coat hooks: 4'-0" above floor. (*)2'-5" allowed for existing stall doors in remodeled facilities.	CAL	MICH	RI	
	COLO	MINN	SC	
	CONN	MISS	SD	FED'L FUNDS
	DEL	MO	TENN	
	FLA	MONT	TEXAS	
	GA	NEB	● UTAH	
	HAWAII	NEV	VT	
	IDAHO	NH	VA	
	ILL	NJ	WASH	
	IND	NM	W VA	
	IOWA	NY	WIS	OTHER
	KANS	NC	WYO	
	KY	ND		

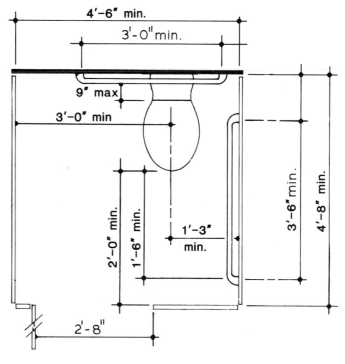

STANDARD STALL

Basis of standard —	APPLICABILITY			
Building Code Advisory Council	ALA	LA	OHIO	GUAM
	ALASKA	MAINE	OKLA	PR
	ARIZ	MD	ORE	VIR IS
Notes —	ARK	MASS	PA	DC
Provide one accessible water closet for every 20 or fraction thereof. Provide 3'-8" min. access to compartment. Top of water closet seat: 1'-4" to 1'-6" above floor.	CAL	MICH	RI	
	COLO	MINN	SC	
	CONN	MISS	SD	FED'L FUNDS
	DEL	MO	TENN	
	FLA	MONT	TEXAS	
	GA	NEB	UTAH	
	HAWAII	NEV	VT	
	IDAHO	NH	VA	
	ILL	NJ	● WASH	
	IND	NM	W VA	
	IOWA	NY	WIS	OTHER
	KANS	NC	WYO	
	KY	ND		

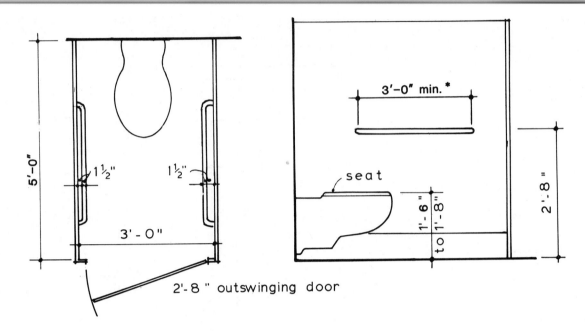

5'-0"

1½"   1½"

3'-0"

2'-8" outswinging door

3'-0" min. *

seat

1'-6" to 1'-8"

2'-8"

TOILET STALLS

Basis of standard —	APPLICABILITY			
Art 10F, Chapter 18, Code of West Virginia	ALA	LA	OHIO	GUAM
	ALASKA	MAINE	OKLA	PR
	ARIZ	MD	ORE	VIR IS
	ARK	MASS	PA	DC
Notes —	CAL	MICH	RI	
Min. of 4' between door and wall where 90° turn is required to enter toilet rooms. Min. 42″ depth and 36″ width in front of stall. If stall is over 3'-6" wide, add rail at rear wall.	COLO	MINN	SC	
	CONN	MISS	SD	FED'L FUNDS
(*)Center bar in line with front of water closet. Fasten at ends and center to withstand 250 lb. load.	DEL	MO	TENN	
	FLA	MONT	TEXAS	
	GA	NEB	UTAH	
	HAWAII	NEV	VT	
	IDAHO	NH	VA	
	ILL	NJ	WASH	
	IND	NM	● W VA	
	IOWA	NY	WIS	OTHER
	KANS	NC	WYO	
	KY	ND		

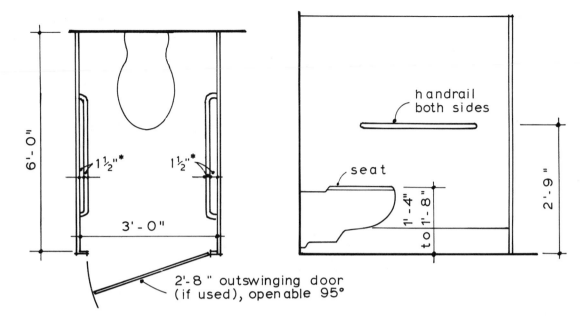

TOILET STALLS

Basis of standard —	APPLICABILITY			
Ind. 52.04, 6 Wisconsin Administrative Code	ALA	LA	OHIO	GUAM
	ALASKA	MAINE	OKLA	PR
	ARIZ	MD	ORE	VIR IS
Notes —	ARK	MASS	PA	DC
4'-0″ wide × 4'-9″ deep stall may be used with grab bar on wall closest to water closet, and with water closet centerline 15″ to 18″ from wall. Door should be diagonally across from fixture. Data not applicable to toilet rooms containing one water closet and one lavatory or to bathrooms containing a water closet, a lavatory and a bathing facility.	CAL	MICH	RI	
	COLO	MINN	SC	
	CONN	MISS	SD	FED'L FUNDS
	DEL	MO	TENN	
	FLA	MONT	TEXAS	
(*)Grabbers may be 1″ to 1½″ o.d., anchored and designed to support 250 lb. load.	GA	NEB	UTAH	
	HAWAII	NEV	VT	
	IDAHO	NH	VA	
	ILL	NJ	WASH	
	IND	NM	W VA	
	IOWA	NY	● WIS	OTHER
	KANS	NC	WYO	
	KY	ND		

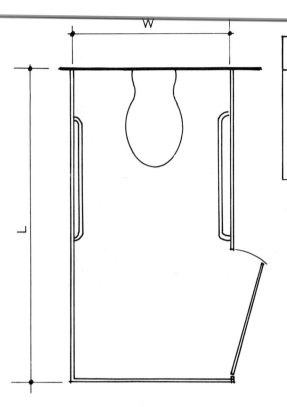

L	W	water closet	hand-rails
6'-6" min	3'-0" min	centered	2
6'-6" min	3'-6" max	centered	2
6'-0" min	4'-0" min	15"-18" to wall	1 - side nearest to w.c.

TOILET STALLS

Basis of standard —	APPLICABILITY			
Ind. 52.04, 6 Wisconsin Administrative Code	ALA	LA	OHIO	GUAM
	ALASKA	MAINE	OKLA	PR
	ARIZ	MD	ORE	VIR IS
Notes —	ARK	MASS	PA	DC
Refer to preceding page.	CAL	MICH	RI	
	COLO	MINN	SC	
	CONN	MISS	SD	FED'L FUNDS
	DEL	MO	TENN	
	FLA	MONT	TEXAS	
	GA	NEB	UTAH	
	HAWAII	NEV	VT	
	IDAHO	NH	VA	
	ILL	NJ	WASH	
	IND	NM	W VA	
	IOWA	NY	● WIS	OTHER
	KANS	NC	WYO	
	KY	ND		

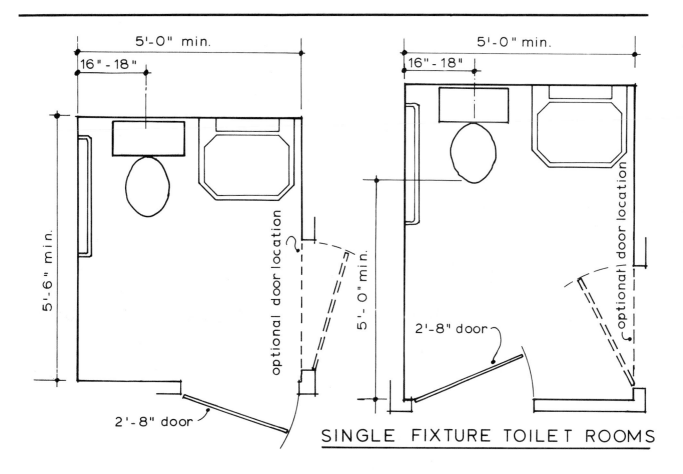

SINGLE FIXTURE TOILET ROOMS

Basis of standard —	APPLICABILITY			
Ind. 52.04, 6 Wisconsin Administrative Code	ALA	LA	OHIO	GUAM
	ALASKA	MAINE	OKLA	PR
	ARIZ	MD	ORE	VIR IS
Notes — Refer to preceding pages.	ARK	MASS	PA	DC
	CAL	MICH	RI	
	COLO	MINN	SC	
	CONN	MISS	SD	FED'L
	DEL	MO	TENN	FUNDS
	FLA	MONT	TEXAS	
	GA	NEB	UTAH	
	HAWAII	NEV	VT	
	IDAHO	NH	VA	
	ILL	NJ	WASH	
	IND	NM	W VA	
	IOWA	NY	● WIS	OTHER
	KANS	NC	WYO	
	KY	ND		

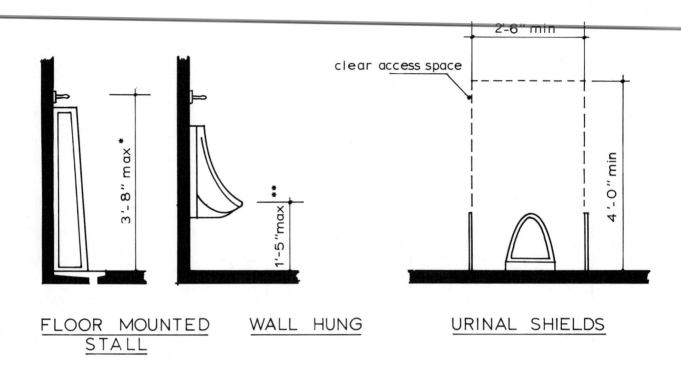

FLOOR MOUNTED
STALL   WALL HUNG   URINAL SHIELDS

Basis of standard —	APPLICABILITY			
ANSI 1980 – 4.18 and others	ALA	● LA	OHIO	GUAM
	● ALASKA	● MAINE	OKLA	PR
	ARIZ	MD	ORE	VIR IS
	ARK	MASS	PA	DC
Notes —	CAL	MICH	● RI	
1. Clear space to adjoin or overlap an accessible route. Wall-hung urinals shall have elongated rims.	● COLO	MINN	SC	
2. Flush shall be hand operated.	CONN	MISS	SD	FED'L FUNDS
Texas:	DEL	MO	TENN	
(*)2'-4″ min. in Texas. Not applicable in Washington.	FLA	MONT	● TEXAS	
(**)Teaxs: 1'-2″ for ages 5 thru 10 or 11; 1'-4″ for ages 11 thru 14 or 15.	GA	NEB	UTAH	
	● HAWAII	● NEV	● VT	
	● IDAHO	NH	● VA	
	ILL	NJ	● WASH	
	IND	● NM	W VA	
	IOWA	● NY	WIS	OTHER
	KANS	NC	WYO	
	KY	ND		

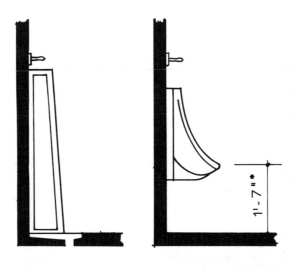

FLOOR MOUNTED   WALL HUNG
STALL

Basis of standard — ANSI 1961 — 5.6.5 and others	APPLICABILITY			
	ALA	LA	OHIO	GUAM
	ALASKA	MAINE	● OKLA	PR
	● ARIZ	MD	ORE	VIR IS
Notes —	ARK	MASS	● PA	DC
Floor mounted urinals shall be level with the main floor of the toilet room.	CAL	MICH	RI	
	COLO	MINN	● SC	
(Connecticut requires stalls to comply with water closet stall requirements.)	CONN	● MISS	● SD	FED'L FUNDS
(*)New York: 1'-9" max. North Carolina permits 1'-3" high standard urinal.	DEL	MO	TENN	
	● FLA	MONT	TEXAS	
	● GA	NEB	UTAH	
	HAWAII	NEV	VT	
	IDAHO	NH	VA	
	ILL	NJ	WASH	
	IND	NM	W VA	
	IOWA	NY	WIS	OTHER
	● KANS	● NC	● WYO	
	KY	● ND		

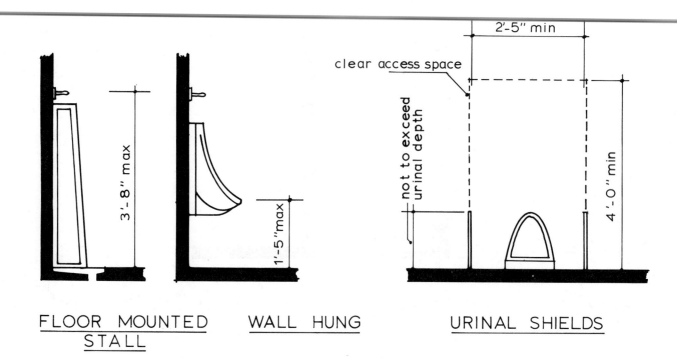

FLOOR MOUNTED STALL   WALL HUNG   URINAL SHIELDS

Basis of standard —	APPLICABILITY			
ATBCB — 1190.150 and others	ALA	LA	OHIO	GUAM
	ALASKA	MAINE	OKLA	PR
	ARIZ	MD	ORE	VIR IS
Notes —	● ARK	MASS	PA	DC
If urinal shield extends beyond front edge of urinal rim, provide 2'-6" min. clear space. Urinals may be floor mounted, stall type or wall hung with elongated rim. Flush shall be hand operated.	CAL	MICH	RI	
	COLO	MINN	SC	
	CONN	MISS	SD	● FED'L FUNDS
	● DEL	MO	TENN	
	FLA	MONT	TEXAS	
	GA	NEB	UTAH	
	HAWAII	NEV	VT	
	IDAHO	NH	VA	
	ILL	NJ	WASH	
	IND	NM	W VA	
	IOWA	NY	WIS	OTHER
	KANS	NC	WYO	
	KY	ND		

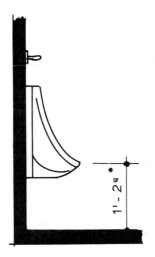

WALL HUNG

Basis of standard —	APPLICABILITY			
Various	ALA	LA	OHIO	GUAM
	ALASKA	MAINE	OKLA	PR
	ARIZ	● MD	ORE	VIR IS
Notes —	ARK	● MASS	PA	DC
Provide at least one urinal as shown where urinals are required.	CAL	MICH	RI	
(*)1'-3″ in Massachussetts and New Hampshire.	COLO	MINN	SC	
	CONN	MISS	SD	FED'L FUNDS
	DEL	MO	TENN	
	FLA	MONT	TEXAS	
	GA	NEB	UTAH	
	HAWAII	NEV	VT	
	IDAHO	● NH	VA	
	ILL	NJ	WASH	
	IND	NM	W VA	
	IOWA	NY	WIS	OTHER
	KANS	NC	WYO	
	KY	ND		

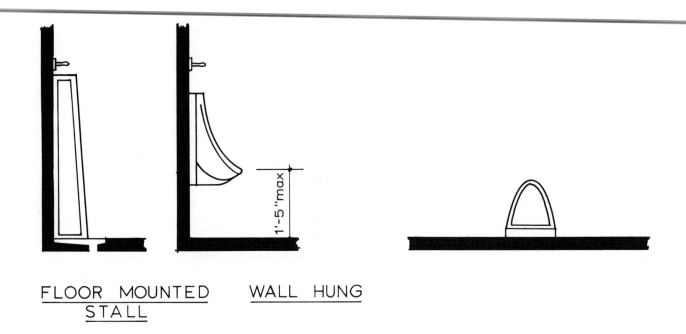

FLOOR MOUNTED STALL   WALL HUNG

Basis of standard —	APPLICABILITY			
Various	ALA	LA	OHIO	GUAM
	ALASKA	MAINE	OKLA	PR
	ARIZ	MD	ORE	VIR IS
Notes —	ARK	MASS	PA	DC
Wall hung urinal shall have elongated rim.	CAL	MICH	RI	
	COLO	MINN	SC	
	CONN	MISS	SD	FED'L FUNDS
	DEL	MO	TENN	
	FLA	MONT	TEXAS	
	GA	NEB	UTAH	
	HAWAII	NEV	VT	
	IDAHO	NH	VA	
	ILL	NJ	WASH	
	● IND	NM	W VA	
	● IOWA	NY	WIS	OTHER
	KANS	NC	WYO	
	KY	ND		

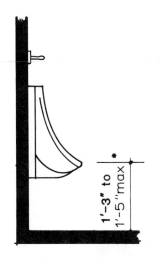

WALL HUNG

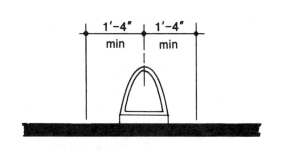

URINAL SHIELDS

Basis of standard — Capital Development Board and others	APPLICABILITY			
	ALA	LA	OHIO	GUAM
	ALASKA	MAINE	OKLA	PR
	ARIZ	MD	● ORE	VIR IS
	ARK	MASS	PA	DC
Notes —	CAL	MICH	RI	
One accessible wall-mounted urinal in every male public toilet room.	COLO	MINN	SC	
(*)Oregon: 1'-4"	CONN	MISS	SD	FED'L FUNDS
	DEL	MO	TENN	
	FLA	MONT	TEXAS	
	GA	NEB	UTAH	
	HAWAII	NEV	VT	
	IDAHO	NH	VA	
	● ILL	NJ	WASH	
	IND	NM	W VA	
	IOWA	NY	WIS	OTHER
	KANS	NC	WYO	
	KY	ND		

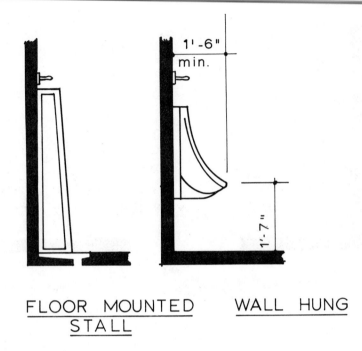

FLOOR MOUNTED   WALL HUNG
STALL

Basis of standard —	APPLICABILITY			
Barrier Free Design Standard	● ALA	LA	OHIO	GUAM
	ALASKA	MAINE	OKLA	PR
	ARIZ	MD	ORE	VIR IS
Notes —	ARK	MASS	PA	DC
Provide at least one urinal in men's toilet rooms as shown. Floor mounted urinals are acceptable if they are at the same level as the main toilet room floor.	CAL	MICH	RI	
	COLO	MINN	SC	
	CONN	MISS	SD	FED'L FUNDS
	DEL	MO	TENN	
	FLA	MONT	TEXAS	
	GA	NEB	UTAH	
	HAWAII	NEV	VT	
	IDAHO	NH	VA	
	ILL	NJ	WASH	
	IND	NM	W VA	
	IOWA	NY	WIS	OTHER
	KANS	NC	WYO	
	KY	ND		

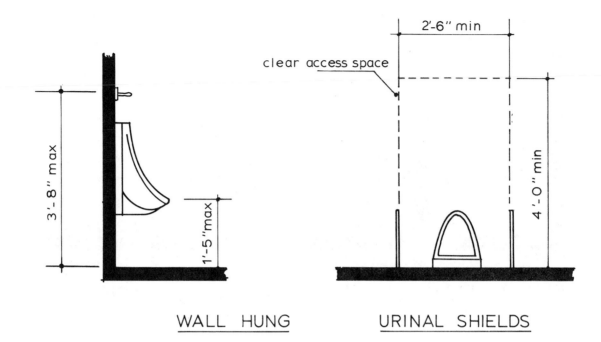

WALL HUNG

URINAL SHIELDS

Basis of standard —	APPLICABILITY			
CAC Title 24, Parts 2 and 5	ALA	LA	OHIO	GUAM
	ALASKA	MAINE	OKLA	PR
	ARIZ	MD	ORE	VIR IS
	ARK	MASS	PA	DC
Notes —	● CAL	MICH	RI	
	COLO	MINN	SC	
	CONN	MISS	SD	FED'L FUNDS
	DEL	MO	TENN	
	FLA	MONT	TEXAS	
	GA	NEB	UTAH	
	HAWAII	NEV	VT	
	IDAHO	NH	VA	
	ILL	NJ	WASH	
	IND	NM	W VA	
	IOWA	NY	WIS	OTHER
	KANS	NC	WYO	
	KY	ND		

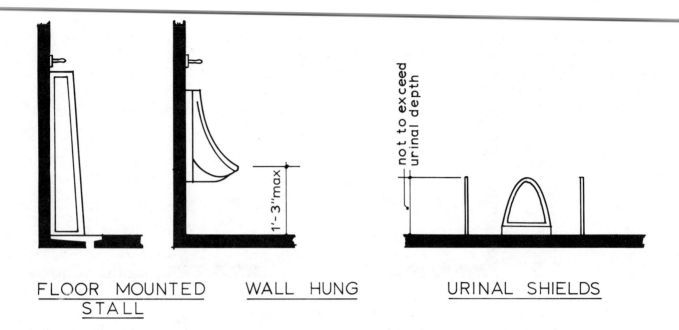

FLOOR MOUNTED   WALL HUNG   URINAL SHIELDS
      STALL

Basis of standard —	APPLICABILITY			
Construction Code Commission	ALA	LA	OHIO	GUAM
	ALASKA	MAINE	OKLA	PR
	ARIZ	MD	ORE	VIR IS
Notes —	ARK	MASS	PA	DC
If urinal is enclosed in stall, the width shall be 3'-0" min., and shall comply with water closet stall requirements.	CAL	● MICH	RI	
	COLO	MINN	SC	
	CONN	MISS	SD	FED'L FUNDS
	DEL	MO	TENN	
	FLA	MONT	TEXAS	
	GA	NEB	UTAH	
	HAWAII	NEV	VT	
	IDAHO	NH	VA	
	ILL	NJ	WASH	
	IND	NM	W VA	
	IOWA	NY	WIS	OTHER
	KANS	NC	WYO	
	KY	ND		

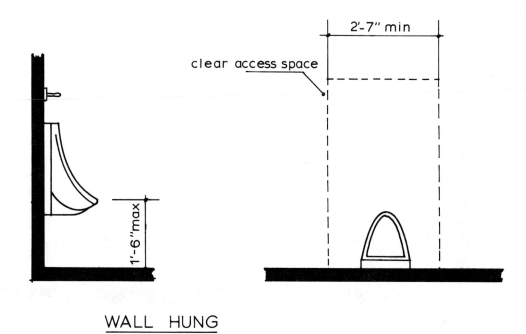

2'-7" min

clear access space

1'-6" max

WALL   HUNG

Basis of standard —	APPLICABILITY			
State Building Code	ALA	LA	OHIO	GUAM
	ALASKA	MAINE	OKLA	PR
	ARIZ	MD	ORE	VIR IS
Notes —	ARK	MASS	PA	DC
	CAL	MICH	RI	
	COLO	● MINN	SC	
	CONN	MISS	SD	FED'L FUNDS
	DEL	MO	TENN	
	FLA	MONT	TEXAS	
	GA	NEB	UTAH	
	HAWAII	NEV	VT	
	IDAHO	NH	VA	
	ILL	NJ	WASH	
	IND	NM	W VA	
	IOWA	NY	WIS	OTHER
	KANS	NC	WYO	
	KY	ND		

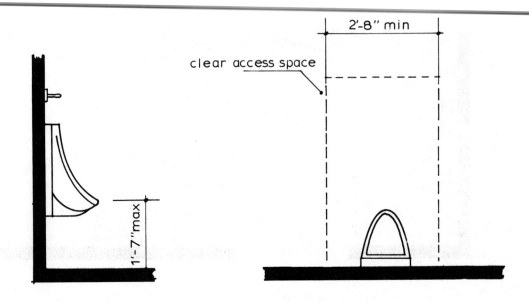

2'-8" min

clear access space

1'-7" max

WALL   HUNG

Basis of standard —	APPLICABILITY			
Nebraska Provisions for the Handicapped	ALA	LA	OHIO	GUAM
	ALASKA	MAINE	OKLA	PR
	ARIZ	MD	ORE	VIR IS
Notes —	ARK	MASS	PA	DC
	CAL	MICH	RI	
	COLO	MINN	SC	
	CONN	MISS	SD	FED'L FUNDS
	DEL	MO	TENN	
	FLA	MONT	TEXAS	
	GA	● NEB	UTAH	
	HAWAII	NEV	VT	
	IDAHO	NH	VA	
	ILL	NJ	WASH	
	IND	NM	W VA	
	IOWA	NY	WIS	OTHER
	KANS	NC	WYO	
	KY	ND		

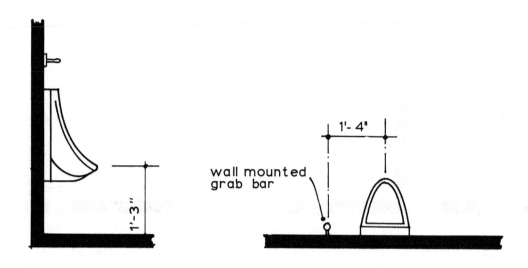

1'- 4"

wall mounted
grab bar

1'- 3"

WALL HUNG

Basis of standard —	APPLICABILITY			
Barrier Free Design Regulations	ALA	LA	OHIO	GUAM
	ALASKA	MAINE	OKLA	PR
	ARIZ	MD	ORE	VIR IS
Notes —	ARK	MASS	PA	DC
Provide wall mounted metal grab bar next to one of	CAL	MICH	RI	
the standard height urinals, approx. 1'-4" from the	COLO	MINN	SC	
centerline of this urinal. Where more than one urinal	CONN	MISS	SD	FED'L
is installed, install handrail between urinals. Vertically	DEL	MO	TENN	FUNDS
installed grab bar shall be 2'-0" long and mounted	FLA	MONT	TEXAS	
2'-0" above floor.	GA	NEB	UTAH	
	HAWAII	NEV	VT	
	IDAHO	NH	VA	
	ILL	● NJ	WASH	
	IND	NM	W VA	
	IOWA	NY	WIS	OTHER
	KANS	NC	WYO	
	KY	ND		

FLOOR MOUNTED STALL   WALL HUNG   URINAL SHIELDS

Basis of standard — Utah State Building Board	APPLICABILITY			
	ALA	LA	OHIO	GUAM
	ALASKA	MAINE	OKLA	PR
	ARIZ	MD	ORE	VIR IS
Notes —	ARK	MASS	PA	DC
Exceptions to the above: for remodeled facilities an existing wall hung urinal that is not elongated may be used if top of rim is 1'-7" max. above floor; for floor mounted urinals if existing urinal has less than 1'-3" depth. Men's toilet rooms with single toilet fixtures and with privacy lock on entrance door need not contain urinal.	CAL	MICH	RI	
	COLO	MINN	SC	
	CONN	MISS	SD	FED'L FUNDS
	DEL	MO	TENN	
	FLA	MONT	TEXAS	
	GA	NEB	● UTAH	
	HAWAII	NEV	VT	
	IDAHO	NH	VA	
	ILL	NJ	WASH	
	IND	NM	W VA	
	IOWA	NY	WIS	OTHER
	KANS	NC	WYO	
	KY	ND		

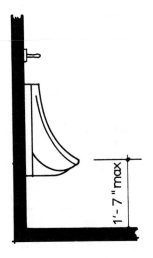

WALL   HUNG

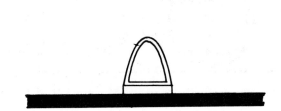

Basis of standard —	APPLICABILITY			
Art 10F, Chapt. 18, Code of West Virginia	ALA	LA	OHIO	GUAM
	ALASKA	MAINE	OKLA	PR
	ARIZ	MD	ORE	VIR IS
	ARK	MASS	PA	DC
Notes —	CAL	MICH	RI	
Where wall mounted urinals are used, install with elongated lip as shown.	COLO	MINN	SC	
	CONN	MISS	SD	FED'L
	DEL	MO	TENN	FUNDS
	FLA	MONT	TEXAS	
	GA	NEB	UTAH	
	HAWAII	NEV	VT	
	IDAHO	NH	VA	
	ILL	NJ	WASH	
	IND	NM	● W VA	
	IOWA	NY	WIS	OTHER
	KANS	NC	WYO	
	KY	ND		

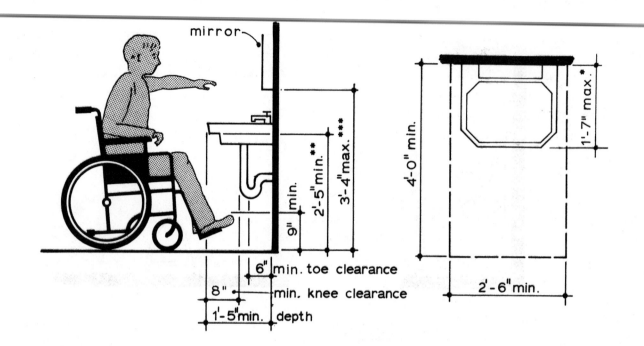

LAVATORY CLEARANCES & CLEAR FLOOR SPACE AT LAVATORIES

Basis of standard — ANSI 1980 — 4.19	APPLICABILITY			
	ALA	● LA	OHIO	GUAM
	● ALASKA	● MAINE	OKLA	PR
	ARIZ	MD	ORE	VIR IS
Notes — Clear floor space to extend 1'-7" max. under lavatory. Insulate hot water and drain pipes under lavatory. Use lever-operated, push-type, electronically controlled mechanisms, or similar for faucets. Self-closing valves are allowed if the faucet remains open at least 10 seconds. (*)For Federal, Arkansas, and Delaware. (**)Texas: 2'-2" for ages 5 thru 10 or 11; 2'-4" for ages 11 thru 14 or 15. (***)Texas: 2'-10" for ages 5 thru 10 or 11; 3'-1" for ages 11 thru 14 or 15. 3'-8" max. to medicine cabinet in residences.	● ARK	MASS	PA	DC
	CAL	MICH	● RI	
	● COLO	MINN	SC	
	CONN	MISS	SD	● FED'L FUNDS
	DEL	MO	TENN	
	FLA	MONT	● TEXAS	
	GA	NEB	UTAH	
	● HAWAII	● NEV	● VT	
	● IDAHO	NH	● VA	
	ILL	NJ	WASH	
	IND	● NM	W VA	
	IOWA	● NY	WIS	OTHER
	KANS	NC	WYO	
	KY	ND		

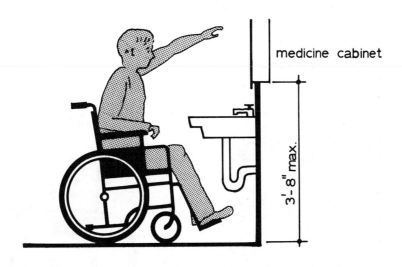

medicine cabinet

3'-8" max.

MEDICINE CABINETS

Basis of standard —	APPLICABILITY			
ANSI 1980 — 4.23.9 and others	ALA	● LA	OHIO	GUAM
	● ALASKA	● MAINE	OKLA	PR
	ARIZ	MD	ORE	VIR IS
	ARK	MASS	PA	DC
Notes —	CAL	MICH	● RI	
If medicine cabinets are provided, locate at least one with usable shelf as shown.	● COLO	MINN	SC	
	CONN	MISS	SD	FED'L
	DEL	MO	TENN	FUNDS
	FLA	MONT	TEXAS	
	GA	NEB	UTAH	
	● HAWAII	● NEV	● VT	
	● IDAHO	NH	● VA	
	ILL	NJ	WASH	
	IND	● NM	W VA	
	IOWA	● NY	WIS	OTHER
	KANS	NC	WYO	
	KY	ND		

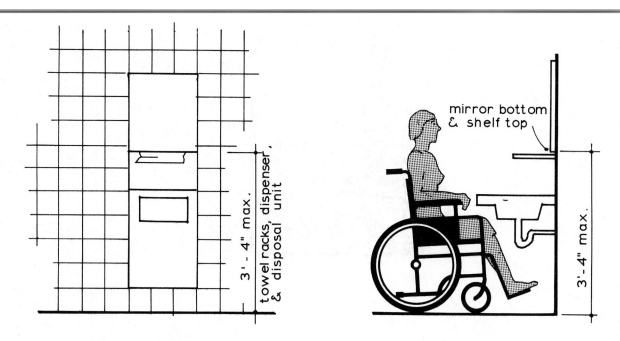

LAVATORIES, MIRRORS, & ACCESSORIES

Basis of standard — ANSI 1961 — 5.6.6 and others	APPLICABILITY			
	ALA	LA	OHIO	GUAM
	ALASKA	MAINE	● OKLA	PR
	● ARIZ	MD	ORE	VIR IS
	ARK	MASS	● PA	DC
	CAL	MICH	RI	
	COLO	MINN	● SC	
Notes — Lavatories at standard height shall have narrow aprons; or mount higher for use by individuals in wheelchairs. Cover or insulate drain and hot water pipes to avoid burn. Some mirrors and shelves shall be mounted at height shown. (Insulation not required in Pennsylvania.)	CONN	● MISS	● SD	FED'L FUNDS
	DEL	MO	TENN	
	● FLA	MONT	TEXAS	
	● GA	NEB	UTAH	
	HAWAII	NEV	VT	
	IDAHO	● NH	VA	
	ILL	NJ	WASH	
	IND	NM	W VA	
	IOWA	NY	WIS	OTHER
	● KANS	NC	WYO	
	KY	● ND		

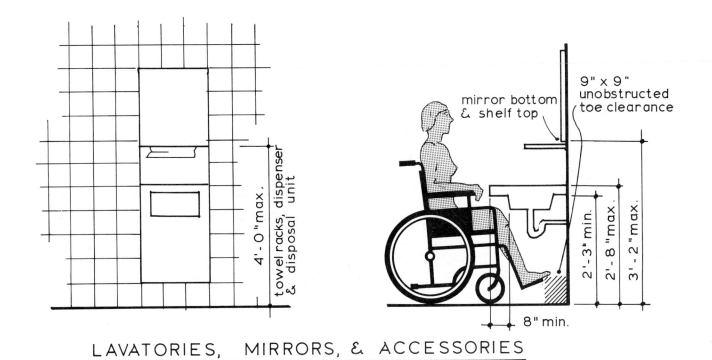

9" x 9"
unobstructed
toe clearance

mirror bottom
& shelf top

2'-3" min.
2'-8" max.
3'-2" max.

8" min.

4'-0" max.
towel racks, dispenser
& disposal unit

LAVATORIES, MIRRORS, & ACCESSORIES

Basis of standard — BOCA – 1978	APPLICABILITY			
	ALA	LA	● OHIO	GUAM
	ALASKA	MAINE	OKLA	PR
	ARIZ	MD	ORE	VIR IS
Notes —	ARK	MASS	PA	DC
	CAL	MICH	RI	
	COLO	MINN	SC	
	CONN	MISS	SD	FED'L FUNDS
	DEL	MO	TENN	
	FLA	MONT	TEXAS	
	GA	NEB	UTAH	
	HAWAII	NEV	VT	
	IDAHO	NH	VA	
	ILL	NJ	WASH	
	IND	NM	W VA	
	IOWA	NY	WIS	OTHER
	KANS	NC	WYO	
	KY	ND		

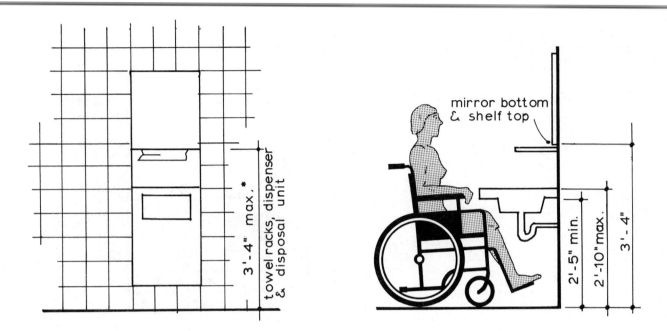

3'-4" max.*
towel racks, dispenser & disposal unit

mirror bottom & shelf top

2'-5" min.
2'-10" max.
3'-4"

LAVATORIES, MIRRORS, & ACCESSORIES

Basis of standard —	APPLICABILITY			
Various	ALA	LA	OHIO	GUAM
	ALASKA	MAINE	OKLA	PR
	ARIZ	MD	ORE	VIR IS
Notes —	ARK	MASS	PA	DC
For Nebraska: insulate supply and drainlines if hot water exceeds 120°F. North Carolina and Tennessee: 8¾" high and 6" deep toe space for toilet room cabinets. (*)4'-0" for Nebraska.	CAL	MICH	RI	
	COLO	MINN	SC	
	CONN	MISS	SD	FED'L FUNDS
	DEL	MO	● TENN	
	FLA	MONT	TEXAS	
	GA	● NEB	UTAH	
	HAWAII	NEV	VT	
	IDAHO	NH	VA	
	ILL	NJ	WASH	
	IND	NM	W VA	
	IOWA	NY	● WIS	OTHER
	KANS	● NC	WYO	
	KY	ND		

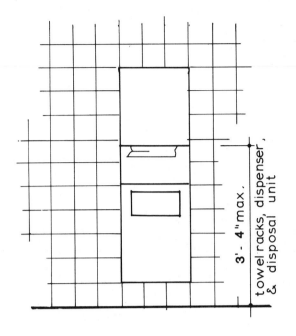

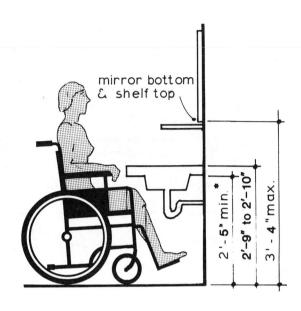

LAVATORIES, MIRRORS, & ACCESSORIES

Basis of standard —	APPLICABILITY			
Building Code Advisory Council and Uniform Building Code	ALA	LA	OHIO	GUAM
	ALASKA	MAINE	OKLA	PR
	ARIZ	MD	ORE	VIR IS
Notes —	ARK	MASS	PA	DC
Washington — Faucets shall be lever type, max. 1'-5" from front edge of lavatory or counter. Recess, insulate, or guard exposed drain pipes and hot water pipes under lavatory when water temperature exceeds 120°F.	CAL	MICH	RI	
	COLO	MINN	SC	
	CONN	MISS	SD	FED'L FUNDS
	DEL	MO	TENN	
Indiana and Montana require clear unobstructed space under lavatories (except for bowls and waste piping projections) 2'-2" wide, 2'-3" high, 1'-0" deep.	FLA	● MONT	TEXAS	
	GA	NEB	UTAH	
In Washington and Montana above requirements are not applicable to Group R, Division 3, Group M, Group R, Division 1 apartment houses and Group B, Divisions 2 and 4 storage occupancies. Indiana exempts Group R, Division 1 apartment houses.	HAWAII	NEV	VT	
	IDAHO	NH	VA	
	ILL	NJ	● WASH	
	● IND	NM	W VA	
	IOWA	NY	WIS	
	KANS	NC	WYO	OTHER
	KY	ND		

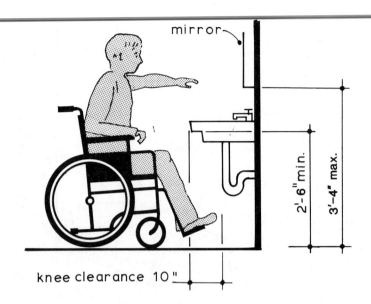

knee clearance 10"

LAVATORY CLEARANCES & CLEAR FLOOR SPACE AT LAVATORIES

Basis of standard — Barrier Free Design Standard	APPLICABILITY			
	● ALA	LA	OHIO	GUAM
	ALASKA	MAINE	OKLA	PR
	ARIZ	MD	ORE	VIR IS
Notes — Cover or insulate drain and water pipes under lavatory. Provide appropriate number of towel racks, towel dispensers, and other dispensers and towel racks at 3'-4" max. above floor. Alabama permits slight forward tilting of mirror to 3'-4" max. height.	ARK	MASS	PA	DC
	CAL	MICH	RI	
	COLO	MINN	SC	
	CONN	MISS	SD	FED'L FUNDS
	DEL	MO	TENN	
	FLA	MONT	TEXAS	
	GA	NEB	UTAH	
	HAWAII	NEV	VT	
	IDAHO	NH	VA	
	ILL	NJ	WASH	
	IND	NM	W VA	
	IOWA	NY	WIS	OTHER
	KANS	NC	WYO	
	KY	ND		

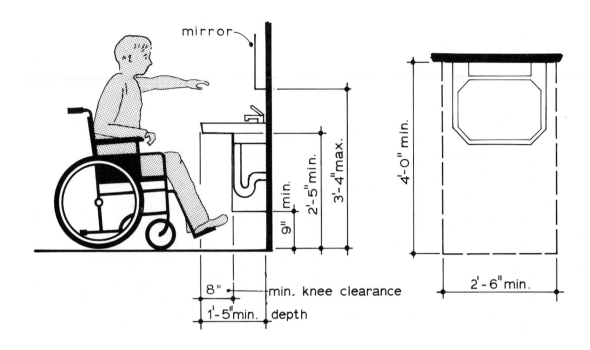

LAVATORY CLEARANCES & CLEAR FLOOR SPACE AT LAVATORIES

Basis of standard —	APPLICABILITY			
CAC Title 24 Parts 2 and 5.	ALA	LA	OHIO	GUAM
	ALASKA	MAINE	OKLA	PR
	ARIZ	MD	ORE	VIR IS
	ARK	MASS	PA	DC
Notes —	● CAL	MICH	RI	
Faucet: lever or push button type, operable with one hand; maximum operating pressure 5 lb. Wrap or cover hot water and drain pipes.	COLO	MINN	SC	
	CONN	MISS	SD	FED'L FUNDS
	DEL	MO	TENN	
	FLA	MONT	TEXAS	
	GA	NEB	UTAH	
	HAWAII	NEV	VT	
	IDAHO	NH	VA	
	ILL	NJ	WASH	
	IND	NM	W VA	
	IOWA	NY	WIS	OTHER
	KANS	NC	WYO	
	KY	ND		

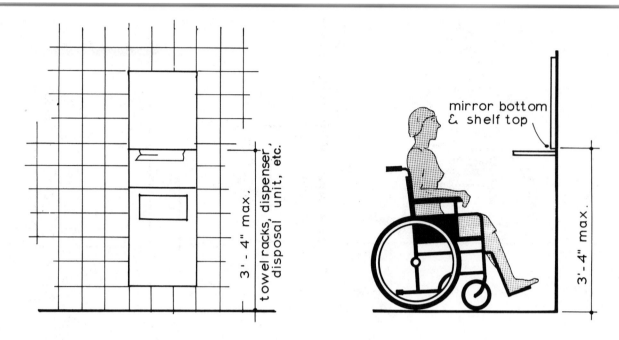

LAVATORIES, MIRRORS, & ACCESSORIES

Basis of standard — CAC Title 24 Part 2	APPLICABILITY			
	ALA	LA	OHIO	GUAM
	ALASKA	MAINE	OKLA	PR
	ARIZ	MD	ORE	VIR IS
	ARK	MASS	PA	DC
	● CAL	MICH	RI	
	COLO	MINN	SC	
	CONN	MISS	SD	FED'L FUNDS
	DEL	MO	TENN	
	FLA	MONT	TEXAS	
	GA	NEB	UTAH	
	HAWAII	NEV	VT	
	IDAHO	NH	VA	
	ILL	NJ	WASH	
	IND	NM	W VA	
	IOWA	NY	WIS	OTHER
	KANS	NC	WYO	
	KY	ND		

Notes —

Provide at least one of each type of accessory included within 40″ of the floor.

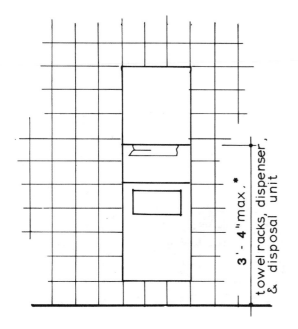
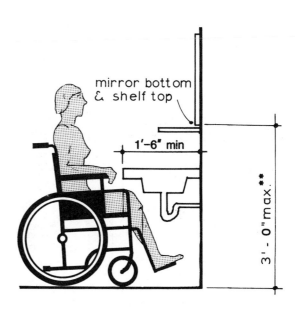

mirror bottom
& shelf top

1'-6" min

3'-4" max.*

towel racks, dispenser, & disposal unit

3'-0" max.**

LAVATORIES, MIRRORS, & ACCESSORIES

Basis of standard —	APPLICABILITY			
Basic Building Code	ALA	LA	OHIO	GUAM
	ALASKA	MAINE	OKLA	PR
	ARIZ	MD	ORE	VIR IS
Notes —	ARK	MASS	PA	DC
Provide single lever control for lavatory. Min. clearance under rim: 2'-4" high by 2'-2" wide. Insulate drain pipes and hot water pipes under lavatory.	CAL	MICH	RI	
	COLO	MINN	SC	
(*)Max. height of coin slot or lever: 3'-4".	● CONN	MISS	SD	FED'L FUNDS
(**)Alternate: full length mirror.	DEL	MO	TENN	
	FLA	MONT	TEXAS	
	GA	NEB	UTAH	
	HAWAII	NEV	VT	
	IDAHO	NH	VA	
	ILL	NJ	WASH	
	IND	NM	W VA	
	IOWA	NY	WIS	OTHER
	KANS	NC	WYO	
	KY	ND		

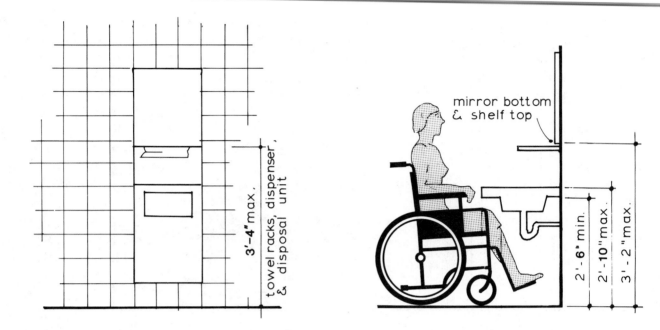

LAVATORIES, MIRRORS, & ACCESSORIES

Basis of standard — Capital Development Board	**APPLICABILITY**			
	ALA	LA	OHIO	GUAM
	ALASKA	MAINE	OKLA	PR
	ARIZ	MD	ORE	VIR IS
Notes —	ARK	MASS	PA	DC
Min. 1'-3" clear width to each side of lavatory center-line to facilitate wheelchair approach. Insulate hot water and drain lines for over 105°F water temperature. Faucets: lever, blade, or multi-arm handle or other design not requiring grasping or wrist twisting as only means of operation. Max. force to activate faucets: 3 lbf. Spring faucets allowed only with delay feature allowing water to run 10 seconds after removing hand from faucet. "Hot" always on left, cold, on right; max. 105°F at faucet. Max. for hot air dryers 105°F.	CAL	MICH	RI	
	COLO	MINN	SC	
	CONN	MISS	SD	FED'L
	DEL	MO	TENN	FUNDS
	FLA	MONT	TEXAS	
	GA	NEB	UTAH	
	HAWAII	NEV	VT	
	IDAHO	NH	VA	
	● ILL	NJ	WASH	
	IND	NM	W VA	
	IOWA	NY	WIS	OTHER
	KANS	NC	WYO	
	KY	ND		

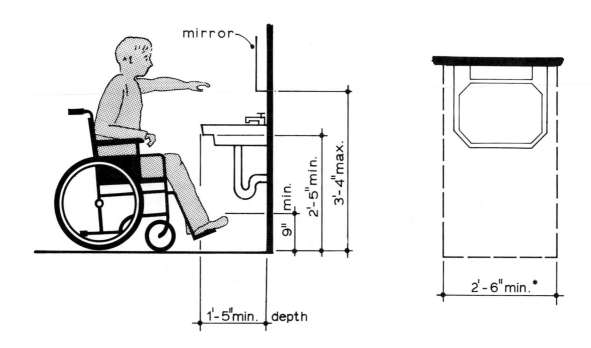

LAVATORY CLEARANCES & CLEAR FLOOR SPACE AT LAVATORIES

Basis of standard —	APPLICABILITY			
Iowa Administrative Code	ALA	LA	OHIO	GUAM
	ALASKA	MAINE	OKLA	PR
	ARIZ	MD	ORE	VIR IS
Notes —	ARK	MASS	PA	DC
Tilt mirrors may be used if bottom is within 3'-8" of floor and provides an equivalent field of view of mirror shown above.	CAL	MICH	RI	
	COLO	MINN	SC	
(*)Bowl and waste piping are excepted from clear space requirement.	CONN	MISS	SD	FED'L FUNDS
	DEL	MO	TENN	
	FLA	MONT	TEXAS	
	GA	NEB	UTAH	
	HAWAII	NEV	VT	
	IDAHO	NH	VA	
	ILL	NJ	WASH	
	IND	NM	W VA	
	● IOWA	NY	WIS	OTHER
	KANS	NC	WYO	
	KY	ND		

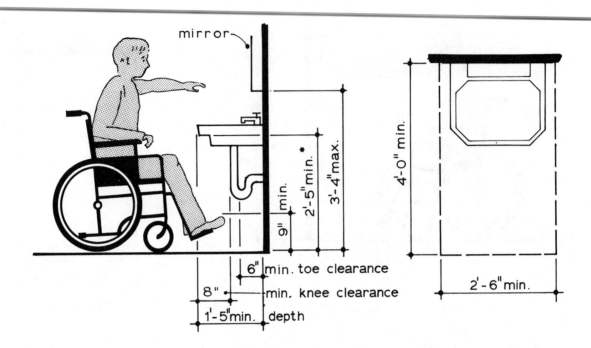

LAVATORY CLEARANCES & CLEAR FLOOR SPACE AT LAVATORIES

Basis of standard —	APPLICABILITY			
815 KAR 7:060	ALA	LA	OHIO	GUAM
	ALASKA	MAINE	OKLA	PR
	ARIZ	MD	ORE	VIR IS
Notes —	ARK	MASS	PA	DC
Faucets: lever, push or electrical.	CAL	MICH	RI	
Pipes: insulated if over 120°F.	COLO	MINN	SC	
(*)2′-3″ allowed where pipes are enclosed.	CONN	MISS	SD	FED'L
	DEL	MO	TENN	FUNDS
	FLA	MONT	TEXAS	
	GA	NEB	UTAH	
	HAWAII	NEV	VT	
	IDAHO	NH	VA	
	ILL	NJ	WASH	
	IND	NM	W VA	
	IOWA	NY	WIS	OTHER
	KANS	NC	WYO	
	● KY	ND		

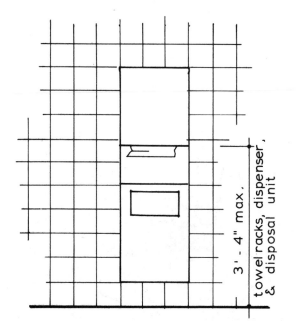

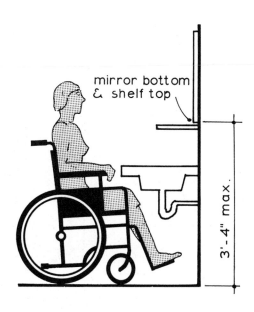

LAVATORIES, MIRRORS, & ACCESSORIES

Basis of standard —	APPLICABILITY			
Maryland Building Code for the Handicapped	ALA	LA	OHIO	GUAM
	ALASKA	MAINE	OKLA	PR
	ARIZ	● MD	ORE	VIR IS
Notes —	ARK	MASS	PA	DC
Insulate, recess or otherwise guard exposed piping.	CAL	MICH	RI	
	COLO	MINN	SC	
	CONN	MISS	SD	FED'L
	DEL	MO	TENN	FUNDS
	FLA	MONT	TEXAS	
	GA	NEB	UTAH	
	HAWAII	NEV	VT	
	IDAHO	NH	VA	
	ILL	NJ	WASH	
	IND	NM	W VA	
	IOWA	NY	WIS	OTHER
	KANS	NC	WYO	
	KY	ND		

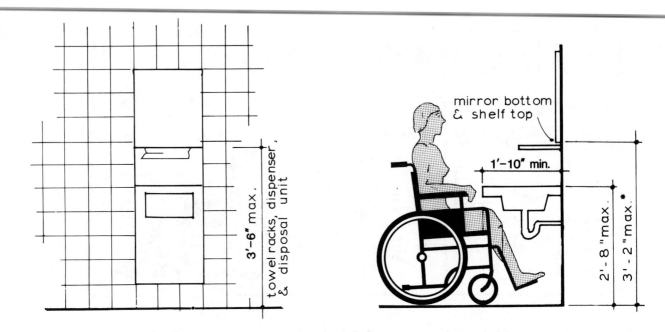

LAVATORIES, MIRRORS, & ACCESSORIES

Basis of standard —	APPLICABILITY			
Architectural Barriers Board	ALA	LA	OHIO	GUAM
	ALASKA	MAINE	OKLA	PR
	ARIZ	MD	ORE	VIR IS
Notes —	ARK	● MASS	PA	DC
In each required toilet room, provide one wall mounted lavatory and dispenser as shown. Provide clear space, 5'-0" diameter, measured 1'-0" above floor to permit wheelchair turning. Recess, insulate or guard drain pipes and hot water pipes. Alternate: counter-type with 2'-6" min. clear open knee space, 27" high. Knob type faucets not allowed. Spring faucets allowed if water running time is 10 seconds as minimum. (*)3'-6" allowed for tilted mirrors.	CAL	MICH	RI	
	COLO	MINN	SC	
	CONN	MISS	SD	FED'L FUNDS
	DEL	MO	TENN	
	FLA	MONT	TEXAS	
	GA	NEB	UTAH	
	HAWAII	NEV	VT	
	IDAHO	NH	VA	
	ILL	NJ	WASH	
	IND	NM	W VA	
	IOWA	NY	WIS	OTHER
	KANS	NC	WYO	
	KY	ND		

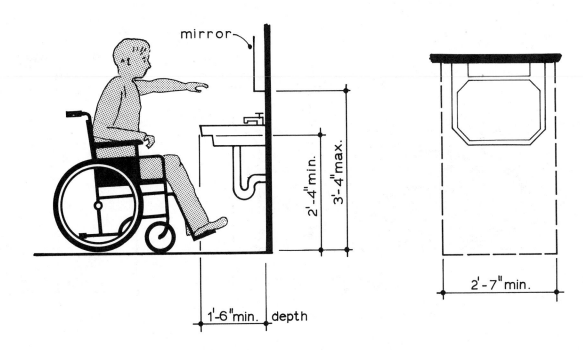

LAVATORY CLEARANCES & CLEAR FLOOR SPACE AT LAVATORIES

Basis of standard —	APPLICABILITY			
Construction Code Commission	ALA	LA	OHIO	GUAM
	ALASKA	MAINE	OKLA	PR
	ARIZ	MD	ORE	VIR IS
Notes —	ARK	MASS	PA	DC
Max. water temperature to outlets: 120°F. Faucets shall be lever or push-button type; when mounted in a counter, the rim shall not be more than 3″ from the front. Mount accessories such as towel dispenser, electric hand dryer, sanitary napkin dispenser, disposal unit, clothes hook, with bottom edge max. 3′-4″ above floor. Provide at least one mirror full length or mount with lower edge max. 3′-0″ above floor.	CAL	● MICH	RI	
	COLO	MINN	SC	
	CONN	MISS	SD	FED'L
	DEL	MO	TENN	FUNDS
	FLA	MONT	TEXAS	
	GA	NEB	UTAH	
	HAWAII	NEV	VT	
	IDAHO	NH	VA	
	ILL	NJ	WASH	
	IND	NM	W VA	
	IOWA	NY	WIS	OTHER
	KANS	NC	WYO	
	KY	ND		

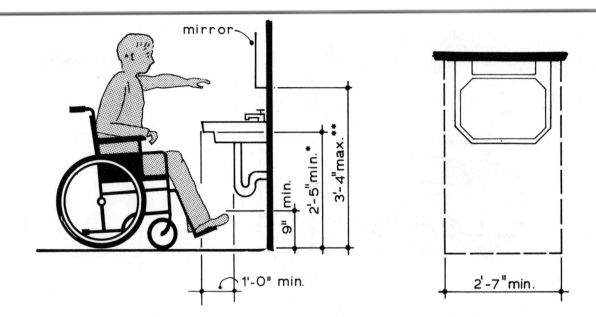

LAVATORY CLEARANCES & CLEAR FLOOR SPACE AT LAVATORIES

Basis of standard — State Building Code	APPLICABILITY			
	ALA	LA	OHIO	GUAM
	ALASKA	MAINE	OKLA	PR
	ARIZ	MD	ORE	VIR IS
Notes — Water control valves shall have lever handles. (*)Max. 2'-10″ to rim of fixture. (**)Dimension also applies to at least one wall-mounted towel racks, dispensers, waste disposal containers or similar appliances.	ARK	MASS	PA	DC
	CAL	MICH	RI	
	COLO	● MINN	SC	
	CONN	MISS	SD	FED'L FUNDS
	DEL	MO	TENN	
	FLA	MONT	TEXAS	
	GA	NEB	UTAH	
	HAWAII	NEV	VT	
	IDAHO	NH	VA	
	ILL	NJ	WASH	
	IND	NM	W VA	
	IOWA	NY	WIS	OTHER
	KANS	NC	WYO	
	KY	ND		

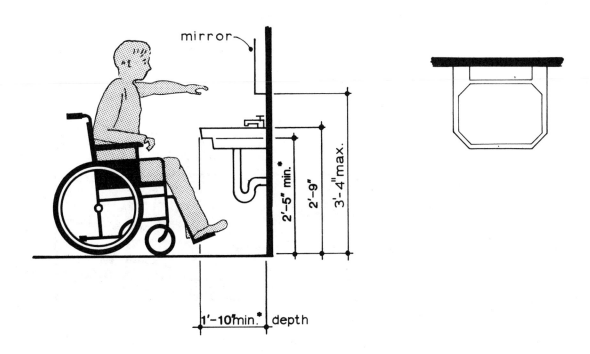

LAVATORY CLEARANCES & CLEAR FLOOR SPACE AT LAVATORIES

Basis of standard —	APPLICABILITY			
Architectural Barrier Free Design Code	ALA	LA	OHIO	GUAM
	ALASKA	MAINE	OKLA	PR
	ARIZ	MD	ORE	VIR IS
Notes —	ARK	MASS	PA	DC
Wall mount without legs or pedestal. Recess, insulate or guard drain and hot water pipes if water tempera-ture exceeds 120°F. Knob type faucets are not allowed. Spring activated faucets allowed only if water running time is at least 10 seconds. Lever handle faucets are preferred. Dispensers and dryers: 3'-4" high.	CAL	MICH	RI	
	COLO	MINN	SC	
	CONN	MISS	SD	FED'L FUNDS
	DEL	MO	TENN	
	FLA	MONT	TEXAS	
(*)Alternate: counter type with clear open knee space of 2'-5" min.	GA	NEB	UTAH	
	HAWAII	NEV	VT	
	IDAHO	● NH	VA	
	ILL	NJ	WASH	
	IND	NM	W VA	
	IOWA	NY	WIS	OTHER
	KANS	NC	WYO	
	KY	ND		

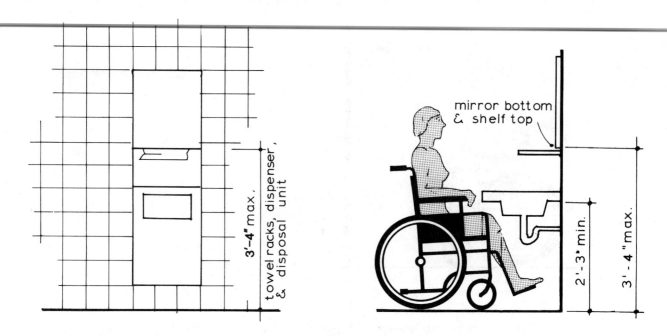

LAVATORIES, MIRRORS, & ACCESSORIES

Basis of standard —	APPLICABILITY			
Barrier Free Design Regulations	ALA	LA	OHIO	GUAM
	ALASKA	MAINE	OKLA	PR
	ARIZ	MD	ORE	VIR IS
	ARK	MASS	PA	DC
Notes —	CAL	MICH	RI	
Vanity type lavatories are acceptable if provided with 6″ deep, 8¾″ high toe space, controls 1′-8″ max. from front edge of vanity top, height of flood rim of lavatory 2′-8″ to 2′-9″ above floor.	COLO	MINN	SC	
	CONN	MISS	SD	FED'L FUNDS
	DEL	MO	TENN	
Faucets shall be operable by the handicapped. Self-closing type to provide metering feature. Insulate or cover drain pipes and hot water pipes under lavatory.	FLA	MONT	TEXAS	
	GA	NEB	UTAH	
	HAWAII	NEV	VT	
	IDAHO	NH	VA	
	ILL	● NJ	WASH	
	IND	NM	W VA	
	IOWA	NY	WIS	OTHER
	KANS	NC	WYO	
	KY	ND		

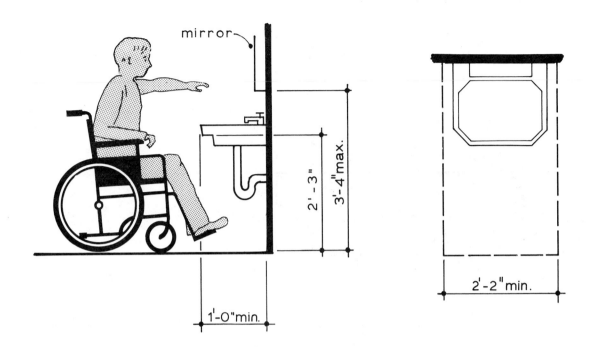

LAVATORY CLEARANCES & CLEAR FLOOR SPACE AT LAVATORIES

Basis of standard —	APPLICABILITY			
Structural Specialty Code	ALA	LA	OHIO	GUAM
	ALASKA	MAINE	OKLA	PR
	ARIZ	MD	● ORE	VIR IS
	ARK	MASS	PA	DC
Notes —	CAL	MICH	RI	
Provide at least one towel and disposal fixtures, where provided, max. 3'-4" above floor.	COLO	MINN	SC	
Data applies to other than Group R, Division 3, Group M, Group R, Division 1 apartment houses and Group B, Divisions 2 and 4 storage occupancies.	CONN	MISS	SD	FED'L FUNDS
	DEL	MO	TENN	
	FLA	MONT	TEXAS	
	GA	NEB	UTAH	
	HAWAII	NEV	VT	
	IDAHO	NH	VA	
	ILL	NJ	WASH	
	IND	NM	W VA	
	IOWA	NY	WIS	OTHER
	KANS	NC	WYO	
	KY	ND		

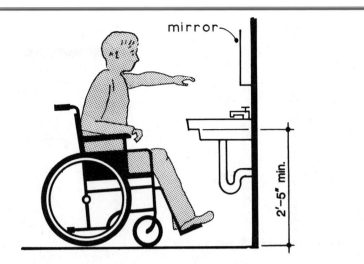

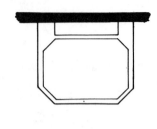

LAVATORY CLEARANCES & CLEAR FLOOR SPACE AT LAVATORIES

Basis of standard — Utah State Building Board	APPLICABILITY			
	ALA	LA	OHIO	GUAM
	ALASKA	MAINE	OKLA	PR
	ARIZ	MD	ORE	VIR IS
Notes —	ARK	MASS	PA	DC
Exception to above: remodeled facilities remodeled with existing lavatories may have less than 2′-5″ bottom clearance. Spring or tension loaded controls are not allowed. Max. hot water temperature shall not exceed 110°F or exposed hot water line and drain shall be fully insulated or protected.	CAL	MICH	RI	
	COLO	MINN	SC	
	CONN	MISS	SD	FED'L
	DEL	MO	TENN	FUNDS
	FLA	MONT	TEXAS	
Provide 11″ high, 6″ deep min. toe space for all cabinets containing a lavatory.	GA	NEB	● UTAH	
	HAWAII	NEV	VT	
	IDAHO	NH	VA	
	ILL	NJ	WASH	
	IND	NM	W VA	
	IOWA	NY	WIS	OTHER
	KANS	NC	WYO	
	KY	ND		

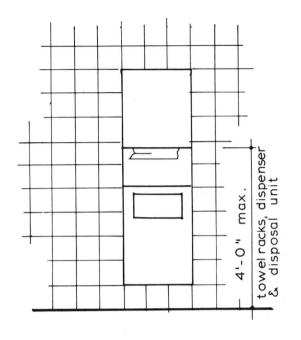

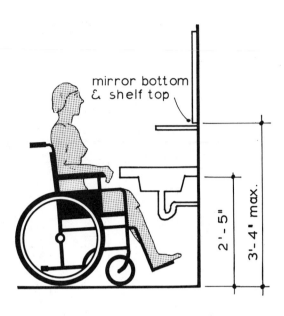

LAVATORIES, MIRRORS, & ACCESSORIES

Basis of standard —	APPLICABILITY			
Utah State Building Board	ALA	LA	OHIO	GUAM
	ALASKA	MAINE	OKLA	PR
	ARIZ	MD	ORE	VIR IS
Notes —	ARK	MASS	PA	DC
See previous page.	CAL	MICH	RI	
	COLO	MINN	SC	
	CONN	MISS	SD	FED'L FUNDS
	DEL	MO	TENN	
	FLA	MONT	TEXAS	
	GA	NEB	● UTAH	
	HAWAII	NEV	VT	
	IDAHO	NH	VA	
	ILL	NJ	WASH	
	IND	NM	W VA	
	IOWA	NY	WIS	OTHER
	KANS	NC	WYO	
	KY	ND		

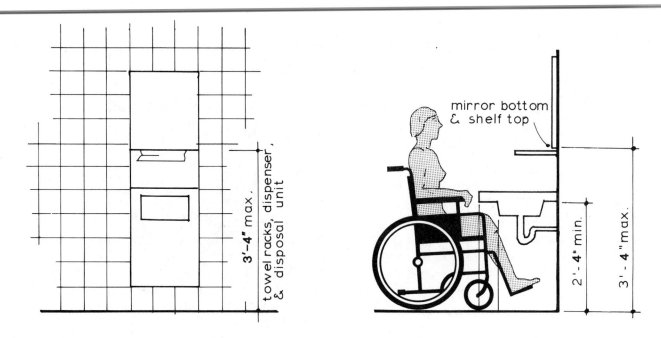

3'-4" max. towel racks, dispenser, & disposal unit

mirror bottom & shelf top

2'-4" min.

3'-4" max.

LAVATORIES, MIRRORS, & ACCESSORIES

Basis of standard — Art 10F, Chapt. 18, Code of West Virginia	APPLICABILITY			
	ALA	LA	OHIO	GUAM
	ALASKA	MAINE	OKLA	PR
	ARIZ	MD	ORE	VIR IS
Notes — Cover and insulate hot water line and trap.	ARK	MASS	PA	DC
	CAL	MICH	RI	
	COLO	MINN	SC	
	CONN	MISS	SD	FED'L
	DEL	MO	TENN	FUNDS
	FLA	MONT	TEXAS	
	GA	NEB	UTAH	
	HAWAII	NEV	VT	
	IDAHO	NH	VA	
	ILL	NJ	WASH	
	IND	NM	● W VA	
	IOWA	NY	WIS	OTHER
	KANS	NC	WYO	
	KY	ND		

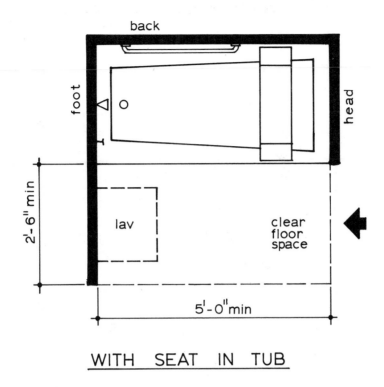

back

foot

head

2'-6" min

lav

clear
floor
space

5'-0" min

WITH   SEAT   IN   TUB

Basis of standard —	APPLICABILITY			
ANSI 1980 — 4.20 and others	ALA	● LA	OHIO	GUAM
	● ALASKA	● MAINE	OKLA	PR
	ARIZ	MD	ORE	VIR IS
Notes —	● ARK	MASS	PA	DC
Mount seats securely so as not to slip during usage.	CAL	MICH	● RI	
For structural strength of seats and attachments	● COLO	MINN	SC	
comply as shown under requirements for ANSI 4.26	CONN	MISS	SD	● FED'L FUNDS
(grab bars and railings). Provide shower spray unit	● DEL	MO	TENN	
with hose at least 60″ long that can be used as a fixed	FLA	MONT	● TEXAS	
shower head or as a hand-held shower. Do not mount	GA	NEB	UTAH	
enclosure tracks on bathtub rim or obstruct controls	● HAWAII	● NEV	● VT	
or transfer from wheelchair into tubs or onto seats.	● IDAHO	NH	● VA	
	ILL	NJ	● WASH	
	IND	● NM	W VA	
	IOWA	● NY	WIS	OTHER
	KANS	NC	WYO	
	● KY	ND		

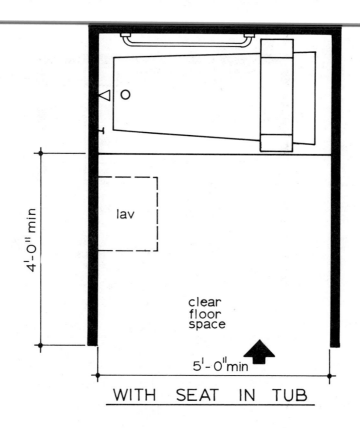

WITH   SEAT   IN   TUB

Basis of standard —	APPLICABILITY			
ANSI 1980 — 4.20 and others	ALA	● LA	OHIO	GUAM
	● ALASKA	● MAINE	OKLA	PR
	ARIZ	MD	ORE	VIR IS
Notes —	● ARK	MASS	PA	DC
Refer to notes on preceding page.	CAL	MICH	RI	
	● COLO	MINN	SC	
	CONN	MISS	SD	● FED'L FUNDS
	● DEL	MO	TENN	
	FLA	MONT	● TEXAS	
	GA	NEB	UTAH	
	● HAWAII	● NEV	● VT	
	● IDAHO	NH	● VA	
	ILL	NJ	● WASH	
	IND	● NM	W VA	
	IOWA	● NY	WIS	OTHER
	KANS	NC	WYO	
	● KY	ND		

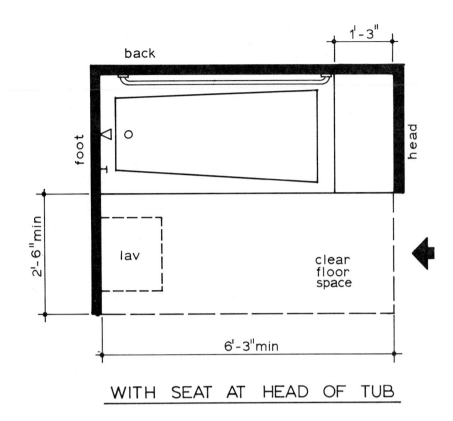

WITH SEAT AT HEAD OF TUB

Basis of standard —	APPLICABILITY			
ANSI 1980 — 4.20 and others	ALA	● LA	OHIO	GUAM
	● ALASKA	● MAINE	OKLA	PR
	ARIZ	MD	ORE	VIR IS
Notes —	● ARK	MASS	PA	DC
Refer to notes on preceding pages.	CAL	MICH	RI	
	● COLO	MINN	SC	
	CONN	MISS	SD	● FED'L FUNDS
	● DEL	MO	TENN	
	FLA	MONT	● TEXAS	
	GA	NEB	UTAH	
	● HAWAII	● NEV	● VT	
	● IDAHO	NH	● VA	
	ILL	NJ	● WASH	
	IND	● NM	W VA	
	IOWA	● NY	WIS	OTHER
	KANS	NC	WYO	
	● KY	ND		

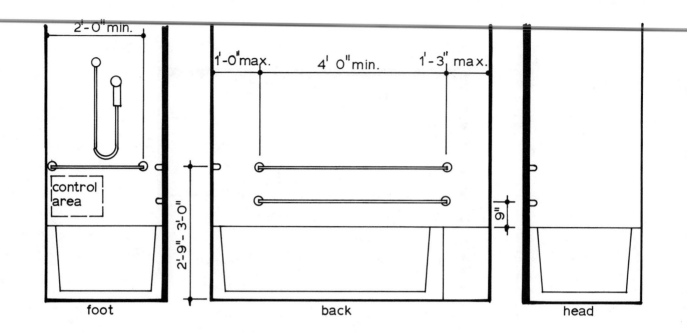

foot   back   head

WITH SEAT AT HEAD OF TUB

Basis of standard — ANSI 1980 – 4.20 and others	APPLICABILITY			
	ALA	● LA	OHIO	GUAM
	● ALASKA	● MAINE	OKLA	PR
	ARIZ	MD	ORE	VIR IS
Notes — Refer to notes on preceding pages,	● ARK	MASS	PA	DC
	CAL	MICH	RI	
	● COLO	MINN	SC	
	CONN	MISS	SD	● FED'L
	● DEL	MO	TENN	FUNDS
	FLA	MONT	● TEXAS	
	GA	NEB	UTAH	
	● HAWAII	● NEV	● VT	
	● IDAHO	NH	● VA	
	ILL	NJ	● WASH	
	IND	● NM	W VA	
	IOWA	● NY	WIS	OTHER
	KANS	NC	WYO	
	● KY	ND		

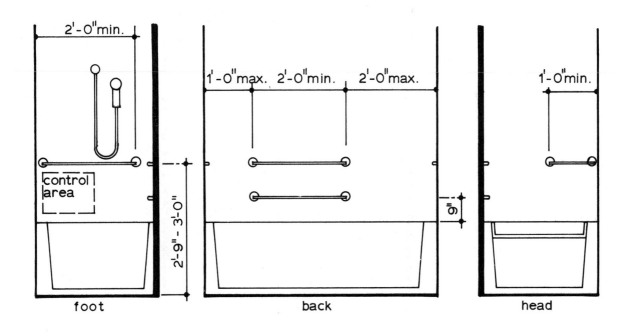

foot   back   head

WITH SEAT IN TUB

Basis of standard —	APPLICABILITY			
ANSI 1980 — 4.20 and others	ALA	● LA	OHIO	GUAM
	● ALASKA	● MAINE	OKLA	PR
	ARIZ	MD	ORE	VIR IS
Notes —	● ARK	MASS	PA	DC
Refer to notes on preceding pages,	CAL	MICH	RI	
	● COLO	MINN	SC	
	CONN	MISS	SD	● FED'L FUNDS
	● DEL	MO	TENN	
	FLA	MONT	● TEXAS	
	GA	NEB	UTAH	
	● HAWAII	● NEV	● VT	
	● IDAHO	NH	● VA	
	ILL	NJ	● WASH	
	IND	● NM	W VA	
	IOWA	● NY	WIS	OTHER
	KANS	NC	WYO	
	● KY	ND		

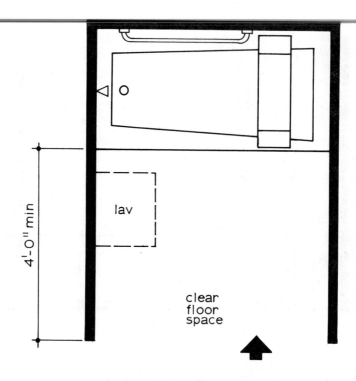

WITH   SEAT   IN   TUB

Basis of standard — CAC Title 24, Part 2	APPLICABILITY			
	ALA	LA	OHIO	GUAM
	ALASKA	MAINE	OKLA	PR
	ARIZ	MD	ORE	VIR IS
	ARK	MASS	PA	DC
	● CAL	MICH	RI	
	COLO	MINN	SC	
	CONN	MISS	SD	FED'L FUNDS
	DEL	MO	TENN	
	FLA	MONT	TEXAS	
	GA	NEB	UTAH	
	HAWAII	NEV	VT	
	IDAHO	NH	VA	
	ILL	NJ	WASH	
	IND	NM	W VA	
	IOWA	NY	WIS	OTHER
	KANS	NC	WYO	
	KY	ND		

Notes —

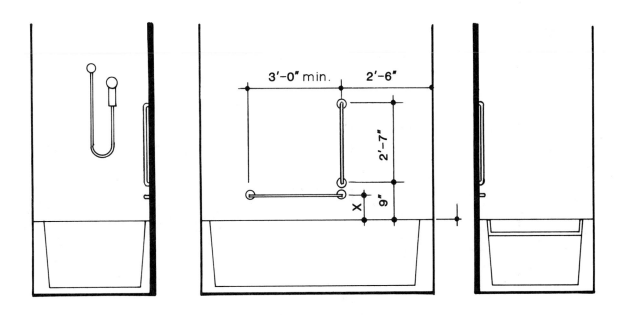

Basis of standard —	APPLICABILITY			
State Building Code	ALA	LA	OHIO	GUAM
	ALASKA	MAINE	OKLA	PR
	ARIZ	MD	ORE	VIR IS
Notes —	ARK	MASS	PA	DC
For bathtubs without showers, provide min. 6'-0" long flexible hose hand shower and vertical height adjustment bar for the shower head at least 4' long. Tub to have folding, retractable or fixed seat min. 17" and max. 20" above tub floor, min. 15" deep and water resistive. Provide 250 lb. capacity grab bars on one side of tub, with 1½" o.d., and 1½" clearance. Water valves to be single lever control, accessible from seat.	CAL	MICH	RI	
	COLO	● MINN	SC	
	CONN	MISS	SD	FED'L FUNDS
	DEL	MO	TENN	
	FLA	MONT	TEXAS	
X = 4" min., 6" max.	GA	NEB	UTAH	
	HAWAII	NEV	VT	
	IDAHO	NH	VA	
	ILL	NJ	WASH	
	IND	NM	W VA	
	IOWA	NY	WIS	OTHER
	KANS	NC	WYO	
	KY	ND		

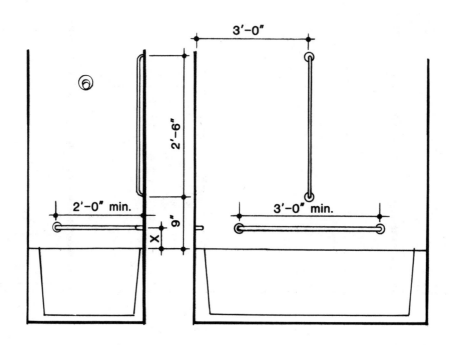

Basis of standard —	APPLICABILITY			
Wisconsin Administrative Code	ALA	LA	OHIO	GUAM
	ALASKA	MAINE	OKLA	PR
	ARIZ	MD	ORE	VIR IS
Notes —	ARK	MASS	PA	DC
Grab bars to support 250 lbs., with approx. o.d. of between 1″ and 1½″ and with 1½″ clearance between wall and rail.	CAL	MICH	RI	
	COLO	MINN	SC	
"x" = 4″ to 6″.	CONN	MISS	SD	FED'L FUNDS
	DEL	MO	TENN	
	FLA	MONT	TEXAS	
	GA	NEB	UTAH	
	HAWAII	NEV	VT	
	IDAHO	NH	VA	
	ILL	NJ	WASH	
	IND	NM	W VA	
	IOWA	NY	● WIS	OTHER
	KANS	NC	WYO	
	KY	ND		

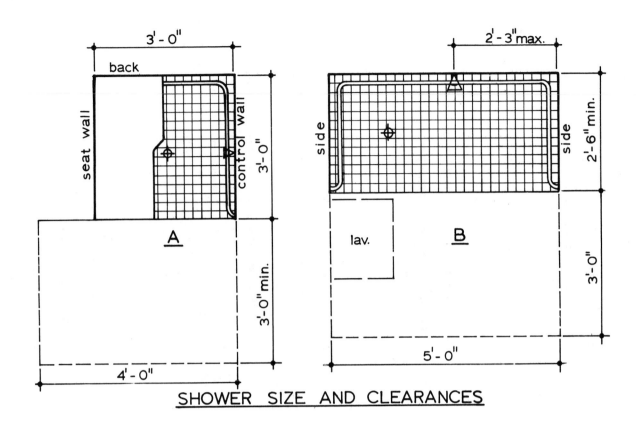

SHOWER SIZE AND CLEARANCES

Basis of standard —	APPLICABILITY			
ANSI 1980 — 4.21 and others	ALA	● LA	OHIO	GUAM
	● ALASKA	● MAINE	OKLA	PR
	ARIZ	MD	ORE	VIR IS
	● ARK	MASS	PA	DC
Notes —	CAL	MICH	● RI	
Provide clear spaces shown.	● COLO	MINN	SC	
	CONN	MISS	SD	● FED'L FUNDS
	● DEL	MO	TENN	
	FLA	MONT	● TEXAS	
	GA	NEB	UTAH	
	● HAWAII	● NEV	● VT	
	● IDAHO	NH	● VA	
	ILL	NJ	WASH	
	IND	● NM	W VA	
	IOWA	● NY	WIS	OTHER
	KANS	NC	WYO	
	● KY	ND		

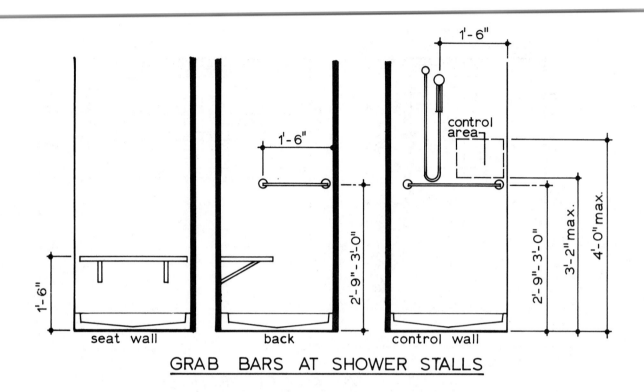

GRAB BARS AT SHOWER STALLS

Basis of standard —	APPLICABILITY			
ANSI 1980 — 4.21 and others	ALA	● LA	OHIO	GUAM
	● ALASKA	● MAINE	OKLA	PR
	ARIZ	MD	ORE	VIR IS
Notes —	● ARK	MASS	PA	DC
Applies to 3'-0" × 3'-0" stall. Threshold: 4" maximum allowed.	CAL	MICH	● RI	
	● COLO	MINN	SC	
	CONN	MISS	SD	● FED'L FUNDS
	● DEL	MO	TENN	
	FLA	MONT	● TEXAS	
	GA	NEB	UTAH	
	● HAWAII	● NEV	● VT	
	● IDAHO	NH	● VA	
	ILL	NJ	WASH	
	IND	● NM	W VA	
	IOWA	● NY	WIS	OTHER
	KANS	NC	WYO	
	● KY	ND		

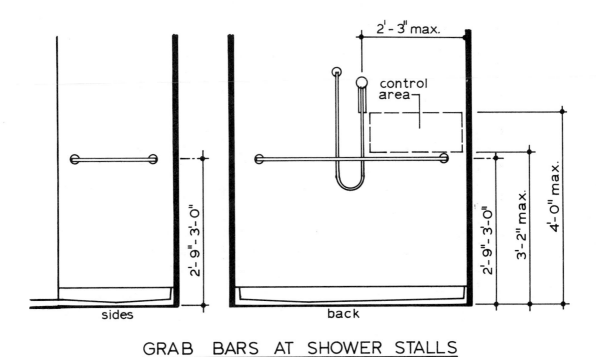

GRAB BARS AT SHOWER STALLS

Basis of standard —	APPLICABILITY			
ANSI 1980 — 4.21 and others	ALA	● LA	OHIO	GUAM
	● ALASKA	● MAINE	OKLA	PR
	ARIZ	MD	ORE	VIR IS
Notes —	● ARK	MASS	PA	DC
Applies to 3'-0" X 5'-0" stall. Threshold: not allowed.	CAL	MICH	● RI	
	● COLO	MINN	SC	
	CONN	MISS	SD	● FED'L FUNDS
	● DEL	MO	TENN	
	FLA	MONT	TEXAS	
	GA	NEB	UTAH	
	● HAWAII	● NEV	● VT	
	● IDAHO	NH	● VA	
	ILL	NJ	WASH	
	IND	● NM	W VA	
	IOWA	● NY	WIS	OTHER
	KANS	NC	WYO	
	● KY	ND		

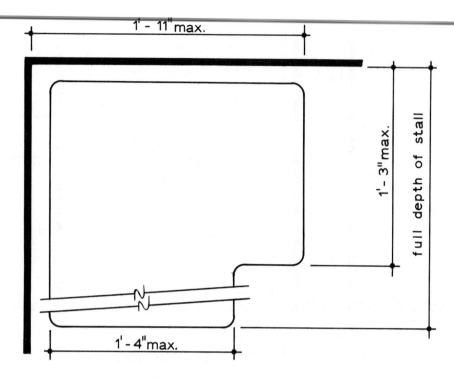

1' - 11" max.

1' - 3" max.

full depth of stall

1' - 4" max.

SHOWER   SEAT   DESIGN

Basis of standard —	APPLICABILITY			
ANSI 1980 — and others	ALA	● LA	OHIO	GUAM
	● ALASKA	● MAINE	OKLA	PR
	ARIZ	MD	ORE	VIR IS
Notes —	● ARK	MASS	PA	DC
Provide seats for 3'-0" × 3'-0" shower stalls, 1'-5" to 1'-7" above floor and extend the full depth of stall. Seat shall be on wall opposite the controls.	CAL	MICH	● RI	
	● COLO	MINN	SC	
	CONN	MISS	SD	● FED'L FUNDS
	● DEL	MO	TENN	
	FLA	MONT	● TEXAS	
	GA	NEB	UTAH	
	● HAWAII	● NEV	● VT	
	● IDAHO	NH	● VA	
	ILL	NJ	WASH	
	IND	● NM	W VA	
	IOWA	● NY	WIS	OTHER
	KANS	NC	WYO	
	● KY	ND		

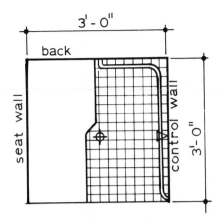

SHOWER

Basis of standard —	APPLICABILITY			
North Carolina State Building Code	ALA	LA	OHIO	GUAM
	ALASKA	MAINE	OKLA	PR
	ARIZ	MD	ORE	VIR IS
Notes —	ARK	MASS	PA	DC
Where showers are provided, 2%, or a minimum of one, whichever is greater, shall comply. No curbs, except for complying thresholds. Height of hinged seat: 1'-7". Single lever control with flexible hand shower spray. Height of soap tray: 3'-4" max. above floor. Floor surface shall be non-slip. Seat: minimum 15" from back wall by 30" in length. Curtains are preferred.	CAL	MICH	RI	
	COLO	MINN	SC	
	CONN	MISS	SD	FED'L
	DEL	MO	● TENN	FUNDS
	FLA	MONT	TEXAS	
	GA	NEB	UTAH	
	HAWAII	NEV	VT	
	IDAHO	NH	● VA	
	ILL	NJ	WASH	
	IND	NM	W VA	
	IOWA	NY	WIS	OTHER
	KANS	● NC	WYO	
	KY	ND		

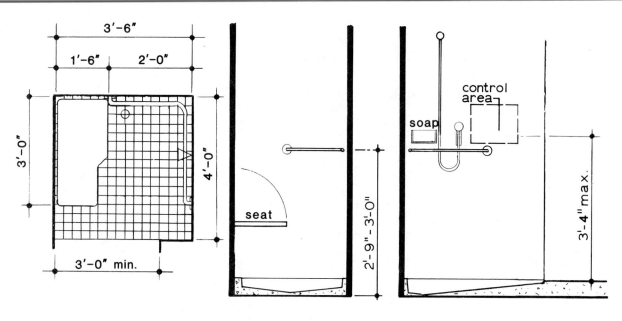

SHOWER STALLS

Basis of standard — CAC Title 24, Parts 2 and 5	APPLICABILITY			
	ALA	LA	OHIO	GUAM
	ALASKA	MAINE	OKLA	PR
	ARIZ	MD	ORE	VIR IS
	ARK	MASS	PA	DC
Notes —	● CAL	MICH	RI	
Controls: single lever design operable with a maxi- mum force of 3 lb. Shower unit: hand held, 60″ hose with head mounting height maximum 48″. (In areas subject to vandalism, two heads may be pro- vided, independently operated with both vertical and horizontal swivel angle adjustment, the lower head at 40″.) Threshold: ½″ maximum, 45° from horizontal. Showers: provide at least one and not less than 1% accessible, where showers are provided. Seat height: 1′-6″. Drain: within 6″ of back wall. Floor slope: maximum ½″ per 1′-0″ (1:24).	COLO	MINN	SC	
	CONN	MISS	SD	FED'L FUNDS
	DEL	MO	TENN	
	FLA	MONT	TEXAS	
	GA	NEB	UTAH	
	HAWAII	NEV	VT	
	IDAHO	NH	VA	
	ILL	NJ	WASH	
	IND	NM	W VA	
	IOWA	NY	WIS	OTHER
	KANS	NC	WYO	
	KY	ND		

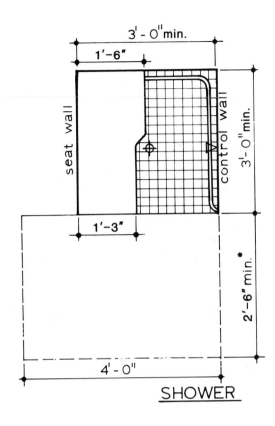

3' - 0" min.

1'-6"

seat wall

3'-0" min.

control wall

1'-3"

2'-6" min.*

4' - 0"

SHOWER

Basis of standard — Capital Development Board	APPLICABILITY			
	ALA	LA	OHIO	GUAM
	ALASKA	MAINE	OKLA	PR
	ARIZ	MD	ORE	VIR IS
Notes — For other than residential, where showers are provided, a minimum of one per sex shall be accessible. (*)4'-0" preferred.	ARK	MASS	PA	DC
	CAL	MICH	RI	
	COLO	MINN	SC	
	CONN	MISS	SD	FED'L FUNDS
	DEL	MO	TENN	
	FLA	MONT	TEXAS	
	GA	NEB	UTAH	
	HAWAII	NEV	VT	
	IDAHO	NH	VA	
	● ILL	NJ	WASH	
	IND	NM	W VA	
	IOWA	NY	WIS	OTHER
	KANS	NC	WYO	
	KY	ND		

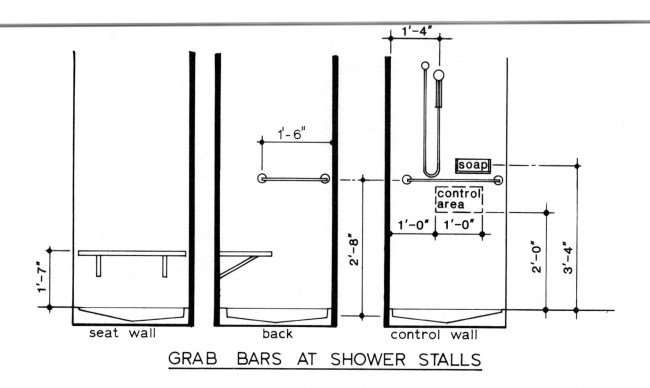

GRAB BARS AT SHOWER STALLS

Basis of standard —	APPLICABILITY			
Capital Development Board	ALA	LA	OHIO	GUAM
	ALASKA	MAINE	OKLA	PR
	ARIZ	MD	ORE	VIR IS
Notes —	ARK	MASS	PA	DC
Water controls shall be of single lever design. Install flexible hand held shower spray permanently with a hook to hold it 3'-4" to 4'-0" above floor. Install diversionary valve to change water flow from hand-held to fixed head shower. Max. temperature of delivered hot water to shower: 105°F. Floor surface to be slip-resistant under wet conditions.	CAL	MICH	RI	
	COLO	MINN	SC	
	CONN	MISS	SD	FED'L FUNDS
	DEL	MO	TENN	
	FLA	MONT	TEXAS	
	GA	NEB	UTAH	
	HAWAII	NEV	VT	
	IDAHO	NH	VA	
	● ILL	NJ	WASH	
	IND	NM	W VA	
	IOWA	NY	WIS	OTHER
	KANS	NC	WYO	
	KY	ND		

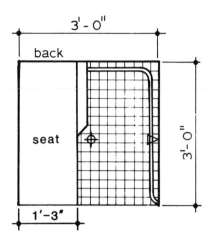

MINIMUM SHOWER SIZE

Basis of standard —	APPLICABILITY			
Barrier Free Design Regulations	ALA	LA	OHIO	GUAM
	ALASKA	MAINE	OKLA	PR
	ARIZ	MD	ORE	VIR IS
Notes —	ARK	MASS	PA	DC
Regulations apply to showers for public use. No curbs except entry threshold with max. ¾″ height and 45° max. slope may be used. Floor: non-slip. Seat height: 1′-5″ to 1′-7″ above floor. Provide 1¼″ to 1½″ wide grab bar, 2′-8″ high, with 1½″ to 2″ wall clearance. For gang showers, provide handrails at a wall intersection adjacent to a shower fixture. Water control: single lever or blade type, with pressure balancing control mounted on wall adjacent or opposite the seat. Soap tray height: 3′-4″ max. adjacent to seat.	CAL	MICH	RI	
	COLO	MINN	SC	
	CONN	MISS	SD	FED'L FUNDS
	DEL	MO	TENN	
	FLA	MONT	TEXAS	
	GA	NEB	UTAH	
	HAWAII	NEV	VT	
	IDAHO	NH	VA	
	ILL	● NJ	WASH	
	IND	NM	W VA	
	IOWA	NY	WIS	OTHER
	KANS	NC	WYO	
	KY	ND		

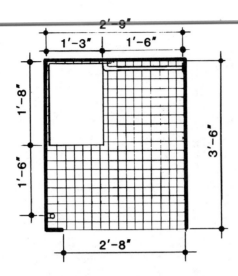

MINIMUM SHOWER

Basis of standard —	APPLICABILITY			
Structural Specialty Code	ALA	LA	OHIO	GUAM
	ALASKA	MAINE	OKLA	PR
	ARIZ	MD	● ORE	VIR IS
	ARK	MASS	PA	DC
	CAL	MICH	RI	
	COLO	MINN	SC	
Notes —	CONN	MISS	SD	FED'L
Applicable to shower room and handicap units in R-1 occupancies. Seat height: 1'-6" to 1'-7", hinged or dismountable. Floor: slip resistant. Water operating controls: 4'-6" max. above floor. Height of back grab bar: 10" above seat. Side grab bar min. 2'-0" long, bottom 3'-0" above floor extending vertically. Shower rooms to have one dressing bench 1'-6" to 1'-8" high and with these min. dimensions: 5'-0" long, 2'-0" wide.	DEL	MO	TENN	FUNDS
	FLA	MONT	TEXAS	
	GA	NEB	UTAH	
	HAWAII	NEV	VT	
	IDAHO	NH	VA	
	ILL	NJ	WASH	
	IND	NM	W VA	
	IOWA	NY	WIS	OTHER
	KANS	NC	WYO	
	KY	ND		

MINIMUM SHOWER

Basis of standard —	APPLICABILITY			
Building Code Advisory Council	ALA	LA	OHIO	GUAM
	ALASKA	MAINE	OKLA	PR
	ARIZ	MD	ORE	VIR IS
Notes —	ARK	MASS	PA	DC
Min. size without seat: 2'-6" × 5'-0". Thresholds: flush with max. beveled edge height of ½", sloped 1:2 max. Min. length of grab bar behind and beneath shower head: 2'-7¾", 2'-11" to 3'-0" above floor. Water control: 3'-4" high; max. water temperature: 120°F; lever operated water control 3'-4" high. Recessed soap tray height: 3'-4". Hand-held shower spray with 5'-0" long hose shall be provided. For 3' × 3' stalls, provide 16" to 18" high full-depth seats capable of supporting 300 lb. Non-slip floor. Where showers are installed, at least 2%, but not less than 1, shall be accessible.	CAL	MICH	RI	
	COLO	MINN	SC	
	CONN	MISS	SD	FED'L FUNDS
	DEL	MO	TENN	
	FLA	MONT	TEXAS	
	GA	NEB	UTAH	
	HAWAII	NEV	VT	
	IDAHO	NH	VA	
	ILL	NJ	● WASH	
	IND	NM	W VA	
	IOWA	NY	WIS	OTHER
	KANS	NC	WYO	
	KY	ND		

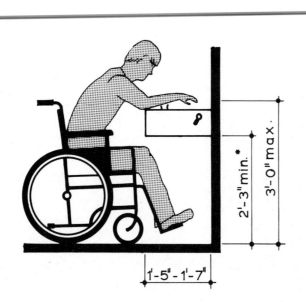

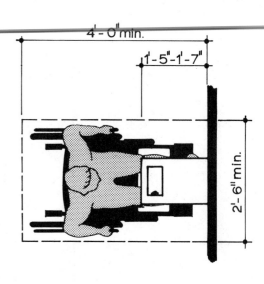

SPOUT HEIGHT AND KNEE CLEARANCE

CLEAR FLOOR SPACE

Basis of standard —	APPLICABILITY			
ANSI 1980 — 4.15 and others	ALA	● LA	OHIO	GUAM
	● ALASKA	● MAINE	OKLA	PR
	ARIZ	MD	ORE	VIR IS
Notes —	● ARK	MASS	PA	DC
If drinking fountains or water coolers are provided, a reasonable number, but always at least one, shall be on an accessible route. Spouts shall be at front of the unit and shall direct the water flow in a trajectory that is parallel or nearly parallel to the front of the unit. Spout shall provide a flow of water at least 4″ high to permit insertion of a cup or glass under the flow of water. (Federal, Arkansas and Delaware requirements: maximum alcove recess: 1′-3″.) New York: where outside fountains are provided, at least one shall be accessible.	CAL	MICH	● RI	
	● COLO	MINN	SC	
	CONN	MISS	SD	FED'L FUNDS
	● DEL	MO	TENN	
	FLA	MONT	TEXAS	
	GA	NEB	UTAH	
	● HAWAII	● NEV	● VT	
	● IDAHO	NH	● VA	
	ILL	NJ	WASH	
(*)Delaware: 2′-5″ min.	IND	● NM	W VA	
	● IOWA	● NY	WIS	OTHER
	KANS	NC	WYO	
	● KY	ND		

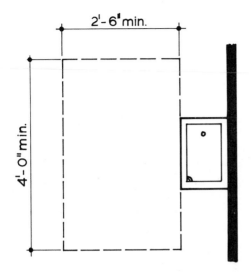

FREE-STANDING
FOUNTAIN OR COOLER

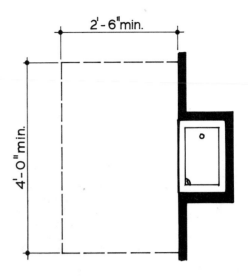

BUILT-IN
FOUNTAIN OR COOLER

Basis of standard — ANSI 1980 — 4.15 and others	APPLICABILITY			
	ALA	● LA	OHIO	GUAM
	● ALASKA	● MAINE	OKLA	PR
	ARIZ	MD	ORE	VIR IS
	● ARK	MASS	PA	DC
	CAL	MICH	● RI	
	● COLO	MINN	SC	
	CONN	MISS	SD	● FED'L FUNDS
	● DEL	MO	TENN	
	FLA	MONT	● TEXAS	
	GA	NEB	UTAH	
	● HAWAII	● NEV	● VT	
	● IDAHO	NH	● VA	
	ILL	NJ	WASH	
	IND	● NM	W VA	
	● IOWA	● NY	WIS	OTHER
	KANS	NC	WYO	
	KY	ND		

Notes —
Clear space shown applies to free-standing or built-in units not having clear space under them to permit parallel approach by person in wheelchair. Texas: 30% of total of all units, strategically located is considered appropriate. Provide min. of one accessible drinking unit on each floor of multi-story building. For children, max. height of spout opening: for ages 5 thru 10 or 11 (grades K thru 5 or 6): 2'-8"; for all ages 11 thru 14 or 15 (grades 6 thru 8 or 9): 2'-10".

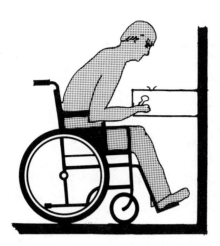

Basis of standard —	APPLICABILITY			
ANSI 1961 — 5.7 and others	ALA	LA	OHIO	GUAM
	ALASKA	MAINE	● OKLA	PR
	● ARIZ	MD	ORE	VIR IS
	ARK	MASS	● PA	DC
	CAL	MICH	RI	
Notes —	COLO	MINN	SC	
Provide an appropriate number useable by the physically handicapped. Provide up-front controls and spouts. Water fountains or coolers shall be hand-operated or hand-and-foot operated. Florida: applies to non-government financed facilities.	CONN	● MISS	● SD	FED'L FUNDS
	DEL	MO	TENN	
	● FLA	MONT	TEXAS	
	● GA	NEB	UTAH	
	HAWAII	NEV	VT	
	IDAHO	NH	VA	
	ILL	NJ	WASH	
	IND	NM	W VA	
	IOWA	NY	WIS	
	● KANS	NC	WYO	OTHER
	KY	● ND		

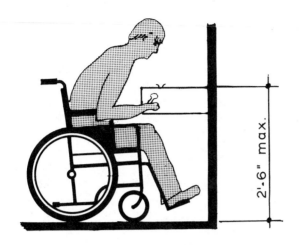

Basis of standard —	APPLICABILITY			
BOCA — 1978 and others	ALA	LA	● OHIO	GUAM
	ALASKA	MAINE	OKLA	PR
	ARIZ	MD	ORE	VIR IS
Notes —	ARK	MASS	PA	DC
Provide 5% of fountains, or min. 1 fountain for physically handicapped persons. Spout and hand control shall be near front. Free standing type shall also be operated by foot pedal.	CAL	MICH	RI	
	COLO	MINN	SC	
	● CONN	MISS	SD	FED'L FUNDS
	DEL	MO	TENN	
	FLA	MONT	TEXAS	
	GA	NEB	UTAH	
	HAWAII	NEV	VT	
	IDAHO	NH	VA	
	ILL	NJ	WASH	
	IND	NM	W VA	
	IOWA	NY	WIS	OTHER
	KANS	NC	WYO	
	KY	ND		

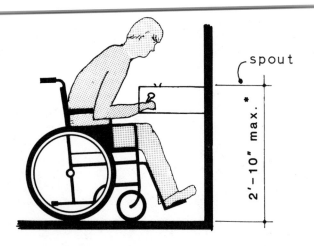

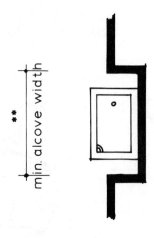

Basis of standard —	APPLICABILITY			
Building Code Advisory Council and others	ALA	LA	OHIO	GUAM
	ALASKA	MAINE	OKLA	PR
	ARIZ	MD	ORE	VIR IS
Notes —	ARK	MASS	PA	DC
Where fountains are provided, at least one per floor shall comply. Spouts up-front with hand operated control. Washington requirements: control to be within 6″ of fountain front. For wall mounted fountains recessed more than 8″, min. alcove width: 4′-0″. Where coolers or floor mounted water fountains are more than 2′-10″ high, provide additional adjacent fountain max. 2′-6″ high. If accessible fountain is recessed more than 8″, provide 2′-0″ clear space from control handle to nearest side wall of alcove. Do not recess accessible fountains more than their depth. (*)Indiana and Montana: 2′-11″ max. to spout. (**)Indiana and Montana: 2′-8″ min.	CAL	MICH	RI	
	COLO	MINN	SC	
	CONN	MISS	SD	FED'L FUNDS
	DEL	MO	TENN	
	FLA	● MONT	TEXAS	
	GA	NEB	UTAH	
	HAWAII	NEV	VT	
	IDAHO	NH	VA	
	ILL	NJ	● WASH	
	● IND	NM	W VA	
	IOWA	NY	WIS	OTHER
	KANS	NC	WYO	
	KY	ND		

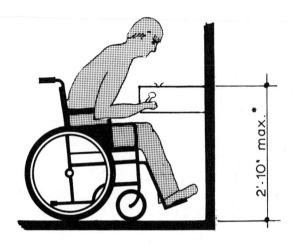

2'-10' max.*

Basis of standard —	APPLICABILITY			
Nebraska Provisions for the Handicapped and others	ALA	LA	OHIO	GUAM
	ALASKA	MAINE	OKLA	PR
	ARIZ	MD	ORE	VIR IS
	ARK	MASS	PA	DC
	CAL	MICH	RI	
	COLO	MINN	SC	
	CONN	MISS	SD	FED'L
Notes —	DEL	MO	TENN	FUNDS
At least one water fountain per floor shall meet these requirements. Spouts and controls shall be up front and shall be hand or hand-and-foot operated.	FLA	MONT	TEXAS	
(*)New Mexico: 2'-8″	GA	● NEB	UTAH	
	HAWAII	NEV	VT	
	IDAHO	NH	VA	
	ILL	NJ	WASH	
	IND	● NM	W VA	
	IOWA	NY	WIS	OTHER
	KANS	NC	WYO	
	KY	ND		

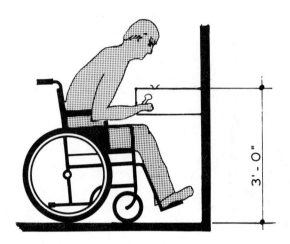

Basis of standard —	APPLICABILITY			
North Carolina Building Code	ALA	LA	OHIO	GUAM
	ALASKA	MAINE	OKLA	PR
	ARIZ	MD	ORE	VIR IS
Notes —	ARK	MASS	PA	DC
Spouts and controls: up-front. Controls: hand or hand-and-foot operated. Where provided, at least one per floor conventional wall or floor mounted water cooler shall have a small fountain mounted on the side of the cooler with a basin height of 2′-6″ max. above floor.	CAL	MICH	RI	
	COLO	MINN	SC	
	CONN	MISS	SD	FED'L FUNDS
	DEL	MO	● TENN	
	FLA	MONT	TEXAS	
	GA	NEB	UTAH	
	HAWAII	NEV	VT	
	IDAHO	NH	VA	
	ILL	NJ	WASH	
	IND	NM	W VA	
	IOWA	NY	WIS	OTHER
	KANS	● NC	WYO	
	KY	ND		

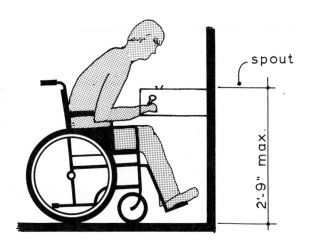

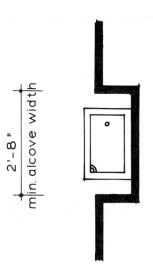

spout

2'-9" max.

2'-8" min. alcove width

Basis of standard —	APPLICABILITY			
Structural Specialty Code and others	ALA	LA	OHIO	GUAM
	ALASKA	MAINE	OKLA	PR
	ARIZ	MD	● ORE	VIR IS
Notes —	ARK	MASS	PA	DC
Where water fountains are provided, at least one shall comply. Controls: up-front, hand-operated. (South Carolina: 2'-6" clear beneath.)	CAL	MICH	RI	
	COLO	MINN	● SC	
	CONN	MISS	SD	FED'L FUNDS
	DEL	MO	TENN	
	FLA	MONT	TEXAS	
	GA	NEB	UTAH	
	HAWAII	NEV	VT	
	IDAHO	NH	VA	
	ILL	NJ	WASH	
	IND	NM	W VA	
	IOWA	NY	WIS	OTHER
	KANS	NC	WYO	
	KY	ND		

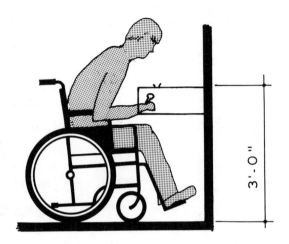

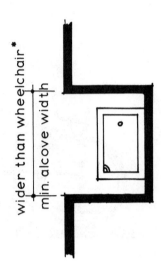

wider than wheelchair*
min. alcove width

Basis of standard —	APPLICABILITY			
ANSI 1961 — 5.7 and others	ALA	LA	OHIO	GUAM
	ALASKA	MAINE	OKLA	PR
	ARIZ	MD	ORE	VIR IS
	ARK	MASS	PA	DC
Notes —	CAL	MICH	RI	
Water fountains shall be accessible and installed at or adapted to a useable height. Conventional floor mounted coolers can be serviceable if a small fountain is mounted on side of cooler 2'-6" above floor. (*)West Virginia	COLO	MINN	SC	
	CONN	MISS	SD	FED'L FUNDS
	DEL	MO	TENN	
	FLA	MONT	TEXAS	
	GA	NEB	UTAH	
	HAWAII	NEV	VT	
	IDAHO	NH	VA	
	ILL	NJ	WASH	
	IND	NM	● W VA	
	IOWA	NY	● WIS	OTHER
	KANS	NC	WYO	
	KY	ND		

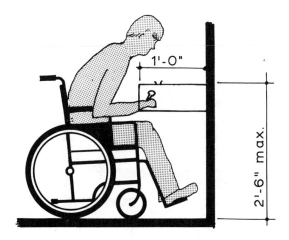

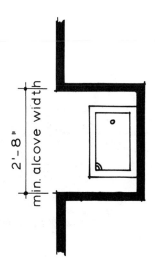

2'-8" min. alcove width

Basis of standard —	APPLICABILITY			
Barrier Free Design Standard	● ALA	LA	OHIO	GUAM
	ALASKA	MAINE	OKLA	PR
	ARIZ	MD	ORE	VIR IS
Notes —	ARK	MASS	PA	DC
Provide at least one fountain at an accessible location on each floor with hand levers or hand and foot operation with up-front water jet and controls. Conventional floor mounted water coolers are preferred and can be made serviceable to individuals in wheel-chairs if a small fountain is mounted on the side of the cooler 30″ above the floor.	CAL	MICH	RI	
	COLO	MINN	SC	
	CONN	MISS	SD	FED'L FUNDS
	DEL	MO	TENN	
	FLA	MONT	TEXAS	
	GA	NEB	UTAH	
	HAWAII	NEV	VT	
	IDAHO	NH	VA	
	ILL	NJ	WASH	
	IND	NM	W VA	
	IOWA	NY	WIS	OTHER
	KANS	NC	WYO	
	KY	ND		

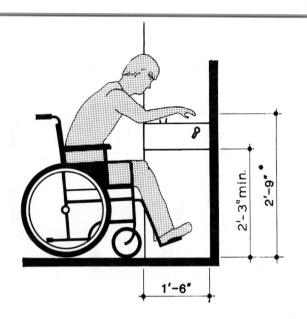

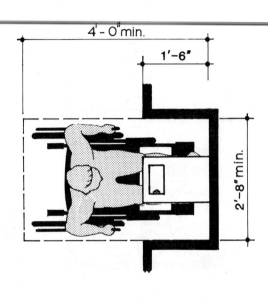

SPOUT HEIGHT AND KNEE CLEARANCE

CLEAR FLOOR SPACE

Basis of standard — CAC Title 24, Parts 2 & 5	APPLICABILITY			
	ALA	LA	OHIO	GUAM
	ALASKA	MAINE	OKLA	PR
	ARIZ	MD	ORE	VIR IS
Notes — (*)No stock manufactured unit presently meets these requirements. Check with enforcing agency to determine if alternate heights (3'-0" to blubbler) might be acceptable.	ARK	MASS	PA	DC
	● CAL	MICH	RI	
	COLO	MINN	SC	
	CONN	MISS	SD	FED'L
	DEL	MO	TENN	FUNDS
	FLA	MONT	TEXAS	
	GA	NEB	UTAH	
	HAWAII	NEV	VT	
	IDAHO	NH	VA	
	ILL	NJ	WASH	
	IND	NM	W VA	
	IOWA	NY	WIS	OTHER
	KANS	NC	WYO	
	KY	ND		

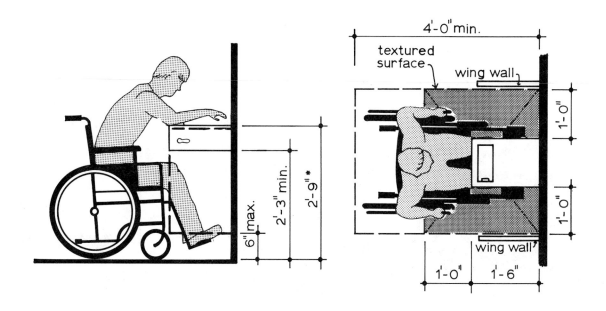

ALTERNATE DRINKING FOUNTAIN

Basis of standard —	APPLICABILITY			
CAC Title 24, Part 2	ALA	LA	OHIO	GUAM
	ALASKA	MAINE	OKLA	PR
	ARIZ	MD	ORE	VIR IS
Notes —	ARK	MASS	PA	DC
Where the enforcing agency approves a finding of	● CAL	MICH	RI	
unreasonable hardship, a textured path or wing walls	COLO	MINN	SC	
may be used in lieu of an alcove. Wing walls shall	CONN	MISS	SD	FED'L
extend to the front of the fountain and shall have	DEL	MO	TENN	FUNDS
minimum 2′-8″ clear between.	FLA	MONT	TEXAS	
(*)See note on previous page.	GA	NEB	UTAH	
	HAWAII	NEV	VT	
	IDAHO	NH	VA	
	ILL	NJ	WASH	
	IND	NM	W VA	
	IOWA	NY	WIS	OTHER
	KANS	NC	WYO	
	KY	ND		

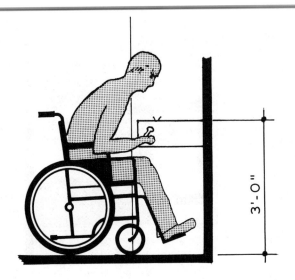
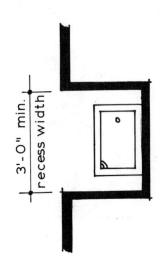

Basis of standard —	APPLICABILITY			
Dept. of General Services	ALA	LA	OHIO	GUAM
	ALASKA	MAINE	OKLA	PR
	ARIZ	MD	ORE	VIR IS
Notes —	ARK	MASS	PA	DC
Florida: applies to government facilities. Provide an appropriate number useable by the physically disabled. Water fountains or coolers shall be hand operated or hand-and-foot operated. Provide up-front controls and spout.	CAL	MICH	RI	
	COLO	MINN	SC	
	CONN	MISS	SD	FED'L
	DEL	MO	TENN	FUNDS
	● FLA	MONT	TEXAS	
	GA	NEB	UTAH	
	HAWAII	NEV	VT	
	IDAHO	NH	VA	
	ILL	NJ	WASH	
	IND	NM	W VA	
	IOWA	NY	WIS	OTHER
	KANS	NC	WYO	
	KY	ND		

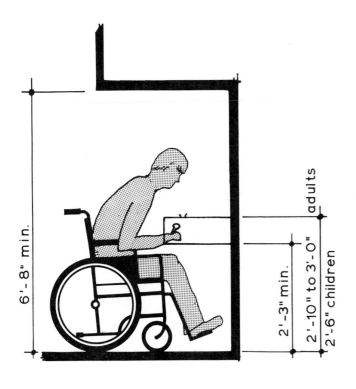

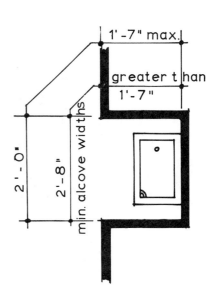

Basis of standard — Capital Development Board	APPLICABILITY			
	ALA	LA	OHIO	GUAM
	ALASKA	MAINE	OKLA	PR
	ARIZ	MD	ORE	VIR IS
	ARK	MASS	PA	DC
	CAL	MICH	RI	
	COLO	MINN	SC	
	CONN	MISS	SD	FED'L FUNDS
	DEL	MO	TENN	
	FLA	MONT	TEXAS	
	GA	NEB	UTAH	
	HAWAII	NEV	VT	
	IDAHO	NH	VA	
	● ILL	NJ	WASH	
	IND	NM	W VA	
	IOWA	NY	WIS	OTHER
	KANS	NC	WYO	
	KY	ND		

Notes —

All fountains to be accessible. For spouts above $3'$-$0''$ height, either have auxiliary fountain or a spigot for cups within $3'$-$0''$ from floor. If a spigot is provided, also provide cup dispenser next to fountain max. $3'$-$4''$ to cups height. Spout to be at front and allow insertion of a $4''$ cup under water flow. Hand controls are required without need for precise grasping, twisting or pinching. Max. force: 3 lbf. Slope front panel inward $2''$ to $3\frac{1}{2}''$ from vertical. $9''$ min. clearance from floor for toes. Locate fountains along accessible path of travel.

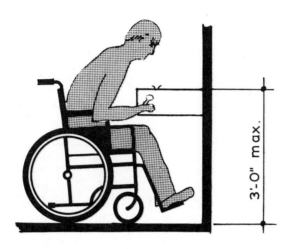

3'-0" max.

Basis of standard —	APPLICABILITY			
Maryland Building Code for the Handicapped	ALA	LA	OHIO	GUAM
	ALASKA	MAINE	OKLA	PR
	ARIZ	● MD	ORE	VIR IS
	ARK	MASS	PA	DC
Notes —	CAL	MICH	RI	
Provide 5%, or not less than 1 for physically handicapped persons. Fully recessed units are not acceptable. Spout and hand control to be near front. Arc of water should be parallel to front. Push bars are acceptable.	COLO	MINN	SC	
	CONN	MISS	SD	FED'L
	DEL	MO	TENN	FUNDS
	FLA	MONT	TEXAS	
	GA	NEB	UTAH	
	HAWAII	NEV	VT	
	IDAHO	NH	VA	
	ILL	NJ	WASH	
	IND	NM	W VA	
	IOWA	NY	WIS	OTHER
	KANS	NC	WYO	
	KY	ND		

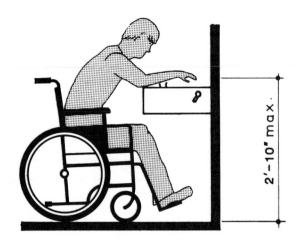

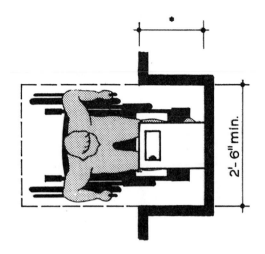

SPOUT HEIGHT

ALCOVE

Basis of standard —	APPLICABILITY			
521 CMR Architectural Barriers Board	ALA	LA	OHIO	GUAM
	ALASKA	MAINE	OKLA	PR
	ARIZ	MD	ORE	VIR IS
Notes —	ARK	● MASS	PA	DC
Provide at least one accessible fountain per floor, hand operated, push button or lever type. Spout shall direct water parallel where possible.	CAL	MICH	RI	
	COLO	MINN	SC	
(*)Where an alcove is used, the alcove shall be no deeper than the fountain.	CONN	MISS	SD	FED'L FUNDS
	DEL	MO	TENN	
	FLA	MONT	TEXAS	
	GA	NEB	UTAH	
	HAWAII	NEV	VT	
	IDAHO	NH	VA	
	ILL	NJ	WASH	
	IND	NM	W VA	
	IOWA	NY	WIS	OTHER
	KANS	NC	WYO	
	KY	ND		

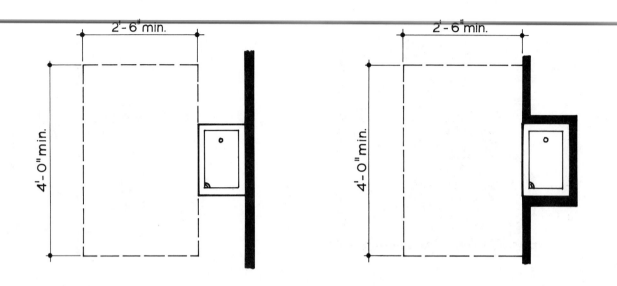

FREE-STANDING
FOUNTAIN OR COOLER

BUILT-IN
FOUNTAIN OR COOLER

Basis of standard —	APPLICABILITY			
521 CMR Architectural Barriers Board	ALA	LA	OHIO	GUAM
	ALASKA	MAINE	OKLA	PR
	ARIZ	MD	ORE	VIR IS
Notes —	ARK	● MASS	PA	DC
See notes previous page.	CAL	MICH	RI	
	COLO	MINN	SC	
	CONN	MISS	SD	FED'L
	DEL	MO	TENN	FUNDS
	FLA	MONT	TEXAS	
	GA	NEB	UTAH	
	HAWAII	NEV	VT	
	IDAHO	NH	VA	
	ILL	NJ	WASH	
	IND	NM	W VA	
	IOWA	NY	WIS	OTHER
	KANS	NC	WYO	
	KY	ND		

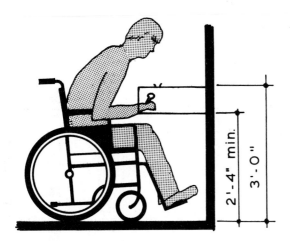

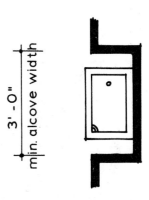

2'-4" min.

3'-0"

3'-0" min. alcove width

Basis of standard — Construction Code Commission	APPLICABILITY			
	ALA	LA	OHIO	GUAM
	ALASKA	MAINE	OKLA	PR
	ARIZ	MD	ORE	VIR IS
	ARK	MASS	PA	DC
Notes — Fountains shall be wall-mounted or semi-recessed. Fully recessed drinking fountains are not acceptable. Provide push button or lever type controls, with controls and spout at front. Floor mounted drinking fountains shall have side-mounted fountain meeting above requirements.	CAL	● MICH	RI	
	COLO	MINN	SC	
	CONN	MISS	SD	FED'L FUNDS
	DEL	MO	TENN	
	FLA	MONT	TEXAS	
	GA	NEB	UTAH	
	HAWAII	NEV	VT	
	IDAHO	NH	VA	
	ILL	NJ	WASH	
	IND	NM	W VA	
	IOWA	NY	WIS	OTHER
	KANS	NC	WYO	
	KY	ND		

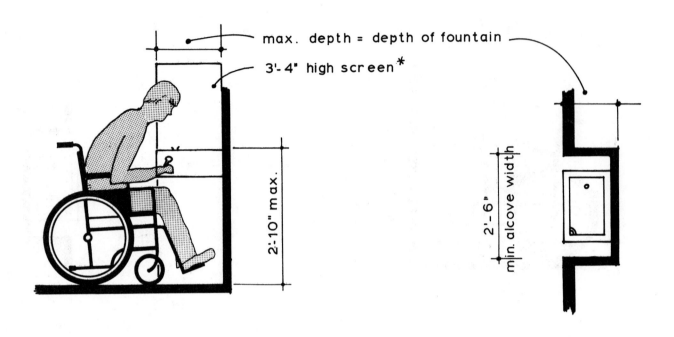

Basis of standard —	APPLICABILITY			
Architectural Barrier Free Design Code	ALA	LA	OHIO	GUAM
	ALASKA	MAINE	OKLA	PR
	ARIZ	MD	ORE	VIR IS
Notes —	ARK	MASS	PA	DC
Provide at least one per floor for wheelchair access. Fountains shall be hand-operated, push button or lever. Controls and spout near front directing water stream as parallel to front as possible. Knob type faucet is not allowed. Other control types may be installed in addition to hand-operated controls. For floor-mounted fountains higher than 2'-10", provide lower fountain or a cup dispenser at 2'-10". (*)Applies to wall mounted fountains.	CAL	MICH	RI	
	COLO	MINN	SC	
	CONN	MISS	SD	FED'L FUNDS
	DEL	MO	TENN	
	FLA	MONT	TEXAS	
	GA	NEB	UTAH	
	HAWAII	NEV	VT	
	IDAHO	● NH	VA	
	ILL	NJ	WASH	
	IND	NM	W VA	
	IOWA	NY	WIS	OTHER
	KANS	NC	WYO	
	KY	ND		

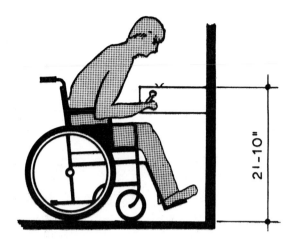

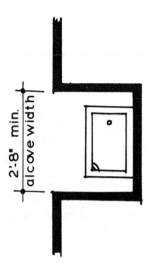

2'-8" min.
alcove width

2'-10"

Basis of standard —	APPLICABILITY			
Barrier Free Design Regulations	ALA	LA	OHIO	GUAM
	ALASKA	MAINE	OKLA	PR
	ARIZ	MD	ORE	VIR IS
Notes —	ARK	MASS	PA	DC
Fully recessed fountains are permitted provided a cup dispenser is part of the unit. Otherwise it shall be free-standing or semi-recessed. Provide up-front controls and spouts. Operation: lever-handle, lever-handle-and-foot, or push button. Where fountains or coolers are higher than 2'-10", they shall have an additional small fountain on the side, or an additional separate cooler, with a 2'-6" high rim.	CAL	MICH	RI	
	COLO	MINN	SC	
	CONN	MISS	SD	FED'L FUNDS
	DEL	MO	TENN	
	FLA	MONT	TEXAS	
	GA	NEB	UTAH	
	HAWAII	NEV	VT	
	IDAHO	NH	VA	
	ILL	● NJ	WASH	
	IND	NM	W VA	
	IOWA	NY	WIS	OTHER
	KANS	NC	WYO	
	KY	ND		

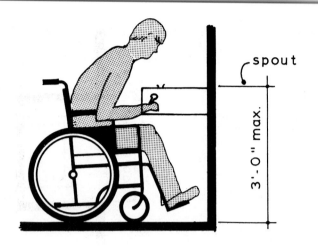

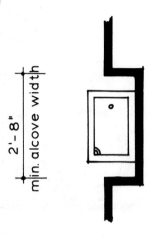

Basis of standard —	APPLICABILITY			
Utah State Building Board	ALA	LA	OHIO	GUAM
	ALASKA	MAINE	OKLA	PR
	ARIZ	MD	ORE	VIR IS
Notes —	ARK	MASS	PA	DC
Where spout height exceeds 3'-0", mount an auxiliary	CAL	MICH	RI	
fountain adjacent or on side of existing unit with a	COLO	MINN	SC	
max. spout height of 2'-9". Provide up-front spouts	CONN	MISS	SD	FED'L
and controls. Controls: hand and foot-operated.	DEL	MO	TENN	FUNDS
Preference is for controls operable by hand without	FLA	MONT	TEXAS	
need for grasping, pinching, twisting or pushing.	GA	NEB	● UTAH	
	HAWAII	NEV	VT	
	IDAHO	NH	VA	
	ILL	NJ	WASH	
	IND	NM	W VA	
	IOWA	NY	WIS	OTHER
	KANS	NC	WYO	
	KY	ND		

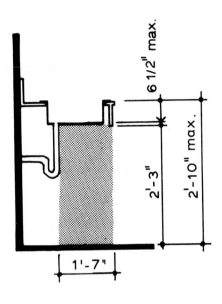

6 1/2" max.

2'-3"

2'-10" max.

1'-7"

SINKS

Basis of standard — ANSI 1980 — 4.24 and others	APPLICABILITY			
	ALA	● LA	OHIO	GUAM
	● ALASKA	● MAINE	OKLA	PR
	ARIZ	MD	ORE	VIR IS
Notes —	● ARK	MASS	PA	DC
Comply with ANSI 1980 — 4.34.6.5 for sinks in accessible dwelling units shaded portion shows knee space. Insulate or otherwise cover hot water and drain pipes under sink. There shall be no sharp or abrasive surfaces under sink. Faucets shall comply with ANSI 1980 — 4.27.4 (lever-operated, push-type, touch-type or electronically controlled mechanisms are acceptable).	CAL	MICH	RI	
	● COLO	MINN	SC	
	CONN	MISS	SD	● FED'L FUNDS
	● DEL	MO	TENN	
	FLA	MONT	TEXAS	
	GA	NEB	UTAH	
	● HAWAII	● NEV	● VT	
	● IDAHO	NH	● VA	
	ILL	NJ	WASH	
	IND	NM	W VA	
	IOWA	● NY	WIS	OTHER
	KANS	NC	WYO	
	● KY	ND		

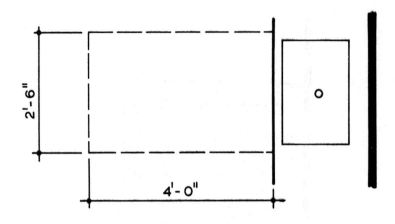

SINKS

Basis of standard — ANSI 1980 – 4.24.5 and others	APPLICABILITY			
	ALA	● LA	OHIO	GUAM
	● ALASKA	● MAINE	OKLA	PR
	ARIZ	MD	ORE	VIR IS
Notes —	● ARK	MASS	PA	DC
Provide indicated clear floor space in front of sink, extending 1'-7" max. underneath sink.	CAL	MICH	RI	
	● COLO	MINN	SC	
	CONN	MISS	SD	● FED'L FUNDS
	● DEL	MO	TENN	
	FLA	MONT	TEXAS	
	GA	NEB	UTAH	
	● HAWAII	● NEV	● VT	
	● IDAHO	NH	● VA	
	ILL	NJ	WASH	
	IND	NM	W VA	
	IOWA	● NY	WIS	OTHER
	KANS	NC	WYO	
	● KY	ND		

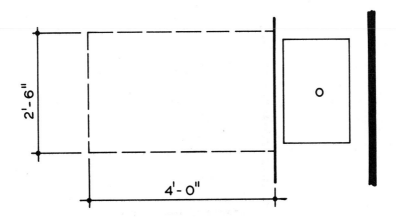

2'- 6"

4'- 0"

O

SINKS

Basis of standard — CAC Title 24, Part 2	APPLICABILITY			
	ALA	LA	OHIO	GUAM
	ALASKA	MAINE	OKLA	PR
	ARIZ	MD	ORE	VIR IS
Notes —	ARK	MASS	PA	DC
	● CAL	MICH	RI	
	COLO	MINN	SC	
	CONN	MISS	SD	FED'L FUNDS
	DEL	MO	TENN	
	FLA	MONT	TEXAS	
	GA	NEB	UTAH	
	HAWAII	NEV	VT	
	IDAHO	NH	VA	
	ILL	NJ	WASH	
	IND	NM	W VA	
	IOWA	NY	WIS	OTHER
	KANS	NC	WYO	
	KY	ND		

SINKS

Basis of standard — CAC Title 24, Part 2	APPLICABILITY			
	ALA	LA	OHIO	GUAM
	ALASKA	MAINE	OKLA	PR
	ARIZ	MD	ORE	VIR IS
Notes —	ARK	MASS	PA	DC
	● CAL	MICH	RI	
	COLO	MINN	SC	
	CONN	MISS	SD	FED'L FUNDS
	DEL	MO	TENN	
	FLA	MONT	TEXAS	
	GA	NEB	UTAH	
	HAWAII	NEV	VT	
	IDAHO	NH	VA	
	ILL	NJ	WASH	
	IND	NM	W VA	
	IOWA	NY	WIS	OTHER
	KANS	NC	WYO	
	KY	ND		

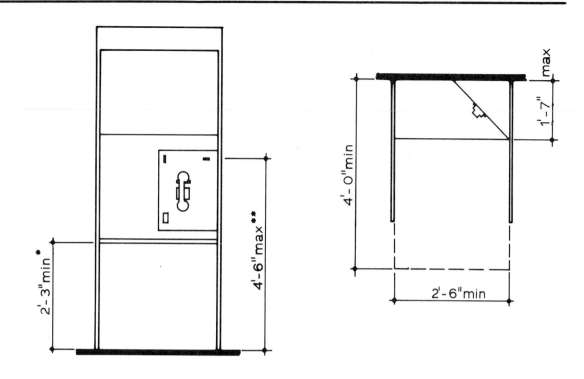

FULL HEIGHT ENCLOSURE

Basis of standard —	APPLICABILITY			
ANSI 1980 — 4.31 and others	ALA	● LA	OHIO	GUAM
	● ALASKA	● MAINE	OKLA	PR
	ARIZ	MD	ORE	VIR IS
Notes —	● ARK	MASS	PA	DC
Federal Arkansas and Delaware requirements provide for max. 4'-0" height for forward and diagonal reach.	● CAL	MICH	● RI	
(*)2'-6" in Illinois except where phones are mounted 4'-0" max. to highest operable part. Minimum illumination at stall: 5 footcandles.	● COLO	MINN	SC	
	CONN	MISS	SD	● FED'L FUNDS
(**)Texas: 4'-0" max. If side panel is deeper than 2'-0", increase clear width to 3'-0".	● DEL	MO	TENN	
	FLA	MONT	● TEXAS	
	GA	NEB	UTAH	
	● HAWAII	● NEV	● VT	
	● IDAHO	NH	● VA	
	● ILL	NJ	WASH	
	IND	● NM	W VA	
	● IOWA	● NY	WIS	OTHER
	KANS	NC	WYO	
	● KY	ND		

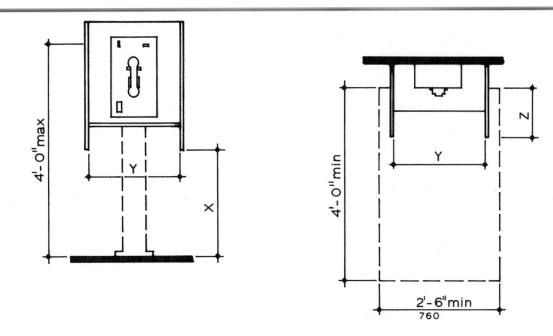

FORWARD REACH REQUIRED

Basis of standard —	APPLICABILITY			
ANSI 1980 — 4.31 and others	ALA	● LA	OHIO	GUAM
	● ALASKA	● MAINE	OKLA	PR
	ARIZ	MD	ORE	VIR IS
	ARK	MASS	PA	DC
Notes —	● CAL	MICH	● RI	
If y < 30″, then x shall be 27″ min. If z > 12″, then y shall be 30″ min.	● COLO	MINN	SC	
Texas: in lieu of 4'-0″ height for children:	CONN	MISS	SD	FED'L FUNDS
	DEL	MO	TENN	
	FLA	MONT	● TEXAS	
	GA	NEB	UTAH	
	● HAWAII	● NEV	● VT	
	● IDAHO	NH	● VA	
	ILL	NJ	WASH	
	IND	● NM	W VA	
	● IOWA	● NY	WIS	OTHER
	KANS	NC	WYO	
	● KY	ND		

Ages 5 thru 10 or 11 (Grades K thru 5 or 6) — Ages 11 thru 14 or 15 (Grades 6 thru 8 or 9)

Front approach 3'-6″ / 3'-9″
Side approach 4'-0″ / 4'-3″

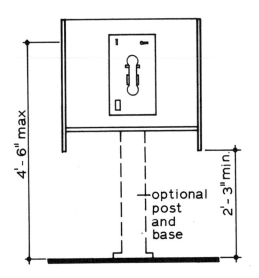
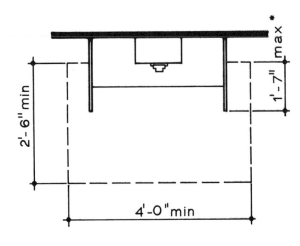

SIDE REACH POSSIBLE

Basis of standard —	APPLICABILITY			
ANSI 1980 — 4.31 and others	ALA	● LA	OHIO	GUAM
	● ALASKA	● MAINE	OKLA	PR
	ARIZ	MD	ORE	VIR IS
Notes —	ARK	MASS	PA	DC
Bases, enclosures, and fixed seats shall not impede	CAL	MICH	● RI	
wheelchair approach to telephones where enclosures	● COLO	MINN	SC	
protrude into walls, halls, corridors, or aisles, comply	CONN	MISS	SD	FED'L
with the section entitled "Protruding Objects", as	DEL	MO	TENN	FUNDS
well. Provide phones with push buttons where such	FLA	MONT	● TEXAS	
equipment is available. Length of cord to handset:	GA	NEB	UTAH	
29″ min.	● HAWAII	⟍ NEV	● VT	
(*)Texas: 1′-0″ max.	● IDAHO	NH	● VA	
	ILL	NJ	WASH	
	IND	● NM	W VA	
	● IOWA	● NY	WIS	OTHER
	KANS	NC	WYO	
	● KY	ND		

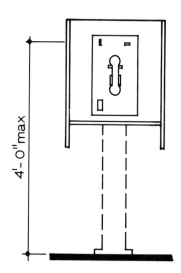

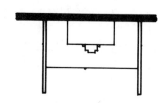

4'-0" max

Basis of standard —	APPLICABILITY			
ANSI 1961 — 5.8 and others	ALA	LA	OHIO	GUAM
	ALASKA	MAINE	● OKLA	PR
	● ARIZ	MD	ORE	VIR IS
	ARK	MASS	PA	DC
	CAL	MICH	RI	
	COLO	MINN	● SC	
	● CONN	MISS	● SD	FED'L
Notes —	DEL	MO	TENN	FUNDS
Provide an appropriate number* of public telephones accessible and usable by the physically disabled; equip for those with hearing disabilities and identify with instructions for use.	● FLA	MONT	TEXAS	
Florida: applies to government facilities and requires at least one in a bank of telephones to comply and to equip for those with hearing disabilities.	● GA	NEB	UTAH	
*The following states specify 5% or no less than one telephone: Connecticut.	HAWAII	NEV	VT	
	IDAHO	NH	VA	
	ILL	NJ	WASH	
	IND	NM	● W VA	
	IOWA	NY	WIS	OTHER
	● KANS	NC	WYO	
	KY	● ND		

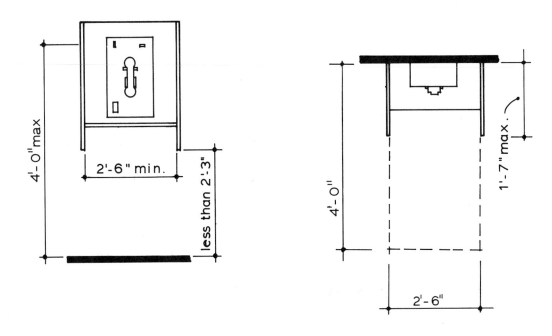

FORWARD REACH REQUIRED

Basis of standard —	APPLICABILITY			
ATBCB 1190.210 and others	ALA	LA	OHIO	GUAM
	ALASKA	MAINE	OKLA	PR
	ARIZ	MD	ORE	VIR IS
Notes —	● ARK	MASS	PA	DC
	CAL	MICH	RI	
	COLO	MINN	SC	
	CONN	MISS	SD	● FED'L FUNDS
	● DEL	MO	TENN	
	FLA	MONT	TEXAS	
	GA	NEB	UTAH	
	HAWAII	NEV	VT	
	IDAHO	NH	VA	
	ILL	NJ	WASH	
	IND	NM	W VA	
	IOWA	NY	WIS	OTHER
	KANS	NC	WYO	
	KY	ND		

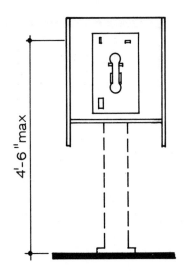

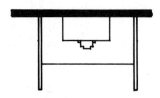

4'-6" max

Basis of standard —	APPLICABILITY			
BOCA — 1978 and others	ALA	LA	● OHIO	GUAM
	ALASKA	MAINE	OKLA	PR
	ARIZ	MD	ORE	VIR IS
Notes —	ARK	MASS	PA	DC
Where a public or pay phone is installed, provide 5%, or not less than one, telephone accessible to, and usable by physically handicapped persons. (Michigan requires such phones to be equipped to assist persons with a hearing disability and so designated.)	CAL	● MICH	RI	
	COLO	MINN	SC	
	CONN	MISS	SD	FED'L FUNDS
	DEL	MO	TENN	
	FLA	MONT	TEXAS	
	GA	NEB	UTAH	
	HAWAII	NEV	VT	
	IDAHO	NH	VA	
	ILL	NJ	WASH	
	IND	NM	W VA	
	IOWA	NY	WIS	OTHER
	KANS	NC	WYO	
	KY	ND		

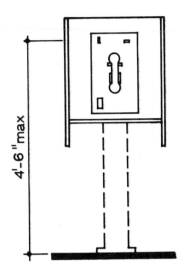

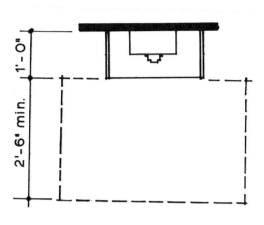

Basis of standard —	APPLICABILITY			
Uniform Building Code	ALA	LA	OHIO	GUAM
	ALASKA	MAINE	OKLA	PR
	ARIZ	MD	ORE	VIR IS
Notes —	ARK	MASS	PA	DC
Provide at least one telephone which complies where public telephones are installed.	CAL	MICH	RI	
	COLO	MINN	SC	
	CONN	MISS	SD	FED'L
	DEL	MO	TENN	FUNDS
	FLA	● MONT	TEXAS	
	GA	NEB	UTAH	
	HAWAII	NEV	VT	
	IDAHO	NH	VA	
	ILL	NJ	WASH	
	● IND	NM	W VA	
	IOWA	NY	WIS	OTHER
	KANS	NC	WYO	
	KY	ND		

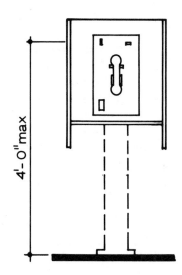

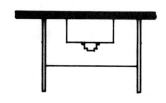

Basis of standard —	APPLICABILITY			
North Carolina Building Code	ALA	LA	OHIO	GUAM
	ALASKA	MAINE	OKLA	PR
	ARIZ	MD	ORE	VIR IS
Notes —	ARK	MASS	PA	DC
All "banks" of public telephones should have at least one telephone useable by the physically disabled. Phone to be provided for those with hearing disabilities with an adjustable volume control for headset and instructions for use. Equip phone with visual and tactile instructions for use, using large tactile letters for instructions. Install at least one complying phone on every floor on which telephones are installed.	CAL	MICH	RI	
	COLO	MINN	SC	
	CONN	MISS	SD	FED'L FUNDS
	DEL	MO	● TENN	
	FLA	MONT	TEXAS	
	GA	NEB	UTAH	
	HAWAII	NEV	VT	
	IDAHO	NH	VA	
	ILL	NJ	WASH	
	IND	NM	W VA	
	IOWA	NY	WIS	OTHER
	KANS	● NC	WYO	
	KY	ND		

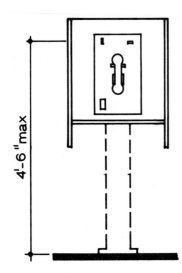

4'-6" max

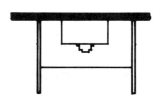

Basis of standard —	APPLICABILITY			
Barrier Free Design Standard	● ALA	LA	OHIO	GUAM
	ALASKA	MAINE	OKLA	PR
	ARIZ	MD	ORE	VIR IS
Notes —	ARK	MASS	PA	DC
Push buttons are preferred. Min. cord length: 3'-0" where public telephones are provided, at least one shall be accessible to wheelchair users. Identify and equip with an amplifier for those with hearing disabilities.	CAL	MICH	RI	
	COLO	MINN	SC	
	CONN	MISS	SD	FED'L FUNDS
	DEL	MO	TENN	
	FLA	MONT	TEXAS	
	GA	NEB	UTAH	
	HAWAII	NEV	VT	
	IDAHO	NH	VA	
	ILL	NJ	WASH	
	IND	NM	W VA	
	IOWA	NY	WIS	OTHER
	KANS	NC	WYO	
	KY	ND		

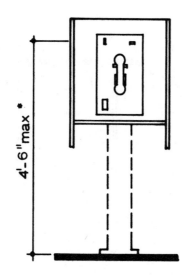

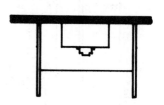

Basis of standard — Capital Development Board	APPLICABILITY			
	ALA	LA	OHIO	GUAM
	ALASKA	MAINE	OKLA	PR
	ARIZ	MD	ORE	VIR IS
Notes —	ARK	MASS	PA	DC
(*)Applies where there is a "dial-tone-first" to get the operator without inserting coins, and located to allow side access for those in wheelchairs. Otherwise, one telephone in the bank shall have highest operable part at 4'-0". Length of handset cord: 2'-6". Provide calling number in raised numerals, or by braille below buttons. Numbers 1/2" high, raised 1/32". Provide adjustable volume control where needed. Telephone receivers shall generate a magnetic field at receiver cap.	CAL	MICH	RI	
	COLO	MINN	SC	
	CONN	MISS	SD	FED'L FUNDS
	DEL	MO	TENN	
	FLA	MONT	TEXAS	
	GA	NEB	UTAH	
	HAWAII	NEV	VT	
	IDAHO	NH	VA	
	● ILL	NJ	WASH	
	IND	NM	W VA	
	IOWA	NY	WIS	OTHER
	KANS	NC	WYO	
	KY	ND		

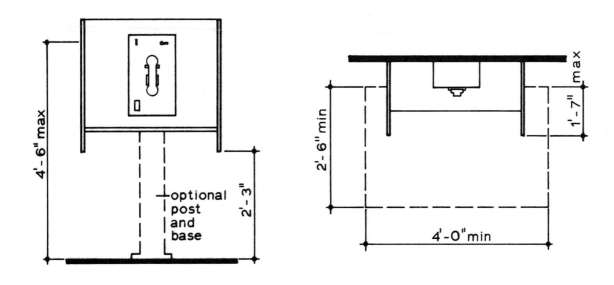

SIDE REACH POSSIBLE

Basis of standard —	APPLICABILITY			
Maryland Building Code for the Handicapped	ALA	LA	OHIO	GUAM
	ALASKA	MAINE	OKLA	PR
	ARIZ	● MD	ORE	VIR IS
Notes —	ARK	MASS	PA	DC
When public or pay phones are installed, 5%, or not	CAL	MICH	RI	
less than one telephone, whichever is more shall be	COLO	MINN	SC	
accessible for use by physically handicapped persons.	CONN	MISS	SD	FED'L
At least one public telephone in each group shall be	DEL	MO	TENN	FUNDS
equipped with a hearing amplification device and	FLA	MONT	TEXAS	
identified with instructions for use.	GA	NEB	UTAH	
	HAWAII	NEV	VT	
	IDAHO	NH	VA	
	ILL	NJ	WASH	
	IND	NM	W VA	
	IOWA	NY	WIS	OTHER
	KANS	NC	WYO	
	KY	ND		

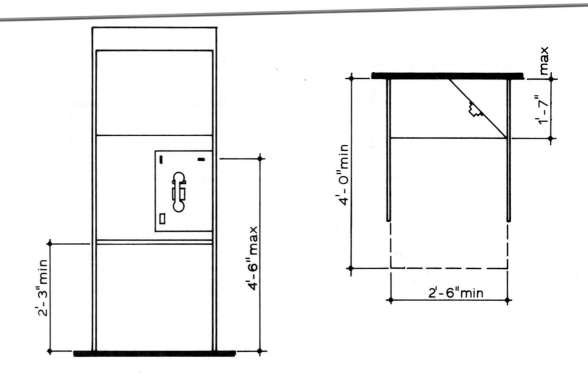

FULL HEIGHT ENCLOSURE

Basis of standard —	APPLICABILITY			
Maryland Building Code for the Handicapped	ALA	LA	OHIO	GUAM
	ALASKA	MAINE	OKLA	PR
	ARIZ	● MD	ORE	VIR IS
Notes —	ARK	MASS	PA	DC
See notes on preceding page.	CAL	MICH	RI	
	COLO	MINN	SC	
	CONN	MISS	SD	FED'L
	DEL	MO	TENN	FUNDS
	FLA	MONT	TEXAS	
	GA	NEB	UTAH	
	HAWAII	NEV	VT	
	IDAHO	NH	VA	
	ILL	NJ	WASH	
	IND	NM	W VA	
	IOWA	NY	WIS	OTHER
	KANS	NC	WYO	
	KY	ND		

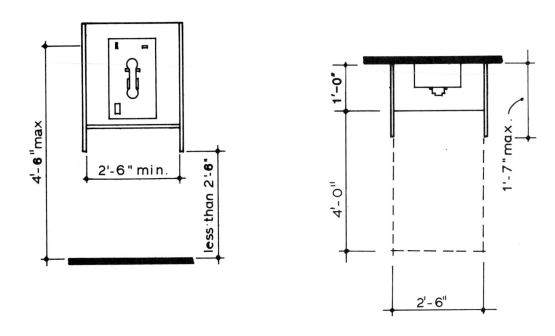

FORWARD REACH REQUIRED

Basis of standard —	APPLICABILITY			
521 CMR Architectural Barriers Board	ALA	LA	OHIO	GUAM
	ALASKA	MAINE	OKLA	PR
	ARIZ	MD	ORE	VIR IS
Notes —	ARK	● MASS	PA	DC
At least one phone shall be accessible, with an inductive coil magnetic field and adjustable volume control. Identify phone with volume control.	CAL	MICH	RI	
	COLO	MINN	SC	
	CONN	MISS	SD	FED'L FUNDS
	DEL	MO	TENN	
	FLA	MONT	TEXAS	
	GA	NEB	UTAH	
	HAWAII	NEV	VT	
	IDAHO	NH	VA	
	ILL	NJ	WASH	
	IND	NM	W VA	
	IOWA	NY	WIS	OTHER
	KANS	NC	WYO	
	KY	ND		

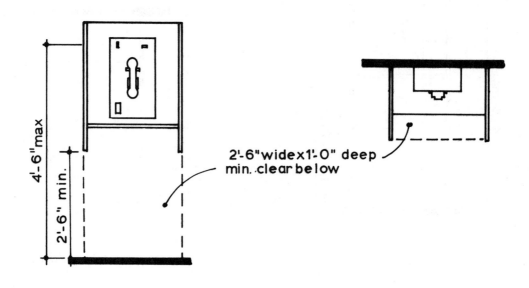

2'-6"wide x 1'-0" deep min. clear below

4'-6" max

2'-6" min.

Basis of standard —	APPLICABILITY			
Architectural Barrier Free Design Code and others	ALA	LA	OHIO	GUAM
	ALASKA	MAINE	OKLA	PR
	ARIZ	MD	ORE	VIR IS
Notes —	ARK	MASS	PA	DC
Public telephones are provided, at least one shall be accessible and usable by a person in a wheelchair. Equip receiver with adjustable volume control, identify controls and provide instructions for use. Provide shelf to allow use of device. Identify area code and telephone numbers by min 1/2″ high raised numerals and 1/8″ thick on the device, and supplement by braille. Identify accessible phones.	CAL	MICH	RI	
	COLO	MINN	SC	
	CONN	MISS	SD	FED'L FUNDS
	DEL	MO	TENN	
	FLA	MONT	TEXAS	
	GA	NEB	UTAH	
	HAWAII	NEV	VT	
	IDAHO	● NH	VA	
	ILL	NJ	WASH	
	IND	NM	W VA	
	IOWA	NY	WIS	OTHER
	KANS	NC	WYO	
	KY	ND		

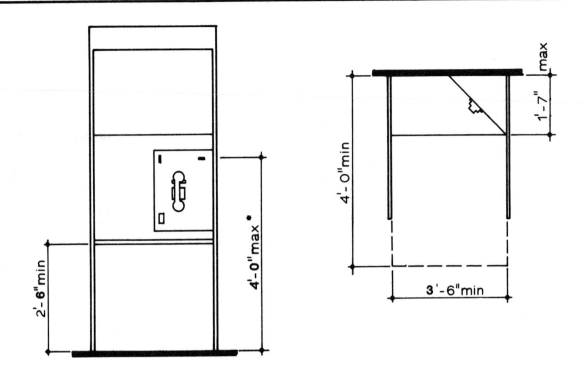

FULL HEIGHT ENCLOSURE

Basis of standard --	APPLICABILITY			
Barrier Free Design Regulations	ALA	LA	OHIO	GUAM
	ALASKA	MAINE	OKLA	PR
	ARIZ	MD	ORE	VIR IS
Notes --	ARK	MASS	PA	DC
Provide at least one complying telephone for all banks of public telephones. Equip with adjustable volume control and instructions for use. Use push-button type dial where available with numbers as large as possible in relief. If door is used provide 32″ clear opening with outswinging, sliding or folding door. If seat is provided it shall fold out of the way. (*)4′-6″ permitted for lateral side reach if not in enclosed booth.	CAL	MICH	RI	
	COLO	MINN	SC	
	CONN	MISS	SD	FED'L FUNDS
	DEL	MO	TENN	
	FLA	MONT	TEXAS	
	GA	NEB	UTAH	
	HAWAII	NEV	VT	
	IDAHO	NH	VA	
	ILL	● NJ	WASH	
	IND	NM	W VA	
	IOWA	NY	WIS	OTHER
	KANS	NC	WYO	
	KY	ND		

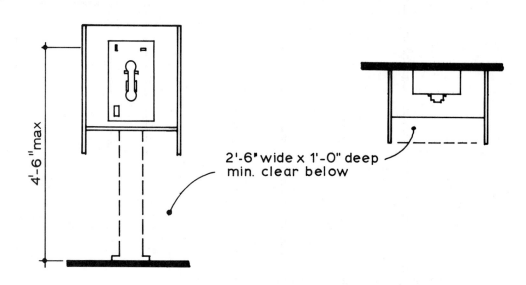

2'-6" wide x 1'-0" deep
min. clear below

4'-6" max

Basis of standard —	APPLICABILITY			
Barrier Free Design	ALA	LA	OHIO	GUAM
	ALASKA	MAINE	OKLA	PR
	ARIZ	MD	ORE	VIR IS
Notes —	ARK	MASS	PA	DC
Where public telephones are provided, install at least	CAL	MICH	RI	
one complying phone. Equip with 3′ min. cord on	COLO	MINN	● SC	
handset and induction coil with operating instructions	CONN	MISS	SD	FED'L
to aid the hearing handicapped.	DEL	MO	TENN	FUNDS
	FLA	MONT	TEXAS	
	GA	NEB	UTAH	
	HAWAII	NEV	VT	
	IDAHO	NH	VA	
	ILL	NJ	WASH	
	IND	NM	W VA	
	IOWA	NY	WIS	OTHER
	KANS	NC	WYO	
	KY	ND		

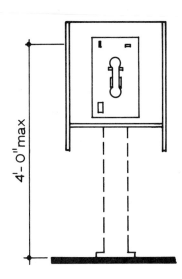

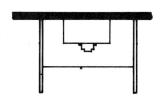

Basis of standard —	APPLICABILITY			
Utah State Building Board	ALA	LA	OHIO	GUAM
	ALASKA	MAINE	OKLA	PR
	ARIZ	MD	ORE	VIR IS
Notes —	ARK	MASS	PA	DC
Where public telephones are provided, one or more phones should comply. All "banks" of public phones shall have at least one to comply. Fixed seats shall not obstruct access to the telephone. Push buttons are preferred. Equip with adjustable volume control on the handset with instructions for use. Telephone instructions shall be in large visual letters. Min. cord length to handset: 2'-5". Minimum clear access: 2'-8" clear.	CAL	MICH	RI	
	COLO	MINN	SC	
	CONN	MISS	SD	FED'L FUNDS
	DEL	MO	TENN	
	FLA	MONT	TEXAS	
	GA	NEB	● UTAH	
	HAWAII	NEV	VT	
	IDAHO	NH	VA	
	ILL	NJ	WASH	
	IND	NM	W VA	
	IOWA	NY	WIS	OTHER
	KANS	NC	WYO	
	KY	ND		

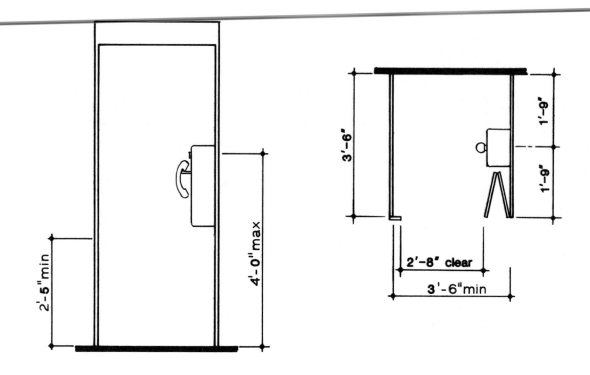

FULL HEIGHT ENCLOSURE

Basis of standard —	APPLICABILITY			
Building Code Advisory Council	ALA	LA	OHIO	GUAM
	ALASKA	MAINE	OKLA	PR
	ARIZ	MD	ORE	VIR IS
Notes —	ARK	MASS	PA	DC
Provide at least one telephone which complies where public telephones are provided. Handset length: 2'-6" min. See following page for alternate arrangement.	CAL	MICH	RI	
	COLO	MINN	SC	
	CONN	MISS	SD	FED'L FUNDS
	DEL	MO	TENN	
	FLA	MONT	TEXAS	
	GA	NEB	UTAH	
	HAWAII	NEV	VT	
	IDAHO	NH	VA	
	ILL	NJ	● WASH	
	IND	NM	W VA	
	IOWA	NY	WIS	OTHER
	KANS	NC	WYO	
	KY	ND		

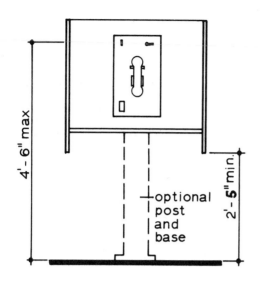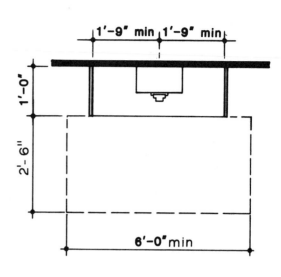

SIDE REACH POSSIBLE

Basis of standard —	APPLICABILITY			
Building Code Advisory Council	ALA	LA	OHIO	GUAM
	ALASKA	MAINE	OKLA	PR
	ARIZ	MD	ORE	VIR IS
Notes —	ARK	MASS	PA	DC
Provide at least one telephone which complies where public telephones are provided. Handset length: 2'-6" min.	CAL	MICH	RI	
	COLO	MINN	SC	
	CONN	MISS	SD	FED'L FUNDS
	DEL	MO	TENN	
	FLA	MONT	TEXAS	
	GA	NEB	UTAH	
	HAWAII	NEV	VT	
	IDAHO	NH	VA	
	ILL	NJ	● WASH	
	IND	NM	W VA	
	IOWA	NY	WIS	OTHER
	KANS	NC	WYO	
	KY	ND		

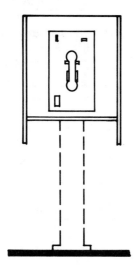

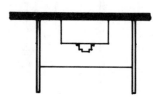

Basis of standard —	APPLICABILITY			
Wisconsin Administrative Code	ALA	LA	OHIO	GUAM
	ALASKA	MAINE	OKLA	PR
	ARIZ	MD	ORE	VIR IS
Notes —	ARK	MASS	PA	DC
Provide minimum one accessible phone where coin telephones are provided. (Recommendation: max. height: 4'-6", max. height of dial: 4'-0", adjustable volume control.)	CAL	MICH	RI	
	COLO	MINN	SC	
	CONN	MISS	SD	FED'L
	DEL	MO	TENN	FUNDS
	FLA	MONT	TEXAS	
	GA	NEB	UTAH	
	HAWAII	NEV	VT	
	IDAHO	NH	VA	
	ILL	NJ	WASH	
	IND	NM	W VA	
	IOWA	NY	● WIS	OTHER
	KANS	NC	WYO	
	KY	ND		

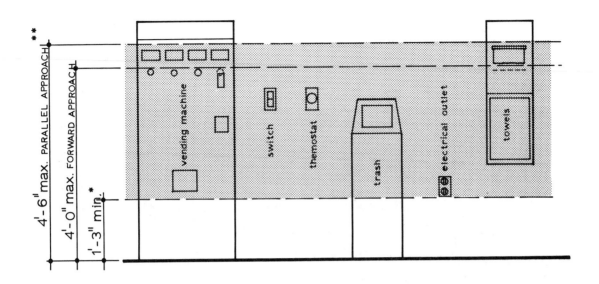

CONTROLS AND OPERATING MECHANISMS

Basis of standard —	APPLICABILITY			
ANSI 1980 — 4.27 and others	ALA	● LA	OHIO	GUAM
	● ALASKA	● MAINE	OKLA	PR
	ARIZ	MD	ORE	VIR IS
	● ARK	MASS	PA	DC
	CAL	MICH	● RI	
	● COLO	MINN	SC	
Notes —	CONN	MISS	SD	● FED'L
For side reach, min. dimension may be 9″. Controls and operating mechanisms shall be operable with one hand and shall not require tight grasping, pinching, or twisting of the wrist. Max. force to activate controls: 5 lbf.	● DEL	MO	TENN	FUNDS
	FLA	MONT	TEXAS	
	GA	NEB	UTAH	
(*)1′-3″ min. applies to electrical and communications system receptacles.	● HAWAII	● NEV	● VT	
(**)Limited to 3′-10″ side reach over an obstruction.	● IDAHO	NH	● VA	
	ILL	NJ	WASH	
	IND	● NM	W VA	
	● IOWA	● NY	WIS	OTHER
	KANS	NC	WYO	
	● KY	ND		

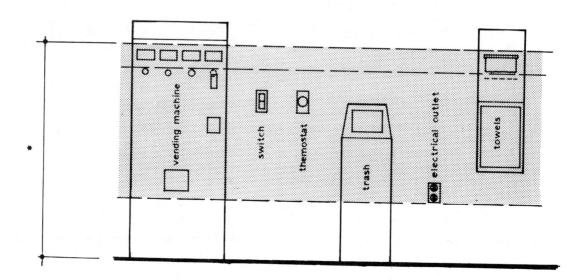

CONTROLS AND OPERATING SYSTEMS

Basis of standard — ANSI 1961 — 5.10 and others	APPLICABILITY			
	ALA	LA	OHIO	GUAM
	ALASKA	MAINE	● OKLA	PR
	● ARIZ	MD	ORE	VIR IS
	ARK	MASS	● PA	DC
	CAL	MICH	RI	
	COLO	MINN	● SC	
	CONN	MISS	● SD	FED'L
	DEL	MO	TENN	FUNDS
	● FLA	MONT	TEXAS	
	● GA	NEB	UTAH	
	HAWAII	NEV	VT	
	IDAHO	NH	VA	
	ILL	NJ	WASH	
	IND	NM	● W VA	
	IOWA	NY	WIS	OTHER
	● KANS	NC	WYO	
	KY	● ND		

Basis of standard —
ANSI 1961 — 5.10 and others

Notes —
Switches and controls for light, heat, ventilation, windows, draperies, fire alarms, and all similar controls of frequent or essential use shall be placed within the reach of individuals in wheelchairs.
(*)4'-6" max. height in West Virginia. 4'-0" in Florida. See "Human Data" for other states.

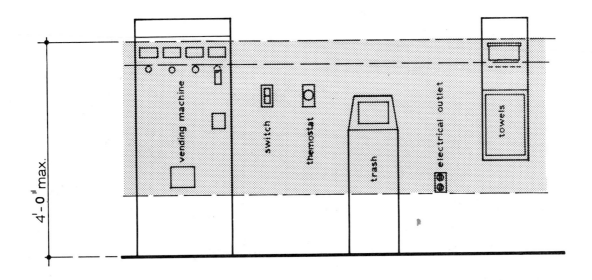

CONTROLS AND OPERATING MECHANISMS

Basis of standard —	APPLICABILITY			
BOCA 1978 and others	ALA	LA	● OHIO	GUAM
	ALASKA	MAINE	OKLA	PR
	ARIZ	MD	ORE	VIR IS
Notes —	ARK	MASS	PA	DC
Washington: window hardware: lever-type or similar, 1′-6″ min. above floor. Min. height for electrical receptacles: 9″, ht.o. (Drying equipment, towel dispensers in toilets to be mounted 3′-4″ above floor max.)	CAL	MICH	RI	
	COLO	MINN	SC	
	CONN	MISS	SD	FED'L FUNDS
	DEL	MO	TENN	
	FLA	MONT	TEXAS	
	GA	NEB	UTAH	
	HAWAII	NEV	VT	
	IDAHO	NH	VA	
	ILL	● NJ	● WASH	
	IND	NM	W VA	
	IOWA	NY	WIS	OTHER
	KANS	NC	WYO	
	KY	ND		

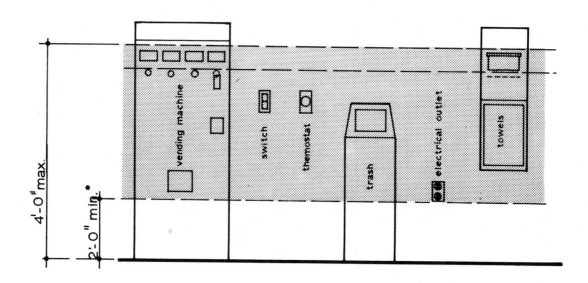

CONTROLS AND OPERATING MECHANISMS

Basis of standard —	APPLICABILITY			
North Carolina Building Code and others	ALA	LA	● OHIO	GUAM
	ALASKA	MAINE	OKLA	PR
	ARIZ	MD	● ORE	VIR IS
Notes —	ARK	MASS	PA	DC
Tennessee and North Carolina applies criteria to	CAL	MICH	RI	
switches and controls operable by occupant and	COLO	MINN	SC	
excludes fire alarm and thermostatic controls from	CONN	MISS	SD	FED'L
the height limit. Wyoming permits 4'-6" max. for	DEL	MO	● TENN	FUNDS
fire alarms.	FLA	MONT	TEXAS	
(*)Applies to Oregon.	GA	NEB	UTAH	
	HAWAII	NEV	VT	
	IDAHO	NH	VA	
	ILL	NJ	WASH	
	IND	NM	W VA	
	IOWA	NY	WIS	OTHER
	KANS	● NC	● WYO	
	KY	ND		

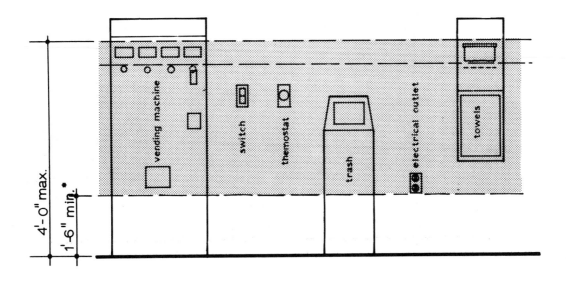

CONTROLS AND OPERATING MECHANISMS

Basis of standard — Basic Building Code and others	APPLICABILITY			
	ALA	LA	OHIO	GUAM
	ALASKA	MAINE	OKLA	PR
	ARIZ	MD	ORE	VIR IS
Notes — Criteria applies to all new construction in Connecticut. (*)Applies to convenience outlets in dwelling units in Connecticut and Michigan and to all outlets in South Carolina.	ARK	MASS	PA	DC
	CAL	● MICH	RI	
	COLO	MINN	● SC	
	● CONN	MISS	SD	FED'L FUNDS
	DEL	MO	TENN	
	FLA	MONT	TEXAS	
	GA	● NEB	UTAH	
	HAWAII	NEV	VT	
	IDAHO	NH	VA	
	ILL	NJ	WASH	
	IND	NM	W VA	
	IOWA	NY	WIS	OTHER
	KANS	NC	WYO	
	KY	ND		

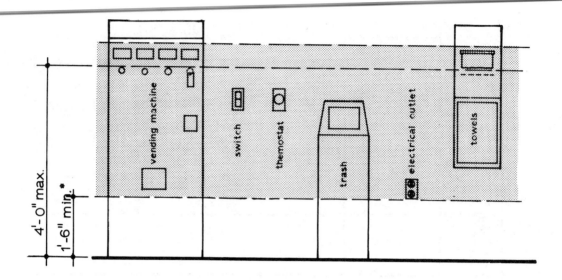

CONTROLS AND OPERATING MECHANISMS

Basis of standard —	APPLICABILITY			
Barrier Free Design Standard and others	● ALA	LA	OHIO	GUAM
	ALASKA	MAINE	OKLA	PR
	ARIZ	● MD	ORE	VIR IS
Notes —	ARK	MASS	PA	DC
All essential controls or frequently used controls shall be located within easy reach of wheelchair users. Fire alarm stations, door, window, and drapery controls shall be placed within the 4′-0″ height limit.	CAL	MICH	RI	
	COLO	MINN	SC	
	CONN	● MISS	SD	FED'L FUNDS
(*)In areas designated specifically for the handicapped use 2′-0″ height for electrical outlets for Alabama.	DEL	MO	TENN	
	FLA	MONT	TEXAS	
	GA	NEB	UTAH	
	HAWAII	NEV	VT	
	IDAHO	NH	VA	
	ILL	NJ	WASH	
	IND	NM	W VA	
	IOWA	NY	WIS	OTHER
	KANS	NC	WYO	
	KY	ND		

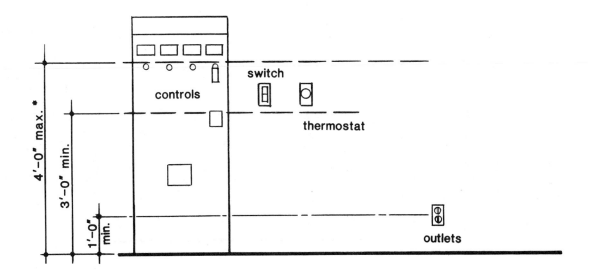

CONTROLS AND OPERATING MECHANISMS

Basis of standard — CAC Title 24, Parts 2 & 3.	APPLICABILITY			
	ALA	LA	OHIO	GUAM
	ALASKA	MAINE	OKLA	PR
	ARIZ	MD	ORE	VIR IS
	ARK	MASS	PA	DC
● CAL	MICH	RI	
	COLO	MINN	SC	
	CONN	MISS	SD	FED'L FUNDS
	DEL	MO	TENN	
	FLA	MONT	TEXAS	
	GA	NEB	UTAH	
	HAWAII	NEV	VT	
	IDAHO	NH	VA	
	ILL	NJ	WASH	
	IND	NM	W VA	
	IOWA	NY	WIS	OTHER
	KANS	NC	WYO	
	KY	ND		

Notes —

(*)3'-4" maximum for toilet accessories.

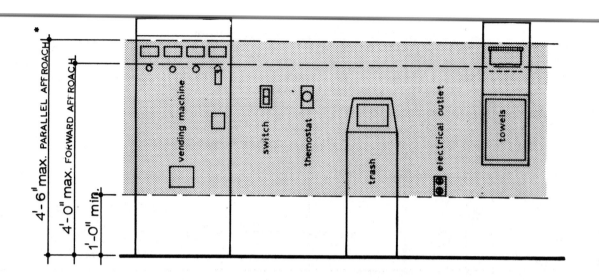

4'-6" max. PARALLEL APPROACH
4'-0" max. FORWARD APPROACH
1'-0" min.

vending machine
switch
thermostat
trash
electrical outlet
towels

CONTROLS AND OPERATING MECHANISMS

Basis of standard —	APPLICABILITY			
Capital Development Board	ALA	LA	OHIO	GUAM
	ALASKA	MAINE	OKLA	PR
	ARIZ	MD	ORE	VIR IS
Notes —	ARK	MASS	PA	DC
Height of fire alarm pulls or buttons: 3'-4" to 4'-0"	CAL	MICH	RI	
to center of device. Controls shall not require tight	COLO	MINN	SC	
grasping or pinching to activate; max. force: 3 lbf.	CONN	MISS	SD	FED'L
Provide 5 footcandle minimum illumination at all	DEL	MO	TENN	FUNDS
controls, dispensers and receptacles. See "Human	FLA	MONT	TEXAS	
Data" for other applicable wheelchair dimensions.	GA	NEB	UTAH	
Illuminate light switches in hotels and motels in the	HAWAII	NEV	VT	
bathroom, bedroom and in the hallways between	IDAHO	NH	VA	
bedrooms and bathroom.	● ILL	NJ	WASH	
(*)In educational buildings, libraries and museums	IND	NM	W VA	
which may include students under 12 years of age use	IOWA	NY	WIS	OTHER
3'-4".	KANS	NC	WYO	
	KY	ND		

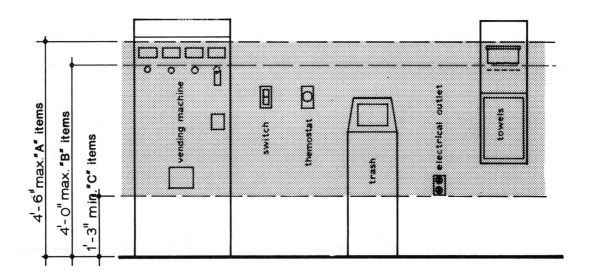

CONTROLS AND OPERATING MECHANISMS

Basis of standard — Architectural Barriers Board	APPLICABILITY			
	ALA	LA	OHIO	GUAM
	ALASKA	MAINE	OKLA	PR
	ARIZ	MD	ORE	VIR IS
Notes —	ARK	● MASS	PA	DC
"A" items: thermostats, intercoms, and fire alarms. "B" items: switches, locks, and controls. "C" item: electrical outlets. "A" and "B" items shall be no lower than 3'-0" above floor. All items shall be at least 1'-6" from corner.	CAL	MICH	RI	
	COLO	MINN	SC	
	CONN	MISS	SD	FED'L
	DEL	MO	TENN	FUNDS
	FLA	MONT	TEXAS	
	GA	NEB	UTAH	
	HAWAII	NEV	VT	
	IDAHO	NH	VA	
	ILL	NJ	WASH	
	IND	NM	W VA	
	IOWA	NY	WIS	OTHER
	KANS	NC	WYO	
	KY	ND		

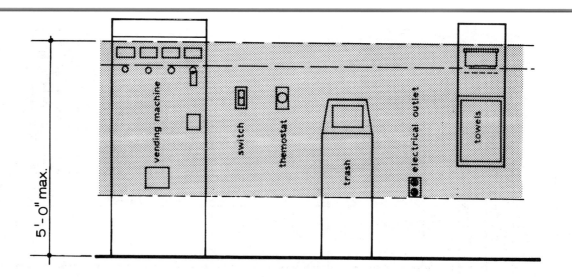

CONTROLS AND OPERATING MECHANISMS

Basis of standard —	APPLICABILITY			
State Building Code	ALA	LA	OHIO	GUAM
	ALASKA	MAINE	OKLA	PR
	ARIZ	MD	ORE	VIR IS
Notes —	ARK	MASS	PA	DC
Applies to elevator controls, thermostats, manual fire alarms and similar equipment, and electrical switches and receptacles in dwelling units, regulated by handi-capped requirements in Minnesota.	CAL	MICH	RI	
	COLO	● MINN	SC	
	CONN	MISS	SD	FED'L
	DEL	MO	TENN	FUNDS
	FLA	MONT	TEXAS	
	GA	NEB	UTAH	
	HAWAII	NEV	VT	
	IDAHO	NH	VA	
	ILL	NJ	WASH	
	IND	NM	W VA	
	IOWA	NY	WIS	OTHER
	KANS	NC	WYO	
	KY	ND		

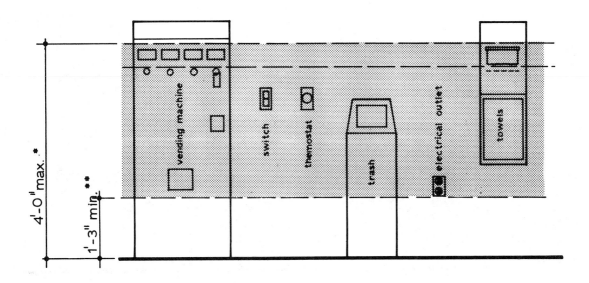

CONTROLS AND OPERATING MECHANISMS

Basis of standard — Barrier Free Design Code	APPLICABILITY			
	ALA	LA	OHIO	GUAM
	ALASKA	MAINE	OKLA	PR
	ARIZ	MD	ORE	VIR IS
	ARK	MASS	PA	DC
Notes —	CAL	MICH	RI	
(*)Applies to switches, locks and controls for public use. Thermostats, intercoms, and fire alarms may be centered 4′-6″ above floor max.	COLO	MINN	SC	
	CONN	MISS	SD	FED'L FUNDS
(**)Applies to centering of electrical outlets. 3′-0″ min. for all others.	DEL	MO	TENN	
	FLA	MONT	TEXAS	
	GA	NEB	UTAH	
	HAWAII	NEV	VT	
	IDAHO	● NH	VA	
	ILL	NJ	WASH	
	IND	NM	W VA	
	IOWA	NY	WIS	OTHER
	KANS	NC	WYO	
	KY	ND		

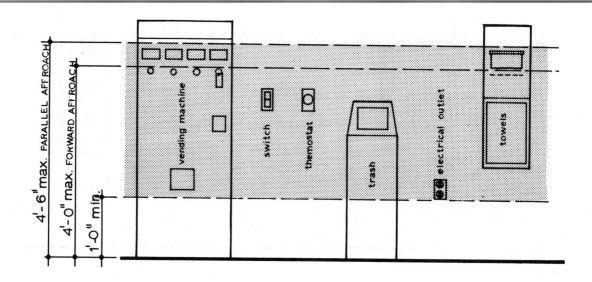

CONTROLS AND OPERATING MECHANISMS

Basis of standard —	APPLICABILITY			
State Purchasing and General Services Commission	ALA	LA	OHIO	GUAM
	ALASKA	MAINE	OKLA	PR
	ARIZ	MD	ORE	VIR IS
Notes —	ARK	MASS	PA	DC
Min. 1'-0" dimension applies to electrical and communication systems receptacles. Controls to be operable without tight grasping, pinching or severe wrist twisting. Max. force to activate controls: 5 lbf. In lieu of heights shown, for children max. shall be:	CAL	MICH	RI	
	COLO	MINN	SC	
	CONN	MISS	SD	FED'L FUNDS
	DEL	MO	TENN	
	FLA	MONT	● TEXAS	
	GA	NEB	UTAH	
	HAWAII	NEV	VT	
	IDAHO	NH	VA	
	ILL	NJ	WASH	
	IND	NM	W VA	
	IOWA	NY	WIS	OTHER
	KANS	NC	WYO	
	KY	ND		

	Ages 5 thru 10 or 11 (Grades K thru 5 or 6)	Ages 11 thru 14 or 15 (Grades 6 thru 8 or 9)
Front approach	3'-6"	3'-9"
Side approach	4'-0"	4'-3"

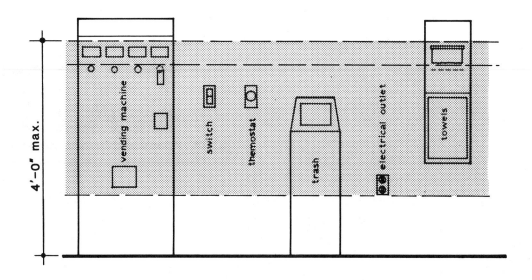

CONTROLS AND OPERATING MECHANISMS

Basis of standard —	APPLICABILITY			
Utah State Building Board	ALA	LA	OHIO	GUAM
	ALASKA	MAINE	OKLA	PR
	ARIZ	MD	ORE	VIR IS
Notes —	ARK	MASS	PA	DC
Data applies to controls designed to be operable by the occupant. Max. height for door knobs, latches and panic hardware: 3'-5". Max. height for deadlocks, and door push and pull plates: 3'-9" to center of hardware. Max. torque allowable for door controls: 8 ft. pounds (5 ft. pounds preferred). Key operated thermostats and switches need not comply. Fire extinguishers may be mounted with their tops max. 5'-0" above floor.	CAL	MICH	RI	
	COLO	MINN	SC	
	CONN	MISS	SD	FED'L FUNDS
	DEL	MO	TENN	
	FLA	MONT	TEXAS	
	GA	NEB	● UTAH	
	HAWAII	NEV	VT	
	IDAHO	NH	VA	
	ILL	NJ	WASH	
	IND	NM	W VA	
	IOWA	NY	WIS	OTHER
	KANS	NC	WYO	
	KY	ND		

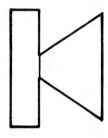

AUDIBLE

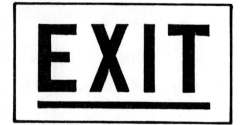

VISUAL

ALARMS

Basis of standard — ANSI 1980 − 4.28 and others	APPLICABILITY			
	ALA	● LA	OHIO	GUAM
	● ALASKA	● MAINE	OKLA	PR
	ARIZ	MD	ORE	VIR IS
Notes —	ARK	MASS	PA	DC
If emergency warning systems are provided, include both audible and visual alarms. Facilities with sleeping accommodations shall have auxiliary visual alarm systems. Audible alarms: sound level exceeding prevailing level in space by at least 15 db or exceeding any maximum sound level with a duration of 30 seconds by 5 db, whichever is louder. Max. sound level for alarm signals: 120 db. Electric internally illuminated exit signs shall flash in conjunction with audible emergency alarms with a flashing frequency of less than 5 Hz. Install on same system as audible emergency alarms if alarms use electricity from building as a power source. Auxiliary alarms: connect visual alarm to building alarm system or provide 110 V receptacle into which such alarm could be connected.	CAL	MICH	● RI	
	● COLO	MINN	SC	
	CONN	MISS	SD	FED'L FUNDS
	DEL	MO	TENN	
	FLA	MONT	● TEXAS	
	GA	NEB	UTAH	
	● HAWAII	● NEV	● VT	
	● IDAHO	NH	● VA	
	ILL	NJ	WASH	
	IND	● NM	W VA	
	IOWA	● NY	WIS	OTHER
	KANS	NC	WYO	
	● KY	ND		

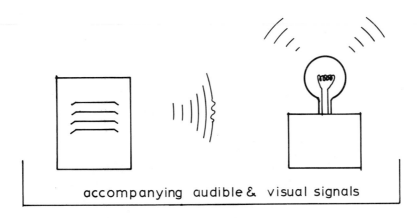

accompanying audible & visual signals

WARNING   SIGNALS

Basis of standard —	APPLICABILITY			
ANSI 1961 — 5.12 and others	● ALA	LA	OHIO	GUAM
	ALASKA	● MAINE	● OKLA	PR
	● ARIZ	MD	ORE	VIR IS
Notes —	ARK	MASS	PA	DC
Connecticut, Iowa, Utah: provide where required by other codes or the authority having jurisdiction.	CAL	MICH	RI	
New Hampshire: max. flashing: 5 cycles per second.	COLO	MINN	● SC	
West Virginia: in areas used by the blind or those with hearing difficulties which do not have direct exit, shall have dual signals.	● CONN	MISS	● SD	FED'L FUNDS
	DEL	MO	TENN	
	● FLA	MONT	TEXAS	
	● GA	NEB	● UTAH	
	HAWAII	NEV	VT	
	IDAHO	● NH	VA	
	ILL	● NJ	WASH	
	IND	NM	● W VA	
	● IOWA	NY	WIS	OTHER
	● KANS	NC	WYO	
	KY	● ND		

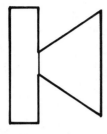

AUDIBLE

VISUAL

ALARMS

Basis of standard — ATBCB – 1190.180 and others	APPLICABILITY			
	ALA	LA	OHIO	GUAM
	ALASKA	MAINE	OKLA	PR
	ARIZ	MD	ORE	VIR IS
● ARK	MASS	PA	DC
	CAL	MICH	RI	
Notes —	COLO	MINN	SC	
If audible alarms are provided, also provide visual alarm device adjacent to or within each exit sign flashing in conjunction and operating on same power source as audible alarms with a flash frequency of less than 5 Hz. Audible alarms to produce sound pressure level exceeding ambient room or space noise by 15 db or any maximum noise level of 30 sec. duration by 5 db, whichever is greater. Mount alarm pull stations as shown for "controls".	CONN	MISS	SD	● FED'L FUNDS
	● DEL	MO	TENN	
	FLA	MONT	TEXAS	
	GA	NEB	UTAH	
	HAWAII	NEV	VT	
	IDAHO	NH	VA	
	ILL	NJ	WASH	
	IND	NM	W VA	
	IOWA	NY	WIS	OTHER
	KANS	NC	WYO	
	KY	ND		

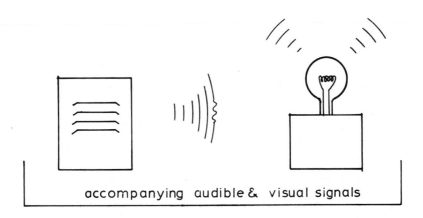

accompanying audible & visual signals

WARNING   SIGNALS

Basis of standard — CAC Title 24, Part 3.	APPLICABILITY			
	ALA	LA	OHIO	GUAM
	ALASKA	MAINE	OKLA	PR
	ARIZ	MD	ORE	VIR IS
	ARK	MASS	PA	DC
● CAL	MICH	RI	
	COLO	MINN	SC	
	CONN	MISS	SD	FED'L FUNDS
	DEL	MO	TENN	
	FLA	MONT	TEXAS	
	GA	NEB	UTAH	
	HAWAII	NEV	VT	
	IDAHO	NH	VA	
	ILL	NJ	WASH	
	IND	NM	W VA	
	IOWA	NY	WIS	OTHER
	KANS	NC	WYO	
	KY	ND		

Notes —
Where audible alarms are provided, visual alarms shall be provided. Visual alarms: lights flashing 60 cycles per minute (maximum 300 cycles per minute allowed).

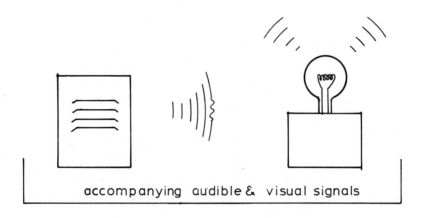

accompanying audible & visual signals

WARNING   SIGNALS

Basis of standard —	APPLICABILITY			
Capital Development Board	ALA	LA	OHIO	GUAM
	ALASKA	MAINE	OKLA	PR
	ARIZ	MD	ORE	VIR IS
Notes —	ARK	MASS	PA	DC
Illuminate exit signs shall flash as a visual emergency alarm with a max. frequency of 5 Hz. Audible emergency alarms to produce sound exceeding normal prevailing sound levels by at least 15 db, with a max. of 120 db. Locate visual emergency alarms so it can be seen anywhere in space. Identify areas or spaces with microwave ovens. Locate fire alarm devices 3'-4" to 4'-0" from floor to center of operable mechanism.	CAL	MICH	RI	
	COLO	MINN	SC	
	CONN	MISS	SD	FED'L FUNDS
	DEL	MO	TENN	
	FLA	MONT	TEXAS	
	GA	NEB	UTAH	
	HAWAII	NEV	VT	
	IDAHO	NH	VA	
	● ILL	NJ	WASH	
	IND	NM	W VA	
	IOWA	NY	WIS	OTHER
	KANS	NC	WYO	
	KY	ND		

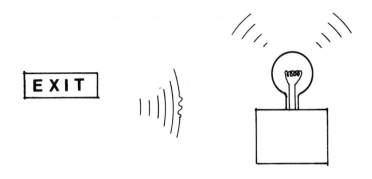

WARNING   SIGNALS

Basis of standard — Maryland Building Code for the Handicapped	APPLICABILITY			
	ALA	LA	OHIO	GUAM
	ALASKA	MAINE	OKLA	PR
	ARIZ	● MD	ORE	VIR IS
	ARK	MASS	PA	DC
Notes —	CAL	MICH	RI	
Provide flashing lights at fire alarm pull boxes which are automatically activated when other fire alarm devices are activated. Flashing exit signs may be used instead of flashing lights.	COLO	MINN	SC	
	CONN	MISS	SD	FED'L
	DEL	MO	TENN	FUNDS
	FLA	MONT	TEXAS	
	GA	NEB	UTAH	
	HAWAII	NEV	VT	
	IDAHO	NH	VA	
	ILL	NJ	WASH	
	IND	NM	W VA	
	IOWA	NY	WIS	OTHER
	KANS	NC	WYO	
	KY	ND		

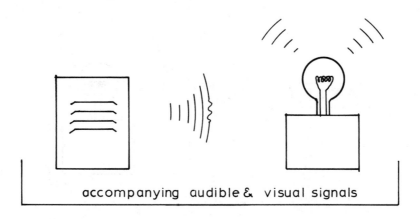

accompanying audible & visual signals

WARNING   SIGNALS

Basis of standard — Architectural Barriers Board	APPLICABILITY			
	ALA	LA	OHIO	GUAM
	ALASKA	MAINE	OKLA	PR
	ARIZ	MD	ORE	VIR IS
Notes — Visual alarms shall flash at max. 5 cycles per second.	ARK	● MASS	PA	DC
	CAL	MICH	RI	
	COLO	MINN	SC	
	CONN	MISS	SD	FED'L FUNDS
	DEL	MO	TENN	
	FLA	MONT	TEXAS	
	GA	NEB	UTAH	
	HAWAII	NEV	VT	
	IDAHO	NH	VA	
	ILL	NJ	WASH	
	IND	NM	W VA	
	IOWA	NY	WIS	OTHER
	KANS	NC	WYO	
	KY	ND		

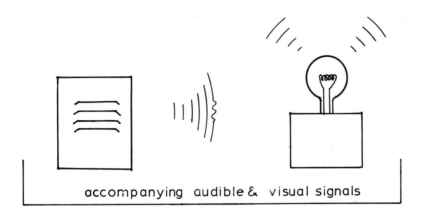

accompanying audible & visual signals

WARNING   SIGNALS

Basis of standard — Construction Code Commission	APPLICABILITY			
	ALA	LA	OHIO	GUAM
	ALASKA	MAINE	OKLA	PR
	ARIZ	MD	ORE	VIR IS
Notes — Operation of any detection device or fire alarm device shall cause all audible and visual alarms to operate, and shall have a distinctive tone not used for any other purpose than that of a fire alarm. Locate as to be effectively heard above all other sounds by all the occupants in every occupied space within the building. Mount visual alarms to be visible from all points of any exitway; bottom of alarm min. 6'-8" above floor.	ARK	MASS	PA	DC
	CAL	● MICH	RI	
	COLO	MINN	SC	
	CONN	MISS	SD	FED'L FUNDS
	DEL	MO	TENN	
	FLA	MONT	TEXAS	
	GA	NEB	UTAH	
	HAWAII	NEV	VT	
	IDAHO	NH	VA	
	ILL	NJ	WASH	
	IND	NM	W VA	
	IOWA	NY	WIS	OTHER
	KANS	NC	WYO	
	KY	ND		

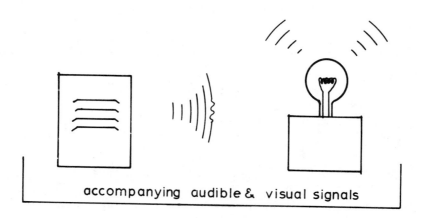

accompanying audible & visual signals

WARNING   SIGNALS

Basis of standard — State of Nebraska Provisions for the Handicapped	APPLICABILITY			
	ALA	LA	OHIO	GUAM
	ALASKA	MAINE	OKLA	PR
	ARIZ	MD	ORE	VIR IS
Notes — Install in central corridors, public areas, and areas of assembly; distribute to be heard effectively above max. noise level of normal conditions or occupancy. Produce audible warning signal distinctive from audible signals used for other purposes in same area. Incandescent, cathode, and strobe visual warning signals shall be legible at 100 feet, and flash at frequency of 45 min. to 120 max. per minute. Project from wall to be readily visible from any point in corridor or locate so no visual light is more than 100 ft. from any individual.	ARK	MASS	PA	DC
	CAL	MICH	RI	
	COLO	MINN	SC	
	CONN	MISS	SD	FED'L FUNDS
	DEL	MO	TENN	
	FLA	MONT	TEXAS	
	GA	● NEB	UTAH	
	HAWAII	NEV	VT	
	IDAHO	NH	VA	
	ILL	NJ	WASH	
	IND	NM	W VA	
	IOWA	NY	WIS	OTHER
	KANS	NC	WYO	
	KY	ND		

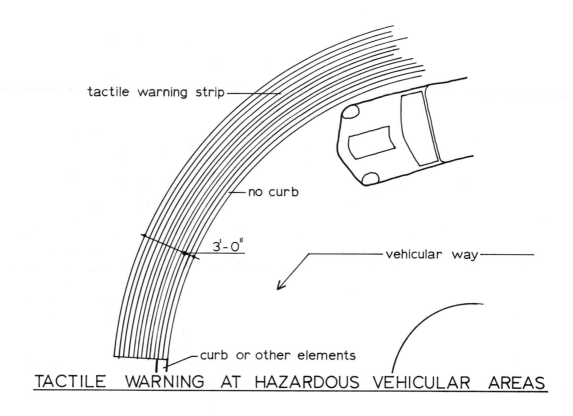

TACTILE WARNING AT HAZARDOUS VEHICULAR AREAS

Basis of standard —	APPLICABILITY			
ANSI 1980 – 4.29.5 and others	ALA	● LA	OHIO	GUAM
	● ALASKA	● MAINE	OKLA	PR
	ARIZ	MD	ORE	VIR IS
	ARK	MASS	PA	DC
	CAL	MICH	● RI	
Notes —	● COLO	MINN	SC	
For walks crossing or adjoining a frequently used vehicular way where there are no curbs, railings or other elements detectable by a person with a severe visual impairment, define the boundary between the areas with a continuous 36″ wide tactile warning texture complying with ANSI 117.1 – 1980, 4.29.2.	CONN	MISS	SD	FED'L FUNDS
	DEL	MO	TENN	
	FLA	MONT	TEXAS	
	GA	NEB	UTAH	
	● HAWAII	● NEV	● VT	
	● IDAHO	NH	● VA	
	ILL	NJ	WASH	
	IND	● NM	W VA	
	IOWA	● NY	WIS	OTHER
	KANS	NC	WYO	
	● KY	ND		

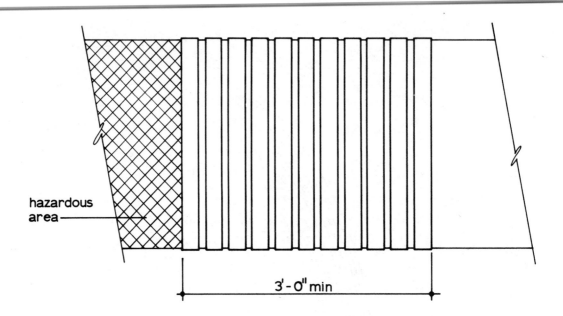

hazardous area —

3'-0" min

PLAN OF TACTILE WARNING SURFACE

Basis of standard —	APPLICABILITY			
ANSI 1980 — 4.29 and others	ALA	● LA	OHIO	GUAM
	● ALASKA	● MAINE	OKLA	PR
	ARIZ	MD	ORE	VIR IS
Notes —	ARK	MASS	PA	DC
See notes on preceeding page.	CAL	MICH	● RI	
Illinois: use 3'-0" width if there is no perceivable	● COLO	MINN	SC	
difference in hardness between the walkway and the	CONN	MISS	SD	FED'L
tactile warning signal. Otherwise use 2'-0" width.	DEL	MO	TENN	FUNDS
Use textured continuous 4" wide strip where vehicular	FLA	MONT	TEXAS	
and pedestrian areas abut at common surface and no	GA	NEB	UTAH	
other barrier is provided, where painted lines define a	● HAWAII	● NEV	● VT	
walk, and for oblique pedestrian crosswalks. Use ¼"	● IDAHO	NH	● VA	
max. size gravel in epoxy, or ¼" thick max. textured	● ILL	NJ	WASH	
resilient surfacing.	IND	● NM	W VA	
	● IOWA	● NY	WIS	OTHER
	KANS	NC	WYO	
	● KY	ND		

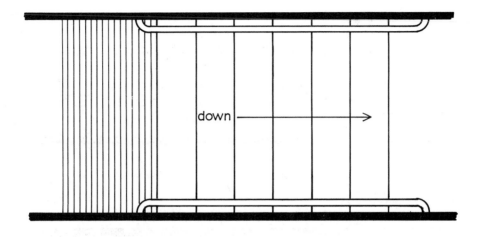

TACTILE WARNING AT STAIRS

Basis of standard — ANSI 1980 – 4.29.4 and others	APPLICABILITY			
	ALA	● LA	OHIO	GUAM
	● ALASKA	● MAINE	OKLA	PR
	ARIZ	MD	ORE	VIR IS
	ARK	MASS	PA	DC
Notes — For all stairs, except those in dwelling units, in enclosed stair towers, or set to the side of the path of travel. For Illinois see also "Stairs".	CAL	MICH	● RI	
	● COLO	MINN	SC	
	CONN	MISS	SD	FED'L FUNDS
	DEL	MO	TENN	
	FLA	MONT	TEXAS	
	GA	NEB	UTAH	
	● HAWAII	● NEV	● VT	
	● IDAHO	NH	● VA	
	● ILL	NJ	WASH	
	IND	● NM	W VA	
	● IOWA	● NY	WIS	OTHER
	KANS	NC	WYO	
	● KY	ND		

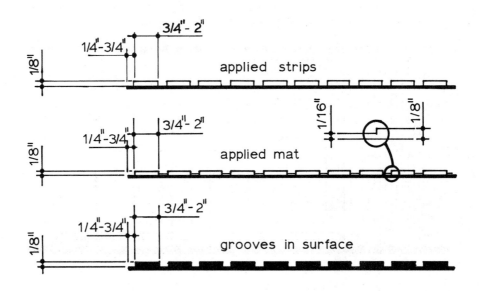

SECTIONS OF TACTILE WARNING SURFACES

Basis of standard — ANSI 1980 — 4.29 and others	APPLICABILITY			
	ALA	● LA	OHIO	GUAM
	● ALASKA	● MAINE	OKLA	PR
	ARIZ	MD	ORE	VIR IS
Notes —	ARK	MASS	PA	DC
On walking surfaces, tactile warning surfaces shall consist of exposed aggregate concrete, rubber or plastic cushioned surfaces, raised strips, or grooves. Textures shall contrast with that of surrounding surface. Grooves may be used indoors only.	CAL	MICH	● RI	
	● COLO	MINN	SC	
	CONN	MISS	SD	FED'L
	DEL	MO	TENN	FUNDS
	FLA	MONT	TEXAS	
	GA	NEB	UTAH	
	● HAWAII	● NEV	● VT	
	● IDAHO	NH	● VA	
	● ILL	NJ	WASH	
	IND	● NM	W VA	
	● IOWA	● NY	WIS	OTHER
	KANS	NC	WYO	
	● KY	ND		

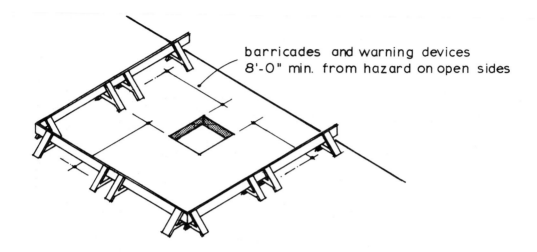

barricades and warning devices
8'-0" min. from hazard on open sides

BARRICADES

Basis of standard — ANSI 1961 — 5.13.2 and others	APPLICABILITY			
	● ALA	LA	OHIO	GUAM
	ALASKA	MAINE	● OKLA	PR
	● ARIZ	MD	ORE	VIR IS
Notes —	ARK	MASS	PA	DC
Provide barricades and warning devices (see "Alarms")	CAL	MICH	RI	
when manholes or access panels are open and in use,	COLO	MINN	● SC	
or when an open excavation exists on a site particularly	● CONN	MISS	● SD	
when it is approximate to normal pedestrian traffic.	DEL	MO	TENN	FED'L
Nebraska does not specify distance. Florida: applies	● FLA	MONT	TEXAS	FUNDS
to non-government financed facilites.	● GA	● NEB	● UTAH	
	HAWAII	NEV	VT	
	IDAHO	NH	VA	
	ILL	● NJ	WASH	
	IND	NM	W VA	
	IOWA	NY	WIS	OTHER
	● KANS	NC	WYO	
	KY	● ND		

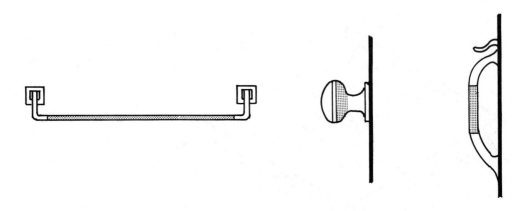

KNURLED DOOR HANDLES AND KNOBS

Basis of standard — ANSI 1961 − 5.11.3, BOCA 1978, and others	APPLICABILITY			
	● ALA	LA	● OHIO	GUAM
	ALASKA	MAINE	● OKLA	PR
	● ARIZ	MD	● ORE	VIR IS
Notes — Provide knurling (or use acceptable plastic, abrasive coating) for doors not intended for normal use to make them quickly identifiable to the touch (i.e., doors to loading platforms, boiler rooms, stages, fire escapes, etc.) Florida: applies to government facilities. New Jersey: alternate: key operated latching mechanisms.	● ARK	● MASS	PA	DC
	CAL	MICH	RI	
	COLO	● MINN	● SC	
	● CONN	MISS	● SD	● FED'L FUNDS
	● DEL	MO	● TENN	
	● FLA	MONT	● TEXAS	
	● GA	● NEB	● UTAH	
	HAWAII	NEV	● VT	
	IDAHO	● NH	● VA	
	● ILL	● NJ	● WASH	
	● IND	● NM	● W VA	
	IOWA	NY	WIS	OTHER
	● KANS	● NC	● WYO	
	● KY	● ND		

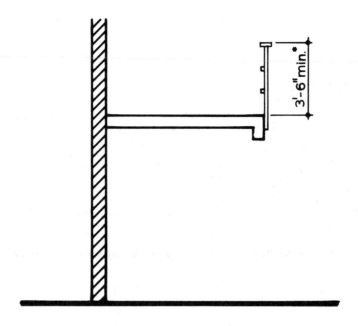

BALCONY RAILING

Basis of standard — BOCA 1978	APPLICABILITY			
	ALA	LA	● OHIO	GUAM
	ALASKA	MAINE	OKLA	PR
	ARIZ	MD	ORE	VIR IS
Notes — Provide guards at open sided floor areas, mezzanines, and landings. (See BOCA 616.5.2 for space between guardrails.) (*)Min. for R-3 and R-4 occupancies: 3'-0".	ARK	MASS	PA	DC
	CAL	MICH	RI	
	COLO	MINN	SC	
	CONN	MISS	SD	FED'L
	DEL	MO	TENN	FUNDS
	FLA	MONT	TEXAS	
	GA	NEB	UTAH	
	HAWAII	NEV	VT	
	IDAHO	NH	VA	
	ILL	NJ	WASH	
	IND	NM	W VA	
	IOWA	NY	WIS	OTHER
	KANS	NC	WYO	
	KY	ND		

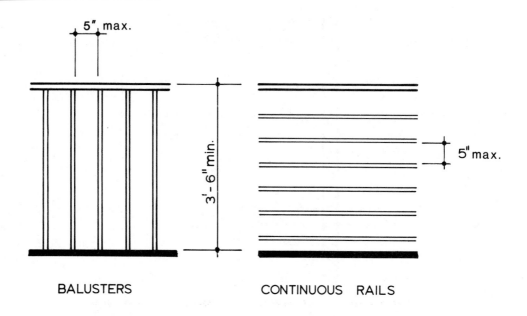

5″ max.

3′-6″ min.

5″ max.

BALUSTERS   CONTINUOUS RAILS

GUARDRAILS

Basis of standard —	APPLICABILITY			
Capital Development Board	ALA	LA	OHIO	GUAM
	ALASKA	MAINE	OKLA	PR
	ARIZ	MD	ORE	VIR IS
Notes —	ARK	MASS	PA	DC
In commercial or industrial occupancies not open to visitors may have space between intermediate rails 10″ apart and open space between balusters may be 6″. Applicable for unenclosed floor openings, and open sides of landings, balconies, accessible roofs or porches. Not applicable to loading side of loading docks. Maybe 3′-0″ in individual dwelling units. Guardrail on a blacony immediately in front of first row of fixed seats not at the end of an aisle maybe 2′-2″ high.	CAL	MICH	RI	
	COLO	MINN	SC	
	CONN	MISS	SD	FED'L FUNDS
	DEL	MO	TENN	
	FLA	MONT	TEXAS	
	GA	NEB	UTAH	
	HAWAII	NEV	VT	
	IDAHO	NH	VA	
	● ILL	NJ	WASH	
	IND	NM	W VA	
	IOWA	NY	WIS	OTHER
	KANS	NC	WYO	
	KY	ND		

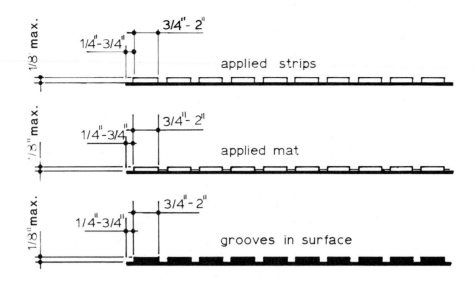

SECTIONS OF TACTILE WARNING SURFACES

Basis of standard —	APPLICABILITY			
Indiana Amendments to Uniform Building Code	ALA	LA	OHIO	GUAM
	ALASKA	MAINE	OKLA	PR
	ARIZ	MD	ORE	VIR IS
Notes —	ARK	MASS	PA	DC
On walking surfaces, tactile warning textures shall consist of exposed aggregate concrete, rubber or plastic cushioned surfaces, raised strips, or grooves. Such tactile warning surfaces shall extend 3'-0" adjacent to areas hazardous to the blind as follows:	CAL	MICH	RI	
	COLO	MINN	SC	
	CONN	MISS	SD	FED'L FUNDS
A. At top of all stair runs except those in dwelling units or in enclosed stair towers.	DEL	MO	TENN	
	FLA	MONT	TEXAS	
B. At hazardous vehicular areas if a walk crosses a vehicular way and if there are no curbs, railings, or other elements separating pedestrian and vehicular areas.	GA	NEB	UTAH	
	HAWAII	NEV	VT	
	IDAHO	NH	VA	
C. At edges of reflecting pools if there are no railings, walks, or curbs.	ILL	NJ	WASH	
	● IND	NM	W VA	
	IOWA	NY	WIS	
	KANS	NC	WYO	OTHER
	KY	ND		

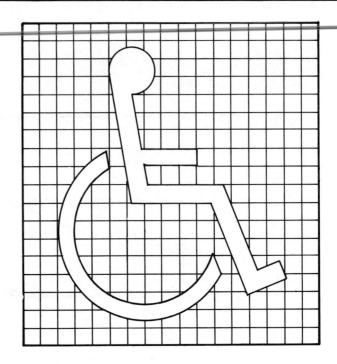

PROPORTIONS

Basis of standard —	APPLICABILITY			
ANSI 1980 — 4.30 and others	ALA	● LA	OHIO	GUAM
	● ALASKA	● MAINE	OKLA	PR
	ARIZ	MD	ORE	VIR IS
Notes —	● ARK	MASS	PA	DC
Refer to following page for display conditions.	● CAL	MICH	● RI	
(Federal Arkansas and Delaware requirements for	● COLO	MINN	SC	
minimum dimensions to display symbol:	CONN	MISS	SD	● FED'L
Size Location Viewing Distance	● DEL	MO	TENN	FUNDS
2½″ Interior Up to 30 ft.	FLA	MONT	TEXAS	
4″ Interior Greater than 30 ft.	GA	NEB	UTAH	
4″ Exterior Up to 60 ft.	● HAWAII	● NEV	● VT	
8″ Exterior Greater than 60 ft.	● IDAHO	NH	● VA	
	ILL	● NJ	WASH	
	IND	● NM	W VA	
	IOWA	● NY	WIS	OTHER
	KANS	NC	WYO	
	● KY	ND		

DISPLAY CONDITIONS

Basis of standard —	APPLICABILITY			
ANSI 1980 — 4.30 and others	ALA	● LA	OHIO	GUAM
	● ALASKA	● MAINE	OKLA	PR
	ARIZ	MD	ORE	VIR IS
Notes —	● ARK	MASS	PA	DC
Letters and numbers on signs — width-to-height ratio between 3:5 and 1:1, stroke width-to-height ratio between 1:5 and 1:10.	● CAL	MICH	● RI	
Color contrast required between characters and symbols and background — light on dark or dark on light.	● COLO	MINN	SC	
Letters and numbers on signs shall be sans serif, and raised or incised 5/8″ min. high and 2″ max. high.	CONN	MISS	SD	● FED'L FUNDS
Stroke width of indented characters or symbols 1/4″ min. Raising or indentation of symbols or	● DEL	MO	TENN	
pictographs 1/32″ min. If accessible facilities are identified, use international accessibility symbol shown.	● FLA	MONT	● TEXAS	
	GA	NEB	UTAH	
	● HAWAII	● NEV	● VT	
	● IDAHO	NH	● VA	
	ILL	● NJ	WASH	
	IND	● NM	W VA	
	● IOWA	● NY	WIS	OTHER
	KANS	NC	WYO	
	● KY	ND		

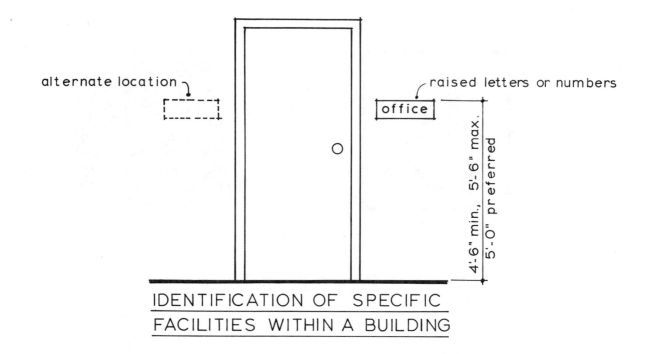

alternate location

raised letters or numbers

office

4'-6" min., 5'-6" max.
5'-0" preferred

IDENTIFICATION OF SPECIFIC FACILITIES WITHIN A BUILDING

Basis of standard — ANSI 1961 — 5.11.1, 5.11.2 and others	APPLICABILITY			
	ALA	LA	OHIO	GUAM
	ALASKA	MAINE	● OKLA	PR
	● ARIZ	MD	ORE	VIR IS
Notes —	ARK	MASS	PA	DC
Florida: above applies to non-government funded facilities and does not specify height. For government buildings use raised or recessed numbers or letters max. 4'-6" above floor.	CAL	MICH	RI	
	COLO	● MINN	● SC	
	● CONN	MISS	● SD	FED'L
	DEL	MO	TENN	FUNDS
	● FLA	MONT	TEXAS	
	● GA	NEB	UTAH	
	HAWAII	NEV	VT	
	IDAHO	NH	VA	
	ILL	NJ	WASH	
	IND	NM	● W VA	
	IOWA	NY	WIS	OTHER
	● KANS	NC	WYO	
	KY	● ND		

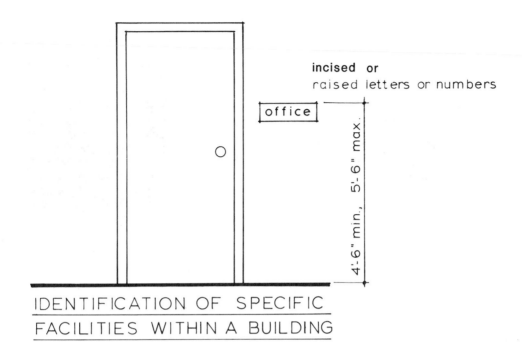

incised or
raised letters or numbers

office

4'-6" min., 5'-6" max.

IDENTIFICATION OF SPECIFIC
FACILITIES WITHIN A BUILDING

Basis of standard —	APPLICABILITY			
ATBCB 1190.200 and others	ALA	LA	OHIO	GUAM
	ALASKA	MAINE	OKLA	PR
	ARIZ	MD	ORE	VIR IS
Notes — ● ARK	MASS	PA	DC
Measure height to centerline of uppermost row of characters. Place signs in a standardized location throughout building or facility. Install exterior signage at entrances and walks to direct individuals to accessible routes and entrances as required.	CAL	MICH	RI	
	COLO	MINN	SC	
	CONN	MISS	SD	● FED'L FUNDS
	● DEL	MO	TENN	
	FLA	MONT	TEXAS	
	GA	NEB	UTAH	
	HAWAII	NEV	VT	
	IDAHO	NH	VA	
	ILL	NJ	WASH	
	IND	NM	W VA	
	IOWA	NY	WIS	OTHER
	KANS	NC	WYO	
	KY	ND		

DISPLAY CONDITIONS

Basis of standard — Various	APPLICABILITY			
	● ALA	LA	OHIO	GUAM
	ALASKA	MAINE	OKLA	PR
	ARIZ	MD	ORE	VIR IS
Notes —	ARK	MASS	PA	DC
Alabama, Utah, New Jersey: display International Symbol of Access at entrances to buildings, parking lots, toilet facilities, etc. for buildings which are accessible to the physically handicapped. New Jersey: Display at accessible building entrances, toilet rooms, and origin of path of travel if not all are accessible. Michigan, Connecticut: buildings and structures, and facilities within buildings and structures, meeting the requirements for barrier free design shall be clearly identified with the International Symbol of Accessibility for the handicapped.	CAL	● MICH	RI	
	COLO	MINN	SC	
	● CONN	MISS	SD	FED'L FUNDS
	DEL	MO	TENN	
	FLA	MONT	TEXAS	
	GA	NEB	● UTAH	
	HAWAII	NEV	VT	
	IDAHO	NH	VA	
	● ILL	● NJ	WASH	
	IND	NM	W VA	
	IOWA	NY	WIS	OTHER
	KANS	NC	WYO	
	KY	ND		

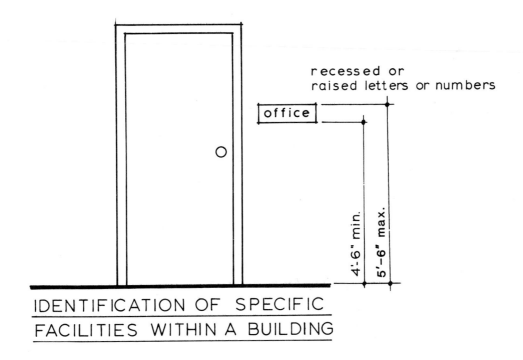

recessed or
raised letters or numbers

office

4'-6" min.

5'-6" max.

IDENTIFICATION OF SPECIFIC
FACILITIES WITHIN A BUILDING

Basis of standard — Various	APPLICABILITY			
	ALA	LA	OHIO	GUAM
	ALASKA	MAINE	OKLA	PR
	ARIZ	MD	ORE	VIR IS
Notes — Provide identification to spaces that would normally be utilized by the visually handicapped.	ARK	MASS	PA	DC
	CAL	MICH	RI	
	COLO	MINN	SC	
	CONN	MISS	SD	FED'L FUNDS
	DEL	MO	● TENN	
	FLA	MONT	TEXAS	
	GA	● NEB	● UTAH	
	HAWAII	NEV	VT	
	IDAHO	NH	VA	
	ILL	NJ	WASH	
	IND	NM	W VA	
	IOWA	NY	WIS	OTHER
	KANS	● NC	● WYO	
	KY	ND		

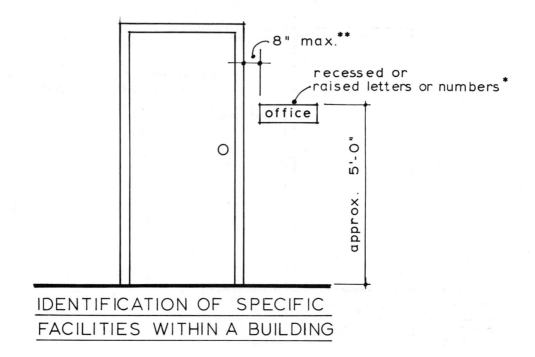

IDENTIFICATION OF SPECIFIC FACILITIES WITHIN A BUILDING

Basis of standard —	APPLICABILITY			
Various	● ALA	LA	OHIO	GUAM
	ALASKA	MAINE	OKLA	PR
	ARIZ	MD	ORE	VIR IS
	ARK	MASS	PA	DC
Notes —	CAL	MICH	RI	
(*)Alabama	COLO	MINN	SC	
(**)Texas	CONN	MISS	SD	FED'L
	DEL	MO	TENN	FUNDS
	FLA	MONT	● TEXAS	
	GA	NEB	UTAH	
	HAWAII	NEV	VT	
	IDAHO	NH	VA	
	ILL	NJ	WASH	
	IND	NM	W VA	
	IOWA	NY	WIS	OTHER
	KANS	NC	WYO	
	KY	ND		

DISPLAY   CONDITIONS

Basis of standard — Various	APPLICABILITY			
	ALA	● LA	OHIO	GUAM
	ALASKA	MAINE	OKLA	PR
	ARIZ	MD	ORE	VIR IS
	ARK	MASS	PA	DC
Notes —	CAL	MICH	RI	
Mississippi: display white on blue background symbol for all public buildings constructed or remodeled which comply or containing facilities which comply with requirements. When a building contains an entrance other than the main entrance which is ramped or level for use by physically handicapped persons, post a sign showing its location at or near the main entrance which shall be visible from the adjacent public sidewalk or way.	COLO	MINN	SC	
	CONN	● MISS	SD	FED'L
	DEL	MO	TENN	FUNDS
	FLA	MONT	TEXAS	
	GA	NEB	UTAH	
	HAWAII	NEV	VT	
	IDAHO	NH	VA	
	ILL	NJ	WASH	
	IND	NM	W VA	
	IOWA	NY	WIS	OTHER
	KANS	NC	WYO	
	KY	ND		

DISPLAY   CONDITIONS

Basis of standard —	APPLICABILITY			
Architectural Barrier Free Design Code and others	ALA	LA	OHIO	GUAM
	ALASKA	MAINE	OKLA	PR
	ARIZ	MD	ORE	VIR IS
Notes —	ARK	● MASS	PA	DC
Display at: special handicapped parking spaces, directional signs showing location of accessible entrances, elevators, and toilet rooms, at accessible entrances to building or facility if not all entrances are accessible, at accessible toilet room entrances if not all toilet rooms in a building are accessible, origins of accessible means of travel to major publicly-used interior spaces if not all means of travel to specific spaces are accessible. Mount no projecting sign lower than 6'-8″ from floor to lower edge of sign.	CAL	MICH	RI	
	COLO	MINN	SC	
	CONN	MISS	SD	FED'L FUNDS
	DEL	MO	TENN	
	FLA	MONT	TEXAS	
	GA	NEB	UTAH	
	HAWAII	NEV	VT	
	IDAHO	● NH	VA	
	ILL	NJ	WASH	
	IND	NM	W VA	
	IOWA	NY	WIS	OTHER
	KANS	NC	WYO	
	KY	ND		

DISPLAY   CONDITIONS

Basis of standard — Uniform Building Code, as amended	APPLICABILITY			
	ALA	LA	OHIO	GUAM
	ALASKA	MAINE	OKLA	PR
	ARIZ	MD	● ORE	VIR IS
Notes —	ARK	MASS	PA	DC
New Mexico: display on all buildings constructed with requirements.	CAL	MICH	RI	
Oregon: designate entrances for use by the physically handicapped in government and public buildings.	COLO	MINN	SC	
	CONN	MISS	SD	FED'L FUNDS
	DEL	MO	TENN	
	FLA	MONT	TEXAS	
	GA	NEB	UTAH	
	HAWAII	NEV	VT	
	IDAHO	NH	VA	
	ILL	NJ	WASH	
	IND	● NM	W VA	
	IOWA	NY	WIS	OTHER
	KANS	NC	WYO	
	KY	ND		

DISPLAY   CONDITIONS

Basis of standard — California Health & Safety Code	APPLICABILITY			
	ALA	LA	OHIO	GUAM
	ALASKA	MAINE	OKLA	PR
	ARIZ	MD	ORE	VIR IS
	ARK	MASS	PA	DC
Notes — When the accessible entrance is other than the main entrance, a sign showing its location shall be posted at the main entrance and visible from adjacent sidewalk. When special toilet facilities are accessible a sign showing their location shall be in the building directory, in the main lobby, and at any specially used accessible entrance.	● CAL	MICH	RI	
	COLO	MINN	SC	
	CONN	MISS	SD	FED'L FUNDS
	DEL	MO	TENN	
	FLA	MONT	TEXAS	
	GA	NEB	UTAH	
	HAWAII	NEV	VT	
	IDAHO	NH	VA	
	ILL	NJ	WASH	
	IND	NM	W VA	
	IOWA	NY	WIS	OTHER
	KANS	NC	WYO	
	KY	ND		

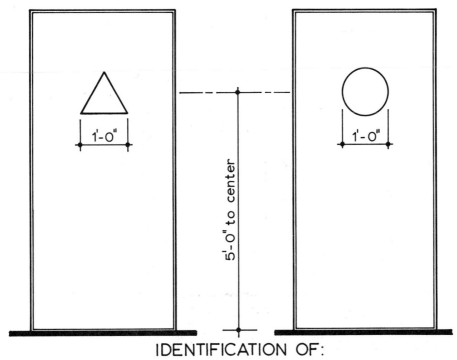

IDENTIFICATION OF:
MEN'S SANITARY FACILITY   WOMEN'S SANITARY FACILITY

Basis of standard —	APPLICABILITY			
CAC Title 24, Part 2	ALA	LA	OHIO	GUAM
	ALASKA	MAINE	OKLA	PR
	ARIZ	MD	ORE	VIR IS
	ARK	MASS	PA	DC
Notes —	● CAL	MICH	RI	
Toilet room signs shall be ¼″ thick material and shall be a contrasting color to the door or background.	COLO	MINN	SC	
	CONN	MISS	SD	FED'L FUNDS
	DEL	MO	TENN	
	FLA	MONT	TEXAS	
	GA	NEB	UTAH	
	HAWAII	NEV	VT	
	IDAHO	NH	VA	
	ILL	NJ	WASH	
	IND	NM	W VA	
	IOWA	NY	WIS	OTHER
	KANS	NC	WYO	
	KY	ND		

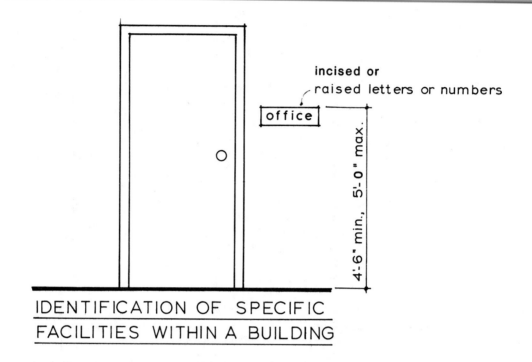

IDENTIFICATION OF SPECIFIC FACILITIES WITHIN A BUILDING

Basis of standard — Capital Development Board	APPLICABILITY			
	ALA	LA	OHIO	GUAM
	ALASKA	MAINE	OKLA	PR
	ARIZ	MD	ORE	VIR IS
Notes — Symbol or name on toilet room door shall be raised 1/32″ min., and be 2½″ min. high. Characters to have stroke width to height ratio of 1:6 to 1:10, and a width to height ratio of 3:5 to 1:1. Locate signs in standardized location throughout building with contrasting colors between characters and background. Characters to be min. 5/8″ high, and 1/32″ min. raised or indented.	ARK	MASS	PA	DC
	CAL	MICH	RI	
	COLO	MINN	SC	
	CONN	MISS	SD	FED'L FUNDS
	DEL	MO	TENN	
	FLA	MONT	TEXAS	
	GA	NEB	UTAH	
	HAWAII	NEV	VT	
	IDAHO	NH	VA	
	● ILL	NJ	WASH	
	IND	NM	W VA	
	IOWA	NY	WIS	OTHER
	KANS	NC	WYO	
	KY	ND		

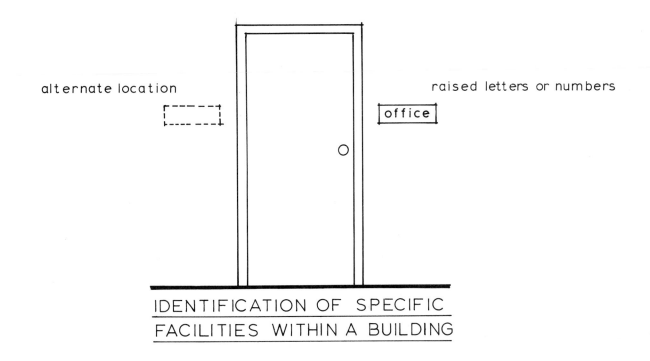

alternate location

raised letters or numbers

office

IDENTIFICATION OF SPECIFIC FACILITIES WITHIN A BUILDING

Basis of standard — Iowa Administrative Code	APPLICABILITY			
	ALA	LA	OHIO	GUAM
	ALASKA	MAINE	OKLA	PR
	ARIZ	MD	ORE	VIR IS
Notes — Use raised or recessed letters or other types of identification in a standard or convenient place.	ARK	MASS	PA	DC
	CAL	MICH	RI	
	COLO	MINN	SC	
	CONN	MISS	SD	FED'L FUNDS
	DEL	MO	TENN	
	FLA	MONT	TEXAS	
	GA	NEB	UTAH	
	HAWAII	NEV	VT	
	IDAHO	NH	VA	
	ILL	NJ	WASH	
	IND	NM	W VA	
	● IOWA	NY	WIS	OTHER
	KANS	NC	WYO	
	KY	ND		

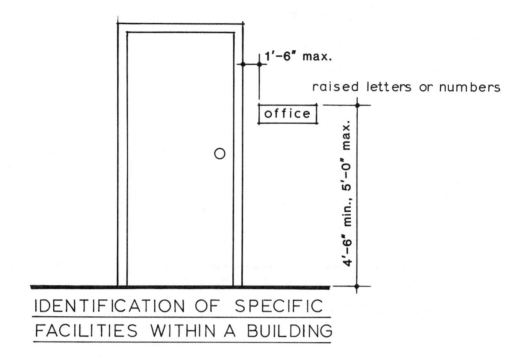

1'-6" max.

raised letters or numbers

office

4'-6" min., 5'-0" max.

IDENTIFICATION OF SPECIFIC FACILITIES WITHIN A BUILDING

Basis of standard — Architectural Barriers Board	APPLICABILITY			
	ALA	LA	OHIO	GUAM
	ALASKA	MAINE	OKLA	PR
	ARIZ	MD	ORE	VIR IS
Notes — When signs are provided in means of egress, fix permanently, raised or recessed, 1¼" high, with contrasting color background. Braille may be used in addition to, but not instead of raised or recessed letters.	ARK	● MASS	PA	DC
	CAL	MICH	RI	
	COLO	MINN	SC	
	CONN	MISS	SD	FED'L FUNDS
	DEL	MO	TENN	
	FLA	MONT	TEXAS	
	GA	NEB	UTAH	
	HAWAII	NEV	VT	
	IDAHO	NH	VA	
	ILL	NJ	WASH	
	IND	NM	W VA	
	IOWA	NY	WIS	OTHER
	KANS	NC	WYO	
	KY	ND		

DISPLAY CONDITIONS

Basis of standard —	APPLICABILITY			
Missouri Revised Statutes	ALA	LA	OHIO	GUAM
	ALASKA	MAINE	OKLA	PR
	ARIZ	MD	ORE	VIR IS
Notes —	ARK	MASS	PA	DC
Prominently display international symbol of accessibility at the main entrance to the building or facility where they are constructed to comply with the requirements.	CAL	MICH	RI	
	COLO	MINN	SC	
	CONN	MISS	SD	FED'L FUNDS
	DEL	● MO	TENN	
	FLA	MONT	TEXAS	
	GA	NEB	UTAH	
	HAWAII	NEV	VT	
	IDAHO	NH	VA	
	ILL	NJ	WASH	
	IND	NM	W VA	
	IOWA	NY	WIS	OTHER
	KANS	NC	WYO	
	KY	ND		

DISPLAY   CONDITIONS

Basis of standard — Nebraska Provisions for the Handicapped	APPLICABILITY			
	ALA	LA	OHIO	GUAM
	ALASKA	MAINE	OKLA	PR
	ARIZ	MD	ORE	VIR IS
Notes — Symbol may be used if building meets all criteria. If building fails to meet all critiera, symbol may be used but must specify which portions of the facility are accessible. Place symbol of access adjacent or attached to a building whichever is most visible to the public.	ARK	MASS	PA	DC
	CAL	MICH	RI	
	COLO	MINN	SC	
	CONN	MISS	SD	FED'L FUNDS
	DEL	MO	TENN	
	FLA	MONT	TEXAS	
	GA	● NEB	UTAH	
	HAWAII	NEV	VT	
	IDAHO	NH	VA	
	ILL	NJ	WASH	
	IND	NM	W VA	
	IOWA	NY	WIS	OTHER
	KANS	NC	WYO	
	KY	ND		

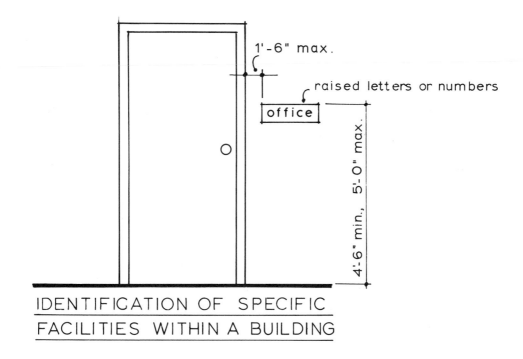

1'-6" max.

raised letters or numbers

office

4'-6" min., 5'-0" max.

IDENTIFICATION OF SPECIFIC FACILITIES WITHIN A BUILDING

Basis of standard — Architectural Barrier Free Design Code	APPLICABILITY			
	ALA	LA	OHIO	GUAM
	ALASKA	MAINE	OKLA	PR
	ARIZ	MD	ORE	VIR IS
Notes —	ARK	MASS	PA	DC
Provide for identification of apartments, offices, room numbers, toilet rooms and elevators. Where provided in means of egress, they shall be permanently fixed, raised 1/8″, 1¼″ min. height, with a contrasting color background. Use braille letters and numbers in addition to raised characters.	CAL	MICH	RI	
	COLO	MINN	SC	
	CONN	MISS	SD	FED'L FUNDS
	DEL	MO	TENN	
	FLA	MONT	TEXAS	
	GA	NEB	UTAH	
	HAWAII	NEV	VT	
	IDAHO	● NH	VA	
	ILL	NJ	WASH	
	IND	NM	W VA	
	IOWA	NY	WIS	OTHER
	KANS	NC	WYO	
	KY	ND		

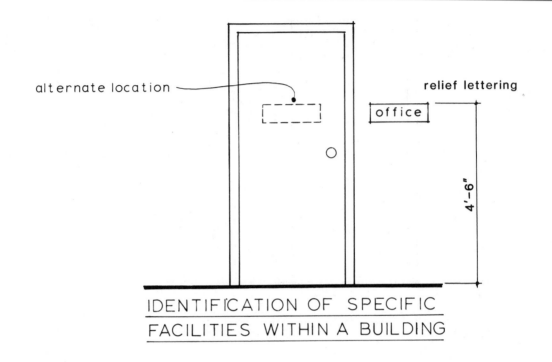

alternate location

relief lettering

office

4'-6"

IDENTIFICATION OF SPECIFIC
FACILITIES WITHIN A BUILDING

Basis of standard — Barrier Free Design Regulations	APPLICABILITY			
	ALA	LA	OHIO	GUAM
	ALASKA	MAINE	OKLA	PR
	ARIZ	MD	ORE	VIR IS
Notes — Lettering symbols: ¾″ min. high, in contrasting colors.	ARK	MASS	PA	DC
	CAL	MICH	RI	
	COLO	MINN	SC	
	CONN	MISS	SD	FED'L
	DEL	MO	TENN	FUNDS
	FLA	MONT	TEXAS	
	GA	NEB	UTAH	
	HAWAII	NEV	VT	
	IDAHO	NH	VA	
	ILL	● NJ	WASH	
	IND	NM	W VA	
	IOWA	NY	WIS	OTHER
	KANS	NC	WYO	
	KY	ND		

DISPLAY   CONDITIONS

Basis of standard —	APPLICABILITY			
Building Code Advisory Council	ALA	LA	OHIO	GUAM
	ALASKA	MAINE	OKLA	PR
	ARIZ	MD	ORE	VIR IS
Notes —	ARK	MASS	PA	DC
White on blue background. Display to identify accessible features including, but not limited to, the following: primary public site entrances, accessible parking facilities, primary public building entrance, accessible toilet rooms, required accessible exits.	CAL	MICH	RI	
	COLO	MINN	SC	
	CONN	MISS	SD	FED'L FUNDS
	DEL	MO	TENN	
	FLA	MONT	TEXAS	
	GA	NEB	UTAH	
	HAWAII	NEV	VT	
	IDAHO	NH	VA	
	ILL	NJ	● WASH	
	IND	NM	W VA	
	IOWA	NY	WIS	OTHER
	KANS	NC	WYO	
	KY	ND		

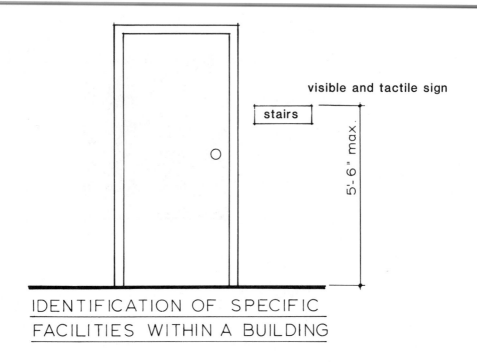

visible and tactile sign

stairs

5'- 6" max.

IDENTIFICATION OF SPECIFIC FACILITIES WITHIN A BUILDING

Basis of standard — Building Code Advisory Council	APPLICABILITY			
	ALA	LA	OHIO	GUAM
	ALASKA	MAINE	OKLA	PR
	ARIZ	MD	ORE	VIR IS
Notes — Identify openings to: public spaces such as reception rooms or toilets, stairs, loading platforms, stages, mechanical equipment rooms, fire escapes, elevators, other areas hazardous to visually disabled persons. Raise or groove lettering 1/16″ min., between 1″ and 2″ high on a background of contrasting value.	ARK	MASS	PA	DC
	CAL	MICH	RI	
	COLO	MINN	SC	
	CONN	MISS	SD	FED'L FUNDS
	DEL	MO	TENN	
	FLA	MONT	TEXAS	
	GA	NEB	UTAH	
	HAWAII	NEV	VT	
	IDAHO	NH	VA	
	ILL	NJ	● WASH	
	IND	NM	W VA	
	IOWA	NY	WIS	OTHER
	KANS	NC	WYO	
	KY	ND		

DISPLAY   CONDITIONS

Basis of standard —	APPLICABILITY			
Art 10F, Chapt. 18, Code of West Virginia	ALA	LA	OHIO	GUAM
	ALASKA	MAINE	OKLA	PR
	ARIZ	MD	ORE	VIR IS
Notes —	ARK	MASS	PA	DC
Display at: ground level entrance or entrance to building having a ramp instead of steps; doorways permitting wheelchair passage (32″ min.), restrooms accommodating wheelchairs, stalls which have grab bars, paper towel dispensers and mirrors 40″ above floor level; water fountains and public telephones within reach of persons in wheelchairs; special parking spaces that are wider and provide room to transfer from auto to wheelchair.	CAL	MICH	RI	
	COLO	MINN	SC	
	CONN	MISS	SD	FED'L FUNDS
	DEL	MO	TENN	
	FLA	MONT	TEXAS	
	GA	NEB	UTAH	
	HAWAII	NEV	VT	
	IDAHO	NH	VA	
	ILL	NJ	WASH	
	IND	NM	● W VA	
	IOWA	NY	WIS	OTHER
	KANS	NC	WYO	
	KY	ND		

DISPLAY   CONDITIONS

Basis of standard —	APPLICABILITY			
Wisconsin Administrative Code	ALA	LA	OHIO	GUAM
	ALASKA	MAINE	OKLA	PR
	ARIZ	MD	ORE	VIR IS
Notes —	ARK	MASS	PA	DC
Use symbol to identify all accessible entrances, toilet facilities, drinking fountains, telephones and parking spaces. Place at all entrances indicating location of the nearest accessible entrance(s) and accessible toilet facilities. Symbol at building exterior shall be legible from adjacent streets, driveways or public works.	CAL	MICH	RI	
	COLO	MINN	SC	
	CONN	MISS	SD	FED'L FUNDS
	DEL	MO	TENN	
	FLA	MONT	TEXAS	
	GA	NEB	UTAH	
	HAWAII	NEV	VT	
	IDAHO	NH	VA	
	ILL	NJ	WASH	
	IND	NM	W VA	
	IOWA	NY	● WIS	OTHER
	KANS	NC	WYO	
	KY	ND		

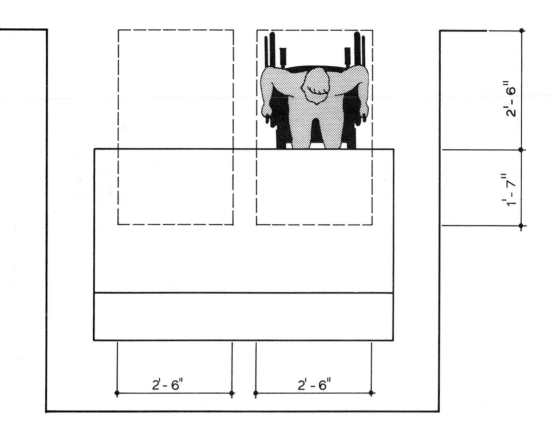

Basis of standard — ANSI 1980 − 4.32	APPLICABILITY			
	ALA	● LA	OHIO	GUAM
	● ALASKA	● MAINE	OKLA	PR
	ARIZ	MD	ORE	VIR IS
	● ARK	MASS	PA	DC
	CAL	MICH	● RI	
	● COLO	MINN	SC	
	CONN	MISS	SD	● FED'L FUNDS
	● DEL	MO	TENN	
	FLA	MONT	TEXAS	
	GA	NEB	UTAH	
	● HAWAII	● NEV	● VT	
	● IDAHO	NH	● VA	
	ILL	NJ	WASH	
	IND	● NM	W VA	
	IOWA	● NY	WIS	OTHER
	KANS	NC	WYO	
	● KY	ND		

Notes —

If fixed or built-in seating, tables, or work surfaces are provided in accessible spaces, a reasonable number, but always at least one of seating, tables or work surfaces shall comply with these requirements. Tops of tables and work surfaces shall be from 28″ to 34″ from floor. Federal and Arkansas require 2′-3″ high knee spaces. Delaware requires 2′-5″ high knee spaces.

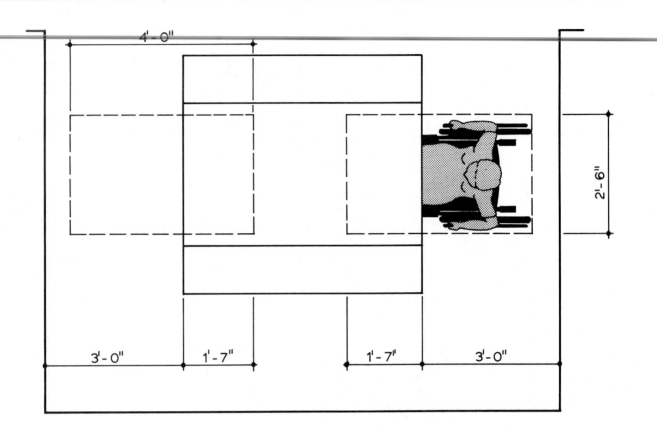

Basis of standard —	APPLICABILITY			
ANSI 1980 — 4.32	ALA	● LA	OHIO	GUAM
	● ALASKA	● MAINE	OKLA	PR
	ARIZ	MD	ORE	VIR IS
	● ARK	MASS	PA	DC
	CAL	MICH	● RI	
	● COLO	MINN	SC	
	CONN	MISS	SD	● FED'L FUNDS
	DEL	MO	TENN	
Notes —	FLA	MONT	TEXAS	
Knee spaces for seating of people in wheelchairs at tables, counters and work surfaces shall be at least 27″ high, 30″ wide, and 19″ deep.	GA	NEB	UTAH	
	● HAWAII	● NEV	● VT	
	● IDAHO	NH	● VA	
	● ILL	NJ	WASH	
	IND	● NM	W VA	
	IOWA	● NY	WIS	OTHER
	KANS	NC	WYO	
	● KY	ND		

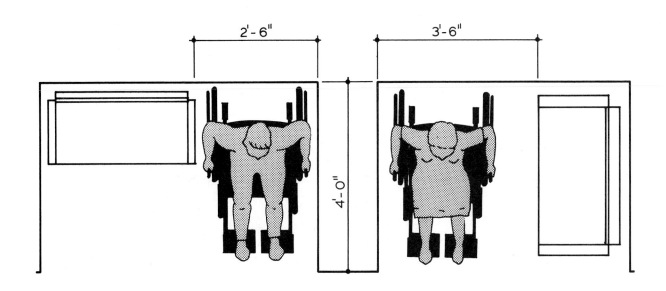

← ACCESSIBLE PATH OF TRAVEL →

Basis of standard — ANSI 1980 — 4.32	APPLICABILITY			
	ALA	● LA	OHIO	GUAM
	● ALASKA	● MAINE	OKLA	PR
	ARIZ	MD	ORE	VIR IS
Notes —	ARK	MASS	PA	DC
	CAL	MICH	● RI	
	● COLO	MINN	SC	
	CONN	MISS	SD	FED'L
	DEL	MO	TENN	FUNDS
	FLA	MONT	TEXAS	
	GA	NEB	UTAH	
	● HAWAII	● NEV	● VT	
	● IDAHO	NH	● VA	
	● ILL	NJ	WASH	
	IND	● NM	W VA	
	IOWA	● NY	WIS	OTHER
	KANS	NC	WYO	
	● KY	ND		

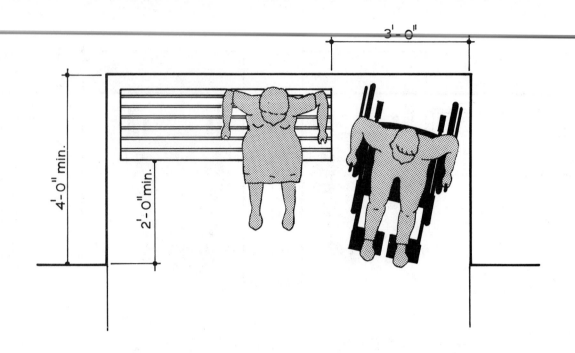

SPACE REQUIREMENTS FOR WHEELCHAIRS ADJACENT SEATING

Basis of standard —	APPLICABILITY			
Capital Development Board	ALA	LA	OHIO	GUAM
	ALASKA	MAINE	OKLA	PR
	ARIZ	MD	ORE	VIR IS
Notes —	ARK	MASS	PA	DC
Where rest areas are provided, include space alongside seating to accommodate those in wheelchairs. Construct seating to support 250 lbf. for each person accommodated and provide back and armrests. Seating shall not hold water.	CAL	MICH	RI	
	COLO	MINN	SC	
	CONN	MISS	SD	FED'L
	DEL	MO	TENN	FUNDS
	FLA	MONT	TEXAS	
	GA	NEB	UTAH	
	HAWAII	NEV	VT	
	IDAHO	NH	VA .	
	● ILL	NJ	WASH	
	IND	NM	W VA	
	IOWA	NY	WIS	OTHER
	KANS	NC	WYO	
	KY	ND		

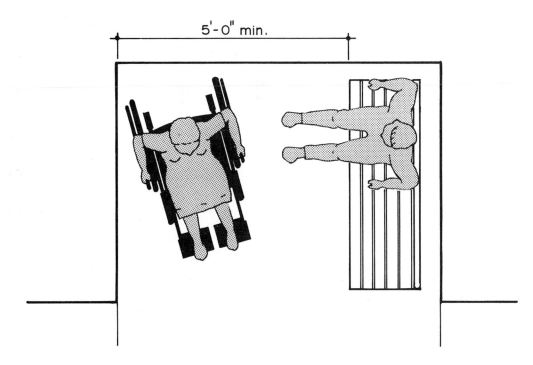

5'-0" min.

SPACE REQUIREMENTS FOR WHEELCHAIRS ADJACENT SEATING

Basis of standard — Capital Development Board	APPLICABILITY			
	ALA	LA	OHIO	GUAM
	ALASKA	MAINE	OKLA	PR
	ARIZ	MD	ORE	VIR IS
Notes — See notes on preceding page.	ARK	MASS	PA	DC
	CAL	MICH	RI	
	COLO	MINN	SC	
	CONN	MISS	SD	FED'L FUNDS
	DEL	MO	TENN	
	FLA	MONT	TEXAS	
	GA	NEB	UTAH	
	HAWAII	NEV	VT	
	IDAHO	NH	VA	
	● ILL	NJ	WASH	
	IND	NM	W VA	
	IOWA	NY	WIS	OTHER
	KANS	NC	WYO	
	KY	ND		

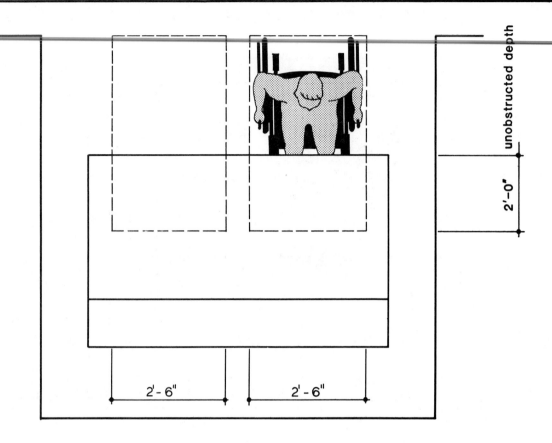

Basis of standard —	APPLICABILITY			
Capital Development Board	ALA	LA	OHIO	GUAM
	ALASKA	MAINE	OKLA	PR
	ARIZ	MD	ORE	VIR IS
Notes —	ARK	MASS	PA	DC
Locate furniture for disabled persons on firm, smooth surfaces of sufficient area to enable maneuvering in wheelchairs. Provide clear space from the ground to underside of table of 2'-6".	CAL	MICH	RI	
	COLO	MINN	SC	
	CONN	MISS	SD	FED'L
	DEL	MO	TENN	FUNDS
	FLA	MONT	TEXAS	
	GA	NEB	UTAH	
	HAWAII	NEV	VT	
	IDAHO	NH	VA	
	● ILL	NJ	WASH	
	IND	NM	W VA	
	IOWA	NY	WIS	OTHER
	KANS	NC	WYO	
	KY	ND		

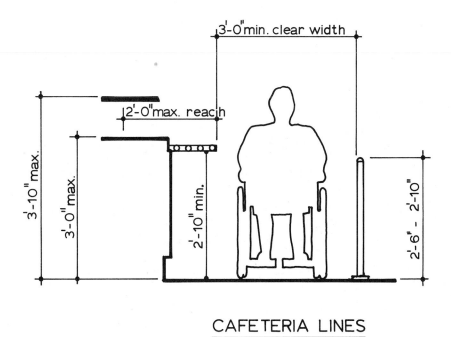

CAFETERIA LINES

Basis of standard — Capital Development Board	APPLICABILITY			
	ALA	LA	OHIO	GUAM
	ALASKA	MAINE	OKLA	PR
	ARIZ	MD	ORE	VIR IS
Notes — Provide at least one, or 5%, of serving counters, seating, fixed tables, or worksurfaces which comply if same are provided in accessible spaces. Top of work surfaces, tables and counters shall be from 2'-4" to 2'-10" high. Where service counters exceed 3'-0" height, provide auxiliary counter or suitable space for the handicapped which complies.	ARK	MASS	PA	DC
	CAL	MICH	RI	
	COLO	MINN	SC	
	CONN	MISS	SD	FED'L
	DEL	MO	TENN	FUNDS
	FLA	MONT	TEXAS	
	GA	NEB	UTAH	
	HAWAII	NEV	VT	
	IDAHO	NH	VA	
	● ILL	NJ	WASH	
	IND	NM	W VA	
	IOWA	NY	WIS	OTHER
	KANS	NC	WYO	
	KY	ND		

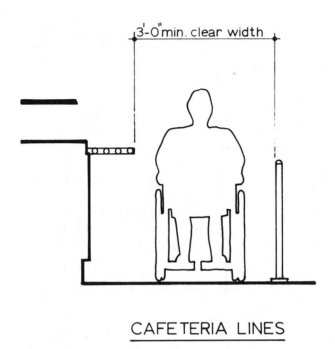

3'-0" min. clear width

CAFETERIA LINES

Basis of standard —	APPLICABILITY			
Architectural Barriers Board	ALA	LA	OHIO	GUAM
	ALASKA	MAINE	OKLA	PR
	ARIZ	MD	ORE	VIR IS
Notes —	ARK	● MASS	PA	DC
Restaurants: provide 3'-0" min. unobstructed means of egress through dining areas. Fixed tables shall have clear space min. 2'-6" wide per seating space, with 2'-3" min. clear height to a depth of 1'-0" from table edge.	CAL	MICH	RI	
	COLO	MINN	SC	
	CONN	MISS	SD	FED'L
	DEL	MO	TENN	FUNDS
	FLA	MONT	TEXAS	
	GA	NEB	UTAH	
	HAWAII	NEV	VT	
	IDAHO	NH	VA	
	ILL	NJ	WASH	
	IND	NM	W VA	
	IOWA	NY	WIS	OTHER
	KANS	NC	WYO	
	KY	ND		

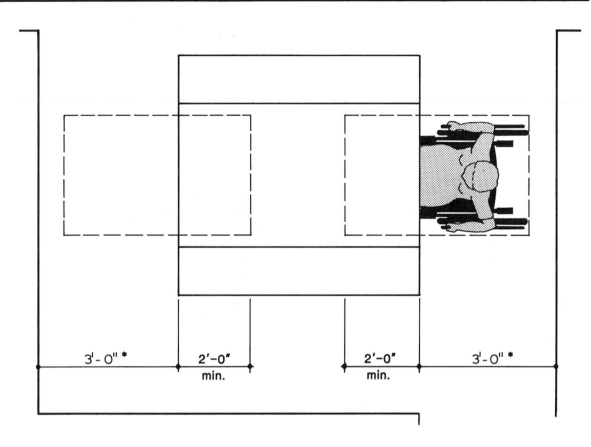

3'- 0" *   2'-0"   2'-0"   3'- 0" *
            min.   min.

Basis of standard —	APPLICABILITY			
Building Code Advisory Council	ALA	LA	OHIO	GUAM
	ALASKA	MAINE	OKLA	PR
	ARIZ	MD	ORE	VIR IS
	ARK	MASS	PA	DC
Notes —	CAL	MICH	RI	
Provide 2'-3" min. clear height beneath fixed tables,	COLO	MINN	SC	
desks, counters and work benches. For movable	CONN	MISS	SD	FED'L
seating within the aisle between fixed equipment,	DEL	MO	TENN	FUNDS
tables, or benches provide 5'-5" min. aisle serving 2%	FLA	MONT	TEXAS	
of such equipment. Max. Slope of aisles: 1:8 except	GA	NEB	UTAH	
as otherwise permitted. Where wheelchair spaces are	HAWAII	NEV	VT	
provided, max. for egress slopes: 1:12.	IDAHO	NH	VA	
(*)3'-6" if serving both sides. Increase 1½" for each	ILL	NJ	● WASH	
5' in length toward exit, cross aisle, or foyer. For	IND	NM	W VA	
continental spacing per U.B.C. sect. 3314 provide	IOWA	NY	WIS	OTHER
side aisle min. of 3'-8" width.	KANS	NC	WYO	
	KY	ND		

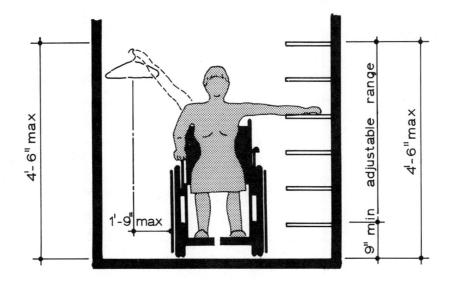

STORAGE   SHELVES   AND   CLOSETS

Basis of standard —	APPLICABILITY			
ANSI 1980 – 4.25	ALA	● LA	OHIO	GUAM
	● ALASKA	● MAINE	OKLA	PR
	ARIZ	MD	ORE	VIR IS
Notes —	● ARK	MASS	PA	DC
Provide min. 2'-6" × 4'-0" clear floor space allowing parallel or forward approach. Reach ranges shall comply with ANSI 4.2.5 and 4.2.6. Hardware to comply with ANSI 4.27 for controls and operating mechanisms. Touch latches and U-shaped pulls are acceptable.	CAL	MICH	● RI	
	● COLO	MINN	SC	
	CONN	MISS	SD	● FED'L FUNDS
	● DEL	MO	TENN	
	FLA	MONT	TEXAS	
	GA	NEB	UTAH	
	● HAWAII	● NEV	● VT	
	● IDAHO	NH	● VA	
	ILL	NJ	WASH	
	IND	● NM	W VA	
	IOWA	NY	WIS	OTHER
	KANS	NC	WYO	
	● KY	ND		

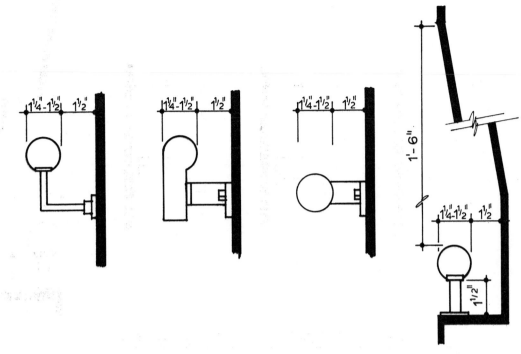

SIZE AND SPACING OF GRAB BARS

Basis of standard —	APPLICABILITY			
ANSI 1980 — 4.26 and others	ALA	● LA	OHIO	GUAM
	● ALASKA	● MAINE	OKLA	PR
	ARIZ	MD	ORE	● VIR IS
	● ARK	MASS	PA	DC
	CAL	MICH	● RI	
Notes —	● COLO	MINN	SC	
Alternate to diameter or widths shown: an equivalent gripping surface. Recess max. 3″ providing recess extends 18″ min. above top of rail. Required structural strength, including fasteners and mounting devices resulting from applying 250 lbf: bending stress induced by max. bending moment: less than allowable stress for the material. Shear stress: less than allowable shear stress for the material. Total direct and torsional shear stresses for combined shear stress if the connection between grab bars and mounting bracket is considered to be fully constrained. Shear force in fastener or mounting: the smaller of the allowable lateral load of fastener or mounting device or the supporting structure. Tensile force of 250 lbf. plus maximum moment of 250 lbf.: less than allowable withdrawal load between fastener and supporting structure. Grab bars shall not rotate in their fittings.	CONN	MISS	SD	● FED'L FUNDS
	● DEL	MO	TENN	
	FLA	MONT	TEXAS	
	GA	NEB	UTAH	
	● HAWAII	● NEV	VT	
	● IDAHO	NH	● VA	
	ILL	NJ	WASH	
	IND	● NM	W VA	
	IOWA	● NY	WIS	OTHER
	KANS	NC	WYO	
	● KY	ND		

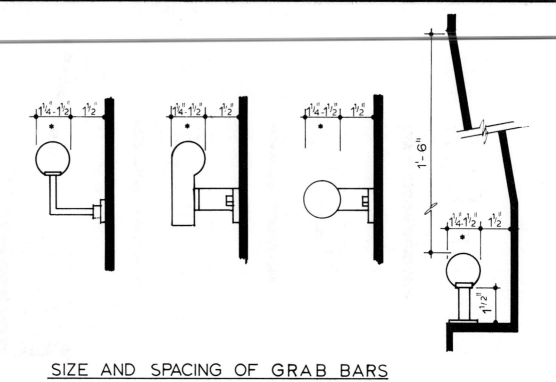

SIZE AND SPACING OF GRAB BARS

Basis of standard — ATBCB 1190.80 and 1190.150, and others	APPLICABILITY			
	ALA	LA	OHIO	GUAM
	ALASKA	MAINE	OKLA	PR
	ARIZ	MD	ORE	VIR IS
	● ARK	MASS	PA	DC
	CAL	MICH	RI	
	COLO	MINN	SC	
	CONN	MISS	SD	
	● DEL	MO	TENN	● FED'L FUNDS
	FLA	MONT	TEXAS	
	GA	NEB	UTAH	
	HAWAII	NEV	VT	
	IDAHO	NH	VA	
	ILL	NJ	WASH	
	IND	NM	W VA	
	IOWA	NY	WIS	OTHER
	KANS	NC	WYO	
	KY	ND		

Notes —
For grab bars: min. strength: 250 lb. concentrated load, not rotating in fittings.
(*)For stairways, handgrip portion of handrail 1¼" min. to 2" max. Unless free standing, provide min. 1/8" radius. Min. strength: momentary concentrated load applied at top edge of 200 lbs. horizontal, and 30% of that load vertical. Increase loading by 50% where railing system is installed in public assembly occupancies. Handrails for stairs: 2'-8" to 2'-10" high.

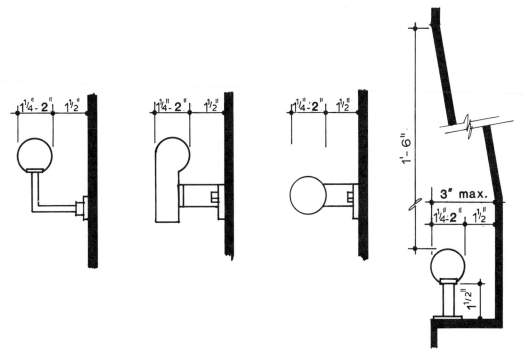

SIZE AND SPACING OF HANDRAILS

Basis of standard — Uniform Building Code	APPLICABILITY			
	ALA	LA	OHIO	GUAM
	ALASKA	MAINE	OKLA	PR
	ARIZ	MD	ORE	VIR IS
	ARK	MASS	PA	DC
	CAL	MICH	RI	
	COLO	MINN	SC	
	CONN	MISS	SD	FED'L FUNDS
	DEL	MO	TENN	
	FLA	● MONT	TEXAS	
	GA	NEB	UTAH	
	HAWAII	NEV	VT	
	IDAHO	NH	VA	
	ILL	NJ	● WASH	
	● IND	NM	W VA	
	IOWA	NY	WIS	OTHER
	KANS	NC	WYO	
	KY	ND		

Notes —
Provide smooth surface with no sharp corners. For ramps with slopes exceeding 1:20 in Washington (1:15 in Montana) as required for stairways (see "Stairs") except that intermediate handrails (over 88″ width) are not required. Indiana does not specify rail width.

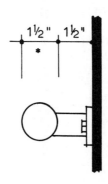

1½"   1½"

GRAB BARS

Basis of standard — Various	APPLICABILITY			
	ALA	LA	OHIO	GUAM
	ALASKA	MAINE	OKLA	PR
	ARIZ	MD	ORE	VIR IS
Notes —	ARK	MASS	PA	DC
Connecticut: handrails for use by the physically handicapped for access and support at plumbing fixtures shall have a ridged or other non-slip surface and shall be securely anchored to withstand a force of 300 lbs.	CAL	MICH	RI	
	COLO	MINN	SC	
	● CONN	MISS	SD	FED'L FUNDS
	DEL	MO	TENN	
Wisconsin: (*)1″ to 1½″, smooth finish, able to support 250 lb. load. Side mounted grab bars to be installed 2′-9″ above floor.	FLA	MONT	TEXAS	
	GA	NEB	UTAH	
	HAWAII	NEV	VT	
	IDAHO	NH	VA	
	ILL	NJ	WASH	
	IND	NM	W VA	
	IOWA	NY	● WIS	OTHER
	KANS	NC	WYO	
	KY	ND		

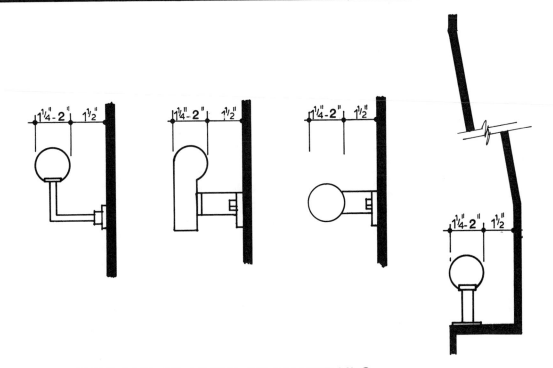

SIZE AND SPACING OF HANDRAILS

Basis of standard — CAC Title 24, Part 2	APPLICABILITY			
	ALA	LA	OHIO	GUAM
	ALASKA	MAINE	OKLA	PR
	ARIZ	MD	ORE	VIR IS
	ARK	MASS	PA	DC
Notes —	● CAL	MICH	RI	
	COLO	MINN	SC	
	CONN	MISS	SD	FED'L
	DEL	MO	TENN	FUNDS
	FLA	MONT	TEXAS	
	GA	NEB	UTAH	
	HAWAII	NEV	VT	
	IDAHO	NH	VA	
	ILL	NJ	WASH	
	IND	NM	W VA	
	IOWA	NY	WIS	OTHER
	KANS	NC	WYO	
	KY	ND		

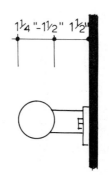

1¼"-1½" 1½"

G R A B   B A R S

Basis of standard — CAC Title 24, Part 2	APPLICABILITY			
	ALA	LA	OHIO	GUAM
	ALASKA	MAINE	OKLA	PR
	ARIZ	MD	ORE	VIR IS
Notes —	ARK	MASS	PA	DC
	● CAL	MICH	RI	
	COLO	MINN	SC	
	CONN	MISS	SD	FED'L
	DEL	MO	TENN	FUNDS
	FLA	MONT	TEXAS	
	GA	NEB	UTAH	
	HAWAII	NEV	VT	
	IDAHO	NH	VA	
	ILL	NJ	WASH	
	IND	NM	W VA	
	IOWA	NY	WIS	OTHER
	KANS	NC	WYO	
	KY	ND		

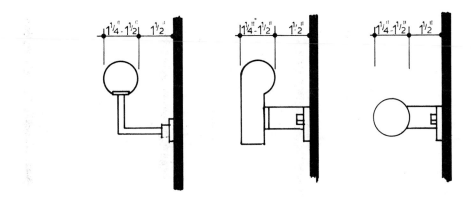

SIZE AND SPACING OF HANDRAILS

Basis of standard —	APPLICABILITY			
Capital Development Board	ALA	LA	OHIO	GUAM
	ALASKA	MAINE	OKLA	PR
	ARIZ	MD	ORE	VIR IS
Notes —	ARK	MASS	PA	DC
Handrails shall permit continuous hand sliding.	CAL	MICH	RI	
Anchor to withstand 250 lbf applied in any direction	COLO	MINN	SC	
at any point on top rail. No sharp edges. Min. edge	CONN	MISS	SD	FED'L
radius: 1/8″. Return projecting ends to wall, floor or	DEL	MO	TENN	FUNDS
post. Place 5/8″ stair raised 1/32″ on top surface of	FLA	MONT	TEXAS	
rail of enclosed stairs at main exit floor.	GA	NEB	UTAH	
	HAWAII	NEV	VT	
	IDAHO	NH	VA	
	● ILL	NJ	WASH	
	IND	NM	W VA	
	IOWA	NY	WIS	OTHER
	KANS	NC	WYO	
	KY	ND		

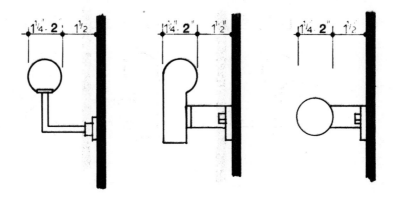

SIZE AND SPACING OF GRAB BARS
AND HANDRAILS

Basis of standard —	APPLICABILITY			
Architectural Barriers Board	ALA	LA	OHIO	GUAM
	ALASKA	MAINE	OKLA	PR
	ARIZ	MD	ORE	VIR IS
Notes —	ARK	● MASS	PA	DC
	CAL	MICH	RI	
	COLO	MINN	SC	
	CONN	MISS	SD	FED'L
	DEL	MO	TENN	FUNDS
	FLA	MONT	TEXAS	
	GA	NEB	UTAH	
	HAWAII	NEV	VT	
	IDAHO	NH	VA	
	ILL	NJ	WASH	
	IND	NM	W VA	
	IOWA	NY	WIS	OTHER
	KANS	NC	WYO	
	KY	ND		

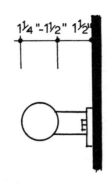

G R A B   B A R S

Basis of standard —	APPLICABILITY			
Building Code Advisory Council	ALA	LA	OHIO	GUAM
	ALASKA	MAINE	OKLA	PR
	ARIZ	MD	ORE	VIR IS
Notes —	ARK	MASS	PA	DC
Supporting capability: 300 lb. live load without permanent deflection.	CAL	MICH	RI	
Height: for water closets: 2'-8" to 3'-0"	COLO	MINN	SC	
for showers: 2'-11" to 3'-0"	CONN	MISS	SD	FED'L
for bathtubs: 2'-11" to 3'-0"	DEL	MO	TENN	FUNDS
for second bar: 9" above tub trim	FLA	MONT	TEXAS	
In adaptable dwelling units, installation of grab bars,	GA	NEB	UTAH	
shower units and in-tub seats may be waived provided	HAWAII	NEV	VT	
structural provision is made for their later installation.	IDAHO	NH	VA	
	ILL	NJ	● WASH	
	IND	NM	W VA	
	IOWA	NY	WIS	OTHER
	KANS	NC	WYO	
	KY	ND		

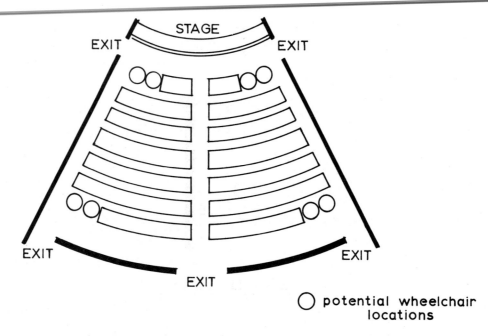

EXIT   STAGE   EXIT

EXIT   EXIT
          EXIT

○ potential wheelchair
   locations

PLACEMENT OF WHEELCHAIR VIEWING LOCATIONS

Basis of standard —	APPLICABILITY			
ANSI 1980 — 4.33	ALA	● LA	OHIO	GUAM
	● ALASKA	● MAINE	OKLA	PR
	ARIZ	MD	ORE	VIR IS
	ARK	MASS	PA	DC
Notes —	CAL	MICH	● RI	
Disperse throughout seating area adjoining an accessible route that also serves as a means of egress in case of emergency and located to provide lines of sight comparable to those for all viewing areas. Connect accessible route with wheelchair locations and performing areas including stages, arena floors, dressing rooms, locker rooms, and other spaces used by performers. If listening systems provided serve individual fixed seats, locate such seats within 50 ft. viewing distance of stage or playing area with complete view of stage or viewing area. Audio loops and radio frequency systems are two acceptable types of listening systems.	● COLO	MINN	SC	
	CONN	MISS	SD	FED'L FUNDS
	DEL	MO	TENN	
	FLA	MONT	TEXAS	
	GA	NEB	UTAH	
	● HAWAII	● NEV	● VT	
	● IDAHO	NH	● VA	
	ILL	NJ	WASH	
	IND	● NM	W VA	
	IOWA	● NY	WIS	OTHER
	KANS	NC	WYO	
	KY	ND		

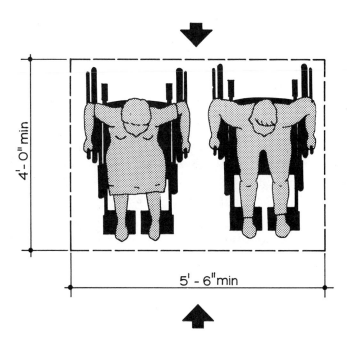

4'- 0" min

5'- 6" min

FORWARD OR REAR ACCESS

Basis of standard —	APPLICABILITY			
ANSI 1980 — 4.33	ALA	● LA	OHIO	GUAM
	● ALASKA	● MAINE	OKLA	PR
	ARIZ	MD	ORE	VIR IS
	ARK	MASS	PA	DC
Notes —	CAL	MICH	● RI	
For assembly areas, provide a reasonable number, but not less than two, of locations for wheelchair users complying with requirements. Each location to provide clear floor area shown, shall be level, and comply with ANSI requirements for floor surfaces.	● COLO	MINN	SC	
	CONN	MISS	SD	FED'L
	DEL	MO	TENN	FUNDS
	FLA	MONT	TEXAS	
	GA	NEB	UTAH	
	● HAWAII	● NEV	● VT	
	● IDAHO	NH	● VA	
	ILL	NJ	WASH	
	IND	● NM	W VA	
	IOWA	● NY	WIS	OTHER
	KANS	NC	WYO	
	KY	ND		

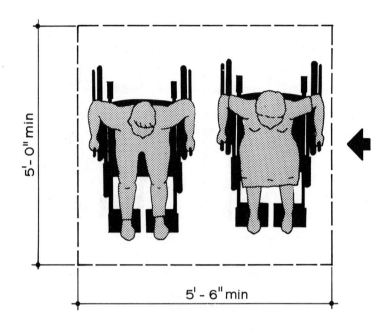

SIDE   ACCESS

Basis of standard — ANSI 1980 — 4.33	APPLICABILITY			
	ALA	● LA	OHIO	GUAM
	● ALASKA	● MAINE	OKLA	PR
	ARIZ	MD	ORE	VIR IS
	ARK	MASS	PA	DC
Notes — See notes on preceding page.	CAL	MICH	● RI	
	● COLO	MINN	SC	
	CONN	MISS	SD	FED'L
	DEL	MO	TENN	FUNDS
	FLA	MONT	TEXAS	
	GA	NEB	UTAH	
	● HAWAII	● NEV	● VT	
	● IDAHO	NH	● VA	
	ILL	NJ	WASH	
	IND	● NM	W VA	
	IOWA	● NY	WIS	OTHER
	KANS	NC	WYO	
	KY	ND		

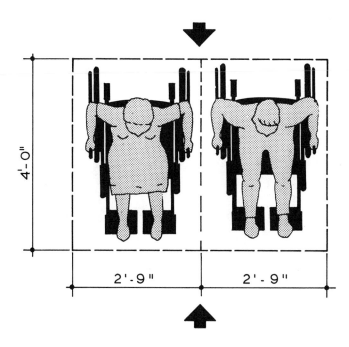

FORWARD OR REAR ACCESS

Basis of standard —	APPLICABILITY			
ATBCB 1190.230 and others	ALA	LA	OHIO	GUAM
	ALASKA	MAINE	OKLA	PR
	ARIZ	MD	ORE	VIR IS
Notes —	● ARK	MASS	PA	DC
Accommodate one occupied wheelchair or one port-able seat (for persons with crutches or leg braces). If only 2 positions are provided, they shall be in adjoining configuration: additional positions may be in single configurations. Provide min. clear floor area shown, level and to comply with requirements for floor surfaces. Provide listening system to assist at least two persons for Federal and Arkansas. If system serves individual seats, locate such seats within 50 ft. of the stage or arena which provide complete view of stage or arena.	CAL	MICH	RI	
	COLO	MINN	SC	
	CONN	MISS	SD	● FED'L FUNDS
	● DEL	MO	TENN	
	FLA	MONT	TEXAS	
	GA	NEB	UTAH	
	HAWAII	NEV	VT	
	IDAHO	NH	VA	
	ILL	NJ	WASH	
	IND	NM	W VA	
	IOWA	NY	WIS	OTHER
	KANS	NC	WYO	
	KY	ND		

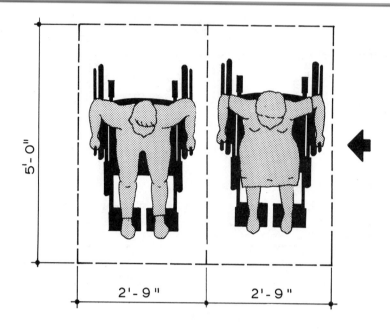

SIDE ACCESS

Basis of standard —	APPLICABILITY			
ATBCB 1190.230 and others	ALA	LA	OHIO	GUAM
	ALASKA	MAINE	OKLA	PR
	ARIZ	MD	ORE	VIR IS
● ARK	MASS	PA	DC
Notes —	CAL	MICH	RI	
See notes on preceding page. Federal and Delaware require:	COLO	MINN	SC	
	CONN	MISS	SD	
	● DEL	MO	TENN	● FED'L FUNDS
	FLA	MONT	TEXAS	
	GA	NEB	UTAH	
	HAWAII	NEV	VT	
	IDAHO	NH	VA	
	ILL	NJ	WASH	
	IND	NM	W VA	
	IOWA	NY	WIS	OTHER
	KANS	NC	WYO	
	KY	ND		

Notes —
See notes on preceding page. Federal and Delaware require:

Capacity of Assembly	Number of viewing positions
1 to 25	1
26 to 50	2
51 to 75	3
76 to 100	4
101 to 150	5
151 to 200	6
201 to 300	7
301 to 400	8
401 to 500	9
501 to 1000	2% of total
Over 1000	20 plus 1 for each 100 over 1000

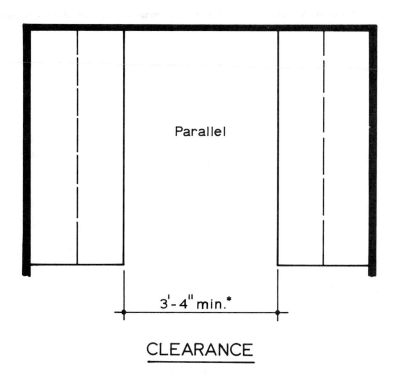

Parallel

3'- 4" min.*

CLEARANCE

Basis of standard —	APPLICABILITY			
ANSI 1980 — 4.34.6.1	ALA	● LA	OHIO	GUAM
	● ALASKA	● MAINE	OKLA	PR
	ARIZ	MD	ORE	VIR IS
	ARK	MASS	PA	DC
	CAL	MICH	● RI	
Notes —	● COLO	MINN	SC	
(*)In Illinois 3'-4" min. applies wall distance for kitchens with countertop only on one side.	CONN	MISS	SD	FED'L FUNDS
	DEL	MO	TENN	
	FLA	MONT	TEXAS	
	GA	NEB	UTAH	
	● HAWAII	● NEV	● VT	
	● IDAHO	NH	● VA	
	● ILL	NJ	WASH	
	IND	● NM	W VA	
	IOWA	● NY	WIS	OTHER
	KANS	NC	WYO	
	KY	ND		

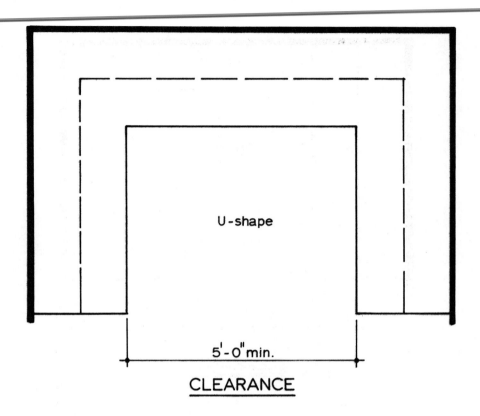

U-shape

5'-0" min.

CLEARANCE

Basis of standard — ANSI 1980 — 4.34.6.1 and others	APPLICABILITY			
	ALA	● LA	OHIO	GUAM
	● ALASKA	● MAINE	OKLA	PR
	ARIZ	MD	ORE	VIR IS
Notes —	ARK	MASS	PA	DC
	CAL	MICH	● RI	
	● COLO	MINN	SC	
	CONN	MISS	SD	FED'L FUNDS
	DEL	MO	TENN	
	FLA	MONT	TEXAS	
	GA	NEB	UTAH	
	● HAWAII	● NEV	● VT	
	● IDAHO	NH	● VA	
	● ILL	NJ	WASH	
	IND	● NM	W VA	
	IOWA	● NY	WIS	OTHER
	KANS	NC	WYO	
	KY	ND		

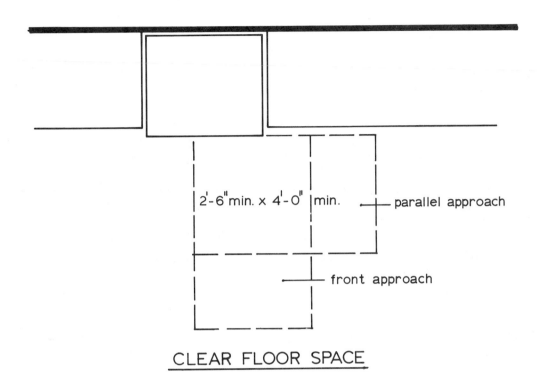

2'-6" min. x 4'-0" min. — parallel approach

— front approach

CLEAR FLOOR SPACE

Basis of standard —	APPLICABILITY			
ANSI 1980 — 4.36.6.2 and 4.34.6.9 and 4.34.7	ALA	● LA	OHIO	GUAM
	● ALASKA	● MAINE	OKLA	PR
	ARIZ	MD	ORE	VIR IS
	ARK	MASS	PA	DC
Notes —	CAL	MICH	● RI	
Provide indicated clearance at all kitchen appliances, including range or cooktop, oven, refrigerator/freezer, dishwasher, and trash compactor. Dishwashers shall have rack space accessible from the front. Laundry facilities shall be on an accessible route, equipment shall be front loading, and controls shall comply with 4.27.	● COLO	MINN	SC	
	CONN	MISS	SD	FED'L FUNDS
	DEL	MO	TENN	
	FLA	MONT	TEXAS	
	GA	NEB	UTAH	
	● HAWAII	● NEV	● VT	
	● IDAHO	NH	● VA	
	ILL	NJ	WASH	
	IND	● NM	W VA	
	IOWA	● NY	WIS	OTHER
	KANS	NC	WYO	
	KY	ND		

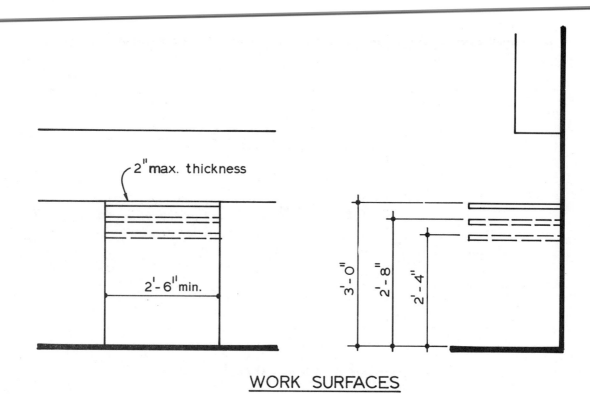

WORK SURFACES

Basis of standard — ANSI 1980 – 4.34.6.4	APPLICABILITY			
	ALA	● LA	OHIO	GUAM
	● ALASKA	● MAINE	OKLA	PR
	ARIZ	MD	ORE	VIR IS
Notes — Counter shall be adjustable or replaceable to provide alternative heights shown. Base cabinets, if provided, shall be removable under the full 30″ min. frontage under the counter.	ARK	MASS	PA	DC
	CAL	MICH	● RI	
	● COLO	MINN	SC	
	CONN	MISS	SD	FED'L FUNDS
	DEL	MO	TENN	
	FLA	MONT	TEXAS	
	GA	NEB	UTAH	
	● HAWAII	● NEV	● VT	
	● IDAHO	NH	● VA	
	ILL	NJ	WASH	
	IND	● NM	W VA	
	IOWA	● NY	WIS	OTHER
	KANS	NC	WYO	
	KY	ND		

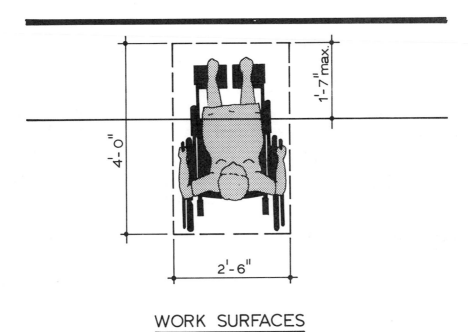

WORK SURFACES

Basis of standard —	APPLICABILITY			
ANSI 1980 — 4.34.6.4	ALA	● LA	OHIO	GUAM
	● ALASKA	● MAINE	OKLA	PR
	ARIZ	MD	ORE	VIR IS
	ARK	MASS	PA	DC
Notes —	CAL	MICH	● RI	
No abrasive or sharp surfaces under counters.	● COLO	MINN	SC	
	CONN	MISS	SD	FED'L
	DEL	MO	TENN	FUNDS
	FLA	MONT	TEXAS	
	GA	NEB	UTAH	
	● HAWAII	● NEV	● VT	
	● IDAHO	NH	● VA	
	ILL	NJ	WASH	
	IND	● NM	W VA	
	IOWA	● NY	WIS	OTHER
	KANS	NC	WYO	
	KY	ND		

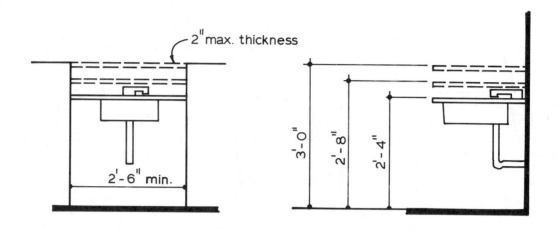

SINKS

Basis of standard — ANSI 1980 — 4.34.6.5	APPLICABILITY			
	ALA	● LA	OHIO	GUAM
	● ALASKA	● MAINE	OKLA	PR
	ARIZ	MD	ORE	VIR IS
	ARK	MASS	PA	DC
	CAL	MICH	● RI	
	● COLO	MINN	SC	
	CONN	MISS	SD	FED'L FUNDS
	DEL	MO	TENN	
	FLA	MONT	TEXAS	
	GA	NEB	UTAH	
	● HAWAII	● NEV	● VT	
	● IDAHO	NH	● VA	
	ILL	NJ	WASH	
	IND	● NM	W VA	
	IOWA	● NY	WIS	OTHER
	KANS	NC	WYO	
	KY	ND		

Notes —

Sink and surrounding counter shall be adjustable or replaceable as a unit to provide alternative heights shown. Locate rough-in plumbing to accept connections of supply and drain pipes for sinks mounted at a 2'-4" height. Max. depth of sink bowl: 6½". (Only one bowl of double or triple bowl sinks needs to comply with max. depth.) Faucets to comply with 4.27.4 (lever-operated or push-type mechanisms are acceptable). Base cabinets, if provided, shall be removable under full 30" min. frontage of sink and surrounding counter.

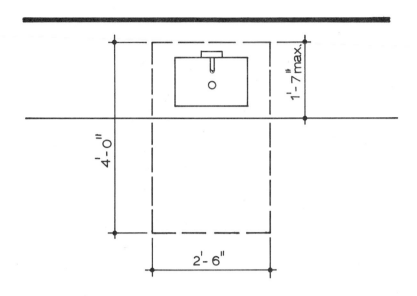

SINKS

Basis of standard — ANSI 1980 — 4.34.6.5	APPLICABILITY			
	ALA	● LA	OHIO	GUAM
	● ALASKA	● MAINE	OKLA	PR
	ARIZ	MD	ORE	VIR IS
	ARK	MASS	PA	DC
	CAL	MICH	● RI	
	● COLO	MINN	SC	
	CONN	MISS	SD	FED'L
	DEL	MO	TENN	FUNDS
	FLA	MONT	TEXAS	
	GA	NEB	UTAH	
	● HAWAII	● NEV	● VT	
	● IDAHO	NH	● VA	
	ILL	NJ	WASH	
	IND	● NM	W VA	
	IOWA	● NY	WIS	OTHER
	KANS	NC	WYO	
	KY	ND		

Notes —

No sharp or abrasive surfaces under sinks. Insulate or otherwise cover hot water and drain pipes under sink.

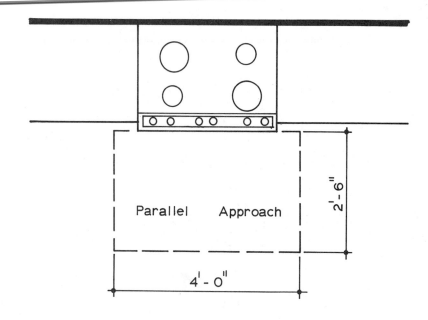

RANGES AND COOKTOPS

Basis of standard — ANSI 1980 — 4.34.6.6	APPLICABILITY			
	ALA	● LA	OHIO	GUAM
	● ALASKA	● MAINE	OKLA	PR
	ARIZ	MD	ORE	VIR IS
	ARK	MASS	PA	DC
Notes — Also comply with 4.34.6.2 for front approach and 4.27 for controls. If knee space is provided, insulate or otherwise protect on exposed contact surfaces to prevent burns, abrasions, or electrical shock. Clear floor space may overlap knee space, if provided, by 1'-7" max. Locate controls so as not to require reaching across burners.	CAL	MICH	● RI	
	● COLO	MINN	SC	
	CONN	MISS	SD	FED'L
	DEL	MO	TENN	FUNDS
	FLA	MONT	TEXAS	
	GA	● NEB	UTAH	
	● HAWAII	NEV	● VT	
	● IDAHO	NH	● VA	
	ILL	NJ	WASH	
	IND	● NM	W VA	
	IOWA	● NY	WIS	OTHER
	KANS	NC	WYO	
	KY	ND		

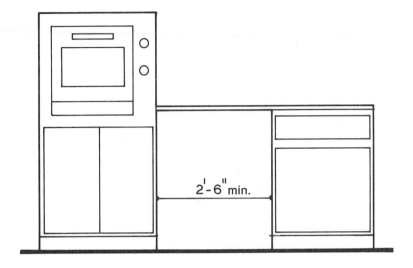

OVENS

Basis of standard —	APPLICABILITY			
ANSI 1980 — 4.34.6.7	ALA	● LA	OHIO	GUAM
	● ALASKA	● MAINE	OKLA	PR
	ARIZ	MD	ORE	VIR IS
Notes —	ARK	MASS	PA	DC
Comply with 4.34.6.2 for clear spaces and 4.27 for controls. Controls shall be on front panels, located on either side of door. Ovens shall be self-cleaning or located adjacent to an adjustable height counter with knee space below (see diagram). For side-opening ovens, the door latch side shall be next to the open counter space, and there shall be a pull-out shelf under the oven pulling out not less than 10″ when fully extended.	CAL	MICH	● RI	
	● COLO	MINN	SC	
	CONN	MISS	SD	FED'L
	DEL	MO	TENN	FUNDS
	FLA	MONT	TEXAS	
	GA	NEB	UTAH	
	● HAWAII	● NEV	● VT	
	● IDAHO	NH	● VA	
	ILL	NJ	WASH	
	IND	● NM	W VA	
	IOWA	● NY	WIS	OTHER
	KANS	NC	WYO	
	KY	ND		

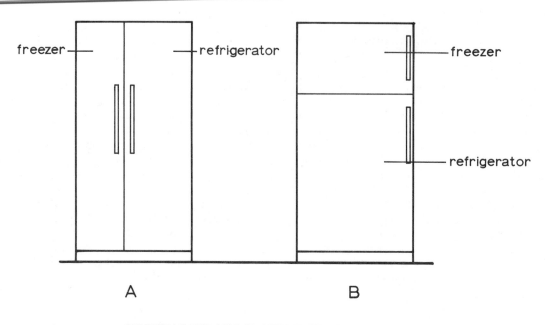

A   B

REFRIGERATOR / FREEZERS

Basis of standard — ANSI 1980 — 4.34.6.8	APPLICABILITY			
	ALA	● LA	OHIO	GUAM
	● ALASKA	● MAINE	OKLA	PR
	ARIZ	MD	ORE	VIR IS
	ARK	MASS	PA	DC
	CAL	MICH	● RI	
	● COLO	MINN	SC	
	CONN	MISS	SD	FED'L FUNDS
	DEL	MO	TENN	
	FLA	MONT	TEXAS	
	GA	NEB	UTAH	
	● HAWAII	● NEV	● VT	
	● IDAHO	NH	● VA	
	ILL	NJ	WASH	
	IND	● NM	W VA	
	IOWA	● NY	WIS	OTHER
	KANS	NC	WYO	
	KY	ND		

Notes —

Comply with 4.27 for controls. Refrigerators shall be type A or B above. For type B: min. 50% of freezer space below 4'-6" above floor and 100% of refrigerator space and controls below 4'-6" above floor. Freezers with less than 100% of storage volume within the limits specified in 4.2.5 and 4.2.6 ("Reaches" — see Human Dimensions) shall be of the self-defrosting type.

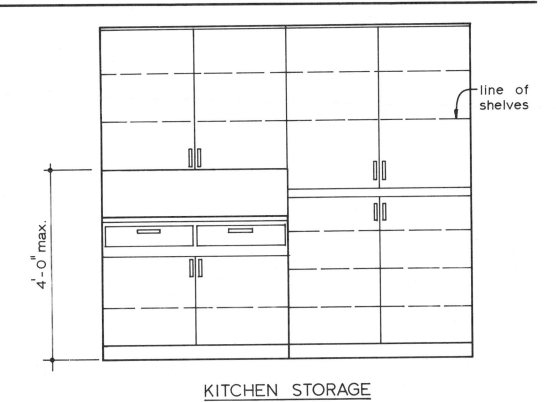

line of shelves

4'-0" max.

KITCHEN STORAGE

Basis of standard —	APPLICABILITY			
ANSI 1980 — 4.34.6.10	ALA	● LA	OHIO	GUAM
	● ALASKA	● MAINE	OKLA	PR
	ARIZ	MD	ORE	VIR IS
	ARK	MASS	PA	DC
Notes —	CAL	MICH	● RI	
Height shown is for at least one shelf of all cabinets and storage shelves mounted above work counters. Mount door pulls or handles for wall cabinets as close to the bottom of doors as possible. Mount door pulls or handles for base cabinets as close to top of cabinet doors as possible.	● COLO	MINN	SC	
	CONN	MISS	SD	FED'L FUNDS
	DEL	MO	TENN	
	FLA	MONT	TEXAS	
	GA	NEB	UTAH	
	● HAWAII	● NEV	● VT	
	● IDAHO	NH	● VA	
	ILL	NJ	WASH	
	IND	● NM	W VA	
	IOWA	● NY	WIS	OTHER
	KANS	NC	WYO	
	KY	ND		

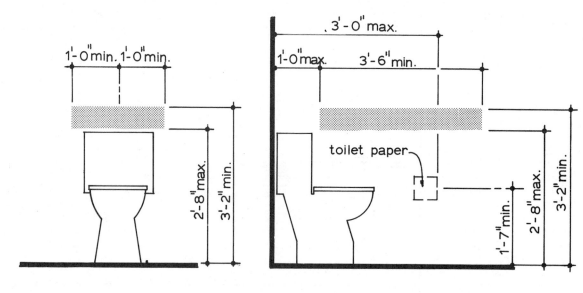

WATER CLOSETS IN ADAPTABLE BATHROOMS

Basis of standard — ANSI 1980 — 4.34.5.2	APPLICABILITY			
	ALA	● LA	OHIO	GUAM
	● ALASKA	● MAINE	OKLA	PR
	ARIZ	MD	ORE	VIR IS
	ARK	MASS	PA	DC
	CAL	MICH	● RI	
	● COLO	MINN	SC	
	CONN	MISS	SD	FED'L FUNDS
	DEL	MO	TENN	
	FLA	MONT	TEXAS	
	GA	NEB	UTAH	
	● HAWAII	● NEV	● VT	
	● IDAHO	NH	● VA	
	ILL	NJ	WASH	
	IND	● NM	W VA	
	IOWA	● NY	WIS	OTHER
	KANS	NC	WYO	
	KY	ND		

Notes —
Shaded areas are reinforced to receive grab bars. Also see section on water closets.

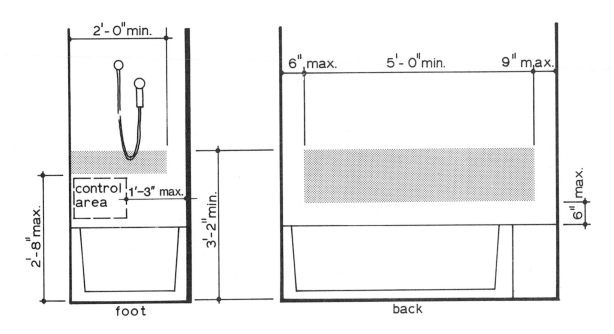

LOCATION OF GRAB BARS AND CONTROLS OF ADAPTABLE BATHTUBS

Basis of standard — ANSI 1980 — 4.34.5.4	APPLICABILITY			
	ALA	● LA	OHIO	GUAM
	● ALASKA	● MAINE	OKLA	PR
	ARIZ	MD	ORE	VIR IS
	ARK	MASS	PA	DC
Notes —	CAL	MICH	● RI	
For bathtubs with seat at the head of the tub. Shaded areas are reinforced to receive grab bars. Also see section on bathtubs. Provide shower spray unit with a 60″ min. hose that can be used as a fixed shower head or as a hand-held shower.	● COLO	MINN	SC	
	CONN	MISS	SD	FED'L
	DEL	MO	TENN	FUNDS
	FLA	MONT	TEXAS	
	GA	NEB	UTAH	
	● HAWAII	● NEV	● VT	
	● IDAHO	NH	● VA	
	ILL	NJ	WASH	
	IND	● NM	W VA	
	IOWA	● NY	WIS	OTHER
	KANS	NC	WYO	
	KY	ND		

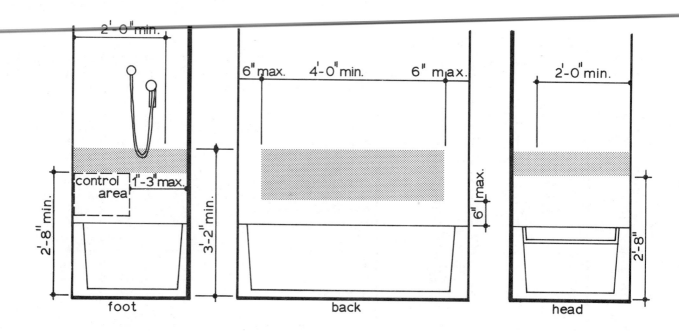

LOCATION OF GRAB BARS AND CONTROLS OF ADAPTABLE BATHTUBS

Basis of standard —	APPLICABILITY			
ANSI 1980 — 4.34.5.4	ALA	● LA	OHIO	GUAM
	● ALASKA	● MAINE	OKLA	PR
	ARIZ	MD	ORE	VIR IS
Notes —	ARK	MASS	PA	DC
For bathtubs with the seat in the tub. Shaded areas are reinforced to receive grab bars. Also see section on bathtubs. Provide shower spray unit with a 60″ min. hose that can be used as a fixed shower head or as a hand-held shower.	CAL	MICH	● RI	
	● COLO	MINN	SC	
	CONN	MISS	SD	FED'L
	DEL	MO	TENN	FUNDS
	FLA	MONT	TEXAS	
	GA	NEB	UTAH	
	● HAWAII	● NEV	● VT	
	● IDAHO	NH	● VA	
	ILL	NJ	WASH	
	IND	● NM	W VA	
	IOWA	● NY	WIS	OTHER
	KANS	NC	WYO	
	KY	ND		

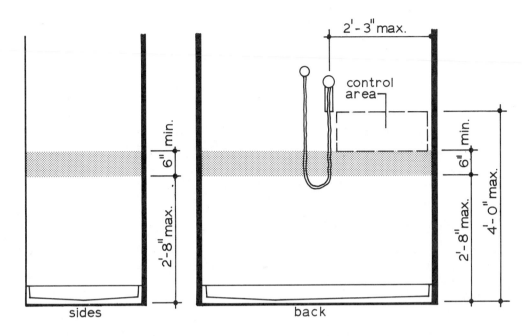

LOCATION OF GRAB BARS AND CONTROLS OF ADAPTABLE SHOWERS

Basis of standard — ANSI 1980 — 4.34.5.5	APPLICABILITY			
	ALA	● LA	OHIO	GUAM
	● ALASKA	● MAINE	OKLA	PR
	ARIZ	MD	ORE	VIR IS
	ARK	MASS	PA	DC
	CAL	MICH	● RI	
	● COLO	MINN	SC	
	CONN	MISS	SD	FED'L
	DEL	MO	TENN	FUNDS
	FLA	MONT	TEXAS	
	GA	NEB	UTAH	
	● HAWAII	● NEV	● VT	
	● IDAHO	NH	● VA	
	ILL	NJ	WASH	
	IND	● NM	W VA	
	IOWA	● NY	WIS	OTHER
	KANS	NC	WYO	
	KY	ND		

Notes —

Shaded areas reinforced to receive grab bars. Also see section on shower stalls. Provide shower spray with a 60″ min. hose that can be used as a fixed shower head or as a hand-held shower. 2′-6″ × 5′-0″ stall is shown.

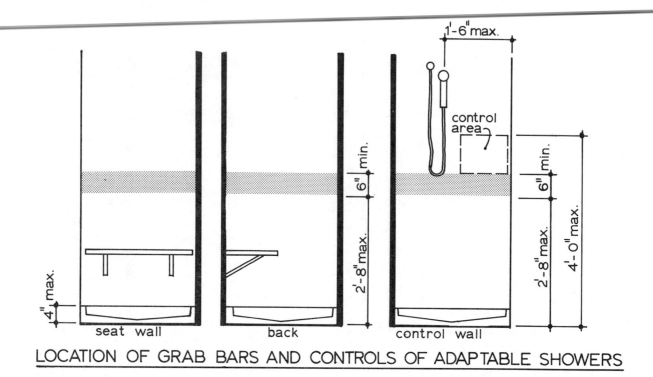

LOCATION OF GRAB BARS AND CONTROLS OF ADAPTABLE SHOWERS

Basis of standard — ANSI 1980 — 4.34.5.5	APPLICABILITY			
	ALA	● LA	OHIO	GUAM
	● ALASKA	● MAINE	OKLA	PR
	ARIZ	MD	ORE	VIR IS
	ARK	MASS	PA	DC
Notes —	CAL	MICH	● RI	
Shaded areas are reinforced to receive grab bars. Also	● COLO	MINN	SC	
see section on showers. Provide shower spray with a	CONN	MISS	SD	FED'L
60" min. hose that can be used as a fixed shower head	DEL	MO	TENN	FUNDS
or as a hand-held shower. 3'-0" X 3'-0" stall is shown.	FLA	MONT	TEXAS	
	GA	NEB	UTAH	
	● HAWAII	● NEV	● VT	
	● IDAHO	NH	● VA	
	ILL	NJ	WASH	
	IND	● NM	W VA	
	IOWA	● NY	WIS	OTHER
	KANS	NC	WYO	
	KY	ND		

INDEX